The upheaval of war

THE
UPHEAVAL
OF WAR

Family, Work and Welfare
in Europe, 1914–1918

Edited by Richard Wall and Jay Winter

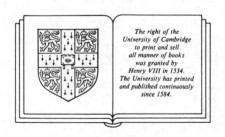

The right of the
University of Cambridge
to print and sell
all manner of books
was granted by
Henry VIII in 1534.
The University has printed
and published continuously
since 1584.

CAMBRIDGE UNIVERSITY PRESS

Cambridge

New York   New Rochelle   Melbourne   Sydney

Published by the Press Syndicate of the University of Cambridge
The Pitt Building, Trumpington Street, Cambridge CB2 1RP
32 East 57th Street, New York, NY 10022, USA
10 Stamford Road, Oakleigh, Melbourne 3166, Australia

First published 1988

Printed in Great Britain at the University Press, Cambridge

British Library cataloguing in publication data
The upheaval of war: family, work and
welfare in Europe, 1914–1918.
1. Europe. Social conditions, 1914–1918
I. Wall, Richard, 1944– ii. Winter, J. M. (Jay Murray)
940.3′1

Library of Congress cataloguing in publication data
The upheaval of war: family, work and welfare in Europe, 1914–1918/
edited by Richard Wall and Jay Winter.
p.   cm.
Bibliography.
Includes index.
ISBN 0 521 32345 2
1. World War, 1914–1918 – Europe. 2. World War, 1914–1918 – Women.
3. Europe – Social conditions – 20th century. 4. Europe – Economic
conditions – 20th century. I. Wall, Richard, 1944– II. Winter, J. M.
D523.U7 1988
940.3′16 – dc 19   88–10229   CIP

ISBN 0 521 32345 2

WD

Contents

CONTENTS

Plates

Sources Plate 1: from Die Frauen-Hilfsaktion, Vienna, 1916; Plates 2–4: from the private collection of R. Sieder; Plates 6–7: from the Women's work collection, Imperial War Museum; Plates 8–23: from the private collection of Marie-Monique Huss.

Plates

Introduction

The impact of the First World War on European political and economic history is a subject which has occupied historians virtually since the guns were silenced in 1918. A vast literature, at once complex, subtle and acrimonious, has emerged about the perennial political questions of war guilt, civil–military relations, and peace-making, the insoluble military problems of tactics and strategy, especially on the Western Front, and the fundamental economic problems of the mobilisation of men and material for war production and of the economic costs of the conflict.

It is only recently, however, that historians have begun to probe the social history of the war years, as a subject standing on its own, rather than as providing necessary background information for the analysis of political and economic developments.

In this field, as in others, French historians have taken the lead. This is in part a function of historiographical trends, in which the *Annales* school has been highly influential. It is not at all surprising that French cultural historians were among the first to examine trends in public opinion in wartime,[1] or to conduct the first systematic investigations of the true nature of war enthusiasm in 1914 and of social stability in the four grim years which followed,[2] or to provide the most profound and moving account of veterans of the First World War.[3] But the richness of recent historical literature about the war period produced by French scholars is also a reflection of the wealth of documentary information, especially from police files, but also from other sources, which are readily available for scrutiny in French archives.

The fact that the vagaries of inclination and evidence have produced a number of fundamentally important works on the social history of wartime France should not detract, however, from similar though scattered contributions made by scholars working on the history of other combatant

1

nations. We have valuable studies of social tensions and social inequality in Germany,[4] of class relations and the workings of social policy in Britain,[5] as well as a growing literature on working-class life in general[6] and on women's history, in particular.[7]

Indeed, it is precisely because there is a range of disparate and important research currently under way on the social history of the war period that we organised a conference on this subject, funded by the Economic and Social Research Council, in Cambridge in 1983. The essays collected here were first presented to this conference and then substantially revised in the light of the ensuing discussion. Not all the original contributions, however, have been included in this volume. Our aim has been to provide a fully comparative framework, and to do so required that each major topic be examined in more than one country. Some essays of real importance on themes not taken up systematically in other parts of the book were, therefore, omitted, or published elsewhere.[8]

Essentially, the issues raised by these papers address the question of the destabilising effects of the First World War on domestic life in a number of combatant countries. The obvious way to begin such a discussion is to examine the direct consequences of wartime mobilisation on the material conditions of the people. Chapters 1 and 2 in part one introduce demographic data on this and related themes. They provide an explicitly comparative perspective whicn enables us to grasp some of the key similarities and differences in the responses of the populations of the major combatant countries to the upheaval of war.

The chapters in part two provide further documentation and discussion of the effects of the war on conditions of life and standards of living. The contrasts in the degree of deprivation suffered by civilian populations on opposing sides are vividly documented for the Central Powers by the essays of Sieder on Vienna, Scholliers and Daelemans on occupied Belgium, Triebel on Germany, and for the Allies by Fridenson for France, and by Dewey and Reid for Britain.

These essays form the foundation for the third and fourth parts of the book, which deal with the role of women in wartime economy and society, and with the efforts of diverse groups, working both within and outside government circles, to promote the stability of the family in wartime. Two central conclusions emerge here. The first is the relatively minor degree to which the sexual division of labour was disturbed by the war. Robert shows conclusively that the war represents not the opening of new opportunities for women, but rather the end of a trend of high female participation rates in extra-domestic employment in France. Similarly, Thom and Daniel offer strong correctives to the view that the war transformed the pattern of women's industrial work in Britain or Germany. It is only in the service sector, that is in white-collar jobs, that we can see the long-term effects of the war in diversifying the occupational distribution of the female labour force.

The second salient argument which arises is the similarity in the pronatalist outlook and policy initiatives of many groups in the major combatant nations concerned with protecting family life from the corrosive effects of the war. Huss's illustrations of the messages contained in pronatalist postcards, Soloway's discussion of the language of the British eugenics movement, Weindling's study of social hygiene and the German medical profession, and Usborne's description of parallel German efforts to promote childbirth as woman's 'active service' all point in the same direction: towards the emergence in wartime of a broadly based campaign to ensure that the war did not undermine traditional patterns of authority within the family or the traditional sexual division of labour.

Reulecke's essay on middle-class youth movements in Germany describes a radically different response to what contemporaries called the 'crisis' of the family in the period of the First World War. The search for a new kind of masculine loyalty antedated the war but took on a new urgency for some unsettled and romantic individuals. This quest for community turned away from the family towards the Männerbund, or heroic men's league. After a relatively quiet phase in the mid-1920s, such groups reappeared in a new and more sinister form. The adoption by the Nazis of facets of this phenomenon, replete with anti-feminine and anti-familial rhetoric, shows that one must not exaggerate the extent to which the war crisis led to a revival of the cult of the family. Those who survived the war spoke in discordant and contradictory voices. Some fled from the family and all it signified, but on the basis of the evidence presented in these essays, more returned to family life readily and with relief.

The demographic impact of these different campaigns for and against the family is very difficult to estimate. We know that nuptiality rates recovered after the wild fluctuations of the war, but in the cases of Britain and France, this may have had less to do with ideological currents than with changes in patterns of emigration and a narrowing of the age and social difference between marriage partners.[9] We know as well that the decline of fertility which had set in well before the war continued at least for another two decades after it.[10] And we know that despite an increase in the divorce rate after the war in a number of different countries, the family life-cycle after the war was not radically different from that before the outbreak of hostilities.[11]

In effect, the cumulative and collective impression of these essays in the social, cultural and demographic history of the 1914–18 war is to reveal the dialectical or contradictory character of the conflict. First, it disturbed family life by military and industrial mobilisation; but secondly, it released social and political forces which helped restore family life in its older forms.

Of course, counter-tendencies and exceptions may be noted. As Reulecke has shown, other forms of masculine bonding and association also emerged in this period. Many such developments were class-specific, requiring us whenever possible to move from the discussion of national to cross-sectional trends, as the essays by Reid and Fridenson on the effect of the war on the British and French working class demonstrate. The way forward is clearly towards more local and regional studies, of the kind presented by Sieder on working-class Vienna, through which the true texture of the war experience may be recaptured.

When such studies are available they will enable us to see to what extent the civilian populations of the major combatant nations sustained the war effort and, despite bereavement, deprivation, and stress of all kinds, still managed to preserve the fundamental features of pre-war family life. The inferences which may be drawn from these studies may go further still. Just as Charles Maier has shown that the power of industrial elites was first challenged and then reinforced by the 1914–18 war,[12] so the essays in this book suggest that the full effect of the war was to restore pre-war social forms rather than to undermine them. Perhaps it was only natural that the catastrophic human losses of the war led to a reinforcement of family life in its aftermath. Perhaps it was understandable that ex-soldiers, many of whom returned home defeated and disillusioned, insisted that their place within the family was preserved or even enhanced. Perhaps some women even welcomed the restoration after 1918; certainly few people asked for their opinion about an issue central to their welfare and their lives. But the weight of evidence from many quarters seems to point towards the view that, in terms of the social history of the European family, the First World War was more a conservative than a revolutionary force.

Richard Wall
Cambridge Group for the History of Population and Social Structure
Jay Winter
Pembroke College, Cambridge

Notes

1 P. Renouvin, 'L'opinion publique et la guerre en 1917', *Revue d'histoire moderne et contemporaine*, 20 (1968). 1–17. J.-J. Becker, 1914. Comment les Français sont *entrés dans la guerre*, Paris, 1977.
2 J.-J. Becker, *The Great War and the French people*, trans. A. Pomerans, Leamington Spa, 1986.
3 A. Prost, *Les Anciens Combattants et la société française*, Paris, 1977.
4 J. Kocka, *Facing total war. German society 1914–18*, trans. B. Weinberger, Leamington Spa, 1984; L. Burchardt, 'The impact of the war economy on the

civilian population of Germany during the First and Second World Wars' in
W. Deist (ed.), *The German military in the age of total war*, Leamington Spa,
1985.

5 B. Waites, *A class society at war*, Leamington Spa, 1987; M. Barnett, *British food
policy during the First World War*, London, 1984; A. Marwick, *The deluge. British
society and the First World War*, 1965; K. Burk (ed.), *War and the state*, London,
1983.

6 P. Fridenson (ed.), *1914–1918: L'Autre Front*, Paris, 1977; J. Hinton, *The first
shop stewards' movement*, London, 1974; D. Englander and J. Osborne, 'Jack,
Tommy and Henry Dubb: the armed forces and the working class', *Historical
Journal*, 21, 1978; D. Gill and G. Dallas, *The unknown army*, London, 1986;
T. Wilson, *The myriad faces of war*, London, 1986.

7 F. Thébaud, *La Femme au temps de la guerre de 14*, Paris, 1986; G. Braybon,
Women workers of the First World War, London, 1981; J.-L. Robert, 'La C.G.T.
et la famille ouvrière 1914–1918, première approche', *Mouvement Social*, 22
(1981).

8 Original contributions to the 1982 conference not included in this volume were:
by George Steiner, Clive Trebilcock, Jonathan Steinberg on the overall cultural,
economic and political background to the war; by Joseph Ehmer on working-
class family life; by David Hiebert on the psychological consequences of the war;
by Eve Rosenhaft on juvenile delinquency in Germany; by Joan Austoker on the
social hygiene movement in Britain; by Miklos Teich on German and British
scientists and food policy; and by Adelheid Grafin zu Castell, Reinhard Spree,
Patrick Festy, and Madeleine Beard on demographic aspects of the war. Festy's
article was published as: 'Effets et répercussions de la première guerre mondiale
sur la fécondité française', *Population*, 39 (1984), 977–1010.

9 J. M. Winter, *The Great War and the British people*, London, 1985, ch. 8;
L. Henry, 'Les Perturbations de la nuptialité résultant de la guerre de 1914–
1918', *Population*, 20 (1966).

10 A. Coale, 'The decline of fertility in Europe since the French revolution' in S. H.
Behrmann (ed.), *Fertility and family planning*, Ann Arbor, 1965.

11 Winter, *The Great War*; and J. Ehmer, 'Family life as a model of working-class
life in Vienna in the period of the Great War', paper delivered to conference on
The European Family and the First World War, Pembroke College, Cambridge,
1983.

12 C. Maier, *Recasting bourgeois Europe*, Princeton, 1977.

I
COMPARATIVE
PERSPECTIVES

I

COMPARATIVE
PERSPECTIVES

1
Some paradoxes of the First World War

J. M. Winter

One of the aims of this book is to examine a previously neglected facet of the social and economic history of the First World War. All too often, the perspective adopted in studies of the conflict has been that of the rulers rather than that of the ruled, of those who fashioned military, economic and social policy rather than of the ordinary men and women who either joined up or who had to make a living, look after their families, and simply survive the varied pressures of war. The official view was promulgated in many of the 128 august tomes commissioned by the Carnegie Endowment for International Peace to describe the domestic war effort. Most of the authors were men whose wartime duties gave them a particularly intimate familiarity with the formulation and implementation of policy in wartime. And while these accounts are essential reading for any student of the 1914–18 conflict, they suffer from the drawbacks of all 'official histories', which usually reflect how history looked to the officials.

This book offers more a complementary than an alternative approach, in the belief that we must go beyond traditional administrative and political studies in order to reach hidden facets of the history of those for whom wartime social and economic policy was fashioned. It is primarily for this reason, therefore, that we have chosen the family unit as the focal point for a discussion of the impact of the First World War on European society.

In the essays which follow, two central themes emerge. They are, first, the way in which the expansion in the power of the state impinged upon virtually all areas of domesticity and community life; and secondly, the way in which a war that destroyed the lives of millions and crippled millions more, created conditions which acted not to weaken but rather to strengthen family ties and the institution of marriage. This opening chapter will discuss some demographic evidence which throws light on the first of these two salient themes.

It is a commonplace to speak of the growth of the power of the state in wartime. Scholars have long been aware of what are known as the concentration and displacement effects of war. That is to say, economic historians have charted the impact of war on the progressive absorption into central government of services and functions previously in private hands. They have shown as well that war changed the level of taxation the population had been prepared to tolerate in order to pay for those services. In other words, the centralisation of economic activity in wartime displaced upward the share of gross national product occupied by the state. Whatever the nature of decontrol following the Armistice or claims about the need to return to the *status quo ante bellum*, these structural changes have been irreversible.[1]

Several of the essays in this book document the complex meaning of these changes for the working and domestic lives of ordinary people in the period of the 1914–18 war. This initial essay will introduce a demographic dimension to this discussion.

We shall argue that one of the central paradoxes of the war is that in the case of Britain, a conflict of unprecedented carnage created conditions – both political and economic – which accounted for a surprising and unplanned improvement in life expectancy among the civilian population. In France, some groups registered improvements; others did not. But on balance life expectancy among French civilians was about the same as it would have been had no war occurred. In a war which severely tested the endurance and economic strength of all combatant, this was no mean achievement, and contrasts sharply with a wide array of evidence about the toll the war took on civilian health in the Central Powers. Indeed, the success of the war effort in Britain and France to defend public health by defending living standards was, we shall argue, one of the prerequisites of military victory.

At the outset, let us note the limitations of this argument, which is intended to be suggestive rather than conclusive. In the space of an essay we simply cannot examine the broad range of demographic data on civilian health in the war period for any one combatant country, let alone for several. Even if space permitted, though, serious gaps in the statistical record preclude comprehensive analysis of the issues raised here. Our intent, therefore, is simply to explore the implications of the analysis of one essential source – life table statistics.

These data are useful in two ways. They permit spatial comparisons, and they enable precise modelling of the way the war deflected pre-war demographic trends. The disadvantage is that similar data are not available for all combatants. German and Austro-Hungarian data are not as complete as those we have used with respect to Britain, France, Belgium (and in the case of non-combatant Sweden). It is therefore impossible to make precise comparative statements about the differing impact of war on the populations of the Central and Allied Powers. What we can offer is an indication of the nature and direction of the wartime deflection of pre-war mortality trends.[2]

Our aim, therefore, is to examine the impact of the wartime state on the survival chances of civilian populations by a simple exercise in comparative demographic history. The structure of our argument is straightforward. First, we present demographic data on mortality rates in wartime Britain and France. Secondly, we contrast them with similar data which describe the deterioration in survival rates in Belgium and in Germany during the war. Thirdly, we examine evidence on mortality patterns in neutral Sweden. Fourthly, we comment on the light this analysis throws on the workings of the war economy in France and Britain, before turning to the more problematic cases of the Central Powers.

It is important to reiterate the real variation in the quality and reliability of the data used in this study. They are most useful in helping to illuminate the British and French experience of the wartime state. Data on Belgium may deepen the discussion, but they cannot contribute decisively to our overall argument. This is essentially for three reasons. First, the invasion, defeat and occupation of Belgium by the German Army were bound to upset vital registration in such a way as to require us to place a substantial margin of error around any calculations using wartime data. Secondly, it is unclear precisely what constituted the 'state' in occupied Belgium. The German Army undertook many key tasks, but some remained in the hands of civilian authorities. Since the Germans claimed initially that they were in Belgium simply to make war on France, we cannot adopt either an 'imperial' model (like British India) or a 'collaborationist' model (like Vichy France) to describe the way political authority operated in Belgium. And thirdly, the fate of an occupied country, milked by Germany of material and human capital, is no sure guide to the demographic situation in Central Europe.

We have already noted the fact that the available German data are incomplete. Still, they do enable us to sketch the outlines of the story of the war's effects on mortality trends, and confirm the overall contrast between conditions on the two sides of the front lines. More systematic studies are required, though, before we may conclude confidently that the underlying source of demographic trends in Germany and Austria-Hungary was a failure of the war economy of the Central Powers as a whole.

However, the preliminary findings reported here are consistent with the view advanced by many scholars using non-demographic evidence that it was precisely on the level of defending civilian living standards that Britain and France succeeded whereas Germany and her allies failed.[3] On both sides, the state took on primary responsibility for the welfare of the home population. In Central Europe, the manifest inability literally to deliver the goods undermined the war effort, discredited ruling circles and brought down governments which had entered the conflict with powerful and wide-spread support. In Britain and France, in part because of the international economic resources they could muster, in part because of their ability to withstand the German blockade, and in part because of the effectiveness of war administration in distributing goods and services as between civilian and military needs, the state succeeded in fielding mass armies without prejudicing civilian living standards. Our demographic analysis tells one side of this story; it is hoped that future studies of a similar kind will illuminate the other.

Mortality patterns in wartime

One of the most difficult problems in assessing the impact of war on life expectancy is to establish a reliable guess as to what mortality levels would have been like had there been no war. Elsewhere we have provided a series of estimates of mortality levels for England and Wales which enable comparisons between a 'war estimate' of actual mortality in 1914–18 and a 'peace estimate' describing a counterfactual situation: the likely pattern of mortality over the war years on the basis of a progression of pre-war trends. The difference between these two estimates is a rough approximation of mortality attributable to the war.[4]

ENGLAND AND WALES

The data on Britain are abridged life tables reflecting the mortality experience of 1913–17 of the working-class male population insured by the Prudential Assurance Company. Unfortunately, no such data exist for the British population as a whole. Still, it is possible to use these data in order to estimate the impact of the war on male life expectancy at ages 16–60 among a sizeable part of the working class.

This exercise enables us to construct reliable estimates of the age-structure of British war losses in the 1914–18 conflict. It also led to the surprising finding that in 1916 and 1917, at ages above which men were likely to see active military service, that is, after ages 40–5, war-related mortality in Britain was either negligible or *negative*. In other words, the survival chances of older men in wartime Britain were actually greater than they would have been had the war never occurred. Figure 1.1 describes the two estimates of actual and hypothetical mortality levels; Figures 1.2 and 1.3 illustrate war-related deaths at ages 16–60 and 40–60 respectively. Positive figures clearly indicate war losses at ages at which men were eligible for

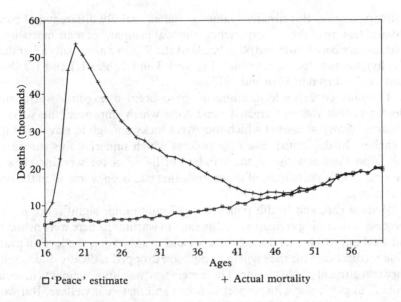

Fig. 1.1. Two estimates of male mortality, 1914–18. England and Wales, ages 16–60

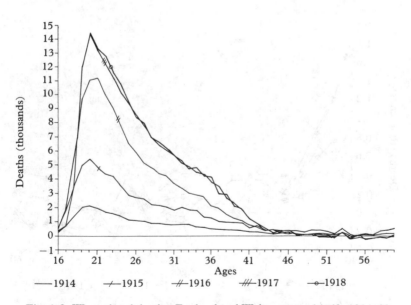

Fig. 1.2. War-related deaths, England and Wales at ages 16–60, 1914–18

military service. But negative values reveal an entirely different and para-doxical feature of the war experience: the 'war estimate' of male mortality at certain ages between 45 and 60 in England and Wales was actually *lower* than the hypothetical 'peace estimate'. Figure 1.3 and Tables 1.1 and 1.2 show that this occurred in 1916 and 1917.

The only conceivable meaning of the concept of *negative* war-related deaths is that the war created conditions which improved the survival chances of men at ages at which they were lucky enough to stay out of the trenches. In the British case, the process which underlay this surprising development was a rise in the standard of living of the working class in general, and in particular, of those strata that had been worst off in the pre-war period.

Medical care and health policy were of only minor significance in this process of declining civilian mortality rates in wartime. There were no major medical improvements during the war, and in any event, the level of avail-able medical care for the civilian population dropped radically due to mili-tary recruitment of physicians. There were wartime improvements in social policy, in particular with respect to infant and maternal welfare. But with the exception of measures (like rationing, control of the liquor trade, or rent control) which directly improved living standards, social policy changes were not behind wartime changes in mortality rates. These developments

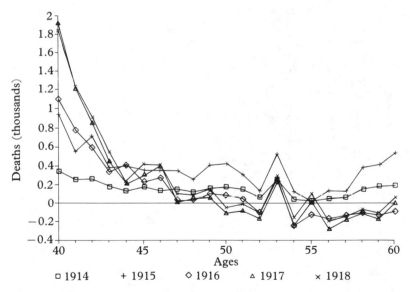

Fig. 1.3. War-related deaths, England and Wales at ages 40–60, 1914–18

Table 1.1. *English and Welsh war-related deaths, male population, ages 16–60, by age cohort*

Age group	1914	1915	1916	1917	1918	1914–18
16–19	4,280	10,753	17,128	16,052	16,339	64,552
20–24	8,803	22,214	48,922	62,899	61,038	203,875
25–29	5,042	12,493	26,699	39,386	38,815	122,435
30–34	3,841	9,599	17,064	26,636	26,082	83,222
35–39	2,300	5,524	9,563	16,368	16,593	50,349
40–44	1,204	2,996	3,217	4,628	4,784	16,829
45–49	753	1,737	665	838	1,159	5,152
50–54	689	1,520	55	−353	−24	1,889
55–60	673	1,601	−759	−715	−355	444
16–60	27,585	68,437	122,554	165,740	164,431	548,747

Table 1.2. *Percentage increase (+) or decrease (−) in deaths in England and Wales attributable to the 1914–18 war*

Age group	1914	1915	1916	1917	1918	1914–18
16–19	95.20	241.32	386.99	365.73	375.52	291.85
20–24	146.13	370.85	824.57	1073.91	1060.98	689.75
25–29	75.63	192.44	420.52	630.68	628.79	383.51
30–34	50.55	128.72	241.77	392.51	402.56	235.23
35–39	25.34	63.31	110.73	194.83	199.87	116.70
40–44	11.36	27.72	30.81	44.74	48.12	32.28
45–49	6.11	14.33	5.39	6.75	9.08	8.31
50–54	4.53	9.72	0.36	−2.36	−0.16	2.50
55–60	3.09	7.31	−3.37	−3.13	−1.52	0.40
16–60	29.41	73.14	132.04	179.68	179.50	118.26

were of importance in the long-term rather than in the short-term history of mortality decline. In sum, the overwhelming weight of evidence is that negative war-related mortality had a material explanation, rooted primarily in the workings of the wartime labour market. In Britain, aggregate earnings kept pace with prices, and the special conditions of wartime enabled the unskilled working class to substantially improve their earnings and thereby their nutritional levels.

There is a host of other demographic and medical evidence to support the view that better nutrition lay behind declining mortality rates in wartime Britain. The general rule is that the poorest gained the most, and that the overall decline in mortality was largely a reflection of a levelling upward of living standards and thereby of survival rates. It should be clear, therefore, why we have termed this unanticipated improvement in civilian health one of the paradoxes of the First World War.[5]

As yet no similar study has been conducted which would enable us to compare rigorously the British case with those of other combatant and non-combatant countries in the period of the First World War. In this chapter we shall provide some of the groundwork for these comparative studies by examining demographic data on three other combatant countries, and on one country which remained neutral throughout the conflict. Using the same procedures, we have replicated our earlier exercise in counterfactual demographic history using French, German, Belgian, and Swedish data. The choice of these countries was simply a function of the existence of comparable annual life-table statistics on which to base our estimates. In all cases, we assumed that the pre-war rates of decline in age-specific death rates continued throughout the war years. The counterfactual estimate of trends in the absence of war therefore takes into account the secular decline in mortality.

FRANCE

As we have already noted, French, Belgian and Swedish annual life tables exist both for male and female populations in this period.[6] It was possible, therefore, to replicate this demographic exercise for both the male and female populations of these countries at ages 16–60.

Let us consider the French case first. Dr Vallin has constructed life tables for the male and female population in the 77 uninvaded departments of France during the war years. These are the basic data used in this part of our study. From them we have derived estimates of the impact of the war on the survival ratios both of those who served in the French armed forces and of the rest of the French population.

Before we describe the results of this exercise, and their implications for our argument, it is necessary to test the reliability of the method we have employed to estimate war-related deaths. Figure 1.4 is a graph comparing the age-structure of male war-related mortality derived by our 'counter-factual' method with the age-structure of French war losses reported in the official military statistics. The fit between the two estimates is remarkably good between ages 20 and 46, despite the fact that the statistics of military losses (notoriously inaccurate anyway) are grouped by recruitment classes – that is when men reached age 20, the age of conscription – while our estimate is based on age at death. Again, if we compare total war losses, we find a striking parallel between the two estimates. We have concluded that male war-related deaths in France in 1914–18 totalled 1,206,213; the official military total is 1,243,500. In other words, we have accounted for 97 per cent of the losses described in the best alternative source on the subject of First World War casualties among the French population.

We may conclude, therefore, that the method we have adopted is an accurate guide to the toll in lives attributable to the war. The results of the analysis of data on the male population of the 77 uninvaded departments of France are presented in Figures 1.5–1.7 and Tables 1.3 and 1.4.

These statistics illustrate clearly a number of key features of this facet of the demographic history of the war. First, the catastrophic shape of male war-related mortality at ages under 40 which appears in Figure 1.1 for Britain looms even larger in the French case. And as we can see in Table 1.4, between ages 20 and 30, the proportional toll of the lives of young Frenchmen was simply staggering: these men suffered up to a tenfold increase in mortality, compared to a maximum seven or eightfold increase in the British case. French losses were also proportionately greater in the age group 30–9, reaching between a three and sixfold increase over the 'peace' estimate.

Secondly, we see as well from the data in Figure 1.7 that in 1916–17, war-related mortality in France turned negative at ages above 45. This *precisely* replicates what we found in the analysis of British data, and constitutes a

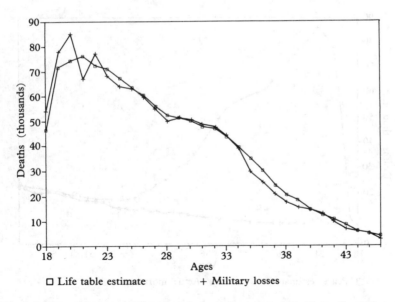

Fig. 1.4. Two estimates of French male mortality at ages 18–46, attributable to the First World War

Table 1.3. *French war-related deaths, male population, ages 16–60, by age cohort*

Age group	1914	1915	1916	1917	1918	1914–18
16–19	45,364	31,285	18,677	12,796	15,961	124,084
20–24	92,942	104,784	68,100	36,825	58,392	361,043
25–29	70,873	79,017	53,053	30,083	50,283	283,308
30–34	55,936	65,622	42,557	22,839	41,002	227,955
35–39	25,355	32,371	23,861	14,307	32,393	128,288
40–44	11,525	14,557	8,766	4,102	14,144	53,093
45–49	1,787	4,048	2,241	590	7,302	15,968
50–54	1,098	1,304	−276	−500	3,756	5,383
55–60	1,705	1,848	523	504	2,500	7,081
16–60	306,585	334,836	217,502	121,545	225,733	1,206,203

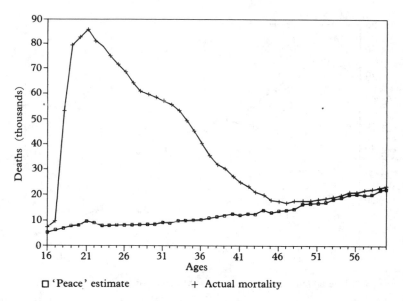

□ 'Peace' estimate   + Actual mortality

Fig. 1.5. Two estimates of male mortality, 1914–18. 77 Departments of France, ages 16–60

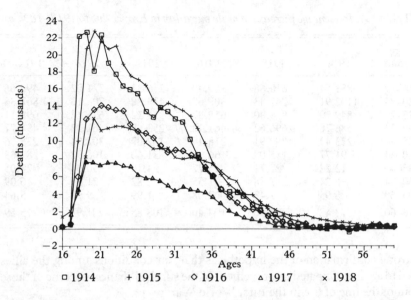

Fig. 1.6. War-related deaths, male population. 77 Departments of France, 1914–18

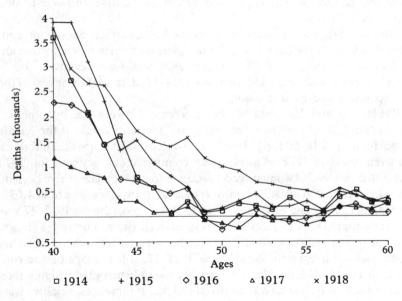

Fig. 1.7. War-related deaths, 77 Departments of France. Male population at ages 40–60, 1914–18

Table 1.4. *Percentage increase in male mortality in France due to 1914–18 War*

Age group	1914	1915	1916	1917	1918	1914–18
16–19	881.54	610.68	369.40	256.33	321.02	490.66
20–24	1102.91	1247.43	809.65	439.28	708.13	862.36
25–29	849.19	974.80	659.37	374.12	625.18	698.11
30–34	586.76	696.62	461.12	253.68	461.32	494.77
35–39	223.49	289.91	218.15	132.07	302.94	233.36
40–44	91.77	115.08	66.90	31.60	108.92	82.63
45–49	12.22	27.71	15.77	4.10	50.04	22.05
50–54	6.24	7.38	−1.55	−2.82	21.35	6.09
55–60	6.95	7.43	2.08	1.99	9.69	5.64
16–60	273.42	298.90	194.40	108.85	201.95	215.59

strong confirmation of the hypothesis that war conditions among the allies led to an unanticipated improvement in the survival chances of some of those out of the line of fire in the First World War.

The British data describe the mortality schedule of the male population in the war years. The French data enable us to discuss the impact of the war on life expectancy among women. This permits us to construct a much more complete picture of the nature and extent of wartime and war-related mortality in France.

On the whole, the analysis of data on the French female population confirms our hypothesis that the war did not increase civilian mortality overall; in fact, at certain ages, totals of war-related deaths are negative. This is clearly the case with respect to the years 1914–17; data on the last year of the war require a separate discussion.

Tables 1.5 and 1.6 describe the difference between the hypothetical 'peace' estimate of mortality and the actual mortality levels of the female population aged 16–60 for 1914–17. War-related deaths are the difference between the two. For example, our counterfactual estimate for 1914 suggested that 86,248 women aged 16–60 would have died had there been no war. In fact, 91,066 actually died; war-related deaths therefore total 4,638, or 5.37 per cent. The total increment to female mortality in 1915–17 was similarly slight: 8, 3, and 2 per cent respectively. But as Figure 1.8 shows, these aggregate statistics obscure the fact that negative war-related mortality was registered irregularly in each year 1914–17. It is perhaps best to conclude that until 1918, total female mortality was only marginally higher than it would have been had no war occurred and that at some ages, negative war-related mortality was registered.

In the final year of the war, though, a marked increase in mortality

Table 1.5. *French war-related deaths, female population, ages 16–60,*
by age cohort

Age group	1914	1915	1916	1917	1918	1914–18	1914–17
16–19	134	435	617	714	6,491	8,390	1,900
20–24	133	432	−126	301	9,998	10,739	741
25–29	152	435	51	271	12,027	12,935	909
30–34	475	740	454	285	12,310	14,263	1,954
35–39	499	809	421	257	8,424	10,409	1,985
40–44	510	792	−71	−187	4,968	6,012	1,045
45–49	694	854	451	27	3,794	5,820	2,026
50–54	845	1,301	492	254	3,666	6,559	2,892
55–60	1,197	971	99	167	1,761	4,195	2,434
16–60	4,638	6,769	2,388	2,089	63,468	79,323	15,885

Table 1.6. *Percentage increase (+) or decrease (−) in female mortality in France*
due to the 1914–18 War

Age group	1914	1915	1916	1917	1918	1914–18	1914–17
16–19	2.78	9.16	13.25	15.62	143.82	36.00	10.11
20–24	1.82	6.05	−1.77	4.31	146.58	30.38	2.60
25–29	1.91	5.60	0.67	3.66	165.29	34.03	2.96
30–34	5.94	9.48	5.91	3.81	167.45	37.22	6.31
35–39	5.73	9.45	5.06	3.13	105.14	24.91	5.88
40–44	5.67	8.85	−0.77	−2.07	55.21	13.31	2.89
45–49	6.82	8.40	4.56	0.27	37.69	11.58	5.04
50–54	6.91	10.68	4.02	2.10	30.57	10.79	5.93
55–60	6.56	5.28	0.54	0.92	9.51	4.57	3.32
16–60	5.37	7.90	2.81	2.48	75.93	18.68	4.66

occurred. This is apparent both in higher male mortality in 1918 (see Figures 1.6–1.7) and in the contrast between the age-structure of female mortality in 1917 and 1918, illustrated in Figures 1.9–1.10. In Figure 1.9, we can see that the counterfactual 'peace' estimate and the actual mortality estimate are virtually identical. But in Figure 1.10, we confront a very different picture. The hypothetical 'peace' estimate is dwarfed by actual mortality. The reason is clear: the 1918 data reflect the special circumstances and age-structure of the pandemic of influenza which afflicted Europe in the war's last year. The disease notoriously struck down young, healthy adults

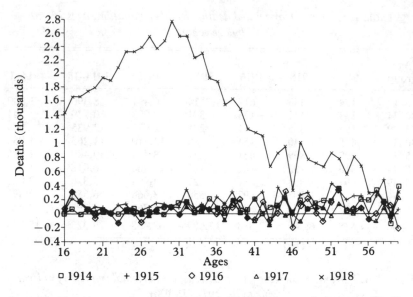

Fig. 1.8. French war-related deaths, 1914–18. Female population, ages 16–60

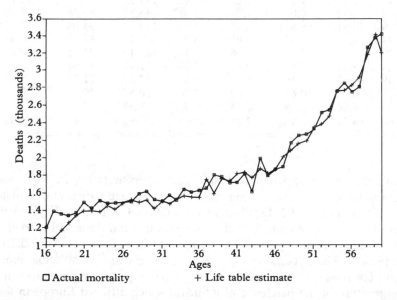

Fig. 1.9. Two estimates of French mortality. Female population, at ages 16–60, 1917

in the prime of life: this we can see in the atypical age-structure of mortality between ages 16 and 40, as well as in the relatively high levels of mortality between ages 40 and 60.

In *The Great War and the British People*, we weighed up the arguments for and against the view that war conditions weakened the resistance of civilians to contagious disease in general and to this killer mutant virus in particular. Our conclusion was that the 'Spanish flu', as it was known, was neither caused by the First World War, nor can its victims be counted among the casualties of the conflict. It is probably best, therefore, to conclude that this modern plague was *sui generis* rather than war-related. Consequently, increased mortality among French women in the last year of the war reflects a 'random shock' to the demographic system rather than the deleterious effects of war on civilian health.

The contrast between the huge increase in female mortality in 1918 and the relatively minor changes of the first three years of the war is illustrated in Figure 1.11. From this histogram, we can see clearly that with the exception of 1918 – a very special case – wartime mortality rates for French women were not uniformly or radically above those which would have been registered in the absence of war.

On the one hand, it is true that total mortality in the 'war' estimate

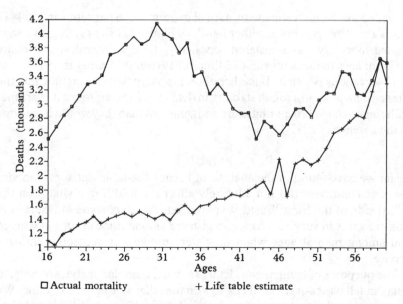

Fig. 1.10. Two estimates of French mortality. Female population, at ages 16–60, 1918

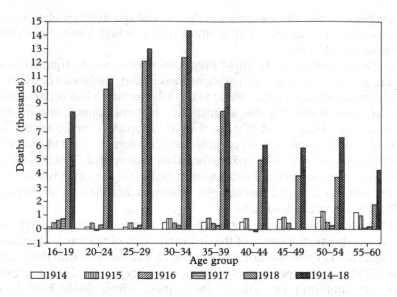

Fig. 1.11. French war-related deaths, 1914–18. Female population, ages 16–60, by cohort

exceeded the 'peace' estimate by a small margin – 4.66 per cent – in 1914–17 (see Table 1.6). But on the other hand, as Figure 1.8 shows, negative war-related mortality was registered repeatedly, though irregularly, at many different ages in the war years: 13 times in 1916 and 14 times in 1917 out of 44 observations per year. It is, therefore, probably best to conclude that the French data point to a rough stability in demographic conditions in wartime, with some groups prospering more and some less than they would have done in the absence of war.

BELGIUM

So far we have found in the analysis of French life-table statistics evidence that war conditions did not adversely affect the health of civilians on the Allied side of the First World War. Indeed, there are some indications of positive gains in survival chances registered among some groups of women and among men at ages when they were unlikely to see active military service.

For purposes of comparison, let us see what a similar analysis of Belgian data can tell us about survival chances on the other side of the front line. We have already admitted some of the intrinsic difficulties in handling such data concerning a country occupied and bled white, in both a human and a

Table 1.7. *Belgian war-related deaths, male population, ages 16–60, by age cohort*

Age group	1914	1915	1916	1917	1918	1914–18
16–19	4,033	3,303	2,621	1,964	1,564	13,485
20–24	7,477	7,469	7,058	6,486	5,582	34,072
25–29	5,553	5,858	6,277	6,683	7,168	31,538
30–34	3,544	3,871	4,231	4,582	4,916	21,145
35–39	2,842	2,894	3,073	3,204	3,414	15,426
40–44	2,124	2,233	2,388	2,524	2,604	11,873
45–49	1,718	1,717	1,672	1,617	1,652	8,376
50–54	1,199	1,130	1,087	1,117	1,125	5,656
55–60	1,292	1,096	919	791	528	4,628
16–60	29,782	29,574	29,326	28,968	28,554	146,200

Table 1.8. *Percentage increase in male mortality in Belgium due to the 1914–18 War*

Age group	1914	1915	1916	1917	1918	1914–18
16–19	390.00	313.68	247.74	182.15	142.74	253.52
20–24	518.87	520.51	491.84	451.98	392.83	475.41
25–29	401.48	430.76	464.30	501.37	539.74	466.75
30–34	209.34	227.84	251.67	274.39	290.51	252.02
35–39	170.69	176.67	190.28	200.66	214.71	190.31
40–44	114.76	120.11	126.21	133.78	139.93	126.99
45–49	77.99	77.64	76.86	74.21	75.34	76.41
50–54	43.91	41.28	39.06	39.32	39.56	40.58
55–60	32.18	26.58	21.58	18.21	11.89	21.86
16–60	165.34	163.28	160.67	157.75	155.03	160.39

material sense. But in two respects, the analysis of Belgian life-table statistics may be of use.

First, we see a case in which war-related mortality for both sexes is unambiguously positive. As we can see in Tables 1.7–1.10, no one can claim that civilian health improved in Belgium during the war. The war increased male and female mortality levels at ages 16–60 by 160 and 127 per cent respectively. This deterioration in public health occurred at all ages and in each war year. In Belgium, it was the German invasion, occupation and sub-

Table 1.9. *Belgian war-related deaths, female population, ages 16–60, by age cohort*

Age group	1914	1915	1916	1917	1918	1914–18
16–19	2,416	2,171	2,004	1,795	1,647	10,038
20–24	3,509	3,454	3,163	2,799	2,975	15,905
25–29	3,590	3,744	3,907	3,800	3,524	18,583
30–34	2,894	3,063	3,333	3,269	3,504	16,099
35–39	2,059	2,119	2,256	2,435	2,574	11,452
40–44	1,673	1,765	1,858	1,945	2,025	9,270
45–49	1,380	1,321	1,270	1,301	1,317	6,565
50–54	1,108	1,084	1,044	1,061	960	5,206
55–60	1,187	1,009	805	707	420	4,037
16–60	19,816	19,730	19,642	19,112	18,846	97,153

Table 1.10. *Percentage increase in female mortality in Belgium due to the 1914–18 War*

Age group	1914	1915	1916	1917	1918	1914–18
16–19	257.03	231.16	216.85	194.22	180.59	216.66
20–24	254.65	252.45	232.07	205.34	220.86	233.41
25–29	278.32	295.72	311.85	303.25	289.56	296.81
30–34	216.44	231.50	256.82	251.82	283.04	249.28
35–39	128.20	133.46	143.26	154.61	164.16	144.88
40–44	107.45	112.25	115.79	121.17	127.52	117.00
45–49	79.84	75.79	73.85	75.65	74.41	75.40
50–54	52.75	51.08	47.86	48.64	42.67	47.82
55–60	37.57	31.09	23.94	21.03	11.85	24.08
16–60	131.27	130.09	128.57	125.10	122.78	127.25

sequent fighting, which increased the death toll among the civilian population long before the influenza pandemic of 1918.

Secondly our results are entirely consistent with the arguments advanced by Scholliers and Daelemans in chapter 4 of this book. Their study shows that the conquest of Belgium opened a harsh period in the life of that country, perhaps even harsher than that of the Nazi occupation 30 years later (see pp. 140–53).

If anything, our estimates suggest that previous scholars may have underestimated the price the Belgian people paid for the war. The best estimate of

SOME PARADOXES OF THE FIRST WORLD WAR

Table 1.11. *Age-structure of German war losses, 1914–19*

Age	1914	1915	1916	1917	1918	1919	Total	%
15–19	10,866	26,105	24,920	38,474	54,052	1,626	155,953	9.22
20–24	99,782	184,512	141,069	104,390	140,126	4,452	674,331	39.86
25–29	74,617	108,927	74,903	53,392	75,491	2,574	389,904	23.05
30–34	36,953	68,018	50,712	37,348	52,748	1,981	247,760	14.64
35–39	14,965	34,359	35,887	27,220	33,579	1,557	147,657	8.73
40–44	2,702	9,700	10,891	16,287	17,744	1,276	58,600	3.46
45+	1,109	2,385	2,044	4,739	5,920	839	17,036	1.01
unknown	349	118	42	55	117	9	690	0.04
Total	241,343	434,034	340,468	281,905	379,777	14,314	1,691,841	100.01

Source: Bewegung der Bevölkerung in den Jahren 1914 bis 1919 Statistik des Deutschen Reichs, Band 276, Berlin, 1922, xlix.

total Belgian deaths in action is around 38,000. In addition, approximately 100,000 Belgian civilians are said to have died of war-related causes.[7] Our estimate of total male war-related deaths is about 146,000, which is close to the above estimate. But to this total we must also add 97,000 female war-related deaths, which seem to have been neglected in official Belgian statistics on war-related deaths. Our total of 240,000 war-related deaths, therefore, appears to be the most comprehensive indication of the deterioration in the condition of the Belgian people during the First World War.

GERMANY
Full life tables are not available for Germany in the period of the First World War. It is impossible, therefore, to offer the same degree of precision about German mortality trends as about those of other combatant countries. Still, with a little ingenuity, it may still be possible to provide some indication of the effect of the conflict on German mortality patterns.

Let us first consider the question of war losses. Over 1.6 million men were killed or died on active service in the German armed forces. In aggregate, this total exceeds that for France (1.3 million), but because of her larger population, Germany's losses as a proportion of men in uniform (15.4 per cent) or of men aged 15–49 (12.5 per cent) were slightly lower than those of France, which lost nearly 17 per cent killed of those who served and over 13 per cent of her male population at military ages.

Table 1.11, which presents aggregate totals of war dead by year and by age group, provides additional data on the extent to which the murderousness of the war was concentrated in cohorts under the age of 30. In Germany fully 40 per cent of the men who died were aged 20–5; the same age group constituted 37 per cent of British war dead.

Table 1.12. *German war-related deaths, male population, 15–59, 1914–18 using hypothetical progression of pre-war trends*

Age	1914	1915	1916	1917	1918	1914–18
15–19	11,826	27,358	27,550	44,550	70,120	181,404
20–24	98,765	180,178	136,052	106,800	145,738	667,533
25–29	73,602	105,844	71,035	55,093	83,601	389,175
30–34	36,428	65,622	47,701	38,947	61,242	249,940
35–39	15,066	32,648	33,162	28,499	39,593	148,968
40–44	2,913	8,602	9,356	17,238	21,370	59,479
45–49	1,493	3,570	3,295	8,644	10,580	27,582
50–54	888	47	89	5,299	7,710	14,033
55–59	−176	254	4,534	5,806	5,822	16,240
15–59	240,805	424,123	332,774	310,876	445,776	1,754,354

Table 1.13. *Percentage increase, German male mortality, 1914–18 over hypothetical progression of pre-war trends*

Age	1914	1915	1916	1917	1918	1914–18
15–19	103.33	237.75	237.75	383.06	603.91	313.96
20–24	757.63	1376.56	1042.46	815.95	1114.03	1021.51
25–29	613.55	883.95	592.01	463.28	705.32	651.74
30–34	301.16	548.68	403.94	332.26	526.86	422.12
35–39	103.44	231.04	240.86	214.97	307.85	217.21
40–44	17.86	52.33	57.35	104.91	130.95	72.70
45–49	8.07	19.74	18.49	48.41	57.51	30.43
50–54	3.81	0.20	0.37	22.01	33.02	11.85
55–59	−0.65	0.92	16.13	20.25	20.09	11.56
15–59	162.36	285.83	223.92	209.19	301.05	236.44

The appalling scale of casualties and the age-structure of war losses are features of the demographic history of the war common to the major combatants. The question remains, though, as to the effects of the war on the life chances of civilian populations. In Tables 1.12–1.15 we present the results of a comparison of a hypothetical 'peace' estimate of mortality trends for males and females in Germany over the years 1914–18 with recorded data on actual mortality in these years.

To make these calculations, we had to construct abridged life tables for German males and females at ages 15–59. There were some serious lacunae in the data used in this exercise, the results of which must therefore be treated with some caution. German statistics report age-structure and

Table 1.14. *German war-related deaths, female population, 15–59, using hypothetical progression of pre-war trends*

Age	1914	1915	1916	1917	1918	1914–18
15–19	400	1,583	2,728	6,138	20,571	31,419
20–24	446	848	2,072	5,107	24,636	33,109
25–29	663	549	1,355	3,847	23,053	29,468
30–34	449	555	1,610	3,627	18,373	24,614
35–39	393	672	1,532	3,934	13,052	19,583
40–44	329	652	1,940	4,944	10,553	18,418
45–49	435	1,111	2,010	3,991	8,380	15,928
50–54	149	−181	522	3,538	9,028	13,056
55–59	−149	−18	1,200	4,605	7,732	13,370
15–59	3,116	5,769	14,969	39,731	135,379	198,963

Table 1.15. *Percentage increase, German female mortality, 1914–18 over hypothetical progression of pre-war trends*

Age	1914	1915	1916	1917	1918	1914–18
15–19	3.98	15.81	27.32	61.58	208.38	62.98
20–24	3.82	7.29	17.93	44.35	215.09	57.26
25–29	5.37	4.45	10.98	31.46	188.57	47.93
30–34	3.56	4.44	12.90	29.09	148.47	39.43
35–39	2.78	4.80	11.09	29.02	97.48	28.43
40–44	2.43	4.76	14.14	35.44	75.19	26.72
45–49	3.01	7.76	13.99	27.40	55.19	21.86
50–54	0.83	−1.00	2.78	18.78	48.58	14.15
55–59	−0.68	−0.08	5.21	19.66	32.79	11.66
15–59	2.42	4.46	11.51	30.44	103.58	30.65

mortality for the war years only in quinquennial groups. Our method of analysis requires data on each year of life, in order to move a population through time. For instance, the counterfactual population aged 20 in 1914 would be 'aged' in our calculations over the following four years, to ages 21, 22, 23, and 24, and would be reduced annually by a specific number of people who would have died each year on the basis of an assumed mortality schedule. We have had to estimate annual totals of males and females at individual ages in order to construct our 'peace' estimate of what mortality patterns might have looked like had there been no war. Some error is bound to enter our calculations of war-related deaths at specific ages, but probably not enough to invalidate the results as a whole.

If we compare the totals in Table 1.12 on male mortality attributable to the war with the official data on war losses in Table 1.11, we can retain some confidence in the utility of the method we have devised to estimate war-related deaths. For instance, German military losses were given as 241,343 for 1914: our estimate of male war-related deaths for that year is 240,805, or over 99 per cent of the registered figure. There is a similar convergence between military statistics and our estimates in 1915 and 1916.

In the last two years of the war, our estimates of war-related deaths for males at ages 15–59 exceed the military statistics for war losses. In 1917, 281,905 Germans lost their lives while on active service; our estimate puts war-related male mortality at 310,876. The gap between the two figures is even greater for 1918: 397,777 war dead, compared to 445,776 war-related deaths. It is apparent that in the last two years of the war, civilian war-related deaths added to the price the German population paid for the war.

The analysis of female mortality statistics shows the same phenomenon. There is no evidence of a major upward deflection of mortality rates in the first two years of the war. Actual mortality totals exceed the hypothetical 'peace' estimates by only 2.4 and 4.5 per cent in 1914 and 1915 respectively. But thereafter the situation clearly deteriorated (1916 totals are 11.5 per cent above normal; 1917, 30.4 per cent, and in 1918, fully 103.6 per cent above the 'peace' estimate for those years).

Even if we discount some of the inflation of mortality totals in 1918 as a product of the influenza pandemic, it is still apparent that the period 1916–18 was one of severely worsening life chances among the civilian population of Germany. Our gross estimates, including flu, suggest that there were about 300,000 excess deaths among civilians aged 15–59 in the war years. Of these 100,000 were men; 200,000 women.

A straightforward comparison of 1913 mortality rates and those for the war years shows that other age groups also suffered an upward deflection in mortality trends. Table 1.16 is an index of German mortality rates for all age groups over the years 1913–23, taking 1913 as the base figure. The rough stability of female mortality trends in 1914–15 is apparent at ages 15–59, but we can already detect an upward trend in 1915 for children under age 15. For instance, female mortality rates at ages 5–9 in 1915 were up 40 per cent over pre-war levels. Similarly inflated rates were registered at these ages in 1916–17, well before the influenza epidemic had arrived. The years 1917–18 were also a time of deteriorating mortality conditions at ages over 60 for both sexes.

Given the absence of full statistical data, it is impossible to provide a reliable estimate of total war-related civilian mortality in Germany. If we reduce our estimate of 300,000 to take account of influenza mortality in 1918, which was not war-related, we must increase it to reflect the worsening

Table 1.16. *An index of mortality rates in Germany, 1913–23 (1913 = 100)*

Age group	1913	1914	1915	1916	1917	1918	1919	1920	1921	1922	1923
1	2	3	4	5	6	7	8	9	10	11	12
					Males						
1–5	100	100	128	116	117	161	136	106	90	83	84
5–10	100	106	143	129	150	189	130	111	89	72	78
10–15	100	107	122	129	154	215	136	119	99	89	90
15–20	100	204	337	315	535	706	186	155	116	108	111
20–25	100	856	1513	1196	997	1330	182	161	133	128	135
25–30	100	710	999	719	607	883	167	146	115	114	116
30–35	100	397	643	501	443	645	143	123	97	93	96
35–40	100	200	318	325	304	390	116	101	88	90	86
40–45	100	116	148	146	192	214	99	87	82	84	80
45–50	100	104	110	107	137	146	93	83	78	84	78
50–55	100	104	100	101	122	128	93	84	78	84	79
55–60	100	100	100	101	122	121	95	86	81	90	83
60–65	100	102	101	102	122	120	96	89	84	94	88
65–70	100	104	103	107	130	128	103	96	89	101	94
70–75	100	103	105	110	132	127	107	99	95	109	103
75–80	100	105	105	113	135	123	109	102	98	114	108
80–85	100	103	106	113	139	124	110	103	98	117	113
85–90	100	109	116	121	148	129	105	104	99	120	119
over 90	100	110	116	128	149	138	108	97	92	104	96
					Females						
1–5	100	99	127	117	119	174	137	104	86	80	83
5–10	100	101	141	133	144	207	133	108	81	68	72
10–15	100	104	124	131	153	239	146	115	89	85	88
15–20	100	103	112	122	156	292	168	136	104	103	106
20–25	100	102	103	110	135	290	156	146	111	115	113
25–30	100	104	101	106	126	272	143	145	108	110	107
30–35	100	103	102	108	124	234	136	132	104	103	97
35–40	100	102	102	107	126	191	125	118	100	99	94
40–45	100	102	103	108	129	165	120	109	97	98	92
45–50	100	101	103	109	126	155	116	106	97	99	96
50–55	100	102	100	105	123	150	114	106	96	99	95
55–60	100	100	100	104	122	135	112	104	95	100	94
60–65	100	101	99	103	118	127	107	99	95	100	94
65–70	100	103	101	107	123	130	111	103	94	103	97
70–75	100	102	102	110	126	132	112	105	97	109	103
75–80	100	106	105	114	133	133	116	107	100	115	110
80–85	100	104	105	112	135	133	119	108	101	116	111
85–90	100	110	111	124	154	141	112	104	99	120	119
over 90	100	106	109	124	150	145	111	106	86	102	104

Source: M. Meerwarth *et al.*, *Die Einwirkung des Krieges auf Bevölkerungs bewegung und Lebenshaltung in Deutschland*, Stuttgart, 1932, Table 20, pp. 60–1

conditions for both old and young dependants at ages under 15 and above 60. On balance, it is probably best to leave our estimate where it stands; after all, the absolute figure is not significant in and of itself. What matters is the unmistakable evidence it provides of a sharp contrast between the effect of the First World War on mortality conditions among Allied populations, on the one hand, and those of the Central Powers, on the other.

SWEDEN

One good test of the robustness of the method we have adopted is to apply it to data on a neutral country in the period of the war. The hypothesis to be tested is that counterfactual analysis will disclose only minor variations in mortality patterns in a country whose economy suffered only indirectly from the vicissitudes of the conflict.

The Swedish Central Statistical Bureau have provided us with the relevant data on pre-war trends and on mortality patterns over the war years. Again, we have assumed in our hypothetical analysis that the pre-war decline in mortality for both sexes continued throughout 1914–18 in a linear trend. Again, we have calculated a set of counterfactual mortality totals at ages 16–60 for both men and women and compared these with actual totals in each year 1914–18. The results of this part of our study may be found in Figures 1.12–1.13 and Tables 1.17–1.20.

As is apparent in Table 1.18, in 1914–17, the deflection of male mortality trends from the expected rate of decline was very slight indeed. The difference between the hypothetical total of male mortality in 1914–17 and the observed total is precisely 0.71 per cent. In the case of female mortality, the deflection was slightly greater, but not significant. Figures 1.12–1.13 show clearly the alternation of positive and negative totals for 'war-related' deaths, which in sum indicate a relatively stable mortality pattern over this period.

These graphs also demonstrate the impact of the influenza epidemic of 1918 on a neutral country. The toll of mortality due to this demographic disaster is evident: mortality was characteristically highest among young adult age groups, and overall, total mortality at ages 16–60 rose by 90 per cent.

These findings confirm two of our central arguments. First, they show that there is nothing in our method which produces the results we have presented. The exploration of the 'null hypothesis' – that is, that war had little or no effect on the mortality pattern of a non-combatant population – can dispose of the claim that our results are merely statistical artifacts. This is another indication that our method of comparing expected and observed age-specific mortality can provide important clues to the impact of war on demographic trends.

Secondly, the evidence we have presented of the huge toll of lives taken by

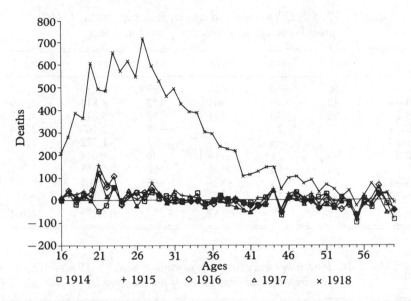

Fig. 1.12. War-related deaths, Sweden. Male population, 1914–18, ages 16–60

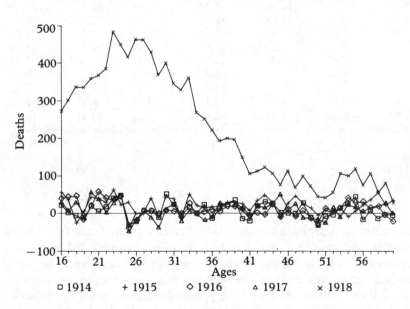

Fig. 1.13. Excess mortality, Swedish women, 1914–18, using hypothetical pro-gression of pre-war trends

Table 1.17. *Swedish war-related deaths, male population, 16–60,*
using hypothetical progression of pre-war trends

Age	1914	1915	1916	1917	1918	1914–18
16–19	40	100	69	69	1,237	1,455
20–24	−48	309	301	172	2,814	3,549
25–29	96	150	171	92	3,011	3,519
30–34	65	78	−39	−38	2,167	2,234
35–39	2	−3	−79	−97	1,272	1,095
40–44	−9	21	−114	−106	644	437
45–49	−29	56	−26	−66	415	350
50–54	13	−15	−144	−105	204	−48
55–60	−187	−79	−72	−208	116	−431
16–60	−58	618	67	−287	11,879	12,161

Table 1.18. *Percentage increase, male mortality, Sweden, 1914–1918,*
over hypothetical progression of pre-war trends

Age	1914	1915	1916	1917	1918	1914–18
16–19	4.12	9.54	6.71	6.62	55.87	23.10
20–24	−3.34	17.06	16.46	9.91	63.76	31.64
25–29	7.42	11.08	12.36	7.03	71.12	36.80
30–34	5.68	6.73	−3.68	−3.49	65.76	28.86
35–39	0.16	−0.24	−7.85	−9.97	54.36	16.84
40–44	−0.84	1.91	−11.54	−10.38	36.16	7.33
45–49	−2.63	4.78	−2.40	−6.25	26.29	5.83
50–54	0.83	−0.97	−10.27	−7.39	12.21	−0.63
55–60	−8.60	−3.47	−3.17	−9.62	4.59	−3.78
16–60	−0.49	4.93	0.56	−2.43	49.41	16.92

the influenza epidemic in a country far removed from the battle fronts helps establish the case that the war had little or nothing to do with the ravages of this killer disease. To establish this point fully, a similar study would have to be undertaken of influenza in other countries remote from the war. But the Swedish data we have presented suggest that these inquiries will further reinforce the view that the demographic history of the First World War and of the influenza pandemic must be strictly separated.

Table 1.19. *Swedish 'war-related' deaths, female population, at ages 16–60, 1914–1918, using hypothetical mortality schedule*

Age	1914	1915	1916	1917	1918	1914–18
16–19	5	75	113	67	1,247	1,506
20–24	131	199	197	171	2,048	2,747
25–29	−50	64	−31	−104	2,139	2,018
30–34	86	137	39	26	1,704	1,991
35–39	80	105	59	54	1,062	1,360
40–44	40	142	31	54	594	861
45–49	18	100	−15	64	431	597
50–54	−2	6	50	−10	345	389
55–60	11	176	59	82	467	795
16–60	318	1,005	502	404	10,036	12,265

Table 1.20. *Percentage increase, female mortality, Sweden, 1914–18, over hypothetical progression of pre-war trends*

Age	1914	1915	1916	1917	1918	1914–18
16–19	0.54	8.27	12.23	7.17	131.16	32.66
20–24	11.77	17.60	17.29	14.79	174.36	48.03
25–29	−3.99	5.05	−2.38	−8.14	165.91	31.63
30–34	7.97	12.68	3.51	2.29	150.74	36.17
35–39	7.61	9.95	5.58	5.15	100.88	25.84
40–44	3.83	13.54	2.90	5.06	54.60	16.22
45–49	1.70	9.61	−1.47	6.16	40.30	11.40
50–54	−0.14	0.47	3.66	−0.76	26.84	5.79
55–60	0.56	8.95	2.97	4.07	22.86	7.97
16–60	2.93	9.25	4.58	3.67	90.57	22.41

Living standards and the political economy of war

Let us consider the implications of these findings for our understanding of the nature of the wartime state. In Britain and France, the war inaugurated a unique and unplanned experiment in state capitalism. This is the most accurate description of the wartime situation, since the state controlled but did not own war-related industry.

The demographic data examined above suggest that in Britain and France the experiment was a success with respect to the well-being of the civilian population. As we have noted, the pre-war trend towards rising life expectancy was not adversely affected by the pressures of war. On the contrary; for some age-groups, gains were registered in advance of those which might have occurred had war not broken out.

These findings suggest that these two states succeeded in maintaining war production without prejudice to the standard of living of the civilian populations. This was achieved in part by social subsidies, among which rent control and separation allowances were crucial. But of even greater importance was the nature of political control over the war economy.

In Britain, the wartime state was never a business state. That is to say, output of war material was assured within a framework which placed national interests above employers' interests. The leaders of business knew this was so, and indeed disquiet about the situation led to the formation of two organisations to defend business interests at this time, the Federation of British Industry in 1916 and the National Confederation of Employers' Organisations in 1919.[8]

For organised labour, the war was a time of recognition and consequently of unprecedented growth in membership. And as Alastair Reid suggests in chapter 7, workers believed – with some justification – that state control of production and prices had improved their bargaining position and thereby had prevented a major deterioration in the purchasing power of their wages in wartime.

These wartime developments were not uniform. In the early phase of the war, perhaps until the end of 1915, when 'business as usual' was the rule, wages fell behind prices. But after mid-1916, when full economic controls were introduced, the gap was closed, and for some groups of workers, real wages rose.

Of course, there were exceptions to the rule that living standards in wartime Britain were maintained or improved during the conflict. Some groups, notably white-collar workers, the elderly, and *rentiers*, failed to benefit from the special conditions of war. But for the bulk of the British population, and especially the manual working class, the wartime state had succeeded where most it mattered, namely, in delivering the goods, both to the men in uniform and to the civilian population.

There are important parallels between British and French management of the war economy. In both cases, it makes little sense to speak of the wartime state apparatus as the 'executive committee of the bourgeoisie'. On the contrary, the history of war administration in France is largely one of the restriction of the power of employers to take advantage of their unusual market position. It is not that they abjured in principle the idea of making weapons of war at the expense of the state and the consumer alike. It is rather that the political economy of war prevented them from doing so.

This was achieved largely through the development of the consortium system, under the control of the Minister of Commerce, Clémentel. This apparatus of controls grew out of the military stalemate and the international character of the Allied war effort. Given the disastrous loss of men, material and industrial potential suffered by France in the first months of the war, there was simply no alternative to a growing reliance on British economic support. The British insisted upon the co-ordination of Allied supply policy, and set up international commissions to oversee wheat, coal, credit and shipping.[9] In effect this structure gave Britain virtual control of essential supplies required by French industry.

What the Allies were forced to do on the international level, Clémentel succeeded in doing within the French economy. He used the fact of French dependence on Britain to justify his control of supply to individual firms, thereby undermining their autonomy and room for manoeuvre.

This was no mean achievement. As one historian has put it, the French war economy was like a poker game, in which one player – the state – had all the chips, and the other – the employers – had all the cards. The businessmen with whom Clémentel dealt were well versed in the techniques of political influence, and on occasion their concern over the position of rivals or competitors seemed to approach or eclipse their anxiety over the outcome of the war. The risks Clémentel faced were substantial. But through the consortium system the essential balance was maintained: production and profits were secured, without undue pressure on prices and thereby on wages. Herein lies the source of the maintenance of living standards in wartime France, and for the fact that 'On the whole, the material circumstances of the French were not too unpleasant during the war.'[10]

Again, as in Britain, the full story was complex and irregular. Conditions later in the war were better than in the early hectic days of the conflict, when the economic and military problems confronting France appeared insurmountable. Even after the threat of early defeat receded, persistent administrative hitches made it a constant struggle for ordinary people to feed, heat and (especially) to clothe their families. As in Britain, housing conditions almost certainly deteriorated during the war.[11]

What is surprising is not that some groups suffered in wartime, but that the majority did not. An important part of the explanation lies in the structure of political control over the war economy, which kept living standards at an adequate level during the conflict. This is the material reality underlying the demographic data presented above.

The full significance of the political economy of war in determining civilian living standards emerges even more clearly when we consider some salient features of the war economy in Germany. As Dr Triebel's chapter shows, there is little doubt that levels of consumption were severely reduced in Germany in the course of the war. This was in part a reflection of the success of the Allied blockade, but it was also an outcome of chronic shortages of supply and administrative chaos leading to rampant price inflation.

Just as in France and Britain, there were those who suffered more under war conditions, and those who suffered less or not at all. Among industrial workers, those employed in munitions factories did best, but even their wages lagged behind soaring prices of consumer goods. Those in civilian production, and white-collar workers generally, were impoverished during the war.[12]

Despite some variation, all series on real wages tell the same story. The series compiled by Jurgen Kocka shows that average real wages were down by one-third in 1918 over the pre-war level. For those in war production, the damage was less: perhaps one-quarter of their purchasing power vanished during the war. But they were the lucky ones: real wages in non-essential industry and among most civil servants dropped by as much as a half during the war.[13] Kuczynski's and Bry's earlier estimates make similarly depressing reading.[14]

Consequently, nutritional levels were severely reduced for most sections of the civilian population. It is not at all surprising, therefore, that age-specific mortality levels at virtually all ages rose sharply after 1915.[15] Whatever the difficulties of making precise comparisons between conditions in Germany and in Britain and France, the overall trend is unmistakable. As the war went on, the Allies succeeded in creating a system which sustained both mass armies and the populations from which they were drawn and supplied; Germany and her allies failed to do so.[16]

It is true that the material resources on which the Allies could call were greater than those available to the Central Powers, and that the economic imbalance became progressively more lopsided as the war went on. The Allied blockade of Germany placed a greater stranglehold on the Central Powers than did the German blockade of the Allies. But the defence of living standards is a question of the successful maintenance of both supply and distribution. And it was primarily the chaotic nature of the wartime system of distribution of goods and services – including labour – which undermined the German war economy from within.

This can be illustrated with respect to two key areas of the management of the domestic economy: food policy and munitions production. Let us take each in turn. The failure of the Ministry of the Interior to ensure food supply in the first phase of the war led to the creation of a kaleidoscope of agencies in Germany, each acting largely on its own. When they felt it to be necessary, Deputy Commanding Generals bypassed the bureaucracy and acted to defend consumer interests in their respective areas. Employers too made it their business to ensure food supply for their labour force, whatever the cost.[17] Mistakes in agricultural policy over such essential questions as pricing or the link between nitrate stocks, fertiliser supply, and output exacerbated these difficulties.[18] In effect, conditions were ripe for a flourishing black market in food and other goods. However hard officials worked to enforce regulations, food prices dwarfed the official maxima. Given the chaos of market forces, and the inevitable irregularities of the harvest and of available transportation, it was inevitable that civilian nutritional levels fell steeply as the war dragged on.

When we turn to more general problems of munitions production, we see a similar absence of effective political control over economic affairs. The Imperial bureaucracy was too cumbersome and inefficient to run the war economy, and the Reichstag was too weak and unprepared. Consequently, from mid-1916, industrialists and the army ran the show by default, as it were.[19]

To understand this development, we must look back at the early stages of the formation of the German war economy. Early in the war, Walter Rathenau, head of the General Electric Corporation (AEG), went to Falkenhayn, then Prussian Minister of War, and sketched out a plan for the organisation of raw materials production. Consequently Rathenau became head of the Kriegsrohstoffabteilung (KRA), or War Raw Materials Department, and produced results by setting up war corporations to handle problems of supply. Rathenau was one of many men in industry who helped harness the benefits of German science – in particular, the Haber-Bosch process of nitrate synthesis – to the needs of war. Given serious shortages of imported saltpetre, essential for the production of explosives, this contribution was of crucial importance for the German war effort.[20]

As the war went on, though, it became apparent that scientific or entrepreneurial ingenuity alone would not win the war. The Allies' industrial strength was brought home forcibly by the Somme offensives of 1916. Allied firepower, more than anything else, convinced Germany's military and industrial leaders that only by a massive and more efficient programme of industrial mobilisation could she win the war.

In 1914, industrialists carried little weight in German politics. Two years later the situation was entirely different. Working closely with the High Command, German industrialists planned a new approach to the war effort. This was the Hindenburg Plan, which arose out of a letter which the Chief of Staff wrote to the Minister of War on 31 August 1916. Hindenburg demanded, among other things, a doubling of the output of machine guns and a trebling of the output of artillery by the spring of 1917.

This gigantic programme was devised and run by industrialists. Any worries they may have harboured about such *étatisme* in economic affairs were allayed by the fact that pricing and profit margins remained their responsibility. Labour too was given incentives to increase productivity: under the Auxiliary Service Law of 5 December 1916 a new framework of industrial bargaining was promulgated, no mean achievement in a country in which trade unions were still regarded by many military men and industrialists with suspicion or contempt. Labour mobility was to be strictly curtailed, but works councils were created to arbitrate disputes over permission to leave work.

This gives in outline what constituted the 'corporatist' solution to Germany's wartime economic difficulties. It left the management of the economy to particular interest groups – the large firms, working under the aegis of the army. The result was total chaos. Labour shortages remained chronic, in part due to the army's demand for more and more men for the front. The big firms benefited from the scheme, at the expense of pre-war competitors and the state. War production did increase, and by 1918 Germany produced more ammunition than at any time during the Second World War.[21] But profits soared, with the costs passed on to the army and then to the consumer, thus ensuring the progressive acceleration of the wartime inflationary spiral, as well as producing a subsistence crisis which undermined the regime itself.

The German war economy of the First World War presents, therefore, one of the earliest and least successful examples of a 'military–industrial complex' in action. The 'corporatist' solution to Germany's economic difficulties was no solution at all. This was because the waging of war – in economic matters as much as in other spheres – is essentially a political matter. However much they juggled the bureaucratic forms, Germany's leaders never established effective political control over the war economy whether in industry or in agriculture. They therefore could not hope to balance the claims of competing sectors for scarce resources. The result was a vast free-for-all, despite the strenuous efforts of the military authorities. As Gerald Feldman has demonstrated, under the pressure of industrial war, the German state dissolved and competing interest groups grabbed what they could get.[22]

The increasingly aggressive campaign of submarine warfare, as well as the exploitation of Belgium, the costs of which for its civilian population we have described above, were attempts to shore up this shaky economic edifice. The same fate that befell Belgium also faced Romania, and would have occurred in Russia, according to the Brest–Litovsk Treaty, had the war lasted until 1919 and beyond. But these policies were ultimately futile, since they could do little other than postpone the demise of a regime which collapsed from within.

In effect, victory in the First World War arose out of the economic resources, political skill and social cohesion of one side and the progressively more damaging shortages, political failures and social divisions within the other. This is the context in which to place the wartime history of the defence of living standards and the contrasting demographic patterns described above.[23]

As we noted at the outset of this chapter, these are issues which can only be rigorously explored in the light of more complete demographic data than are currently available. But when such data are examined, they will help establish both the full human costs of the war and to elucidate the complex political and economic parameters of the social and demographic history of the First World War. This task is in urgent need of attention, for, to paraphrase Clemenceau, the history of the wartime state is too serious a matter to be left to the political historians.

Notes

1 A. Peacock and J. Wiseman, *The growth of public expenditure in the United Kingdom*, Cambridge, 1967. See also A. L. Bowley, *Some economic consequences of the Great War*, London, 1927, pp. 116ff., for comments on tax levels before and after the war. On the French economy, see R. Delorme and C. André, *L'Etat et l'économie, un essai d'explication de l'évolution des dépenses publiques en France 1870–1980*, Paris, 1983, and F. Bock, 'L'Exuberance de l'Etat en France de 1914 à 1918', *Vingtième Siècle*, 1 (July 1984), 41–51.

2 Thanks are due to Dr A. Vallin of INED in Paris and Professor R. Spree of Berlin for advice on this point. Other basic demographic data on Germany may be found in: *Bewegung der Bevölkerung in den Jahren 1914 bis 1919, Statistik des Deutschen Reichs, Band 276*, Berlin, 1922; M. Meerwarth *et al.* (eds.), *Die Einwirkung des Krieges auf Bevölkerungsbewegung und der Lebenshaltung in Deutschland*, Stuttgart, 1932; and P. Marschalk, *Bevölkerungsgeschichte Deutschlands im 19. und 20. Jahrhundert*, Frankfurt am Main, 1984.

3 J. Kocka, *Facing total war. German society 1914–1918*, trans. B. Weinberger, Leamington Spa, 1984; J.-J. Becker, *The Great War and the French people*, trans. A. Pomerans, Leamington Spa, 1986; J. M. Winter, *The Great War and the British people*, London, 1985, esp. ch. 7.

4 Winter, *The Great War*, statistical appendix.

5 Winter, *The Great War*, chs. 5–7.

6 J. Vallin, *La Mortalité par génération en France, depuis 1899*, Institut National d'Etudes Démographiques, Travaux et Documents, Cahier no. 63, Paris, 1973; D. Veys, *Cohort survival in Belgium in the past 150 years*, Sociologische Studien en Documenten, vol. 15, Louvain, 1983.

7 The Belgian data do not reflect pandemic influenza mortality.

8 J. Turner, 'The politics of "organized business" in the First World War' in J. Turner (ed.), *Businessmen and politics. Studies of business activity in British politics, 1900–1945*, London, 1983.

9 D. P. Silverman, *Reconstructing Europe after the Great War*, Cambridge, Mass., 1982, ch. 1; K. Burk, *Britain, America and the sinews of war, 1914–18*, London, 1985.

10 J. F. Godfrey, *Capitalism at war. Industrial policy and bureaucracy in France 1914–18*, Leamington Spa, 1987.
11 Becker, *The Great War*, p. 325.
12 Becker, *The Great War*, p. 326.
13 Kocka, *Facing total war*, pp. 23, 89.
14 G. Bry, *Wages in Germany 1871–1945*, Princeton, 1960, pp. 305ff.; and J. Kuczynski, *Die Geschichte der Lage der Arbeiter unter dem Kapitalismus*, 38 vols., Berlin, 1967, vol. IV, pp. 329, 350. See also W. Zimmermann, *Die Einwirkung des Krieges auf Bevölkerungsbewegung, Einkommen und Lebenshaltung in Deutschland*, Stuttgart, 1932, pp. 200ff.
15 P. Marschalk, *Bevölkerungsgeschichte*, Table 3.18, p. 169.
16 L. Burchardt, 'The impact of the war economy on the civilian population of Germany during the First and Second World Wars' in W. Deist (ed.), *The German military in the age of total war*, Leamington Spa, 1985.
17 G. D. Feldman, *Army, industry and labor in Germany 1914–1918*, Princeton, NJ, 1966.
18 J. J. Lee, 'Administrators and agriculture: some aspects of German agricultural policy in the First World War' in J. M. Winter (ed.), *War and economic development*, Cambridge, 1975.
19 Feldman, *Army, industry and labor, passim*.
20 H. Pogge van Strandmann (ed.), *Walther Rathenau. Industrialist, banker, intellectual and politician. Notes and diaries 1907–22*, Oxford, 1985, introduction and entries for 1915; and L. F. Haber, *The poisonous cloud*, Oxford, 1986.
21 I am grateful to Hartmut Pogge van Strandmann for bringing this to my attention.
22 Feldman, *Army, industry and labor, passim*.
23 Burchardt, 'Impact', p. 61, and *passim*, for interesting comments on the ways in which the Nazis learned from the errors of 1914–18.

2
English and German families and the First World War, 1914–18

Richard Wall

The First World War separated and then estranged millions of young men from their society, past and present. The uniformity of this experience, it has been claimed,[1] underlays the many differences of rank, nationality and temperament that divided soldier from soldier, but the impact of the war on those not directly involved in the fighting is likely to have been even more diverse. The general direction of change is clear: the reorganisation of the economies of the combatant nations to meet the needs of war, the work of absent men taken over by women and youths, the collapse of living standards in many countries as more resources were poured into the production of machinery of war.[2] Less is known about the extent to which such changes operated evenly across society or were implemented with the same speed in different countries. The selection of the essays for the prevent volume was largely motivated by a wish to throw more light on such issues. Armin Triebel, for example, in chapter 5, questions whether the economic privations of the war years in Germany in any way lessened inter-class differences in consumption patterns, while, in chapter 7, Alastair Reid argues that there is no sign in Britain of the major erosion of the wage differential between skilled and unskilled that some scholars have seen as a marked feature of the war years.

Inevitably, comparative research which advances on such a broad front to cover differences in living conditions, relations between trade unions, employers and the state, changing work practices and social policy and family ideology will encounter difficulties: difficulties arising from the absence of comparative data, difficulties resulting from differences of approach.[3] The ideology of the war years makes the task of the historian doubly difficult as efforts were mounted to portray events in a particular way, leaving the reality obscured. Deborah Thom pertinently remarks, in chapter 11, that even the surviving pictorial evidence is not untainted by the exigencies of war propaganda.[4]

It is also a fact that the records of individual pressure groups are relatively more abundant and are certainly more accessible than are the experiences of 'ordinary' families. The dilemma for the historian is particularly acute when popular behaviour diverges widely from the ideal pattern being promoted by particular interest groups, as in the case of the campaign for larger families waged by the pronatalists. Even when it would appear that the population at large accepted the official ideology as when they bought post-cards whose message was flagrantly pronatalist, it is difficult to reconcile this acceptance with the continued sharp fall in marital fertility.[5]

One solution is to interview the dwindling band of survivors of the period. Oral history is represented in the present collection by Richard Sieder's chapter on working-class family life in wartime Vienna. Ways were found, concludes Sieder, to maintain the principle of the dominance of male authority within the family even in the absence of the father at the front. This is a useful corrective to claims that the patriarchal family was destroyed by the First World War,[6] and it is to the effect of the war on the family that the rest of this chapter will be devoted. The most obvious influence to discuss is the change in the composition of families and households resulting from the loss of so many millions of young men. But consideration will also be given to the impact on the quality of family life of the new employment opportunities that became available for women and the relationship between living standards and child health. To pursue the comparative approach we will consider Germany as well as England, drawing in particular on the censuses and surveys of the employment of women in war industries carried out by the Bayerisches Statistisches Landesamt,[7] and the papers of the Children's Care Sub-Committee of the London County Council. This immediately suggests a problem, which is that neither London nor Bavaria is likely to be fully representative of the national situations. The justification for proceeding in this way is simply that the data lay ready to hand. For obvious reasons, censuses are rarely taken during a war, while judged from the prominence given to child health in London by the Chief Medical Officer of the Board of Education in his reports covering the war period, the system of producing reports on the health of the school child was more fully maintained in London than elsewhere.[8]

The health of the school child

LONDON

There can be no doubt that living standards in Britain were less adversely affected by the war than were those of Germany. This much is clear from the contributions of Armin Triebel and Peter Dewey (chapters 5–6 below),[9] but it is not immediately apparent how great was the difference. Nor is it clear how quickly the difference was established, although in chapter 1 Jay Winter suggests that the life expectancy of the British working-class male, old enough to escape war service, had by 1916 improved on the pre-war situation. Even before 1916, however, we can now report there were signs of an improvement in the health of children attending public elementary schools in London.

Throughout the war, as indeed before it, the London County Council prepared weekly lists of the numbers of necessitous children fed at its expense during the school year.[10] These lists would appear to provide a more sensitive indicator of the changes over time in the level of need of an important section of the general population than is likely to emerge from an examination of the occasional survey of household budgets or annual data on mortality. But is the evidence of the lists entirely trustworthy?

Before presenting the data, their accuracy should not go unchallenged. The first and most obvious point concerns the process by which a child came to be defined as 'necessitous' and placed on the list. The initial selection was made by the child's teacher,[11] but a detailed investigation then followed into the circumstances of the family using the services of the School Care Committee, the School Attendance officer and the National Society for the Prevention of Cruelty to Children. The father's sickness or disability, intermittent employment or desertion of his family and the mother's 'immorality' or low earnings if she was the principal economic supporter of the family, could all result in a child being classed as 'necessitous'.[12] Much more, therefore, was involved than a subjective assessment of the child's nutritional state. In fact a report to the Children's Care Sub-Committee in March 1915 estimated that only about half of the necessitous children had subnormal nutrition and that not all of these were identified until they had undergone a medical examination. Furthermore, the ill-nourished children defined as 'necessitous' represented no more than a third of all the ill-nourished children on the Council's books.[13] There was also some delay in removing children from the list when circumstances changed. The policy was to review all cases every six months, but in March 1916 it emerged that some of the Woolwich case files contained no information other than original applications made sometimes a year earlier.[14] On the other hand, there are records of parents voluntarily withdrawing their children from the feeding list when the circumstances of the family improved.[15]

It would seem not unreasonable therefore to see the number of children on the Council's feeding lists as offering an approximate indicator of the degree of poverty in the community and, with more certainty, whether the incidence of poverty had increased over time. Prior to the war the Council was responsible for the feeding of some 35,000 children (see Figure 2.1). Immediately following the outbreak of war the total stood at 50,000 and rose rapidly to a peak of 75,000 in late September. Thereafter began a steady decline. By February 1915 fewer children were on the list than in February 1914; by September there were only slightly more than half the number of September 1913. Further advances followed. September 1916 represented a 30 per cent improvement over September 1915, and although the Autumn of 1917 was much as 1916, some 10 per cent fewer children were being fed in September 1918. The war also virtually suppressed the seasonal variation in the number of needy children. It had been customary prior to the war for the numbers of children on the feeding lists to fall during the spring and summer and rise during the autumn and winter, reflecting probably the cycle of economic activity.[16] During the war years this pattern was scarcely visible so strong was the downward movement in numbers.

For the first years of the war some further information is available. A rather complicated classification scheme had been devised to observe the effect of the war on the numbers of necessitous children, according to which each case was variously classified as 'chronic', military or directly or

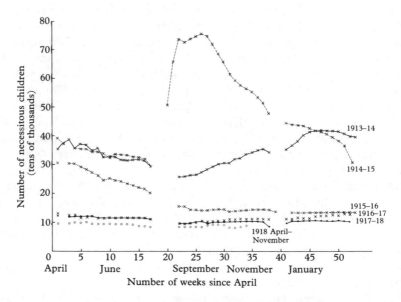

Fig. 2.1. Number of necessitous children fed by the London County Council, April 1913–November 1918. *Sources* 1913–14: London County Council Annual Report, vol. IV, Education, chapter XXX. Other years: Children's Care Sub-Committee, *passim*.

indirectly arising from the war. Too much credence in such a categorisation is perhaps unwise[17] and a summary only is presented in Table 2.1. Two months into the war in the average London borough, factors associated with the war had explained the presence on the Council's feeding lists of about 60 per cent of the families with necessitous children. Three months later war-related factors only accounted for some 38 per cent. On both occasions there was a very considerable variation in the experience of different London boroughs, no doubt reflecting the differing extent to which their local economies had been disturbed and the number of their inhabitants who had enlisted. How such factors may have altered the ability of families to support themselves will be considered later.[18] At this point we need only note that the evidence of the feeding lists indicates a major improvement during the war in the economic circumstances of some of the poorest sections of society. From a responsibility for the feeding of approximately 5 per cent of the school children prior to the war and just over 10 per cent of all school children in September 1914, the Council's obligations had been limited to 1.2 per cent of school children by September 1918.

Even in the autumn of 1914, however, only a small minority of school children were included on the feeding lists and for information on the health of the school child population in general, it is necessary to look elsewhere. Fortunately, throughout the war the Council continued its standard monitoring of the health and social conditions of all the children on the school rolls.[19] The nutritional status of three groups of children, entrants (who would have been aged between four and six), intermediate (aged eight) and leavers (aged twelve) is considered in Table 2.2. Again some apology is in order concerning the quality of the data. The classification of nutritional status relied on such bland categories as 'excellent' and 'subnormal', terms which it was difficult to define consistently between one inspection and another. These issues were widely recognised at the time. To cite one example from many, in 1914 the School Medical Officer for London observed that comparisons between districts in the standard of nutrition were particularly suspect due to differences of view between examiners and the definition of 'standard' as the perceived 'average' nutrition in the area concerned.[20] However, there is a case to be made against so complete a rejection of this evidence on nutritional standards. First, there are some regularities in the data for different areas that ought not to exist if assessments of nutritional level were so variable. For example it is noticeable that in areas as disparate as Cumberland, Cambridgeshire, Cardiff and London more boys than girls were reported as malnourished.[21] Secondly, it is worth noting that a special study of nutritional and health standards in London and Bedfordshire schools in 1917, which avoided many of the pitfalls of the routine inspection in that it involved a surprise visit to the schools, and the

Table 2.1. *War-associated poverty among London families with schoolchildren, 1914–15*

		3 October 1914 War-associated poverty[a] (%)	16 January 1915 War-associated poverty[a] (%)
1	Holborn	85	44
2	Westminster	75	—
3	Shoreditch	74	56
	Camberwell	74	39
5	Southwark	71	26
6	Bethnal Green	70	53
7	Hackney	67	35
	Wandsworth	67	—
9	Chelsea	66	—
10	Stoke Newington	65	50
11	Paddington	64	39
12	Poplar	63	12
13	Hammersmith	61	—
14	St Pancras	60	28
15	Battersea	59	29
16	Bermondsey	56	45
17	Stepney	54	38
	Fulham	54	—
19	Finsbury	52	42
20	Deptford	47	12
21	City	44	22
22	Kensington	43	—
	Islington	43	37
24	Lewisham	42	18
25	Hampstead	40	22
26	St Marylebone	35	41
27	Woolwich	33	12
28	Greenwich	32	16
29	Lambeth	28	39
	London	60	38

Note
[a] The category 'war-associated poverty' subsumes cases initially classified as 'military' or directly or indirectly due to the war, cf. notes 12 and 17. The percentages represent the incidence of war-associated poverty among all families with necessitous children.

Source
London County Council, EO/WEL/1/4, Report of Children's Care Organisers and Divisional Superintendents on unemployment and distress. The information was derived from the records kept on the families whose children were fed at the expense of the London County Council.

Table 2.2. *Nutritional standard of London school children, 1913–19*

| | Percentage with excellent nutrition | | | | | |
| | Boys | | | Girls | | |
	Entrants[a] (aged 4–6)	Intermediate (aged 8)	Leavers (aged 12)	Entrants[a] (aged 4–6)	Intermediate (aged 8)	Leavers (aged 12)
1913	31	22	26	33	25	31
1914	31	20	26	32	23	30
1915	32	21	29	32	23	33
1916	—	24	29	—	26	31
1917	31	21	27	31	22	29
1918	31	20	25	31	21	27
1919	29	20	26	29	22	28

| | Percentage with subnormal nutrition | | | | | |
| | Boys | | | Girls | | |
	Entrants[a] (aged 4–6)	Intermediate (aged 8)	Leavers (aged 12)	Entrants[a] (aged 4–6)	Intermediate (aged 8)	Leavers (aged 12)
1913	11	16	15	9	14	14
1914	8	10	13	7	9	12
1915	5	9	7	5	8	6
1916	—	9	7	—	8	6
1917	5	9	6	5	8	6
1918	5	7	5	4	7	5
1919	6	8	5	6	7	5

Note
[a]Third term only in 1917
Source
London County Council, Annual Report of Council 1915–19, vol. III, Public Health

examination by one competent Medical Officer of a random set of children according to a common schedule and including children temporarily absent, yielded results which were considered broadly compatible with those of the routine inspection.[22] Unfortunately the sample was a small one; no more than 273 London children, all leavers, were actually examined and the results on close scrutiny are somewhat different from those of a general inspection in that far fewer children were classed as enjoying no more than 'fair nutrition'.[23]

It would appear prudent, therefore, to consider the percentages of children with subnormal or excellent nutrition in Table 2.2 as indicative of the variation in the state of nutrition from year to year, rather than as defining a specific nutritional standard. In fact there is very little sign of a trend in the proportion of children considered to enjoy excellent nutrition, no more than hints of an increase between 1914 and 1915, followed by a subsequent fall in the later years of the war. It is quite otherwise with the much smaller group of children with subnormal nutrition which shrank quite markedly between 1913 and 1914 and 1914 and 1915, stabilised in 1916, only to experience a further decline in 1918. This is the group that most closely approximates to the children included on the Council's feeding lists and it is reassuring that both sets of figures imply that there was an improvement in the nutritional state of disadvantaged children during the First World War.

It may also be the case that the circumstances of the poorest children improved more quickly than those of children in general. Such a 'catching-up' process is implied by the absence of any marked change in the percentage of children considered as enjoying 'excellent nutrition'.[24] Nor is it likely that the improvement was confined to the mere quantity of food consumed. The relationship of nutrition to health is notoriously complex. In his 1915 Report the Chief Medical Officer of the Board of Education stressed the unsuitability rather than the insufficiency of food as the cause of poor nutrition and went on to list other factors to which consideration needed to be given. Amongst these were a lack of fresh air, exercise and sleep, uncleanliness, premature employment and disease.[25] For nutritional standards to have risen, therefore, it seems likely that there was some reduction in the incidence of ill health, acting in combination with improvements in the quality of child care.

From other records on schoolchildren maintained by the London County Council it would appear that this was indeed so. Table 2.3 presents information on the degree of cleanliness of the heads and bodies of London schoolchildren between 1913 and 1919. Those children deemed to have clean heads were free of infestation with either nits or vermin while clean bodies excluded both those infested with vermin and the merely dirty and the number of such 'clean' children rose steadily between 1913 and 1915 and again after 1917. This striking improvement in the standard of cleanliness could be taken as a sign of the success of the Council's efforts to enforce parental compliance with its own definitions of acceptable cleanliness, but it is difficult to see how such an improvement could have been maintained in the absence of any parallel change in the standards of home care. A similar case could be made out in connection with dentition, where the proportion of twelve-year-old children with four or more decayed teeth declined steadily from one in ten in 1913 to one in twenty in 1919 (Table 2.4). More direct parental involvement is evident in the quality of children's clothing and footwear (Table 2.5), and it is significant that again the most obvious signs of improvement occurred before 1916 and after 1917.[26]

Table 2.3. *Cleanliness of London schoolchildren 1913–19*

| | Percentage whose heads were found to be clean | | | | | |
| | Boys | | | Girls | | |
	Entrants[a] (aged 4–6)	Intermediate (aged 8)	Leavers (aged 12)	Entrants[a] (aged 4–6)	Intermediate (aged 8)	Leavers (aged 12)
1913	87	87	87	73	67	67
1914	88	87	89	74	66	69
1915	90	88	91	76	69	73
1916	—	89	91	—	69	71
1917	90	89	91	75	69	70
1918	93	92	92	80	71	73
1919	93	93	93	81	74	74

| | Percentage whose bodies were found to be clean | | | | | |
| | Boys | | | Girls | | |
	Entrants[a] (aged 4–6)	Intermediate (aged 8)	Leavers (aged 12)	Entrants[a] (aged 4–6)	Intermediate (aged 8)	Leavers (aged 12)
1913	78	72	73	77	74	75
1914	82	75	75	81	78	78
1915	82	77	78	81	78	81
1916	—	79	79	—	81	82
1917	83	80	79	82	81	82
1918	90	86	84	89	85	85
1919	92	89	88	91	90	89

Note
[a]Third term only in 1917
Source
London County Council, Annual Report of Council 1915–19, vol. III, Public Health

There can be little room for doubt, therefore, that there was an improvement during the war in the health of school children, and, if the information on clothing is reliable, in the ability of their parents to provide for them. The changes were general encompassing cleanliness, dentition and nutrition and a number of related illnesses. One further piece of evidence, however, needs to be presented. The analysis up to this point has relied on cross-sectional data, but it was not just the case that each successive school year was better fed and better cared for than its predecessor. Data on a cohort of London school children, aged eight in 1915 and twelve in 1919 indicate that the circumstances of this particular group of children had altered for the better during the course of the war (Table 2.6).[27] For example the percentage

Table 2.4. *Dentition of London schoolchildren,*
1913–19

Percentage of leavers[a] with four or more decayed teeth		
	Boys	Girls
1913	10	9
1914	9	8
1915	7	7
1916	7	6
1917	6	6
1918	7	7
1919	5	4

Note
[a]Aged 12
Source
London County Council, Annual Report of Council
1915–19, vol. III, Public Health

Table 2.5. *Clothing standard of London schoolchildren, 1913–19*

	Percentage with good clothing and footwear					
	Entrants[a] (aged 4–6)	Intermediate (aged 8)	Leavers (aged 12)	Entrants[a] (aged 4–6)	Intermediate (aged 8)	Leavers (aged 12)
1913	54	48	49	55	51	52
1914	56	48	53	57	52	56
1915	58	51	53	58	55	58
1916	—	52	54	—	56	59
1917	56	52	51	56	54	55
1918	58	51	51	58	55	55
1919	60	54	51	60	56	56

Note
[a]Third term only in 1917
Source
London County Council, Annual Report of Council 1915–19, vol. III, Public Health

suffering from defective nutrition had almost halved, 74 per cent of girls now had clean heads against 69 per cent in 1916 and 89 per cent now had clean bodies, whereas formerly 78 per cent had been in this fortunate position. Some of the documented changes are not unexpected. The arrival of the second dentition would naturally reduce the extent of dental decay, at

Table 2.6. *Comparative health of a cohort of London schoolchildren at ages 8 and 12*

Percentage with	Boys (aged 8)	Boys (aged 12)	Girls (aged 8)	Girls (aged 12)
Nutrition: excellent	21	26	23	28
defective	9	5	8	5
Clean heads	88	93	69	74
Clean bodies	77	88	78	89
Teeth: all sound	46	55	47	57
>4 decayed	11	5	11	4
Vision poor	18	22	20	23
Enlarged tonsils	11	9	12	11
Heart defects and anaemia	3	4	3	5
Deformities (excluding rickets)	2	2	2	3

Source
Report of School Medical Officer to London County Council, 1919 as cited in *Annual Report of the Chief Medical Officer to Board of Education*, 1919, Cd 995, 1920, p. 28

least initially, and there are signs that school leavers were generally better fed and cleaner than were eight-year-olds. Nevertheless the improvement in the cleanliness of this cohort of children between 1915 and 1919 and in the numbers within it with subnormal nutrition, exceed what might have been anticipated from a comparison of this group with those who were already twelve years old in 1915.[28] Similarly, successive groups of entrants appear to have been in better circumstances when they reached the age of eight than were earlier cohorts.[29]

GERMANY

If we now turn to the health of German children during the war a very different picture presents itself. Direct comparison is difficult because of the subjective nature of the assessments of satisfactory nutritional status. Nevertheless the surveys of two schools in the Saxon city of Chemnitz (now KarlMarxstadt) in 1916 and 1918 indicate clearly a marked decline in the health of school children. Cases where the nutritional status of the child was deemed unsatisfactory rose from 11 per cent to 17 per cent in the one school and from 5 to 16 per cent in the other. By December 1918 over half of all the children were showing signs of anaemia compared with just a third two years previously (see Table 2.7). Tuberculosis was also on the increase.[30] This is in sharp contrast to the situation in London where in the latter stages of the

Table 2.7. *Incidence of unsatisfactory nutrition, anaemia, and tuberculosis among schoolboys, Chemnitz, Saxony, 1916–18*

Percentage of boys with given condition	Brühlvolksschule		Andresvolksschule	
	December 1916	December 1918	December 1916	December 1918
Nutrition: unsatisfactory	11	17	5	16
Anaemia	37	51	34	53
Tuberculosis	4	6	3	5

Source
Thiele in Max Rubmann (ed.), *Hunger*, Berlin, 1919, as cited by Johannes Lehmann, 'Untersuchungen über Gewicht, Grosse und Hämoglobingehalt des Blutes der Kinder einer Bürgerschule in Löbau', *Zeitschrift für Schulgesundheitspflege*, 33(3) (1920), p. 68.

war nutritional standards were only subject to a gentle decline and actually rose for the most disadvantaged (see above, Table 2.2).

How soon in the war the health of German children could be affected is evident from data on children in another Saxon town, Weissenfels, in 1915 and 1916 (Table 2.8). The sample was a small one but as early as 1916 two of the three measures proffered as a guide to nutritional status (height and weight) indicated a worsening situation. The more subjective assessment, the classification of the children according to whether their nutrition was considered good, average or bad, did not indicate any decline in the standard of nutrition.[31] Clearly, the evidence from these schools is totally insufficient to establish any general conclusion as to the state of health of German children in wartime. This must await the analysis of surveys from other towns. However, it is equally clear that the percentage of Saxon children whose nutrition was thought to be unsatisfactory was increasing up to threefold at a time when the percentage of London children of below normal nutrition was declining. And in this regard there is no reason to consider the London position as unrepresentative of the English wartime experience.[32]

The employment of women in wartime

BRITAIN

A major development during the war years in Europe was the number of women drawn into new employment, moving moreover into sectors of the economy previously dominated by men and frequently into jobs vacated by men. One view would be to see the expansion of female employment as a

Table 2.8. *Nutritional standards of school entrants, Weissenfels, Saxony, 1915–16*

	Boys (N = 62)		Girls (N = 62)	
	1916	1918	1916	1918
Mean weight (kg)	19.2	17.9	17.5	17.0
Mean height (cm)	106.0	105.0	105.0	102.0
Mean nutritional score[a]	1.3	1.4	1.5	1.6

Note
[a]Mean score on a scale where 1 = good; 2 = average; 3 = bad
Source
Oschmann, 'Der Einfluss der Kriegkost auf die Schulkinder', *Zeitschrift für Schulgesundheitspflege*, 30(2) (1917), p. 58

great emancipating process, a precondition for the award of the right to vote, and a harbinger of the increased participation in the labour force in later decades.[33] An alternative view is that the changes were not that dramatic and their impact questionable. Thus, it has been pointed out that many of the new jobs existed only for the duration of the war and that women who were employed on them did not feel that their lives had been fundamentally altered through employment on war work.[34] A closer look at the statistics on women's wartime employment in Britain suggests other reasons why such conflicting interpretations could arise.[35] We may consider first women's share in the workforce in particular industries and services. In July 1914 certain occupations not surprisingly were dominated by women. For example more than two-thirds of those employed in hospitals, the clothing trades, teaching, in certain textile industries such as linen and silk, and in the tobacco industry, were women. At the other extreme women constituted negligible proportions of the workforce in engineering, dockyards and arsenals, transport, iron and steel, shipbuilding, mines and quarries, the building trades, and docks and wharves. Four years later the situation was essentially unchanged. The ten employments that had contained the largest proportions of female workers in July 1914 did so again in November 1918 while of the ten employments with fewest female workers in 1914, no more than two had moved out of this category by 1918. The absence of significant change is explained easily enough. During the war most sections of the economy gained female workers but few added them in sufficient numbers to alter their position relative to other sectors. Indeed the only employments to become significantly more feminised between 1914 and 1918[36] were the civil service, factories, dockyards and arsenals, municipal tramways, banking and finance, other tramway and bus operations, the Post Office and the cycle, motor and aircraft industry.

A different perspective is suggested by considering the number of women working in each employment sector in November 1918 relative to the number so employed in July 1914.[37] For every 100 women employed in 1914, 150 were employed four years later, but much greater increases were recorded in certain sectors than others. In 24 sectors, out of a total of 62, the number of women more than doubled, in 12 it more than quintupled and there was more than a hundredfold increase in the numbers employed in factories, dockyards and arsenals. Without doubt it was changes such as these that captured the imagination of contemporary observers, and others. The perspective may be shifted again, however, by focusing on the numbers of women who had entered the different employment sectors between July 1914 and November 1918.[38] From the point of view of the woman war worker this must be the most relevant record of her war service and it emerges that the record was a most diverse one. Some 23 per cent of all women had entered the commercial sector and close on 16 per cent had joined the workforce in the factories, dockyards and arsenals. Much smaller percentages, though more than 5 per cent of all women entering employment between 1914 and 1918, had joined the civil service, or taken up employment in the engineering or miscellaneous metal trade sectors (which included the ordnance and small arms factories). Otherwise the 'additional' women workers were liberally spread around all the remaining sectors with the important exception of some 'traditional' female employments within the clothing, textile, paper and food trades which occupied fewer women at the end of the war than at the beginning.

A fair conclusion would be, therefore, that during the First World War many women moved into a broad range of employments. By November 1918 the number of women employed had increased by some 50 per cent compared with July 1914, but although certain employments had proved more popular than others, only a handful had become significantly more 'feminised' during the course of the war. However, no data considered so far can throw any light on how many women entered employment for the first time. For information on this point it is necessary to turn to a much smaller survey of working mothers conducted in 1917 by the Chief Education Officer of the London County Council for the Children's Care Sub-Committee.[39] The survey was probably conducted in a hurry in that only nine of the London boroughs were included and the category 'working on account of the war' seems to have been interpreted differently in different areas. For example it is difficult to believe, particularly given the results for the other boroughs, that none of the mothers of school-age children in Wandsworth had been in employment prior to the war. If, therefore,

Table 2.9. *Employment of mothers with school-age children in selected London schools, 1917*

School district	Children on roll	Mother working outside home (%)	Per cent of all working mothers		
			Employed in munitions	Working on account of war	Working prior to war
Bow	1,500	17	0	66	34
Poplar					
(1)	1,552	9	18	82	—
(2)	857	14	0	85	15
Bethnal Green					
(1)	868	33	2	49	49
(2)	991	10	10	90	—
Fulham	736	14	10	42	48
Chelsea	271	39	6	73	20
Kensington					
(1)	826	21	21	33	46
(2)	560	39	12	58	30
Hammersmith					
(1)	544	46	22	40	38
(2)	1,162	25	29	37	34
Wandsworth					
(1)	710	11	5	95	—
(2)	772	11	22	78	—
(3)	611	13	17	83	—
(4)	474	8	21	79	—
(5)	899	12	15	85	—
Woolwich					
(1)	596	7	—	—	—
(2)	1,078	6	—	—	—
(3)	406	6	—	—	—

Source
London County Council, Report of Education Officer to Children's Care Sub-Committee, 30 March 1917

Wandsworth is excluded from consideration together with the school districts in other boroughs for which the data could be suspect, it would appear that it was the war that had provided the first extra-domestic salaried work experience for approximately two-thirds of the working mothers (Table 2.9, columns 4 and 5).[40] On the other hand the mother working regularly for a wage was still the exception. In none of the areas was a majority of mothers employed outside of the home.[41] The highest percentage was recorded in Hammersmith where 46 per cent of the mothers of school-age children worked away from the home, but the average (median) was only 13 per cent and in Woolwich, despite the proximity of the armaments factory, just 6 per cent of the mothers reported work of this nature.

From time to time anxieties surfaced concerning the increasing neglect and consequent indiscipline of children arising from their mothers being out at work. For example this was one of the factors considered relevant by a conference on juvenile delinquency held in Lambeth in February 1917.[42] The survey of 30 March 1917 reported a range of opinions. For Bow it was stated that there were no cases of children being locked out of the home through their mother being at work, nor was there any special sign of neglect in Poplar apart from some difficulty in supervising children over the lunch hour (1–2 p.m.). On the other hand mothers in Woolwich were said to have had great difficulty in finding anyone to look after their children and that children were being kept away from school, presumably to care for their young siblings. Nevertheless in October 1917 working mothers were still being held responsible in part for the prolonged absence from school of certain children.[43]

On the assumption that this survey of March 1917 does provide an accurate guide to the extent and nature of married women's employment in wartime London, these fears would appear to be greatly exaggerated, at least for this mid-war period. Unfortunately no hard evidence is available on how the situation may have varied either side of March 1917. All that we know at present is that in the two Bethnal Green districts rather more mothers could be expected to be employed in 'normal times' than the 33 per cent and 10 per cent respectively, recorded in March 1917; that there are suggestions of married women refusing work once they had received the separation allowance from the War Office; and that other women were pressurised out of work by health officers concerned for the welfare of their children.[44] It is also clear that in the early stages of the war, it was rather the lack of employment for women that was the problem.[45] Further discussion of the significance of issues such as these for the nature of the family economy will be reserved for later. What does deserve emphasis here is that even when women were employed on munitions, the work differed from their normal work in terms of product and location but remained routine and unskilled. In 1915, for example, the Apprenticeship and Skilled Employment Association argued against the employment of boys in munitions factories on the grounds that there was an adequate supply of female labour for unskilled work such as cartridge testing. Boys, the Association maintained, should be reserved for skilled work for which they received no training in the munitions factories.[46] There may be an element of special pleading in this particular case, but it illustrates clearly the attitude that younger males should be trained for skilled, and eventually more highly paid work. By contrast it was considered acceptable for women to perform the necessary unskilled tasks with of course no prospect of continued employment, let alone advancement, once their services were no longer required for the war effort.

Table 2.10. *Pre-war employments of women*
employed in Bavarian war industries, 1917

	Women employed	
Employment sector	no.	(%)
Agriculture	1,057	1
Commerce: office workers	904	1
shop assistants	1,865	2
Industry: factory workers	37,421	41
seamstresses	4,214	5
Hotels and inns	1,134	1
Day labour	2,296	3
Domestic service	16,697	18
High status[a]	243	0
Without employment	25,034	28
Total	90,865	100

Note
[a]*im gehobenen Beruf*
Source
Die Frau in der bayerischen Kriegsindustrie, Beitrage zur
Statistik Bayerns, 92, Munich, 1920, p. 12. All four
Armeekorpbezirks are included (Munich, Würzburg,
Nuremberg and Ludwigshafen)

GERMANY

The pattern of female employment in wartime Germany, may be illustrated from the detailed occupational censuses conducted in 1917 and 1918 by the Bayerisches Statistisches Landesamt.[47] Table 2.10 shows that more than four in ten of all the women employed in war industries in Bavaria in 1917 had had previous experience of factory work. Another 18 per cent were former domestic servants, which English evidence shows was one of the least preferred employments.[48] It needs to be stressed, however, that in certain key respects the census differs from the survey conducted by the Education Officer of the London County Council for the Children's Care Sub-Committee (cf. Table 2.9) in that all women were included providing they were employed in war industries. The London survey was restricted to mothers of school-age children by no means all of whom were involved in war work. It is difficult to know, therefore, what to make of the fact that in Bavaria only 28 per cent of the women employed in the war industries had not been employed prior to the war whereas of the London working women, two-thirds were apparently drawn into the labour market by the war. At first

Table 2.11. *Pre-war employments and employment expectations of women working in 21 war factories, Bavaria, November–December 1918*

| | Munich Armeekorpbezirk | | | | Würzburg Armeekorpbezirk | | | |
	Expected employment after the war no.	(%)	Pre-war employment no.	(%)	Expected employment after the war no.	(%)	Pre-war employment no.	(%)
Agriculture	36	0	161	2	19	1	30	2
Commerce: office worker	377	4	278	3	2	0	5	0
shop assistant	112	1	242	3	6	0	32	2
Industry: factory worker	4,197	46	2,005	22	63	4	101	6
seamstress	497	5	712	8	163	10	183	12
Hotels and inns	138	2	460	5	7	0	36	2
Day labour	193	2	500	6	136	9	102	7
Domestic service	812	9	2,656	29	50	3	156	10
High status	37	0	91	1	16	1	44	3
Home-keeping[a]	716	8	1,390	15	182	12	823	53
Undecided	2,019	22	—	—	923	59	—	—
Unemployed	—	—	46	0	—	—	13	1
Not previously employed	—	—	593	6	—	—	42	3
Total	9,134	100	9,134	100	1,567	100	1,567	100
Same employment as pre-war	3,501	38			430	27		
Change of employment	3,151	35			197	13		
Not previously employed[b]	463	5			17	1		
Undecided	2,019	22			923	59		
Total	9,134	100			1,567	100		

Notes
[a] Not otherwise employed
[b] i.e. too young for employment pre-war
Source
Die Frau in der bayerischen Kriegsindustrie, Beiträge zur Statistik Bayerns, 92, Munich, 1920, pp. 74–5. Due to rounding, the percentages may not always sum to 100.

sight it would appear that the war marked less of a turning-point in the employment histories of the Bavarian women than it did for these London mothers. However, it should perhaps be stressed again that the majority of mothers in the London County Council's survey were not employed.[49]

In 1918 the Bayerisches Statistisches Landesamt conducted a further census of female employment in two of its administrative divisions (Armeekorpbezirks).[50] This second census is of particular interest in that on this occasion a question was asked concerning employment expectations after the war and the results are presented in Table 2.11. In the Munich

Armeekorpbezirk, for instance, more than a third of the women expected to continue in the same employment as pre-war. Just over another third anticipated a change of employment while more than a fifth remained undecided. The situation in the Würzburg Armeekorpbezirk was somewhat different in that only a quarter intended to retain their pre-war employment and just over a tenth to change with nearly 60 per cent remaining uncertain. Compared with the position prior to the war, in both Munich and Würzburg, many more women expected to be involved in industry and many fewer in domestic service and in home-keeping, not otherwise employed.[51] What this seems to imply is acceptance of industrial employment by considerable numbers of women who had occupied service or domestic roles prior to the war. But appearances in this case are deceptive. In their commentary on the results of the census prepared during the course of 1919, the Statistisches Landesamt noted how women's employment expectations had not been realised with the increasing likelihood of unemployment. The result was that in 1919 the 'traditional' female task of housewifery featured much more prominently in women's roles than they had anticipated in 1918.[52] The most convincing interpretation would appear to be the following. Since these women were reacting to the volatility of the labour market, their previous anticipation of industrial work was no more 'modern' than their acceptance in 1919 of a more domestic role was 'traditional'. Rather the women were presumably adopting a flexible approach to employment opportunities consistent with their family obligations. In this respect their abandonment of employment, and the substitution of one job for another can be seen as part of a quite different tradition, visible in both the eighteenth-century village, where depending on the season women combined agricultural and craft tasks, and in the decades following the Second World War, when women moved frequently between part-time employments within the burgeoning service sector of the economy.

The Statistisches Landesamt also collected information on the arrangements that women employed in war industries had made for the care of their children. They were no doubt prompted in this by similar concerns to those that motivated the Children's Care Sub-Committee of the London County Council (cf. above, Table 2.9). The results should have given some degree of satisfaction to those concerned about a decline in the standards of parental care during the war. According to the Landesamt's survey, a little over a tenth of all children under the age of 19 were left unsupervised and just under a fifth of all children without any provision having been made for their meals during the day (see Table 2.12). Only a handful of children were reported as being alone at night. The survey also helps to identify the significance of the informal care networks on which working mothers could rely. Almost 30 per cent of their children were cared for in their own homes,

RICHARD WALL

Table 2.12. *Child care arrangements of mothers employed in Bavarian war industries in Munich and Würzburg Armeekorpbezirks, 1917*

Care category (%)	Children[b]	
Boarded out	31	
At home, in care of relatives[a] or neighbours	29	
Self-supporting or apprenticeship	8	83
Dayboard	5	
Institution: with board	10	
Institution: no board	3	
Supervised: no board	2	18
Unsupervised	13	
Alone at night	0	
	100	
Total number	30,000	

Notes
[a] Principally grandparents
[b] Aged <19, where mothers were employed in Bavarian war industries
Source
Die Frau in der bayerischen Kriegsindustrie, Beiträge zur Statistik Bayerns, Munich, 1920, p. 63. The mothers in the survey worked in the first (Munich) and second (Würzburg) Armeekorpbezirks. Due to rounding, percentages may not sum to 100

mainly by grandparents but also by neighbours. A considerable amount of informal care may also be hidden within the 31 per cent of cases of 'boarding out', as institutional provision is separately noted.[53] It is likely that child care arrangements in England were equally 'informal'. What little evidence there is points to the traditional practice of having older siblings, usually sisters, care for the younger (cf. above). The use of children as child supervisors seems not to have been envisaged in the Bavarian survey.

The impact of the war on the family and household

The more general issue of the relationship between the war and the changing composition of the family and household has been bedevilled by a general lack of data. After 1861 the Registrar-General in Britain, unlike his continental counterparts, abandoned any attempt to use the decadal censuses to

62

Table 2.13. *Distribution of household by number of persons, Bavaria, 1910 and 1916*

Household size	1910 (%)	1916 (%)	Change 1910–16 (1910 = 100)
1	6	9	135
2	14	16	118
3	16	18	113
4	17	17	103
5	15	14	95
6	11	10	88
7	8	7	83
8	5	4	79
9	3	2	77
10	2	1	77
⩾11	2	2	72
	100	100	
Total households	1,431,693	1,446,383	101

Source
Die Kriegs-Volkszählungen vom Jahre 1916 und 1917 in Bayern, Beiträge zur Statistik Bayerns, 89, Munich, 1919, p. 108

measure family and household structure as opposed to their size, and it was only after the Second World War that interest in the topic was resumed.[54] Such information as there is suggests rather lower headship rates (fewer adults heading households) in 1921 than in 1911 but leaves unresolved the other major issue, which is how much change arose directly from the war and how much was determined by developments that would have occurred anyway, or were only loosely connected to the wartime situation. The more detailed information that has recently become available on household membership in four English communities in 1911 and 1921 makes it clear for the first time how residence patterns changed during the decade that spanned the war.[55] At the same time it has to be admitted that the assignment of any change specifically to the war remains a matter of probability rather than of proof. In the absence of documents which enable one to trace families and households through the war this must inevitably be so.[56]

GERMANY

In the case of Germany some additional information is available owing to a census being taken in Bavaria at the end of 1916.[57] A comparison of the distribution of households by size in 1916 with that at the time of the last census in 1910 indicates that at this mid-point of the war, households were considerably smaller on average than six years earlier (Table 2.13). There were

Table 2.14. *Distribution of persons by household size, Bavaria, 1910 and 1916*

Household size	Males			Percentage female		Females		
	1910 (%)	1916 (%)	Index of change 1910–16 (1910 = 100)	1910	1916	1910 (%)	1916 (%)	Index of change 1910–16 (1910 = 100)
1	1	1	90	66	77	2	3	159
2	5	6	97	57	64	6	8	133
3	10	12	94	54	62	11	14	129
4	14	16	88	52	59	15	16	117
5	16	16	82	51	58	16	16	107
6	15	15	78	51	57	14	14	98
7	13	12	74	50	55	12	10	92
8	9	8	72	50	55	9	7	87
9	6	6	70	50	54	6	5	84
10	4	4	71	49	53	4	3	83
≥11	6	5	65	47	51	5	4	77
All	100	100	—	51	58	100	100	—
Total number	3,231,142	2,590,861	80			3,427,605	3,590,063	105

Source

Die Kriegs-Volkszählungen vom Jahre 1916 und 1917 in Bayern, Beiträge zur Statistik Bayerns, Munich, 1919, pp. 106, 111. Due to rounding the percentages may not always sum to 100.

substantially fewer persons living in large households. In fact the larger the household the greater the reduction.[58] Conversely, more persons in 1916 were living in households of four persons or less with the greatest increase, of more than a third, involving persons who lived on their own. On the other hand these changes were not dramatic enough to alter significantly the distribution of households according to size. Even in 1916 only 9 per cent of households consisted of one person compared with 6 per cent of all households in 1910 (see Table 2.13, columns 2–3).

This analysis can be supplemented by taking into consideration the number of persons of each sex present in each size category of household (Table 2.14). Not surprisingly there were fewer males present in 1916 than in 1910. Males had departed from households of all sizes but particularly from the larger households. This too is not particularly surprising since, on average, there would have been more males originally in such households. It may be noted, however, that there was little overall effect on the proportion of either males or females living in households of various sizes (Table 2.14, columns 2–3 and 7–8). Nor was there a marked change in the proportion of females in each size category of household. This was despite the fact that there were some 60 per cent more women living alone in 1916 than in 1910. It is a moot point as to whether the stability in the distribution of households by size or the increase in the number of women living alone is the more significant. The latter represents the 'expected' outcome of the war situation but in fact the nature of the household as a consumption unit, as reflected in the way adults were distributed between households, changed little despite the pressures war imposed on the household budget.[59] The mean size of the household itself only fell a modest 9 per cent between 1910 and 1916.[60] On the other hand it needs to be emphasised that significant changes in the composition of households are not precluded by the lack of major changes in the distributions of households by size or persons per household. Indeed the Statistisches Landesamt considered it probable that despite the general fall in household size, certain households had expanded during the war to take in married daughters or daughters-in-law who were temporarily separated from their spouses. In the absence of any direct evidence, however, this can only be conjecture.[61]

ENGLAND

As was intimated earlier, different issues have to be broached in the case of England. Although detailed information is now available on the composition of English households in 1911 and 1921, since no census was taken during the war, the nature of the wartime household and the precise impact of the war on family and household forms remain obscure. Nevertheless it will be argued below that there is sufficient evidence to suggest that the war

had a fairly limited impact on family and household patterns. A useful first
step is to consider the change in the sex ratio at those ages where losses in the
war were highest (cf. above, chapter 1). Figure 2.2 shows that in England
and Wales in 1921 the sex ratio between the ages of 15 and 45 was at its lowest
at age 24, when there were only 81 men to every 100 women. Thereafter it
moved erratically upwards but was still registering just over 92 men per 100
women at age 45. The shortfall of men was at its most severe in the cohort
born in 1896 and 1897 and aged between 17¼ and 18¼ on the outbreak of
the war, was only marginally less severe on all the cohorts born between

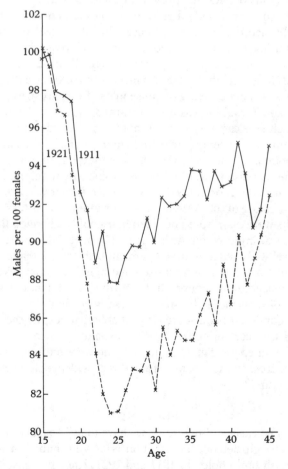

Fig. 2.2. Number of males per 100 females of same age, 1911 and 1921, England and
Wales. *Source* Census of England and Wales, 1911, vol. VII, PP 1912–13, cxiii,
Cd 6610. Ages and conditions as to marriage, Table 1, p. 461. Census of England and
Wales 1921, General Tables, 1925, Table 32, p. 127.

1890/1 and 1898/9,[62] and generally could be said to affect all those who were between 19 and 45 in 1921. Not all of this should be attributed to the war, however, as a glance at the sex ratio in 1911 makes clear. Even in 1911 the sex ratio fell below 90 for those cohorts then in their mid- or late twenties and remained under 94 at most ages up to 45. The effect of the war, therefore, even on the assumption that all the change between 1911 and 1921 could be ascribed to its influence, was only to intensify an existing imbalance within the resident population.

Even less change is apparent in marriage patterns. Figures 2.3a and 2.3b illustrate the percentages of men and women in 1911 and 1921 remaining unmarried at single years of age up to 45. Earlier marriage by men and somewhat later marriage by women might have been anticipated given the loss of so many young men, but it is clear that women as well as men were able to marry earlier in 1921 than had been the case in 1911. The proportion of younger men who remained unmarried in 1921 was some 4 per cent less than in 1911 at each year of age between 20 and 32 declining to negligible differences after the age of 42. The proportions of women who remained unmarried fell less markedly but there was still a 4 per cent decrease registered for women between the ages of 21 and 24 with more modest decreases up to age 38. It was also the case that in 1921 as in 1911, more women than men remained unmarried at the age of 45 although the point at which there ceased to be more men than women unmarried occurred earlier (at the age of 30 instead of at 33 as in 1911). One can only conclude, therefore, that any tendency towards later marriage by women resulting from the loss of so many young men was more than outweighed by other factors, themselves perhaps linked directly with the war, which promoted earlier marriage.

Stability in marriage patterns coexisted, however, with considerable increases between 1911 and 1921 in the number of persons in particular marital status and age groups. For example few contemporaries could have been unaware of the increase in the number of younger widows. Figure 2.4 indicates that in 1921 there were more than twice as many widows at all ages between 20 and 33 than in 1911, with a threefold increase being recorded for women born in 1893 and 1894 (aged 27 at the time of the 1921 census). There was also a quite dramatic change in the number of widows relative to the number of widowers of the same age (see Figure 2.5). In 1911 there had been just over half as many widowers in their early twenties as widows, relatively more widowers in their mid-twenties but increasing proportions of widows thereafter. 1921 not surprisingly shows a much greater imbalance with widows in their mid-twenties outnumbering widowers almost five to one. The sex ratio in fact was at its lowest point at ages 25 and 26 and only began a sustained move upwards after age 33.

In the analysis of family and household patterns in 1911 and 1921, particular attention will be devoted to the residence patterns of younger widows since it is here that most change can be expected. It may be noted now, however, that the ratio of 'marriageable' females to 'marriageable' males, that is the number of single, widowed and divorced women per 100 single, widowed and divorced men, changed a lot less dramatically than the sex ratio of the widowed population. Women under the age of 30 who had no spouse in 1921 exceeded the number of men in this position but only by a small amount: 1,154 women to 1,000 men aged 25–9 and 1,043 to 1,000 men aged 20–4 compared with a slight surplus of 'marriageable' men in 1911 (see

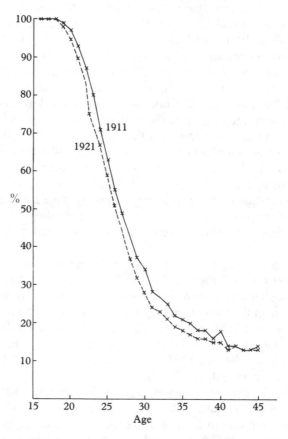

Fig. 2.3a. Percentage of males never married at single years of age (15–45), England and Wales, 1911, 1921. *Sources* Census of England and Wales 1911, vol. VII, PP 1912–13, cxiii, Cd 6610, Ages and condition as to marriage, Table 1, p. 461. Census of England and Wales 1921, General Tables, 1925, Table 32, p. 127.

Table 2.15). Finally, the overview of the change between 1911 and 1921 in the distribution of population according to age, marital status and sex confirms the spectacular increase in both the number of younger widows and in younger married persons of both sexes (see Table 2.16).

Less immediately obvious but of considerable significance is the substantial ageing of the population that had occurred during the decade. Those who have argued for a collapse of the patriarchal family during the war would appear to have overlooked the fact that the numbers of older men were increasing substantially at a time when younger male cohorts had been depleted.[63] The age group which experienced the major loss was 25–34 (men

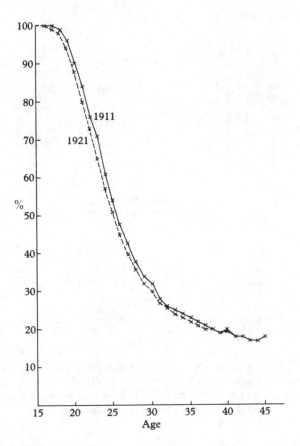

Fig. 2.3b. Percentage of females never married at single years of age (15–45), England and Wales, 1911, 1921. *Sources* Census of England and Wales 1911, vol. VII, PP 1912–13, cxiii, Cd 6610, Ages and condition as to marriage, Table 1, p. 461. Census of England and Wales 1921, General Tables, 1925, Table 32, p. 127.

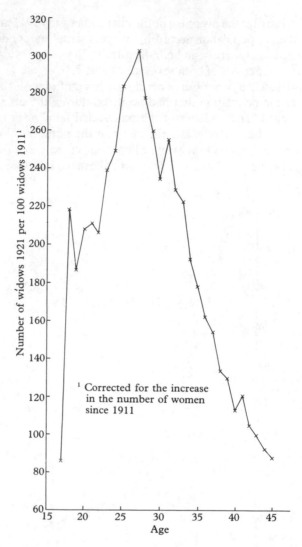

Fig. 2.4. Number of widows in 1921 per 100 widows 1911, England and Wales. *Source* Census of England and Wales 1911, vol. VII, PP 1912–13, cxiii, Cd 6610, Ages and condition as to marriage, Table 1, p. 461. Census of England and Wales 1921, General Tables, 1925, Table 32, p. 127.

Table 2.15. *Number of marriageable^a females per 1,000 marriageable^a males, England and Wales, 1911 and 1921*

Age group	1911	1921
20–24	984	1,043
25–29	990	1,154
30–34	1,111	1,470
35–44	1,366	1,683
45–54	1,726	1,768
55–64	1,960	2,038
≥65	2,147	2,263

Notes
[a]Single, widowed and divorced
Source
1921 Census General Report, Table xl, p. 82.

Fig. 2.5. Widowers per 100 widows, England and Wales, 1911 and 1921. *Sources* Census of England and Wales 1911, vol. VII, PP 1912–13, cxiii, Cd 6610, Ages and condition as to marriage, Table 1, p. 461. Census of England and Wales 1921, General Tables, 1925, Table 32, p. 127.

Table 2.16. Changes to marital and age distribution of the population, England and Wales, 1911–21

	Males				Females			
				Percentage increase or decrease (−) from 1911				
Age group	Single	Married	Widowed and divorced	Total	Single	Married	Widowed and divorced	Total
<15	-4.4	—	—	-4.4	-5.5	—	—	-5.5
15–19	4.2	117.7	90.9	4.4	5.0	54.9	119.1	5.6
20–24	-7.6	20.1	18.3	-3.6	-2.3	13.8	146.4	1.8
25–29	-16.6	0.3	16.5	-8.0	-5.7	1.6	187.9	-0.2
30–34	-20.9	-1.7	3.3	-6.9	-2.8	-0.7	129.0	1.2
35–44	-4.9	9.7	-5.3	6.8	11.2	12.4	40.2	13.6
45–54	24.7	28.0	0.6	25.9	29.5	26.9	7.5	24.7
55–64	34.0	30.8	4.3	27.4	46.3	29.5	9.7	26.1
65–74	29.9	25.7	8.3	21.1	38.6	26.3	11.8	20.5
≥75	29.3	28.6	14.0	21.2	39.4	35.7	23.9	27.7
Total	-3.7	15.1	5.7	3.6	-0.4	14.5	19.4	6.4

Source
1921 Census General Report, Table xxxix, p. 81

aged 25–9 in 1921 were 8 per cent fewer than in 1911; men aged 30–4 some 7 per cent fewer, see Table 2.16, column 5, rows 4 and 5). This contrasts sharply, however, with the increase of at least 20 per cent in the number of males in age groups from 45–54 through to 75+. Other factors being equal, this trend towards an older population can only have served to strengthen the power of the older generation, many of whom would have been family heads.

Against this background we must now seek to interpret the patterns of family composition and household composition in the four chosen local populations. Since the selection of these particular communities was guided in part by the desire to include as wide a range of local economies as was possible,[64] with the object thereby of capturing most of the variability in family and household types, it is obviously desirable to examine each community separately even at the expense of a considerably extended analysis. Furthermore it must be self-evident that no 'national' composite picture of English household and family patterns is likely to emerge from such a small set of communities even had they been selected at random. To make the most of the new data, therefore, the emphasis in what follows will be on the degree of variation in certain key aspects of family and household composition among the four communities. Of these, one, Bolton in Lancashire, was urban, the second, Pinner in Middlesex, was rapidly becoming suburban, and the other two, Saffron Walden in Essex and Morland in Westmorland, were completely rural.[65]

The first point to establish is whether it is possible to identify in all four the same increase in the number of younger widows and younger married persons of both sexes that was so visible in the national level data. Three of the four communities do in fact show some rise between 1911 and 1921 in the proportion of women younger than 35 who were widowed but in no case could it be claimed that the change was dramatic.[66] There was less consistency in the pace of marriage formation. Only in Bolton were fewer men aged 20–4 unmarried in 1921 than in 1911; yet fewer men aged 30–4 remained unmarried in all four communities in 1921. Between 1911 and 1921 the singulate mean age at marriage[67] for men rose in both Pinner and Saffron Walden in opposition to the national trend (cf. above, Figure 2.3a). Admittedly the singulate mean age at marriage for women did fall in three of the communities (Bolton, Morland and Saffron Walden) but again the proportion remaining unmarried did not decline across all age groups.[68] Given the closeness of the association between age at marriage and household formation,[69] there would be good reason to expect, therefore, an equivalent degree of variation in the pattern of household formation, although the differential impact of the housing crisis on the ability of the population to form new households could be a complicating factor.[70]

The composition of the household can be measured in a multitude of different ways: in terms of kinship structure, generational depth, combinations of different persons present (children, relatives, servants) and, of course, size. For a simple overview, however, it is sufficient to describe the total population by age, sex and relationship to the household head. Figure 2.6a offers a cross sectional perspective of the male life cycle in Bolton in 1911.

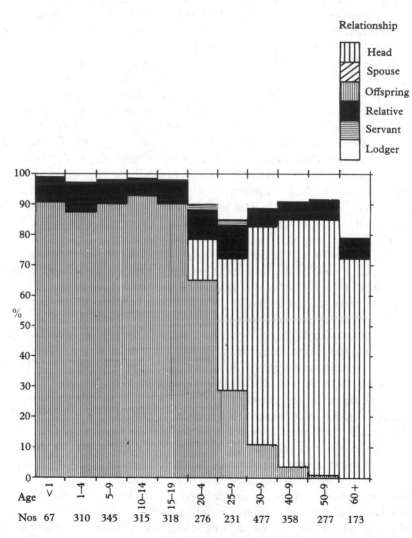

Fig. 2.6a. Bolton 1911. Male population by age and relationship to household head

Close to nine in every ten younger males were sons of household heads. Most older males, more than 80 per cent of those in their forties and fifties were themselves heads of households with the main movement into headship occurring during the late twenties. Few males were related to the head other than as never-married sons and the fact that such relatives represented a fairly constant proportion of each age group implies that there was no par-

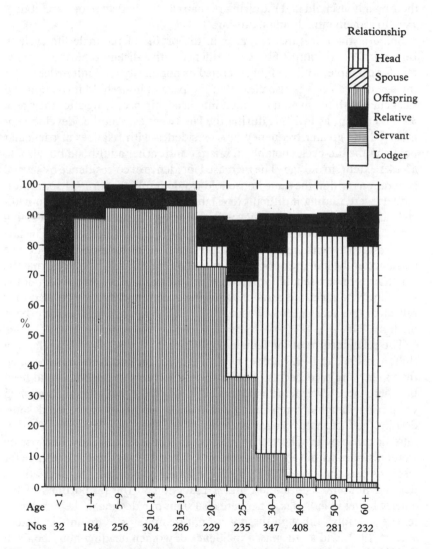

Fig. 2.6b. Bolton 1921. Male population by age and relationship to household head

ticular point in their life cycle when males needed to seek a home with more distant relatives. Of considerably greater significance was lodging, particularly for adult males. A number no doubt required accommodation on a temporary basis near their work, but since the incidence of lodging also peaked in the 60+ age group, while the headship rate (i.e. the proportion of males who were household heads) fell, it could be argued that movement into lodgings was also the recourse of older males no longer able to maintain their own household and requiring perhaps a certain degree of 'care' if they were to remain outside an institution.[71]

Some of these features reappear in the profile of the male life cycle in Bolton in 1921 (Figure 2.6b). Co-residence with a distant relative remained rare for example, while lodging retained its popularity for adult males under the age of 60. Yet it is also clear that the pace of household formation had slackened with the main movement into headship occurring after the age of 30 rather than, as in 1911, during the late twenties. Another development involved the greater frequency of co-residence with relatives at particular points in the life-cycle, notably in infancy and earlier adulthood but also, to a lesser extent, in old age. The increased incidence of co-residence by several generations within the same household would imply that in 1921 some individuals were finding it difficult to establish their own households immediately after marriage and that they were resolving the situation by co-residing for a time with relatives, at least until the birth of their first child. The fact that residence with relatives was preferred over lodgings, despite the existence of the lodging option within the community might suggest that the constraints on household formation involved an inability on the part of the new family to meet the costs of acquiring accommodation more than they reflected the shortage of housing to which reference has already been made.[72]

The relationships of the female population to the heads of household in Bolton in 1911 and 1921 are set out in Figures 2.6c and 2.6d. More women than men were recorded as relatives and as servants of the household head but there were fewer female lodgers. It is also clear that after the age of 25 unmarried daughters remaining with their parents outnumbered sons, despite the fact that by marrying earlier than men, women moved earlier into the role of wife of head than men became household heads. Comparing women's roles within the household in 1911 and 1921, there is evidence for 1921, as was the case with men, of increased co-residence with relatives, delayed household formation and a reduction in the proportions of the elderly living in lodgings. There are also signs of a decline in the number of female servants, although there were not many female servants in Bolton even in 1911, and an increased incidence of women heading households in their late twenties and thirties. Yet apart perhaps from the changed pace of household formation, it would be difficult to claim that there had been any drastic change to the pattern of relationships within the household between 1911 and 1921. A greater degree of change, however, might be expected elsewhere, particularly where, prior to the war, large numbers of women had been in service. We need in other words to consider relationships within households in our other chosen communities: Saffron Walden, Pinner and Morland.

Figure 2.7a sets out the relationships of the male population to the household heads in rural Saffron Walden in 1911. Much higher proportions of older males occupied the position of head of household in this largely agricultural population than in Bolton. There was little lodging with the exception of a few men in their twenties, and an even lower incidence of living with relatives. On the other hand sons were generally older when moving out of the parental household. Almost half the males aged between 25 and 29 were recorded as sons of household heads compared with under 30 per cent in Bolton. As regards the female population (Figure 2.7c), the most notable contrast with the situation in Bolton is the much greater prominence of what are known as life-cycle servants,[73] large numbers of younger women residing as servants in the homes of their employers. In Saffron Walden about 35 per cent of women in the age group 15–19 were in service and about one quarter of those aged 20–4. Other differences from Bolton were the much larger part of the female life-cycle which was spent as the wife of the household head and, conversely, the lower proportion of women who headed their own households.

The main purpose of our enquiry, however, is to consider the degree of change in household patterns between 1911 and 1921. Comparison of Figures 2.7a with 2.7b and 2.7c with 2.7d would suggest that the pattern of relationships across the life-cycle both for males and females in 1921 closely resembled that found in 1911. There is little sign, for example, of the delay in household formation noted in Bolton. Although there were fewer men and women aged 20–4 in Saffron Walden heading households or married to household heads in 1921 than in 1911, considerably higher 'headship' rates were recorded in 1921 for the 25–9 age group. As at Bolton, however, there were more women in their late twenties and thirties heading households in 1921 than in 1911. There was also some increase in the frequency of co-residence with relatives but in this latter case the increase was less marked than in Bolton and not consistent across all age groups. Of much greater significance undoubtedly is the fact that there was very little diminution between 1911 and 1921 in the proportion of Saffron Walden women entering domestic service. The peak age for employment as a live-in servant remained within the 15–19 age group but small numbers of much older women also continued in service.

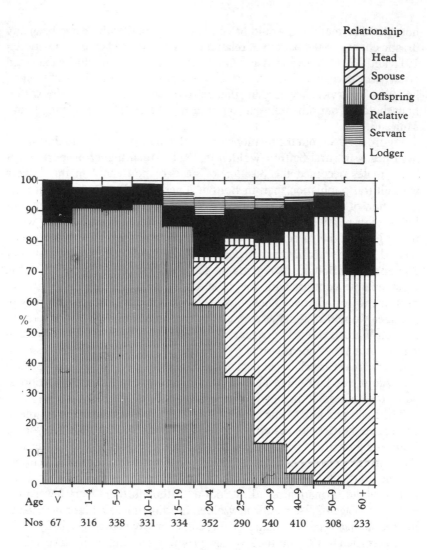

Fig. 2.6c. Bolton 1911. Female population by age and relationship to household head

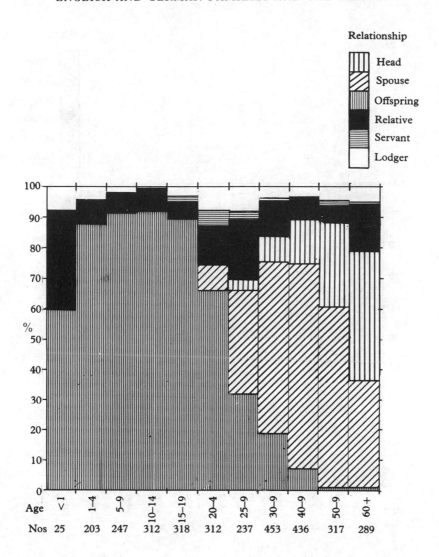

Fig. 2.6d. Bolton 1921. Female population by age and relationship to household head

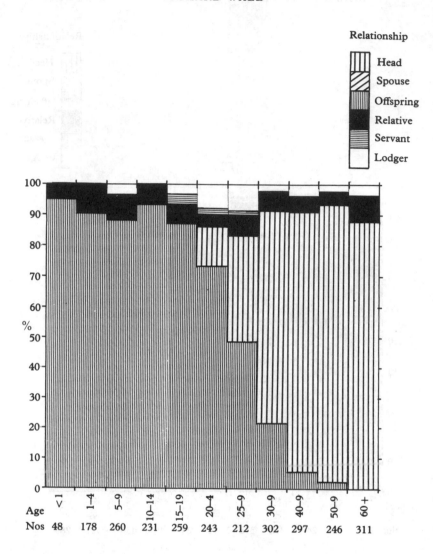

Fig. 2.7a. Saffron Walden 1911. Male population by age and relationship to house-hold head

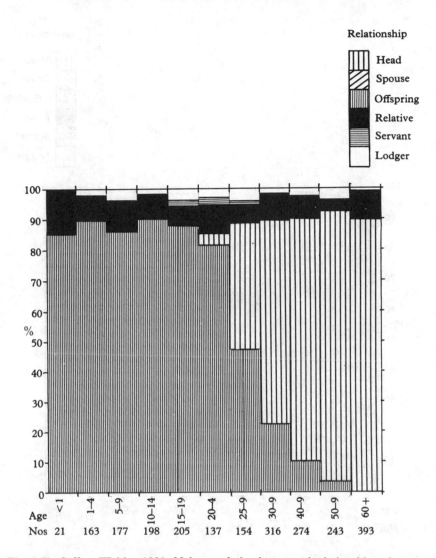

Fig. 2.7b. Saffron Walden 1921. Male population by age and relationship to house-hold head

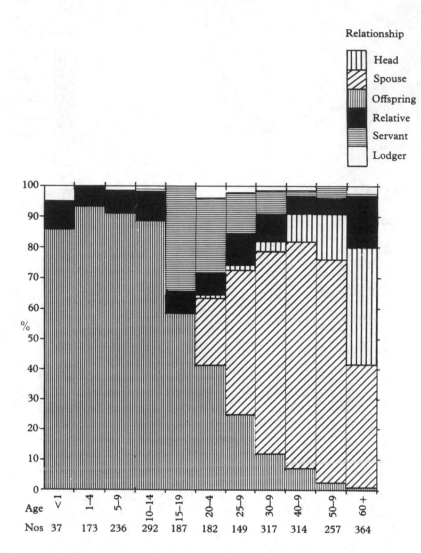

Fig. 2.7c. Saffron Walden 1911. Female population by age and relationship to household head

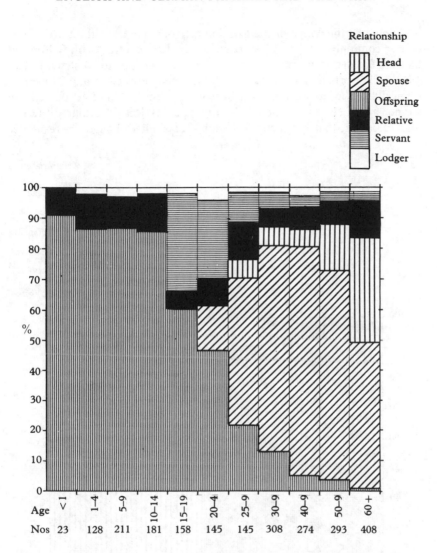

Fig. 2.7d. Saffron Walden 1921. Female population by age and relationthip to household head

Pinner, on the fringe of the London metropolitan area, the third of our chosen communities, provides a particularly sharp contrast with Bolton and Saffron Walden in terms of both its social and occupational structure. In 1911 well over half of all women in Pinner aged between 15 and 24 were in domestic service as were a third of women aged 25–9 and 10 per cent of women aged between 30 and 60 (see Figure 2.8c). It is particularly interesting, therefore, that between 1911 and 1921 similar changes in residence

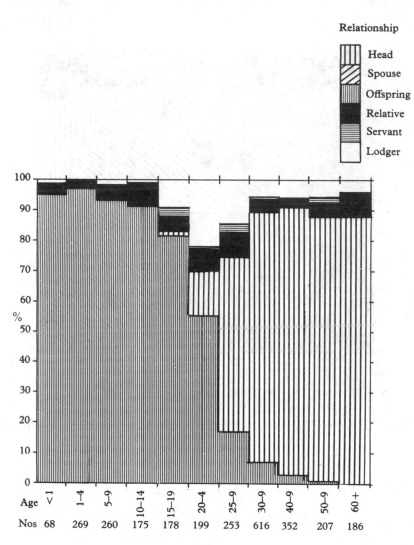

Fig. 2.8a. Pinner 1911. Male population by age and relationship to household head

patterns can be identified to those occurring in Bolton (compare Figures 2.8a, 2.8b, 2.8c, and 2.8d). For example, as at Bolton, men and women moved later into positions of responsibility in the household in 1921 than in 1911. Also in evidence is the increased incidence of co-residence with relatives in 1921 and its more pronounced 'life-cycle' character as residence in the household of a relative became more likely in infancy and, for men, in early adulthood and old age. The increase in younger women heading

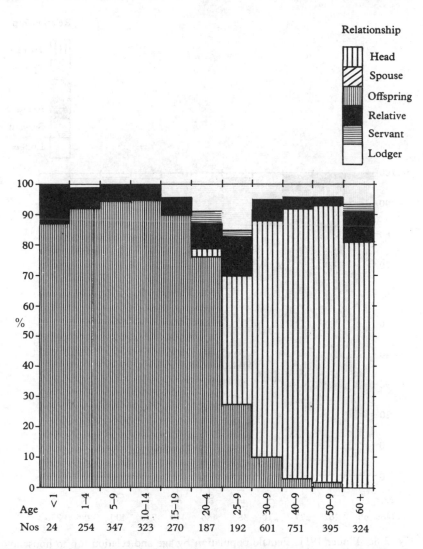

Fig. 2.8b. Pinner 1921. Male population by age and relationship to household head

households, which was noted elsewhere appears in Pinner to be confined to women in their thirties. But in Pinner the major change between 1911 and 1921 has to be the decline in the incidence of domestic service. Whereas in 1911 more than half of the women aged 15–24 had been resident as servants in the households of their employers, by 1921 servants accounted for no more than one third of the 15–19 age group and just over 40 per cent of those aged 20–4. Considerably smaller declines were registered for older age

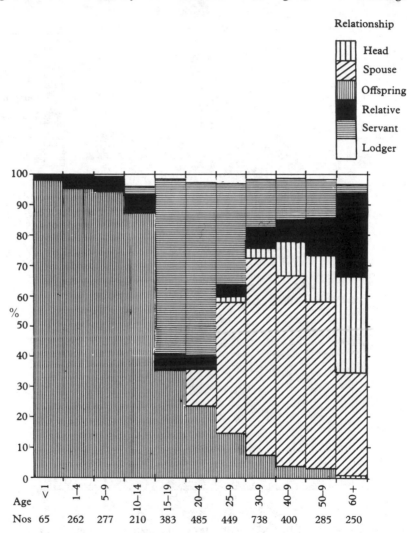

Fig. 2.8c. Pinner 1911. Female population by age and relationship to household head

groups suggesting that it was particularly the younger women who were forsaking domestic service. Before all this is imputed to the effects of the war in broadening women's employment horizons there is the rapidly changing social character of Pinner during this period to be considered. Although we are not yet in a position to measure this directly, it is clear that the north-ward push of suburbia was having an ever greater impact with the immi-gration of many new households.[74]

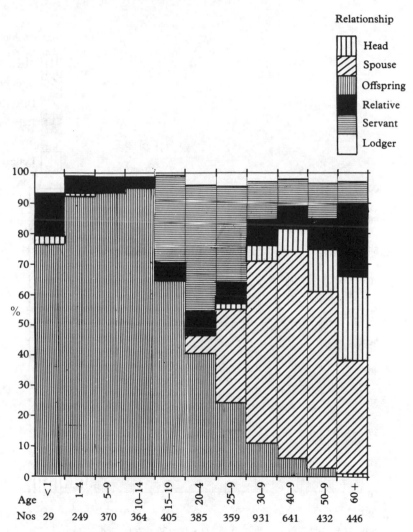

Fig. 2.8d. Pinner 1921. Female population by age and relationship to household head

The last population to be surveyed here is that of Morland, covering a large part of the county of Westmorland east and north of the Lake District. The principal distinguishing characteristic of the social structure was the survival of farm service for males. This form of life-cycle service by men was most likely between the ages of 15 and 30 and would appear to have survived the war although in a somewhat attenuated form (compare Figures 2.9a and

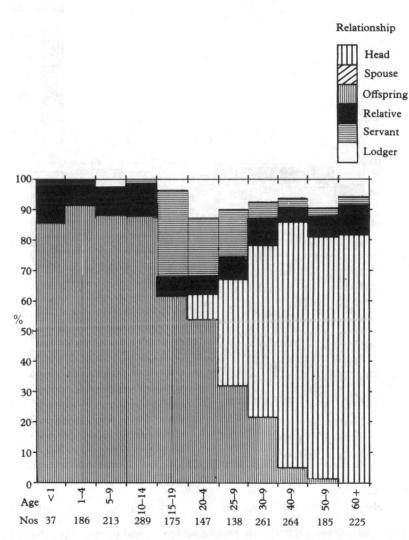

Fig. 2.9a. Morland 1911. Male population by age and relationship to household head

2.9b). On the other hand, and contrary to the trend elsewhere, somewhat higher proportions of women were in service in 1921 than in 1911 (Figures 2.9c and 2.9d). The change was most marked within the age group 15–19, 45 per cent of whom were in service in 1921 compared with approximately a third in 1911, but there was a slight decline in the proportion of women in service in their twenties. Other changes we have seen elsewhere: delayed

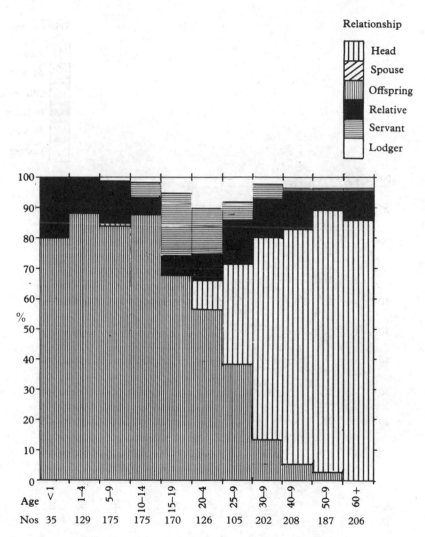

Fig. 2.9b. Morland 1921. Male population by age and relationship to household head

household formation in 1921, and a rise in the proportion of women in their twenties heading households and in the frequency of living with relatives at particular points in the life-cycle.

That these three trends can be identified in communities with such diverse social structures as Bolton, Pinner and Morland suggests they may have some general applicability. However, the fact that changes in general

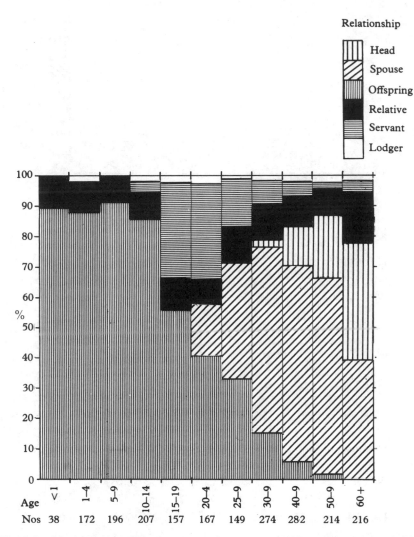

Fig. 2.9c. Morland 1911. Female population by age and relationship to household head

were frequently limited and that when they did occur, were not always uni-directional, indicates the need for caution. Above all there is no sign of the war or the altered conditions of the 1920s having curtailed the frequency with which women entered life-cycle service in Saffron Walden, and men and women became servants in Morland.

Major change might seem most likely in the case of the residence patterns

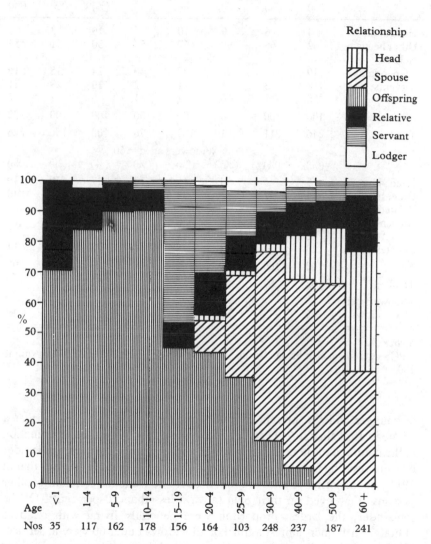

Fig. 2.9d. Morland 1921. Female population by age and relationship to household head

Table 2.17. *Household position of widowed persons aged <60, 1911 and 1921*

	Bolton		Morland		Saffron Walden		Pinner	
	1911 (%)	1921 (%)	1911 (%)	1921 (%)	1911 (%)	1921 (%)	1911 (%)	1921 (%)
Widows aged <60								
Head alone	4	6	9	10	5	16	3	5
Other heads	62	66	58	57	57	50	51	53
Related dependants	19	17	22	20	30	24	15	19
Servants	8	3	11	11	7	10	29	21
Inmates	8	8	0	2	1	0	1	2
All	100	100	100	100	100	100	100	100
Total	246	211	91	105	76	100	156	226
Widowers aged <60	(%)	(%)	(%)	(%)	(%)	(%)	(%)	(%)
Head alone	5	5	4	15	13	17	10	19
Other heads	44	42	42	38	52	42	33	40
Related dependants	26	31	19	26	23	33	29	24
Servants	2	0	12	14	2	0	12	3
Inmates	23	22	23	8	10	8	15	14
All	100	100	100	100	100	100	100	100
Total	102	91	57	50	61	52	48	110
Widowers per 100 widows	41	43	63	48	80	52	31	49

Source
OPCS data file at Cambridge Group. Due to rounding percentages may not sum to 100.

of younger widows, present in much larger numbers in the country as a whole in 1921 than in 1911 (cf. above, Figure 2.4). A detailed examination of the nature of the households in which widows, and widowers, aged under 60 were residing in our chosen communities (see Table 2.17) reveals that in 1911 the majority of the widows headed households containing other persons. Few lived on their own (always less than 10 per cent). Of the remainder, the largest proportion were generally living with relatives although in Pinner, almost a third of all widows under 60 were in service. Unlike widowers they were rarely found in lodgings but were more likely to be in service or head households containing two or more persons. Between

1911 and 1921 there was some increase in the proportion of widows aged under 60 living on their own but this apart, there was no pattern of change that embraced all four populations and in three of the four the proportion of younger widowers living alone also increased. Clearly there is nothing here to indicate a major transformation in family patterns between 1911 and 1921. War widows, to the extent that they are identified in our figures,[75] seem not to have created a special type of household in 1921.

Authority in the wartime family and the economics of family life

The census, as is well-known, can reveal the pattern of relationships within households but not the quality of these relationships. In his imaginative portrayal of wartime Vienna, based on interviews with those who were children at the time of the war, Reinhard Sieder has been able to suggest how certain families were able to compensate, socially if not economically, for the absent patriarch by promoting into his place of authority, the oldest of the male children or another more distant male relative.[76] The very different sources called upon in the present chapter have other strengths. They indicate for example that the years of war brought about an economic restructuring of families, a process which would also seem to have implications for the lines of authority within families. Certainly, worries were voiced from time to time between 1914 and 1919 about the unfortunate consequences of the new-found economic independence enjoyed by women and children as a result of the war. Yet it is much easier to illustrate the moral outrage of the middle-class observer, for example, about the consumption of alcohol by women or about children running riot, than it is to assess whether their concern was justified.

An obvious first point (and here we will be focusing exclusively on the English evidence) is that the impact of the war varied widely from area to area, from year to year and from family to family. As was shown in Table 2.1 above, the incidence of poverty in London in October 1914 directly or indirectly attributable to the war ranged from 85 per cent of the families with necessitous children in Holborn to 28 per cent in Lambeth. It is evident, too, that in the early stages of the war, rather than more women being drawn into the labour market through new employment opportunities, many of the existing jobs for women and girls were either lost or put under threat with the collapse of the service sector of the economy. Dressmakers, laundresses and charwomen in a number of London boroughs suddenly found themselves out of work or on short-time[77] and when these women were the sole or principal earners for their families, the loss of their earnings would have been devastating.[78]

Precisely how many families were of this type is unknown.[79] Perhaps rather more at the outbreak of the war than in 'normal' times, given the numbers of men enlisting, but those families relying on the earnings of women and girls to supplement those of the breadwinner would have consti-tuted the largest number of losers. When the male breadwinner in these families did not enlist or when there were younger males to take advantage of the opportunities opening up for them in the job market (and these appeared as early as the first months of the war),[80] families were reasonably well protected. Nevertheless, even the loss of secondary earners was a serious matter for families living on the margin of poverty, with one report of October 1914 specifically attributing the increase in the proportion of children being included on the London Council's feeding list to older girls having lost their positions as dressmakers.[81]

Male employment was less seriously threatened even in the early stage of the war, and the unemployed were among the first to enlist.[82] However, the initial months of the war did also see a certain amount of male unemploy-ment and underemployment in particular trades and in particular areas. In August 1914 unemployment was reported among French polishers and piano makers in St Pancras. Five months later came the claim from Marylebone that the fried fish trade was in serious difficulty as a result of the near impossibility of obtaining fish, as were the vendors of cat meat owing to the high price of horse flesh. In Fulham it was said that the takings of cab-drivers had fallen, in Hammersmith that shopkeepers were doing less well, this apparently because so many young lodgers and boarders had enlisted.[83]

Differences such as these although difficult to quantify help to explain some of the variation between London boroughs in the proportions of chil-dren on the London County Council's feeding lists (Table 2.1). Moreover, pockets of hardship remained even as living conditions in general improved during the later stages of the war (cf. above, Figure 2.1); 24 per cent of the families whose children were classed as 'necessitous' in Islington in March 1916 and 28 per cent of such families in St Pancras in May 1916 were dependent on a male breadwinner who was unemployed or on short time due to age, infirmity or incompetence.[84]

A further distinction was made in the case of St Pancras between those families who were in difficulty because of what were termed the 'educational problems' of the male breadwinner (20 per cent of the total) as opposed to specific economic factors (8 per cent). Within the former category were included those men who were on half pay or less; a few because, in the opinion of the Committee, they were worthless, workshy, inclined to drink or gambling; others because they were crippled, deformed, elderly, weak or muddled and unable, except in the exceptional circumstances of the war, to command more than a 'boy wage'. The second type of case, more 'distinctly economic', involved those who stuck steadfastly to their trades despite the fall in demand, such as the employees of the best furniture shops, the makers of tennis rackets and of hunting breeches and the French polishers, together with those who, as aliens, were unable to practise their trade.

For those families dependent on what a woman could earn, the disparity between the earnings of a man and a woman was so great that even on an 'average' wage for a woman, it was impossible for a widow to support herself and her children. The problem was more than just one of attempting to earn sufficient to support a family. As the Shoreditch Local Association noted in its report to the Children's Care Sub-Committee of the London County Council in March 1916 on families reliant on the mother's earnings, 'the necessity was due to the whole burden of the support and care of the family being thrown upon the woman; it is manifestly impossible that both these duties can be performed adequately by one person'.[85] Where the bread-winner had enlisted there was supposed to be no problem as the War Office would arrange for a weekly allowance to reach his dependants. However, in the first weeks of the war the scheme did not always work smoothly, and there were complaints about late payments.[86] There also seems to have been some difficulty in agreeing allowances for those who were dependent on someone other than a husband or a father. Not all families were of this type. Widows in particular might be supported by adult sons or other relatives and the allowance system operated by the War Office appears to have lacked the flexibility to cope with such situations.[87]

Nevertheless, as the war progressed, it was principally the problems posed by unexpected affluence, the product of a buoyant labour market and regular allowances from the War Office, that came to exercise the attention of the members of the Children's Care Sub-Committee of the London County Council. In November 1915 and again in January 1916 they considered the evidence on the alleged increase of alcohol consumption by women.[88] The problem was seen in the following way. With the arrival of the war allowance, large numbers of women had more money at their disposal than ever before. According to one estimate the allowances to wives and dependants 'in numerous instances' exceeded by sums varying from five to twenty shillings the usual amounts received from their husbands when in work, and from which of course they no longer had to maintain the husband.[89] In addition, it was reported that most of the former employers of their husbands were supplementing the allowance in the form of a pension. But even the allowance by itself was sufficiently generous, or so it was claimed, that many women felt no need to work.[90] Furthermore, the allowances were paid on Mondays, said to be the usual day off for many women, and what could be more natural than that, having collected their allowances from the Post Office, they should adjourn to a neighbouring public house to treat each other and gossip.

Yet in practice it proved difficult to establish that excess drinking had occurred. There were individual cases that could be cited, plenty of stories of women drinking at home and evading the regulations by sending men and youths as messengers to the pubs to ensure their supply of alcohol, but the principal argument was that the serious increase in drinking had occurred soon after the start of the war. Significantly, this was not only prior to the imposition of restrictions on the hours when alcohol could be sold but also predated the period when the Committee was likely to have had direct evidence. Might we conclude, therefore, that the 'moral outrage' about excessive drinking was considerably out of proportion to the scale of the problem? The Charity Organisation Society in their earlier study of the alleged increase in drinking certainly thought so.[91] Only a comparatively small percentage of women, in their opinion, were drinking more alcohol than prior to the war, with the majority 'doing remarkably well by their families and homes'. There was a problem but this was because those women who did drink made in the aggregate a large number and were concentrated in particular areas of London and in specific localities within those areas.

A little later in 1916, the Children's Care Sub-Committee came to consider some of the consequences for the family of the strong demand for juvenile labour.[92] The position was complex. There was certainly some occupational mobility. Numbers of boys were reported to have moved into men's jobs and more girls were taking up clerical work and serving on bookstalls. The greater degree of independence that they both gained was noted, not always with total approval. Boys were accused of taking time off whenever they felt that they had money in their pockets and there were the conventional charges of an increase in crime and in gambling, and a breakdown in discipline within the home. Having raised these issues, the report presented to the Committee went on to argue that the activities of a restless minority should not be allowed to colour the whole picture, and in fact the extent of change was strictly limited. Despite the great ease of entry into skilled trades, there was evidence that dull mechanical jobs nearer home were often preferred over more attractive work further away. Boys did not always choose skilled work but replaced men as porters and van drivers, tasks for which no training was required. The sex-typing of jobs also remained intact.[93] The first experience of employment for boys might be the delivery of papers or milk, the running of errands or the minding of a stall. Girls would most often assist a neighbour, mind the baby or, like the boys, run errands. Indeed the demands of maintaining the family during the war may actually have intensified the process by which the tasks of earning money and providing care were allocated on the basis of the gender of the child. Boys, it was noted, were taking up the new job opportunities in greater numbers than were girls, as many girls were needed at home to help their mothers.[94] This could and did lead to tensions between brothers and sisters, as Richard Sieder has been able to demonstrate for working-class Vienna (below, chapter 3).

What is also clear, however, from the details on juvenile employment provided to the Children's Care Sub-Committee, is that different families had responded in different ways to the increased prosperity of the war years. The Committee was very much concerned to learn whether there had been an increase in the proportion of children who took on a job while still at school. The evidence pointed to an increase in the employment rate when London was considered as a whole. But some schools could detect no change whatsoever compared with the position prior to the war, while others reported an actual decrease in the proportion of children in employment, owing to the improvement in the standard of living. The explanation that was proffered to the Committee was that while increased prosperity was encouraging some parents to let their children stay on longer in the elementary school, or even to attend secondary school, others were tempted by the high wages that were available to take their children out of the school at the age of 14, when previously they would have allowed them to continue until 15. The implication was that need, as represented by a family's proximity to the poverty line, was no longer the primary determinant of whether parents would encourage their children to seek work. To support the arguments some inquiries were made of children in the upper standards of one 'better class' school. Forty children, out of a total of 132, were found to have started work, just 13 of them out of necessity. By contrast in two 'poorer class' schools in South London no more than 37 out of a total of 494 children were at work. The evidence could hardly be termed conclusive but there seems less reason to doubt the more general point on the flexibility of the family's response to the opportunities provided by work and school.[95]

If prosperity was encouraging a variety of fresh approaches to child employment, there is also much evidence that many behavioural patterns were too deeply entrenched to be much shaken even by the First World War. It has already been established in the case of Bavaria that women's employment expectations were subject to extreme variations depending on the state of the labour market.[96] To this can be added the fact that their options were extremely limited by their need to combine a continued presence in the labour market, if at all possible, with their duties in the home.[97] Within the working-class family, resistance to official direction, from whatever quarter, remained strong. In London the Children's Care Sub-Committee battled hard to see that a widow removed herself from the labour market the better to care for her children, as they saw it. The Committee succeeded but could not persuade her to provide glasses for her girls.

'They don't look nice', she said, 'and other children laugh at them.'[98] In another case a man objected to the cutting of his daughter's hair as part of the treatment for head lice, expressing himself in a nationalistic vein he thought appropriate for the time, 'What do you think we are – Germans, that you can do as you like with?'[99]

This was by no means the only occasion on which the insistence of the school medical service that they had the ultimate responsibility for a girl's cleanliness, failing parental care, resulted in disputes with the parents. Nevertheless, in due course, the Committee came to feel that the school medical service was gradually winning the battle in regard to personal cleanliness. By February 1920 they could report that they were treating children who would not have been treated in earlier years and that girls were now clean *even on Friday afternoons*.[100] It would have been only natural for the Committee to consider the rising standards of cleanliness during the war years (cf. Table 2.3) as an occasion for self-congratulation, but the effectiveness of their campaign is difficult to separate from the consequences of general improvements in the standard of living. Even with this problem solved to their satisfaction, however, others remained. The battle to mould the working-class family into a form acceptable to those who considered themselves responsible for its welfare would continue into the 1920s and beyond.[101]

Notes

1 Eric J. Leed, *No man's land*, Cambridge, 1979, pp. 2, 4.
2 Arthur Marwick, *The deluge, British society and the First World War*, London, 1966, esp. pp. 289–99.
3 Family policy in Germany looks very different when told from the point of view of the women it affected (see chapter 14) as opposed to that of parts of the medical profession (see chapter 15). Each approach is perfectly valid.
4 Moreover, illustrations that would have served perfectly well in the English context, such as that of the *munitionette* were suppressed in France (cf. below, chapter 9, p. 265). However, perhaps the greatest distortion of the events of the war years was the idea of a lost generation, the absence from post-war society of men of talent and ability when the more dramatic change was that eldest sons of the pre-war elite no longer found themselves in a world they could rule. See Robert Wohl, *The generation of 1914*, Cambridge, Mass., 1979, esp. pp. 120–1.
5 For an imaginative use by Marie-Monique Huss of the evidence of the postcard to indicate popular attitudes towards pronatalism in France and England, see chapter 12 below. On the pronatalist campaign in Britain from the standpoint of the Eugenics Society see Richard Soloway in chapter 13.
6 See for example M. Ferro, *The Great War 1914–18*, London, 1970, p. 225.
7 The analysis of the Bavarian employment and population censuses was undertaken during a period as a Visiting Fellow at the Max Planck Institut in Göttingen in the winter of 1986.

8 It was the opinion of the Chief Medical Officer to the Board of Education that schoolchildren in London enjoyed better health than those in other parts of the country because of the large number of relief agencies operating in the capital. Report for 1914 as communicated to the London County Council, Children's Care Sub-Committee, 15 October 1915. Now in the London Record Office (Greater London Council).

9 Peter Scholliers and Frank Daelemans (chapter 4) and Patrick Fridenson (chapter 8) suggest that living standards in Belgium were considerably below living standards in France and somewhat below those in England.

10 Separate lists were kept of children fed during the holidays. These lists have not been used in this chapter. Nor has any reference been made to the type of meal taken by the children (breakfasts, dinners, suppers) on which statistics were also kept. At one point a campaign was mounted for the substitution of dinners by breakfasts. See the Report by Chief Education Officer on Hanover Street Care Committee, Children's Care Sub-Committee, 26 February 1915.

11 Children's Care Sub-Committee, 18 June 1915, comment on Chief Medical Officer's report to Board of Education 1914.

12 Children's Care Sub-Committee, 18 June 1915. Report by Education Officer on 'chronic cases' in Lewisham. Chronic cases concerned children who had been on the feeding list for at least six months.

13 Children's Care Sub-Committee, 21 March 1915.

14 Children's Care Sub-Committee, 17 March 1916.

15 London County Council Education Officer, EO/WEL/1/5, 16 February 1915. Report on unemployment and distress in Bethnal Green. Also of interest in this connection is the review of the Council's agreement for feeding children over the Christmas holiday in 1914. This review established that of the children who had failed to attend when expected, one-quarter were absent because the parents were in work and the children no longer necessitous. A further 9 per cent had been withdrawn following the receipt of the allowances from the army and 4 per cent because the children had found work. The remainder were reported as absent through ill health (one-fifth), and other factors not obviously connected with the improvement of the war economy. See Children's Care Sub-Committee, 10 February 1915, summary of reports from school care committees.

16 It was decided not to risk cluttering up Figure 2.1 by including data on more than one year before the war, but the Annual Report of the LCC Education Officer for 1914 indicates that trends during 1911–12 and 1912–13 were similar to those of 1913–14, except that the summer months of 1912 saw more children on the feeding list than had the spring of that year.

17 Military cases were presumably those where the head of the family or its chief economic supporter had enlisted and there was some difficulty over the allowance. However, the distinction between the cases directly and indirectly due to the war remains obscure. For chronic cases see above, note 12.

18 See pp. 93–4 . Space constraints obviously preclude a detailed account of employment trends in individual London boroughs although there are useful indications in the reports by Children's Care Organisers and Divisional Superintendents on individual London boroughs in EO/WEL/1/4 and EO/WEL/1/5. For example, the report on Hammersmith of 3 October 1914 reported the slackness of business in a cigarette factory dependent on trade with Germany.

19 One exception was the abandonment of the detailed examination of all entrants after November 1915 but the third term of 1917 saw a return to the earlier procedure on the grounds that a number of important health defects had gone undetected. See Children's Care Sub-Committee, 11 November 1915 and 29 June 1917, reports on entrants' medical examination.

20 Report of County Medical Officer and School Medical Officer for 1914, in LCC, Annual Report of the Council for 1914, vol. iii, p. 87.

21 The nutritional standards of Cardiff and Cambridgeshire school children were detailed in the Annual Reports of their School Medical Officers beginning in 1909 and 1910 respectively; for Cumberland see Board of Education, *Annual Report of the Chief Medical Officer of the Board of Education 1910*, PP 1911, xvii, Cd 5925, pp. 28–9; and for London, Table 2.1. Whether girls were less likely than boys to suffer from subnormal nutrition is a question to which I intend to return elsewhere, but a preliminary airing of the issue is to be found in my paper 'Inferring differential neglect of females from mortality data', *Annales de démographie historique* (1981), p. 126.

22 Board of Education, *Annual Report of Chief Medical Officer of Board of Education 1917*, PP 1918, ix, Cd 9206, pp. 22ff. The results were communicated to the Children's Care Sub-Committee on 15 January 1919.

23 The effect was that the percentage of children reported as having poor nutrition was about double that of a routine inspection, for boys 10 per cent as against 6 per cent, for girls 13 per cent as against 6 per cent. Considered to have good nutrition were 37 per cent of the boys and 44 per cent of the girls against 27 per cent and 29 per cent with 'excellent' nutrition according to the routine inspection (see Table 2.2). However, some differences are to be anticipated from the routine inspection relying on the terms 'excellent', 'normal' and 'subnormal' while the special enquiry adopted the terms 'good', 'fair' and 'poor' to classify nutritional status.

24 For evidence that points in a different direction see the contribution of Alastair Reid below, chapter 7, pp. 224–5.

25 Board of Education, *Annual Report of the Chief Medical Officer of the Board of Education 1915*, PP 1916, viii, Cd 8338, p. 32 and cf. the 1914 Report, PP 1914, xviii, Cd 8055, p. 69 where attention is drawn to the unhealthiness of certain schools as well as to the lack of facilities and neglect at home.

26 It will be noted that in regard to both clothing and cleanliness, intermediate children would appear to be more disadvantaged than either entrants or leavers and that girls fared better than boys with the notable exception of head infestations which were difficult to avoid with long hair.

27 According to the Report of the School Medical Officer for London in 1919 the same children were examined in 1919 as in 1915. The similarity of the results to those on all children examined in these years (see above Tables 2.2 and 2.3) suggests, however, that movements into and out of the cohort as a result of migration were ignored. Dr Hammer's report of 1919 is summarised in the *Annual Report of the Chief Medical Officer of the Board of Education 1919*, PP 1920, xv, Cmd 995, p. 29.

28 Not all the evidence, however, indicates improvement. Comparison of the proportion of children enjoying excellent nutrition in 1915 at age eight and 1919 at age twelve (Table 2.2) and possessing clothing and foot wear that could be classed as good (Table 2.5) suggests on the contrary that this particular cohort had not caught up with those who had already reached the age of 12 in 1915.

29 This point is based on a comparison of the situation of entrants in 1915 with those of the intermediate group, two and four years later (see Tables 2.2, 2.3 and 2.5). Exact comparison is not possible because entry was not at a set age and variously two, three or four years could elapse before an entrant appeared in the intermediate group. In addition it should be stressed that the progression from entrant to intermediate, unlike that from intermediate to leaver, did not involve an absolute improvement in the circumstances of the cohort but rather that the deterioration was not as severe as to reduce them to a condition of the intermediate group at the time of their own entry into school (cf. above note 26).

30 Few cases of tuberculosis were identified at the routine examination of London schoolchildren as possible cases of tuberculosis were also considered at special investigations. See the summary of the Report of School Medical Officer for London 1919 in Board of Education, *Annual Report of the Chief Medical Officer of the Board of Education 1919*, PP 1920, xv, Cmd 995, p. 150. From the figures given by Dr Hammer it would appear that at least 1 per cent of London children had been diagnosed as having one or other forms of tuberculosis. In England as a whole tuberculosis *mortality* increased steadily between 1914 and 1917 within the age groups 5–9 and 10–14. By 1917 the rate per 1,000 living aged 5–9 was 0.19 for phthisis and 0.49 for other tuberculosis against 0.14 and 0.42 in 1914 and for the age group 10–14 0.38 and 0.35 against 0.31 and 0.28. Information on anaemia in London children is included in Table 2.6. The trend is upwards between 1915 and 1919 but the marked difference in the percentages, a maximum of 5 per cent against a minimum of 34 per cent in the Saxon schools implies a major discrepancy in the identification of anaemia. In the Gloucestershire study (see below note 32) the incidence of anaemia declined to parallel the improvement in nutrition.

31 A considerable effort would appear to have been made by the author of the report to discount any impression that the health of the children was adversely affected by the wartime shortages. This interpretation of the data was corrected by later commentators. Compare Oschmann, 'Der Einfluss der Kriegkost auf die Schulkinder', *Zeitschrift für Schulgesundheitspflege*, 30 (2) (1917) with the summary in Johannes Lehmann, 'Untersuchungen über Gewicht, Grosse und Hämoglobingehalt des Blutes der Kinder einer Bürgerschule in Löbau', *Zeitschrift für Schulgesundheitspflege*, 33 (3) (1920). However, height and weight are also not entirely satisfactory indicators of nutritional status. In 1920, for example, the School Medical Officer for Gloucestershire reported a 1–2 per cent decline in weight comparing 1916–20 with 1908–15 despite an increase in the percentage of children whose nutrition was 'above average', cf. note 32.

32 In 1920 for example the School Medical Officer for Gloucestershire was reporting an extraordinary increase in 'above average' nutrition comparing the period 1916–20 with 1908–15. Among leavers, on the other hand, the percentage with 'below normal' nutrition remained unchanged at 17 per cent. See Board of Education, *Annual Report of the Chief Medical Officer of the Board of Education 1920*, PP 1921, xi, Cmd 1522, p. 55.

33 See for example the claims cited below by Deborah Thom, chapter 11, p. 297, and for employment trends between 1911 and 1931, Diana Gittins, *Fair sex, family size and structure 1900–39*, London, 1982, pp. 45, 70. In other European countries the context may have been quite different. For example, as J.-L. Robert makes clear in chapter 9, in France the war marked the start of a secular downturn in the proportion of women in the labour force.

34 A number of women who had been employed on munitions work during the war were interviewed by Deborah Thom. Her findings are reported below, pp. 307, 315–17.

35 The following account is based on the data on women's employment in July 1914 and November 1918 and summarised below in chapter 11, Appendices I and II, pp. 318–23.

36 Indicated by an increase of at least five positions in terms of the proportion of the labour force that was female, see below, chapter 11, Appendix I, pp. 318–20.

37 Below chapter 11, Appendix II, column 3, pp. 321–3.

38 Below chapter 11, Appendix II, column 4, pp. 321–3.

39 Report of Education Officer to Children's Care Sub-Committee, 30 March 1917.

40 The proportion varied, however, from area to area ranging from more than eight of every ten working women in one school district in Poplar to just over half in one of the districts in neighbouring Bethnal Green (see Table 2.9).

41 Many mothers of course may have been employed but able to work at home. For the importance of this in the German context see the contribution of Ute Daniel, below, chapter 13, pp. 276–8.

42 Other factors thought to have promoted delinquency were irregular attendance at school, the general excitement occasioned by the war and undue leniency by the courts. Among the remedies proposed were controls on sensational hoardings and a prohibition on the presence in cinemas after 8 p.m. of those under the age of 14. See Children's Care Sub-Committee, 10 February 1917. Also to be noted is the very different context of the opposition of some German youth to the family as an institution before, during and after the war, as recounted below by Jürgen Reulecke, chapter 16, pp. 439–52.

43 Children's Care Sub-Committee, 30 March 1917, 21 October 1917. For the arrangements made by Bavarian working mothers for the care of their children see below Table 2.12.

44 For Bethnal Green see Children's Care Sub-Committee, 30 March 1917. The withdrawal of married women from the labour market is reported for Paddington in February 1915 in EO/WEL/1/5. The attitude of the officials to a working widow can be followed through the Care Committee reports on the Deane family, Children's Care Sub-Committee, 16 July 1916. This last case is also discussed below, pp. 97–8.

45 See for example the reports of unemployment amongst seamstresses and tailoresses in Hammersmith in October 1914 in EL/WEL/1/4. Unemployment amongst women and girls was also reported in neighbouring districts of West London.

46 Children's Care Sub-Committee, 22 October 1915.

47 Regional Office of Statistics, Munich, *Die Frau in der bayerischen Kriegsindustrie*, Beiträge zur Statistik Bayerns, 92, Munich, 1920. The same source is used below by Ute Daniel in her broader account of women's wartime employment in Germany, see chapter 10, pp. 271–4.

48 This is implied, for example, in the report on employment in Fulham in 1914 where it was noted that with the workforce in factories and laundries gradually returning to full-time or three-quarters time, several girls had turned down positions as domestic servants. See EO/WEL/1/4. Report on unemployment and distress in Fulham, 3 October 1914.

49 Between 1914 and 1918 women's share of the total British workforce rose from 24 per cent to 38 per cent. See the contribution of Deborah Thom, chapter 11, Appendix I, p. 320 and for the situation in Germany, Ute Daniel, chapter 10, pp. 268–74, 276–8.

50 Regional Office of Statistics, Munich, *Die Frau in der bayerischen Kriegsindustrie*, pp. 74–5.

51 Cf. Table 2.11, rows 4, 8 and 10. Declines from modest pre-war positions are also suggested for such 'traditional' female employments as shop assistant, seamstress, and catering. The proportion expecting employment in agriculture was also lower than had been employed in this sector before the war but as Ute Daniel makes clear in chapter 10 the extent of agricultural work by women, being often ancillary to other tasks, is often underestimated in employment censuses. The Statistisches Landesamt also stated that women themselves may have under-reported their expectation of returning to agricultural employment because of the ease with which this could be achieved. See Regional Office of Statistics, Munich, *Die Frau in der bayerischen Kriegsindustrie*, p. 62.

52 Regional Office of Statistics, Munich, *Die Frau in der bayerischen Kriegsindustrie*, pp. 69, 76, but see also 88–9. Whereas the emphasis in the account of the Munich Armeekorpbezirk was on the numbers of women returning to housework who had expressed a preference for factory work, the report on employment in the Würzburg Armeekorpbezirk pointed to the numbers of women formerly without employment who would now be compelled to consider remaining within the labour market.

53 However the distinction between 'boarded out' and 'day board' remains obscure.

54 The long-term trends in household structure in Britain are set out in R. Wall, 'Regional and temporal variations in the structure of the British household since 1851' in T. C. Barker and M. Drake (eds.), *Population and society in Britain 1850–1980*, London, 1982, pp. 62–99.

55 The data come from a larger set covering 13 communities between 1891 and 1921. Names and addresses were not included but otherwise comprehensive information was available on age, sex, marital status, occupation, employment status and birthplace. I would like to express my gratitude to the Office of Population Censuses and Surveys for their willingness to make the data available. I am also indebted to my colleague Kevin Schurer for having written the computer programmes that generated the tables on household structure.

56 Countries with population registers may eventually provide such information. For a positive view of these registers see David I. Kertzer, *Family life in central Italy 1880–1910*, New Brunswick, NJ, 1984, p. 11 and references.

57 Regional Office of Statistics, Munich, *Der Kriegs-Volkszählungen vom 1916 und 1917 in Bayern*, Munich, 1919.

58 For example there were only 72 persons for every 100 in households of 11 persons or more in 1916 compared with 1910, but 83 for every 100 in households of size 7 and 95 for every 100 in households of size 5.

59 Cf. below Armin Triebel, chapter 5.

60 Calculated from Table 2.14. Mean household size was 4.65 in 1910 and 4.27 in 1916.

61 To the regret of the Statistisches Landesamt, the topic had not been selected for analysis. *Der Kriegs-Volkszählungen vom Jahre 1916 und 1917 in Bayern*, pp. 109–10.

62 Misstatements of age, particularly the rounding of ages to 30 and 40 by females depress the observed sex ratio at these ages at the expense of the immediately surrounding years (see Figure 2.2).

63 M. Ferro, *The Great War*, p. 225.

64 Another major reason for selection was the ready availability of further information on family patterns in that community at a later date. This was true, for example, in the case of Swansea, York and Banbury. The full list of communities selected for analysis was Abergavenny, Axminster, Banbury, Bethnal Green, Bolton, Earsdon, Morland, Pinner, Saffron Walden, Stoke, Swansea, Walthamstow and York. A preliminary set of results, prepared in association with Peter Laslett and Kevin Schurer, was presented to a conference of the British Society for Population Studies in February 1987.

65 Within these areas certain enumeration districts only were selected for analysis because of the costs of keying in and then analysing large quantities of data. Even so, the total population across all census years and all 13 districts was 401,116. In 1921 there were on average 8,458 persons per district ranging from 4,202 in Morland, to 14,521 in York. Saffron Walden (the town of Saffron Walden was not itself included) contained 4,777, Bolton 5,997 and Pinner 9,032. Every effort was made to ensure that the enumeration districts selected in successive census years encompassed the same area but since enumeration district boundaries were frequently subject to radical revision and the maps that were prepared of them have not survived, it proved impossible to achieve a perfect match of area from census to census.

66 The exception is Morland where in 1921 under 1 per cent of women under 35 were recorded as widowed against 2 per cent in 1911. In none of the four were more than 5 per cent of women in 1921 widowed at any single year of age under 35.

67 Calculated from the proportion of each age group not yet married in 1911 and 1921. The method is that of John Hajnal, see J. Hajnal 'Age at marriage and proportions marrying', *Population Studies* , 7 (1953), 111–36.

68 For example in all the communities there were actually higher proportions of women aged 20–4 unmarried in 1921, than in 1911. Lower proportions unmarried in the age group 25–9 were found in Bolton and Saffron Walden and lower proportions in the age group 30–4 in Pinner and Saffron Walden.

69 For an illustration of the strength of this relationship in some English pre-industrial populations see Wall 'The household: demographic and economic change in England 1650–1970' in Richard Wall, Peter Laslett and Jean Robin (eds.), *Family forms in historic Europe*, Cambridge, 1983, p. 494.

70 Two measures suggest that household formation was constrained in 1921: the ratio of adults to household and the comparison of the actual number of households with the number that could have been formed had the age, sex and marital status specific headship rates of 1951 applied. The evidence is summarised in Wall 'Regional and temporal variations in the structure of the British household since 1851', pp. 85–6.

71 The institutional population is excluded from the present study as there is no way of reallocating to the districts selected for analysis those former inhabitants resident in an institution at the time of the census. For long-term trends in the proportion of the elderly population resident in institutions in England see Wall, 'Residential isolation of the elderly, a comparison over time', *Ageing and Society*, 4 (1984), p. 487.

72 Cf. note 70 above.
73 Service as a stage in the life-cycle for both males and females is readily discernible in pre-industrial English society, see Peter Laslett, *Family life and illicit love in earlier generations*, Cambridge, 1977, p. 34. It was Laslett who first coined the term 'life-cycle servant'.
74 The area of Pinner included in our study, for example, contained 9,032 people in 1921 whereas in 1911 there were just 6,719.
75 The ideal target group for our purposes would be widows under the age of 40 rather than widows under the age of 60 but the first set of results did not permit a finer breakdown. From just four populations there are difficulties too over the small number of cases falling within any particular sub-population, difficulties which would only multiply were the widowed group in question slimmed down to those under 40.
76 See below chapter 3, pp. 115–17, 129–30.
77 LCC EO/WEL/1/4, Reports on unemployment and distress in Chelsea and Fulham, 3 October 1914; EL/WEL/1/5 Report on unemployment and distress in Fulham, 16 February 1915.
78 The absence of a male breadwinner by itself was sufficient to push a family deep into poverty. More than half of all the families in Islington whose children had been on the London County Council's feeding lists for at least six months in March 1916 lacked a father either through death (45 per cent) or separation or desertion (6 per cent) and the position in other London boroughs such as St Pancras and Finsbury was not dissimilar. See LCC Children's Care Sub-Committee, 17 March 1916, 19 May 1916 and 23 June 1916 and cf. below on the Shoreditch Local Association, note 85.
79 A number of them no doubt are represented in the cases brought before the Children's Care Sub-Committee and classed as military, or directly or indirectly owing to the war, see note 17 above.
80 EL/WEL/1/4. Reports on unemployment and distress in Chelsea and Fulham, 3 October 1914, EO/WEL/1/5. Report on employment and distress in Fulham, 16 February 1915.
81 EO/WEL/1/4. Report on unemployment and distress in Chelsea, 3 October 1914.
82 EL/WEL/1/4. Report on unemployment and distress in Hammersmith, 3 October 1914. Cf. J. M. Winter, *The Great War and the British people*, London, 1985, p. 36, although Winter also notes an early rush to enlist from most well-paid occupations, p. 34.
83 EL/WEL/1/4. Report on unemployment and distress in St Pancras, 3 October 1914 and Hammersmith, 16 January 1915; EL/WEL/1/5. Report on unemployment and distress in Fulham, 16 February 1915.
84 Children's Care Sub-Committee, details of 'chronic cases' presented by the Islington Association, 17 March 1916 and by the St Pancras Chronic Cases Sub-Committee, 19 May 1916.
85 Children's Care Sub-Committee, details of 'chronic cases' presented by the Shoreditch Local Association, 17 March 1916. See also note 78.
86 EO/WEL/1/4. Report on unemployment and distress in Kensington, 3 October 1916.
87 See for example EO/WEL/1/5. Reports on unemployment and distress in Kensington and Lewisham, 16 February 1915.
88 Reports on this subject are amongst the papers of the Committee for

19 November 1915 and 21 January 1916. The first is in the form of a statement from M. Frere on a conference called by the Charity Organisation Society to discuss the alleged increase of drinking by women. The Society's evidence was derived from its own district committees, the Committees of the SSFA, house agents and a magistrates court. By January the Children's Care Sub-Committee had available the results of its own enquiry derived from the reports of Divisional Superintendents and School Attendance Officers.

89 Children's Care Sub-Committee, 21 January 1916. Except where otherwise stated, the account in the text is derived from this report.

90 Similar claims had been made before, see for example EO/WEL/1/5, Report on unemployment and distress in Paddington, 16 February 1915. Other factors inducing increased drinking by women according to the January 1916 enquiry were the excitement, and sometimes the worry, of having a husband in the army, and the desire to give relatives and friends a good send-off.

91 Children's Care Sub-Committee, 19 November 1915 and see note 88 above.

92 Children's Care Sub-Committee, 14 July 1916. The information available to the Committee was based on an analysis of the After Care Index, a record of jobs held by children after leaving school, the half yearly reports of the After Care Workers, supplemented by special enquiries among care workers, head teachers and club managers. Six districts which reported directly to labour exchanges were not included in the study.

93 The focus here is on the juvenile labour market. For the situation in general see above pp. 54–8 and also the contribution of Deborah Thom, below, pp. 301–10.

94 For the proportion of mothers with school-age children in certain of the London school districts, who worked outside the home, see above Table 2.9.

95 For the flexibility of the family's response to opportunities in the labour market see my account of the adaptive family economy, 'Work welfare and the family: an illustration of the adaptive family economy' in L. Bonfield, R. M. Smith and K. Wrightson (eds.), *The world we have gained*, Oxford, 1986, pp. 261–94. On the allocation of family tasks to daughters to accommodate two years of schooling, see Mary Russell Mitford's sketch of the early stage of the female life-cycle, *Our village*, Everyman Editions, London, 1936, pp. 135–6.

96 Cf. above and see Regional Office of Statistics, Munich, *Die Frau in der bayerischen Kriegsindustrie*, p. 69.

97 *Ibid.*, pp. 83–4.

98 Reports of the case are in the papers of the Children's Care Sub-Committee of 16 July 1915.

99 Reported to the Children's Care Sub-Committee, 19 March 1915.

100 Children's Care Sub-Committee, 13 February 1920. The emphasis is my own.

101 For the situation in Vienna see the contribution of Reinhard Sieder, below, chapter 3, pp. 132–4, and for Germany, David F. Crew, 'German socialism, the state and family policy, 1918–33', *Continuity and Change*, 1 (1986), 235–62.

II
CONDITIONS OF LIFE AND STANDARDS OF LIVING

3

Behind the lines: working-class family life in wartime Vienna

Reinhard J. Sieder

Whilst we have detailed information on military events in the years 1914–18, research on the social effects of the First World War is – at least in Austria – still in its preliminary stages.[1] Early attempts at social and cultural history like the *History of Mores in the First World War*, brought out by Magnus Hirschfeld and Andreas Gaspar[2] in 1929, have not been taken further. The four volumes of the first edition were amongst the first books burnt by Goebbels after the Nazi seizure of power.

This chapter discusses those social developments which occurred far behind the front: in the houses and dwellings of the workers, where in the war years women, children, the elderly and youths waged a battle to survive. The primary focus will be on four particular issues. First, we need to consider how working-class families found food and fuel in the years of dearth during the war and the early post-war period. This leads to the second issue which is whether the destitute working-class women's stubborn struggle to survive in any way undermined established patriarchal values. Thirdly, there is the question of whether the considerable contribution of young people to this struggle for survival succeeded in reducing their strict subjugation to the authority of their parents. Did young people rebel against the defeated society of their fathers? And finally we must ask what the experience of the trenches meant for working-class men. If they returned at all, could it be that they frequently did so as 'disabled patriarchs' – crippled, sick and depressed? The final hypothesis will be that the collapse of the Austro-Hungarian Monarchy was in fact the collapse of a male society – the old Emperor dead, his young successor in flight, the Church robbed of its power and prestige, particularly amongst the workers.

Information about everyday life in the cities far behind the lines is rarely recorded. Yet much is retained in the memories of people still alive who

REINHARD SIEDER

lived through those war years and can still be brought to light even at this late date. With the help of historical interviews, it is possible to preserve from oblivion a piece of history about the 'people in the street', in a difficult phase of their life. This is the history in which the shabby reality rather than the great battles is to be recorded, the ersatz coffee and infested clothes, the dropsy of the returned husband or the marriage broken up by the war. In this sense, it is a small piece of history from below.

Our account of everyday life on the 'home front' will be based partly on the evidence of the sparse cultural and social histories of the First World War, partly on the analysis of contemporary debates and partly on the personal testimony of those who lived through the war.[3] The focus is necessarily on the memories of childhood and early youth since the persons interviewed were only born around the year 1900. It follows, too, that we will be concerned with working-class families in a certain stage of their life-cycle. At the outbreak of war most of the people quoted on the following pages were between four and fifteen years old. Their parents to whom they refer would then have been aged between 24 and 40. There is no information, therefore, on those families whose fathers were of such an age that they were exempted from military service and whose sons became soldiers. The difficulties experienced by those families in wartime conditions cannot be assessed.

On the other hand, our sample of 60 Viennese working-class families does represent the typical working-class family involved in the 1914–18 war. Figures published in June 1918 show that 72 per cent of all Viennese soldiers killed in action were between 20 and 40 years old. Of all Viennese soldiers killed 60 per cent were members of the working class; 70 per cent of them were married. Their widows had to take care of their children.[4] Thus our evidence does represent the typical case of a working-class family, where the father was either at the front, or employed in war production. The soldier's wife was at home looking after small children or working in war industry, and the children went through the daily struggle for subsistence at home.

Foraging for food and fuel

As mentioned earlier, the first question at issue is this: where did working-class families find food and fuel in the war years? If one asks working-class people, who were then in their childhood, what was their experience of the war years and which memories they retain most vividly, all answer: it was a time of queuing for hours on end, of scrounging for food and gathering firewood, of 'war bread' which fell apart in one's hands, and of turnips; it was a time of hunger and freezing cold.

When the Austro-Hungarian Monarchy declared war on Serbia on 28 July 1914, the government as well as the people were only prepared for a

110

short war. When it became obvious, however, that the campaign would be a long one, people realised that the war was not only to be fought on the battlefields but would encompass also both war industries and the food supply of the civilian population.

Admittedly, in peacetime the Austro-Hungarian Monarchy was more self-sufficient in food production than the German Reich, France or Great Britain. However, for agricultural products, the Austrian half of the Monarchy was principally dependent upon Hungary. The latter, the *Kornkammer* (granary) of the Monarchy, had produced a surplus of grain which could easily compensate for the structural weakness of grain production in the Austrian part of the monarchy. After the outbreak of war, however, Hungary reduced its deliveries of grain and refused to release details on the real figures of its grain production.[5] Additionally there was sabotage, mainly in the Slavic areas of the *Vielvölkerreich* (multi-national empire). The decrease in grain production was also partly caused by military disturbances (Galicia, Bukowina, Gorz), the decline in the peasant population because of military conscription, and the confiscation of horses and oxen by the army. Grain produced in the Austro-Hungarian Monarchy fell from 9.2 million tons in 1914 to 6.2 million tons in 1917 and to 5.3 million tons in 1918.[6] The amount of grain required was estimated to be about 10 million tons per year. The deficit in grain production became all the more serious as other foodstuffs like rice, which were a potential substitute, were also in short supply because of the restriction on trade introduced by the *Entente*.

This naturally affected the cities and the industrial areas of Austria, above all the capital of the Empire, Vienna, with its two million inhabitants. The extensive purchase of foodstuffs, put in hand by the army, resulted in a rapid rise in prices – particularly in grain and flour. Widespread hoarding aggravated the situation. As early as October 1914, the *Entente*'s hunger blockade began to be felt and henceforth as much as 30 per cent and more of the flour for bread was derived from barley, maize and potato. All those whom I interviewed clearly remember the maize bread which fell apart in one's hands when one wanted to cut it. Karl Bauer for instance, born in 1911, said:

Until 1914, I cannot remember what food was like. But, then, when the war began, maize bread. Then we got half a loaf of bread a day between everybody[7] and mother sat in a meadow in summer – there she sat on a stool – and then, because the bread always came in the afternoon, one of us went to get the bread and put it in Mother's apron – since it fell apart – and everyone got a handful of these crumbs. Well, we were often very hungry, very hungry.

(Interview 52, p. 7)

From February 1915 the state began to purchase grain directly from the producers by means of the 'War-Grain-Transport Organisation' and distributed it at fixed prices. The aim was to halt the continuous rise in prices and suppress the free play of market forces. This innovation marked the launch of the Austrian war economy. In early 1915 ration-cards for bread and flour were introduced and further rationing of foodstuffs with ration-cards and 'shopping-cards' followed. In May 1915 two 'meatless days' per week were introduced – a farce for most working-class families which had long since been unable to afford meat. The caloric value of the food obtainable with these cards was minimal. For example, the card of a worker in heavy industry permitted a daily intake of 1,292.7 calories. however, such a worker normally consumed 3,900 or more calories per day.[8] Clearly had the working class been exclusively dependent upon the official food allowance, they could not have been able to survive. Yet given the conditions of a war economy, it was no easy task to obtain more food. At this point the capacity for ingenuity and craftiness in the organisation of survival, and for flexibility in the struggle for food, fuel and clothing came into play.

At weekends many working-class women, young people and children went out to the harvested fields in the countryside around Vienna to gather up the remaining ears of corn. This, for example, is the story of Anton Srmcka, who was born in 1902 and began an apprenticeship in a strategic industrial plant in 1917. His father and his elder brother were at the front. Anton lived with his mother in one of those 'one-room-plus-kitchen flats', the common experience for the majority of working-class families at the time:

I came home one Saturday. My mother sat there, she cried, she said, I can't give you anything, I've got nothing to eat! We went straight off to the fields in Schwechat and picked ears of corn in the fields, even though they'd already been harvested. Of course, there wasn't much left by then. We weren't the first ones. *Hundreds* went picking them, and we gathered the ears of corn.

And then I went, because those bundles of corn were all around, you know, they hadn't been gathered in yet, as I can still remember it, you know, and I was on the look-out all the time to see if anyone was about and I didn't see a soul, not a soul. So I went up to a bundle and like broke off a couple of ears. Didn't a policeman just have to see me and take me off?! He saw it from a distance . . . so, my mother cried and of course begged him not to take me away, she needed me. So he saw sense.

We went home with the ears of corn we'd collected and my mother put them in a pillow-case and threshed them, so that the little grains didn't fall out, you know . . . threshed the ears, like beat them, so the grains fell out of the ears, and we ground the little grains in the coffee-grinder, and she made a soup out of it. And that was our food for that Saturday.

(Interview 8, pp. 5–6)

It was customary for the Viennese poor to visit the fields of estate owners in the south-west of the city to collect remaining ears of corn. This was tolerated but frequently policemen and the owners tried to protect the corn bundles, which had not yet been collected in, from 'predatory attacks' by ordinary people. The incident involving the policeman is one of many examples of the danger of criminal charges, to which, in the struggle to survive, children and young people were especially exposed. This applied equally to the collection of ears of corn, the attempt to gather firewood in the Wienerwald and the smuggling of hoarded foodstuffs past police checkpoints.

For many young working-class people this probably constituted a decisive early experience in their dealings with uniformed authority – an authority which represented the state, a class state which aimed at protecting the property of the rich, however needy the poor. From early childhood they learnt to outwit uniformed authority. In peacetime, in the alleys of the working-class districts, they used to warn each other of approaching policemen by means of coded signals. During the hunger riots of 1911 they had learnt to avoid mounted soldiers, or, more innocuously, to outwit the uniformed park attendant, the guardian of the Vienna River and so forth.[9] In the period of famine during the First World War, these skills became necessary for survival.

The way in which the mother of Anton Srmcka threshed the ears of corn, which they had collected, in a pillow-case may either have been her own innovation or the result of knowledge that had been passed on by neighbouring women, the knowledge of the destitute. Frau Weiss, the wife of a brewery worker, used a rolling-pin to 'thresh' grain, from which she then baked bread. Her daughter, who was born in 1903, recalls:

During the war . . . we went picking ears of corn, and it was dried and threshed and ground and then we had something to eat . . . in the farmyard or . . . in the field, something was spread out and the ears of corn were put on it and we had a rolling-pin and we banged away with it, but that was good fun.
. . . we had a sort of grinder . . . a sort of gristmill, you know, which we fixed to the table and then we ground it and . . . my mother made a loaf, and she sifted it through, and a bit of flour came out and it was very tasty.
(Interview 17, p. 19)

Each day, the struggle for each little morsel of food was repeated. Even in peacetime working-class household budgets could not be planned far in advance and the short-term nature of the planning became more pronounced in the war years. The changes resulting from the war may be judged by considering the family life of the working class as it was before the war. Forward planning had still been a possibility through cooking two or three days ahead. In peacetime, when working-class fathers came back from work every day, the evening meal was the most important one of the day, during the working week. On weekdays, it was the only short period which parents and children spent together. The daily ritual of the working man's return home symbolised patriarchal authority in the family. Whilst at midday wife and children usually ate something light, the communal evening meal was cooked:

... for the evening, because then you had to cook proper. Because father came home then and then you had to cook a proper meal and not just heat something up.

(Interview 19, p. 9)

In the evening we [the mother and the children] were all waiting for my father to come home. Everything had to be ready and in place, so that he could have his meal at once. That was the most important event of the day!

(Interview 27, p. 34)

In peacetime the husband and father was the central figure at every meal that the family ate together. This was clearly expressed in the way that portions were served. The children and sometimes the wife, too, were expected to wait their turn after the father and husband, when a piece of meat was being divided up:

When we were small, there was a big bowl of noodles with poppy seed and sugar in the middle of the table and we often used to look at our father's plate when he got a piece of meat. They [the parents] said: 'Now children, when you're earning a living, then you can have a bit of meat, too!'

(Interview 4, p. 2)

But when there was sufficient meat for everyone, the father was always given the biggest piece, 'That's obvious!' (Interview 2, p. 17).

It was similar with the beer drunk at the midday meal on Sundays. Anna Neumann, born 1903 as the daughter of a skilled worker, a lithographer, recalls the very symbolic way in which her father and mother shared a pint of beer:

On Sundays then it wasn't bottled beer, I always ran with a mug, I can remember, my mother was allowed to bite it off[10] and then my father emptied it.

(Interview 3, p. 5)

The priority that was clearly accorded the working-class man as the head of the family reflected general recognition of the logic that the first task of the worker's family had to be to strengthen the 'breadwinner'. This way of distributing food should be understood as the result of a situation where such necessities were notoriously scarce. Furthermore, this was one of the few opportunities where the family man's desire for authority could be recognised and reinforced. The working-class wife did everything to support her husband's claim to be the master in the home and provider of food for the family, even at her own cost and at the cost of their children.[11]

If, then, prior to the war, the structure of the working-class family was clearly authoritarian, what did the outbreak of war, the initial high unemployment and the drafting of the men into the army, mean for the distribution of authority in the working-class family?

The retention of patriarchy

The abrupt cessation of exports, and the failure of raw materials to reach their intended destination led initially to numerous cases of factories working at reduced capacity, or having to close. In August 1914, the first month of the war, 566 Viennese factories involved in the metal industry were closed, affecting 10,102 workers.[12] In most instances the regulations that there should be notice of the closure, were ignored. However, with the adaptation of industry to the needs of war, initial unemployment was soon transformed into a labour shortage. On the one hand, all the factories which could adapt to the production of strategic items such as foodstuffs, weapons, munitions, medicines and bandaging material experienced an economic upturn.[13] On the other hand, conscription began to take its toll. In the Austrian half of the Empire, a total of approximately 4.3 million men were conscripted into the army. That was around 60 per cent of the male population between the ages of 18 and 53. The number of Austrian soldiers killed in action was about 810,000.[14] According to the statistics referred to above,[15] the majority of Viennese soldiers were members of the working class. At least the statistics give the impression that members of the working class and the lower strata of the white-collar workers (Angestellte) were exposed to the highest risk of losing their lives at the front. Of all Viennese men killed in action 88 per cent were workers or had white-collar jobs and were in general scarcely in better circumstances than the workers. Only 11 per cent of the dead were described as self-employed, officials or academics.

If the exorbitant rise in prices, the shortage of food, and unemployment at the beginning of the war undermined the working-class family, it was further thrust into a situation of extreme misery by the calling up of family members old enough to do military service. The relief given by the state to the wives of the soldiers was one-and-a-half Kronen at maximum, frequently it was just 85 Heller a day. In 1919, however, a loaf of bread cost 32 Heller. Working-class families lost not only the greater part of their monetary income, but also the head of the family who, as we have seen, constituted the primary focus of attention in the family's every-day life. His place at the kitchen table was now empty. Now, one or two of his children slept in his bed next to the forsaken wife. Josef N., born in 1901, the eldest son of an unskilled factory hand, recalls:

So when my father had to go to the front, I lay in his bed beside my mother. My younger sister slept between us. I was only fourteen years old at the time and I felt very grown-up. I thought, somebody must be father while he is not there. And each Saturday my mother and I worked out how we could get by on the little sum of money which I earned.

(Interview 63, p. 43)

As the mother had previously waited for her husband to return home from work, now she waited for her son. As she had done so before, she considered it to be her duty, first and foremost, to put something tasty on the table for him. Older sons moved suddenly into the position of the father and found themselves confronted with an increase in authority and responsibility. Daughters were drawn into the running of the household, more so than in peacetime. And one of the most important tasks here, as we shall note below, was to queue for hours on end for potatoes, margarine and horsemeat. It was usual, too, in working-class families in Vienna during the decades before the war, for daughters to be taught to do housework, and for most of the income of children who worked to be used to support the family. Only a small amount of pocket money was handed back to them. The new development was the larger share of their contribution to the family budget, the increased importance of their diverse activities aimed at securing the family's physical survival and – not least – the growing son's partial filling of the authority-vacuum created by the father's absence.

For the wives of the absent working-class men and the mothers of elder sons who were recruited by the army, shouldering the burden of leadership in the family was possible only to a limited degree. At least, sections of certain interviews point in this direction. It would appear that the women were so thoroughly conditioned to feel inferior in relation to their menfolk, that they were not able to make the wartime absence of their husbands or eldest sons the occasion for creating autonomous positions. If at all possible, a man – their father, father-in-law or a son – temporarily assumed the leadership of the family. When her husband was sent to the front, Maria S.'s father-in-law, a widower, came to stay with the family, because 'there must be a man in the family in times like that' (Interview 9, p. 25). Grete Fischer, who was born in 1905, the daughter of a skilled worker, was reprimanded by her mother when she refused to clean her elder brother's shoes:

She said that I should be happy that we had a man at home, now that Dad was at the front. Give him his due!

(Interview 16, p. 42)

Whilst before the war it was a widely accepted practice for boys to let themselves be attended to by their sisters, this tendency was accentuated during the war, when the family needed a wage and the father was at the front. Frau Bauer, who was born in 1902 and grew up in a Vienna working-class district with two brothers, recalls:

Table 3.1. *Real wages during the First World War (in* Kaufkronen, *i.e. nominal weekly wage in Kronen divided by an inded of the cost of living)*

Profession	July 1914	July 1915	July 1916	July 1917	July 1918
Mason	34	21.52	10.71	5.37	5.16
Metal-worker (turner)	40	31.65	16.67	9.84	6.37
Printer (typesetter)	40	25.32	13.69	8.94	8.61
Coachman	28	21.52	11.90	6.86	3.96
Baker	38	24.68	11.61	8.35	4.82

Source
W. Winkler, *Die Einkommensverschiebungen*, p. 141

Well, my eldest brother, he was a rogue. He worked at Werner & Pfleiderer.[16] He came home, took off his overalls, threw them down, well, and then he went and he had a wash; well, half the kitchen was under water, wasn't it, and then he got dressed. I says to him: well, and who's going to clean that up? He says: What are you here for, then? Once he threw the water pot at me, right into the bedroom, because I talked back. He was always like that, so violent.

(Interview 7, p. 14)

Income losses and the increase of women's employment

The development of the war economy led to a serious decline in income for the masses. Real income declined between 60 and 90 per cent during the war. The rise in prices made the situation virtually intolerable. Price inflation amounted to 121 per cent in 1915 and rose to more than 200 per cent in 1916.[17] The gap between inflation and income grew so rapidly that the reproduction of the wage-dependent parts of the population was endangered. Cost-of-living allowances were authorised and a 'family allowance' (*Familienzulage*) was established to help the families of workers to survive the difficult conditions (see Table 3.1).[18]

At the beginning of the war the need for army uniforms brought thousands of women into outwork. The Kriegsfürsorge and the Viennese Communal Women's Help Organisation (uniting most of the women's organisations) opened *Näh- und Strickstuben* (see Plate 1) which distributed working material to the outworking women. By January 1916, 29 *Nähstuben* had been opened, employing 2,000 to 8,000 women, most of them as homeworkers.[19] Very soon, however, the raw materials vanished and most of the women were forced to move to the munition plants or to the *Verkehrsbetriebe* (communal traffic enterprises). This was supported by

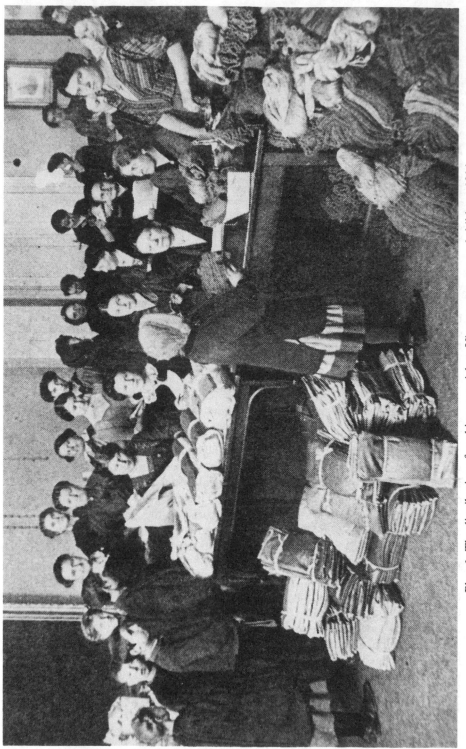

Plate 1. The distribution of working materials to Viennese women and children, 1916

Table 3.2. *Proportion of female workers in Viennese
metal industries*

Year	Total workforce	Female workers	% female
1913	65,789	12,180	18.51
1914	69,065	15,407	22.31
1915	78,068	20,767	26.60
1916	70,124	24,401	34.80
1917	86,807	31,401	36.17

Source
According to the statistics of the *Wiener Allgemeine Arbeiter
Krankenkasse* as cited by V. Stein, 'Die Lage der österreichischen
Metallarbeiter', p. 252.

several measures taken by the local authorities. The Commissions which
granted separation allowances (*Kriegsunterstützungen*) to those women
whose husbands had been conscripted were instructed to refuse support to
all women who did not care for small children. In this way, it was intended
married women would be forced into the war industries.[20]

Unfortunately, in the absence of an occupational census for the war years,
only figures for certain branches of the economy are available. For example,
the number of female employees in the Vienna Tramway Company
(Städtische Straßenbahnen) rose from 287 in June 1914 to 7,490 in June
1918.[21] That was 54.1 per cent of all employees of the Tramway Company.
In the metal industries the number of employed women rose rapidly during
the course of 1915 as well. Even jobs which had been seen as typical men's
jobs like welding, cutting, pressing, the handling of boring-machines and
lathes, etc., were taken over by women.[22]

According to the statistics of the industrial, trading and transport sectors
in the service of the Imperial and Royal Military Administration, a total of
363,970 women and 920,702 men were employed in 1916. In the same year,
61,573 women worked in the armaments and munition factories alongside
160,900 men.[23] For some of the munition plants it is said that up to 78 per
cent of the workers were female. The overall increase in the female labour
force during the war has been estimated as around forty per cent, representing about one million women entering the labour force in Austria during the
First World War.[24]

In general, women were less well paid than men. Even for the same kind
of work, women frequently earned just a third of the male wage. When a
male worker was replaced by a female one, the wage bill of the employer
declined sharply.[25] The majority of women who entered the factories during

the war did not join a union. By the end of 1916 the proportion of all workers (male and female) who were members of a trade union had fallen by sixty per cent. Only in the last two years of the war did large numbers of women enter trade unions.[26]

The role of the children

Whilst many women worked in the war industries, in the transport system, and so forth, or did domestic piece-work, the burden of organising food and fuel frequently fell on the children and those young people who did not already have a job. Queuing for hours in front of food shops and coal dumps, gathering firewood in the Wienerwald, and so on, are amongst their most frequent and evidently indelible memories. Once again let us listen to the war children talking about those days. Anna Müller, born in 1905:

We children had to queue for potatoes and everything, you know . . . so they queued in front of shops, and as we moved forward to the door, the grown-ups said, go to the back, you jumped the queue, and it wasn't even true . . .and we did it a second time . . . we were half frozen to death, because we queued in winter, too, and by the time we'd moved up to the door, the potatoes were all gone.

(Interview 18, p. 12)

Anton Smrcka, born in 1902:

We often stood for whole nights in front of the shops, and finally, early in the morning – there were hundreds standing there, they didn't have that much, you know. When the policeman came: finished! And we'd stood there for half the night and now we had to go back home and hadn't got a thing.

(Interview 8, p. 4)

Again and again one of the children would be sent when word got around that in this or that shop potatoes, dripping or horsemeat would be on sale the following morning, and the less success people had, the earlier they would start queuing the next time. Even in winter, children were sent to queue. They tried to keep going through the long, cold nights, with blankets and stools, which they had brought along:

In the night there were a few of us girls. We took some blankets and a foot stool to sit down on. Maybe two hundred people were standing in rows of three. They all had blankets and stools, so that you could have a bit of a rest . . . when we got to the door, it was finished. So we started going more often at seven at night, and joined the queue so that we'd be right at the front.

(Interview 12, p. 19)

The disastrous distribution of foodstuffs and the rise of a clandestine black-market trade made social inequality more visible. Whilst the monied sections of the population could buy more or less anything on the thriving black market, even if it was at exorbitant prices,[27] the destitute labouring population was particularly affected by the shortage of foodstuffs. Their attempts to barter some of their belongings for food from the farmers remain as some of the most vivid memories of the years during and immediately after the war.

Every Sunday the station and railway trains were overflowing with people who were going to the farmers in the countryside, so as at least to cadge a piece of meat, bacon or sausage, a few eggs or the odd half-pound of butter or dripping.[28]

But the workers did not have any signet-rings or porcelain services to exchange for food. They offered their best remaining clothes (coats, suits, shoes) and when they had nothing more, they begged. Frau Bayer, who was born in 1902, remembers the attempts of her mother to get potatoes, milk and bread from farmers in the area:

And she took a rucksack and went off somewhere in the countryside. Well, if she got a drop of milk through charity somewhere or a little bit of bread, she was really happy . . .

And did she exchange anything for this?

Well, people did barter, you know, but we didn't have anything to barter!

(Interview 7, p. 24)

Frau Lintner remembers that, as a twelve-year-old, she begged for milk for her newly born brother, before going off to school, running from one milk shop to the next with a two-litre milk jug:

I went out every day for him at five in the morning with a two-litre milk jug . . . work it out yourself how many milk shops I had to go to get about two litres, if each one only gave me an eighth of a litre!

(Interview 29, p. 4)

In the years of war, hunger and food ration-cards, it paid to have relatives in the countryside. In times of greatest need, many farming families were ready to help out relatives in the town with things like a sack of potatoes:

My mother came from the Waldviertel . . . and this way we had some support, because relatives of ours were all still farmers.[29] They all got together, you know, and we got a sack of potatoes from them in the autumn . . . So, as far as I can remember, we had 6–8 sacks of potatoes, you know, they put them on the train and we had to fetch the potatoes from the station at Zwischenbrücken. We children had to take the trolley there and fetch the potatoes . . .

In February, March there wasn't any more left and then the really hard times started and lasted till the new harvest.

(Interview 8, p. 8)

Apart from the struggle against hunger, working-class families had to contend with the cold and freezing conditions of the war winter. In this case, too, the official arrangements for fuel distribution were far from adequate.

Plate 2. Foraging for fuel: 1

We had to go off picking up bits of coke and ears of corn. Do you know where? Down to the Danube, on foot. They brought the burnt stuff from the gas-works to the Danube, to the place where the barracks are today . . . They brought it there and my mother and us, my brother – who's still alive – and then the family next to us, they had two children of our age, together with them we went along this path and picked up the bits of coke, so that we had something to burn in the stove . . .

What did you carry them in?

In sacks, in potato sacks, we dragged them, on our backs. Nobody can talk to me about heavy work!

(Interview 17, p. 10)

At one station on the urban railway (*Stadtbahn*), there was a storage space for various coal companies. From time to time, brown coal was sold to the ordinary people. As in the case of foodstuffs, hundreds of Viennese queued during the night to be able to purchase a sack of brown coal. Anton Smrcka recalls:

We stood there at two o'clock in the morning and the whole breadth of the pavement was taken up by a packed crowd of people, right down to Währingerstrasse, and next day in the early morning, they began to sell the coal, you know . . . I can't remember now if we got twenty or thirty kilos, I'm not sure any more . . . You had to bring sacks, and they weighed them there . . . Mostly we got them back home with those sugar crates, with two wheels off a pram.

(Interview 8, p. 7)

Collecting firewood in the Wienerwald, too, was frequently the task of children and young people. Willi Horvath, the son of a construction worker who was born in 1906, asserts:

So I can only say that I walked for kilometres in the woods, looking for firewood.

(Interview 20, p. 39)

But in the freely accessible woods in the west and south-west of Vienna, there was hardly any 'picking wood' (i.e. branches lying on the ground) left after the first winter of the war. The Viennese had long since carried it off home on their backs. Willi Horvath and two friends knew a few tricks: they climbed over a fence into park which surrounded a country house, which, at the time, still belonged to an aristocratic family. They threw the picking wood, which was abundantly present there, over the fence and carried the wood home in bundles on their backs:

Outside the fence we didn't find a single bit of picking wood, you know . . . I can remember, sometimes we used to go up there twice a day to get wood, and each one of us carried down what we used to call a 'bundle' . . .

Wasn't that dangerous?

Well, you know, I can remember that once a gamekeeper ran after us with his dog,

Plate 3. Foraging for fuel: 2

Plate 4. Foraging for fuel: 3

but we made it over the fencing . . . and the gamekeeper didn't do anything about it
. . . I stood there shaking outside.

(Interview 20, pp. 39–40)

Karl Auer was born in 1907, the son of a plasterer whose wife worked as
an umbrella-maker. They lived in the working-class district of Ottakring.
Young Karl was also somebody who knew a few tricks: when there were no
more branches left on the ground, he climbed the trees and broke off individual branches with his feet. Of course, this was strictly prohibited and he
could not afford to let himself get caught doing it. But how else was he to get
firewood? Almost daily he marched off to the wood and clambered about
nimbly in the trees. His ankles and hands were soon raw from so much
scrambling about.

Popular disturbances and the official response

The longer the war lasted, the worse the situation became for the people.
The food supply was poor in 1917 and became dramatically worse in 1918.
In several areas of Austria, particularly in Vienna and the industrialised
region in the south-east of the city, hunger appeared. When there was no
longer any flour in the supply depots, the government ordered that ships on
the Danube *en route* to Germany should be stopped in order to divert the
flour for the inhabitants of Vienna. On the other hand, peasants and landowners maintained secret quantities of grain and vegetables in order to sell
them illegally at high prices to the wealthy citizens and their agents.

Working-class people who could not afford black market prices suffered
more severely. They were increasingly forced to take action on their own
initiative. In 1916 41.5 per cent of all strikes in Austria were so-called
'Hungerstrikes'; in 1917 they constituted 70.2 per cent. In May 1917,
42,000 Viennese industrial workers protested against the poor distribution
of food and against war by going on strike. Strikes reached a peak in January
1918. At the beginning of the year, food supply had reached its lowest point.
The negotiations in Brest–Litovsk had disappointed hopes for peace. When
the daily ration of flour was once again reduced, the employees of the
Daimler-Motorenwerke in Wiener Neustadt went on strike. Within a few
days nearly a million workers in Vienna, Lower and Upper Austria, Upper
Styria, Trieste, Krakau, Brünn and Budapest joined the strike, the biggest
in the history of the Austrian workers' movement. The workers passed a
series of resolutions demanding an improvement in the distribution of food
but also more serious negotiations for peace in Brest–Litovsk. Left-wing
radicals called for the installation of workers' and soldiers' councils
(Arbeiter- und Soldatenräte) as in Russia. The strikes were primarily con-

cerned with economic issues. The Social Democratic Workers' Party and the trade unions, however, persuaded the workers to abandon the strike, which eventually ended without any real success.[30]

Hunger constantly drove the Viennese into the countryside. At the end of 1918, approximately 30,000 people entered the rural parishes in the north of Vienna, to acquire potatoes from the farmers, who refused to sell any, pointing out that it was prohibited by the government. Thereupon, the crowd of mainly women and children went to the fields and took for themselves what the farmers refused to give them. Uniformed soldiers on leave tried to protect the women and children from the attacks of the peasants and the police. Finally, the crowd was dispersed with the help of the army and some police units.[31]

The more serious the popular disturbances became, the more the government attempted to relieve the situation of the worst affected poorer sections of the population. From July 1918, the Emperor-Karl-Welfare programme, called 'Children-to-the-countryside', organised two-month holidays with Hungarian farmers for approximately 100,000 children.[32] Heated rooms were made available for the large number of working-class people who, on account of the fuel shortage, were no longer able to heat their dwellings. They were at least able to spend a few hours in these rooms on cold winter days.

At the end of June 1918, the 'War Kitchens Campaign' was launched. This arranged for the provision of meals at low prices.[33] The Emperor visited such kitchens several times in an attempt to rescue the Monarchy's crumbling image. According to the head of the 'Communal Food Committee', General Landwehr, 'In spite of the fear . . . that the Emperor might be exposed to an affront, if not a more serious danger, if he went to these establishments in working-class districts when meals were being served . . . the Emperor and Her Majesty the Empress often visited the kitchens in the most decidedly working-class areas. An embarrassing incident never occurred.'[34] The table where they ate, always a place which in a curious way combined misery and authority for working-class people, was evidently, even in the dire situation of the second half of 1918, still not a scene of revolt against the crumbling old order and its highest representatives.

On account of an acute shortage of milk, many working-class women tried to keep a goat. However, at that time, goats were very difficult to acquire. Thousands of goats were transported from the Balkans to Vienna by the 'Communal Food Committee'. Many of them, unfortunately, did not survive the journey. Nevertheless, in the last years of the war, goats came to be extensively kept, especially in the outer districts of Vienna, and in the city's rural hinterland. This continued into the early post-war period.

As early as the first years of the war, many Viennese began cultivating small gardens in which they grew vegetables and fruit for their own consumption. Emperor Karl made available 200,000 square metres of land for allotments in the district of the Prater. A total of approximately 1,000 families acquired small gardens there. In addition, large areas in the Schmelz district and Simmering Heath were later brought under cultivation. In 1917, approximately 34,000 people were involved in this 'war-gardens movement' in Vienna and in the autumn of 1918 this rose to 157,300.[35] Even after the war had ended, large numbers of people from the working class, the civil service and small business, continued to obtain some of their food from these small gardens.

Whereas at the beginning of the war the general enthusiasm seemed to cover up the rifts in class society, the social gap widened continuously in the following years. When in summer 1918 it became obvious to the masses that the war was lost, the social standing of officers of the army declined rapidly. They were seen now by an increasing part of the population as belonging to the privileged class of the monarchy. Several insults to representatives of the army were reported. On 30 October 1918, the Social Democrats organised a big demonstration, in which 10,000 workers are said to have marched through the city of Vienna.[36] When the demonstration was officially over, groups of soldiers attacked army officers and stripped them of the emblem of the Monarchy. Some hundred soldiers marched to the Rossauerkaserne (the main barracks of the police) and demanded the release of deserters. On 31 October, a crowd stopped the car of the Minister of War, insulted him and destroyed his cockade.[37] How much the authority of the monarchy and its uniformed representatives had already been undermined may be judged from one of the recollections of the persons interviewed. Emil Huk, born in 1911, remembers an incident which happened to his father in the last months of the war:

Shortly before the end of the war, my father had a holiday. But he deserted and did not go back to his unit, along with many others. They knew what was to come and they saw that the war would not last much longer . . . In the first district, there was a public house which was used as a war kitchen at the time. There one could get a soup or vegetable scraps [*Gemüseschnitzel*] . . . And it was on one Sunday that my father and I drove there to eat vegetable scraps. Whoever wore a uniform was served first and he could ride on the trams free. So, he wore a uniform. A lot of people were queuing in front of the public house. Suddenly, a military policeman arrived. I remember an officer on his horse and behind him two figures with bayonets, just like Schwejk. When the officer saw my father, he stopped and summoned him. So my father went to him and showed the officer, on his request, his expired leave pass. Suddenly, there was a deafening noise, the officer cursed and his cheeks grew bigger. My father became terribly angry and he cried out: 'You *Tachinierer* [shirker]! In the country they lord it about!' and he started to attack the officer. The horse began to neigh; the officer tried to draw his sword . . . But the people were against him and they started to scream and shout and curse and throw stones at the officer. The officer turned and he galloped away and disappeared without trace. People were very angry. There was a policeman nearby who did not react at all. All this was possible then as it was a few days before the end.

(Interview 53, p. 9)

A constantly growing section of the suffering masses grew angry about the class in power, symbolically represented by the rich, the entrepreneurs, the dealers, the public authorities and the officers of the unsuccessful army. As the actual conflict of material and political interests between the classes intensified, social tensions grew as well. The political thinking of the labouring masses, however, was still rather diffuse and remote from revolutionary class consciousness.

The return of the wounded patriarchs

Reports of soldiers' experiences of the front indicate that the First World War, with the first use of artillery and trench tactics on a large scale, transformed a war of movement into a static war, leading all too frequently to an anonymous death in what Ernst Jünger called the 'storm of steel'.[38] Industrialised war devoured the soldiers physically and mentally. It would be

Plate 5. The soldier's return

pointless to attempt to elicit their numbers from any statistics, unless one were to limit oneself to the registered physical injuries. Global statistics for the First World War read: '13 million dead, 11 million crippled, 6 billion shells and 50 billion cubic metres of gas in four years . . . '[39] When a large number of angry, crippled war veterans occupied the old imperial summer residence, the Schönbrunn Palace in Vienna, Social Democratic functionaries hurried to head them off with a large group of children from the *Kinderfreunde* movement, with the object of utilising the rooms for a children's home. If the Palace were to be occupied, then it should be for the children, the hope for a better tomorrow, the classical paradigm of social democracy,[40] not for the cripples of the war, a war with which the Social Democratic leaders had initially concurred, and of which the cripples were an unwelcome reminder.

The celebration of the virtues of physical prowess and pugnacity, the ridiculing of anxious, helpless and 'weak' men, contrasted with the damaged patriarchs, returning home from the war, made relations within families more difficult than they had been before. Numerous marriages, arranged quickly under the extraordinary circumstances of wartime, ended in divorce. Suicides and attempted suicides followed with the experience of the trenches. Anna Lechner born in 1903, and working as a battery solderer in the last years of the war, recalls several suicide attempts by her father, after his return from the war:

Then the story was that he had been in the Balkan struggles and he'd fallen from a rock there and was unconscious for three days. The Captain's dog had found him there, and the story was that it had come from that!

(Interview 10, p. 6)

Veterans had become used to drinking and refused to take care of their children when they came back home.[41] The experience of the 'industrialised' killing of the war had clearly traumatised many soldiers.[42] Now the veterans came home and carried their traumas into the family. Many of the men who returned from the trenches were 'weak' men: the opposite of those whom the military bands, the women and girls with songs and flowers had sent off to the war. They were often more a burden than a source of help for their families. If they were physically disabled, they received only a meagre invalid's pension. Their claim to authority in the family often appeared to be threatened.

Alienated from their wives and children and not knowing what would await them at home, they returned to their families as losers in every sense. In many cases, the father had trouble reoccupying his former place in the family. During his absence power and authority had passed to others and not infrequently he had to displace his eldest son or his father or father-in-law from the position he now wished to reoccupy. Frau Freitag, 13-years-old at the end of the war, remembers the return of her father in late autumn of 1918:

It was night and someone suddenly pounded on the door. We got up, Mother and we children – all from the parents' bed. Mother lit the paraffin lamp and opened the door. There was a strange man with a beard in a dirty soldier's overcoat.

What does this man want in the middle of the night?

'Children, this is your father', Mother said.

'That's our father?' We did not get used to him for a long time.

(Interview 19, p. 23)

In spite of this, or perhaps because of it, many men tried to compensate for their damaged authority by trying to dominate their wives and children. Hermine Kohn, the daughter of a factory worker, recounted in detail the various forms of her father's oppression. For instance, he beat his wife when a button was missing from his shirt; he dragged his eight-year-old daughter across the staircase by her plaits because the lentils, which the girl had cooked him for his evening meal, were too hard. Hermine Kohn attributes her father's behaviour to the consequences of war:

Of course he is, of course he was sick from the war. He had had malaria, he had bouts of fever for the rest of his life, you know, and shivering fits. Actually he was pitiful, a pathetic figure. But the worse he felt, the more he played the master and we were all the more afraid of him.

(Interview 25, p. 10)

When the end of the war came, the material distress of working-class families was far from over. Austrian agricultural production could not even supply half the needs of the population. Prices soared and wages lagged behind.[43] Considerable loss in real income was the result for the wage-earning masses. In addition, many a patriotic working-class saver, who had invested in war-bonds, lost his savings. In the first months of the Republic, the number of unemployed rose very sharply. In December 1918, 24,503 people were unemployed in Vienna, while by February 1919, the number had increased to 113,905 and by May of the same year to 131,500.[44]

High unemployment aggravated the problem of integrating the demobilised soldiers into the economy. Many of the women who had taken over the jobs of conscripted men, now found themselves displaced as the men returned. They returned to the home, or moved out of those branches of industry which, traditionally, had been a male preserve, into 'typical women's' occupations. The policies of the Republic's first government (a coalition of Christian Socialists and Social Democrats) aimed at achieving precisely this. In a decree of 14 February 1919, the National Bureau for

Social Welfare, led by the Social Democrat, Ferdinand Hanusch, instructed all labour exchanges, that what they 'were to aim at, was that, of the numerous women who had made a distinguished contribution to the war industry, as many as possible were to return to the household'.[45] As early as 1917, the *Catholic Working Women's Newspaper* considered that it was 'a matter of course, that after the war female workers should not keep a job to which a male worker was coming back'.[46] This view appears to have been shared by a large part of the working-class population. Frau Stupek, the daughter of a furrier's assistant, thought that men should have been given back their old jobs; something she found right then, as she does today:

My grandfather said, women must go back to the family now that the men are coming home from the war. And we found that all quite right. You can't have a man without work and his family goes hungry because a woman has got his job!

(Interview 27, p. 13)

Karl Pollak, a skilled metal worker and long-standing works committee member, recalls:

Then the women slowly disappeared. The women slowly disappeared. Firstly, their husbands came back and the husband more or less took over the reins, took care of the income and so on.

(Interview 6/2, p. 7)

As a member of the works committee, Karl Pollak knew the mood of the workers very well. When the workers' freedom of association was reinstated after the de-militarisation of the factories, conflicts constantly erupted, as attempts were made to prevent the recruitment of women for jobs which had previously been monopolised by men:

What I remember is that, for example, in factories where women had been taken on, after the war there were even small strikes. Because the workers then made really sure that their jobs wouldn't be put at risk by the women. For example, they refused to work next to a woman. They refused . . . They wouldn't have women doing their work.

(Interview 6/2, p. 7)

On the other hand, for many women, not even a march back to the household remained open, for they had lost their husbands in the 'field of honour'. The war had left approximately 6,800 widows and 11,534 orphans in Vienna alone.[47]

After the war: the family as part of the new political realm

The old pillars of society had collapsed: the Church, the aristocracy, the bourgeoisie and the highest echelons of the bureaucracy. The demise of the monarchy and the revolutionary gesture of the proletariat had robbed them of political and psychological power. Insecurity and confusion, in the relations between men and women, between parents and their children as well, gripped sections of the middle class and petty bourgeoisie.[48] However, after the first revolutionary thrust had been dissipated and the revolutionary energy of the workers councils had been subverted by the Social Democratic leadership, the demobilised soldiers reintegrated themselves into society and the working class entered upon a phase of order and reconstruction. Although the old establishment and its father-figures had fallen from power, the Social Democratic leaders presented themselves in the chaos of the first post-war years as new father-figures. For numerous members of the working class, who were used to authoritarian structures, 'the vision of a future socialist state contained a message of salvation which replaced that of the Church. The organisations gave them brothers and fathers and a new sense of security', the psychoanalyst, Paul Federn wrote in 1919.[49] If the revolutionary councils replaced the old principle of authority with the postulate of fraternity, Social Democracy, on the other hand, soon developed marked hierarchical characteristics. Through the symbols of its political propaganda and its structure and organisations, it communicated to the masses a sense of disciplined order, cleanliness, health and hierarchy.

After four years of war in which the state had removed the male bread-winners from their families and from their workplaces in order to make them soldiers, and after the state had moved women and youths into industry more frequently than ever before, the state now took on new responsibility for the endangered families of the masses. In running a war economy in the fields of food and fuel supply, the allocation of dwellings, orphans' welfare and so on, new political issues had been raised which could no longer be suppressed. When the Social Democratic Workers Party came into power at the first General Election in the spring of 1919, it based its new role and its programme as a partner in government precisely on the political issues which the war had raised. In the opening article of its monthly review *Der Sozialdemokrat* the Party's leaders proclaimed:

The war had a revolutionary effect. In its reality, the war made clear what the state means nowadays for the life of every single person and every family. This state, whose command forced millions to leave their families and their homes in order to sacrifice their lives, became the almighty power in society, and to control it is of prime importance.[50]

The extended field of political intervention is also clearly discernible in the Social Democratic conceptions of working-class marriage and family life. It could be established that it was the effects of the war which led Julius Tandler, the city councillor in charge of 'Welfare Services' in 'Red Vienna', to place special emphasis on what he termed the 'moral climate' in working-class families. The various measures introduced as part of the health and welfare service, which became known internationally in the inter-war period as the 'Vienna System', aimed at establishing an ordered family life in the working class, in particular better methods of raising and educating children in workers' families, as well as higher living standards.

The ideal of Social Democratic policies was the nuclear family, which was contrasted in propaganda with the semi-open family forms of the workers in the big tenement blocks (*Zinkasernen*) built in the second half of the nineteenth century.[51] The plans of the so-called 'City Fathers' (*Stadtväter*) – the leading Social Democratic city councillors – were based on the ideas of the middle-class social reformers of the late nineteenth century, whose consciences had been disturbed by the conditions in the *Zinskasernen* and the potential threat to the integrity of the family posed by alcoholism, lodgers, and people who only rented beds (*Bettgeher*). In their place, the Social Democratic City Fathers wanted to build hygienic, clearly separated small flats, with the maximum amount of sunlight and green courtyards, with bathing and central washing facilities, with kindergartens for future generations of socialists, and with reading rooms to permit the acquisition of knowledge previously a virtual monopoly of the middle class. They continued the legal rent control (*Mieterschutz*) which had been introduced in 1917 to alleviate the hardships suffered by soldiers' families, and they kept housing rents low in order to give more stability and security to the lower classes.[52]

The experience of the First World War contributed to the fact that the mass of working-class people scarcely questioned the ideal of the family and the establishment of 'order and cleanliness' by means of socialist municipal government. Their programme spanned welfare and health services, the construction of 60,000 flats, primarily for working-class people, inspection of workers' accommodation and educational advice. As large sections of these plans came to fruition, the mass of the working population, particularly the skilled workers, considered that their opinions were reflected by this policy of order. If it occurred at all, resistance to the municipal government's intervention in the conditions of everyday life was found only amongst the sub-proletarian strata of society. In this case, however, social workers sometimes required the protection of the police when they removed a child to one of the municipal children's homes, on the grounds that the flat in which it lived with its parents seemed too dirty.[53] The challenge to traditional values of marriage and family, articulated on occasion by particular intellectuals and psychoanalysts, was rarely taken up by the working class. In the final instance, everything was focused on the children, the future generation. Even for proletarian women, motherhood was considered to be their highest duty. *Der Sozialdemokrat*, just a few days before the elections for the Viennese city council, in May 1919, announced:

Protection of women, protection of mothers! This also will protect children. In the interests of national health, not only good hygienic flats are necessary; houses for the people must be furnished in a way that all comfort is introduced which reduces housework in every single household. Houses with a central kitchen, kindergartens, playrooms and reading rooms are a necessity.[54]

However the plan to relieve women of heavy household work through the provision of communal arrangements in council homes was, in the end, carried out only half-heartedly. The burden of household work and childcare continued to fall on the women. Moreover, standards in these fields rose, further increasing the demands on women. The only *Einküchenhaus* which was built in Vienna was ridiculed and ignored by most workers. It reminded many of the 'war kitchens' (*Kriegsküchen*), which were associated with hard times and bad food. Working-class men wanted to be served the food of their choice personally by their own wives, and would have nothing to do with the professionalisation of household work which was attempted in the *Einküchenhaus*.[55]

After his experience of the war and in view of the daily struggle for survival and the reduction in his ability to work, the male worker wanted to have 'his order' restored. And in this connection, he placed most stress on his family life, regular meals and the attentive care of his wife. The tense mood of fundamental change which unsettled parts of the middle class (in particular, the intellectuals), and which led them to question the traditional values of marriage and family, did not filter down to the average worker. In the aftermath of a period of hunger and misery, he was too absorbed with making sure that his primary needs were satisfied.

Notes

1 This seems also to be true for Germany, as Jürgen Kocka has noticed; see J. Kocka, *Klassengesellschaft im Krieg. Deutsche Sozialgeschichte 1914–1918*, Göttingen, 1973, p. 1.
2 Magnus Hirschfeld and Andreas Gaspar (eds.), *Sittengeschichte des Ersten Weltkrieges*, Hanau, 1929.
3 Most of the interviews referred to in this chapter were conducted by the author in the years 1982, 1983 and 1984. Interviews 52–3 were conducted by Hans Schafranek and Hans Witek, respectively. The original tapes and transcripts are held by the Institute for Social and Economic History at the University of Vienna. The method used was the open-ended in-depth interview following the course of a life history. For methodological problems see Reinhard Sieder, 'Bemerkungen zur Verwendung des Narrativinterviews für eine Geschichte des Alltags', *Zeitgeschichte*, 15 (1982), and R. Sieder, 'Geschichten erzählen und Wissenschaft treiben' in Gerhard Botz and Josef Weidenholzer (eds.), *Mündliche Geschichte und Arbeiterbewegung*, Vienna, 1984, pp. 203–21.

4 *Census of the soldiers killed in action*, June 1918, Vienna, cited in *Blätter für das Wohlfahrts- und Armenwesen*, December, 1918.
5 See R. Riedl, *Die Industrie Österreichs während des Krieges*, Vienna, 1932, p. 20; General Landwehr, *Hunger. Die Erschöpfungsjahre der Mittelmächte 1917/18*, Vienna, 1931, p. 9.
6 G. Gratz and R. Schüller, *Der wirtschaftliche Zusammenbruch Österreich-Ungarns*, Vienna, 1930, p. 46.
7 The mother and six children. The father was a skilled worker, an assistant gilder who became a member of the fire brigade of the Heereskonservenfabrik, Inzersdorf on the outbreak of war.
8 See H. Hautmann, 'Hunger ist ein schlechter Koch', in G. Botz *et al.* (eds.), *Bewegung und Klasse. Studien zur österreichischen Arbeitergeschichte*, Vienna, 1978, p. 669. The system of the ration-cards differentiated *Selbstversorger* (self-sufficient people, i.e. peasants), *Nichtselbstversorger* (those not self-sufficient, i.e. non-peasants) and *Schwerarbeiter* (workers in heavy industry). Cards for this last category were issued to the majority of industrial workers, miners, brickmakers, blacksmiths, tool makers and male workers in strategic industries and to all railway workers and policemen.
9 For more details see R. Sieder, 'Gassenkinder', *Aufrisse*, 4 (1984), 8–21, and H. Safrian and R. Sieder, 'Gassenkinder – Strassenkämpfer. Zur politischen Sozialisation einer Arbeitergeneration in Wien 1900 bis 1938' in L. Niethammer and A. Plato (eds.), *'Wir kriegen jetzt andere Zeiten'. Auf der Suche nach der Erfahrung des Volkes in nachfaschistischen Ländern*, Bonn and Berlin, 1985, pp. 117–51.
  Incidents with policemen like the one quoted in the text indicate the questionable nature of those interpretations of criminal statistics which indiscriminately attribute the rising criminality amongst youths during the war to such factors as the 'deprivation of young people', cf. the unpublished paper by Eve Rosenhaft presented to the conference on the European family and the First World War, Cambridge, 1983.
10 That is, she was allowed to drink the head on the beer.
11 For more details see R. Sieder, ' "Vata, derf i aufstehn?" Childhood experiences in Viennese working-class families around 1900', *Continuity and Change*, 1 (1986), 53–88. Cf. R. S. Rowntree, *Poverty. A study of town life*, London, 1901, p. 55, in which he cites a woman from York: 'If there's anything extra to buy, such as a pair of boots for one of the children, me and the children goes without dinner – or mebbe only 'as a cup o' tea and a bit o' bread, but Jim ollers takes 'is dinner to work, and I never tell 'im.'
12 Fritz Klenner, *Die österreichischen Gewerkschaften*, vol. 1, Vienna, 1951, p. 401. V. Stein, 'Die Lage der österreichischen Metallarbeiter im Kriege' in F. Hanusch and E. Adler (eds.), *Die Regelung der Arbeitsverhältnisse im Kriege*, Vienna, 1927, pp. 222–62.
13 E. Adler, 'Das Arbeitsrecht im Kriege' in Hanusch and Adler, *Die Regelung der Arbeitsverhältnisse im Kriege*, p. 28.
14 W. Winkler, *Die Totenverluste der österreichisch-ungarischen Monarchie nach Nationalitäten*, Vienna, 1919. W. Winkler, *Berufsstatistik der Kriegstoten der österreichisch-ungarischen Monarchie*, Vienna, 1919.
15 Above, note 4.
16 Werner and Pfleiderer was a metal firm in the Viennese working-class district, Ottakring.

17 W. Winkler, *Die Einkommensverschiebungen in Österreich während des Weltkrieges*, Vienna, 1930, p. 40; Hanusch and Adler, *Die Regelung der Arbeitsverhältnisse im Kriege*, p. 400.

18 J. Deutsch, *Geschichte der österreichischen Arbeiterbewegung*, Vienna, 1947, p. 88. Gratz and Schüller give data on the rise of the living costs of a worker's household. With July 1914 = 100, the comparable figures for each succeeding July during the war were 179, 382, 616 and 1,560. In October 1918 they reached 1,876. See Gratz and Schüller, *Der wirtschaftliche Zusammenbruch*, p. 184.

19 *Die Frauen-Hilfsaktion*, Vienna, 1916, p. 32.

20 E. Freundlich, 'Die Frauenarbeit im Kriege' in Hanusch and Adler, *Die Regelung der Arbeitsverhältnisse*, p. 401.

21 W. Winkler, *Die Einkommensverschiebungen*, p. 31.

22 V. Stein, 'Die Lage der österreichischen Metallarbeiter', p. 250.

23 E. Freundlich, 'Die Frauenarbeit im Kriege', p. 399.

24 W. Winkler, *Die Einkommensverschiebungen*, p. 31.

25 V. Stein, 'Die Lage der österreichischen Metallarbeiter', p. 251.

26 See F. Klenner, *Die österreichischen Gewerkschaften*, p. 410.

27 Even in the years of extreme hunger and misery of the lower strata, parts of the bourgeoisie celebrated feasts and consumed most expensive foodstuffs; J. Kocka, *Klassengesellschaft im Krieg*, p. 44.

28 H. Hautmann, 'Hunger ist ein schlechter Koch', p. 668.

29 They were small farmers with two or three cows.

30 Vorwärts-Verlag (ed.), *Um Friede, Freiheit und Recht! Der Jännerausstand des innerösterreichischen Proletariats*, Vienna, 1918, p. 5 and p. 8; H. Hautmann, *Die Anfänge der linksradikalen Bewegung und der Kommunistischen Partei Deutsch-Österreichs 1916–1919*, 1970, p. 24; J. Deutsch, 'Radikale Strömungen', *Der Kampf*, 11 February 1918, pp. 71–8. The Social Democratic Leaders called on the workers not to join the strike in the *Arbeiterzeitung* 17, 17 January 1918, p. 1: 'In the interests of the whole population, we urge workers in all food industries, miners, workers on the railway, trams and other transport industries, gas and electricity works not to stop work. Such strikes would heighten the predicament of the whole workforce and must therefore be avoided.'

31 R. G. Plaschka, H. Haselsteiner and S. Suppan, *Innere Front. Militärassistenz, Widerstand und Umsturz in der Donaumonarchie 1918*. Vienna, 1974, p. 42.

32 General Landwehr, *Hunger*, p. 236.

33 General Landwehr, *Hunger*, p. 255; on 27 June 1918, a *Kriegsküche* was opened which served food to 100,000 persons, see Gratz and Schüller, *Der wirtschaftliche Zusammenbruch*, p. 80.

34 General Landwehr, *Hunger*, p. 236.

35 General Landwehr, *Hunger*, p. 72.

36 G. Botz, *Gewalt in der Politik*, Vienna, 1976, p. 25.

37 G. Botz, *Gewalt in der Politik*, p. 26; see also Plaschka, Haselsteiner, and Suppan, *Innere Front*, p. 42. 'As the car passed the Schwedenplatz some hundred people ran to the car, coming from the Taborstrasse. Shouting and insulting the officers, they blocked the street and smashed the car's windows. The generals had their caps ripped off their heads . . . A call to the driver: "Well, now you can drive on, you stupid chap! Hail the Republic!"'. Cf. the officers' memories: C. Freiherr von Bardolff, *Soldat im alten Österreich. Erinnerungen aus meinem Leben*, Vienna, 1936 and 1943, p. 343.

38 Ernst Jünger, *In Stahlgewittern*. 'The messenger boys fell dead under the storm of steel, the telephone wire, hardly connected, was already hacked into small pieces. Even the flashing lights of the signal lights failed in the country over-clouded by steam and dust. Behind the front line there was a kilometre-wide zone governed by explosives . . . here courtesy disappeared, it had to give way to the intensive speed of the battle, like all noble and personal feelings must give way, where machines won control. Here the new Europe also showed itself for the first time in the battle.' Quoted from E. Jünger, 'Der Krieg als inneres Erlebnis' in R. Winter (ed.), *Auszüge aus seinen Schriften*, Frankfurt am Main, 1933, pp. 11–12. The term 'new Europe' can be understood in this connection as indicating 'industrialised Europe'.

39 P. Sloterdijk, *Kritik der zynischen Vernunft*, Frankfurt, 1983, vol. 2, p. 791.

40 W. Benjamin, *Über den Begriff der Geschichte*, in *Illuminationen. Ausgewählte Schriften*, Frankfurt, 1977, p. 257.

41 In 1921 a number of members of the Vienna City Council complained that working-class men were no longer willing to care for their children. For this they were inclined to blame the war. 'This is a peculiarity that some people unfortunately seem to have acquired in the war, that is to say we are dealing with a kind of moral defect imposed on them by the war.' Gemeinderatsprotokoll, 22 June 1921, p. 893; cf. R. Sieder, 'Housing policy, social welfare, and family life in "Red Vienna", 1919–1934', *Oral History*, 13/2 (1985), 35–49.

42 Cf. 'Zur Psychoanalyse der Kriegsneurosen', *Internationale psychoanalytische Bibliothek 1* with an introduction by Sigmund Freud, and a report by Ferenczi on the psychoanalysis of war neuroses, given at the 5th International Congress for Psychoanalysis in Budapest, 28 and 29 September 1918. See also the unpublished paper by David Hiebert presented to the conference on the European Family and the First World War, Cambridge, 1983.

43 Benedikt Kautsky, 'Löhne und Gehälter' in Julius Bunzel (ed.), *Geldentwertung und Stabilisierung in ihren Einflüssen auf die soziale Entwicklung Österreichs* (Schriften des Vereins zur Sozialpolitik 169), Vienna, 1925, pp. 105–31.

44 Karl Pribram, 'Die Sozialpolitik im neuen Österreich', *Archiv für Sozialwissenschaft und Sozialpolitik*, 48 (1920/21), 615–80, p. 634.

45 Käthe Leichter, *Frauenarbeit und Arbeiterinnenschutz in Österreich*, Vienna, 1917, p. 16.

46 *Arbeiterinnenblatt*. Mitteilungen der katholischen Arbeiterinnenvereine, 1917/3–5, p. 35.

47 See *Witwen- und Waisenfond. Offizielle Monatsschrift*, 1919/21, p. 10.

48 Cf. A. Pfoser, 'Verstörte Männer und emanzipierte Frauen' in F. Kadrnoska (ed.), *Aufbruch und Untergang*, Vienna, 1982, p. 205.

49 Paul Federn, *Psychologie der Revolution – Die vaterlose Gesellschaft*, Leipzig, 1919, p. 28. Cf. P. Loewenberg, *Decoding the past. The psycho-historical approach*, Berkeley, 1985, p. 268.

50 *Der Sozialdemokrat. Monatsschrift der Organisation Wien*, 1 January 1919, p. 3.

51 See Gottfried Pirhofer and R. Sieder, 'Zur Konstitution der Arbeiterfamilie im Roten Wien' in Michael Mitterauer and R. Sieder (eds.), *Historische Familienforschung*, Frankfurt, 1982, p. 326.

52 Pirhofer and Sieder, 'Zur Konstitution der Arbeiterfamilie', p. 330.

53 See Reinhard Sieder, 'Housing policy, social welfare, and family life', pp. 35–48.

54 'Was bedeuten die Gemeinderatswahlen für die Frauen?', *Der Sozialdemokrat*, vol. 1, no. 5, May, 1919, p. 6.
55 Pirhofer and Sieder, 'Zur Konstitution der Arbeiterfamilie', p. 331; and Sieder, 'Housing policy, social welfare and family life', p. 46.

4

Standards of living and standards of health in wartime Belgium

Peter Scholliers and Frank Daelemans

Introduction

There is a vast literature about the wartime destruction and disturbance of social and political trends in Central and Eastern Europe where regimes collapsed and revolutions followed with varying degrees of success. There is an equally impressive literature about the less traumatic but undeniably significant developments in France, Britain and the Netherlands.

What do we know about Belgium, a country occupied by the Germans for over fifty months? Contemporaries witnessed the vast devastation of Belgian towns and factories, the theft of cattle, the fleeing masses, the hunger and starvation in large parts of the kingdom and the general discontent. During the immediate aftermath of war, contemporaries witnessed the quasi-revolutionary days of November 1918, the rapid growth of trade unions, the entry of socialists into government, the carelessness of farm labourers (formerly religious, exhausted and poor workers), the decline of traditional moral values, the changes in fashion and the noisy troop of merry-makers dancing to wild music. This (incomplete) sketch might suggest that the war was a total caesura for Belgian society. Fifty months of occupation seemed indeed to have brought about significant discontinuity.

Questions arise, however, concerning the character and origins of social instability. Firstly, it can be questioned whether such discontinuity pervaded all levels of society. What about capital investments, profit rates, employments, standard of living, health, nuptiality, nutrition and other items which were not so obvious to contemporaries? Secondly, it can be asked to what extent did the war itself cause certain changes. Were there forces within society which would have led to changes even without the impact of war, or did war merely accelerate developments?

The standard of living during the occupation

The present study concentrates on the influence of the war and the occupation on demography and on the standard of living. Both are indicative of changes in the economic, social and political structure and enable approximate measurement of the immediate impact of war. It will be argued that war and the German occupation did change some aspects of Belgian society, but that other features continued to develop along pre-war lines.

J. M. Keynes was, in our opinion, completely wrong when, in his *Economic consequences of the peace* of 1919, he advanced the thesis that Belgium had suffered relatively little during the war period. According to him, 'It will turn out that . . . Belgium has made the least relative sacrifice of all the belligerents except the United States'.[1] In fact, living conditions in Belgium during the war were far worse than Keynes suggested.

Following the German invasion of 4 August, the country suddenly faced the insuperable task of ensuring its own essential supplies. Indeed the Allies' intention was to put a quick end to war through economic measures: all trade with the enemy *and* occupied territories was suspended. The supremacy of the British Navy guaranteed a strict enforcement of this blockade. Belgium, being dependent on imported wheat – by far the most important food item – for 80 per cent of its wants,[2] found itself cut off from this vital import and was unable to ensure its own supply except for a very short period. Neither the successful harvest drive of 1914, nor the considerable stocks which Belgium as a transit country always held, could prevent the first shortages appearing as early as Christmas 1914.

Shortages caused price increases, notwithstanding the price freeze which had been decreed by the Belgian government one day before the invasion and which was later re-imposed by the German authorities. In fact, the Germans themselves caused a systematic aggravation of the shortages by requisitioning provisions for their troops from August 1914. Since voluntary deliveries to the Germans were understandably slow to come, occasional looting of foodstuff depots (such as the wheat stocks in the harbour of Antwerp) soon followed. This, together with the mass transfer of food to Germany, drained the diminishing stocks even faster.[3]

It soon became apparent that what had started as shortages in 1914 would evolve into severe famine during the summer or autumn of 1915. The Germans, having an interest in maintaining law and order in occupied territory (and, if possible, in diverting even more Belgian resources to the German economy) issued a series of decrees exhorting the Belgians to resume trade, factory work and harvesting. There was, however, less and less merchandise to be traded, especially as several factories had been closed down either for lack of raw materials or because their machinery had been stolen. Only agriculture could still provide sufficient employment. Otherwise, the Germans simply maintained order by means of the military and by issuing decrees which ruined both the monetary system, through imposed exchange rates, and financial activity, through the withdrawal of small currency and credit facilities.[4] International agreements stipulated that an occupying power had to assure the food supply for the inhabitants of occupied territory, yet the Germans would not provide such supplies unless the Allied blockades were raised. It was not, and shortages in Belgium grew worse and worse as German requisitions continued. Without special measures of some kind, famine was unavoidable.

In the absence of the Belgian government (which had fled to the north of France), financiers and industrialists decided to raise funds in order to alleviate the misery of the poor. Already by the end of August 1914 the first distributions of free soup rations were organised in the Brussels area. In this small-scale private charity are to be found the roots of the semi-official Comité National de Secours et d'Alimentation, which countered the effects of the blockade by organising an efficient system of food distribution and supply. After an agreement had been reached between Great Britain and the German Empire through the mediation of the United States, the Netherlands and Spain, which ensured the effective passing-on of the food to its intended destination (i.e. Belgian stomachs), a relief system came into being.[5] This happened as early as October 1914, thanks to international solidarity on the one hand and to the nation-wide co-operation of financiers, industrialists, politicians and trade union leaders on the other.[6] The German authorities were thereby relieved of trouble and responsibility; in fact they even skilfully used the Comité National to reduce social agitation to a minimum. The Comité National, which included bankers and employers among its founders, may have been equally satisfied with this result as charity was put to the purpose which it had served of old.[7]

The Comité National organised food aid in close co-operation with the Commission for Relief in Belgium. For various reasons, however, the volume of imported goods never nearly reached the level of normal times. The start in 1915 had been promising; but never thereafter was the import of that first year equalled (see Table 4.1).[8]

The extent of the shortfall is vividly brought out when the level of imports during the war period is set against that of normal years. The *Annuaire Statistique de la Belgique* (1920, p. 220) quoted a figure of 3,960,752 tons of food imported in 1913. This exceeded the total secured by the Comité National during the four war years. In 1915 food imports amounted to 24 per cent of the 1913 standard; and the three succeeding years were worse with imports reaching only 21.4 per cent, 15.9 per cent and 18.7 per cent, respectively, of the 1913 level. Shipment of goods was the main problem. In

Table 4.1. *Total food imported by the*
Comité National

	kg	Index (1915 = 100)
1915	955,207,239	100
1916	848,016,465	89
1917	631,165,234	66
1918	743,039,835	78
Total	3,177,428,773	

Source
A. Henry, *Le Ravitaillement de la Belgique*, p. 71

February 1917, Germany launched its U-boat campaign and sank no less than 12 'Relief in Belgium' ships during that very year alone. The Comité National could therefore never really compensate for dearth. It could, however, prevent excessive price rises in 1915 and 1916 through its import programme, even if this satisfied no more than 25 per cent of the actual needs. The Comité also largely succeeded in achieving an equitable distribution of imported food, transferring it principally to Public Assistance Institutions, unemployment funds, hospitals, and the like. Initially, the high-income classes were excluded from this assistance: they could take care of their own supply by purchasing goods on the black market.

In addition to falling food imports, domestic production itself was found wanting, firstly because yields fell short of the pre-war average and secondly because the distribution system functioned badly and arbitrarily. Some arable land was unavailable for agriculture purposes through West Flanders having become the front. In addition, there was a shortage of manpower with refugees having fled to the Netherlands and to Great Britain, with soldiers under arms, and with approximately 120,000 people compelled to join the 90,000 voluntarily employed in Germany and Northern France (see figures on agriculture output Appendix 4.1).

Defective distribution, on the other hand, arose principally from German interference with the stocking and distribution process. Belgian experts estimated that the potato harvest of 1917 had yielded 400 g of potatoes per head and per day; in reality, people received no more than 190 g. The combined effect of production and distribution failures resulted in shortages of *all* home-produced food. For example, the Brussels metropolitan area, where 240,000 litres of whole milk were consumed in 1914, received only 90,000 litres of skimmed milk in 1917. Belgian production, which was

Table 4.2. *Official prices of some basic foodstuffs, 1914–17 (Belgian francs)*

Commodity[a]	1914	1916	1917	Increase 1916–17 (%)
Butter	3.37	6.43	8.35	29
Bread	0.23	0.48	0.61	27
Flour	0.27	0.42	0.64	52
Potatoes	0.79	1.35	2.25	66
Fruit	0.68	2.10	3.50	66
Cheese	0.25	1.00	1.92	92
Meat	1.60	4.56	9.20	101
Eggs	0.10	0.25	0.58	128
Milk	0.17	0.37	0.85	129
Bacon	2.73	9.41	25.30	168
Peas	0.35	0.74	2.36	218

[a]All prices per kilo except in the case of milk (litres) and eggs (one)
Source
P. Scholliers, 'Koopkracht en indexkoppeling. De Brusselse levensstaandard tijdens en na de Eerste Wereldoorlog, 1914–1925' (Purchasing power and price index-linking. The Brussels standard of living during and after the war), *Revue Belge d'Histoire Contemporaine* (1978), 354, 375–6

insufficient to meet domestic demand even in normal times, suffered considerably during the occupation.[9]

During the winter of 1916–17 the situation became disastrous. Shopkeepers with a talent for usury saw their chance to sell wares hoarded in the course of the year at rates at least twice those of August 1914. Fodder potatoes were distributed for human consumption and kohlrabi was eaten on a large scale. A typical famine situation as had repeatedly occurred before the beginnings of the mass import of food, seemed imminent by the end of 1917. Seed stocks were used up, hungry crowds clamoured for charity, and the mortality rates rose. The famine of 1917 and 1918 was a small-scale replica of the great crisis of the mid-nineteenth century which, in Flanders and Ireland in particular, had claimed thousands of victims. The exorbitant price rise in 1917 bears testimony to the scarcity of commodities in that the average price of food reached almost double that of 1916. This figure represents the increased price of meat and cheese. Much higher rises were recorded for peas, eggs, milk and bacon, whereas butter, bread, potatoes and flour prices increased relatively less. These details are set out in Table 4.2 (while Table 4.3 places the rise in food prices in the context of the increases in other main expenditure categories).

The figures quoted here do not take into account the black-market prices current in 1917 and 1918 which were undoubtedly higher. A professor at the

Table 4.3. *An index of price increases in the Brussels region (1914 = 100)*

Expenditure category	1915	1916	1917	1918
Food	134	215	422	578
Clothing	114	132	191	682
Lighting/heating	122	137	172	270
Housing	110	116	126	161
Miscellaneous	131	180	253	466
Total	131	191	341	520

Source
P. Scholliers, 'Koopkracht en indexkoppeling', p. 354

University of Ghent carefully recorded the extraordinarily high prices on the Brussels black market. A 5 kg bag of potatoes was 10 to 15 times more expensive than in 1914, whereas the official price increase suggested a factor of no more than three or four. A poor-quality bread made of spelt and potato flour cost 18 francs in clandestine traffic, the official price being 0.83 francs! A black-market price index of domestic produce would indicate the following rates of increase based on prices in April 1914: in 1915, 67 per cent, in 1916, 252 per cent, in 1917, 684 per cent; in 1918 – beating all records – 1,200 per cent. These figures, it must be emphasised, relate to domestic products. To take into consideration the price of imported goods would boost such an index even more. Actually, the 'average' Belgian citizen very quickly lacked the necessary wherewithal to make purchases on the black market. The regular customers, i.e. the wealthier classes and the Germans, were being thoroughly fleeced by various sorts of dealers who made huge profits.[10] The existence of such an extensive black-market trade greatly hindered the fair apportionment of necessities. Before long two price levels were simultaneously in existence: a high level reflecting conditions on the well-supplied black market, and another controlled by the Comité National.

The price boom severely disrupted the pattern of demand. Beginning in the spring of 1915, the average menu came to look quite different from what it had been before the war: cheap 'calories' were purchased instead of expensive ones, and far less meat, butter, eggs, fat and milk were consumed. Potatoes became the principal source of calories. The typical pattern of food consumption in the last quarter of 1916 now resembled the menu of the 1860s. Expenditure on food, and on potatoes and bread in particular, was relatively high.[11]

No budget enquiries were conducted during the war.[12] The serious situation faced by certain families may nevertheless be illustrated by means of a family budget drawn up by miners in September 1919 (see Table 4.4).[13]

Table 4.4. *Proportional expenditure of miners' families and composition of their food basket*

Expenditure category	%		Consumption per head[a] and per day	
Food	84.6	of which	Bread	590 g
Clothing	2.3		Potatoes	890
Housing	7.3		Butter	71
Lighting/heating	2.6		Meat	133
Miscellaneous	2.6		Milk	267 cl
			Sugar	35 g
	100.0			

[a] Not standardised for age. Elsewhere in this volume, Triebel (chapter 4, n. 3) and Dewey (chapter 5) apply different definitions in their accounts of consumption patterns in Germany and Britain.
Source
P. Scholliers, 'Verschuivingen in het arbeiderconsumptiepatroon', p. 288

The salient features of this budget are the large share of food relative to other items of expenditure, and the marked lack of variety in a menu entirely dominated by bread and potatoes. There can be no doubt that these characteristics must have been shared by many wartime budgets. It should be emphasised, however, that the wartime food basket failed to provide either the quality or the quantity of food required by a given individual. Several pieces of evidence imply the occurrence of nutritional deficiencies. For example, as was shown in Table 4.1, the Comité National was unable to implement its full importation programme. A more detailed breakdown, however, can be presented (Table 4.5) indicating for the most important kinds of imported food, the disparity between the estimated requirements and the quantities effectively distributed.[14]

The prognoses of the Comité National envisaged a daily caloric intake of 1,220 calories per head; clearly the corresponding food assortment was intended as a supplement only. In fact, imported foodstuffs could never have provided more than 950 calories at best. The low point in 1917 deserves our particular attention.

As mentioned above, domestic food production which was insufficient even in normal times, was further reduced through the loss of arable land, food export to Germany, lack of manpower, and crop failures. The resultant shortages were reflected in the variation of the bread ration first imposed in September 1914. Set initially at c. 500 g of bread per head and per day, the ration was sharply cut back to 250 g in September 1914 and reached successive lows between February and July 1917 (225 g) and between March and October 1918 (190 g).[15]

Table 4.5. *Imported foodstuffs: estimated requirements and quantities distributed by the Comité National per head and per day*

	Estimated requirements (grams per head per day)	Quantities actually distributed (grams per head per day)			
		1915	1916	1917	1918
Wheat	288	202	246	165	183
Bacon and fat	30	8	14	13	21
Peas	16	11	4	8	16
Rice	25	18	21	10	11
Maize	16	38	48	9	16
Miscellaneous	18.5	15	3	18	25
Total nutritional value (calories)	1,220	788	951	658	794
Food distributed as percentage of requirements	100	64.6	77.9	53.9	65.1

Source
A. Henry, *Le Ravitaillement de la Belgique*, p. 192

Statistics on the sale of bread by consumer co-operative associations also throw some light on the reduction of bread rations by more than half. In Ghent, the co-operative Het Volk saw its annual bread sales (on a per capita basis and at current prices) dwindle by 40 per cent during the war years.[16] In the same co-operative, per capita sales of groceries dropped by 82 per cent between 1914 and 1918![17] The combined effects of the inefficient distribution of food, shrinking bread rations and dwindling retail sales was, of course, a drop in the caloric and protein intake per head and it was the latter which provided the best measure of living conditions during the occupation (see Table 4.6).

It should be emphasised that, depending on the type of activity, rations of 2,800–3,500 calories were considered adequate for an adult male. This would imply a deficit of 1,300–2,000 calories for working people and 1,400 calories for unemployed people in September 1917.[18] For the sake of comparison, we may take the caloric intake in Great Britain as reported in Beveridge's wartime report. Here, the pre-war figure of 3,442 calories was exceeded in 1914, 1915 and 1916 and all but equalled in 1917 and 1918.[19] The British deficit in 1917 was 3.5 per cent against 56 per cent in Belgium. This huge difference was due in the first place to the restrictions of food imports into Belgium. Nevertheless, Great Britain also owed a good deal of its relative 'prosperity' during this period to its war economy. This not only

Table 4.6. *Per capita daily caloric intake*

	Calories	Protein (grams)	Study population
December 1915	1,928	57.1	Unemployed workers in Brussels
April 1916	1,860	54.8	Unemployed workers in Brussels
September 1917	1,387	54.3	Unemployed workers in Brussels
September 1917	1,500	57.0	Employed workers in Brussels

Source
J. Demoor and A. Slosse, 'L'Alimentation des Belges pendant la guerre et ses conséquences', *Bulletin de l'Académie Royale de Médecine* (1920), 464–72.

absorbed unemployment but also effectively increased the proportion of women in employment – thereby increasing family incomes.[20] Nothing of the sort happened in Belgium, where nearly *all* factories were operating on half-time or less since raw materials were in short supply and/or machinery had been pilfered. Heavy industry was affected by the second handicap in particular. In the industrial centres of Liège, Mons, Verviers, Charleroi, Ghent and Antwerp, unemployment rose to unprecedented levels, with up to 90 per cent of industrial workers becoming jobless. Moreover, the salaries of those who remained in employment were never adjusted in line with inflation. The result was a steady loss of purchasing power: a drop of 70 per cent between 1914 and 1918. The financial situation of employed and unemployed actually differed very little in the end. In September 1917, for example, their caloric rations were 1,500 calories and 1,387 calories respectively: a difference of only 113 calories. During the first years of the war, the gap had undoubtedly been greater (see Table 4.6).

As a result of all this, even more people were forced to have recourse to public and private charity (cf. Figure 4.1). 'Traditional' dole-drawers such as the sick, poor, elderly and unemployed were now joined by employed workers and as the war continued, their ranks were increased by persons on small fixed incomes derived from pensions, the letting of property or other small investments. Any with savings saw their value wiped out by rampant inflation. Shopkeepers had to close their businesses for lack of stocks and/or clientele. White-collar workers, like labourers, had their purchasing power eroded by inflation. Classes which had never come into contact with public charity now found themselves on the dole. In the course of 1917, for the first time in history, *all* Belgians had access to it.

Initially, the relief distribution scheme included bread and soup for lunch, and meat and vegetables for supper. In the course of time, however, the level of food imports became so inadequate that of this programme only the distribution of soup remained. One serving provided on average *c.* 300 calories, but sometimes as little as 130 calories. Soup distribution was organised in 74 per cent of the Belgian communes and was used by some 40 per cent of the population. When the soup distribution schemes are examined province by province, it is clear that it was the industrial regions which were worst affected (see Table 4.7).[21]

In some parts of the country 90 per cent of the population received some form of public assistance; only an upper-class minority remained independent. Never before, and never thereafter, has institutional relief work been so universal as during the First World War. The Belgian situation in those days stands in glaring contrast to J. Burnett's conclusion with respect to the British food situation during the war:[22] 'If the Great Depression (1871–1895) marks the first step by the working classes of England towards material comfort, the First World War, for all its horrors and miseries, marks the second.' Famine reigned in Belgium at this time.

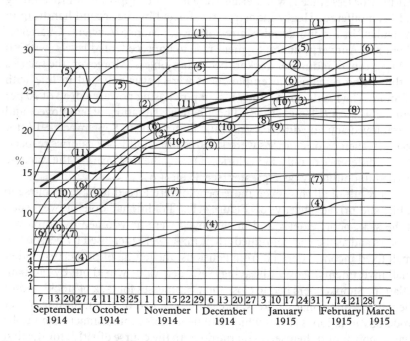

Fig. 4.1. Numbers receiving public assistance in the Brussels area as a percentage of the total number of inhabitants during the first months of war. *Source* Archives du Palais Royal, Secretary of the King, 1914–18, no. 605. 1. Brussels 2. Anderlecht 3. Etterbeek 4. Ixelles 5. Laken 6. Molenbeek 7. Saint-Josse 8. Saint Gilles 9. Schaarbeek 10. Uccle 11. all districts.

Table 4.7. *Attendance at soup kitchens as a percentage of the total population of each province*

Province	Numbers attending (%)[b]
Antwerp	40
Brabant	36
Brussels	29
Hainaut[a]	65
Liège[a]	56
Limburg	38
Luxembourg[a]	5
Namur	36
East Flanders (S)	45
East Flanders (N)	37

[a] Hainaut and Liège are regions of heavy industry, Luxembourg an agricultural region
[b] Percentages of the total population of each province
Source
A. Henry, *Le Ravitaillement de la Belgique*, pp. 124–5

To complete the picture, let us reiterate that the quality of available food deteriorated continually. Wheat was all but wanting in bread; potato flour, spelt and cattle-fodder were used instead. In addition, this bread rotted readily. Potatoes were used as a substitute, but these were stunted, waxy and black. Milk was diluted and meat was lean and scanty. The better-off classes largely limited their meat consumption to bacon, which had been the food of the poor before the war. The average annual consumption of meat per head before and after the war is illustrative of the hard times during the occupation. In 1913 consumption had stood at about 30 kg, yet in 1919 it amounted to no more than 17.3 kg.[23]

The demographic consequences of war and malnutrition

If this picture of living conditions under the German occupation is only approximately correct, some increase in the mortality of the civilian population during the years of war is to be expected. Unfortunately, little research has been carried out into the impact of scarcity on demographic trends between 1914 and 1918. The material collected immediately after the war and published in 1922[24] contains only totals of vital events although on

Table 4.8. *Annual totals and indices of births, marriages and deaths, Belgium, 1910–21*

	Births	Marriages	Deaths ≤1	1–4	≥5	Total
1910	176,414	58,776	23,646	9,792	79,388	112,826
1911	171,802	59,370	28,608	9,264	74,971	122,843
1912	171,187	61,278	20,525	8,541	83,312	112,378
1913	171,099	61,096	22,241	7,835	81,151	111,227
1914	156,389	41,095	20,333	6,669	81,718	108,720
1915	124,291	24,654	15,544	7,898	77,232	100,674
1916	99,360	30,458	11,522	7,693	81,799	101,044
1917	86,675	32,974	12,147	8,527	104,150	124,824
1918	85,056	43,558	11,377	11,282	134,681	157,340
1919	123,314	97,084	12,241	6,925	94,566	113,732
1920	163,738	106,514	16,960	4,179	81,366	102,505
1921	163,333	88,456	18,833	4,756	79,319	102,908
Indices						
1910	100	100	100	100	100	100
1911	97	101	121	95	94	109
1912	97	104	87	87	105	100
1913	97	104	94	80	102	99
1914	89	70	86	68	103	96
1915	70	42	66	81	97	89
1916	56	52	49	79	103	90
1917	49	56	51	87	131	111
1918	48	74	48	115	170	139
1919	70	156	52	71	119	101
1920	93	181	72	43	102	91
1921	93	150	80	49	100	91

Source
Annuaire statistique de la Belgique et du Congo belge, Ghent, 1934

occasion distinguishing the number of births, deaths and marriages in individual provinces or administrative districts. During the war the German governments had forbidden the gathering of information by which annual population trends could be estimated. The material was collected by R. Olbrechts in 1926 and published in a study of the post-war recovery of Belgium[25] and later studies and summaries have relied almost completely on Olbrechts' research.[26]

Particularly marked, as Table 4.8 makes clear, was the impact of the war on nuptiality. By the end of 1914, the average number of marriages celebrated each month had declined to 1,200 from 5,000 in August 1914, representing a fall of more than 75 per cent. However, it was 1918 that recorded the lowest annual marriage total and by 1919 three-quarters of the mean number of the pre-war period 1911–13 had been reached.

Olbrechts interpreted the relatively fast recovery in the number of marriages as a 'progressive adaptation of the population to the abnormal conditions caused by the war'.[27] Nevertheless, even the marriage boom of 1920 and 1921 failed to compensate for the number of marriages that had been 'lost' during the years of war. Mobilisation, the flight of thousands of people, and the prevailing unemployment all had their part to play in reducing the number of marriages. Certainly, unemployment was high and it may be significant that the number of marriages fell steeply even in those areas such as Limburg which were far away from the front line.[28]

By contrast with the trend in marriages, the number of births continued to decline during the whole period of the German occupation, so that in 1918 only half the number of children were born compared with the average of the period 1911–13. This represented a loss of 340,000 births or 40 per cent.[29] Regional differences were also more marked than was the case with the number of marriages. West Flanders was hit harder than other provinces, naturally enough since it contained the front line. The *arrondissement* of Diksmuide, in the middle of the battlefield,[30] registered a birth rate some 83 per cent lower in 1916–18 than in 1911–13. The least changes occurred in the province Luxembourg where there were just some 29 per cent fewer births in 1918 than in 1914. Next came Namur with a fall of 35 per cent and then Limburg with 36 per cent. In the other provinces the decrease was close to the national average of 49 per cent. A distinction can also be observed between the heavily urbanised and industrialised areas and the more agricultural ones. Between 1916 and 1918 the decline in the number of births was less pronounced in the latter than in the former.[31]

Various explanations can be advanced to account for these differences. It is possible that the Church's condemnations of birth control were more heeded in rural areas. However, the role of malnutrition in rendering numbers of women temporarily infecund should also be given careful consideration. A report on the medical situation in the country, intended for King Albert I, mentions the undernourishment of the mothers as the main cause of the fall of the birth rate: 'The weakness of the women, resulting from undernourishment, can be judged the principal cause of the evil [i.e. the fall in the number of births] without taking into account that voluntary abstinence was largely to be explained by the anxiety and fear of not being able to provide for any offspring.'[32] In rural areas, however, both factors were probably less significant since the inhabitants could supplement their diets from the produce of their gardens.

Two periods stand out in regard to the trend in the number of deaths during the war (see Table 4.8). The first, lasting until 1916, reflected a continuation of the mortality decline of the pre-war period. Between 1881 and 1890, the crude death rate still averaged 20.7 per thousand but the rate decreased gradually to 15.2 per thousand for the years 1911–13 and fell further to 13.1 per thousand for 1915 and 1916. The latter fall was contrary to what might have been anticipated, given the very rapid deterioration in food supplies that followed the outbreak of war (cf. above). It can, however, largely be seen as an artifact of the extraordinarily high emigration of the early years of the war, the decline in the number of births, with a consequent impact on a significant component of total mortality – the number of infant deaths, and the incomplete registration of deaths. Yet it may be significant that the level of infant mortality also appears to have declined until 1916. About this there is more certainty as the infant mortality rate is calculated by relating the number of deaths within the first year of life to the number of births and not to an estimate of the total population. In 1916 the infant mortality rate stood at 116 per thousand births compared with 139 per thousand in the immediate pre-war period. During 1916 and 1917, however, the infant mortality rate was once again at 140 per thousand. This was in spite of the many attempts carried out by all sorts of charitable institutions for the benefit of babies and young children, and forces a reappraisal of the effectiveness of their campaigns. Of the scale of their activities there can be no doubt. Even in the smallest villages, consultation offices were established where young mothers were advised about healthy feeding and supplied with food. Before the war, only 97 such offices had been in existence whereas by the end of December 1918, there were 768 infant welfare centres of the *Goutte de lait* run by middle-class women, 435 canteens serving undernourished children and 474 centres for young mothers. In this month the *Goutte de lait* had 86,332 children on their books, the canteens were providing for 132,381 children and the centres for 22,037 young or expectant mothers.[33]

All these measures did in fact improve children's health and the impact on the level of infant mortality, while not capable of precise measurement, can at least be roughly assessed. In the three provinces where charitable organisations functioned to the fullest extent, the infant mortality rate fell throughout the war. Thus in Brussels an infant mortality rate of 143.8 per thousand live births declined to 119.6, representing a fall of 17 per cent by 1916–18 over the opening years of the war. In Antwerp, there was a more substantial decrease of 20 per cent over the same period and in the province of Hainaut a decrease of 13 per cent. On the other hand, in those provinces where the infant welfare movement was weakened or totally non-operational, infant mortality increased greatly, as in the province of Luxembourg where infant mortality increased by 28 per cent and in the province of West Flanders where it increased by 24 per cent.

It has already been hinted above that the most significant factor affecting the trends in mortality between 1914 and 1918 is likely to have been the varying degree of success in maintaining the flow of imported foodstuffs. An indication of the severity of the wartime food shortage is that whereas before the war, it had been customary for children to be breastfed until they were nine months old, after 1916 breastfeeding was not prolonged beyond seven months, in spite of the supplementary meals which were given free to expectant mothers, two or three months before their delivery, in the Cantines maternelles or in other private charitable institutions.[34] The curtailment of breastfeeding meant that babies failed to make the expected gains in weight. One report spoke of a weight rise of 50 grams per week as against 180 grams in the period before the war.[35] However, even at the moment of birth, many children were underweight as a consequence of the poor nutritional state of their mothers. Data from the Antwerp maternal hospital (Ste-Anne) indicate that the majority of children were very weak at birth, assuming the appearance of babies born prematurely whose weight and size were below average. In fact, those born at full term weighed on average no more than 2,500 grams and measured 19 inches as against a normal weight in the region of 3,000–3,500 grams and a normal length of 20 inches.[36]

Confirmation of the link between the mortality level and the supply of imported food is provided by a comparison between the number of deaths in Brussels, collected quarterly, and the figures also produced quarterly on total imports (see Figure 4.2). In order to emphasise the degree of correlation between the two series, use was made of the inverse index of the import data. The correlation coefficient between the two variables was calculated as -0.525, indicating that one half of the trend in the death series could be explained by changes in the volume of imports, with an increase in the number of deaths corresponding to a decrease in imports. The relationship was particularly close, as Figure 4.2 makes clear, in three particular periods: the first half of 1916, the second quarter of 1917 and the first quarter of 1918. Less clear and even contrary are the trends during the third quarters of 1915 and 1917 and it is possible that the decrease in imports in these periods may have been made good, at least in part, by the produce of the domestic harvest, however small this may have been. Nevertheless, the conclusion is inescapable that the underlying deterioration of the food situation did in general determine the course of mortality during the four and a half years of the war. Indeed, at times when the food crisis became acute, as at the beginning of 1917, the margin of safety was so small that food shortages were immediately converted into deaths.

Conclusion

Fifty months of arduous occupation influenced Belgian society in different ways and on different levels. Of course, the war had a direct impact on standards of living and health between August 1914 and November 1918. The population, cut off from the vitally important in-flow of foreign food and faced with the failures of domestic production and distribution, plunged into misery and malnutrition. People fled, mortality increased from the end of 1916, nuptiality decreased from the beginning of the war and the number of births fell by almost 40 per cent.

If the consequences of the German occupation on living conditions during the war seem self-evident, it is far more difficult to assess the possible influence of the war on trends in the standard of living. The post-war recovery brought an increase in the average 'spending potential'. This, reinforced by changes in social policy, changed nutritional patterns by ending the traditional preponderance of vegetable foodstuffs in the average diet. Still, there can be no doubt that such progress would have occurred even if there had been no war. This is clearly attested by the relative improvements in the quality of the diet of the working class between 1890 and 1913. War accelerated this transition. Progress continued to be made until 1930, but thereafter

Fig. 4.2. Relation between imports of food and number of deaths in Brussels (quarterly figures; January–March 1915 = 100)[37]

a downward phase in the business cycle restricted the possibility of further improvements.[38]

A recovery is also evident with regard to the demographic situation. War losses and the decrease of nuptiality and births naturally introduced gaps in the age-structure of the population. However, marriage and birth rates, and the expectation of life, not only rapidly returned to the levels of the pre-war period but soon came to exceed them. In the longer term, the effect of the war on demographic changes seems fairly minimal. The only discontinuity to appear involved migration trends, where a net in-migration came to replace a net out-migration.

The war and the German occupation undoubtedly did cause changes on different levels of Belgian society, but most of these lay within the parameters already established in pre-war society. In many ways the war merely accelerated certain existing tendencies, although an exception would have to be made for the transformation of the role of the state in social and economic life. Continuity, however, predominated.

Appendix 4.1
Agricultural output in Belgium, 1913–19

	1913	1919	Decline 1913–19 (%)
Agricultural output[a]			
Wheat	25.2	20.7	18
Rye	22.0	17.4	21
Oats	25.6	17.5	32
Graincrop	24.2	18.4	24
Vegetables	22.7	17.7	22
Sugarbeet	265.5	225.3	4
Potatoes	206.5	180.1	13
Cattle-fodder	50.5	45.2	20
Second crop	266.4	188.9	29
Livestock			
Horses	267,160	161,619	40
Horned cattle	1,849,484	1,295,956	31
Pigs	1,412,293	770,201	46

[a]Quintals per hectare
Source
G. Bublot, 'Période 1914–1980', in A. Verhulst and G. Bublot (eds.), *L'Agriculture en Belgique. Hier et aujourd'hui*, Brussels, 1980, p. 56

Notes

We are indebted to Marc Bergmans, Hans Behaegel and Karla Oosterveen for the translation into English of the original Dutch text.

1 J. M. Keynes, *The economic consequences of the peace*, 1919, included in *The collected writings of John Maynard Keynes* (ed.) E. Johnson, vol. XVI, London, 1971, p. 79.

2 Domestic production accounted for 84.4 per cent of the total Belgian wheat consumption in 1845, 87.6 per cent in 1860, 67.7 per cent in 1875, 39.6 per cent in 1890, 22.9 per cent between 1910 and 1913, 28.9 per cent between 1924 and 1929 and 32.0 per cent between 1936 and 1939. These computations are based on production statistics and per capita consumption rates for wheat.

3 L. Schepens, 'Belgie in de Eerste Wereldoorlog' (Belgium during the First World War) in *Algemene Geschiedenis Nederlanden*, Bussum, 1979, vol. 14, pp. 22–3.

4 F. Baudhuin, *Histoire économique de la Belgique, 1914–1939*, Brussels, 1946, part 1, pp. 39–46.

5 A. Henry, *Le Ravitaillement de la Belgique pendant l'occupation allemande*, Paris, 1924, p. 43.

6 Literary sources are abundant as regards the Comité National and the Commission for Relief in Belgium, e.g. V. Kellogg, *Headquarters nights*, New York, 1919; H. Hoover, *An American epic, vol. 1, The relief of Belgium and Northern France, 1914–1930*, Chicago, 1959; B. Whitlock, *Belgium under the German occupation*, London, 1919; G. Gay, *The commission for relief in Belgium: Statistical review of relief operations*, Stanford, 1925. The most complete data however are to be found in the *Rapport général sur le fonctionnement et les opérations du Comité National de Secours et d'Alimentation 1914–1919*, 5 vols., Brussels, 1920–7.

7 For the functions of charity, see F. Piven and R. Cloward, *Regulating the poor. The functions of public welfare*, London, 1974.

8 A. Henry, *Le Ravitaillement de la Belgique*, p. 71.

9 *Rapport spécial sur le fonctionnement et les opérations de la section agricole du Comité National de Secours et d'Alimentation, 1914–1919*, Brussels, 1920, pp. 62–3.

10 Ch. De Lannoy, 'Quelques données rétrospectives sur les prix de détail à Bruxelles de août 1914 à octobre 1918', *Revue du Travail* (1919), 642–62.

11 See the collection of Belgian budget inquiries: G. Avondts and P. Scholliers, *Prices and house rents in Ghent and budget inquiries in the nineteenth and twentieth centuries*, vol. 5 of the series, *Textile workers in Ghent in the nineteenth and twentieth centuries*, Brussels, 1981, pp. 157–63. Expenditure on food represented 75 per cent of the total expenditure during the years 1840–60. From the 1880s the percentage of expenditure devoted to food declined to 60 per cent and was still at this level in the inquiries instigated by the British Board of Trade in 1910. *Report of an enquiry by the Board of Trade into working-class rents, housing, retail prices and standard rates of wages in the principal industrial towns of Belgium*, PP 1905, XCV Cd 5065.

12 The survey of the employed and unemployed in Brussels, to which reference is made in the text (cf. Table 4.6), was based on medical reports indicating caloric intake and did not detail family expenditure as would a 'classic' budget-based enquiry.

13 P. Scholliers, 'Verschuivingen in het arbeidersconsumptiepatroon, 1890–1930' (Changes in the labourer's consumption pattern, 1890–1930), *Revue belge d'histoire contemporaine*, 13 (1982), p. 288. These figures for expenses were checked and, minor corrections apart, confirmed by the Ministry of Labour.
14 A. Henry, *Le Ravitaillement de la Belgique*, p. 192.
15 *Ibid.*, p. 82.
16 Archives of the co-operative store 'Het Volk'.
17 *Ibid.*
18 Inquiries into the nutrition of the occupied part of the north of France revealed that the caloric intake was the same as it was in occupied Belgium. In the city of Lille, per capita intake varied between 1,800 calories during the winter of 1915, 1,340 calories during the summer of 1917 and 1,540 calories during the spring of 1918. See P. Collinet and P. Stahl, *Le Ravitaillement de la France occupée*, Paris New Haven, 1928, pp. 64–5.
19 W. H. Beveridge, *British food control*, London, 1928, p. 313.
20 J. Burnett, *Plenty and want*, London, 1979, p. 282.
21 A. Henry, *Le Ravitaillement de la Belgique*, pp. 124–5.
22 J. Burnett, *Plenty and want*, p. 282.
23 For information on meat consumption in 1913 see C. Vandenbroeke, 'Kwantitatieve en kwalitatieve aspecten van het vleesverbruik in Vlaanderen' (Quantitative and qualitative aspects of meat consumption in Flanders), *Tijdschrift voor sociale geschiedenis*, 8 (1983), p. 251. Comparable data for 1919 and 1922 is to be found in Ministère de l'Agriculture, *Consommation de la viande de boucherie*, Publication du Service des Associations et de la Statistique, Brussels, 1919–22.
24 *Annuaire statistique de la Belgique et du Congo belge, Quarante-sixième à cinquantième année, 1913–1915*, 46 (Brussels, 1922).
25 R. Olbrechts, 'La Population' in E. Mahaim (ed.), *La Belgique restaurée. Etude sociologique*, Brussels, 1926, pp. 1–66.
26 G. Dooghe, 'De bevolking', *Twintig eeuwen Vlaanderen*, part 8, Hasselt, 1978, pp. 11–128.
27 R. Olbrechts, 'La Population', p. 19.
28 In Limburg the number of wartime marriages was some 39 per cent below the number in pre-war years whereas in West Flanders, where the fighting was severest and most prolonged, marriages fell by 63 per cent.
29 R. Olbrechts, 'La Population', p. 22.
30 Cf. map of the destruction in *Resurgam, La Reconstruction en Belgique après 1914*, Brussels, 1985, p. 76.
31 R. Olbrechts, 'La Population', pp. 23–9; H. Pirenne, *La Belgique et la guerre mondiale*, Paris–New Haven, 1928, pp. 113–19; G. Dooghe, 'De bevolking', p. 21.
32 Archives of the Royal Palace, Secretary of the King and Queen, no. 614, p. 16.
33 G. Rency and A. Stassar, *La Belgique et la guerre, vol. 1, La vie matérielle de la Belgique pendant la première guerre mondiale*, Brussels, 1920, pp. 75–6.
34 *Ibid.*, p. 256, *Rapport général sur les opérations, troisième partie*, vol. 1, *Rapport*, 1920, p. 81.
35 G. Rency and A. Stassar, *La Belgique et la guerre*, chapter XI, 'La protection de l'enfance', p. 75; Archives of the Royal Palace, Secretary of the King and the Queen, no. 614, pp. 74–5.

36 *Ibid.*
37 Sources to Fig. 4.2: *Rapport général sur le fonctionnement et les opérations du Comité National*, vol. II, 1921, pp. 276–81; Archives de la ville de Bruxelles, Régistres de déces, 1914–18.
38 For data on per capita food consumption during the inter-war years see P. van den Eckhout and P. Scholliers, 'De hoofdelijke voedselconsumptie in Belgie, 1831–1939' (Per capita food consumption in Belgium, 1831–1939), *Tijdschrift voor sociale geschiedenis*, 8 (1983), 298–301.

5

Variations in patterns of consumption in Germany in the period of the First World War

Armin Triebel

Introduction

In the memory of our elders, the years of the First World War and its aftermath live on as a period of mourning for sons and fathers, brothers and friends, of challenges to established values, and of increasing hardship. The long war and the collapse of the Empire, opened for most people an episode of major changes in their very lives. They encountered phenomena never thought of before, and had to muddle through new and difficult situations.

One such was the subsistence crisis of 1916–19. We will not dwell upon the fact that the supply of consumer goods became worse for the masses, both in quantity and quality as the war went on. We need only ask those who lived through these times for their memories of turnip winters (especially the fateful *Kohlrübenwinter* of 1916/17) and of all sorts of substitutes that appeared in the shops. Yet despite all these privations they tell us that really hard times set in after the Armistice and lasted until the end of the post-war inflation.

Our main concern is not with the deterioration of living standards, but rather with the question as to whether the best way to interpret the war experience is in terms of relative deprivation and class antagonism. In other words, did the pre-war cleavages between social classes in respect of living standards survive the upheaval of war? Besides levelling differentials between skilled and unskilled workers to a certain degree, the war created disparities in other respects between war and civilian industries, large and small towns, and large and small families.

To test these hypotheses we shall attempt to assess changes in the stratification of social classes as measured by consumption differentials. Although

ARMIN TRIEBEL

the information on private household budgets cannot cover all relevant matters, they are still the best available for historical research of this kind.

The economic background

Shortly after the war, the Prussian Statistical Office tried to quantify the increase in the cost of living during the war.[1] Standard food consumption per month and person was assessed as consisting of 18 kg of potatoes, 10 kg of bread, 0.5 kg of other pastry, 1.5 kg of flour and farinaceous products, 8 litres of milk, 0.5 kg of butter, 0.4 kg of other fats, 2 kg of meat, 1.4 kg of sugar and 8 eggs.

These basic foods together with some minor ingredients were estimated to yield 2,400 or 2,700 calories per day, irrespective of whether they were purchased legally or on the black market. The lowest grade within the officially fixed scale of food requirements for workers was 2,400 calories, the highest category being 3,500 calories for miners working at the pit-face. The food supply situation took a turn for the worse in 1916, when, in the towns, most of the important foodstuffs were rationed. The authorities set out to provide animal foodstuff equal to 20 per cent of the total calorie intake. In fact, only 6.2 per cent of the requisite animal calories could be procured in 1916, 15.3 per cent in 1917 and 3.3 per cent in 1918.[2] The total monthly per capita expenditure on food was variously estimated at between 21 and 26 marks in 1914 depending on the area concerned compared with between 55 and 65 marks at the end of 1918, indicating a rise of around 150 to 200 per cent.

It is no simple matter, however, to calculate the average expenditure per head. In the absence of sufficient data, experts merely extrapolated the expenditure, food apart, for the average-sized family. Using a variety of sources, it was estimated that blue-collar workers needed to expend per consumption unit ('head') the amounts set out in Table 5.1.[3] A per capita figure for rent is of course artificial. Rent largely depended upon size of town, the status of the people living in the district, and the storey of the dwelling.[4] Coal prices rose two or three times in the course of the war. So did prices of clothing, especially in 1918, whereas the increases of the remaining minor items appear to have been moderate.

Nevertheless, it has been argued recently that the major part of the working class was doing reasonably well by the end of the war. Not only had their income improved relative to that enjoyed by civil servants but, unlike employers, they also profited by the subsequent inflation.[5] This argument has been mainly applied to the period between 1920 and 1923, and the main indicator, the compound real income rate (*Kumulierte Reallohnposition*) has

Table 5.1. *Estimated cost of essentials per month and per consumption unit ('head') for blue-collar workers in certain parts of Germany, 1914–18 (marks)*

Category of expenditure	1914 (January)	1916 (April)	1917 (September)	1918 (October)
Food	21–26	37–46	43–46	55–65
Rent	—	6	7–9	5–9
Heating and light	2.40	2	5	6
Clothing	—	5	6	20
Taxes and other expenditure	—	12–15	15–17	22–25
Total				
Berlin	46	—	—	125
Danzig	44	—	—	110
Saxony	43	—	—	112
Rhineland	50	—	—	122

Source
Quante, 'Lohnpolitik und Lohnentwicklung im Kriege', pp. 366–8

been derived from macroeconomic statistics which indicate productivity in the industrial sector. So far, such assertions remain unproven.

The notion that other classes experienced greater losses as a result of the war than did blue-collar workers is not new. As a consequence of wartime casualties, the relative value of manpower in the factories at home rose, as did the bargaining power of their political representatives. G. D. Feldman has argued that the industrialists and the workers employed in war industries were the only two groups who derived material benefits from the war. Feldman gave much emphasis to the 'proletarianisation' of the middle class, particularly the junior civil servants[6] and the white-collar employees, who could not afford to buy on the black market and who 'unlike a goodly number of workers' did not always have relatives in the countryside. In addition to declining real incomes, they experienced a loss of status. Under such conditions, an increase in social tension was very likely. But the quantification of relative gains and losses should not obscure the fact that the real earnings of almost all sections of the labour force were lower in the immediate post-war years than they had been in 1914. Male workers in civilian industries earned in real terms no more than 55 per cent of what they had previously, female workers in war industries, 88 per cent. There is no evidence that the rise in wages compensated for the rise of prices.[7]

This was accepted at the time by informed observers. Various experts attempted estimates of necessary household expenditure as a poor substitute for a cost of living index which was established in 1920. Table 5.2

Table 5.2. *Minimum cost of living estimated for a four-person working-class family, per month, in certain parts of Germany, 1914–18*

	1914 (pre-war)	1916 (April)	1917 (September)	1918 (October)
Greater Berlin				
minimum cost of living [mark]	180	370	380	500
minimum necessary wage per hour [pfennig] (in brackets: working hours)	75 (10)	180 (8) 170 (9)	185 (8) 175 (9)	240–250 (8) 225 (9)
Danzig				
minimum cost of living [mark]	175	295	335	440
minimum necessary wage per hour [pfennig] (in brackets: working hours)	70 (10)	135 (8–9)	155 (8–9)	200 (8–9)
Saxony				
minimum cost of living [mark]	170	335	360	445
minimum necessary wage per hour [pfennig] (in brackets: working hours)	70 (10)	155 (8–9)	165 (8–9)	200 (8–9)
Rhineland				
minimum cost of living [mark]	200	360	415	485
minimum necessary wage per hour [pfennig] (in brackets: working hours)	80 (10)	165 (8–9)	190 (8–9)	220 (8–9)

Source
Quante, 'Lohnpolitik und Lohnentwicklung im Kriege', pp. 369ff.

summarises one of these fairly well-known indicators, i.e. the so-called minimum cost of living per month for a four-person working-class family and the hourly wages that were required to provide it.

In Berlin, the pre-war standard of 180 marks per month was reached by nearly all skilled and semi-skilled workers. Unskilled workers, however, may have been obliged to find supplementary earnings. In the first years of the war, wages were insufficient to keep pace with inflation even in high-wage industries such as the metal, chemical and wool industries and in government-owned enterprises. Pay did not improve until the Hindenburg Plan was implemented in 1916 with the aim of increasing munitions output regardless of cost. Even then, workers in the textile industries remained poorly paid.

With a few exceptions, the situation in Danzig, Saxony and the Rhineland was worse, for in these areas wages did not keep pace with prices in the long run, as Quante maintained. On the Rhine, only the wages of the best-paid metal-workers kept pace with prices. On balance, most wage-earners and salaried workers suffered a sharp decline in real wages in the first years of the war, a decline that was reversed, and then only in part, through government measures from 1917 onwards. Even food allowances awarded by individual entrepreneurs to their workers provided only temporary relief and, in any case, were designed only for the workers themselves, not for their families. Public soup kitchens fed scarcely 8 per cent of the population.[8]

Professor Briefs, who at the time held the chair of political science in Giessen University, attested in 1917 that 'the German household' was living on the poverty line.[9] Before the war, 42 per cent of all fats consumed, 28 per cent of total albumen, 8 per cent of total carbohydrate supply, and 20 per cent of total calorie input had been imported. Germany could produce all the potatoes that she required for her own consumption, but only 90 per cent of the bread, 75 per cent of the milk, and 60 per cent of the meat. When international trade ceased with the war, the demand had to be supplied from home – or done without. It is reported that some households passed a year during the war without sight of an egg. Meat consumption fell to the level of the 1800s. Housewives had to manage with poor substitutes ('Ersatz') and with household utensils to which they were not accustomed in order to save energy. They prepared food which, formerly, would have been purchased, and started the cultivation of small vegetable gardens. Again, the petty bourgeoisie and, more generally, the inhabitants of the towns were worst affected, especially if they had young children.[10]

Unfortunately, effects of this kind, important as they were, are not easily quantified. Not only was official planning of calorie supply and distribution upset by unforeseen shortages and the disruption of the transport system, but also there must be major reservations about the accuracy of the estimates of caloric requirements. What, for example, were the caloric requirements of housewives who had to queue for hours in order to obtain a half pint of milk? Crude quantification of caloric requirements may be particularly wide of the mark in times of acute social stress. Seemingly hard figures may well present us with fictitious images of the past.[11] With such reservations in mind, let us turn, therefore, to the evidence of actual household account books.

Consumption patterns from household budgets

Extensive, and indeed well-known, investigations yield a considerable quantity of data on consumption patterns before and after the war. For

Table 5.3. *Principal expenditure categories of household budgets included in surveys undertaken before the First World War*

Area	Year	Social group	Food (%)	Clothing (%)	Housing (%)	Total expenditure[d] (marks)
Nuremberg	1900	Workers	50–59	9	14–15	700–2,200
Hamburg	1903	Teachers	37	11	19	3,314
Deutsches Reich[a]	1907/08	Diverse occupations	48	12	18	2,234
DMV	1908	Metalworkers	53[b]	13[b]	14	1,825
Halle	1909/10	Workers	56 (26–74)	14	14	1,482
Saarland	1910[c]	Miners	47	12	11	2,477
Deutsches Reich	1912/13	Post Office clerks	50	13	16	2,054

[a] The Statistical Office reported 46 per cent for food and 13 per cent for clothing which may be due to a miscalculation
[b] Any expenditure on the replacement of household goods was also included here. *320 Haushaltungsrechnungen*, p. 31.
[c] According to Hoffmann, wages in mining and salt-works averaged about 1,300 marks. See Walter G. Hoffmann, Franz Grumbach and Helmut Hesse, *Das Wachstum der deutschen Wirtschaft seit der Mitte des 19. Jahrhunderts*, Berlin, 1965, p. 461.
[d] All budgets were maintained for 12 months.

example, in 1903, 908 working-class households in Berlin were asked for details of their annual expenditure. Regardless of occupation and number of family members, out of an average total expenditure of 1,768 marks, 56 per cent was devoted to food, 8 per cent to clothing and 20 per cent to housing. One household budget maintained between 1896 and 1905 was published as a typical example of lower-middle-class experience. The head of this household was a book-keeper, at first salaried, later self-employed, and then became an insurance agent. This 'representative' expended 2,391 marks on average per annum, 33 per cent on food, 10 per cent on clothing and 17 per cent on housing.[12]

These figures corroborated existing expectations concerning the characteristic differences between the working and middle classes.[13] The former were said to attach too great an importance to food. The latter were praised for their effort to be dressed respectably. The expenditure on housing also increased with status.

Differentials of a similar order appear in Table 5.3. From the turn of the century, many budget surveys were carried out, most of them frequently cited, some of them extensive. Without exception, the originators and editors maintained that the budgets collected, though not representing the whole population, would nevertheless present 'interesting' insights into the way of life of the low-income classes. However, the average income of the households in Table 5.3, as indicated by total expenditure, make it clear that, on the whole, the respective households were not particularly impoverished.[14] All accounts were kept over a period of twelve months and based on daily notes. So were the budgets from 44 workers' families in Nuremberg and from 14 elementary teachers in Hamburg.[15] In 1907, the Reich's Statistical Office collected the budgets of 852 families of white- and blue-collar workers and civil servants. In the following year the metal-workers' union (DMV) collected 320 budgets.[16] The Statistical Office of the town of Halle published the budgets of 49 skilled and unskilled working-class families covering the years 1909–10.[17] Then in 1910, the managing director of a coal mine in the Saar asked over a hundred 'reliable' miners' families to keep a written account of income and expenditure.[18] The Saar miners are known to have been wealthier than the miners in the Ruhr district in that many of them owned their own cottages. In addition to metal-workers and miners, a third group much represented in budget surveys were civil servants, especially in the postal administration. For example, the budgets of 127 lower-grade post office clerks were collected by their Federation in 1912 and 1913.[19]

These data provide a pre-war base against which to measure subsequent developments. Twenty years later, the President of the Statistical Office of the town of Hamburg reviewed the chief features of living standards before

Table 5.4. *Principal expenditure categories of household budgets included in the major surveys of the 1920s and 1930s*

Area	Year	Social group	Food (%)	Clothing (%)	Housing (%)	Total expenditure (Reichsmarks)[c]
Deutsches Reich	1927	Diverse occupations	40	13	16	4,235
Deutsches Reich	1937	Diverse occupations	46	9	16	2,399
Deutsches Reich	1925/26	Shoe-making: workers and artisans	54	10[a]	7	2,409
Hamburg	1925	Diverse occupations	46[b]	13	12	3,234[b]
Deutsches Reich	1926	Clerks	37	12	14	4,446
Deutsches Reich	1929	Railway: clerks and officials	38	12	14	4,429

[a] The shoe-makers association reported 12 per cent which is probably a calculation error.
[b] The editors reported 45 per cent for food and 3,233 marks respectively.
[c] All budgets were maintained for 12 months.

the war. Varying according to prosperity of the individual household, 30–50 per cent of total expenditure, pre-war, went on food, 6–18 per cent on rent, 3–5 per cent on heating and light, and 10–15 per cent on clothing. The wealthier classes, in particular, spent up to 30 per cent of their total expenditure on cultural needs.

The President of the Statistical Office then went on to itemise expenditure on food. Town dwellers concentrated on animal foodstuff (such as meat, fat, butter, eggs, and milk). These alone accounted for half of the total expenditure on food, indicating, in his opinion, that with increased resources, people were anxious to turn away from a vegetable-based diet. His somewhat subjective conclusion was that 'the standard of living was that of culturally refined people who, on the whole, were well nourished and had something left for intellectual and social needs.'[20]

To provide a perspective on longer-term trends, we have derived similar statistics from the official inquiries of 1927 and 1937[21] and some smaller investigations (300 workers in a shoe-factory, 80 households in Hamburg, 43 budgets of white-collar workers, and 120 budgets of workers and officials employed by the railway).[22] It is not easy to find signs of a significant shift in expenditure patterns over time, the only exception being the reduced expenditure on housing reported in the surveys conducted during the 1920s. However, it should be noted that again the households belonged to the upper ranges of the income scale.[23] Conversely, the low expenditure on clothing reported in some surveys, in 1900 and 1937 for example, probably reflects the inclusion of relatively large numbers of low-incomes families.

Household budgets in war-time

The budget surveys of the War Committee for Consumers' Interests (Kriegsausschuss für Konsumenteninteressen hereafter, KAKI)[24] from April 1916 were taken on the initiative of W. Zimmermann. He claimed that shortages affected all people living in towns in a similar way, and that this had lessened but not eliminated social differentials in living standards.[25] The reduction of social distinctions to a common level of scarcity may have deepened a sense of relative deprivation on the part of the middle- and upper-classes. On the other hand, the democratisation of dearth did not ease the situation of the greater part of the white-collar and blue-collar labour force. They found themselves in an even more restricted purchasing position in that they had to cope with a proportion of rationed food to non-rationed food of 7 or 9:1 whereas the upper classes enjoyed a proportion of 2:1. Zimmermann asserted that legally specified rations could not satisfy the needs of a single family. Yet by 1918, it was admitted officially that non-rationed food other than vegetables and preserved food had disappeared

Table 5.5. *Average food consumption per head and month, in grams, 1907–18*

	Pre-war Deutsches Reich 1907/08		DMV metal workers 1908	War-time War Committee for Consumers' Interests		
	Workers	Civil servants		1916	1917	1918
Bread and pastry	—	—	13,155	8,770[a]	8,352	9,374
Flour	—	—	1,110	1,445	1,876	1,593
Potatoes	7,666	8,400	10,590	16,793	12,025	21,807
Butter, other fats	1,116	1,175[b]	525[c]	862	507	614
Meat[f]	2,291	2,808[d]	2,064[e]	1,901	1,829	1,710
Fish[g]	—	—	—	857	311	777
Eggs	340	520	425	600	300	450
Milk[f]	10,560	13,800	11,160	9,870	11,000	9,000
Cheese	316	225	—	363	448	397
Vegetables and fruit[h]	—	—	—	2,573	1,938	3,671
Sugar	—	—	—	1,184	907	844

[a] Rubner, 'Ernährungswesen', 1928, p. 8, reported, for January 1915, 7,600 g war bread made from wheat, rye, and potatoes
[b] Butter only
[c] No animal fat
[d] Meat only, without sausages
[e] Animal fat included
[f] Includes preserved foods of the same type
[g] Includes smoked and preserved fish
[h] Includes tinned greens and jam
Source
Tyszka, 'Hunger und Ernährung', p. 347 and for War Committee for Consumers' Interests (KAKI), cf. below Table 5.6.

from the market. The 1918 report on the last budget survey surmised that about one-half of the observed families consumed food purchased on the black market at prices and in quantities higher than was officially authorised.[26]

The President of the Statistical Office of the town of Hamburg, Carl von Tyszka, indicated a number of specific changes to the differentials in consumption that had been taken for granted prior to the war. First came the rise in food prices, the growing shortage of food supplies, and the emergence of black markets which resulted in a rise in the proportion of income spent on food. With about half of the income of all major social groups now devoted to food, the consumption patterns of certain social classes, who had considered themselves different from each other, converged. Secondly, the middle class curtailed their social expenditure during the war to a level in line with the norms formerly typical of the lower classes. Thirdly, the war brought an end to the advantages the town-dweller had enjoyed over the

Table 5.6. *Principal expenditure categories of household budgets included in the inquiries of the War Committee for Consumers' Interests (KAKI)*

Date of survey	Number of families	Food (%)	Clothing (%)	Rent (%)	Total expenditure (marks per 'head')[a]
April 1916	858	52	8	11	74.87
April 1917	342	51	0	11	75.58
April 1918	249	48	7	8	107.56

[a]1 'head' = 1 grown-up or two children aged 1–11
Sources
Reichs-Arbeitsblatt, 15, 2, 1917, p. 147 (183 workers, 166 clerks, 63 junior civil servants, 114 middle-ranking civil servants, 48 senior civil servants, 284 diverse); *Beiträge . . . drittes Kriegsjahr*, 1917, pp. 7 & 26 (100 workers, 81 clerks, 31 junior civil servants, 81 middle-ranking civil servants, 9 senior civil servants, 40 professionals and war-widows); *Beiträge . . . viertes Kriegsjahr*, 1919, pp. 9 & 28 (118 workers, 32 clerks, 20 junior civil servants, 61 middle-ranking civil servants, 4 senior civil servants, 14 pensioners and professionals).

rural population, such as a steady supply of diverse articles and some competition among tradesmen. As the war went on town-dwellers poured into the countryside and begged from farmers whom they envied for their well-stocked barns. Foreign trade statistics confirmed that agrarian producers retained a considerable proportion of their produce, thus aggravating the privation in the towns.[27]

Between 1916 and 1918 not only did the amount spent on food increase but, as we can see in Table 5.5, the composition of the diet deteriorated compared with the situation before the war, away from high-standard animal food to potato-dominated, low albumen foods. While consumption of meat declined by 40 per cent, expenditure on potatoes increased by 300 per cent. Expenditure on vegetables and fruit fell, the increase in 1918 presumably reflecting the introduction of the much-hated turnip meals (for example, turnips in the form of pap, stewed, or as an ingredient in bread).[28]

Quantitative information on the type and quantity of food and other goods consumed by the masses during the war years is scattered, inexact, and grossly deficient. So is information on expenditure. The only official sources are the budget inquiries undertaken by KAKI which, however, only covered one month (Table 5.6). The individual budgets have not survived. We shall try to offer a fresh perspective on the characteristics of differential consumption during the last years of the war by presenting data for certain income and occupational groups (Tables 5.7–5.9). These findings will be compared with computations for the pre-war and post-war periods derived from the Berlin Data File. First, however, some comment is in order on the nature of the various KAKI surveys.

The first inquiry commenced only in April 1916. Families were asked to write down their income derived from salaries or wages for that month. No receipts from subletting, relief payments, interests on capital and the like were registered. Average expenditure per 'head' was calculated for each category of monthly 'income', regardless of socioeconomic status. Details of expenditure per income group and occupational class were given only for a small number of select families of four without an explicit statement of the selection criterion. Judged from the context it has been assumed that these families actually comprised four persons, i.e. parents and two children. This was the case later, in the 1917 survey, when 'standard families' were identified. No standard families comprising two children were sifted out in the last survey of April 1918, there being too few of them for effective analysis.[29] The second survey, taken in July 1916 and limited to expenditure on food, has to be excluded from further consideration here.

Fortunately, however, the documentation of the following two inquiries was more exhaustive. Expenditure per 'head' (consumption unit, cf. below, note 3), was set out according to income and, at the same time, differentiated by occupational class. The expenditure figures for senior civil servants with an income of 50–75 marks per head in 1917 which are based only on two families demonstrate the principle of the consumption per head computation. These two families contained altogether 12 'heads'. For example, from this information, the following family composition can be inferred for each family: parents, two children over 11 years old, two children under 11, and one maid servant, and a total income in April 1917 of between 300 and 450 marks.

Given that the 1917 and 1918 classifications relate to consumption units while the 1916 figures refer to standard families, the income and expenditure figures of the latter need to be recalculated in the following way. Assuming that the families from 1916 were 2-child families, i.e. families with three consumption 'heads', and choosing from the 1917 data the class of 50–75 marks income per 'head' (the lowest income class that allows comparison between five social classes), the appropriate income-per-family class for 1916 turns out to be 50–75 multiplied by 3, or approximately 150–225 marks. Within the 1918 data there were no senior civil servants with 50–75 marks income per head per month, but the war-inflationary rise in wages provides independent justification for substituting the next highest income class.

It was decided not to reproduce in Tables 5.7–5.9 all the expenditure categories in the original source, but to omit expenses for heating and light, taxes, fares, gifts, and 'miscellaneous items' together with those items within

Table 5.7. *Differential consumption during the First World War: four-person families, April 1916, income per family 100–200 marks, expenditure per month and consumption unit ('head'), in marks*

	Civil servants			Workers	
	Senior	Middle-rank	Junior (N = 19)	White-collar (N = 6)	Blue-collar (N = 16)
Total expenditure	.	.	74.36	71.69	73.10
Rent	.	.	8.87	7.54	6.63
Household equipment	.	.	0.48	0.45	0.49
Clothing (including shoes)	.	.	6.74	5.60	4.49
Detergents	.	.	1.65	1.87	1.65
Servants, gratuities[a]	.	.	0.06	2.25	0.25
Insurance	.	.	1.29	1.69	1.73
Social expenses, i.e.	.	.	1.95	1.93	2.55
Books, newspapers, etc.	.	.	0.95	0.71	0.94
Amusements, sports	.	.	0.40	0.16	0.56
Associations, trade unions	.	.	0.60	1.06	1.05
Personal care, i.e.	.	.	2.38	1.15	1.56
Medical provision	.	.	1.87	0.78	1.24
Barbers, baths	.	.	0.51	0.47	0.32
Food, e.g.	.	.	42.31	41.33	46.64
Bread and rolls	.	.	4.25	4.03	4.76
Potatoes	.	.	2.07	2.58	3.51
Butter / Fats, other than butter	.	.	5.26	5.49	5.69
Meats and sausage	.	.	6.41	8.15	7.04
Meats, preserved	.	.	1.44	1.65	0.90
Milk, fresh	.	.	3.25	2.80	2.32
Milk, preserved	.	.	0.62	—	—
Vegetables and fruit, fresh	.	.	1.28	1.87	1.55
Vegetables and fruit, preserved	.	.	0.52	0.50	0.93
Restaurants (meals and beverages)	.	.	1.81	1.29	1.27

[a] Includes small sums or gifts to neighbours and others in return for services rendered.
 . indicates no data available.
Source
'Einkommen und Lebenshaltung', 1917, pp. 150ff.; converted into expenditure per consumption unit ('head') by the author. The sources refer to the selection of families of 4 heads or 'standard families' and we made two assumptions: first, that the selection criterion used in this context was indeed 4 persons and, secondly, that apart from the parents, the remaining members of the household were children. This was the case in the majority of four-person households known. Accordingly, we arrived at the expenditure per consumption unit by dividing the reported expenditure by three. If one of the two children was in fact approaching 16 years old, the divisor ought instead to have been 3.5 and the figures in this table reduced accordingly.

Table 5.8. *Differential consumption during the First World War: families of 5 social classes. April 1917, income per 'head' and month 50–75 marks, expenditures per month and consumption unit, in marks*

	Civil servants			Workers	
	Senior (N = 2)	Middle-rank (N = 25)	Junior (N = 14)	White-collar (N = 27)	Blue-collar (N = 42)
Total expenditure[a]	74.34	74.90	72.05	68.32	67.03
Rent	8.42	8.49	8.55	8.71	5.19
Household equipment	0.96	1.03	1.11	0.79	0.82
Clothing (including shoes)	5.92	6.87	7.01	6.60	6.62
Detergents	0.71	1.97	1.70	1.76	1.86
Servants, gratuities[b]	1.20	1.16	0.09	0.27	0.08
Insurance	1.30	1.46	1.14	1.87	1.11
Social expenses, i.e.	4.88	2.64	2.30	2.31	1.84
Books, newspapers, etc.	2.25	1.97	1.67	1.58	1.06
Amusements, sports	1.20	0.11	0.21	0.22	0.13
Associations, trade unions	1.43	0.56	0.42	0.51	0.65
Personal care, i.e.	0.85	1.71	1.03	1.18	0.81
Medical provision	0.28	1.42	0.56	0.81	0.54
Barbers, baths	0.57	0.29	0.47	0.37	0.27
Food, e.g.	34.06	36.97	39.58	34.47	39.88
Bread and rolls	1.80	3.33	3.32	3.30	3.61
Potatoes	1.81	1.45	1.46	1.36	1.43
Butter	1.88	1.62	1.75	1.50	1.79
Fats, other than butter	1.04	1.05	1.52	1.22	1.73
Meats and sausage	6.67	7.81	8.00	7.83	8.34
Meats, preserved	—	0.18	—	0.21	0.27
Milk, fresh	1.33	2.02	2.43	2.06	1.82
Milk, preserved	—	0.65	0.30	0.49	0.38
Vegetables and fruit, fresh	1.70	1.51	2.06	1.16	1.67
Vegetables and fruit, preserved	0.80	0.61	0.56	0.57	0.60
Restaurants (meals and beverages)	3.98	2.11	3.11	1.59	3.58

[a] Since the figures reported in the survey of 1917 clearly indicate expenditures per head (i.e. per consumption unit), they represent the average of expenditures across families of all sizes.
Mean family sizes per social class in this sample:
senior civil servants   5.0
middle-ranking civil servants 4.1
junior civil servants   3.9
white-collar workers   4.0
blue-collar workers   4.3
[b] Includes small sums or gifts to neighbours and others in return for services rendered.
Source
Beiträge, 1917, pp. 31–6

Table 5.9. *Differential consumption during the First World War: families of 5 social classes. April 1918, income per 'head' and month 75–100 marks, expenditures per month and consumption unit, in marks*

	Civil servants			Workers	
	Senior (N = 1)	Middle-rank (N = 13)	Junior (N = 5)	White-collar (N = 5)	Blue-collar (N = 35)
Total expenditure[a]	136.75	106.68	103.40	76.54	96.30
Rent	9.14	11.60	8.25	8.25	7.16
Household equipment	1.13	1.70	1.48	5.05	1.46
Clothing (including shoes)	13.75	15.21	12.62	12.38	13.82
Detergents	2.12	1.83	3.33	1.17	3.09
Servants, gratuities[b]	—	1.05	0.51	—	0.56
Insurance	6.75	2.66	1.07	2.99	1.96
Social expenses	5.97	4.16	6.79	2.37	3.24
Books, newspapers, etc.	3.97	3.00	5.19	1.60	1.52
Amusements, sports	—	0.51	0.99	0.29	0.51
Associations, trade unions	2.00	0.65	0.61	0.48	1.21
Personal care, i.e.	1.12	3.48	3.01	1.55	1.43
Medical provision	—	2.94	2.22	0.86	0.90
Barbers, baths	1.12	0.54	0.79	0.69	0.53
Food, e.g.	69.48	46.23	50.09	31.94	51.71
Bread and rolls	3.20	3.80	3.79	4.21	4.74
Potatoes	2.72	3.69	3.67	4.17	3.86
Butter	3.38	2.27	2.24	1.70	2.74
Fats, other than butter	1.04	3.05	2.28	0.53	2.01
Meats and sausage	13.80	5.97	6.05	4.23	7.89
Meats, preserved	1.94	0.24	0.06	0.16	0.21
Milk, fresh	1.16	3.28	2.97	2.45	2.95
Milk, preserved	—	0.31	0.66	0.59	0.22
Vegetables and fruit, fresh	1.35	2.52	1.57	1.23	2.87
Vegetables and fruit, preserved	2.86	0.61	0.38	0.21	0.78
Restaurants (meals and beverages)	6.49	2.29	3.69	1.74	3.57

[a] Cf. Note to Table 5.8. Mean family sizes per social class in this sample were:

senior civil servants	4.0
middle-ranking civil servants	4.3
junior civil servants	3.6
white-collar workers	3.8
blue-collar workers	4.2

[b] Includes small sums of gifts to neighbours and others in return for services rendered.
Source
Beiträge, 1919, pp. 50–5.

the general category of food which in my view do not reflect social class differentials or, as with heating and light, are subject to seasonal distortion. Proportions of overall expenditure on other items of consumption have been calculated and are presented below in Tables 5.12–5.18. We should, in addition, take account of some of the features considered at the time as typifying household budgets in wartime: notably the higher proportions of expenditure devoted to food which reached nearly 60 per cent in the lower-income groups and the extremely low variation rates from one income level to the next (8 to 10 per cent) in expenditure on 'cultural needs' such as household articles, medical care, hygiene and sport, insurance, amusements, books, journals, and newspapers, together probably with educational fees.

The wartime household budgets in perspective

It remains to try to place the war years within the context of the long-term development of differential consumption patterns in Germany. Since the 1950s, different methods have been developed to uncover the long-term structural changes in patterns of consumption. Most of them use national accounting statistics. The micro-economic approach was, in most cases, confined to the calculation of elasticity of demand. But elasticity does not tell us much about structural changes of private consumption unless interpreted in relation to the performance of other macro-economic variables, which is rarely the case.[30] Only recently have there been some attempts to reinterpret the long-term change in consumption from a sociological and historical point of view.[31] Sociological research centres around the distinction drawn between individual productivity and a worker's life-style choices. The skills of an individual are measured by their value on the labour market. Individual attributes are interpreted as status variables, on the other hand; that is, they reflect differences in life-style independent of the individual's position in the labour market.

In the case of the First World War, variations in life styles have been seen in terms of changes in the structure of social inequality during the conflict. According to this view the war reduced differences between and among strata within the workforce. But so far neither the historical nor the sociological approach has been able to address the question of wartime changes in the system of consumption differentials itself.

It is appropriate, therefore, that we should return to the question posed at the beginning of this chapter and examine differences in consumption behaviour as evidence of the extent of social inequality over the war period. Did social class differentials diminish or, alternatively, were they unaffected by the war? In order to compare household budgets before 1914, 1914–18, and in the 1920s we must establish the type of households represented by the KAKI inquiries. These were households of four persons including two children within an income range of 50–100 marks per 'head' per month. According to Professor Tyszka this income class in 1914/18 was, before the war, equivalent to the income bracket up to 2,000 marks per annum. The equivalent income in 1927 would approach 3,600 Reichsmarks per annum.[32] Controlling for other variables such as dwelling-place and age of parents and children would be desirable, but is impractical because the sources do not provide the relevant information.

Tables 5.10 and 5.11 illustrate the circumstances of the relevant households selected from the Berlin Data File of household accounts. They represent the special household type of two parents with two children within a medium income range living mostly in towns. This limitation is serious, but the data can still be used to measure temporal changes in expenditure patterns. For the first time we have also been able to break down the previously undivided civil servant aggregate into its constituent ranks.

The first impression is certainly one of continuity in consumption patterns over time. Some class characteristics remained stable from before the war through the years 1914/18 until the stabilisation period in the late 1920s. As we can see by comparing Table 5.10 with Table 5.7 above, the figures for differential consumption after two years of war were strikingly similar to the established features of pre-war consumption patterns, differentiated along social class lines. It was still the blue-collar workers who spent least on rent and clothing, and most on food. White-collar workers and junior civil servants spent far less on food, but more on clothing. The six white-collar families in the survey seem to have occupied rather cheap housing, parsimoniously lit and heated and poorly furnished (although the low rate for household equipment is not unambiguous). On the other hand, they recorded the highest expenditure, in absolute figures, on detergents. Junior civil servants spent the most on clothes, rent, heating, and light. Their medical expenses were also considerable, although these may have been distorted by illnesses among the particular families under consideration. In general, junior civil servants and white-collar workers laid equal stress on hygiene and health (drawing on the services of the barber, physician and chemist).

The Report of the 1916 survey made special reference to the fact that all families spent twice as much on 'books, newspapers, etc.' as on 'amusements and sports'. This was interpreted as encouraging evidence that even under the unfavourable circumstances of the war these families preferred to cultivate mind and morale than to make a hullabaloo.[33] In fact, as the war progressed, newspapers became more and more important for all people as a means of obtaining vital information about special rations and changes in

Table 5.10. *Differential consumption, 1902–12: 2-child families, income per family up to 2,000 marks, expenditures per month and consumption unit, in marks*

	Civil servants			Workers	
	Senior	Middle-rank (N = 1)	Junior (N = 17)	White-collar (N = 1)	Blue-collar (N = 99)
Total expenditure[a]	.	61.57	45.14	40.03	44.21
Rent	.	13.89	5.55 (14)	2.78	5.34 (18)
Household equipment	.	.	3.15 (2)	0.32	1.51 (26)
Clothing (including shoes)	.	6.26	5.28	5.22	4.78
Detergents	.	.	0.61 (12)	.	.
Servants (only)	.	.	— (4)	.	0.03 (90)
Insurance	.	.	1.36 (4)	.	1.77 (90)
Social expenses I[b] (excluding education)	.	.	0.94 (5)	.	1.51 (95)
e.g. associations	.	.	0.47 (12)	.	1.32 (5)
Social expenses II[c] (excluding associations)	.	.	0.79 (12)	.	.
e.g. amusements	.	.	0.19 (13)	.	0.34 (7)
e.g. education	.	.	0.33	.	0.14 (95)
Personal care, i.e.	.	.	1.03	.	0.62 (95)
Medical provision	.	.	1.06 (13)	.	0.25 (8)
Barbers, baths	.	.	0.26 (13)	.	0.35 (8)
Food, e.g.	.	24.51	22.05	22.53	22.85
Bread and rolls	.	3.08	3.63	.	3.84 (95)
Potatoes	.	.	0.82	.	0.83 (94)
Butter	.	.	2.72	.	1.68 (95)
Fats, other than butter	.	.	1.02	.	1.03 (95)
Meat	.	4.86	5.66	.	5.59 (95)
Milk	.	.	2.19	.	2.70 (95)
Vegetables and fruit	.	.	0.95	.	1.02 (94)
Restaurants (meals and beverages)	.	.	0.41	.	1.34 (95)

[a] Amounts represent the annual averages divided by 12. The figures in brackets represent the number of cases, if different from the numbers indicated at the head of the column.
[b] 'Social expenses I' comprise expenditure on amusements, subscriptions for associations and trade union membership, short journeys, books, journals, writing materials, and postage.
[c] 'Social expenses II' comprise education fees and other outlays on education including adult education, job training, books, journals, writing materials, postage, journeys, expenditure on holidays, entertainment including films, fun-fairs, purchase costs of musical instruments.
· indicates no data available

Table 5.11. *Differential consumption, 1925–8: 2-child families, income per family up to 3,600 Reichsmarks, expenditures per month and consumption unit, in Reichsmarks*

		Civil servants		Workers	
	Senior	Middle-rank (N = 8)	Junior (N = 11)	White-collar (N = 20)	Blue-collar (N = 139)
Total expenditure[a]	.	93.33	86.12	85.82	80.06
Rent	.	15.18	9.11	9.33	8.55
Household equipment	.	5.28	4.68	4.05	2.85
Clothing (including shoes)	.	11.00	11.44	11.07	9.63
Detergents	.	.	.	.	.
Servants (only)	.	—	—	—	—
Insurance	.	3.10	2.87	7.48	6.48
Social expenses I[b]					
(excluding education)	.				
e.g. associations	.	0.83	0.81	1.25	1.85
Social expenses II[c]					
(excluding associations)	.	3.51	3.81	3.53	2.66
e.g. amusements	.	0.90	0.90	0.43	0.49
e.g. education	.	2.09	1.82	1.61	1.45
Personal care, i.e.	.	1.32	1.87	1.30	1.13
Medical provision	.	.	.	.	5.14(1)
Barbers, baths	.	.	.	.	.
Food, e.g.	.	35.88	36.64	36.23	37.18
Bread and rolls	.	4.45	4.92	5.59	5.14
Potatoes	.	1.13	1.74	1.25	1.65
Butter	.	2.91	2.39	2.60	1.79
Fats, other than butter	.	1.40	2.23	1.90	2.22
Meat	.	8.82	8.29	8.17	8.39
Milk	.	4.66	4.38	4.02	4.34
Vegetables and fruit	.	3.11	2.60	2.78	2.77
Restaurants (meals and beverages)	.	0.26	0.30	0.78	0.57

[a] Amounts represent the annual averages divided by 12. The figures in brackets represent the number of cases, if different from the numbers indicated at the head of the column.

[b] 'Social expenses I' comprise expenditure on amusements, subscriptions for associations and trade union membership, short journeys, books, journals, writing materials, and postage.

[c] 'Social expenses II' comprise education fees and other outlays on education including adult education, job training, books, journals, writing materials, postage, expenditure on holidays, journeys, entertainment including films, fun-fairs, charges for radio, and purchase costs of musical instruments.

. indicates no data available.

the system of allowances. Variations in differential consumption nevertheless, are clearly visible in the next higher income class (families earning more
than 200 marks, not illustrated in Table 5.7), with civil servants and white-
collar workers spending more than 4 marks, and workers barely 3 marks on
books and newspapers per family (i.e. 1 mark or so per consumption unit).

A somewhat puzzling piece of evidence is the low expenditure on amusements of the white-collar workers in the 100–200 mark income range. By
contrast, their expenditure on gifts and tips and the keeping of domestic servants was the highest, even compared with the notoriously high expenditure
of middle-ranking civil servants (evident in the income class 200–300 marks:
1.14 marks per consumption unit).

The high level of workers' expenditure on amusements and sports corre-
sponds perfectly with conventional expectations concerning their life-style.
In a striking way, so, too, does the low expenditure of the households of
middle-ranking civil servants in the 200–300 mark income class (0.68 marks
compared with 0.75 and 0.77 marks per consumption unit for white-collar
and blue-collar workers respectively).

If the horizon is now extended to encompass the evolution of consumption
patterns over the longer term, certain patterns are seen to persist from the
pre-war period through to the post-war period (compare Tables 5.7–5.11).
These elements of regularity are, incidentally, welcome evidence that the
figures we have computed represent real differences in consumption
patterns and do not simply reflect chance variations arising from the fact that
the households in Tables 5.7–5.11 are not the same. Instead, certain common features transcend the individual characteristics of households.

Trends over the war years reflect in part, it is true, changes in the availability of certain goods in urban areas, and in the purchasing power of the
majority of the urban population. In 1916, all households were forced to
reduce their expenditure on clothing as a proportion of their total expenditure, while the expenditure of blue-collar workers declined even in absolute
terms. A shortage of milk was apparent for all classes (except in the case of
the junior civil servants in 1916). The proportion of the budget allocated to
the purchase of milk was curtailed vigorously and returned to its former
level only after the war. In 1917 households generally reduced their
expenditure on amusements and spent markedly less on bread and potatoes
and (the white-collar workers apart) more on meat (cf. Table 5.8). Yet overall, the quantity of meat consumed decreased (cf. Table 5.5). During 1918,
while the average amount of meat consumed continued to decrease, expenditure on meat fell sharply (Table 5.9). Expenditure on and consumption of
bread was at its lowest in 1917, but it was the following year before the most
obvious substitute (potatoes) was purchased in appreciably greater
quantities (cf. Table 5.5). Indeed, on average, fewer potatoes were con-

sumed in 1917 than had been the case in 1916. A more curious feature of consumption patterns was the marked rise between 1917 and 1918 in expenditure on clothing, amusements and personal care (both physicians' fees and personal hygiene). During the 1920s, expenditure on these items was to remain generally high (cf. Table 5.11).

Expenditure on rent as a proportion of total expenditure, reached record lows in 1918. White-collar workers and junior civil servants actually spent less in absolute terms than they had in 1917. Other classes did increase their expenditure on rent; for example blue-collar workers spent 2 marks more, on average, but their other expenditure increased at an even faster rate. By the later 1920s, however, expenditure on rent had increased yet again, both absolutely and relatively, for all social classes.

Generally, there were only modest inter-class differences in expenditure on clothing and shoes, although blue-collar workers tended to spend less than other groups. This was reversed in 1917 and 1918. In most years, junior civil servants spent most on clothing, closely followed by the white-collar workers. It may well have been that civil servants felt that they had to buy stylish clothes to maintain their position in society, as their spokesmen were inclined to argue. By contrast, blue-collar workers, from a smaller budget, had to clothe on average more children and had higher clothing expenses resulting from the nature of their employment. Clothing and personal care expenditure combined, provides an appropriate indicator of life-style and outer appearance. One continuity in this respect was the low relative expenditure of the blue-collar worker. Of all social classes, the blue-collar worker regularly spent least on clothing and personal hygiene. The exception is for 1918, when such items constituted a lower proportion of the expenditure of junior civil servants, and white-collar workers expended the smallest sums (see Table 5.12). In fact, the difference between blue-collar workers and junior civil servants in the proportion of their expenditure allocated to outward appearance, lessened appreciably after 1916, having initially widened compared with the pre-war situation. Differences between white- and blue-collar workers in this respect were also at their lowest in 1917, although unfortunately, in this case, we lack pre-war data.

Inter-class differences in expenditure on personal care, considered separately, are difficult to detect. Civil servants generally spent more than blue-collar and white-collar workers but the differences were much lower in the 1920s than had been the case earlier. On hygiene alone (expenditure on barbers or on public baths, for example) blue-collar workers generally spent less than other groups between 1916 and 1918, although the differences were slight.

Experts at the time considered that the consumption of valuable and expensive butter, as opposed to cheap fats of all other sorts, served to dis-

Table 5.12. *Expenditure on clothing and personal care as a percentage of total expenditure*

	Civil servants			Workers	
	Senior (%)	Middle (%)	Junior (%)	White-collar (%)	Blue-collar (%)
Pre-war	—	—	14.0	—	12.2
1916	—	—	12.3	9.4	8.3
1917	9.1	11.6	11.2	11.4	11.1
1918	10.9	17.5	15.1	18.2	15.8
1925/8	—	13.2	15.6	14.4	13.4

Source
Derived from Tables 5.8–5.11 above

tinguish the upper from the lower classes. Support for this view comes from considering both the absolute and relative expenditure on these items in both the pre- and post-war periods, even when income is controlled as in Tables 5.7–5.11. This is something of a surprise given the stress placed in the recollections of the period on how frequently the butter, as well as milk, purchased by women of the lower classes was adulterated. In the late 1920s, for example, families of junior civil servants had a higher expenditure on butter than the families of blue-collar workers (2.39 marks representing 2.8 per cent of total expenditure compared with 1.79 marks representing 2.2 per cent of total expenditure). On the other hand, blue-collar families had higher expenditure on margarine, dripping and lard than the former (2.22 marks representing 2.8 per cent of total expenditure compared with 2.23 marks representing 2.6 per cent of total expenditure in the case of junior civil servants). The inversion of the social class hierarchy when these two classes are ranged according to their expenditure on fats other than butter, can be considered a classic representation of the different consumption patterns of the various classes. The same situation, blue-collar workers first, junior civil servants second in the case of fats of inferior quality, and the converse in the case of butter, can be identified in the budgets of 1902–12, although in the case of fats, the amounts expended were almost identical.

This pattern set in peacetime was, it would appear, disturbed during the war, although even in 1917, the rank order of the classes according to the amount spent on fats other than butter was the same as it was to be in the late 1920s: blue-collar workers, junior civil servants, white-collar workers and, finally, middle-rank civil servants (compare Tables 5.8 and 5.11).[34] On the other hand, there were two stable elements in the consumption of fats during

Table 5.13. *Expenditure on insurance and associations as a percentage of total expenditure*

	Civil servants			Workers	
	Senior (%)	Middle-rank (%)	Junior (%)	White-collar (%)	Blue-collar (%)
Pre-war	—	—	4.0	—	7.0
1916	—	—	2.5	3.8	3.8
1917	3.7	2.7	2.2	3.5	2.6
1918	6.4	3.1	1.6	3.2	3.3
1925/8	—	4.2	4.3	10.2	10.4

Source
Derived from Tables 5.7–5.11 above

the war. The first was the high absolute amount expended by senior civil servants on butter and the low amount they expended on other fats. The second was that blue-collar workers maintained relatively high expenditure on butter despite the shortages of wartime.

Class-specific consumption patterns

This leads us to another continuity in consumption behaviour,[35] namely the persistence of class-specific consumption patterns. To simplify matters, we can consider two contrasting kinds of consumption behaviour, associated with blue-collar workers and civil servants respectively. The predominant traits of blue-collar consumption involved low expenditure on rent, and education, but high expenditure on insurance and a series of commitments to trade unions and clubs (burial funds, consumers' co-operatives and the like). Tables 5.7–5.11 corroborate this view. Of all classes, blue-collar workers had the highest expenditure on associations whereas white-collar workers in all years except 1916, made considerably greater use of insurance agencies than did blue-collar workers. Combining the expenditure on insurance premiums and association fees, reveals that in general, white- and blue-collar workers set aside similar proportions of their expenditure for such items (see Table 5.13). Civil servants, on retirement, received a subsidised state pension. In consequence, their average expenditure on insurance and associations was seldom greater than four per cent. Nevertheless, by the 1920s, all classes had markedly increased such expenditure, indicative perhaps of the extension of social insurance benefits under the Weimar Republic.

It was often stated by upper-class critics of working-class consumption patterns that blue-collar workers spent less on clothing and more on amusements than other social groups. It is difficult, however, to see clear evidence of this in our data. There were years when blue-collar workers spent more on clothing than other social groups (in 1918, for instance, see above) and less on amusements (in 1917 and the later 1920s). More distinctive, and in line with contemporary perceptions, were the food purchases of blue-collar workers. This is not true in the sense that their food was low in quality and substantial in quantity, but was a reflection of the fact that they spent considerable amounts both on low-standard foods, such as bread and potatoes, and on valuable foods, such as vegetables and fruit. Their consumption of bread may, in fact, have increased due to the allocation of additional allowances to all those involved in heavy manual labour. Both before and after the war, blue-collar workers spent relatively more on milk than did other social classes, whereas between 1916 and 1918, they spent relatively less than other classes, except for the senior civil servants, of whom there were only a few.

The second set of consumption characteristics were those of civil servants, whose pattern of expenditure emphasised housing and education. Average expenditure on housing came to between 10 and 12 per cent of total expenditure. Expenditure on household equipment showed no clear differences by social class. Only in enquiries of the 1920s, did the expenditure of blue-collar workers fall below that of all other groups. One problem in regard to measuring expenditure on education is that such expenditure was not separately itemised in the wartime budgets, although it may be included in the category referred to as 'books, newspapers, etc.'. On this basis, the families of civil servants had the highest expenditure on education of all classes in 1917 and 1918, the only years for which information is available on all three civil service grades (see Table 5.14). We should not conclude, from our evidence, that civil servants were necessarily the best-educated group, although this may well have been the case, but rather interpret their high expenditure as indicative of the importance they attached to keeping themselves 'informed'. By contrast, as was made clear earlier (cf. Table 5.13), civil servants spent relatively little on insurance.

The civil service pattern of consumption was, however, not a homogeneous one. Some differences between the ranks should be noted. In the case of insurance expenditure, for example, the junior civil servants seemed to have followed a pattern of their own. In 1917 and 1918 they spent less, both absolutely and relatively, than the other ranks, and less than both white- and blue-collar workers in 1918. The same general point applies if association fees and insurance premiums are combined as in Table 5.13. Association fees on their own contributed little to the differences between

Table 5.14. *Expenditure on education and on books and newspapers as a percentage of total expenditure*

	Civil servants			Workers	
	Senior (%)	Middle-rank (%)	Junior (%)	White-collar (%)	Blue-collar (%)
Pre-war	—	—	0.7	—	0.3
1916	—	—	1.3	1.0	1.3
1917	3.0	2.6	2.3	2.3	1.6
1918	2.9	2.8	5.0	2.0	1.6
1925/8	—	2.2	2.1	1.9	1.8

Source
Derived from Tables 5.7–5.11 above. It has been assumed that between 1916 and 1918 expenditure ascribed to books and newspapers included expenditure on education.

the ranks. It would seem, therefore, that even when the lower ranks enjoyed approximately the same income as their more senior colleagues, they placed less value on protection against future risks. Where did their money go instead? It is impossible to be certain, but it may be significant that junior civil servants raised their outlay on books, newspapers, and schooling five-fold. The trend of their expenditure in these years differed markedly from that of other civil servants although it has to be remembered that information on all ranks is available only for the last two years of the war. That the other grades scarcely increased expenditure at a time of inflation must have meant they spent less in real terms. Although blue-collar workers also expanded their expenditure on education tenfold, they did not achieve the same level of expenditure as did the families of civil servants. White-collar workers doubled their expenditure from the level of 1916 and, after the war, joined the blue-collar workers with just under two per cent of their total expenditure devoted to education, still somewhat below that of the civil service ranks for which we have information (Table 5.11).

Two other features of the consumption patterns of junior civil servants also require consideration: their expenditure on personal care, and on food. For example, the proportion of their expenditure devoted to personal care not only exceeded that of blue-collar workers but was also above that of senior civil servants in 1917 and 1918, the only years for which there are comparative data.[36] On food, the amount expended by junior civil servants and its share in their overall expenditure never quite matched that of blue-collar workers, but was greater than that spent by other civil servants (cf.

Table 5.15. *Expenditure on food as a percentage of total expenditure*

	Civil servants			Workers	
	Senior (%)	Middle-rank (%)	Junior (%)	White-collar (%)	Blue-collar (%)
Pre-war	—	39.8	48.8	56.3	51.7
1916	—	—	56.9	57.7	63.8
1917	45.8	49.3	54.9	50.4	59.5
1918	50.8	43.3	48.4	41.7	53.7
1925/8	—	38.4	42.5	42.2	46.4

Source
Derived from Tables 5.7–5.11 above

Table 5.15). If high expenditure on food was a characteristic of working-class consumption patterns, the lower-rank civil servants might be called the 'workers' of the German civil service. In addition, the constituents of their diets differed markedly. The diet of junior civil servants was generally frugal, with some high-quality elements in it. They economised on bread and, in certain years, expended relatively less on potatoes than did blue-collar workers (see Table 5.16). After the war, the share of their expenditure devoted to butter was less than that of other civil servants. In 1917 and 1918, blue-collar workers still preferred to consume butter, but had to economise on this item. Conversely, junior civil servants regularly spent more than middle-rank and senior civil servants on fats other than butter, their expenditure in this regard equalling that of blue-collar workers. Junior civil servants also economised on vegetables and fruit, although 1917 was an obvious exception, and, in 1917 and 1918, they spent proportionately less on meat than did blue-collar workers.

Long-term changes in consumption patterns

The war disturbed what was otherwise an enduring set of class-specific consumption patterns. This is clear even though we lack full information for the period before the war. Our remarks are based on the principal expenditure categories, i.e. the low-standard foodstuffs (bread, potatoes, and fats excluding butter), the high-standard ones (meat, butter and milk), vegetables (primarily turnip during the war), rent, schooling and books, amusements, association and trade union membership, insurance, and personal care.

The constituent elements of the middle-class consumption pattern, high

Table 5.16. *Expenditure on particular food products as a percentage of overall expenditure on food*

		Civil servants			Workers	
Period	Product	Senior (%)	Middle-rank (%)	Junior (%)	White-collar (%)	Blue-collar (%)
Pre-war	Bread	—	12.6	16.5	—	16.8
	Potatoes	—	—	3.7	—	3.6
	Butter	—	—	12.3	—	7.4
	Fats	—	—	4.6	—	4.6
	Meat	—	19.8	25.7	—	24.5
	Vegetables	—	—	4.3	—	4.5
1916	Bread	—	—	10.0	9.8	10.2
	Potatoes	—	—	4.9	6.2	7.5
	Butter	—	—	—	—	—
	Fats	—	—	—	—	—
	Meat	—	—	18.6	23.7	17.0
	Vegetables	—	—	4.3	5.7	5.3
1917	Bread	5.3	9.0	8.4	9.6	9.0
	Potatoes	5.3	3.9	3.7	3.9	3.6
	Butter	5.3	4.4	4.4	4.4	4.5
	Fats	3.1	2.8	3.8	3.5	4.3
	Meat	19.6	21.6	20.2	23.3	21.6
	Vegetables	7.3	5.7	6.6	5.0	5.7
1918	Bread	4.6	8.2	7.6	13.2	9.2
	Potatoes	3.9	8.0	7.3	13.1	7.5
	Butter	4.9	4.9	4.5	5.3	5.3
	Fats	1.9	6.6	4.6	1.7	3.9
	Meat	22.7	13.4	12.2	13.7	15.7
	Vegetables	6.1	6.8	3.9	4.5	7.1
1925/8	Bread	—	12.4	13.4	15.4	13.8
	Potatoes	—	3.1	4.7	3.5	4.4
	Butter	—	8.1	6.5	7.2	4.8
	Fats	—	3.9	6.1	5.2	6.0
	Meat	—	24.6	22.6	22.6	22.6
	Vegetables	—	8.7	7.1	7.7	7.5

Source
Derived from Tables 5.7–5.11 above

expenditure on rent and education, low expenditure on food, associations, and insurance, are persistent features throughout this period. This pattern should not, however, be called a civil service pattern, given that the junior civil servants adopted some specific consumption strategies. Their consumption of bread, potatoes and fats resembled that of blue-collar workers,

Table 5.17. *Expenditure on membership of associations as a percentage of overall expenditure*

	Civil servants			Workers	
	Senior (%)	Middle-rank (%)	Junior (%)	White-collar (%)	Blue-collar (%)
Pre-war	—	—	1.0	—	3.0
1916	—	—	0.8	1.5	1.5
1917	1.9	0.8	0.6	0.8	1.0
1918	1.5	0.6	0.6	0.6	1.2
1925/8	—	0.9	0.9	1.5	2.3

Source
Derived from Tables 5.7–5.11 above

although it needs to be borne in mind that in some years, white-collar workers spent relatively more than junior civil servants on bread and potatoes. Finally, when in the food crisis of 1918, the blue-collar workers markedly increased their relative consumption of vegetables and fruit, white-collar workers had the lowest proportional expenditure of all classes on these items (cf. Table 5.16).

A shift in consumption preferences also took place with regard to other budget items. Expenditure on amusements provides a telling example. Our data suggest that prior to 1917, civil servants, shop assistants and other white-collar workers all restricted their outlay on entertainments. Not so the workers. In 1917, all classes had low levels of expenditure. By the late 1920s, a high expenditure on amusements and education and low expenditure on insurance and subscriptions to associations separated civil servants from both other classes. Civil servants were also distinct in spending less on insurance (Table 5.11). In the late 1920s, their expenditure was no more than 3 Reichsmarks per head and month or 3.3 per cent of overall expenditure, while white-collar workers were spending 7.5 Reichsmarks, representing approximately 9 per cent of their total expenditure. The differences are of the same order even if expenditure on insurance and subscriptions is combined (cf. Table 5.13). The position is more complex if expenditure on associations is considered in isolation (as in Table 5.17). In 1916, blue-collar workers and white-collar workers had fairly high expenditure. After the war, however, white-collar families spent less than the families of blue-collar workers, and civil servants the least. As we have no data on white-collar families in the pre-war period, it is difficult to exclude the possibility

Table 5.18. *Expenditure on rent as a percentage of overall expenditure*

	Civil servants			Workers	
	Senior (%)	Middle-rank (%)	Junior (%)	White-collar (%)	Blue-collar (%)
Pre-war	—	22.6	12.3	6.9	12.1
1916	—	—	11.9	10.5	9.1
1917	11.3	11.3	11.9	12.7	7.7
1918	6.7	10.9	8.0	10.8	7.4
1925/8	—	16.3	10.6	10.9	10.7

Source
Derived from Tables 5.7–5.11 above

that they were simply returning to an expenditure pattern that had been in force before the war.

Let us now turn to the question of expenditure that went on the payment of rent. It will be seen from Table 5.18 that over time expenditure patterns of junior and middle-rank civil servants diverged.[37] Expenditure of middle-rank civil servants was after the war some 50 per cent higher than before the war, although again the pre-war pattern rests on the experience of just one family. At the same time, they reduced their relative expenditure on rent from 22.6 to 16.3 per cent of their overall expenditure, still involving a net increase of 1.50 marks. Nevertheless, their rent payments were the highest of all groups included in the surveys of the late 1920s.

In the 1920s junior civil servants made 'common cause' with blue-collar and white-collar workers. Should we interpret this as symptomatic of the proletarianisation of the junior civil servants? Of course, one key factor in favour of equalising expenditure was the policy of public rent control partially enacted during the Weimar Republic. As for the blue-collar workers and junior civil servants, similarities in expenditure also existed. Overall pre-war expenditure patterns moved in parallel in this period. During the 1920s, total expenditure for blue-collar workers was some 80 per cent above the pre-war level and that of junior civil servants some 90 per cent higher, again not indicative of any marked change (cf. Tables 5.10 and 5.11).

Nevertheless, some social class differences can be discerned. If we examine the trend, only white-collar workers raised their proportional expenditure on rent during the war. While expenditure of all other classes declined or remained stable (as in the case of junior civil servants) theirs peaked in 1917 at a level above that of all other classes. The one white-collar employee included in the pre-war enquiries, entered no more than 100 marks into his account book, an extraordinarily low amount (cf. Table 5.3). Taken at face value, this would suggest a threefold increase in expenditure on rent from 2.78 marks pre-war to 9.33 Reichsmarks in the late 1920s. Yet even setting this aside, it is still remarkable that it was the white-collar workers who valued housing so highly.

The special features of consumption in the war years stand out as a drawing together of class-specific behaviour to an extent that had been unknown before and was not to recur. This can be observed in the case of the expenditure on rent by middle-rank civil servants and white-collar workers in 1917 and 1918, by contrast with the situation before and after the war (cf. Table 5.18). In addition, during the war, but not later, a roughly equal share of their total expenditure went on membership of associations and on some basic foods. This picture is the more remarkable as clearly it did not apply to blue-collar workers. Their expenditure patterns were usually distinct. After the war, the only budget items on which the blue-collar and white-collar workers spent comparable amounts, were education, entertainment, and bread.[38] In general, the budget of the blue-collar worker retained its class-specific features during the war years: i.e. the blue-collar budgets involved a relatively high proportion of expenditure on associations as well as on meat, potatoes, bread, and fats, but a relatively low proportion of expenditure on rent, butter and education.

Conclusion

On balance, therefore, it would be difficult to claim that between the 1890s and the 1920s, there was either a heightening or a reduction of the social divide as far as consumption patterns were concerned. Matters were not so simple. Although only a small number of household budgets have been examined, we would like to advance the following hypothesis: both a middle-class and a proletarian pattern of consumption behaviour survived the war. The first was characteristic of middle-ranking and senior civil servants, the second of blue-collar workers. The consumption patterns of junior civil servants and white-collar workers can be seen as blends of the varying elements of middle-class and proletarian consumption strategies. Further analyses would be necessary in order to test this hypothesis. Methodologically, this kind of study has shown that consumption patterns are not homogeneous structures, clearly demarcating social classes. In fact, classes which seem disparate in respect of one item in their budget, were found to resemble each other in other respects. There is also an overriding need for more systematic investigations into the social meanings to be attached to certain commodities. Our investigations here should only be the first of many. Above all, it would be useful to disaggregate amorphous categories such as 'blue-collar workers'.

Finally, let us reassess some of the background data presented in the first part of this chapter. The proportion of total expenditure on the main budget items in Table 5.10, though calculated per consumption unit and month, match fairly well the average expenditure of households for the pre-war period set out in Table 5.3. The same is true of the 1920s (compare Tables 5.4 and 5.11), but total expenditure and food expenditure were a little higher in the majority of the post-war surveys of household account-books. The data on differential consumption in 1916 and 1917 (Tables 5.7–5.8) give an idea of the fall in living standards during the war: families spent less on food, in both absolute and relative terms in 1917 than they had done in 1916. Of all the war years, 1917 would appear to be worst. Households had at their disposal less money than in 1916 or 1918. In 1917, expenditure on major items, such as bread and potatoes, medical care, and entertainment declined, although the expenditure of white-collar workers went against the trend in the latter case.

On average no class achieved the level of expenditure which the experts of the time considered necessary for survival (cf. Table 5.2). The same point can be made using the information on the prices of essentials given in Table 5.1. If contemporary estimates were in any way realistic, the actual figures, especially in 1917 and 1918, imply a near disastrous situation (cf. Tables 5.8 and 5.9). Even in households following strict budgets, the average family had available in 1917 no more than 40 marks per head for food instead of the 43–6 marks which were considered 'necessary'. In 1918, with the exception of one senior civil servant's family, the averages of total expenditure in all classes were considerably lower than the expenditure that seemed to be necessary to purchase basic commodities. This shared level of absolute deprivation was the material reality of the war for most of the German population. It is to be hoped that further investigations will throw even more light on the impact of inflation, on the strain that the war imposed on social life, and on the ways people managed to make ends meet.

Notes

1 Peter Quante, 'Lohnpolitik und Lohnentwicklung im Kriege', *Zeitschrift des Preussischen Statistischen Landesamtes*, 59 (1919), 364ff., citing Reports of the Industrial Inspection Boards; petitions of the metal workers' trade union and others; price lists from official price series. Some of the material they used also appears in *Beiträge zur Kenntnis der Lebenshaltung im dritten Kriegsjahre. Auf Grund einer Erhebuing des Kriegsausschusses für Konsumenteninteressen, Sondarheft zum Reichs-Arbeitsblatte*, 17, Berlin, 1917, *Beiträge zur Kenntnis der Lebenshaltung im vierten Kriegsjahre. Auf Grund einer Erhebung des Kriegsausschusses für*

Konsumenteninteressen, Sondarheft zum Reichs-Arbeitsblatt, 21, Berlin, 1919; 'Einkommen und Lebenshaltung. Die Erhebungen des Kriegsausschusses für Konsumenteninteressen über die Lebenshaltung im Kriege. Die Erhebung vom April 1916', *Reichs-Arbeitsblatt,* 15, 2 (1917); Carl von Tyszka, 'Die Veränderungen in der Lebenshaltung städtischer Familien im Kriege', *Archiv für Sozialwissenschaft und Sozialpolitik,* 43 (1916/17), 841ff. The ranks in the German army were to receive up to three times more of the said quantities, cf. Fritz Hartmann, *Die Heeresverpflegung (Beiträge zur Kriegswirtschaft* 11), Berlin, 1917, pp. 22ff. By contrast, in the third week of September 1917 the actual ration in Greater Berlin consisted of (recalculated into monthly figures): 7.8 kg of bread, 1 kg of meat, 0.2 kg of butter, 0.12 kg of margarine, 0.8 kg of farinaceous products, cf. Goetz Briefs, 'Entwicklung und Verfassung der Hauswirtschaft innerhalb der Volkswirtschaft' in Goetz Briefs, Martha Voss-Zietz and Maria Stegemann-Runk, *Die Hauswirtschaft im Kriege (Beiträge zur Kriegswirtschaft)* 25, Berlin, 1917, p. 33.

2 For details see Max Rubner, 'Ernährungswesen' in F. Bumm (ed.), *Deutschlands Gesundheitsverhältnisse unter dem Einfluss des Weltkrieges,* (Wirtschafts- und Sozialgeschichte des Weltkrieges (ed.) James T. Shotwell) Deutsche Serie Stuttgart, 1928, pp. 14 and 19ff.; Richard Lenz, 'Die Lebensmittel-Zulagen für die schwerarbeitende Bevölkerung' in A. Stegerwald, R. Lenz, L. Wiernik, *Die Schwerarbeiterfrage (Beiträge zur Kriegswirtschaft* 26/27), Berlin, 1917, pp. 11–41.

3 Cf. note 1. Richard Calwer, who ran a private Bureau of Economic Observation, recorded living costs that from 1916 were slightly higher, but were based on the needs of a family of five persons. See Richard Calwer, *'Monatliche Übersichten über Lebensmittelpreise'* vols. 1ff., Berlin, 1911. 'Head' was defined in such a way that every adult and child over the age of eleven or every two children aged between one and eleven counted as one head. However, if there was only one child in the family, this child on its own was counted as the equivalent of one head. Children below one year often were not counted at all. See, 'Einkommen und Lebenshaltung', p. 145; *Beiträge,* 1917, pp. 5 and 11.

4 Some examples may serve as illustrations. The metalworkers' trade union (DMV) reported average monthly rents about 1910 ranging from 9.50 marks in Zwickau, Saxony to 30 marks in Stuttgart for two rooms and a kitchen for a blue-collar worker. In Berlin, rents averaged between 25 and 33 marks and in Munich around 20 marks. See *320 Haushaltungsrechnungen von Metallarbeitern,* p. 29 (see note 16 for full reference); von Tyszka, 'Hunger und Ernährung' in R. Allers (ed.), *Soziale Physiologie und Pathologie,* Berlin, 1927, p. 341, footnote 1; Zimmermann, 'Die Veränderungen', p. 335; Rosa Kempf, *Das Leben der jungen Fabrikmädchen in München,* Leipzig, 1911, p. 107.

5 Werner Abelshauser, 'Verelendung der Handarbeiter? Zur sozialen Lage der deutschen Arbeiter in der grossen Inflation der frühen zwanziger Jahre' in Hans Mommsen and Winifried Schulze (eds.), *Vom Elend der Handarbeit,* Stuttgart, 1981, pp. 445–76. Carl-Ludwig Holtfrerich, *Die deutsche Inflation 1914–1923. Ursachen und Folgen in internationaler Perspektive,* Berlin and New York, 1980, pp. 246–60, takes only a cursory glance at the sources and applies, somewhat superficially, alleged laws of consumption to the war years. For a discussion of the problem of real incomes with respect to the period of inflation (1919–24) based on the experiences of civil servants in Hamburg, see Andreas Kunz, 'Verteilungskampf oder Interessenkonsensus? Zur Entwicklung der Realein-

kommen von Beamten, Arbeitern und Angestellten in der Inflationszeit 1914–1924' in Gerald D. Feldman *et al.* (eds.), *Die deutsche Inflation. Eine Zwischenbilanz*, Berlin and New York, 1982, pp. 346–84.

6 The German civil service was highly differentiated. Within it there were three separate careers, namely the careers of the junior civil servant, the middle-rank civil servant, and the senior civil servant. These were differentiated on the basis of educational achievement, and the barriers between them were strict. In addition, different ranks (*Klassen*) existed within each of these careers, and promotion from one to another was possible in accordance with the level of seniority and degree of responsibility. In 1909 some 80 ranks were established (*Reich-Gesetzblatt*, 1909, pp. 573ff.). The tripartite system of the German civil service survived the 1918 revolution and continued to be the basic pattern during Weimar. See H. Völter, 'Die deutsche Beamtenbesoldung' in W. Gerloff (ed.), *Die Beamtenbesoldung im modernen Staat*, Munich and Leipzig, 1932, pp. 3–105.

7 Gerald D. Feldman, *Army, industry and labor in Germany, 1914–1918*, Princeton, NJ, 1966. Quante, 'Lohnpolitik und Lohnentwicklung im Kriege', p. 369. For a detailed and well-balanced assessment of the available sources and the main trends in living standards see Gerhard Bry, *Wages in Germany, 1871–1945*, Princeton, NJ, 1960, and pp. 197–214 especially Tables 53 and A-41.

8 L. Wiernik, *Die Arbeiterernährung in der Kriegsorganisation der Industrie (Beiträge zur Kriegswirtschaft 26/27)* Berlin, 1917, pp. 42–87; Rubner, 'Ernährungswesen', p. 13.

9 Briefs, Voss-Zietz and Stegemann-Runk, *Die Hauswirtschaft im Kriege*, pp. 28ff., 32ff. and 48ff.

10 Rubner, 'Ernährungswesen', pp. 5 and 9. See also Hans Stadthagen, *Die Ersatzlebensmittel in der Kriegswirtschaft (Beiträge zur Kriegswirtschaft 56–8)*, Berlin, 1919. Political implications are discussed in the following case study concerning Berlin, Robert Scholz, 'Ein unruhiges Jahrzehnt: Lebensmittelunruhen, Massenstreiks und Arbeitsloskrawalle in Berlin 1914–1923' in Manfred Gailus (ed.), *Pöbelexzesse und Volkstumulte in Berlin. Zur Sozialgeschichte der Strasse (1930–1980)*, Berlin, 1984, pp. 79–124.

11 Bry, *Wages in Germany*, pp. 209ff., gives an instructive example when he cites three time series describing average weekly real wage rates of skilled workers in 1913–18. The decline ranges from 17–46 per cent. The real wages of unskilled railway workers, on the other hand, are reported for 1918 as no more than 0.2 per cent below those of 1913, but as 26 per cent below the 1913 level in 1917, implying an increase between 1917 and 1918. Bry, however, was suspicious of the data. 'Increases . . . are probably fictitious. The economic circumstances of the last war could scarcely have permitted improvements in real wages.'

12 Statistisches Amt der Stadt Berlin, *Lohnermittelungen und Haushaltsrechnungen der minder bemittelten Bevölkerung im Jahre 1903*. Berliner Statistik, Part 3, Berlin, 1905, p. 54*; 'Wirtschaftsrechnungen von Karl von K'. *Zeitschrift für die gesamte Staatswissenschaft*, 62 (1906), 701–38. Food is defined here, and elsewhere, as inclusive of luxury foodstuffs. Unfortunately, the sources often do not make it clear what they understand by luxuries, but generally people reported tea, coffee, liquor, beer, and sugar as luxury foodstuffs. Expenditure on housing excludes the costs of heating and light. Cf. Armin Triebel, 'Ökonomie und Lebensgeschichte' in C. Conrad and H.-J. von Kondratowitz (eds.), *Gerontologie und Sozialgeschichte*, Berlin, 1983, pp. 273–317. Also relevant is a British inquiry into living standards in German towns, *Cost of living in German*

towns. Report of an enquiry by the Board of Trade into working class rents, housing and retail prices, together with the rates of wages in certain occupations in the principal industrial towns of the German empire, London, 1908, which is comparable with the 'Lohnermittelungen' and full of valuable information, although the issue of social differentials was not investigated.

13 During the Kaiserreich, there were many complaints about the workers' excessive consumption of alcoholic beverages (the 'Alkoholfrage') and of tobacco and of the waste, in time and money, that resulted from the inefficient way in which the workers and their wives made their purchases of food. See the documents collected by Klaus Saul et al. (eds.), *Arbeiterfamilien im Kaiserreich. Materialien zur Sozialgeschichte in Deutschland 1871–1914*, Königstein, 1982, pp. 100ff. Also typical of contemporary thinking is a paragraph from the Annual Report of the Chamber of Commerce of Chemnitz (1889), p. 112. The assertions of Ernst Günther, 'Haushalt des kleinen Mittelstandes und der Arbeiter', *Schmollers Jahrbuch* 34 (1910), 253–77, commenting upon the official survey of 1907/8, esp. pp. 265–70, are representative of many others. The editors of this survey describe the differences between working-class and middle-class consumption in exactly the same way: 'Erhebung von Wirtschaftsrechnungen', pp. 58*–65*, esp. p. 60*.

14 Hoffmann et al., *Das Wachstum der deutschen Wirtschaft seit der Mitte des 19. Jahrhunderts*, Berlin, 1965, pp. 470ff., suggests 1,000–1,100 marks as average annual earnings of those employed in trade and industry. For more recent estimates, see Toni Pierenkemper, 'Die Einkommensentwicklung der Angestellten in Deutschland 1880–1913', *Historical Social Research*, 27 (1983), 69–92. The author emphasises that wage differentials were extremely large. According to his account, income varied from less than 1,000 marks in the case of female shop assistants to about 2,000 marks for technicians with the male shop assistants being in the upper range (1,700 marks). See also: Toni Pierenkemper, *Arbeitsmarkt und Angestellte im Deutschen Kaiserreich, 1880–1913*, Münster, 1984.

15 A. Braun, *Haushlatungs-Rechnungen Nürnberger Arbeiter. Ein Beitrag zur Aufhellung der Lebensverhältnisse des Nürnberger Proletariats*, Nuremberg, 1901. Statistische Kommission der 'Gesellschaft der Freunde des vaterländischen Schul- und Erziehungswesens' (ed.), *Haushaltungsrechnungen hamburgischer Volksschullehrer*, Hamburg, 1906.

16 *Erhebung von Wirtschaftsrechnungen minderbemittelter Familien im Deutschen Reiche*, Berlin, 1909. Vorstand des Deutschen Metallarbeiter-Verbandes (ed.), *320 Haushaltungsrechnungen von Metallarbeitern*, Stuttgart, 1909, reprint (ed.) Dieter Dowe, with an introduction by Jens Flemming and P.-Ch. Witt, Berlin and Bonn, 1981; cf. the review by A. Triebel in *Historical Social Research*, 24 (1982), 97ff. The *Erhebung* of 1909 is incorporated in the Berlin Data File of household budgets. This data file, which contains about 5,100 individual household account books, was created at the Max Planck Institute for Education and Human Development between 1980 and 1984 thanks to the initiative of Professor Reinhard Spree, to whom I am much obliged.

17 Statistisches Amt der Stadt Halle a.S., *Wirtschaftsrechnungen kleiner Haushaltungen in Halle a.S. und Umgebung 1909/10* (Beiträge zur Statistik der Stadt Halle a.S. 13), Halle, 1911.

18 E. Herbig, 'Wirtschaftsrechnungen Saarbrücker Bergleute', *Zeitschrift für das Berg-, Hütten- und Salinen-Wesen in dem preussischen Staat*, 60 (1912), 451–613. This inquiry is also incorporated in the Berlin Data File of household budgets.

19 *Wirtschaftsrechnungen von unteren Post- und Telegraphenbeamten*, Berlin, 1916. This inquiry, too, forms part of the Berlin Data File. Unfortunately, the editors of this survey were somewhat careless, though at first sight their edition looks satisfactory enough. The processing of the data for entry into the Berlin Data File revealed that the editors had made errors of calculation or transferred figures incorrectly. Two budgets had to be omitted because certain sections were so confused that the correct order could not be reconstructed. No reliance should be placed on the editors' own calculations of average expenditure (food 63 per cent, clothing 16 per cent, housing 19 per cent, total expenditure 2,055 marks).
20 von Tyszka, 'Hunger und Ernährung', pp. 345ff.; and for a similar position: Briefs, 'Entwicklung und Verfassung der Hauswirtschaft'.
21 *Die Lebenshaltung von 2,000 Arbeiter-, Angestellten- und Beamtenhaushaltungen. Erhebungen von Wirtschaftsrechnungen im Deutschen Reich vom Jahre 1927/28*, Berlin, 1932; *Wirtschaftsrechnungen. Verbrauch in Arbeiterhaushalten 1937*, Stuttgart and Mainz, 1960. Both surveys form part of the Berlin Data File.
22 Vorstand des Zentralverbandes der Schuhmacher, *300 Haushaltungsrechnungen von Arbeitern der Schuhindustrie und des Schuhmacher-Gewerbes in Deutschland*, Nuremberg, 1928; *Die Lebenshaltung minderbemittelter Familien in Hamburg im Jahre 1925*, Hamburg, 1926; *Die Lebenshaltung des Deutschen Reichsbahnpersonals. Ergebnisse einer Erhebung von Wirtschaftsrechnungen unter den Arbeitern und Beamten der Deutschen Reichsbahngesellschaft*, Berlin, 1930, especially p. 113. The first two surveys are included in the Berlin Data File.
23 According to Hoffmann et al., *Das Wachstum der deutschen Wirtschaft*, average annual earnings in industry varied between 1,600 and 2,000 Reichsmarks, and between 1,500 and 2,400 Reichsmarks for miners; cf. note 14. Surveys that reported a relatively low percentage of expenditure on clothing (the Nuremberg workers in 1900, the 1937 survey) may have included higher proportions of low income families.
24 In Germany, relief in cash and kind for the lower income brackets was principally organised by the state authorities. Soon a chaos of competing regulations and bureaucratic administrations, military and civilian, came into being, of which the War Committee for Consumers' Interests (KAKI) was one.
25 The *Reichs-Arbeitsblatt*, 15, 3 (1917), p. 244, commented in a similar vein, comparing the KAKI April and July surveys of 1916 and stating that governmental control had had equalising social effects. The same view was expressed by von Tyszka, 'Die Veränderungen' but this is only to be expected since von Tyszka was a leading figure in the production of the KAKI investigations and prepared its 1917 survey for publication. Whenever he set pen to paper, he argued strongly that it was the middle classes who had suffered the greater losses, both materially and in terms of self-confidence.
26 Rubner, 'Ernährungswesen', p. 11. Nevertheless, even turkeys sold for 100 marks on the clandestine market; Waldemar Zimmermann, 'Die Veränderungen der Einkommens- und Lebensverhältnisse der deutschen Arbeiter durch den Krieg' in Rudolf Meerwarth, Adolf Günther and Waldemar Zimmermann, *Die Einwirkung des Krieges auf Bevölkerungsbewegung, Einkommen und Lebenshaltung in Deutschland. (Wirtschafts- und Sozialgeschichte des Weltkrieges*, ed. James T. Shotwell, Deutsche Serie), Stuttgart and New Haven 1932, p. 431; *Beiträge*, 1919, pp. 5 and 21.
27 von Tyszka, 'Die Veränderungen', pp. 874ff.
28 The decreases would appear even greater if we were to rely on the calculations of

other well-known statisticians, who assessed the consumption of meat, e.g. per head and month in 1912/13, as 4,020 g and vegetables and fruit as 10,740 g. On this basis consumption in 1918 would have been only 60 per cent and 66 per cent, respectively, of the level of 1912/13. Conversely, according to their estimates the consumption of potatoes increased by up to a third; R. Kuczynski and N. Zuntz, 'Deutschlands Nahrungs- und Futtermittel', *Allgemeines Statistisches Archiv*, 9 (1915), 107–88.

29 *Beiträge*, 1919, p. 21.

30 Amongst a number of influential recent studies see, Helga Schmucker, 'Die angfristigen Strukturwandlungen der Verbrauchs der privaten Haushalte in ihrer Interdependenz mit den übrigen Bereichen einer wachsenden Wirtschaft' in Fritz Neumark (ed.), *Strukturwandlungen einer wachsenden Wirtschaft*, vol. I (Schriften des Vereins für Sozialpolitik, new series, vol. 30/I), Berlin, 1964, pp. 106–83; esp. pp. 106ff. and tables on pp. 160–3; Hoffmann et al., *Wachstum*, pp. 618–703; Ekkehard von Knorring, 'Strukturwandlungen des privaten Konsums im Wachstumsprozess der deutschen Wirtschaft seit der Mitte des 19. Jahrhunderts' in Walther G. Hoffmann (ed.), *Untersuchungen zum Wachstum der deutschen Wirtschaft*, Tübingen, 1971, pp. 167–91.

31 Anthony Giddens, *The class structure of the advanced societies*, London, 1981; Max Haller, *Theorie der Klassenbildung und der sozialen Schichtung*, Frankfurt and New York, 1983; Jürgen Kocka, *Klassengesellschaft im Krieg. Deutsche Sozialgeschichte, 1914–1918*, Göttingen, 1973, pp. 4ff., 12ff., 33, 51, and 80ff. The only recent investigation which provides a detailed treatment of differential consumption patterns is Sandra Coyner, *Class patterns of family income and expenditure during the Weimar Republic*, New Brunswick, 1975. The author re-analyses the results of the large survey of household budgets produced by the Statistical Office of the Reich at the end of the 1920s (*Lebenshaltung*, 1932). Many of her arguments are very interesting, but some are not supported by her analysis.

32 von Tyszka, 'Veränderungen', p. 853; H. Schmucker, 'Die langfristigen Strukturwandlungen', p. 113, 156, 160ff.; W. G. Hoffmann and J. H. Müller, *Das deutsche Volkseinkommen*, Tübingen, 1959, p. 14; Hoffmann et al., *Wachstum*, pp. 464, 470ff., and 494ff.; the *Statistical Yearbook of the German Reich* (1930), p. 532ff., calculated a rise of 30 per cent from 1913 till 1927 for national income per capita (750 marks – 1,000 Reichsmarks).

33 'Einkommen und Lebenshaltung', 1917, p. 150.

34 The year 1916, unfortunately, has to be excluded from consideration because the consumption of different types of fat was not differentiated within the budget.

35 This is the sort of continuity Sköllin had in mind when pointing out that consumption styles ('Lebenshaltung') had not changed much between 1907 and 1925. 'Die Lebenshaltung minderbemittelter Familien in Hamburg im Jahre 1925' in H. Sköllin (ed.), *Statistische Mitteilungen über den Hamburgischen Staat*, 20, Hamburg, 1926, pp. 22ff.

36 Expenditure on personal care represented 2.3 per cent of all expenditure by junior civil servants in the pre-war period, 3.2 per cent in 1916, 1.4 per cent in 1917, 3.0 per cent in 1918 and 2.2 per cent between 1925 and 1926. Blue-collar workers' expenditure in the same years was 1.4 per cent, 2.1 per cent, 1.2 per cent, 1.5 per cent and 1.4 per cent. Senior civil servants devoted 1.1 per cent of their total expenditure in 1917 and 0.8 per cent in 1918 to personal care. All percentages have been derived from the information given in Tables 5.7–5.11.

37 Unfortunately, only one middle-ranking civil servant was included in the pre-war enquiries.
38 Comparability of expenditure was defined, totally arbitrarily as to include all categories where the proportional expenditure of the two classes differed by less than one-tenth.

6

Nutrition and living standards in wartime Britain

P. E. Dewey

Current talk is chiefly about Food and Peace. The former is an increasing muddle, partly through general shortage, but quite as much through unsound maximum prices and an increase of wages which allows people to eat more than they ever have before.

(J. M. Keynes, 30 January 1918)[1]

The history of food consumption in the UK during the First World War is notable in several respects. Most obvious and important is that the average level of nutrition did not fall very much below that of pre-war. Allied to this is that policy, when it finally tackled the problems of food, was on the whole strikingly successful. In particular, food rationing, when it was imposed in the last year of the war, seems to have worked well. Finally, it is by no means certain that the poorer sections of the nation suffered the most from wartime shortages. These elements form the themes of this paper, which will begin by examining pre-war patterns of food consumption.

I

By 1914, the science of nutrition had reached the stage where it was possible to make accurate statements about the adequacy or otherwise of the diets of individuals or groups of any size or composition. The energy value of a diet could be measured in calories (a unit familiar to nutritionists, if not to the lay public) and the three basic nutritional elements in food (protein, fat and carbohydrate) were also known and measurable. The science of vitamins, however, was as yet almost unknown.[2]

These developments in scientific knowledge were of comparatively recent origin; in analysing the energy value of different foods, for example, it was usual to base statements on the pioneering work of Atwater in the USA,

Table 6.1. *Daily food supply in the UK, 1909–13, average per head*

Survey	Protein (g)	Fat (g)	Carbohydrate (g)	Calories
Royal Society	87	100	440	3,091
Thompson	86	96	422	2,980

which had appeared in 1906.[3] It is perhaps this that accounts for the odd fact that, although much concern had been expressed before 1914 about the possible interruption of food imports in wartime (there had even been a Royal Commission on the subject),[4] there had not been undertaken before the war, in any of the belligerent nations, a comprehensive study of the size and composition of the national diet in nutritional terms. When the war broke out, Germany was first off the mark in this respect, and a committee was formed to survey the German food supply. The report of the committee, referred to as the Eltzbacher report, was written in 1914, and was translated into English in 1915.[5] The first British work on the subject appeared in a paper by W. H. Thompson in March 1916.[6] Later in that year, the previously formed Food (War) Committee of the Royal Society performed a similar exercise. Thompson was a member of the committee, and reworked his earlier calculations to provide a comparison with the committee's own estimates (see Table 6.1).[7]

The two estimates, which were worked from independent data, clearly agree quite closely. However, they had to be modified to take account of the sex and age composition of the population. How many 'average men' could the population be said to contain? On the basis of equivalents suggested by Atwater, the man-value of the population was 0.77, so that the pre-war population of some 45.2 millions had a man-value of only 34.9 millions. To convert the above figures into amounts available per average man, they were thus divided by 0.77, so that the food supply was much more substantial than appeared at first sight.[8] However, it became more usual by the end of the war to use a more rigorous standard, by which the man-equivalent of the population was 0.84. This more rigorous standard, suggested by Lusk, and adopted by the Inter-Allied Scientific Commission (and also by Beveridge in his history of wartime food control), when applied to the above figures, shows this result (see Table 6.2).[9]

These estimates may be compared with the later estimate of the Ministry of Food, quoted by Beveridge, that the national calorie supply was 3,442 per average man per day in 1909–13.[10] This is slightly lower than the others, but still gives well over 3,000 calories per day. As far as the adequacy of this diet

Table 6.2. *Daily food supply in the UK (1909–13 average) per 'average man'*

Survey	Protein (g)	Fat (g)	Carbohydrate (g)	Calories
Royal Society	104	119	524	3,680
Thompson	102	114	502	3,548

is concerned, contemporary opinion was that the average man required per day at least 100 g of protein, 100 of fat, and 500 of carbohydrate;[11] on this basis, the diet was just adequate, assuming even distribution. As far as energy supply is concerned, the Inter-Allied Scientific Commission later estimated that the average man required 3,300 calories per day. This seems to be met, but the figures are on different bases. The first two estimates (cf. Table 6.1) are those of gross supply, i.e. without making allowance for losses in transport, storage and food preparation. The IASC standard was for food 'as eaten', i.e. without allowing for such losses, which might be of the order of several hundred calories per day.[12] In addition, such calculations as these are subject to a certain amount of error. Bearing these problems in mind, it seems safer to say that the national diet before 1914 was only barely adequate in nutritional terms. But the broad division between the major food elements was about right; there was at least a bare sufficiency of protein and carbohydrate, and a rather more adequate supply of fat. Also, given that the diet was a well mixed one, a sufficient proportion of the protein was of the first-class type (i.e. from animal sources), and the supply of vitamins would have been adequate.

In spite of the overall adequacy of the pre-war diet, both in terms of quantity and quality, it was clear to contemporaries that the distribution of foods between different social groups was very uneven. From the later years of the last century, social investigators such as Rowntree and Booth had drawn attention to the fact that the diet of the working classes was distinctly inferior to that of other classes. Such an observation was hardly new. What was new was the greater degree of attention paid to the phenomenon, and the determination of investigators to measure precisely the quantities involved. Stimulated by such work, official surveys followed, most notably in the form of the first large-scale survey of working-class diet ever undertaken; the 1904 survey by the Board of Trade of 1,944 family budgets.[13] The results of this and earlier surveys have been collated and analysed in nutritional terms by Oddy and his analysis shows that the pre-war nutritional level of working-class families was much below the national average. While the average intake of calories in the working-class families was only 2,398 per head per

Table 6.3. *Food consumption per week expressed in terms of lbs per head*

	Bread	Potatoes	Sugar	Fats	Meat	Milk (pints)
UK average 1904–13	6.9	3.6	1.5	1.4	2.2	4.1
Working-class 1902–12	6.6	3.0	1.0	0.5	1.2	1.8

day on average during 1902–13, the national intake per head was 3,171 calories (average during 1904–13); the working-class intake was thus only 76 per cent of the national average. This comparatively low energy intake was accompanied by a further source of uneven distribution within the family, since it was noted that working-class husbands tended to obtain a disproportionately large share of the available food.[14]

Adequacy of diet was obviously a function of income. Opinions varied as to the point at which income sufficed to produce an acceptable level of nutrition, but it was apparent that undernourishment was not confined merely to those households where the (unskilled) head of the household earned £1.00–£1.25 per week; the Board of Trade estimated that the daily calorie intake per average man was only 2,670 in households whose weekly income was less than 25 shillings (£1.25), but did not rise to the level of 3,300 until income reached 40 shillings (£2.00), which was in the upper reaches of the skilled working class.[15]

The lower than average calorie intake of working-class families was also accompanied by differences in the quantities of specific foodstuffs consumed. Broadly, as might be expected, working-class diet was relatively more dependent upon foods which supplied energy comparatively cheaply, such as bread and potatoes. This is not to say that the absolute amounts of such foods consumed were greater than the national average; they were in fact slightly lower (at least in Oddy's analysis). The difference lay in the much lower intake of 'superior' foods (chiefly those from animal sources) (see Table 6.3).[16]

As well as this broad pattern, it was noted that the working-class diet was marked by a low intake of fresh fruit, and to some extent fresh vegetables. Thus as well as being deficient in quantity it was inadequate in quality; the protein intake was relatively more dependent upon second-class protein (chiefly from cereals), and the 'protective' foods such as dairy produce, fruit, eggs and vegetables were also lacking to some extent. The greatest sufferers from these shortages were working-class children, whose general development and resistance to disease were impaired, and who were much more prone to what was later recognised as vitamin deficiency disease (e.g., rickets) than children from other social classes.[17]

II

The outbreak of war did not lead to any immediate concern about the food supply. This might seem surprising, since it was well known that the UK depended upon imports for much of its food supply (in terms of calories, about 60 per cent). In particular, concern had often been expressed before the war about the wheat supply, of which about three-quarters came from abroad.[18] Yet little alarm was felt until 1916, since the carrying power of the merchant marine remained substantially unimpaired by the first German submarine campaign of 1915–16, and policy remained one of relying on the Royal Navy to keep the sealanes open. The only executive action of note in the first eighteen months of the war was the establishment of a Sugar Commission (August 1914), whose main task was to rectify the situation caused by the disappearance of imports from Europe, which before the war had supplied some two-thirds of the sugar consumed in the UK.[19]

Nor, in this early period, can it be said that this generally *laissez-faire* approach was ill-founded. At this time, the main problems concerning food were not, except for sugar, those of supply, but those of price. This partly reflected the generally inflationary nature of war finance, but also the high cost of imports, which reflected in turn the rapid rise in shipping rates. The well-known index of Isserlis shows freight rates rising from 60 in 1909–13 to 365 in 1916 and 751 in 1918.[20] Thus the price level in general, in particular that of food, and especially imported food, rose rapidly. By October 1916, the general level of retail prices was 150–155 (July 1914 = 100); that of food alone was 168. By that date also, the prices of, for example, British wheat and beef had risen by 73 and 68 per cent, but imported beef had risen by 87 per cent, and imported wheat (Canadian Manitoba No. 1) by 111 per cent.[21]

At this point, policy underwent a dramatic and radical change. The *laissez-faire* approach was abandoned, and a comprehensive set of interventionist policies adopted. The reasons for this were partly political, being concerned with the intrigues surrounding the fall of the Asquith government and its replacement by the Lloyd George coalition. Yet concern for the food supply antedated this event, and grew rapidly during the summer of 1916; the alleged neglect of the food question was one of the political criticisms made of the Asquith administration in its last months. From the early autumn concern grew as it was realised that the harvest in North America and the UK had been poor.[22] It was also felt that the curbing of food price rises was overdue. Finally, it was suspected that the German submarine fleet would pose a much more serious challenge in the future, and this latter fear was realised with the announcement at the end of January 1917 that from 1 February an Aunlimited' sinking campaign would commence. Henceforth all shipping in British waters, including that of neutrals, would be subject to attack on sight.

By that time, policy towards food had already substantially changed.[23] One of the last acts of the Asquith government had been to announce the appointment of a Food Controller, although the first Controller (Lord Devonport) was not appointed until after Lloyd George had become Prime Minister.[24] The early work of his office was mainly concerned with controlling food prices; thereafter it moved on to rationing, which commenced effectively at the beginning of 1918. The other main development was the establishment of a Food Production Department, with the aim of expanding home food production.[25] Finally, imports became subject to strict control, in order to economise on shipping. The end result of all these changes was that the import, production and sale of most of the national food supply became strictly controlled. This process took some time, and was not complete even at the Armistice, but there is no doubt of the substantial break with previous policy which occurred.

From the consumers' point of view, these changes had certain consequences. Firstly, they succeeded in slowing down the rate of inflation in food prices. This process was first apparent in July 1917. In September, the price of bread was stabilised by the application of a subsidy. This remained in force for the rest of the war, and the price of bread (which was never rationed) remained constant until September 1919. Largely as a result of price control, the retail food price index remained almost unchanged from November 1917 to June 1918.[26] The second major consequence was that the composition of the national diet altered in favour of cereals, potatoes and other crops, at the expense of livestock products. This was due to the rationale behind the policies of food production and food control, which was that, since livestock are wasteful converters of crops into food, the nation's energy supply would be maximised by consuming more crops directly, instead of via meat and milk. In this way, the supply of energy stored in human food would be increased. Provided that the national diet remained sufficiently mixed, the main nutritional elements would be available in adequate amounts.[27] In furtherance of this aim, the home production of crops rather than livestock was encouraged, the use of grain for brewing and distilling was restricted, and the extraction rate for flour was raised so as to utilise a higher proportion of the wheat grain. The final consequence was rationing in 1918, when the food intake of the better-off classes was curtailed, with a view to minimising unnecessary shortage amongst the working classes.[28]

Taking the period as a whole, the supply of energy in the national diet was adequate throughout. While it is clear that there was some slight decline in 1915–17, this was checked in the last year of the war. By the Armistice, the

Table 6.4. *UK food supply 1909–18*

	1909–13 average	1914	1915	1916	1917	1918
Calories per average man per day	3,442	3,454	3,551	3,418	3,320	3,358
Ratio (1909–13 = 100)	100	100	103	99	96	97

energy supply was only marginally lower than in the pre-war period; for this comparatively favourable situation the new policies of 1917–18 must take a large part of the credit.[29]

Even this comparatively favourable picture may be too pessimistic for the mid-war period. An estimate for 1916 by the Food (War) Committee of the Royal Society suggested that the food supply in that year was actually slightly higher than in 1909–13, by about 2 per cent (see Table 6.4).[30]

Whichever estimate is preferred, it is clear that the total energy supply was maintained almost unchanged during the war, in sharp contrast to the position in the Central Powers. However, this picture of near-stasis conceals important changes in the relative supply of various commodities. The largest change affecting a major food was in the case of sugar, all of which had been imported before the war. Some of the loss attendant on the absence of European supplies was made good, but by the end of the war the total UK supply was only about two-thirds that of peacetime. Since before the war sugar had accounted for some 13 per cent of the entire energy supply of the national diet, this alone was a problem of great importance.[31] A further consideration was that it was a relatively cheap way for the consumer to obtain energy (if nothing else of nutritional importance). Imported butter was also sharply reduced; the supply had fallen to one-half by 1918. This was also the loss of a concentrated source of energy, which had the additional advantage of making other foods palatable (in particular, bread). The supply of eggs, large numbers of which had previously come from Russia, was also sharply curtailed. Amongst foods largely supplied domestically, the greatest falls were in meat and milk. This was partly due to the policy of encouraging crops at the expense of livestock, but mainly to the shortage of feed (especially imported concentrates) in the last year or so of the war. The largest reduction was in pork, which fell to only one-quarter of its pre-war level. The supply of mutton and lamb fell by about one-third, that of beef by one-quarter. The milk supply also fell by about a quarter.[32]

These losses were to some extent offset by changes in other elements of the food supply. The most notable, in the last two years of the war, was the increased supply of flour. This increase was partly due to the use of a higher

PETER DEWEY

Table 6.5. *Composition of UK diet 1914–18*[a]

	Protein (g)	Fat (g)	Carbohydrate (g)	Calories	Calories ratio (1909–13 = 100)
1909–13	99	115	469	3,398	100
1914	99	115	473	3,414	100
1915	98	123	489	3,551	105
1916	96	118	458	3,369	99
1917	99	108	469	3,333	98
1918	99	105	487	3,379	99

[a] Quantities per average man per day calculated from Beveridge, *Food Control*, p. 361. The totals are slightly different from those given by him on p. 313.

extraction rate, and partly due to the eking out of the flour supply by admixture with flour made from other cereals (chiefly barley), rice, and potatoes. Admixture was carried on to a considerable extent, and could have been carried further. But for the Armistice, observed Beveridge, the bread of 1919 would have consisted largely of potatoes.[33] The potato supply itself expanded considerably in the last two years of the war, as the new food production policy got into its stride. A side-effect of the policy was the encouragement of allotment keeping. This must have added materially to the supply of fresh vegetables (and, again, potatoes) in 1917–18, but the actual yields involved can only be guessed roughly.[34] The shortage of butter was offset by the expansion of the margarine supply from an early stage, as consumers turned to the cheaper substitute. Imported bacon came in from the USA in large amounts in 1918. It was generally considered to be of lower quality than the home or imported bacon which it replaced, but it did have the virtue of rectifying some of the deficiency in meat and fat consequent on the decline in the overall meat supply. Finally, the supply of condensed milk grew, and went a little way to offset the decline in the fresh milk supply.

In sum, the national dietary changes may be described as the maintenance of energy intake, and a shift in composition away from livestock products towards cereals and potatoes. These changes had implications for the nutritional balance of the national diet. In particular, while such adjustments could do much to maintain the intake of protein and carbohydrate, they could do little to repair the loss of fats implied by the decline in livestock products (see Table 6.5).

Protein intake declined slightly in 1915–16, reflecting the beginning of the decline in the supply of livestock products, but was restored subsequently as the output of cereals and potatoes rose, and imports of bacon increased. On balance, however, protein quality was reduced, as first-class animal protein was replaced by second-class vegetable protein. The drop in fat, although small in comparison with that of Central Europe, was yet the most serious and intractable of the food problems encountered during the war. Initially due to the decline in butter imports, it was exacerbated by the reduction of meat and milk output which was a concomitant of the new policies of 1917–18, and was only inadequately offset by the import of American bacon. The carbohydrate supply was barely affected by the decline in livestock products, since these do not, except for milk, contain significant amounts. Above all, its supply was a function of the availability of sugar, cereals and potatoes. The supplies of the latter two were well maintained for most of the war (although the Scottish potato crop failed in 1916),[35] and actually increased in the last two years. Whereas the average man derived 41 per cent of his energy intake from cereals and potatoes in 1909–13, this rose to 50 per cent in 1918.[36] As Table 6.5 shows, this shift in dietary composition permitted carbohydrate intake to actually rise above the pre-war level in 1918, in spite of the increasing shortage of sugar, for which the new policies held no solution.

On balance, these changes in the broad composition of the national diet were not particularly alarming. On the conventional contemporary assumption that the average man required 100 g of protein and fat, and 500 g of carbohydrate per day, the intake of both protein and fat was still sufficient. The carbohydrate intake was below the norm, but it had already been so before the war, and finished in 1918 slightly above the pre-war level.

However, the national diet was still, as in pre-war days, only barely adequate, both in quantity and quality, for the population as a whole. To what extent did the uneven distribution which had been such a marked feature of the pre-war period persist in wartime, and to what extent, if any, was it altered?

For most of the war there was little study on any scale of this question. A small survey of working-class families in Glasgow compared the diet of 48 families in 1911–12 with that of 40 families (not previously studied) in 1915–16, and re-examined 10 of those 40 in early 1917. These are clearly small samples, which are not necessarily representative of larger working-class groups, but they do show that the families concerned were probably maintaining the energy value of their diets, although some deterioration in quality is evident. Thus the 48 pre-war families had an intake of 2,899 calories per average man per day; the 40 families of 1915–16 an intake of 3,059. Of those 40, 10 had a calorie intake of 2,899 and when these families were re-surveyed early in 1917, their calorie intake was 2,878 per average man per day. As far as quality is concerned, the 40 families of 1915–16 had a poorer diet than the 48 pre-war families; only 80 g of meat per average man per day, compared to 110 g before the war. There was also by then a substan-

Table 6.6. *Principal changes in daily calorie supply per average man in working-class diet, June 1914 and June 1918*

	Losses		Gains
Sugar	178	Bread and cereals	42
Butter and margarine	47	Potatoes	44
Cheese	28	Milk	31
Eggs	9		
	−262		+117

tial shift to margarine in place of butter. In 1911–12, it had been used by few families, but in 1915–16 was used by 70 per cent of the families. This change accounted for the rise in fat intake, from 76 g per average man per day before the war, to 84 g in 1915–16. As a result of the decline in meat consumption, protein intake per day had fallen from 101 g to 95 g.[37]

The only large study made of wartime diet was conducted for the Sumner Committee in 1918. The Committee had been asked to estimate the increased cost of living to the working classes during the war. In order to form an estimate of working-class expenditure in 1914, it used the results of the 1904 Board of Trade survey referred to above,[38] and adjusted them to take account of changes in consumption and prices in the period 1904–14. For 1918, the Committee conducted a fresh survey, which entailed making a large collection of household budgets. In all, 1,306 were made, chiefly relating to household expenditure in the first week of June 1918. Of these, 104 budgets proved on examination to be from the families of clerks; the rest were from working-class households, comprising 231 from families where the chief wage-earner was away on military service, 566 from skilled men's households, 139 from semi-skilled, and 266 from unskilled men's households.[39]

The survey (which did not consider food consumption in 1915–17) showed that the overall energy intake per average man had changed little between June 1914 and June 1918. For all working-class households grouped together (excluding the 'on service' class), calorie intake per average man had fallen by about three per cent (from 3,130 to 3,040 per day). This fall is the same as that suggested by Beveridge from different sources in his history of food control. However, the Sumner data showed that different types of household had different experiences. In skilled men's households, calorie intake had fallen by about 6 per cent, in semi-skilled ones it had fallen only 'very slightly', and in unskilled ones it had *risen* by about 3 per cent (and now stood at about 2,900 per day).[40]

This near-stasis in energy supply concealed certain quite substantial

Table 6.7. *Weekly working-class family food consumption, 1914–18*

	July 1914	December 1917	June 1918[a]
Bread and flour (lb)	32.0	32.0	34.5
Potatoes (lb)	17.0	17.0	20.0
Bacon (lb)	1.4	1.1	2.5
Milk (pints)	10.0	8.3	11.7
Sugar (lb)	5.6	3.2	2.8
Meat (lb)	6.5	5.3	4.0

[a]*Sources:* PRO MAF 60/104, 3, and for 1918, Sumner Committee, pp. 15–16

changes in dietary composition. In calorie terms, the greatest loss was due to the loss of sugar, other changes being minor by comparison (see Table 6.6).[41]

However, the omission of reference to the intervening years 1915–17 is a serious one, since the situation was almost certainly more acute then for working-class families than at the time of the Sumner survey, by which time a good deal of remedial action had been taken. The Glasgow survey cited above suggests that families were having to make quite large adjustments to their diets as early as 1915–16, although the energy value of the diet was being roughly maintained. Moreover, the general problems of food supply became more acute in 1916–17, and there is the possibility that the energy value of working-class diets declined by more than is indicated in the national estimates presented by Beveridge. This is suggested in a rough way from a memorandum issued by the second Food Controller (Lord Rhondda) in January 1918.[42] This contains an analysis of working-class food consumption in December 1917 (from Ministry of Food sources) compared with July 1914. This list of commodities is not exhaustive, but contains the major foods. Analysing the list in terms of currently accepted calorie-equivalents,[43] and expressing the result in terms of average men, the daily calorie intake in July 1914 was 2,539, and in December 1917 it was 2,249 – a fall of nine per cent.[44] This estimate is necessarily a rather rough one, and it has not been possible to check the original data. However, it may perhaps indicate the likely size of the fall in working-class energy intake at what was probably the most difficult period of the war, after the supply of sugar and certain livestock products (mainly butter) had fallen considerably, and before such losses had been largely offset by the new policies of food control and food production. Clearly the position was in certain respects worse than it was to be at the time of the Sumner enquiry six months later (see Table 6.7).[45]

Thus by December 1917, although consumption of bread and potatoes had been maintained, all the other foods had fallen quite sharply. Further

Table 6.8. *UK working-class and national food consumption levels, 1914 and 1918*

	Working-class 1914	UK 1914	Ratio A[b]	Working-class 1918	UK 1918	Ratio B[c]	Index Ratio B/Ratio A
	(lb per average man per week)						
Bread and flour	7.33	5.07	1.44	7.55	5.80	1.30	0.90
Meat (sold by weight)[a]	1.49	2.36	0.63	0.96	1.53	0.63	1.00
Bacon and ham	0.26	0.41	0.63	0.56	0.56	1.00	1.59
Lard, suet, etc.	0.22	0.13	1.69	0.17	0.18	0.94	0.56
Eggs (number)	2.80	2.40	1.17	1.99	1.52	1.31	1.12
Fresh milk (pints)	2.01	3.94	0.51	2.56	2.90	0.88	1.72
Cheese	0.18	0.17	1.06	0.09	0.14	0.64	0.60
Butter	0.37	0.36	1.03	0.17	0.20	0.85	0.83
Margarine	0.09	0.16	0.56	0.20	0.27	0.74	1.32
Potatoes	3.41	5.12	0.67	4.38	6.34	0.69	1.03
Rice and tapioca	0.31	0.24	1.29	0.28	0.32	0.87	0.67
Oatmeal	0.28	0.21	1.33	0.31	0.33	0.94	0.71
Sugar	1.29	1.78	0.73	0.62	1.11	0.56	0.77

[a] Includes sausages

[b] $\text{Ratio A} = \dfrac{\text{Column 1}}{\text{Column 2}}$

[c] $\text{Ratio B} = \dfrac{\text{Column 4}}{\text{Column 5}}$

losses of sugar and meat were to be experienced by June 1918, but by then they were offset by increases in bread and potatoes, which helped to make up some of the energy losses, although entailing qualitative deterioration in the diet. On the other hand, this was counter-balanced by increases in bacon and milk. The table shows a fall in meat supply after December 1917 which is probably exaggerated, since in that month consumption was unseasonally high consequent upon the heavy slaughterings of that autumn.[46]

More detailed comparison of the Sumner report with Beveridge's figures for national food consumption levels enables a view to be taken of the ratio of working-class consumption to the national average in 1914 and 1918, and thus the extent to which working-class standards of diet varied relative to national averages at the beginning and at the end of the war (see Table 6.8).[47]

In Table 6.8, Ratio A is the ratio of working-class consumption to the national average in 1914, Ratio B that in 1918. The index in column 7 is obtained by dividing Ratio B by Ratio A, to obtain an indication of the change in working-class relative to national consumption levels between 1914 and 1918. An index number above unity shows that working-class consumption rose between 1914 and 1918 relative to the national average; an index number below unity shows that it had fallen. The main caveats are that the working-class data refer to the summer and exclude Ireland while the national data are yearly averages and include Ireland.

From this comparison, the relative position of the working-class consumer in respect of individual commodities appears as very variable. To take first the important item of bread (including flour), it is clear that working-class consumption was quite substantially above the national average in 1914,[48] and rose slightly in absolute terms by 1918, yet non-working-class consumers raised their absolute level of consumption even more, so that working-class consumption actually fell in relative terms. As regards meat, the relative position of the working-class consumer was unchanged. The amount consumed both by working-class and other consumers was sharply curtailed, in both cases by a similar proportion. This presumably reflects the imposition of meat rationing in 1918. On the other hand, the position of the working-class consumer in respect of bacon had improved substantially in relation to the national average. However the comparatively low esteem in which the imported bacon of 1918 was held by many consumers might account for this.[49] The relative working-class position as regards the supply of animal fats (butter, lard, suet, etc.) clearly deteriorated, although working-class consumers made up for this loss to a greater extent than did other consumers by resorting to margarine. Indeed the absolute loss of butter to the working class was almost made good by this means. In the cases of eggs and milk the relative working-class position improved – quite substantially in the case of milk. Relative working-class potato consumption was maintained, and the absolute intake increased (as it did for the nation as a whole). Minor cereals (rice, tapioca, oatmeal) became less important in the diet of the working-class consumer, but the absolute amounts are too small to be of material concern. Finally, there is the important case of sugar, where working-class consumption had been much lower than the national average before the war, and fell during it relatively more than did the national average. By 1918, working-class intake was only about half that of 1914, and was about the same as the official ration (8 oz per head per week). The national average was about twice as high. However, it must not be necessarily concluded that non-working class consumers were evading rationing, since the national sugar consumption figures given here include sugar used in manufacturing (mainly alcohol and confectionery), and so are not strictly comparable to the working-class consumption figures, which include only sugar purchased as such.

On balance, it would seem that working-class diets in wartime were almost the same in energy value by 1918 as they had been in 1914, although there was a decline in the years in between which may have been as much as the 9 per cent indicated in Lord Rhondda's memorandum. It is, however, by no means certain that the working-class diet deteriorated qualitatively any more than that of the nation as a whole. In the cases of the two most important pre-war foods (bread and meat) consumption levels were maintained (or nearly so) relative to the national average. The two most significant losses were those of sugar and butter. However, the loss entailed by the former was wholly one of energy, and this was almost entirely made good from other sources. The loss of energy and nutrition from the latter was largely made good through the increased consumption of margarine. The Sumner Report also showed that working-class milk consumption had increased in absolute terms between 1914 and 1918. This finding may perhaps be unreliable. It is clear that the national intake of milk fell sharply, and there seems no evidence which would account for the working-class share of the milk supply increasing so much at a time of general shortage. However, there seems little doubt that it was the working-class which benefited most from the large supply of imported bacon in 1918, and although not regarded highly by higher income groups, there seems no reason to doubt the beneficial effect which it had on working-class diet, both in quantitative and qualitative terms.

III

There was therefore, in comparison with other belligerent nations, no serious food shortage in the UK during the war. This is clearly so if national aggregates are used to measure food supply. Even if one considers the working class alone, as being most vulnerable to shortages and high prices, it does not appear that energy intake fell by more than about 9 per cent by late 1917, and this was reduced to a loss of about 3 per cent by the summer of 1918. It is of course arguable that this was in itself a serious shortfall, in view of what has been said about the pre-war working-class diet, but the shortfall does not seem to have lasted long enough to have had adverse physical consequences, and there is a case for saying that the health of the civilian population actually improved during the war.[50]

If the overall energy supply was adequate; if the supply of the major foods was not seriously impaired (except for sugar); and if the national diet remained sufficiently varied to avoid particular nutritional and vitamin deficiencies[51] – and these assertions are all valid – then in what respect can there be said to have been a food problem during the war? The answer is that the food problem was of an altogether less serious order than that experienced in Europe, and consisted in the forced change of customary standards of consumption, leading to what may be described as loss of consumer satisfaction, which yet stopped well short of actual privation. Before considering this further, it may be useful to place food consumption as a whole within the context of changes in the standard of living in wartime.

The ability of consumers to maintain their standard of living (defined as the maintenance of real consumption levels of goods and services of unchanged quality) depends upon two factors: the maintenance of real income, and of the supply of goods and services of standard quality. As far as real income is concerned, this was probably maintained fairly well. There were several reasons for this. The most important was probably the existence of full employment. After the first few months, when disruption of the export trades caused some concern, it became apparent that the huge demands of the armed forces for men and *matériel* had created a fully employed economy for the first time in living memory. Whilst the pre-war economy had run on average at about 6 per cent unemployment,[52] there was virtually no unemployment during the war.[53] This was a material factor in improving the well-being of those groups formerly prone to cyclical or seasonal unemployment – one of the major causes of poverty in the pre-war period. Secondly, high labour demand meant that there was plentiful overtime work available, as well as extra bonus and piece payments.[54] Thirdly, official 'separation allowances' were given to wives, children and other dependants of servicemen; in total, these payments were substantial (£113 million in the financial year 1917–18, for example).[55]

These sources of enhanced income have to be set against the rapid rise of prices during the war, and the somewhat lower rise in wage-rates. By July 1917, Bowley's index of wage-rates stood at 135–140, with the cost of living index at 160–180 (July 1914 = 100). But it would be misleading to conclude that real wages necessarily fell. The existence of overtime and the other factors mentioned above probably sufficed to keep actual earnings roughly in step with the cost of living. Bowley even hazarded a guess that household earnings may often have risen faster than prices.[56] It should be said, however, that these comments do not necessarily apply to all households, since individual household situations could differ markedly, depending upon such things as changes in the number of children or (especially early in the war) whether wage-rates had yet caught up with prices.[57] In the case of those families whose former main earner had gone on military service, there was probably a reduction in household real income per 'man'. Such families were surveyed by the Sumner committee in 1918. It was found that, notwithstanding separation allowances, the diet of such families was in general inferior to that of non-service families in that it contained more bread and margarine, and less meat. It was also noted that the service families spent much less on food per 'man' than did other families. The explanation for this seems to be twofold; the non-service families usually had two earners each (the service families only one), and separation allowances did not keep pace

PETER DEWEY

Table 6.9. *Consumers' real expenditure, 1914–18 (1913 = 100)*

	1914	1915	1916	1917	1918
Food	98	100	96	90	88
Drink and tobacco	99	97	87	65	47
Housing	101	102	102	102	103
Fuel and light	99	104	104	101	90
Clothing	86	93	65	60	58
Durable household goods	97	92	75	71	75
Other goods	99	103	101	98	107
Transport and communications	94	97	97	81	92
Other services	101	95	85	78	77
All goods and services	98	98	90	83	81

with inflation. The rate for the wife of a private or corporal with two children was 14s. 7d. per week in September 1914, and had risen to 24s. by July 1918. This was a rise of some 65 per cent, compared with a rise in the cost of living of some 100 per cent.[58]

On the whole, however, it seems that real incomes for consumers were maintained during the war. The cost of the war to consumers was largely felt in the diminution of the supply of goods and services, and a deterioration in their quality. The impact of this process on consumers can be roughly assessed by using estimates of consumer spending on goods and services at current prices, and deflating these by the appropriate price indexes for each group of commodities. When this is done, it may be seen that real standards of consumption fell by about one-fifth overall, but that the reduction in consumption fell unevenly on different types of goods and services (see Table 6.9).[59]

Clearly consumers succeeded in maintaining real consumption levels of what may be described as essential goods (food, housing, fuel and light) better than less essential items such as drink and tobacco and clothing.[60] In the case of these latter goods, there were specific forces making for a reduction in supply. In the case of drink, the government intervened as early as 1915 in order to curtail the supply of alcohol to consumers, allegedly to reduce industrial absenteeism induced by drunkenness. This policy became more effective as time went on, and by 1917 was reinforced by the need to save imported cereals, and to divert grain formerly used for brewing and distilling directly to human consumption.[61] The import of tobacco was restricted in the second half of the war to save shipping space. The clothing industry (at least the civilian side) was also subject to restriction to save foreign exchange; the function of the Cotton Control Board, established in 1917, was to reduce capacity in the cotton industry.[62]

In addition to these specific cases, there was the general tendency of the economy to shift towards the production of military goods and services at the expense of the civilian consumer. As manpower and raw materials moved into the military sector, either in the shape of the forces themselves or of industries serving them, less was available for the consumer who wished to maintain the pre-war pattern of consumption. In particular, the service sector could be curtailed quite substantially in order to release manpower (if little else) for the forces or for other, more 'essential' industries.[63] The significance of this was that services were second only to food as items of expenditure before the war. While food accounted for 29 per cent of consumers' expenditure in 1913, services had accounted for 21 per cent.[64]

The overall impression left by considering real consumption levels must be a certain surprise that they held up so well during a war which made such large demands on the productive powers of the economy. Some suggestions as to how this was achieved were made in a report by the Board of Trade in July 1918. Commenting on the great increase in the sector of the economy supplying military requirements, it drew attention to the comparatively favourable situation of the civilian consumer, who appeared to be:

. . . not less well fed and clad than before the war, though (it is) doubtless worse housed, and less adequately warmed and lit, especially the relatively well-to-do classes, and less copiously provided with newspapers and books, and many minor necessities and luxuries.

The report pointed to two reasons why this should be so. The first was that the nation as a whole had gone without services rather than goods – the services of retail tradesmen, domestic servants, transport and postal workers being specifically cited. Secondly, the high pressure of demand for labour had led to a considerably increased output per head, partly through more individual effort on the part of the workforce, but also through the better organisation of factories. The result was that the nation had been enabled to achieve 'an almost unbelievable expenditure of effort on the war without this entailing any large amount of suffering to the civilian population.'[65]

Overall, then, consumers found their living standards cut by the end of the war by about one-fifth, and food consumption in real terms fell by somewhat less. In order to make some estimate of the loss of satisfaction implied to the consumer of food, this fall in the real level of food consumption may be taken as the yardstick, since it effectively measured the gap between the rate of increase of food prices and expenditure on food; in this case a shortfall of some 12 per cent. However, this measurement may be refined by taking a more complete set of data on food prices and consumption; in this case they are those assembled by Prest and Adams (see Table 6.10).[66]

The derivation of the food price index is that of the retail price of all foods,

Table 6.10. *An index of UK retail food prices and food consumption, 1914–18 (1909–13 = 100)*

	Retail food prices	UK food consumption
1909–13	100	100
1914	101	101
1915	128	128
1916	158	146
1917	202	173
1918	231	197

weighted according to the pattern of national expenditure on them in 1909–13. Thus the wartime price index measures the extra cost to consumers as a whole had they been able to purchase exactly the same foods in the same quantities during the war as during those pre-war years. The food expenditure index shows the degree of variation from the maintenance of that standard. There is, in overall terms, no gap between the two series until 1916, when it is 8 per cent. The gap becomes much bigger in 1917, at 14 per cent, and is 15 per cent in 1918.

For the nation as a whole, then, the loss of satisfaction implied in the forced dietary changes of wartime was at the end of the war of the order of one-sixth. However, for the working class it was distinctly less. In the case of this group, the appropriate price index to use is not the national average of Prest and Adams, but the official index of food prices, which was based on pre-war working-class consumption. This index rose more slowly than the national average index, especially towards the end of the war, when it stood only at 205 (July 1914 = 100), compared with 231 for the national price index above.[67] While the price rises facing working-class consumers were thus not as steep as the national average by the end of the war, working-class food expenditure had risen almost as fast as the national average; the Sumner Committee thought that it had risen by 82–90 per cent.[68] In contrasting the price rises and level of expenditure by working-class households Bowley thought that the loss of satisfaction to working-class food consumers might, using the same method as above, be put at about 8½ per cent – 'To put the result more crudely, the urban workman spent 90 per cent more on food and got 8½ per cent less in return.'[69]

The above measurements are a rough approximation of the extent to which food consumers suffered through an enforced change of customary standards of consumption. There are other forms of satisfaction loss which are not measured thereby. In particular, it is assumed that food qualities are unchanged, and this is clearly not the case. Nor can this technique take

Table 6.11. *UK food consumption per 'average man', 1880–1954,*
expressed in terms of lbs per week

	1880	1909–13	1914	1915	1916	1917	1918	1924–8	1934–8	1954
Wheat flour	6.4	5.3	5.1	5.0	5.2	5.7	5.8	4.7	4.7	4.5
Meat[a]		2.3	2.4	2.3	2.2	2.0	1.5	2.0		
Bacon	2.1	0.4	0.4	0.5	0.5	0.4	0.6	0.5	3.4	3.0
Potatoes	6.8	5.2	5.1	5.4	4.9	4.7	6.3	4.7	4.2	5.3
Milk (pints)	3.7	4.2	3.9	3.9	3.6	3.3	2.9	4.0	4.0	6.1
Eggs (number)	2.0	2.5	2.4	2.1	1.9	1.7	1.5	2.9	4.8	5.8
Butter	0.3	0.4	0.4	0.3	0.3	0.2	0.2	0.4	0.6	0.3
Cheese	0.2	0.2	0.2	0.2	0.1	0.1	0.1	0.2	0.2	0.2
Margarine	—[b]	0.1	0.2	0.2	0.3	0.3	0.3	0.3	0.2	0.4
Sugar	1.5	1.8	1.8	1.9	1.5	1.2	1.1	2.0	2.5	2.5

[a] Includes ham, except for 1909–19, when it is included with *bacon*
[b] = no data

account of what might be termed psychological deprivation, in the form of resentment at the enforced alteration of standards. But insofar as loss of consumption standards can be measured, this is probably as near as we can get to a quantitative assessment. Assuming that losses of this rough magnitude were sustained, they remain essentially trivial in comparison with the real nutritional shortages which were suffered in Europe.

IV

The wartime changes in food consumption patterns are placed in the longer-run context in Table 6.11, which covers the period 1880–1954.[70] From this it is apparent that in most cases the war had only a temporary effect upon consumption patterns. Well before 1914, consumption had begun to shift away from 'inferior' foods (cereals, potatoes) towards 'superior' ones (mainly meat and dairy produce). This process reflected mainly the rise in average real income which became apparent from about 1850 but it was also related to the greater availability of certain foods, and in some, but not all cases, a lowering of the price of individual commodities. This broad shift continued in the period after 1918, although the process may have been slowed by the high unemployment of the inter-war period, and is not fully reflected in the 1954 figures due to contemporary shortages of certain foods (sugar, meat and fats).

In nearly every case, the experience of the war was that most foods showed temporary reversals of the already established long-term trend. This is so for wheat flour (and thus bread), meat, potatoes, milk, eggs, butter and sugar.

The data on bacon is inadequate. In the case of cheese, there appears to be a temporary decline from a long-run position of stability. Finally, margarine provides the only exception to the general experience; an unimportant commodity before 1914, it was given a substantial boost by the high cost and shortage of butter. Thereafter consumption fell back in the inter-war period, but the war had served to establish it as a cheap and competitive substitute for butter, and the long-term trend thereafter was clearly upwards (see Table 6.11).

V

In comparison to the experience of certain other nations, the UK during the First World War suffered in only minor respects from food shortages. To what can this comparatively fortunate experience be attributed?

Undoubtedly the most fundamental basis of this success was the maintenance of imported supplies.[71] These were certainly curtailed to some extent, partly by circumstance and partly by deliberate design in 1917–18, but without their substantial continuation questions of food control would have been entirely academic. While technically it would have been just possible to have squeezed enough calories from the soil of the UK to feed the entire population, such a change could not have been achieved in the time available from the military point of view.[72] In its most fundamental form, the comparative immunity of the UK from food shortages depended upon the broader course of the military and naval conflict.

Given an adequate degree of provisioning from outside, there were yet considerable problems of food supply, which remained for domestic administrators and politicians to solve. Before the end of 1916 there could not be said to be a food problem in any but a rather superficial sense. After that, what turned out to be a comparatively trivial degree of hardship could undoubtedly have been made much worse by a substantial political and administrative failure. In this context, the accession of the Lloyd George coalition was important, since it generated various policies which contributed materially to the easing of a potentially serious situation. In particular, it gave full political support to various measures of food control, which culminated in rationing in 1918, and inaugurated the new policy of home food production. The latter, although a minor contribution to the overall food supply, was yet of some material assistance.

Given the political will, the next requirement was administrative competence. This seems to have been forthcoming. Mistakes were certainly made, but they were either not serious or were retrieved before too much damage had been done.[73] They were certainly minor in comparison with the complete unreality and sheer incompetence of German food policy.[74] In particular, the administrators in the UK had the benefit of informed scientific opinion, which was taken into account in framing policy (although the first Food Controller seems to have been relatively immune to such opinion).[75]

Finally, the rock on which successful administration rested was public consent. Without the substantial measure of public acquiescence in the policies of food control and production which actually occurred, such policies would have been inoperable. Thus considerations of administrative competence must eventually give way to wider questions concerning public opinion and political unity.

Notes

1 J. M. Keynes, *The collected writings of John Maynard Keynes*, (ed.) E. Johnson, vol. XVI, London, 1971, pp. 270–1.
2 The contemporary state of dietetic theory is found in E. H. Starling, *The feeding of nations*, London, 1919.
3 W. O. Atwater and A. P. Bryant, *The chemical composition of American food materials*, US Department of Agriculture, Bulletin No. 28, revised edition, Washington, 1906.
4 *Royal commission on the supply of food and raw material in time of war*, PP 1905, xxxix, Cd 2643.
5 P. Eltzbacher, *Die deutsche Volksernahrung und der englische Aushungerungsplan. Eine Denkschrift von Friedrich Aereboe*, Braunschweig, 1914; English trans. by Sir S. Russell Wells, *Germany's food; can it last*, London, 1915.
6 W. H. Thompson, 'The food value of Great Britain's food supply', *The Economic Proceedings of the Royal Dublin Society*, II, no. 11, March 1916.
7 Royal Society, *The food supply of the United Kingdom*, PP 1916, ix, CD 8421, p. 3, Appendix Ib.
8 *Ibid.*, p. 4.
9 This standard is detailed in W. H. Beveridge, *British food control*, London, 1928, pp. 392–3. The Lusk/IASC Standard is used as the basis for the man-equivalent calculations presented in this chapter.
10 *Ibid.*, p. 313.
11 Royal Society, *Food supply*, pp. 3–4.
12 For the IASC standard, see Beveridge, *Food control*, pp. 392–3. It was usual to reckon that the average man needed to digest 3,000 calories' worth of food per day, and that this could be obtained by supplying 3,300 calories in the form of purchased food, Starling, *Feeding of nations*, p. 30.
13 Board of Trade, *Consumption and cost of food in workmen's families in urban districts in the United Kingdom*, PP 1905, lxxxiv, Cd 2337.
14 D. Oddy and D. Miller (eds.), *The making of the modern British diet*, London, 1976, pp. 224–5.
15 Starling, *Feeding of nations*, p. 46.
16 Oddy and Miller, *British diet*, p. 221.
17 *Ibid.*, pp. 228–9.
18 The first full examination of the relative contribution to the nation's energy supply of home production and imports did not, however, occur until Thompson published his article in 1916 (see above, note 6).
19 Beveridge, *Food control*, p. 6.

20 L. Isserlis, 'Tramp shipping, cargoes and freights', *Journal of the Royal Statistical Society*, new series, 101 (1938), 53–134.
21 A. L. Bowley, *Prices and wages in the United Kingdom, 1914–1920*, Oxford, 1921, pp. 70, 200.
22 For evidence of Cabinet concern, see PRO, CAB 42/22/12, Memorandum G.91 of 30 October 1916, 'Food prospects in 1918; memorandum by the President of the Board of Agriculture and Fisheries', and the War Cabinet discussion of 13 November 1916, PRO, CAB 42/24.
23 The growing submarine threat seems to have been instrumental in initiating the policy of home food production; D. Lloyd George, *War memoirs*, I, London, 1933, p. 677.
24 On 11 December 1916: Beveridge, *Food control*, p. 31.
25 On 1 January 1917; T. H. Middleton, *Food production in war*, Oxford, 1923, p. 166.
26 Bowley, *Prices and wages*, pp. 44–5, 52; Beveridge, *Food control*, pp. 230, 322.
27 Middleton, *Food production*, pp. 49–50; Beveridge, *Food control*, pp. 312–13.
28 See, for example, the list of rationed foods and the amounts involved in Beveridge, *Food control*, pp. 224–5.
29 *Ibid.*, p. 313.
30 Royal Society, Food (War) Committee, *The food supply of the United Kingdom, 1916*, London, 1916, p. 2.
31 Calculated from Beveridge, *Food control*, p. 313.
32 Supply figures from *ibid.*, p. 361.
33 *Ibid.*, p. 98, n. 2.
34 The number of allotments in England and Wales increased during the war from 570,000 to over 1,400,000; *War Cabinet. Report for the year 1918*, PP 1919, xxx, Cmd 325, p. 240.
35 Middleton, *Food production*, p. 155.
36 Calculated from Beveridge, *Food control*, p. 313.
37 M. Ferguson, 'The family budgets and dietaries of forty labouring class families in Glasgow in war time', *Proceedings of the Royal Society of Edinburgh*, 37 (1916–17), pp. 121–2, 134.
38 Cf. above n. 13.
39 *Report of the Committee appointed to enquire into and report upon (i) the actual increase since June 1914, in the cost of living to the working classes, and (ii) any counterbalancing factors (apart from increases of wages) which may have arisen under war conditions*, PP 1918, vii, Cd 8980 (hereafter Sumner Committee), pp. 10–15.
40 Sumner Committee, pp. 16–19.
41 Calculated from Sumner Committee, p. 17, using the standard family sizes on p. 14.
42 Public Record Office (PRO), MAF 60/104, *Expenditure on food since 1914; memorandum by the Food Controller*, 2 January 1918.
43 Calorie-equivalents from Royal Society, *Food supply*, Appendix 1a, supplemented by A. B. Callow, *Food and health*, Oxford, 1938, pp. 46–57.
44 PRO, MAF 60/104, p. 3.
45 Sources for calorie equivalents are as in note 43.
46 Beveridge, *Food control*, pp. 144–6.
47 Beveridge, *Food control*, pp. 311, 362–3; Sumner Committee, p. 18. Both these sources include ham under 'bacon'. Eggs are calculated at 2 ounces each, and 1 pint of milk at 20 ounces. Cf. Callow, *Food and health*, p. 155.

48 Although the estimate of Oddy (cf. Table 6.3 above) is that it was actually slightly lower; Oddy and Miller, *British diet*, p. 221.

49 J. C. Drummond and A. Wilbraham, *The Englishman's food; a history of five centuries of English diet*, revised edn, London, 1957, p. 438.

50 J. M. Winter, 'The impact of the First World War on civilian health in Britain', *Economic History Review*, 2nd series, 30, 3 (1977), especially section III.

51 Although Hollingsworth considers that the incidence of rickets probably rose (in Drummond and Wilbraham, *Englishman's food*, p. 439), there is little firm evidence on the subject.

52 J. H. Clapham, *An economic history of modern Britain; machines and national rivalries (1887–1914)*, Cambridge, 1938, pp. 543–4.

53 S. Pollard, *The development of the British economy 1914–1950*, London, 1962, p. 79.

54 *Ibid.*

55 War Office, *Statistics of the military effort of the British Empire during the Great War 1914–1920*, London, 1922, p. 570.

56 Bowley, *Prices and wages*, pp. 90, 106.

57 See, for example, the small number of detailed budgets for November and December 1915 in V. de Vesselitsky, *Expenditure and waste; a study in war-time*, London, 1917, ch. 3.

58 War Office, *Regulations for the issue of Army Separation allowance, allotments of pay and family allowances during the present war*, London, 1916 (dated November 1916), pp. 5–6; PRO, War Cabinet minutes, CAB 23/1, 31, Appendix II, CAB 23/6, 449 (15); Bowley, *Prices and wages*, p. 70.

59 Calculated from C. H. Feinstein, *National income, expenditure and output of the United Kingdom 1855–1965*, Cambridge, 1972, Tables 24 and 25.

60 But there was an increasing degree of housing shortage, not revealed by such types of measurement. On the other hand, the real cost of existing housing was sharply reduced by the introduction of rent control in 1915. See Pollard, *British economy*, p. 84.

61 Average UK beer consumption in 1909–13 was 35.1 million bulk barrels per annum. This had fallen to 21.4 millions in 1918; A. R. Prest and A. A. Adams, *Consumers' expenditure in the United Kingdom 1900–1919*, Cambridge, 1954, p. 76.

62 See H. D. Henderson, *The Cotton Control Board*, Oxford, 1922.

63 P. E. Dewey, 'Military recruiting and the British labour force during the First World War', *Historical Journal*, 27 (1984), 219, 222.

64 Feinstein, *National income*, Table 24.

65 Board of Trade, *Report on the state of employment in the United Kingdom in July 1918*, p. 14.

66 Prest and Adams, *Consumers' expenditure*, pp. 1–74. Other calculations give slightly different results; Feinstein, *National income*, Table 24, estimates expenditure as rising to 204 in 1918 (1909–13 = 100). A reworking of the food prices in Prest and Adams yields a higher index figure (237) for 1918 than is shown here. The differences, however, are not large enough to alter the broad picture.

67 Average level of food price index (retail) in 1918; Bowley, *Prices and wages*, p. 70.

68 Sumner Committee, p. 6.

69 A. L. Bowley, 'The measurement of changes in the cost of living', *Journal of the Royal Statistical Society*, new series, 82, 3 (May 1919), p. 351.

70 *Sources:* 1880, 1954: Hollingsworth, in Drummond and Wilbraham, *English-*

man's food, p. 430; 1909–13: Royal Society, *Food supply*, Appendix 1a; 1914–18: Beveridge, *Food control*, p. 363; 1924–28: A. W. Flux, 'Our food supply before and after the war', *Journal of the Royal Statistical Society*, n.s., 93, 4 (1930), 552–3; 1934–38: E. M. H. Lloyd, 'Food and money; some reflections on changes in food consumption and farm prices', *Journal of Proceedings of the Agricultural Economics Society*, 10, 2 (1953), 174–91, esp. p. 183.

71 The relative contributions of imported and home supplies are examined in P. E. Dewey, 'Food production and policy in the United Kingdom, 1914–1918', *Transactions of the Royal Historical Society*, 5th series, 30 (1980).

72 For example, the policy advocated in K. Mellanby, *Can Britain feed itself?*, London, 1975, chs. 6, 9.

73 The most serious error of food control was probably the meat price policy of Autumn 1917, which led initially to a glut of meat, and was followed by a serious scarcity early in 1918; Beveridge, *Food control*, pp. 146–8.

74 See J. J. Lee, 'Administrators and agriculture; some aspects of German agricultural policy in the First World War' in J. M. Winter (ed.), *War and economic development; essays in memory of David Joslin*, Cambridge, 1975.

75 The Royal Society was frequently critical of the lack of scientific basis to the policies of the first Food Controller, Lord Devonport; Report 28 (h) of the Food (War) Committee (24 April 1917) was especially damning. Lord Devonport resigned on 2 June on grounds of ill-health, and his position as Food Controller was filled by Lord Rhondda on 15 June 1917.

7

The impact of the First World War on British workers

Alastair Reid

Most of the recent literature on the impact of the First World War on British workers has tended to conform to one of two main models which might be labelled the 'social democratic' and the 'revolutionary'. Both have been based on the assumption that the working population was becoming more homogeneous in the long run (i.e. was becoming a real 'working class') and both have seen the experience of the war as a major catalyst in this process. The usual picture has assumed that both the lower middle class and skilled workers were experiencing a severe deterioration in their position while the unskilled were experiencing a marked improvement. Thus, in this view, teachers, clerks and other white-collar workers on relatively fixed incomes suffered most from inflationary price rises and so began to drop their pre-war attitudes of deference and to participate in labour organisations for the first time. Meanwhile, skilled workers, especially in the metal industries which had been the pre-war stronghold of the 'craftsman', found that their claims for special treatment were being undermined by the introduction of machinery which could be operated by less skilled men and even women, and this is said to have pushed some of them towards a revolutionary expression of their discontent. Finally, many of those at the bottom of the heap moved into better-paid sectors or more highly skilled jobs, while the gap in incomes between those still classified as 'unskilled' and those above them is supposed to have narrowed.[1]

However, while sharing a common interpretation of the levelling impact of the war on social hierarchies, the two models have diverged in their assessment of power relations. Proponents of the 'social democratic' view, most notably Arthur Marwick, have argued that mass participation in a collective effort generated a new sense of social solidarity, seen especially clearly in the wartime co-operation between trade unions, employers and the state. This in turn created a new willingness on the part of those in power to concede reforms from above and, given the increasingly homogeneous nature of popular needs which is taken for granted, it was accompanied by a greater ease in their implementation: thus the basis was laid for mass housing, mass schooling and mass health care.[2] By contrast, proponents of the 'revolutionary' view, most notably James Hinton, have seen the war as providing an opportunity for big business to take tighter control of the apparatus of government, to dupe trade union officials into a closer collaboration and to use this new position of advantage to force through unpopular measures of mass compulsion and the forcible reorganisation of labour. However, given the assumed impact of the war on social hierarchies, this initiative was opposed by increasing unity among the rank and file, and the basis was laid for an international crisis which found its sharpest manifestation in the Bolshevik Revolution.[3]

Despite their political opposition, these two viewpoints turn out on closer analysis to be two sides of the same historical coin. For they are brought together not only by their common assumptions about the increasing homogeneity of experience of the workforce but also by a shared exaggeration of the coherence and effectiveness of response of dominant political groups, and by a shared exaggeration of the degree of co-operation between the official organisations of labour and industrial employers. The benign corporatism of the one shades over into the sinister incorporation of the other.[4] The rest of this chapter will strike out in a different direction: firstly, by rejecting the common assumption that there was a long-run tendency towards the creation of a homogeneous working class and consequently making a more cautious and complex analysis of the economic and social changes brought about by the war and, secondly, by taking a different view of the relationship between the state and trade unions and, in a sense, bringing the two previous approaches together where they most diverge. This is, in effect, to combine the 'social democratic' emphasis on the openness of the state to genuine reforms with the 'revolutionary' emphasis on the persistence of serious conflicts of interest between employers and workers. Real changes did take place during the war, but largely because organised labour was strong enough to demand them and, since this strength itself depended heavily on the peculiarities of wartime political and economic conditions, most of the changes were temporary.

Wage rates, earnings and the social hierarchy

Turning then to the question of the impact of the war on social hierarchies it does seem likely that salaried workers were more seriously hit by price inflation as a result of their employers' unwillingness to grant increases in earnings, but it would be wrong to interpret this in terms of an unprecedented levelling down. In the first place, their rates of pay had already been relatively poor in comparison with those of well-paid skilled workers, their working conditions and chances of upward mobility had already been deteriorating for several decades, and there had been many indications of the weakness of deferential attitudes before the war, especially among white-collar workers in industry and among municipal employees.[5] In the second place, it would be mistaken to think of teachers, clerks and shopworkers before 1914 as a social group completely separate from 'the working class' for many of them, particularly in industrial areas, were recruited from families of manual workers and their social attitudes remained profoundly ambiguous: for each example of snobbery there can be found a counter-example of continued loyalty to their origins.[6]

Before reaching firm conclusions about the impact of the war on these occupations we would need to know a great deal more about their experiences than is currently the case. For example, it would be important to have more precise information on the proportion of white-collar workers who came under government control during the war and a more detailed analysis of their response. Further, remarkably little is known about wartime developments in private sector financial, commercial and retailing workplaces even though it was these that underwent the greatest changes as a result of the higher than average rates of enlistment of employees and the subsequent, and permanent, influx of female labour. However, what already seems very likely is that one of the most important changes which the war brought to the salaried occupations was the rapid spread of trade unionism and, moreover, it also seems likely that this was more a result of the ideological and political context than a straightforward reflex response to changing material conditions. After all, as the experience of other European countries indicates, there are several alternative forms of collective organisation available to non-manual workers and in Britain itself there was a marked reversion to professional associations in the 1920s. Some of the most important wartime influences on the 'lower middle class', then, were the example of the growing strength and effectiveness of trade unionism among manual workers, the political impact of the major increases in state intervention in the economy, and the more diffuse ideological impact of military and civilian mismanagement in a time of crisis and personal sacrifice. Thus the Association of Engineering and Shipbuilding Draughtsmen, formed on the Clyde in 1913 grew rapidly in the war years and still proudly proclaimed on its twenty-first birthday that:[7]

the Association, in its early stage of development, deliberately set its face against any suspicion of a third-party policy, throwing in its lot whole-heartedly with the trade union world, as a union determined to exercise its industrial power, at once for the economic improvement of its own members and for the good of the working class in general.

The other section of the workforce about which we know too little is that usually referred to as the 'unskilled'. Here again the standard picture, this time of improving job opportunities and rising pay, makes sense only at the most general level and should not be confused with a process of unprecedented homogenisation. For, once again, the extent of the pre-war gulf between the groups concerned, this time between unskilled and skilled manual workers, has generally been exaggerated. Though there were important differences between them before the war, few workers in British industry had absolutely no skills and all grades of the workforce adopted broadly similar forms of organisation or indeed were members of the same trade unions. A large number of men with lesser skills could expect to be gradually upgraded during the course of their working lives through plant seniority systems, and many of those permanently restricted to the role of assistants to the fully skilled were given a reasonable share in work group earnings.[8]

If the size of the pre-war gulf has usually been exaggerated so too has the degree of its closure during the war, mainly as a result of excessive reliance on national data on engineering wage rates. Certainly the differential in rates between skilled and unskilled workers was reduced by the tendency to make flat-rate cost of living increases across the board to the whole spectrum of grades, with the same sum then becoming a greater proportional increase for the less well-paid. However, the extent to which unskilled workers caught up varied significantly between sectors and the engineering improvement on differentials of 14 per cent was unusually high: the average for other heavy industries being nearer 7 per cent (see Appendix 7.1).

Whether or not either of these figures proves the existence of substantial homogenisation is open to interpretation and it must be noted immediately that they do not represent actual incomes, let alone standards of living. It is important in this field to distinguish between standard rates set as a result of local or national collective bargains and the actual sums paid out to individual workers at the end of each week, which will be affected by overtime, bonuses and above all by the extent of payment by results as opposed to payment by the hour. It would be expected that similar increases in pay would have disproportionately large effects on workers paid by results in a period of high demand for their products and unlimited opportunities for hard work. Initially there would seem to be good a priori reasons for thinking that this would contribute even further to the narrowing of differentials between skilled and unskilled workers in wartime industry, for in most engineering shops those with lesser skills were paid by results while the highly skilled toolmakers and toolsetters were usually paid by the hour. However, as well as formal national bonuses like the 12½ per cent bonus to time workers in 1917, there were also innumerable informal bonuses set up on a shop-by-shop basis to protect scarce skills and, in fact, from late in 1916 there was also a marked spread of piecerates into the highly skilled grades of the engineering workforce; all of these measures being consciously intended to offset any erosion of pre-war differentials.[9] Moreover, the whole picture was quite different outside the engineering shops for in steel and shipbuilding the pattern of wage payment was reversed, with the fully skilled workers having their earnings linked to output by sliding scales and piecerates while those on time wages, and likely to lose out in a period of high output, were the already less well-paid unskilled workers. Thus more fully considered a priori reasoning indicates that the relative improvement in earnings made by unskilled engineering workers would have been no more than and would probably have been less than the improvement indicated by the figures for wage rates, while in other metalworking sectors we would expect to find an actual deterioration in unskilled workers' earnings positions. Unfortunately reliable data on take home pay is very scarce, which is why so much attention has to be paid to a priori assumptions. However, an important Engineering Employers' Federation survey of regional take home pay indicates that the average improvement in unskilled earnings was indeed significantly lower than the parallel improvement in wage rates, increasing by 11 per cent as opposed to 14 per cent. Meanwhile, data from one Clydeside shipyard shows a tendency for the differential between skilled and unskilled earnings to *widen* by up to 6 per cent (see Appendix 7.2).[10]

The wartime experience of unskilled workers as measured by changes in their position in the hierarchy of incomes is therefore likely to have been quite diverse, with some groups experiencing improvement and others deterioration. Moreover in assessing the significance of those cases in which differentials were reduced it is important to note in most of them the pre-war pattern was very rapidly restored after 1918. Indeed one of the most striking features of the pay structure in Britain has been its long-term stability, within which short-term disruptions have been tolerated by the better paid as temporary concessions to prevent real suffering inperiods of high price inflation.[11] Thus it would seem likely that feelings of profound threat or of a strong increase in common interests would have been substantially diluted even in sectors with significantly narrowed wartime wage differentials. As in the case of white-collar workers, then, what is striking about the experience of the unskilled is not so much a straightforward change in their economic and social position as the massive extension of trade unionism throughout their ranks. Perhaps, indeed, the appearance of a major improvement in their position was largely a reflection of the sudden strengthening of their institutional presence and the reactions which it provoked, for during the war the unskilled had stronger trade unions, more substantial recognition from employers and a much better position in formal collective bargaining than they had ever had before.

In any case the assessment of the overall impact of the war on unskilled workers depends very heavily on our assumptions about what was happening to the skilled. Here we have a far more substantial body of historical writing but unfortunately it has almost all contributed to an exaggeration of the degree to which skilled workers were downgraded by wartime dilution and mechanisation. Most research has focused on the engineering industry, which certainly makes sense given its centrality to war production and the political interest of the shop stewards' movement. However, too much credibility has been given to the claims of revolutionary currents among the engineers and it has too often been assumed that engineers were the paradigm case.[12] Whatever was going on in engineering, research into shipbuilding brings to light a very different picture. Here the unions were so strong both in the yards and at district level that the dilution of labour with women and unskilled men was almost negligible, and when machinery was introduced it was largely on terms set by the skilled men. The employers tacitly recognised the centrality of skilled labour to production by focusing on attempts to increase its mobility through the relaxation of demarcation lines between skilled occupations, but here too the unions were strong enough to restrict changes to levels acceptable to their members.[13]

There seems to have been equally little change in the position of skilled workers in coal and steel, and in engineering itself the impact of the war needs to be carefully reconsidered. In the first place, the extent of dilution has been exaggerated: far from being general throughout metalworking it was focused squarely on the production of motors, guns and above all shells. In the second place, its signiffcance has generally been misunderstood, for the main aim was not to downgrade skilled men but on the contrary to release them from more menial tasks so that they could be moved to areas of activity in which their training could be more extensively used. For some this meant enlistment into the military technical corps, but for many it meant a marked upgrading to supervisory, toolmaking and toolsetting positions. In fact, just like the employers' attempts to increase mobility in shipbuilding, the focus on dilution was a tacit recognition of the continued indispensability of skilled labour in British industry. Finally, the degree to which the introduction of female labour was felt as a threat to skill has been exaggerated. Though it was indeed an initial shock, it soon became clear that most women were going to be working either on unskilled tasks or in separate shell shops which would be closed after the war. That small proportion which did encroach on pre-war definitions of tradesmen's work soon came to be seen as advantageous by the skilled unions for it was expected that they would be more easily pushed out after the war because differences in levels of skill would be highlighted by the clarity of sexual differences.[14]

Given the general stability of their position in the division of labour it would seem highly unlikely that skilled workers lost out substantially on the wages front. No doubt the margin of advantage was reduced in some cases but on the whole their collective bargaining position was strong enough to guarantee that they could win it back again quite quickly. For even though the organisational strength of the skilled men was less novel and increased less dramatically, it too was on the increase. It was the skilled unions who led the way in the first two years of the war on both the industrial and the political fronts and it was always the skilled men who were most involved in bargaining and consultation with the government.

Unions and the state

There was, then, no simple overall impact of the First World War on the social and economic position of British workers for the forces in operation did not all act in the same direction. There were tendencies, counter-tendencies and movements off at a tangent, and in all this complexity it should be stressed that there was both more continuity and more sectoral unevenness than has usually been acknowledged. What working people shared during the war was not an increasingly homogeneous class position but rather a common experience of institutional changes.

Thus the one persistent thread running through all the occupational experiences discussed so far has been the wartime expansion of trade unionism, a point which can hardly be stressed enough. Following the famous explosion of organisation in 1889, trade union growth had only been gradual and had faltered in many sectors during the 1900s, only beginning to increase rapidly again during the 1911–13 boom. Labour therefore entered the war in an optimistic and aggressive mood and the whole wartime experience, as well as the brief post-war boom, confirmed a major advance in its economic and organisational power. Figures for total union membership indicate an increase from 2.5 million to 4.0 million during the pre-war boom, from 4.0 to 6.5 million during the war itself, rising again to over 8.0 million by 1920, that is, a more than threefold increase over the decade 1910 to 1920.[15] Growth rates were, of course, most spectacular in those sectors with the lowest starting points, like the white-collar workers and unskilled labourers, but rates of expansion were also high among those already fairly well-organised, with the Amalgamated Society of Engineers, for example, growing at an above average rate. Even more crucially, the skilled unions were able to raise their membership subscriptions and so build up enormous welfare and strike funds during the war years: the Boiler-makers' Society, for example, increased its reserves to over £750,000, while the engineers built up a phenomenal fund of £2.5 million.[16]

The significance of this increase in the strength of the unions was greatly magnified by wartime changes in the nature of the state. Even before 1914 industrial employers had been surprisingly marginal to government decision-making: the wealthiest and most powerful property owners in Britain were almost always landowners and bankers, and civil servants were normally formed in the London–Oxford–Cambridge triangle, quite remote both geographically and culturally from the centres of heavy industry.[17] The war made the products of that industry even more vital to the survival of the nation and its owners were able to make vast profits out of the urgency of demand and their own ability to manipulate prices on government con-tracts. However, paradoxically, the consideration of their interests became even more marginal to the process of government policy formation for the main goal of the state was no longer to maintain stability within a privately-owned market economy but rather to defend national sovereignty by any means available. As the war dragged on, market mechanisms and the free-dom of property holders were more and more undermined by the develop-ment of a set of highly centralised government regulations which eventually spread to cover the supply of the bulk of food and raw materials, the allocation and wages of labour, and the output norms of most major industries.[18]

This suspension of the habitual assumptions of political economy gave even more room for manoeuvre to all elements within the civil service which had become sceptical of the virtues of *laissez-faire*, in particular to those radical Liberals and ex-trade unionists who had been responsible for labour policy within the pre-war Board of Trade. The influence of this group began to increase early in 1915 when Board of Trade arbitrators were asked for reports on industrial problems, leading rapidly to the formation of the 'Committee on Production', then to the wholesale transfer of Board of Trade officials into the Labour departments of the Ministry of Munitions in the summer of 1915 (where they insisted on a wartime tax on profits), and eventually to the creation in 1916 of a separate Ministry of Labour with ambitious goals for social reform. Throughout this whole process the main aim of these officials was to subordinate employers' demands firmly to the national interest and to engage in the most extensive and sympathetic con-sultations with trade unionists at both national and local levels.[19]

These changes in the nature of the state during the war had a dual effect on British workers. In the first place, they felt a marked increase in their power, not only because of the urgent need for labour in war industries, the extremely low levels of unemployment and the growth in the strength of

THE IMPACT OF THE WAR ON BRITISH WORKERS

trade unions, but also because the official administration of labour policy was biased decisively towards their interests. This did not mean that there were no conflicts between trade unions and the government nor did it eliminate friction within the unions between leaders and members, and it certainly did not prevent industrial disputes. But it did mean that all of these tensions were acted out within a framework of extensive union influence on government labour policy.[20] In the second place, British workers' experience of the wartime state was largely formulated in terms of 'war collectivism'. This was probably greatest in the case of those working in 'controlled establishments' in engineering and shipbuilding, for here many workers now felt themselves for the first time to be direct employees of the state and almost all were entering into the new experience of successful bargaining with the government over wages, hours and working conditions. Something of this was also felt by employees in the coal mines, on the railways and in shipping and as a result there was a general tendency for organised labour to drop its pre-war separation of 'economic' and 'political' issues. Thus the unions most centrally involved in the war effort began very rapidly to raise non-industrial issues when they made demands on the government (perhaps most marked in the case of house rents), there was a slowly growing acceptance among all trade unionists that the election of Members of Parliament could have a direct effect on industrial conditions, and there was a marked increase in trade union support for the permanent nationalisation of key industries, above all coal mining and railways. Furthermore, even those not immediately involved in war production could see demonstrated for the first time on a national level the validity of the socialist claim that private enterprise was not the only viable form of economic organisation, and the growing interest in socialist ideas was consolidated and heightened by the dramatic events in Russia in 1917. Even after the Bolshevik seizure of power in October most strands of socialist opinion in Britain continued to support the Soviet experiment and to benefit from the excitement which it generated.

Our knowledge of government intervention in the British war economy is still rather sketchy and superficial and we need more research on the diverse influences which helped to shape policy. For example, it would be valuable to know more about the influence of the City of London on the decision to finance the war by borrowing rather than by taxation. For this would seem to have had a vital effect both on the fairly high levels of popular consumption permitted during the war and on the period of severe government stringency and reluctance to finance expensive social reforms after 1921. There is also a great deal more to be uncovered about the relations between industrialists and the state, for it seems likely that one reason for their truculent acceptance of a very unfavourable labour policy was the allocation of contracts on a cost-plus basis, which meant that profits rose in direct proportion to increases in wage bills; and there are several indications of widespread collusion and corruption to increase gains on munitions contracts.

What has, however, become clearer as a result of recent research is that industrial employers did not control government labour policy, nor did they approve of the direction it was taking in the hands of the metropolitan liberal-radicals. If the state is seen as a set of institutions responsive to pressure from powerful social groups then the war years saw a significant shift in the balance of power towards organised labour. And this wartime combination of increases in labour's strength and political influence along with the changes in popular attitudes towards state intervention, goes a long way towards explaining the emergence of a separate Labour Party in the immediate post-war years, without recourse to doubtful arguments about a major shift towards the increasing homogeneity of workers' economic and social experiences.

The wartime advantage of labour was, however, a temporary phenomenon and the story of the 1920s was one of continuous defeats, wage reductions and organisational decline as the employers clawed back all, and more, that they felt they had lost. At the same time the political legacy of the war was more long-lasting, for it had demonstrated the feasibility of collectivism, given real life to the idea of socialism and helped to set the Labour Party on its feet as the largest element in the parliamentary opposition. Organised labour therefore found itself faced with an unfortunate combination of political growth and industrial collapse which was to be the strategic weakness of both the inter-war Labour governments. The legacy for society at large was equally mixed. Despite the very rapid dismantling of economic controls there were some lasting advances in welfare, most notably the 1919 Act which laid the basis for publicly financed housing, and there was also a permanent decline in domestic service and other purely menial tasks. At the same time, however, the economy was being locked ever more firmly into a pattern which was increasingly inappropriate for the rapidly changing international context. Wartime investment subsidies, cost-plus contracts and particularly the post-war boom had encouraged a huge flood of capital into the traditional heavy industries, involving even the banks for the first time, and this fresh wave of investment posed a very substantial barrier to all attempts at industrial reorganisation during the inter-war years. The legacy of the First World War, then, was that paradox which has dogged Britain throughout the twentieth century: gradual social advance and accelerating economic decline.

Appendix 7.1
Changes in standard wage rates 1914–18

Engineering: weekly rates (shillings)

	Fitters and turners	Labourers	Labourers' rates as % of fitters'	Change 1914–18 (%)
1914	38.91	22.83	58.7	—
1918	67.33	48.66	72.3	+13.6

Shipbuilding: weekly rates (shillings)

	Platers	Labourers	Labourers' rates as % of platers'	Change 1914–18 (%)
1914	40.33	22.83	56.6	—
1918	77.83	48.66	62.5	+5.9

Coal: shift rates (shillings)

	Hewers	Screenmen	Screenmen's rates as % of hewers'	Change 1914–18 (%)
1913	8.41	4.50	53.5	—
1918	16.33	9.83	60.2	+6.7

Source
A. L. Bowley, *Prices and wages in the United Kingdom, 1914–1920*, Oxford, 1921

ALASTAIR REID

Appendix 7.2
Changes in earnings 1914–18

Engineering: national average weekly earnings (shillings)

	Fitters	Labourers	Labourers' earnings as % of fitters'	Change 1914–18 (%)
1914	43	26	60.5	—
1918	104	74	71.2	+10.7

Source
R. A. Hart and D. I. Mackay, 'Engineering earnings in Britain, 1914–68', *Journal of the Royal Statistical Society*, 138 (1975), 32–50

Shipbuilding: average earnings at Connell's yard on the first pay day in April (shillings)

	Platers	Labourers	Labourers' earnings as % of platers'	Change 1914–18 (%)
1914	34	20	58.8	—
1918	59	31	52.5	−6.3

Source
C. Connell Pay Books in Strathclyde Regional Archives (T – CO 25)

Notes

1 For a comprehensive survey see B. A. Waites, 'The effect of the First World War on class and status in England, 1910–20', *Journal of Contemporary History*, 11 (1976), 27–48.
2 A. Marwick, *Britain in the century of total war*, London, 1970, pp. 95–127.
3 J. Hinton, *The first shop stewards' movement*, London, 1974, pp. 23–100; J. E. Cronin, 'Labour insurgency and class formation: comparative perspectives on the crisis of 1917–1920 in Europe' in J. E. Cronin and C. Sirianni (eds.), *Work, community and power*, Philadelphia, 1983, pp. 20–48.
4 For an explicit attempt to combine both views see Waites, 'Effect of the First World War', pp. 41–5.
5 For the example of draughtsmen in shipbuilding see A. J. Reid, 'The division of labour in the British shipbuilding industry, 1880–1920', Cambridge PhD, 1980, pp. 75–82.
6 For example, the social background of activists in the West of Scotland before the war which makes it clear that the leadership of the labour movement was dominated by the 'lower middle class', especially school teachers, journalists, small employers and shopkeepers, see W. Knox (ed.), *Scottish labour leaders, 1918–*

1939, Edinburgh, 1984 for entries on Patrick Dollan, William Haddow, David and George Hardie, Thomas Johnston, James MacDougall, John Maclean, James Maxton, James Stewart and John Wheatley.

7 G. W. Thompson, *Short history of the Association of Engineering and Shipbuilding Draughtsmen*, London, 1934, p. 6.

8 For a general argument about the structure of the workforce before 1914 see A. J. Reid, 'The division of labour and politics in Britain, 1850–1920' in W. J. Mommsen and H.-G. Husung (eds.), *The development of trade unionism in Great Britain and Germany 1880–1914*, London, 1985, pp. 150–65; and for the cases of steelworkers, flintglass makers and shipbuilders see F. Wilkinson, 'Collective bargaining in the steel industry in the 1920s' in A. Briggs and J. Saville (eds.), *Essays in labour history 1918–1939*, London, 1977, pp. 102–32; T. Matsumura, *The labour aristocracy revisited. The Victorian flint glass makers 1850–80*, Manchester, 1983, pp. 199–211; Reid, 'Division of labour', 1980.

9 G. D. H. Cole, *Workshop organisation*, Oxford, 1923, pp. 61–3.

10 For evidence of increasing differentials in steel see Wilkinson, 'Collective bargaining', especially pp. 115–21.

11 G. Routh, *Occupation and pay in Great Britain 1906–60*, Cambridge, 1965, pp. 147–8, 150–1.

12 Hinton, *Shop stewards' movement, passim*.

13 A. J. Reid, 'Dilution, trade unionism and the state in Britain during the First World War' in S. Tolliday and J. Zeitlin (eds.), *Shop floor bargaining and the state*, Cambridge, 1985, pp. 46–74.

14 *Ibid.*; I. McLean, *The legend of red Clydeside*, Edinburgh, 1983, pp. 28–110; H. A. Clegg, *A history of British trade unions since 1889. Volume II 1911–1933*, Oxford, 1985, pp. 139–41.

15 H. Pelling, *A history of British trade unionism*, London, 1972, pp. 288–9.

16 United Society of Boilermakers and Iron and Steel Shipbuilders *Annual Report*, 1931, pp. xx–xxi; Amalgamated Engineering Union *Financial Report*, 1931, pp. 120–1.

17 W. D. Rubinstein, 'Wealth, elites and the class structure of modern Britain', *Past and Present*, 76 (1977), 99–126; M. J. Wiener, *English culture and the decline of the industrial spirit 1850–1980*, Cambridge, 1981.

18 R. H. Tawney, 'The abolition of economic controls, 1918–1921', *Economic History Review*, 13 (1943), 1–30.

19 R. Davidson, 'The Board of Trade and industrial relations 1896–1914', *Historical Journal*, 21 (1978), 571–91; R. Lowe, 'The Ministry of Labour, 1916–1924: a graveyard of social reform', *Public Administration*, 52 (1974), 415–38.

20 Reid, 'Dilution, trade unionism and the state'; Clegg, *History Volume II*, pp. 163–8.

8
The impact of the First World War on French workers

Patrick Fridenson

It has long been held that the period of the First World War was an interruption or temporary deflection of trends in the economic and social history of France. But even short-term developments have lasting effects, and some of the transformations affecting French industry and society in 1914–18 were so deep that they persisted well into the inter-war decades. Thus a new interpretive framework is necessary, in which more stress is placed on the far-reaching ramifications of the war experience.

The subject of the impact of the war on the French working class is a difficult one with which to test the relative merits of interpretations stressing continuity and discontinuity in the war decade. Data on wages are scattered and incomplete. Official statistics on strikes are unreliable. The mail, the press, and printed books all bear the marks of censorship. There are only a few studies of the war years in particular areas or industries.

Still, it is hard to deny the significance of the war experience in some areas, for instance, in terms of the growth of the foreign labour force, the emergence of the Communist party, and the changing role of the state in economic life. Each proceeded from the dynamics of wartime industrial mobilisation, which modified the composition of the labour force, changed conditions of life at home and at the workplace, and transformed the power of the state and perceptions of its appropriate role in French society. It is to these issues that we shall address these general remarks.

The composition of the labour force

The geographical distribution of the French working class changed during the war. New sources of labour were mobilised. The predominance of skilled labour was severely reduced. Clearly the trend was towards a more heterogeneous working class.

A NEW GEOGRAPHY OF WORK

The German invasion of the north and east of France, coupled with the expansion of war production, led to a major relocation of industry. The main beneficiaries were the cities and environs of Rouen, Tours, Bourges, Bordeaux, Marseilles, Lyons, and Grenoble.[1] They received both firms located in occupied territory and new branches of expanding or newly created companies.[2] These new workplaces made it inevitable that labour mobility would increase substantially. Some workers moved with their factories. Others were conscripted, and then sent to work far from their pre-war homes; this was especially true with respect to the southern half of the country.[3]

These mobile workers added elements of homogeneity and diversity to the indigenous workforce which they joined. They spread the customs and traditions of their original industrial centre, especially in terms of unionisation and syndicalism. But they often had trouble in mixing with the local labour force and its leaders.[4]

These developments also affected some older industrial cities. For example, the region of Paris received displaced firms and developed new trades, such as spinning mills. This turned a metropolis of specialised crafts into a centre of mass production industries. This is one trend that proved irreversible after the war.[5]

NEW SOURCES OF LABOUR

The war effort required more than a simple transformation of the geography of production. In addition, a major influx of new workers was inevitable, as soon as the stalemate of 1915 began. For this purpose, national reserves of labour were tapped: adolescents, women, and disabled men. Employers gradually used them all. They also drew upon new resources provided by the war itself: foreign refugees and prisoners of war.

Again, this was not enough.[6] The only option left was a massive recourse to foreign workers.[7] Like women, immigrants formed a sizeable part of the labour force before 1914. France sheltered two million residents at the outbreak of the war. During the conflict, a further 500,000 entered the country. Some were foreign (Polish, Belgian, Italian, Spanish, Portuguese, Serbian, Greek, Turkish, Chinese) or colonial (Tunisian, Algerian, Moroccan, Madagascan, Indo-Chinese). Thirty-five per cent came from Spain, and 33 per cent from China and French colonies.

This ethnic mix was quite different from that pertaining in the pre-war period. But of even greater importance was the fact that the war made

France the second greatest receiver of immigrants in the world, trailing only the United States. The results were on occasion turbulent. Migrant workers had trouble acclimatising to French culture, its food, climate and language, as well as its traditionally low levels of pay. In return, French workers frequently met these newcomers with fear and suspicion, which on occasion spilled over into hostility.

We shall not dwell on the subject of women's work, which is addressed by Jean-Louis Robert (see below, chapter 9). Suffice it to say that by 1916, women, adolescents and foreign workers made up fully half of the workforce in munitions.

A REDISTRIBUTION OF SKILLS

On the whole, the working class had become more diverse socially and ethnically during the war. The new sources of labour were also less skilled than was the pre-war labour force. Before 1914, skilled workers accounted for the majority of the labour force. This was true in most trades, although not in the textile sector. During the war some groups – miners, railwaymen and printers – did not experience major changes in the skill composition of the labour force.[8] But most others did.

Some qualifications are needed here. Some new skilled trades were created, and a few older ones prospered and grew, such as tool and die-makers or machine setters. But such developments affected only a minority of the working class.[9] For the majority, deskilling was the rule. Both the number and the relative weight of semi-skilled labour in industrial work soared. The sources of this change were clear: the collapse of traditional import channels, the shortage of labour, the proliferation of army orders. They all prompted the spread of new machines, the reorganisation of space within factories, and the introduction of new products. They also provided a favourable setting for rationalising the labour process.

Some historians claim that the 'scientific management' of work in the workshop – or Taylorism, as it came to be called after the American engineer, Frederick W. Taylor, who set out the principles of workshop management – was not well-developed during the war, coming in only after the Armistice. Recent research, though, points to the variety of methods derived from Taylorism, frequently variants of the original, applied in wartime in a number of sectors of the economy.[10] In munitions factories, semi-skilled labour made up largely of women, foreigners, and adolescents, predominated. In other places, where production tasks remained complex, the preponderance of skilled labour declined, but at a slower pace.

This change in the skill composition of the labour force had three distinct effects. First, it widened existing divisions within the French labour force. In September 1917, Hyacinthe Dubreuil, a machinist and union activist, wrote a pamphlet pointing to the 'fracture' between 'workers in the private sector' – metalworkers, builders, clothing workers, chemical workers – and those in 'regulated trades' – railwaymen, transport workers, men enrolled in ship construction, match-makers, gas workers, municipal workers, hospital employees, and postmen. Not only did these latter trades enjoy the protection of their *statuts*, rules granting favourable terms of employment which had been obtained from their employers and which applied nation-wide, but they also experienced a slower and less severe shift in the role of skilled labour in their work.[11]

Secondly, trade unions consistently concentrated on the defence of the interests of the skilled worker. They always asked for the maximum use of skilled men in every factory. They insisted on imposing controls on the labour process: apprenticeship had to be protected, the skilled worker's wage differential and time-rates had to be preserved, work rhythms had to be maintained and not intensified, time and motion studies had to be limited, and average bonuses guaranteed.[12]

Thirdly, dilution opened up new job opportunities for male adolescents and for elderly men. The 1921 census shows that 70 per cent of French men were at work; the highest proportion of the male population in employment at any point in the twentieth century. This is explained in part by conscription and in part by the growing opportunities for work for men under age 18 and over age 60.[13]

Undoubtedly the French working class in wartime was more diverse than it had been in 1914. But war conditions presented all workers with similar problems of having to cope with wartime shortages and annoyances. It is to the subject of conditions of ordinary life that we turn next.

Conditions of life

A number of local surveys describe daily life on the home front.[14] They show that there was considerable variation in the difficulties workers' families faced with respect to wages and basic supplies. They also describe the compensatory effects of welfare work and other aspects of state intervention which partly compensated for wartime shortages.

BASIC COMMODITIES OF CONSUMPTION

Food was obviously the key issue in wartime. Since the days of the *Ancien Régime*, everyone knew that the absence of a minimum supply of food could threaten the legitimacy of the state. During the war, food production in France declined by at least one-third. New channels for imports had to be found, but even when located, these were fragile and far from abundant.

The food situation in France, though, never became critical. It is true that most workers' families knew deprivation in wartime, but no one starved. Families had recourse to voluntary restrictions on consumption and on new dietary patterns. The state supported the creation of new market-gardens in the cities. In addition, rationing of selected foodstuffs began only in 1917, and was generalised only in 1918.

Protests about the food situation abounded in wartime. Housewives complained in market places and in shops about prohibitive prices, poor quality and insufficient supplies of various goods. Men voiced their discontent in public meetings, in which the subject of the bread supply featured prominently. Food clearly became a matter of widespread concern, though not of anger.

The coal situation was worse. Hardship caused by high prices, queues and rationing for coal describes the lot of most French families from January 1917 on. Yet the setting of a complex inter-Allied supply machinery in co-operation with private companies finally solved the problem.[15]

Perhaps the most worrying feature of war conditions on the home front was housing. Here the situation deteriorated and stayed bad throughout the war. Rents for private accommodation climbed to unprecedented levels, which both ensured overcrowding and posed a real threat to living standards. The rapid growth of numerous urban industrial centres also accounted for the proliferation of shabby tenements. Tenants' associations agitated for the extension to the entire population of the rent moratorium of August 1914, covering soldiers' households. But on this subject, more primary research needs to be done.[16]

REAL WAGES IN WARTIME

The same must be said of the crucial subject of wages. Some basic data can be derived from the records of the Ministry of Labour and the early publications of the Carnegie Foundation on the economic and social history of the war.[17] These data are very incomplete. Local studies and business histories yield better evidence, but they are still too scattered to form a representative sample. We must, perforce, stick to the conventional wisdom on wages, though these remarks may well be superseded in the light of future research.

The available data support the view that on average real wages declined by 20 per cent between 1914 and 1918. This reflected three developments. The first is that early in the conflict, employers actually reduced nominal wages. From 1915 to mid-1917, nominal wages rose again, but not as rapidly as did prices. In the last year of the war, wages rose substantially and closed much of the inflationary gap. But even then, such relative progress did not mean that living standards rose. Rationing and the exigencies of the black market were too powerful for that. Thus we can conclude that as consumers, workers were hard hit by the war.

Some qualifications are in order here. First, let us consider the subject of women's wages. Partly because of trade union action and partly because of state intervention, the gap between male and female wages narrowed during the war, as Jean-Louis Robert points out in chapter 9 of this book. Secondly, the wage differential between unskilled, semi-skilled and skilled workers was eroded, especially from 1917 on. Thirdly, munitions workers generally were better paid than their comrades, although even these well-paid men and women had severe housing problems.[18]

We can further qualify this interpretation by reference to local studies.[19] Wages in the provinces rose more rapidly than in Paris. Mobilised workers earned less than did men out of uniform. Unions everywhere demanded across-the-board increases to meet the rising cost of living, which narrowed wage differentials. But in some places, skilled men thought this went too far and made counter-claims. Employers remained reluctant to bargain with unions and shop stewards. Consequently, the mediation of a state official or representative of a municipality was sought by the workers. Many strikes were launched simply to gain the right to bargain with employers, who defended their authority and believed that workers had sufficient resources to mitigate the difficulties of wartime life.

WELFARE WORK IN WARTIME
Social provision soared during the war, producing a modernised version of older forms of French industrial paternalism.[20] Employers wanted to stabilise the volatile workforce and to counteract the difficulties of adjustment to industrial routines faced by newcomers. They also aimed to create an ambience of consent and co-operation at the workplace.

Lodgings had to be built for war workers, to prevent their disappearance to more favourable areas. A special effort was made to create special quarters for women workers.[21] These workmen's neighbourhoods or blocks often had their own shops selling goods at reduced prices. Some firms did what they could to help foster co-operative stores. In addition, companies created or sponsored a range of sports facilities and clubs, as had occurred in the United States. In France, grants were also available for those interested in music, which alongside sport, was deemed to be a useful way of maintaining high morale and of encouraging workers to emulate the leisure patterns of other classes and to compete with each other.

At work, employers sanctioned lectures, posters and company newspapers. They developed leisure activities, such as libraries and even in a few cases, cinemas. They also built industrial canteens.[22] They paid particular attention to the needs of women workers, and especially those with young children. Infirmaries and other medical provisions were made available, in the interest of better hygiene.

In sum, French employers followed two paths to industrial welfare in wartime. The first was a liberal approach of support for co-operatives and workers' societies; the second was a more authoritarian and paternalistic attitude, according to which employers sought direct control over these social activities. In the latter case, conflict ensued, in which on occasion workers successfully wrested control of co-operatives which employers had founded.[23]

Of equal, or perhaps of greater, importance was the spread of family allowances to every railway company, every coal mine and to some metal-working firms in eastern France, such as in Montbéliard and Grenoble. These developments were soon followed by the creation of what were known as 'equalisation funds' in particular trades, to even out disparities between family allowances paid to workers in the same region.[24]

It is perhaps best to characterise as ambivalent workers' responses to this proliferation of social provision. They welcomed the efforts some managers made to alleviate the domestic difficulties they and their dependants faced. At the same time some resented the fact that in wartime their whole lives seemed to wind up under managerial supervision. Finally, these developments directed workers' attention to the role played in welfare by the state and by local authorities, which acted in concert with employers and some labour organisations in wartime to build up a network of support for working men and women.

Perceptions of the state

Changes can be discerned in workers' attitudes to the state in this period not only among activists and leaders but also within the rank and file. According to some historians, this was a natural reflection of the secular growth of labour organisations.[25] But there are at least two specific facets of the war effort which suggest that the war itself changed workers' perceptions of the political realm and its bearing on their lives. The first is the role of the state in economic mobilisation, primarily as a positive force in securing recognition and a hearing for workers' grievances. The second is the coercive role of the wartime state, primarily as a guarantor of internal order and controller of dissent.

The role of the state in economic mobilisation between 1914 and 1918 earned it the admiration of most of the labour movement. The policies of two Ministries, the Ministry of Commerce, under Clémentel, and the Ministry of Munitions, under Thomas and Loucheur, determined wartime developments in the world of industrial relations and production. Both of these ministries were largely wartime creations, which by and large worked with great efficiency. Their achievement was to make it possible to expand munitions production without damaging the civilian economy. In addition, they were influential formulators of reconstruction policy for the post-war period.

This major expansion of the economic power of the state led the trade unions and the Socialist party to formulate a grand scheme for the remodelling of the French economy, when the war was won. Completed in 1916, this programme envisioned long-term economic planning, state management of the economy, and the creation of a mixture of state monopolies and nationalised industries.[26] In effect, the state became the agent of labour's cult of production, upon which the future economic life of the country would rest.

Wartime developments seemed to reinforce this optimism about the beneficent character of the state. During the conflict, the state protected individual workers' liberties in the factory, and encouraged the collective expression of working-class demands in trade unions and other organisations. It even tolerated pacifism to a certain extent.[27] It regulated the recruitment and placement of the labour force and helped to direct to appropriate places the growing influx of female and foreign workers.[28]

In addition, the state protected the worker as a consumer, by controlling prices or improving supply; some municipalities or departmental councils even set up their own butcher shops. It promoted co-ops and helped defer rent payments.[29] Moreover, it helped the worker as producer. By setting up minimum wages for specific trades in specific regions, by creating agencies of compulsory arbitration, and by securing recognition for shop stewards, the state facilitated the conclusion of collective agreements, regulated conditions of work, and helped resolve disputes before they threatened the war effort.[30]

This was the positive side of the story. But the repressive side of the state's powers did not disappear in wartime. It emerged out of the shadows only when socialist ministers left the government in autumn 1917, at the time that Clemenceau, known for his anti-union policies, became Premier. Strict censorship was imposed on news reports of industrial relations. Mobilised workers who played a leading part in their trade unions or in pacifist agitation were recalled to their regimental depots or sent to the front. The state took these decisions after consulting employers; indeed, some recall notices were clearly issued at employers' request. In addition, some activists were laid off by employers when army service was not an option; others, who were pacifists, were prosecuted for their stand against the war.

This intensification of repression should not be exaggerated. It was carried out half-heartedly, full of inefficiency and beset by all kinds of limitations, especially at the time of the massive outbreak of strikes in 1917–18 which coincided with military difficulties at the front.[31] Beyond these moments of conflict was the dominant policy of Taylorism and scientific management, both in state-owned firms and in private companies engaged in munitions production. This approach to management accorded well with negative images of the state developed by revolutionary syndicalists and some socialists in the pre-war period.[32]

But whatever the intention of some ministers to coerce labour and control the labour force, the growth of workers' organisations had a dynamic of its own which lay behind changing perceptions of the state. As we have noted, workers organised as consumers. Tenants' associations created new branches and registered a tenfold increase in membership to a total of 100,000 by the beginning of 1919. As impressive as this was, it was dwarfed by the expansion of the co-operative movement, from 800,000 in 1914 to over two million in 1918. And this takes no account of the fact that one-third of the pre-war membership of co-operatives lived in the occupied north-east of France, and were therefore lost to the movement during the conflict. To be sure, this development was not solely a product of workers' initiatives. It was also deliberately promoted by the state, the municipalities and some employers dedicated to 'social peace'. Yet co-operative organisations provided workers with an important venue for the exercise of workers' management of their own affairs.[33]

Union organisation was also strengthened during the war. Before the war, only a minority of workers were affiliated to the Confédération Générale du Travail (CGT). Total strength in 1913 was 355,000, falling to only 50,000 in the turbulent first months of the war. But by 1918, CGT membership had soared to 600,000, which was the highest level in the organisation's history.

Most of the organised rank and file were young people, who had never been in unions before and who were very eager to get results through industrial action.[34] Most activists in the labour movement had direct knowledge of the positive side of the state's activities, including participation in bipartite commissions with employers and in tripartite commissions with employers and higher civil servants. But many activists knew as well of the state's repressive potential.[35]

It was inevitable that during the war, the unions would come to feel a marked increase in their power. Yet the major strike waves of 1917 and 1918 did not arise out of any centralised initiative; indeed the unrest challenged the strategy of the union leadership. This sense of workers' agitation arising from below is reinforced by considering the eclipse of the Socialist party in wartime. Of course, trade unionism and socialist politics were worlds apart in France, but it is surely revealing to note that party membership fell from 100,000 in 1914 to about 30,000 throughout the war. We do not yet know who remained in the party, and how many newcomers filled the gaps of those who dropped away.[36] But even after having added to the Socialist party the wartime membership of various left-wing groups, we still do not approach the pre-war total. We may conclude, therefore, that wartime militancy did not develop through politics and political channels; rather it grew via the unions and other workers' associations, whose essential counterpart was a more robust and more powerful state apparatus.

Conclusion

French society and its economic base withstood the upheaval of war. So did the health of the French people. This was largely due to the involvement of the state in the production and distribution of most goods, and in industrial relations down to the shop-floor level. Workers' wartime experiences varied considerably, but whenever the occasion arose to raise a voice of protest, over wages, working conditions, or the question of peace, it was to the state that they directed their attention and their pleas.

Reformists and revolutionaries in the labour movement derived contrary lessons from this experience. The ranks of the reformists swelled. The image of the state managing the economy for the sake of growth, consumption and welfare was no longer seen simply as an invention of French intellectuals and civil servants or of allegedly declining *petits-bourgeois* or even as an alien import of Central European ideas. Reformism had henceforth much deeper roots in the working class, a part of which during the war broke with its earlier anti-statist views. Some union leaders did not approve of some of the specific institutional reforms which emerged during the conflict. But they saw the state as the agent which had made collective bargaining possible and which in future might give further responsibilities to the working class.

At the same time, the ranks of revolutionaries also swelled. Their experience of industrial conflict, of the new role of the state, and of the protracted nature of the war radicalised another section of the labouring population and added to their will to socialise the Republic. For some of them, and for some radical soldiers returned from the front, a Communist commitment followed as a logical consequence of war experiences. And just like reformists within the union movement, who had formed their Committee of Action, those soon to join the nascent Communist movement saw the possibilities of wider political alliances.

This bifurcation of labour politics and union activity arose out of a very peculiar set of circumstances. The combination of industrial conscription, state regulation of labour, and industrial relocation produced a circulation of ideas and, simultaneously, a development of new industrial cities. This is the origin of the leadership of the new mass unionism of the immediate post-war years, which in many towns contrasted sharply with pre-war patterns of unionisation and militancy. Before the war the unions had only a minimal representation in large-scale companies. There had been no 'mass unionisation' outside of the printing trades and the docks, and only a minority of workers had been members of unions.

This upsurge of organisational strength did not survive long into the post-war years.[37] Two years after the Armistice, membership had dwindled, but the bifurcation of the labour movement was maintained and has lingered to this day. Perhaps this attests to the robust qualities of political ideas and traditions in France. Perhaps it reflects as well changes in the composition of the labour force induced or accelerated by the war. More than ever, heterogeneity was at the heart of the experience of class.

Notes

Thanks are due to Jay Winter and John Horne.

1 J. W. Dereymez, 'Les Usines de guerre (1914–1918) et le cas de la Saône et Loire', *Cahiers d'Histoire*, 26 (April–June 1981), pp. 156–81. P. Dogliani, 'Stato, imprenditori e manodopera industriale in Francia durante la prima guerra mondiale', *Rivista di storia contemporanea*, 20 (1982), 527–31. J. Bond-Howard, 'The Syndicat des Métallurgistes de Bourges during the 1914–1918 war: a study of a minoritaire trade union', PhD, London, 1985.
2 A. Dantan, 'Le Développement de l'industrie dans les cantons de Sotteville et de Grand-Couronne 1914–1939', *Etudes Normandes*, 24 (July–December 1974), 3–8. G. Declas, 'Les Usines Berliet 1895–1921' *De Renault Frères constructeurs d'automobiles à Renault Régie Nationale*, 10 (June 1979), p. 268. R. Colinet, 'Un site industriel: Nouzonville. Une dynastie industrielle de la métallurgie ardennaise: les Thomé', MA, University of Nancy II, 1979. O. Hardy-Hémery, *De la croissance à la désindustrialisation*, Paris, 1984, pp. 92–3. C. Omnès, *De l'atelier au groupe industriel*, Paris, 1980, p. 116.
3 E. Hug and P. Rigoulot, *Le Croque-rave libertaire*, Paris, 1980, p. 77. Dereymez, 'Les Usines de guerre', pp. 166–9. B. Frachon, *Pour la C.G.T.*, Paris, 1981, pp. 56, 60.
4 D. Reid, 'Guillaume Verdier et le syndicalisme révolutionnaire aux usines de Decazeville (1917–1920)', *Annales du Midi*, 96 (April–June 1984), p. 175.
5 M. C. Volovitch, 'Essai sur l'évolution et la composition de la main d'oeuvre industrielle pendant la guerre de 1914–1918', MA, University of Paris, 1968, pp. 84–98. J. P. Brunet, *Saint-Denis la ville rouge*, Paris, 1980, chapter 7.
6 H. D. Peiter, 'Les patrons, les mutilés de guerre et la France', *Recherches*, 13 (September 1978), 443–7. Volovitch, 'Essai', pp. 129–50.
7 Volovitch, 'Essai', pp. 151–69. J. van der Stegen, 'Les Chinois en France, 1915–1929', MA, University of Paris X – Nanterre, 1974. G. Hatry, *Renault usine de guerre 1914–1918*, Paris, 1978. G. Cross, 'Towards social peace and prosperity: the politics of immigration in France during the era of the First World War', *French Historical Studies*, 11 (Fall 1980), 610–32. Dogliani, 'Stato', pp. 543–50. J. Horne, 'Immigrant workers in France during World War I', *French Historical*

Studies, 14 (Spring 1985), 57–88. M. Favre-Le Van Ho, 'Un Milieu porteur de modernisation: travail et travailleurs vietnamiens en France pendant la première guerre mondiale', PhD, Ecole des Chartes, Paris, 1986.

8 M. B. Stein, 'The meaning of skill: the case of the French engine-drivers, 1837–1917', *Politics and Society*, 8 (1978), 425–7. D. Reid, *The miners of Decazeville*, Cambridge, Mass., 1985, pp. 161–3.

9 P. Fridenson, 'Automobile workers in France and their work, 1914–83' in S. L. Kaplan and C. J. Koepp (eds.), *Work in France*, Ithaca, NY, 1986, pp. 518, 522.

10 Dogliani, 'Guerra e mobilizatione industriale in Francia' in G. Procacci (ed.), *Stato et classe operaia in Italia durante la prima guerra mondiale*, Milan, 1983, pp. 333–4. For a different interpretation see A. Moutet, 'La première guerre mondiale et le taylorisme' in M. de Montmollin and O. Pastré (eds.), *Le taylorisme*, Paris, 1984, pp. 64–76, Moutet, 'Ingénieurs et rationalisation 1914–1929' in A. Thépot (ed.), *L'Ingénieur dans la société française*, Paris, 1985, pp. 71–90. See also G. C. Humphreys, *Taylorism in France 1904–1920*, New York and London, 1986, pp. 145–224.

11 H. Dubreuil, *La Vraie Cassure*, Paris, Comité de défense syndicaliste, 1917, pp. 3–4, 7.

12 E. H. Lorenz, 'The labour process and industrial relations in the British and French shipbuilding industries from 1880 to 1970', PhD, Cambridge, 1983, p. 81. J. Cavignac, *La Classe ouvrière bordelaise face à la guerre (1914–1918)*, Bordeaux, 1976, pp. 128, 130. Moutet, 'La Première Guerre', pp. 78, 80. Minutes of the Executive Committee of the Metalworkers' Federation, 24 July 1915, Paris, National Archives, 14 AS 21bis.

13 J. L. Robert, 'Nouveaux éléments sur les origines du P.C.F.', *Cahiers d'histoire de l'Institut de Recherches Marxistes*, 14 (October–December 1980), p. 16.

14 The list given by J. J. Becker in *The Great War and the French people*, Leamington Spa, 1986, is far from complete. Among others should be added: D. Charrier, 'La Vie quotidienne des Nantais pendant la première guerre mondiale', MA, University of Nantes, 1978. C. Pollet, 'La Vie quotidienne des Rouennais pendant la guerre de 1914–1918', MA, University of Rouen, 1974. J. Daniel, 'La Vie quotidienne à Rennes et en Ille et Vilaine de juillet 1918 à juin 1919', MA, University of Rennes II, 1977. J. Blot, 'La Sarthe, un département de l'arrière pendant la grande guerre', MA, University of Le Mans, 1976. J. M. Bonnefoy, 'Les Mineurs de Montceau, les mines et les métallurgistes de Chalon sur Saône pendant la grande guerre', MA, University of Dijon, 1974.

15 Becker, *La Première Guerre mondiale*, Paris, 1985, pp. 153–4. J. Gallois, 'Quelques aspects de la vie en France pendant la guerre de 1914–1918 vus à travers *L'Illustration* et quelques autres périodiques', MA, University of Reims, 1977. F. Thébaud, *La Femme au temps de la guerre de 14*, Paris, 1985, pp. 211–25. S. D. Carls, 'Louis Loucheur: a French technocrat in government, 1916–1920', PhD, Minnesota, 1982, pp. 119–37, 198–216, 255–78. Cavignac, *La Classe ouvrière*, pp. 28–48. R. F. Kuisel, *Capitalism and the state in modern France*, Cambridge, 1981, pp. 39–48. H. Néant (ed.), *La Sarthe 1914–1939*, Le Mans, 1979, documents I/11 and 12.

16 See note 14. Also, National Archives, F22 536, report by Lieutenant Meurdra, 24 May 1918. Cavignac, *La Classe ouvrière*, p. 38. Becker, *The Great War*, p. 326. Dogliani, 'Stato', pp. 534–5. Thébaud, *La Femme*, p. 180. C. Sorba, 'Edilizia popolare nella regione parigina: il caso dell' "Office Public d'Habitations à Bon Marché du Département de la Seine" (1915–1939)', *Storia Urbana*, 26 (1984),

82–3, 86–7. A. Luquet, *La Législation sur les loyers de guerre*, Paris, 1919, pp. 5–19.

17 L. March, *Le Mouvement des prix et des salaires pendant la guerre*, Paris, 1925. W. Oualid and C. Picquenard, *Salaires et tarifs. Conventions collectives pendant la guerre (1914–1918)*, Paris, 1928.

18 G. Hardach, 'Guerre, état et main d'oeuvre', *Recherches*, 13 (September 1978), 298–301. J.-L. Robert, 'Les Luttes ouvrières en France pendant la première guerre mondiale', *Cahiers d'histoire de l'Institut de Recherches Marxistes*, 11 (October–December 1977), 41–3, 48. Robert, 'Nouveaux éléments', pp. 14–15.

19 E. Pelé, 'Le Mouvement ouvrier lyonnais pendant la première guerre mondiale', MA, University of Lyon II, 1970, pp. 22–46, 155–8. Volovitch, 'Essai', pp. 191–223. Cavignac, *La Classe ouvrière*, pp. 5–12, 135–6. Hatry, *Renault*. Reid, 'Guillaume Verdier', pp. 181, 184. Lorenz, 'The labour process', p. 84.

20 A. Citroën, 'L'Organisation du travail, les règles de l'hygiène et du repos dans l'usine moderne', *La Science et la Vie*, 6 (December 1917–January 1918), 61–70. H. Godfroid, 'Les Oeuvres sociales à l'usine', *Chimie et Industrie* (September–October 1918), 341–5. M. Didier, 'Recherches pour servir à l'histoire des établissements Bessonneau à Angers des origines à 1939', MA, Paris – I, 1976, pp. 61ff. S. Schweitzer, *Des Engrenages à la chaîne*, Lyon, 1982, pp. 100–3. Hatry, *Renault*. Dogliani, 'Stato', pp. 551–5. Thébaud, *La Femme*, pp. 182–5.

21 S. Sulger-Buel, 'Les Cantonnements féminins pendant la première guerre mondiale', MA, University of Paris – VII, 1976.

22 National Archives, F22 536, report of Medical Officer Landowski, 18 February 1918.

23 National Archives, F22 532, letter from Undersecretary of State Louis Loucheur to Captain Bouffartigue, 5 October 1916. Y. Cohen, 'Quand les masses viennent au syndicat: moralisation et représentativité', *Révoltes logiques*, 5 (Summer 1979), 28–51.

24 J. Hochard, 'Les Origines françaises des allocations familiales avant 1920', in Comité d'histoire de la sécurité sociale (ed.), *Colloque sur l'histoire de la sécurité sociale*, Paris, 1984, pp. 106–11. J. P. Goux, *Mémoires de l'enclave*, Paris, 1986, p. 37.

25 Becker, *The Great War*, p. 327.

26 H. Dubreuil, *Employeurs et salariés en France*, Paris, 1934, pp. 79–81. Kuisel, *Capitalism*, pp. 34–57. J. Horne, 'Le Comité d'Action (CGT–PS) et l'origine du réformisme syndical du temps de guerre (1914–1916)', *Le Mouvement Social*, 24 (January–March 1983), 33–60. J.-L. Robert, 'Les "Programmes minimum" de la CGT de 1918 et 1921', *Cahiers d'histoire de l'Institut de Recherches Marxistes*, 18 (January–March 1984), 58–70.

27 V. Daline, *Hommes et idées*, Moscow, 1983, pp. 308–41. N. Papayanis, *Alphonse Merrheim*, Dordrecht, 1985, pp. 88–98, 105–9. Robert, 'Les luttes', p. 45. Reid, 'Guillaume Verdier', p. 177.

28 Horne, 'Immigrant workers', *passim*. Thébaud, *La femme*, pp. 169–85. Carls, 'Loucheur', pp. 77–86. Lorenz, 'The labour process', pp. 78–80. Papayanis, *Merrheim*, p. 106.

29 J. Felician, 'Remarques sur le travail des femmes dans les Bouches du Rhône pendant la première guerre mondiale' in *Colloque sur l'histoire de sécurité sociale*, Paris, 1985, p. 24. Dogliani, 'Stato', p. 535. T. Stovall, 'The urbanization of Bobigny 1900–1939', PhD, University of Wisconsin at Madison, 1984, pp. 81, 211.

30 H. Grossheim, *Sozialisten in der Verantwortung. Die französischen Sozialisten und Gewerkschaften im ersten Weltkrieg 1914–1917*, Bonn, 1978. J. Vichniac, 'Industrial relations in historical perspective: a case study of the French iron and steel industry (1830–1921)', PhD, Harvard, 1981, pp. 261–92. Volovitch, 'Essai', pp. 230–5. Lorenz, 'The labour process', pp. 81–3. Hatry, 'Les Rapports gouvernement, armée, industrie privée pendant la première guerre mondiale: le cas des usines Renault' in G. Canini (ed.), *Les Fronts invisibles*, Nancy, 1984, pp. 182–7. D. Gallie, *Social inequality and class radicalism in France and Britain*, Cambridge, 1983, pp. 224–50.

31 Robert, 'Les Luttes', pp. 45–6. Becker, 'Dalla sorpresa alla protesta: classi popolari francesi di fronte alla guerra (1914–1918)', *Movimento operaio e socialista*, 20 (September–December 1982), 395–9. Vichniac, 'Industrial relations', pp. 293–8. Pelé, 'Le Mouvement ouvrier lyonnais', pp. 224–6, 240–1. Frachon, *Pour la C.G.T.*, pp. 71–4. G. Hatry, 'Les Délégués d'atelier aux usines Renault' in P. Fridenson (ed.), *1914–1918: l'autre front*, Paris, 1977, pp. 232–4. J. P. Depretto and S. V. Schweitzer, *Le Communisme à l'usine*, Roubaix, 1984, pp. 54–9. Volovitch, 'Essai', pp. 141–3, 224–9. J. M. Salmon, 'Essai sur la lutte ouvrière dans les usines de guerre de la région parisienne en 1917 et 1918', MA, University of Paris, 1967. J. Lojkine and N. Viet-Depaule, *Classe ouvrière, société locale et municipalités en région parisienne*, Paris, 1984, pp. 231–2. G. Declas, 'Recherches sur les usines Berliet (1914–1949)', MA, University of Paris I, 1977, pp. 123–5. Carls, 'Loucheur', pp. 249–55. Reid, 'Guillaume Verdier', pp. 179–80.

32 Hardach, 'Guerre', pp. 292–4. Moutet, 'La Première Guerre', pp. 73–6.

33 Lojkine and Viet-Depaule, *Classe ouvrière*, p. 230. S. Magri, 'Le Mouvement des locataires à Paris, 1919–1925', *Le Mouvement social*, 27 (October–December 1986), p. 57. Dogliani, 'Stato', pp. 550–4.

34 J.-L. Robert, *La Scission syndicale de 1921*, Paris, 1980.

35 F. Bock, 'L'Exubérance de l'Etat en France de 1914 à 1918', *Vingtième Siècle*, 1 (July 1984), 41–51. Amdur, *Syndicalist legacy*, Urbana–Champaign, Illinois, 1986, chapter 4.

36 Robert, 'Nouveaux éléments', pp. 18–19, 23. Cavignac, 'La Classe', pp. 138–73.

37 D. Gallie, *Social inequality*; J. C. Guillaume, *Guillet. Histoire d'une entreprise 1847–1879*, Auxerre, 1986, pp. 97–113; A. Rossiter, 'Experiments with corporatist politics in Republican France, 1916–1939', DPhil, Oxon., 1986, pp. 9–81; J. F. Godfrey, *Capitalism at War*, Leamington Spa, 1988.

III
WOMEN AND WORK

9

Women and work in France during the First World War

Jean-Louis Robert

The subject of this chapter is salaried and urban work by women in France during the First World War, and more particularly, work in factories involved in the war economy. The prior organisation of women's labour and the reaction of social forces (state, employers, workers' movements) to the expansion of the female labour force during the war will be treated as subordinate themes in this brief overview of female labour in wartime.

Some salient features

HOW MANY?

Although it may seem surprising, answering the question 'Were there more women at paid work in France during the war?' is an extremely difficult matter. There is no rigorous or exhaustive census collection available; the one that was planned for 1917 was cancelled on the eve of the appointed date.

The best information is that contained in 15 surveys conducted by Work Inspectors in war plants. Seven of these surveys provide data on women's work, but particular care must be exercised in handling these statistics. Some important branches of the economy are not covered, such as railways or state-owned firms. Data are, therefore, restricted to the following trades: food, chemicals, book production, textiles, clothing, earthenware production, leather, wood, building, metalwork, transport and commerce. In all, these surveys cover a very large number of workshops and factories (between 40,000 and 50,000 establishments) employing in the order of 1.5 million workers on the eve of the war. This constitutes approximately one-quarter of the labour force engaged in industry and commerce in 1914; we have, therefore, a not inconsiderable sample to evaluate. In addition, these data cover a wide range of work situations: the vast majority report on firms

Table 9.1. Total employed and total labour force in France, 1914–1920, according to seven surveys of the Works Inspectorate

		Date of survey						
		July 1917	January 1918	July 1918	January 1919	July 1919	January 1920	October 1920
July 1914	All	1,524,959	1,469,588	1,384,049	1,272,160	1,548,410	1,372,408	1,313,377
	Female	487,474	474,342	454,642	410,729	502,261	436,398	392,393
August 1914	All	518,729	497,346	469,746	439,346	565,436	525,891	482,001
	Female	199,107	188,117	179,398	167,653	228,357	209,190	183,173
January 1915	All	—	848,055	—	291,854	744,145	666,949	691,818
	Female	—	333,020	—	—	—	263,410	264,574
July 1915	All	1,050,744	—	901,994	—	938,219	864,406	933,384
	Female	418,579	—	352,034	—	388,684	345,520	355,341
January 1916	All	—	1,185,176	—	1,037,064	—	—	—
	Female	—	475,151	—	419,035	—	—	—
July 1916	All	1,380,866	—	1,215,838	—	1,162,764	1,039,627	1,133,354
	Female	546,701	—	488,609	—	470,308	405,801	422,720
January 1917	All	1,500,016	1,432,846	—	1,226,480	—	—	—
	Female	600,759	573,499	—	481,894	—	—	—
July 1917	All	1,559,393	1,491,638	1,344,634	—	1,291,731	—	—
	Female	626,881	600,063	543,025	—	529,245	—	—
January 1918	All	—	1,481,986	1,351,646	1,281,215	1,265,666	1,085,866	1,197,870
	Female	—	595,370	548,589	527,132	515,945	423,586	444,470
July 1918	All	—	—	1,318,903	—	1,171,710	—	—
	Female	—	—	533,523	—	458,504	—	—
January 1919	All	—	—	—	1,233,158	—	1,064,468	1,162,990
	Female	—	—	—	492,800	—	399,849	412,870
July 1919	All	—	—	—	—	1,241,090	1,140,476	—
	Female	—	—	—	—	458,898	408,155	—
January 1920	All	—	—	—	—	—	1,285,540	1,326,619
	Female	—	—	—	—	—	452,056	439,585
July 1920	All	—	—	—	—	—	—	1,380,373
	Female	—	—	—	—	—	—	442,124

employing fewer than 30 labourers, which means that we have a broad base of evidence on small workshops as well as large factories.[1]

In Tables 9.1–9.3, we present data contained in these surveys. In Table 9.1, we find statistics of total labour force and total female labour force in July/August of 1914 and in January and July of the subsequent five or six years. Table 9.2 converts these data into index figures, with totals in July 1914 as the standard of comparison. Table 9.3 considers the female labour force as a percentage of the total labour force over the war period.

The first point to notice is the variation among the seven surveys in their estimates of the growth of the female labour force in wartime. For instance, one survey finds female labour 23 per cent above the 1914 level by January 1917; another puts female labour at 7 per cent below the 1914 level. One inspector notes that female labour in metallurgy has grown by 900 per cent during the war; another puts the figure at about 250 per cent. Clearly we must allow for a substantial margin of error in these data.

Nevertheless, it is still possible to draw at least one important inference from these data. It is that the wartime increase in female labour was not as explosive as some contemporaries believed it to be.

The logic of continuity over the war period is based on two premises. First, women had already worked in great numbers before the war. The French economy was characterised by a relatively high level of female participation rates in paid labour on the eve of the war. According to some estimates, the female participation rate in France stood at 35–40 per cent, which was one of the highest rates in the world.[2] Indeed, it may not be too fanciful to suggest that France was *the* land of women workers at the beginning of the twentieth century.

The importance of women's work in France is related, without doubt, to the structure of her industrial revolution. The significance of the textile industry, and the employment of women from the onset of mechanisation in most sectors of the economy, help to account for this phenomenon.[3] One early text explicitly refers to the desirability of recruiting male and female labour to nascent industrial production.

By wisely ordered instruction, it is possible to spread among the weaker sex the knowledge and talents which will create the most advantageous links between male and female labour.[4]

Indeed, throughout the nineteenth century, employers followed a clear strategy of recruiting an abundant female labour force, a phenomenon which soon enough provoked considerable comment from workers themselves.

The second reason why it is reasonable to note elements of continuity in female labour participation rates over the war period is that the 1914 level of

Table 9.2. *An index of total female labour force in France, 1914–1920 according to seven surveys of the Works Inspectorate (1914 = 100)*

	Date of survey						
	July 1917	January 1918	July 1918	January 1919	July 1919	January 1920	October 1920
July 1914	100	100	100	100	100	100	100
August 1914	41	40	39	40	45	47	46
January 1915		70		71		60	67
July 1915	86		77		65		
January 1916		100		102		79	90
July 1916	112		107		93		
January 1917	123	120		117		93	107
July 1917	129	126	119		105		
January 1918		125	121	128		97	113
July 1918			117	119	102		
January 1919				104	91	91	105
July 1919					91	93	103
January 1920						103	112
July 1920							113

Source
See note 1 and Table 9.1

overall industrial activity in France was not reached even by the last year of the conflict. This means that the increased feminisation of a section of the workforce occurred at a time of economic instability after the departure of many men for military service. Furthermore we must place women's work patterns in the general context of economic developments in a country which lost an important industrial region to an invading army in the first weeks of the war.

WHEN?

With these qualifications in mind, it is still apparent that there was a sizeable rise in female participation rates in industry in the early part of the war, after the initial disruption of mobilisation in 1914. Even before the government acted to encourage the recruitment of female labour into war industry in 1915, the influx of women workers is striking. Private effort therefore preceded state initiatives, a fact confirmed by other studies of the different strategies of state-owned and private firms (see Table 9.4).

As early as January 1915, female labour in the metal trades exceeded that of July 1914, and this demand for women's labour proceeded apace as the war economy grew. The peak in the demand for female labour was reached in late 1917 or early 1918 (see Table 9.2) and was followed by fluctuations

Table 9.3. *Percentage of women in the French labour force, 1914–1920, according to seven surveys of the Works Inspectorate*

	Date of survey						
	July 1917	January 1918	July 1918	January 1919	July 1919	January 1920	October 1920
July 1914	32	32	33	32	32	32	30
August 1914	38	38	38	38	40	40	38
January 1915		39		39		39	38
July 1915	40		39		41		
January 1916		40		40		40	38
July 1916	40		40		40		
January 1917	40	40		39		39	37
July 1917	40	40	40		39		
January 1918		40	41	41		39	37
July 1918			41	40	41		
January 1919				36	39	38	36
July 1919					37	36	35
January 1920						35	33
July 1920							32

Source
See note 1 and table 9.1

Table 9.4. *An index of female labour employed in munitions factories in France during the First World War*

	Private factories[a]	State factories[a]
January 1916	100	100
April 1916	178	123
September 1916	289	196
January 1917	358	241
January 1918	388	295

[a] January 1916 = 100
Source
Bulletin de Ministère du Travail, January–February 1918

linked to the exigencies of the war economy, in particular to the fall in demand following the Armistice, a feature of this subject not adequately illustrated in Tables 9.1–9.3. By January 1919, the index of female participation rates was again close to that of 1914 (Table 9.2). This is supported by the evidence of a survey of 952 war factories which showed a total female labour force of 110,000 in November 1918 and only 48,000 in early March

Table 9.5. *Wages of some workers in munitions factories in France, 1917–18, in francs per hour*

Category	March 1917	January 1918	August 1918
1 Girls under age 16	0.30	0.30	0.30
2 Boys under age 16	0.40	0.40	0.40
3 Girls aged 16–18	0.50	0.50	0.60
4 Boys aged 16–18	0.60	0.60	0.70
5 Labourers (female)	0.75	0.85	0.95
6 Labourers (male)	1.00	1.10	1.25
7 Semi-skilled workers (female)	0.75	0.95	1.05
8 Semi-skilled workers (male)	1.00	1.10	1.25
9 Skilled workers (male)	1.33	1.47	1.70

Source
Ministère du Travail, Tarifs des salaires et conventions collectives pendant la guerre (1914–1918), Paris, 1923

1919.[5] Within two years of the Armistice, the return of enlisted men to work brought the proportion of women among the factory labour force back to roughly the 1914 level. The wartime feminisation of work thus appears to be no more than an interlude. We shall return to this point below.

WHERE?

This query is best approached in two parts: (1) in what branches of the economy was there a real increase in women's labour? and (2) in what parts of France did such increases occur? The answer to the first query is well known: the most substantial increases in women's labour were registered in the chemical, wood and transport sectors, that is, in the production and supply of war material. Less pronounced was the growth in women's work in the textile, clothing and earthenware industries. Of course, this is what one would expect given the diversified nature of economic activity during the war.

So far we have considered absolute increases in the number of female employees. As to the proportion of women in the overall labour force, feminisation occurred in all branches of the economy, without exception. In some cases, the rise was sudden, for example in the case of metallurgy, where fully one-quarter of the 1918 labour force is female compared to one-twentieth in 1914. But the basic rule was that the hierarchy of 'feminisation' – or the proportion of women in the overall labour force – was not altered by the war, and this is true in sectors where employment grew rapidly, such as in the munitions factories, and in areas where absolute levels of employ-

Table 9.6. *An index of wages of some workers in munitions factories in France, 1917–18*

	March[a] 1917	January[a] 1918	August[a] 1918
1 Girls under age 16	100	100	100
2 Boys under age 16	100	100	100
3 Girls aged 16–18	100	100	420
4 Boys aged 16–18	100	100	113
5 Labourers (female)	100	113	127
6 Labourers (male)	100	110	125
7 Semi-skilled workers (female)	100	127	140
8 Semi-skilled workers (male)	100	110	125
9 Skilled workers (male)	100	110	128

[a]March 1917 = 100
Source
Ministère du Travail, *Tarifs des salaires et conventions collectives pendant la guerre (1914–1918)*, Paris, 1923

ment fell, such as in the book or leather industries. The clothing trades remain staffed with large numbers of women, while few were ever employed in the building trades.

The one unmistakable trend in wartime was the marked increase in women's labour, both absolute and relative, in trade, banking and insurance. This phenomenon, also visible in wartime Britain, certainly survived the termination of hostilities, and may be taken to be an important and lasting legacy of the 1914–18 conflict.

On the one hand, we confront a diversity of evidence on sectoral changes; on the other hand, we must attend to the diversity of local conditions. We can see a clear distinction between districts such as Paris, Dijon, Rouen, Bordeaux and Lyon, where women's work grew rapidly – for example, there was a 100 per cent increase in the capital – and other districts, particularly in the south, such as Toulouse and Marseilles, where the total female labour force declined and the proportion of women in the overall labour force rose slowly. With respect to the Marseilles area, the lack of progress in the mobilisation of women into the paid labour force persisted after the war. Works Inspectors' reports account for this by referring to employers' refusal to employ women, deemed to be low quality workers, and to managerial preference for hiring young male labour. The evolution of wages may help clarify the forces underlying this situation. Tables 9.5–9.6 summarise the data derived from inquiries of the Ministry of Munitions.[6] It is clear that the increase in women's wages outstripped the increase in the wages of young male operatives.

One of the reasons why women's wages increased more rapidly than those of other low-paid workers is that the Minister of Munitions made it a matter of policy to produce a more equitable balance between male and female wages. But of equal importance in the upward movement of women's pay is the impact of the strikes of May–June 1917, the incidence of which was directly related to the condition of women workers. In Paris alone there were 60 strikes in May and June 1917; the first 19 of them, breaking out after 25 May, arose out of the grievances of the female labour force.[7] Their success was not unnoticed by the Ministry of Munitions.

WHO?

Unfortunately, data do not exist to enable us to compare the origins of female war workers in France and Britain. We have only a few limited studies which describe a handful of factories. But on the basis of this evidence, we can suggest that the new women workers of the First World War period were older than the pre-war average and likely to be married. In 1914, half of the single women recruited to industry had already had paid employment, whereas only one-quarter of the newly hired married women had been at work previously.[8] We are therefore faced with a double stream: first, of women who returned to work they had already done; and secondly, women who found a new kind of job. Within this process two other trends are visible: from textiles (the *midinette*) to munitions work (the *munitionnette*); and from domestic housework to the workshop. Unfortunately the precise dimensions of these changes remain unknown to us.

JOBS?

What sort of job? A rough answer to this question would suggest that, with the exception of a few skilled tasks demanding great physical strength and some white-collar jobs, women worked at all levels of every trade during the First World War. The characteristic form of labour was in running machines of all types, for example: presses (hydraulic, printing, sealing); furnaces (in biscuit factories, iron works, etc.); saws (hand saws, chain saws, etc.); cranes (overhead, electrical); paste grinders (for the cardboard industry); lathes of all types (for shell production). Machining of the largest shells was the only job rarely performed by a woman.

Then we encounter all types of handling tasks, and other tasks requiring more physical strength. We can find many instances of women loading and unloading wagons and ships, or handling shells and spare parts within war factories. Some carried a 155 mm shell along a 15 metre passage. Others performed all kinds of arduous labour related to cutting up clothes, kneading in the food industry, nail driving and packing.

As early as 1915, women were employed at control and inspection jobs which they came more or less to monopolise. These delicate tasks were, on occasion, extremely skilled. For example, the gauging of parts is done by means of delicate instruments of calibration, such as the micrometre gauge. And even if very few people engaged in this sort of work, they occupied a crucial position in the labour process. In this way, some women (admittedly relatively few) came to be given a part in the supervision of male workers.

We have emphasised the machine-calibration, handling and inspection jobs as the three key functions of women war workers, but the range of tasks they performed was much wider still. Nevertheless, the most skilled jobs remained entirely out of the reach of women workers: there were no women typographers, tailors, cabinet-makers, mechanics, tool-makers, and (as in the building trades) some less skilled jobs remained still solely within the male preserve.

Pay differentials and relativities. There is some evidence supporting the contention that the gap between male and female workers' wages for comparable jobs narrowed during the war (see Tables 9.5–9.6). In fact, the greatest relative gains were made in the lowest paid jobs in the traditionally female branches of the clothing trades. This was due in part to the operation of the Act of July 1915 establishing a minimum wage for home workers (or 'cottage' workers). It was also a result of competition with the relatively high wages paid by employers in munitions factories.

In 1917, an experienced semi-skilled woman worker employed in the manufacture of shells earned twice as much as a woman worker in the clothing trades. This differential compelled employers to raise the wages of low-paid women workers, simply to keep them from leaving their employment.

In addition, some concessions were granted late in the war over the question of hours of work. The working day in 1917 averaged ten hours, although there were cases exceeding this figure. There was provision for two days off per month, but these were unpaid, since much munitions work was done on the piecerate basis. After the strikes and disturbances of May 1917, women workers were granted a 'weekly rest' (one day off per week, usually Sunday) and/or 'the English week' (half day off on Saturday and all day off on Sunday).

Some salient consequences

TECHNOLOGICAL ASPECTS

One way to look at women's work in wartime is as a phenomenon leading to the deskilling of the labour force as a whole. Several qualifications are necessary before accepting this contention. It is true that the presence of women in the factory compelled employers to alter the organisation of work somewhat and to think in a more elaborate manner about the labour process. Thus the distribution of tasks between men and women, though it was partial or temporary, led to the reorganisation of teams within the shop, the formation of mixed, more reliable teams, for example, ten women on a lathe, with one or two men adjusting. Another case is that of shell machining, involving 75 women to 155 men, organised in separate shops, specialising in different sizes of shells. When production is largely a man's job and inspection, a woman's, it is easy to see that a high degree of precision is needed in organising the workshop.[9]

Women's labour had another effect, perhaps of even greater importance: it led to greater and more efficient modes of mechanisation. This meant mechanisation of transportation inside the factory, with the use of inclined planes, rolling assembly lines, railheads, all designed to facilitate some tasks which women were said to find difficult or unnecessarily demanding. Motorising some machines such as hand presses, or improving some tools to reduce the strain on the wheel, helped an increasingly feminine labour force. But these steps also contributed to technical progress overall. The conclusion is, therefore, that women's work may have been deskilling, in that traditionally skilled jobs were done by people previously excluded from them, but it was also progressive in leading to greater efficiency (and hence productivity) of labour.

SOCIAL ASPECTS

Prior to the war, trade unionists were among the wide community which believed that women's entry into the labour market dragged down men's wages. What such opinion ignored was that in the area of working conditions, women's work constituted, on the contrary, a very effective instrument of reform.

The need to take care of female workers, originating either in a pronatalist attitude or in a particular perception of women's 'needs', is a constant preoccupation of state policy attitudes during the 1914–18 war.

There was also what might be termed a 'spin-off' effect whereby reforms originating out of a wide-spread concern over the supposedly special problems of women's work tended to benefit general working conditions. Consider the characteristic and influential example of Albert Thomas, the socialist Minister of Munitions. Thomas issued a memorandum in July 1917 'related to women's labour in war factories'. The memorandum states in its preamble that 'national interest demands that [women's labour] be used rationally and with great care, for it represents a reserve for the future which must be safeguarded in its entirety'. From this starting point, he developed a strategy which went well beyond the problem of women workers. On the one hand, some issues concerned women alone, such as the prohibition of night work for girls under age 18, and the protection of married and pregnant women, such as job guarantees, maternity leave, special rooms for feeding babies and the provision of crèches. But on the other hand, some measures clearly concern the labour force *tout court*. I have in mind the sanitary condition of workers' housing, health and safety of the workplace, and medical services. The case for safety or sanitation did not rest on the presence of women in the factory, but their war work was bound to raise such issues of importance to labour as a whole.[10]

As we have noted elsewhere, the possibility that women's work helped ameliorate working conditions for all was not accepted by the French labour movement, preoccupied as it was with a struggle to maintain the purchasing power of wages and to defend the working-class family against exploitation.[11] On these grounds, trade unionists virtually unanimously objected to women's labour.

In effect, at the core of the policy of the Confédération Général du Travail (CGT) during the war we find the defence of the working-class family. This meant above all the universalisation of separation allowances, increase in maternity allowances, regulation of adolescent labour. But underlying these measures lay a wider belief in the crucial importance of family life in what may be called class education, or the transmission of the conscience of the working class. In this context it was the objective of working-class leaders to defend women's crucial place in the regulation of the home. This mixture of fear that women's work would force down men's wages and would undermine working-class family life is encapsulated in a statement by Renaudel, Paris regional secretary of the clerks' union. In July 1919, he stated that 'A man's wage must be a family wage, sufficient to cover the needs of a family and a woman must cease work to dedicate herself to her social roles of wife and mother'.[12]

The strikes of women workers in May–June 1917, which in most cases were not followed by any lasting surge in trade union membership, did not help narrow the gap between the perceived interests of male and female workers. Let us take the case of the executive of the Federation of Metalworkers, which engaged in extended discussions of the problem of women's work in 1916 and early 1917. Suddenly, after July 1917, the executive ceased to discuss this issue. Why? Because the union's national council decided then to oppose the further introduction of women into metalwork. Its grounds were organisational, as one branch secretary, Labe, declared: 'We have seen the women go out on strike without a clear aim, obtain benefits, and then leave the very organisations from which they have profited'.[13]

The pacifist wing of the labour movement also added their criticism of women's war work in the war effort. By making munitions, they were

Table 9.7. *Employed women as a percentage of all persons employed, France, 1896–1962*

Employment sector	1896	1901	1906	1911	1918	1921	1926	1931	1936	1946	1954	1962
Agriculture	33.0	32.5	37.9	38.0	—	44.2	41.7	41.8	40.8	—	—	—
Industry and transport	32.4	33.7	34.8	34.8	(40.0)	31.3	27.8	26.9	26.1	—	—	—
Trade	34.9	37.1	37.7	40.6	(55.0)	43.5	40.0	42.5	42.0	—	—	—
Services	23.6	28.8	28.3	27.5	—	37.0	36.4	38.3	39.3	—	—	—
Domestic	81.0	82.0	81.6	83.0	—	87.0	86.0	86.0	87.0	—	—	—
All sectors	32.6	35.6	38.2	38.2	(46.0)	42.3	37.2	37.3	37.1	38.3	34.2	33.3

Source
Résultats statistiques des recensements. Estimates are bracketed.

Table 9.8. *Percentage of women in employment in France, 1901–62*

	1901	1906	1911	1918	1921	1926	1931	1936	1946	1954	1962
As per the census	—	39.0	38.7	(47.0)	39.6	37.5	37.1	34.2	—	—	—
Revised[a]	36.0	36.0	35.5	(47.0)	35.5	33.0	33.0	30.5	32.0	30.0	27.5

[a]See note 2
Source
See Table 9.7. Estimates are bracketed.

deemed to have opted for nation rather than for class, thus prolonging the war itself. The validity of this criticism is, of course, debatable, but the attitudes which lay behind it help reinforce the view that women's work raised highly controversial issues in the course of the First World War.

REFLECTIONS ON LONGER-TERM CONSEQUENCES

The First World War marks a divide between two aspects of the long-term history of women's labour in France. Until 1914, the trend is towards an increase in the proportion of women who work and in the proportion of the labour force that is female. After 1918, the trend is reversed. The war, therefore, marks both the zenith of the secular trend of women's work and the onset of a 50-year pattern of decline in the role played by women in the French labour force.

Data on this phenomenon are presented in Tables 9.7 and 9.8. Some doubt remains as to the accuracy of these statistics, in particular with respect to agriculture. The years 1906 and 1921 appear from these data to have been years when women's work in agriculture increased, but this is probably untrue, reflecting the looseness of the statistical criteria employed therein. At other dates, for instance in 1911 and after 1954, more rigorous criteria are applied to the classification of women's work, particularly in agriculture. Therefore, the sizeable increase of women's jobs as a share of all jobs, from 38.2 to 42.3 per cent, probably reflects the evolution of the agricultural rather than of the industrial world.

With such qualifications in mind, it is still possible to see in these data evidence that the First World War marks the beginning of a secular decline in women's employment in France. There is a dip in female participation rates as early as 1921 in the 15–54 age group. Equally clear was a rise in the labour force participation rates of males, no doubt to compensate for war losses. With the exception of the Second World War, this decrease in women's labour persisted for a full half-century. The percentage of all persons who were women increased from 32.6 per cent in 1896 to 38.2 per cent in 1911, and reached 46 per cent during the war. The rate then declined to 37.1 per cent in 1936 and 33.3 per cent in 1962 (Table 9.7). The most severe and most rapid decline was registered in the industrial and transport sectors where women who had represented 35 per cent of all those employed in these sectors in 1911 (and 46 per cent during the war) accounted for no more than 26 per cent of the labour force in 1936. The data in Table 9.8 are more difficult to interpret since variations in women's labour force participation rates are affected by a variety of factors, some demographic, some educational. Nevertheless the trend in female labour force participation rates lends strong support to the above conclusions, since the rate was steady prior to the war and in a continuous decline thereafter.

Of course, we must note that this trend is related primarily to the overall decline in manpower in the two most important sectors of female employment: the textile and clothing trades. This long-term trend towards the disappearance of the 'conventional' nineteenth-century female worker clearly more than outweighed the movement of women into other branches of the economy.

With respect to women's work, therefore, the economic exigencies of war had little permanent impact. Consider the case of metallurgy: in 1911 5.5 per cent of the labour force was female; about the same as in 1906. By 1918 this had risen to 25 per cent only to fall back to 9.5 per cent in 1921, at which level it more or less remained throughout the inter-war period. In other words, the proportion of women in this one sector of the labour force did indeed rise, but only slightly. The same applies to virtually all branches of industry that employed women during the war.

The major contrast is with respect to the service sector. The professions, trade and the general category of services are the growth areas of female employment during the war which continued to grow in the inter-war years. Consider the case of banking and insurance: in 1906 5.5 per cent of the workers were female (roughly the same as in metalwork); in 1921, 28 per cent were female; and in 1931, 31 per cent. It is clear that the longer-term impact of the First World War on women's work must be sought here. The office worker, the masculine prototype in the world of Balzac and other nineteenth-century writers, turns feminine in the first half of this century, and has remained so to this day.

In sum, the First World War is the apogee of a trend towards increased women's labour which had been in motion since the middle of the nineteenth century. By 1914 this trend was somewhat running out of steam. After the war and for half a century, women's participation rates declined, and so did the degree of feminisation of the labour force. Of course it is possible that this reversal of trend would have occurred even without the experience of war. But the war, in sharpening the trend towards female labour, led many to see a number of negative connotations in this phenomenon, and thereby contributed to its reversal. After the First World War, the housewife outnumbered the worker/housewife described by Michelle Perrot as a characteristically nineteenth-century figure.[14] The 1914–18 war, which dragged hundreds of thousands of women to the factory for a few years, did not impose this pattern of activity on their lives in subsequent decades.

In the post-war period a strengthened workers' movement retained deep reservations about women's work while employers were left by their war experience hesitant and doubtful as to their own interests. Meanwhile both the government and society were imbued with pronatalist values, naturally strengthened in a country counting the human costs of war in terms of 1.3 million dead and a further decline in the birth rate. It is scarcely surprising, therefore, that the culture was still receptive to the conventional imagery of women's tasks. Not a single illustration of the *munitionette* had appeared in the popular press during the war.[15] Some demobilised soldiers were exasperated by women who wanted to retain the jobs they had taken on during the war,[16] and who seemed to refuse to accept the obligations of the 'warriors' rest'. All these trends run in the same direction: towards a resounding 'no' to female labour, 'no' to the woman worker.

Those most directly concerned largely kept silent. Above all, women had withstood the challenges of their stay in the factory. Many had known both the freedom of financial independence and community alongside the hardships of difficult and exhausting labour. In any event, no one asked them for their opinions on the upheaval of war. Only a few militants carried the memories with them into peacetime struggles.

Notes

Translated by Jay Winter.

1 The major sources for this study are the statistics and other evidence found in the issues for the war years of the following journals: *Bulletin du Ministère du Travail*; *Bulletin de la statistique générale de la France*; and *Bulletin des usines de guerre*. Specific references to articles or tables found therein have not been provided. For an overview of the situation of women during the war, see M. Frois, *La Santé et le travail des femmes pendant la guerre*, Paris, 1926 and F. Thébaud, *La Femme au temps de la guerre de 14*, Paris, 1986.

2 *Résultats statistiques de recensement général de la population, mars 1911*, Paris, 1913. Census figures have been revised by J.-J. Carre, P. Dubois, E. Malinvaud, *La Croissance française, un essai d'analyse économique causale de l'après-guerre*, Paris, 1972.

3 *Statistique de la France. Publiée par le ministère de l'Agriculture et du Commerce*, Paris, 1846, introduction, no. xviii.

4 C. Dupin, *Forces productives et commerciales en France*, Paris, 1827, p. 97.

5 Cf. *Bulletin du Ministère du Travail*, May–June 1919.

6 See *Tarifs des salaires et conventions collectives pendant la guerre (1914–1918)*, Paris, 1923.

7 J.-L. Robert, 'Les Luttes ouvrières en France pendant la première guerre mondiale', *Cahiers d'histoire de l'Institut de Recherches Marxistes*, 11 (1977), 28–65.

8 M. Zancarini, 'Etude du registre de la main d'oeuvre feminine aux Forges et Aciéries de la Marine de Saint-Etienne' in Université de Vincennes colloquium on 'Les Femmes et la classe ouvrière', December 1978.

9 The same point could be made in relation to conditions in the 1960s. See M. Guilbert, *Les Fonctions des femmes dans l'industrie*, Paris, 1965. This may be connected with the same division of labour within French peasant families. See M. Segalen, *Sociologie de la famille*, Paris, 1981.

10 Circulaire du Ministre de l'Armement, en date du 1 Juillet 1917, relative a la

restriction de la main d'oeuvre feminine dans les usines de guerre, BMT, June 1917.

11 J.-L. Robert, 'La CGT et la famille ouvrière, 1914–1918, première approche', *Mouvement social*, 22 (1981), 47–66.

12 Archives Nationales (AN) F7 1372;, cited in *ibid.*, p. 59.

13 Comptes rendus de la Commission executive de la Fédération des Métaux, 6 Juin 1917, déposés au Centre de Recherches d'Histoire des Mouvements sociaux et du Syndicalisme, Université de Paris I.

14 M. Perrot, 'La Ménagère dans l'espace parisien au xixe siècle', *Nouvelles annales de la recherche urbaine* (December 1980), and her 'La Ménagère et la classe ouvrière' in the Vincennes colloquium on 'Les Femmes et la classe ouvrière', December 1978.

15 Cf. the contribution below of Marie-Monique Huss on the infrequency with which girls were portrayed in the active role of nurses on the postcard literature of France during the war, esp. note 96.

16 Teaching was one of the professions which some women refused to abandon. In the post-war period, there was serious conflict between schoolmasters and schoolmistresses, reflected in the formation of the (male) 'Groupe d'action des instituteurs de la Seine', the stated purpose of which was to require that school-mistresses limit their activities to the nursery schools, for children under six years of age. See *Bulletin du Groupe d'action des Instituteurs Publics de la Seine*, no. 1, May 1918.

10

Women's work in industry and family: Germany, 1914–18

Ute Daniel

'Today seamstresses, laundresses, shopgirls and, by far the most numerous, women who have never worked before are showering bombs and grenades on the enemy; the men have been replaced by thousands of former maids who help keep the wheels of our national economy turning.'[1] That is how contemporary observers saw it, and this view has been repeated in many of the histories of the war, even the most recent ones. The German war economy of 1914–18 is said to have increased female employment to unprecedented levels and to have brought about lasting changes in its structure: 'The First World War represented an important, if not the most important leap in the development of women's work in Germany.'[2]

Against this, I would like to put forward the following arguments. First, the First World War was not accompanied by any spectacular increase in women's work in Germany. The number of women who had never worked before and who went into employment for the first time during the war remained relatively small. One major reason for this was the fact that most of the women who had never gone out to work previously, had not actually been unemployed: they had worked – and continued to work – in the family, and during the war they were needed there more than ever before. Secondly, where there was an above average increase in the proportion of women in employment, it took place not in the factories of the war industry, but within the confines of home and family. The majority of those women who during the war took up employment for the first time ever preferred homework to factory work. In this way they were able to combine domestic tasks with wage labour; a double role which became extremely hard to fulfil as the war made housework increasingly intensive and complicated. Thirdly, wartime social policy was obliged to take account of women's family ties. It institutionalised a system of material support for the families of conscripted

267

soldiers and for the unemployed, who were, in the main, women. This system of state, local government and private assistance was something completely new in terms of scale and, inadequate though it was, it actually enabled many women to stay out of industry, even though this went against the interests of the state. The attempt to use social policy as a political instrument for regulating the labour market and inducing more women to go and work in the factories was a failure.

The first part of the following account gives a sketch of developments in women's employment and housework. The second section concentrates on wartime social policy towards women and the family.

Female wage work and housework in wartime

The most reliable information about the quantitative development of female employment during the First World War is provided by the reports of the statutory sickness insurance authorities on the number of women paying compulsory contributions. Besides being the most representative and continuous source, these reports have been drawn on by studies in support of their argument that there was a great increase in women's employment during the war. The compulsory insurance provisions applied to male and female workers, clerks, with an annual income of less than 2,500 marks, servants and agricultural labourers. Together with clerks of public works, the last two categories of worker could be exempted from the obligation to contribute under certain circumstances. Likewise, not all male and female homeworkers were registered because their obligation to insure was abolished as of 1 September 1914 and not reintroduced everywhere by local statute. The totals for those covered by statutory provisions were themselves probably still too low, because the insurance offices did not always provide full information: there are only rare reports from the Post Office, the miners' welfare institutes were exempted from giving reports and other offices managed only intermittent reports during the war. As a result, the published statistics included only about 70 per cent of all workers obliged to contribute. On the other hand, male workers were over-represented because all those soldiers were kept on the books for whom the employer, local authority or trade union continued to pay contributions.[3] For this reason, the relative figures can tell us more about changes in the number of women paying contributions than the absolute figures can, if one wants to take this number as an indicator of developments in women's employment in the war.[4] Here, we are less interested in the ratio of female to male contributors (where percentage fluctuations reflect not only developments in the pattern of female employment but also and above all the conscription of male contributors) than in the percentage increase in the number of women workers between 1914 and 1918 to whom the statutory insurance provisions applied.[5]

As Table 10.1 shows, between June 1914 and June 1918 the index number of compulsorily insured woman workers rose to 117.4 (with June 1914 = 100), i.e. an increase of around 17 per cent in recorded female employment in this period. The argument that the war saw a significant growth of women's employment rests upon this figure in particular, which represents the culmination of the percentage increase in recorded female employment – leaving aside the temporarily higher figures for November/December 1917.

However plausible this may sound at first, the significance of this figure is beset with problems the moment one recalls that rates of increase only make sense when seen in relation to other data. No conclusions can be drawn from this 17 per cent rate of increase until it is compared with the corresponding pre-war rate. Between 1889 and 1913 the following pattern emerges (at four-year intervals to correspond to the duration of the war) (see Table 10.2).[6]

Between 1889 and 1913 the rate of increase in the number of female contributors declined slightly (although the numbers of women employed continued to rise) and the 1914–18 rate of around 17 per cent is consistent with this pattern. Far from indicating that the war had a great effect on the development of women's employment, these insurance figures suggest that the impact of the war was remarkably small. This somewhat surprising result is reinforced by the results of a population and employment census carried out in Bavaria on 1 December 1916.

Table 10.3 actually suggests a decline in female employment between 1907 and 1916, but this is probably an artifact of the under-recording of female agricultural 'helpers' in 1916 compared to their 'over-recording' in 1907.[7] Nevertheless, it is reasonable to conclude that in Bavaria, too, there was no noticeable above average rise in female employment, either overall or in industry in particular. Once and for all we should abandon the image of the hordes of women who supposedly appeared on the labour market for the first time between 1914 and 1918.

This prompts the question; if they were not drawn from among the ranks of women who had never worked hitherto, what were the origins of the female workers in war industry? By 'war industry' is meant in particular the metal, engineering, electrical and chemical industries, for here beyond all doubt there was an extraordinarily large increase in the number of women employed. Taking March 1914 as 100, the index number of women working in the metal industry in September 1918 was 846.7, in engineering 3,520.4, in the electrical industry 813.8 and in chemicals 436.2.[8] The rise in the absolute number of women working in war industry was also considerable:

Table 10.1. *An index of persons paying sickness insurance contributions, 1914–19 (membership on 1 June 1914 = 100)*

Membership on 1st of:	No. of insurance offices in 1919	Males 1914–19						Females 1914–19						Total 1914–19					
	1919	1914	1915	1916	1917	1918	1919	1914	1915	1916	1917	1918	1919	1914	1915	1916	1917	1918	1919
January	4,814	—	72.3	62.3	60.1	60.4	66.6	—	85.3	97.1	107.5	116.5	—	—	76.8	74.5	76.9	80.4	79.0
February	3,898	89.4	71.6	62.1	59.4	60.3	73.8	88.9	85.9	97.3	107.8	115.4	101.5	89.3	76.6	74.5	76.5	80.0	82.0
March	5,175	92.4	71.5	61.7	59.5	60.4	77.5	92.2	88.2	97.8	108.5	115.1	97.2	92.3	77.3	74.4	76.9	79.9	83.7
April	5,245	95.2	70.8	61.5	60.1	60.3	81.4	94.3	90.0	99.4	109.9	115.2	95.3	95.1	77.5	74.8	77.7	79.8	86.4
May	4,276	98.8	71.7	62.9	61.9	62.0	85.5	98.4	93.3	101.7	113.0	117.8	95.7	98.6	79.2	76.5	80.0	81.7	89.8
June	4,157	100.0	70.7	63.6	62.0	62.8	88.8	100.0	94.1	103.3	114.9	117.4	97.9	100.0	78.9	77.6	81.1	81.8	92.8
July	5,384	99.8	69.3	63.6	61.1	60.8	90.3	99.7	94.4	102.9	115.1	116.7	100.2	99.8	78.1	77.4	80.2	80.8	93.8
August	4,310	98.0	67.9	63.3	60.8	59.8	91.1	97.8	95.6	103.3	115.3	115.4	100.5	98.0	77.6	77.4	80.1	79.7	94.2
September	4,888	71.5	66.8	63.0	60.9	60.4	91.8	80.0	96.4	104.0	116.1	116.6	100.3	74.4	77.1	77.4	80.5	80.5	94.7
October	5,309	71.8	65.7	62.2	60.9	60.2	92.3	80.6	96.4	104.4	116.6	116.0	100.4	74.9	76.5	77.0	80.7	80.1	95.0
November	4,096	73.1	64.5	61.9	61.2	58.1	92.9	83.6	98.1	106.1	117.5	110.7	100.9	76.8	76.4	77.5	81.2	76.8	95.6
December	4,609	73.6	63.5	60.5	61.3	59.3	93.8	85.4	98.8	108.1	118.5	108.7	101.9	77.8	75.9	77.3	81.7	76.8	96.5

Source
Reichsarbeitsblatt, 18, 1920, p. 4

Table 10.2. *Female members of the compulsory sickness insurance scheme, annual averages 1889–1913*

	Total	Rate of increase (%)
1889	1,195,662	
1893	1,549,425	30
1897	1,886,995	22
1901	2,288,270	21
1905	2,834,697	24
1909	3,444,425	22
1913	4,127,401	20

In 1903 compulsory insurance was extended to cover clerks and apprentices with an annual income of up to 2,000 marks.
Source
Statistik des Deutschen Reiches, new series, vol. 189, Berlin, 1921, p. 55*. Rates of increase were calculated by the author.

Table 10.3. *Female employment in Bavaria, 1882–1916*

	1882	1895	1907	1916
Total females employed[a]	956,797	952,114	1,413,718	1,235,611
In agriculture	674,116	522,540	873,030	616,415
Percentage of total	60.9%	46.6%	53.2%	42.3%
In industry	102,017	156,267	215,366	258,051
Percentage of total	9.2%	13.9%	13.2%	17.7%
Total female population	2,699,411	2,949,056	3,363,981	3,616,182
Percentage of total female population in employment	35.5%	32.3%	42.1%	34.2%

[a]Including domestic service, excluding 'self-employed, without profession'.
Source
Die Kriegsvolkszählungen vom Jahre 1916 und 1917 in Bayern, Beiträge zur Statistik Bayerns, 89, published by the Regional Office of Statistics, Munich, 1919, pp. 128–34, 139ff.

UTE DANIEL

Table 10.4. *Previous employment experience of employed females, Bavaria, 31 July 1914–1 December 1916, by employment sector*

Employment sector	Women workers on 1 December 1916	Not in that sector or position on 31 July 1914	Not previously employed	
			No.	%
Agriculture	614,585	69,963	48,249	7.9
Forestry	1,830	314	200	10.9
Mines	1,436	495	241	16.8
Minerals	9,577	1,316	929	9.7
Metalworking	11,879	2,331	1,420	12.0
Engineering	13,866	2,960	1,427	10.3
Chemicals	31,596	17,436	7,143	22.6
Lighting, etc.	1,109	213	129	11.6
Spinning	29,625	2,001	1,344	4.5
Paper	5,073	826	585	11.5
Leather	2,109	498	277	13.1
Wood and carving	12,066	2,604	1,645	13.6
Foodstuffs	26,597	4,317	3,278	12.3
Clothing	81,960	9,455	6,971	8.5
Cleaning	13,240	772	533	4.0
Building	1,294	220	146	11.3
Printing	3,567	336	250	7.0
Arts and crafts	681	21	17	2.5
Manufacturers, unspecified factory work	12,376	1,477	1,060	8.6
Commerce	80,515	6,534	5,273	6.5
Insurance	854	95	67	7.8
Transport	9,315	2,357	1,806	19.4
Hotel and catering	30,789	2,156	1,409	4.6
Domestic services, etc.	185,093	13,833	6,633	3.6
Military, court service, etc.	54,579	4,494	2,776	5.1
No trade/unspecified	222,678	11,015	7,233	3.2
Total	1,458,289	158,039	101,041	6.9

Source
Die Kriegsvolkszählungen vom Jahre 1916 und 1917 in Bayern, Beiträge zur Statistik Bayerns, 89, published by the Regional Office of Statistics, Munich, 1919, pp. 195–202, 208. Percentages calculated by author.

a trade union survey of 2,594 metalworking firms conducted in August/September 1916 counted 266,530 women, whereas the same firms employed only 63,570 women before the war.[9]

The fullest information about the provenance of woman industrial workers is provided once again by the Bavarian employment census of 1916 (see Table 10.4). Of the female employees registered on 1 December 1916,[10] 158,039 had ceased to work in the same sector of the economy or position they had occupied on 31 July 1914; of these, 101,041 ha never been employed prior to the war. That means that of all the women in Bavaria on 1 December 1916, only 6.9 per cent had never worked before the war. Moreover, this category includes all the young girls who would have entered working life quite independently of war breaking out.[11] The increase in the number of women entering employment for the first time, only part of which in turn benefited the war industry (both in the narrow and wider sense), was thus far too small to be able to explain the large increase in women working in war industry, both in Bavaria and in the rest of Germany.[12] War industry recruited additional labour not from the women who had not worked hitherto, but from some of those women who had previously been employed in other trades and industries. This is borne out by a closer examination of the provenance of women workers in the Bavarian chemical industry, where the intake of previously non-working women was high, in both absolute and percentage terms (7,143 or 22.6 per cent of all the women employed on 1 December 1916). Exact figures are available for the Bavarian gunpowder industry (see Table 10.5).

Almost half the women working in the powder-mills had already had experience of factory work before the war, a good 8 per cent had been in service, almost 3 per cent in agriculture, and about 1 per cent had been shopworkers. Included in the 27 per cent who had not worked hitherto were all those girls who had entered work in the meantime. Only the women left in this category once these young first-time workers have been subtracted could be said to have taken up work as an 'unscheduled' consequence of the war situation.

The above average rise in the number of women working in war industry was thus not the result of women taking up employment for the first time ever, but of the recruitment of women who had hitherto been working in other industries or non-industrial occupations. This conclusion is confirmed by both Bavarian and non-Bavarian sources of other provenance.[13] Previous studies of women's work in the First World War are correct insofar as they emphasise the displacement of female employment brought on by the war.[14]

At this point in our investigation, we must reformulate our questions: how did the many female dependants of conscripted soldiers earn their living, if they did not go out to work in the expanding war industries? And why did only a relatively small number of them take advantage of war industry's offer of a job? To answer these questions, we must remind ourselves of the 'obvious'. Then as now, women who were not in paid work were not, in most cases, 'unemployed'. Most of them, especially – but not exclusively –

Table 10.5. *Former occupations of female labour force in Bavarian powder mills, December 1916*

Employment sector		Occupation	No.	%
Industry			11,121	48.8
	of which:	Powder mills	8,488	37.3
		Metalworking	645	2.8
		Spinning	430	1.9
		Factory work (unspecified)	386	1.7
		Weaving	344	1.5
		Sewing	313	1.4
		Engineering	311	1.4
		(Metal) toy manufacture	204	0.9
Domestic service			1,839	8.1
	of which:	Servants	1,398	6.1
		Paid service work	222	1.0
		Cleaners	219	1.0
Agriculture			633	2.8
Shopworkers			257	1.1
Unspecified			540	2.4
Not previously employed			6,053	26.6
Other			2,319	10.2
		Total	22,762	100.0

All occupations with fewer than 200 women are excluded
Source
Die Kriegsvolkszählungen vom Jahre 1916 und 1917 in Bayern, Beiträge zur Statistik Bayerns, 89, published by the Regional Office of Statistics, Munich, 1919, p. 204

those who were married, had family and household work to do. Then as now, a large part of their time was taken up by housework and looking after children and relatives. Wartime conditions made these demands upon women considerably more intensive. An analysis of women's work, even in industry, is bound to be incomplete if it does not take these factors into account, because women's attitude to employment can only be understood once their role as workers in the home and family is established.

During the war the household economy, which had previously functioned as part of the consumer goods market, virtually degenerated together with that market into what was in reality a subsistence economy – a development which was noted by contemporary observers.[15] There is more to this than the simple fact that many households went over to producing their own food instead of buying it. Shopping and dealing with consumer goods in general made far greater demands on time and energy than before: buying was no longer just a matter of buying. Even the military authorities sometimes accepted the widespread complaints about 'the large amount of time it took to obtain food and the difficulties involved in running the home'[16] as a valid excuse for what they saw as the otherwise criminal non-availability of women for other work. How exactly did the various aspects of housework alter? Changes were most obvious in the very act of buying, presumably because of the public nature of the activity, where the most striking phenomenon were the so-called *polonaises*: the queues outside food shops, shoemakers' and other shops. To quote Goetz Briefs,

Keeping a watchful eye on supplies, fighting for goods, queuing up for hours on end, are all things which appeared for the first time with the war. The same tribulations, and others besides, are to be endured when one tries to get hold of one's allocation of rationed goods. Visits to the local authorities, the difficulties of managing and using ration cards, having one's name put down on the customer roll, keeping track of coupons, standing patiently in queues – all this definitely requires a good deal of calm, ingenuity and effort, as well as imposing a completely different division of labour when seeing to all those household tasks which have to take second place to these wartime problems.[17]

Another problem with which housewives had to contend was the rapid deterioration in the quality of food. At an executive meeting of the Bavarian association of municipal authorities held in July 1917, Mayor Gessler of Nuremberg remarked of wartime flour that 'sometimes you have to take a pickaxe to it',[18] and this characterisation of his was by no means an isolated example. A flood of food substitutes, from 'packet cow' (dried milk substitute) to guaranteed fish-free fishcakes, set in and gradually defied all efforts to keep abreast of it. The quality of these substitutes was dubious if not actually harmful, and housewives were often left to guess at their nutritional value. As food supplies grew scarcer, so the number of items placed on ration rose.[19] The consequence was that what women bought was often dictated by what happened to be on offer at the time. They had to cope with foodstuffs previously unknown in their region[20] and problems of distribution meant that people never knew when they would get their rations:

The people find it particularly disturbing – and rightly so – not to know by the middle of the month what food is going to be available for the month then current and in what quantities the various foodstuffs are going to be allocated . . . Orderly housekeeping is plainly out of the question if one cannot plan supplies. This applies above all to the households of less well-off workers, where stores have not been laid by from preceding months. One hears these classes complaining vociferously about how bad the situation is, and it has led the unions to fear unrest in the factories, where everything has been quiet up till now.[21]

Changes in another aspect of housework, the use of consumer goods in general, were less visible to the outside observer. 'Make do and mend' had to take the place of buying new clothes and food supplies, refuse had to be prepared for recycling and many households went over to making their own preserves.[22] Many urban households began producing their own food for the first time ever, and even in large towns it was by no means exceptional to see pigs and rabbits kept in cellars and on balconies, while the cultivation of allotments or 'war gardens', as well as the increased extra work done by women on smallholdings, were noted everywhere.[23]

Last of the factors which made housework more complicated to be singled out here was rationing and its vagaries. These made themselves felt in every single household, either in the form of gas or electricity rationing, which made it impossible to do housework early in the morning or in the evening,[24] or in the guise of state surveillance of individual household consumption. In many towns state inspectors monitored the consumption of potato supplies. If it was deemed to be too high the result could be a warning, refusal to allow replacement supplies or potatoes or turnips or even, in some cases, outright confiscation of potatoes stored in cellars.[25] In some instances veritable campaigns of expropriation were waged against whole sections of the population, depriving them of the potato supplies they had just been allotted.[26]

An additional factor which made housework more intensive was that the longer the war went on, the more often city dwellers were forced to go into the countryside and obtain food directly, by purchase, barter or even theft. All these extra chores, which usually fell to the women in addition to their 'normal' household and child-rearing duties, meant that working in a factory was totally out of the question for many women. Insofar as they relied on earned income, there was, however, an alternative open to them: they could bring in some money by doing homework; the army authorities in particular put out a huge amount of such work. In fact many women, especially those with young children or absolutely no experience of factory work, resorted to this option, which in turn meant that a large number of women were engaged in homework for the army administration while the civil and military authorities waited in vain for them to go into war industry.[27]

Together with the degeneration of housework into a quasi-subsistence economy, the spread of homework suggests that a differentiated view of the development of the 1914–18 war economy is called for. There is a peculiar contrast between 'modernising' tendencies, such as mass production and new production techniques on the one hand, and anachronistic features, so to speak, on the other. Modes of production which had long been rendered obsolete by advances in technology and in the division of labour enjoyed a new lease of life. Roughly speaking, wartime homework displayed two different tendencies. Some of its traditional associations with certain regions and production processes waned away to insignificance as the war went on. Either raw materials or demand were lacking, or the workforce transferred to agriculture or war industry. By contrast, those types of homework which

Table 10.6. *Membership of
the Women Homeworkers
Union, 1913–19*

1913	8,385
1914 (January)	8,400
1915 (March)	10,100
1916 (January)	12,915
1917 (January)	16,106
1918 (March)	17,100
1919 (January)	19,644

Sources
Elisabeth Martha Gravert, 'Der
Einfluß der wirtschaftlichen
Demobilmachung auf die
Entwicklung der Frauen-
arbeit', Dissertation, Ham-
burg, 1924–5, p. 131 (for 1913);
Charlotte Lorenz, 'Die
gewerbliche Frauenarbeit
während des Krieges' in Paul
Umbreit and Charlotte Lorenz,
*Der Krieg und die Arbeits-
verhältnisse*, Stuttgart, 1928,
p. 356 (for 1914–19)

were able to adapt to the needs of military production or which were actually called into existence by such needs, underwent expansion.[28] The men and, above all, the women who found employment in this area were engaged in the production of gunlock covers, baskets for shells and cartridges, military belts, gasmasks, fur coats, sandbags, uniforms and shoes among other items. Women homeworkers in the corset industry manufactured tent squares and biscuit-bags. Women working in the Black Forest clock industry produced munitions instead of clocks, and others soon learned to make complete uniforms.[29]

There are no available statistics for the total extent of homework in the period 1914–18, though the increase in women doing such work can be demonstrated on a regional basis. In Hamburg, for instance, there were almost 8,400 homeworkers registered in 1914, roughly two-thirds of them women. During the war, it has been estimated that their number rose to an average of 15,000, of whom about 10,000 were women.[30] In the Prussian administrative district of Kassel the number of women homeworkers rose from 1,010 in May 1914 to over 7,500 in September 1918.[31] The growing membership of the Women Homeworkers Union is a further indicator of the increase in women doing homework (see Table 10.6).

Women and families in wartime social politics

Let us recapitulate, first, the main points made above. There was no excessive rise in female employment in the First World War. Where armaments factories enlarged their female workforce or took on women for the first time ever, they did so by recruiting workers predominantly from among the ranks of women who were already in employment, more particularly from service and other industries. Family ties stand out as the factor which prevented more women from going out to work in war industry. It proved impossible to cope both with looking after children and dependants and a 'second' job. As the consumer goods market collapsed, women set increasingly greater store on having time and energy at their disposal than on the higher income to be earned in industry. For this reason, and also because for women who had never worked before, going to work in a factory meant a much more radical break, large numbers of women preferred to take in homework.[32]

The military and civil authorities were naturally not unaware of this state of affairs. They attempted to remedy the increasingly alarming wartime labour shortage by, amongst other things, mobilising women, and in so doing they were continually hindered by the limits posed by women's family obligations. In the words of Marie-Elisabeth Lüders, whom the Prussian Kriegsamt (War Office),[33] entrusted with mobilising women for war work in late 1916:

The conditions under which women live and work are indissolubly linked, and this means that . . . any attempt to recruit women by force in an emergency stands no chance of success . . . Forcible recruitment is bound to fail because of the physiological, psychological and sociological conditions of women's existence, and whoever tries to enforce demands which are impossible by their very nature will be repaid with defeat.

Therefore, she argued, it was necessary to find ways and means of paying due regard to these conditions of existence – and this led directly to a social policy aimed specifically at women and the family.[34]

Social policy in place of forced labour: this was the programme with which Lüders and her colleagues tried, within the framework of wartime economic organisation, to solve the dilemma posed by women's obligations to their families. Setting up nurseries, employing welfare workers to look after working women and their families, making it easier for women workers in the armaments industry to obtain food; these and a battery of other measures were aimed at making it easier for women to work in the factories and look after their families at the same time.[35]

Welfare provisions for female industrial workers began in late 1916. In the Prussian Kriegsamt, itself established on 1 November 1916 under the direction of Lieutenant General Wilhelm Groener, a Frauenreferat (Women's Department) and a Frauenarbeitszentrale (Women's Labour Office) were set up, the first being responsible for mobilising women for war work, the second for their general welfare. At the same time, Groener inaugurated a parallel organisation, the Nationaler Ausschuß für Frauenarbeit im Kriege (National Committee for Women's War Work), which brought together the most important women's and welfare organisations. A Frauenreferat was also set up in each of the Kriegsamtsstellen, the regional subdivisions of the central Kriegsamt which, like the central Frauenreferat and Frauenarbeitszentrale, were headed by women. At the beginning of 1918 the Kriegsamt and its subsidiary bodies employed about 1,000 women in the organisation of women's work and welfare.[36]

An especially intensive effort was made to institute factory nurses (*Fabrikpflegerinnen*) in all firms employing large numbers of women. Before the war, these nurses – a kind of industrial social worker – had existed in only a few firms.[37] Sometimes known as 'company housewives', their duties involved ensuring the welfare of women inside the factory (for example, safety measures and hygiene facilities) and outside (living conditions and use of leisure time). They paid housecalls, visited the sick and had to take care of the problems women workers encountered in arranging for their children to be looked after and, increasingly, with food and transport. They were also responsible for the running of hostels for women workers who did not live locally. In early 1917 the Prussian and Bavarian Ministries of War decreed that the Kriegsamtsstellen should advise large firms to employ a factory nurse, and in the summer of the same year it became compulsory for state-owned firms to appoint one. Thereafter, the number of factory nurses rose steadily. Whereas in November 1917 521 firms throughout the Reich with a total female workforce of 507,066 employed 482 factory nurses, by November 1918 1,248 firms with a female workforce of 778,426 employed 752 such nurses. In just under three-quarters of all the firms the appointment had been arranged by the Kriegsamtsstellen, and 469 of the 752 nurses had undergone a course of training with the Frauenarbeitszentrale.[38] Compared with the 20 factory nurses employed in the entire Reich at the outbreak of war,[39] this was a rapid expansion of this particular element of social policy. Even so, in relation to the size of the female workforce, the number of factory nurses was not great.

The ambitious programme of the Frauenfererate, the planned extent of which would have been a credit to any welfare state in the second half of the

UTE DANIEL

Table 10.7. *Factory welfare, November 1917–November 1918*

Year and month	1	2	3	4	5
1917					
November	521	495	507,066	482 (325)	1,052
December	875	538	425,501	540 (364)	788
1918					
January	698	588	546,294	545 (378)	1,002
February	822	702	605,427	627 (384)	966
March	1,004	866	648,772	669 (407)	970
April	1,090	835	569,863	638 (417)	893
May	1,131	854	642,330	762 (432)	843
June	1,169	890	716,837	781 (439)	918
July	1,176	893	733,846	789 (443)	930
August	1,184	894	736,171	707 (443)	1,041
September	1,195	904	751,773	703 (449)	1,069
October	1,235	941	759,888	741 (456)	1,025
November	1,248	957	778,426	752 (469)	1,035

Column 1: Number of firms employing a factory nurse
Column 2: Number of them doing so at the instigation of the Frauenreferate
Column 3: Total number of females employed in the firms with a factory nurse
Column 4: Number of factory nurses (in brackets: number who had attended a training course)
Column 5: Number of females employed per factory nurse
Source
Frieda Wunderlich, 'Fabrikpflegerinnen', *Archiv für Frauenarbeit*, 8, 1920, p. 101

twentieth century, failed nevertheless to meet expectations.[40] There can be no doubt, however, that it had a positive effect on the morale of women already working in the factories, where conditions were sometimes appalling. Health and safety regulations for women at work had been suspended *de facto* since the outbreak of war,[41] but for there to have been a real impact on the mobilisation of women workers it would have been necessary to bring about a 'revolution in all conditions of existence',[42] namely the dissolution of the family as a social institution. A radical solution like that was, of course, out of the question – for political, economic and also ideological reasons.

There was, however, a much more pragmatic cause for the failure of the rather more modest steps actually taken in this direction, namely that wartime social policy towards women and the family had a double aspect. On the one hand, the policy (or rather, the institutions which supported it – the state, local authorities, private societies) attempted to free women from their family duties in order to mobilise them for war industry; on the other hand, it created a system of social security which made it possible for women to provide for themselves and their families without going to work in the factories. The following is a brief outline of the two most important social policy programmes.

ASSISTANCE FOR TEXTILE WORKERS

The textile industry was one of the sectors of the economy which laid off workers during the war. The cause of the high unemployment among textile workers was the shortage of raw materials. From the middle of 1915, cotton, the textile industry's most important raw material, could no longer be imported, and had production continued at its previous rate, the existing stocks would have run out in another six months.[43] In order to secure these scarce supplies for army requirements, the government issued a series of decrees in 1915 and 1916 reducing production and hours of work in the textile industry. Since unemployment in this sector was thus the direct result of state intervention, both central government and the individual provinces recognised that they had a responsibility to support those without work – the scope of which was something completely new in the history of social policy.

Central government accompanied production restrictions with the introduction of state assistance for textile workers. The provisions extended to workers in the textile and garment industries who were unemployed or on short time, and were conditional on need. The local authorities were to determine eligibility for assistance in each case.[44] In order to grasp the full implications of this measure, both in financial terms and as an aspect of labour market politics, it is necessary to take a look at the number of workers – predominantly women – who were affected. What follows is an examination of the textile industry in the Rhineland, Westphalia and the Kingdom of Saxony with a view to this question.

In September 1915 the Rhineland chambers of commerce announced that at least 30,000 textile workers would be made redundant in their area, of whom about 17,500 were women.[45] Before the war the textile and garments industry in Westphalia[46] had employed about 70,000 workers in all, almost half of them women. A survey conducted in September 1915 by the organisation of Westphalian employment agencies, covering 349 textile firms in the province, revealed the following changes in the workforce, compared to the position before the war.

The number of male workers had fallen by 11,852 or 41 per cent, female workers by 3,309 or 15 per cent. If we project these percentages onto the workforce as a whole, then in September 1915 the Westphalian textile industry would have employed just under 30,000 women, but only 17,000 men; the other male workers had either already been called up or had transferred to other firms or regions. While there was no male unemployment to speak

Table 10.8. *Number employed in the Westphalian textile industry in September 1915, and before the war*

District	Firms	Employed before the war			Employed on 18 September 1915		
		Total	Males	Females	Total	Males	Females
Münster	205	35,739	20,891	14,848	24,616	12,570	12,046
Minden	52	9,601	4,150	5,451	8,004	2,678	5,326
Arnsberg	92	6,088	3,895	2,193	3,644	1,833	1,811
	349	51,428	28,936	22,492	36,264	17,081	19,183

Source
Association of Westphalian labour agencies, 6 December 1915; Report on the survey conducted by the Association of Westphalian employment agencies, on unemployment in the Westphalian textile industry, Staatsarchiv Münster, Oberpräsidium 4124

of in September 1915, some of the women were already unemployed or on short-time. In January 1916 unemployment among woman textile workers rose to around 50,000 as production restrictions were implemented.[47]

Production restrictions had a particularly serious effect in the Kingdom of Saxony, dominated as it was by the textile industry. Of the 380,000 or so people employed in the textile and garment industry there before the war, roughly 280,000 were women.[48] Whereas about one-third of the men had been called up or had changed occupation by autumn 1915, four-fifths of the women were still employed in July 1915. In other words, a good 220,000 women were working in firms directly affected by the production restrictions. Allowing for workers who could be found jobs in other firms, the government of Saxony reckoned on more than 100,000 unemployed persons who would be needing assistance, the majority of them women.

That the newly introduced system of unemployment benefit became, in the main, a system of assistance for unemployed women cannot be entirely ascribed to the fact that a high proportion of the workers in the textile and garment industry were women. A further reason was that women were unwilling to move, above all because of their family ties.[49] Their particular role as workers in the family was allowed for. Marriage or children were accepted as valid reasons for women refusing to move to another region to work and they continued to receive unemployment benefit.[50] Yet another factor reinforced this lack of mobility among woman textile workers. Many families of textile workers owned their own house and/or a plot of arable land and were therefore not prepared to move.[51] Despite various attempts[52] to get

Table 10.9. *Family allowance expenditure in selected months in Prussia, 1914–18 (in millions of marks)*

	1914	1915	1916	1917	1918
April		47.9	79.5	108.0	104.4
August	16.3	56.5	78.8	107.0	100.8
December	38.6	80.2	131.5	117.7	

Source
Information on family allowance payments made by the central government, Zentrales Staatsarchiv Merseburg, Rep. 77, Tit. 323g, Nr. 27, Beiheft 3, Bd. 1–7. The totals represent the expenditure on the portion of the allowance which was refunded to local authorities by the Reich.

at least some of these women to transfer to war industry, the problem persisted into the second half of 1916. This 'hardly satisfactory state of affairs',[53] whereby thousands of proficient woman textile workers fell prey to state-subsidised unemployment while the arms industry was suffering from an increasingly acute shortage of labour did not alter until employment opportunities in the textile and garment industry improved again with the introduction of pulp yarn processing.[54] Women who could not or had no wish to wait for this development, availed themselves of the opportunities afforded by homework.[55] In all, it appears that only a quarter of unemployed woman textile workers transferred to war work.[56]

FAMILY ALLOWANCES

Immediately after the outbreak of war the state and local authorities began paying allowances to support the families of conscripted soldiers, the so-called 'warrior families' (*Kriegerfamilien*). The basis for these payments was a law dating from 28 February 1888 and 4 August 1914 concerning support for the families of men in military service.[57] It obliged local authorities to grant a certain measure of financial support to 'warrior families' in need, part of which would be refunded by the central government.[58] Since the number of families to whom such payments were made was quite considerable (it has been estimated that by the end of 1915 some four million families, i.e. about eleven million individuals, were receiving allowances),[59] expenditure on family allowance rose to a fairly high level.

In Prussia between August 1914 and October 1918, a total of 4,166,300,000 marks was spent on the portion of family allowance refundable by the central government alone, leaving aside the additional payments made by local authorities.[60] Yet actual sums received by individual families were not very great. Calculations based on the individual records kept by the

Berlin family allowance authorities reveal the following picture of how the circumstances of 'warrior families' changed once they made the transition from earned income to family allowance. The average monthly income of a skilled worker's family with one child fell from 128.52 marks to 30 marks, just 23.34 per cent of its former level. With a larger number of children, the ratio improved somewhat, so that the family of a skilled worker with four children received as much as 49.56 per cent of the husband's previous earnings. Families of unskilled workers with one child who drew on the allowance saw their average income drop from 99.62 marks to 30 marks, some 30.11 per cent of their former income. Unskilled workers with four children retained 69.73 per cent of their previous income while families of unskilled workers with at least nine children belonged to the rare category of workers whom the war welfare authorities blessed with 'income supplement': they received 116.31 per cent of the husband's previous earnings.[61]

It is clear, therefore, that the families in question were unable to make ends meet from the family allowance on its own. State and local government benefits between them usually covered little more than the cost of the rent.[62] But if one takes into account the rent reduction imposed by the authorities[63] and the extra payments made to the families of conscripted soldiers by their former employers,[64] then most families had just about sufficient money to buy what few things were available in the shops. The income of working-class families living in their own house and producing some of their food themselves – by no means rare in the countryside and small towns – proved to be perfectly adequate.[65] By contrast with the situation before the war, the financial circumstances of many women and their families was further improved by the fact that once the husband had been called up no more money had to be spent on him. The Bavarian local government office in Augsburg, to cite one example out of many, remarked that it was quite true

that many soldiers' wives, especially those with large numbers of children, had never had as much cash to spend on the household as they have now. Many of them have admitted this to me personally, referring to their husbands in very strong language indeed and remarking that they no longer have to slave away as they used to before the war, when their husbands spent nearly all their wages on drink and left next to nothing for their wives and children.[66]

As a result, many of the women who received the family allowance were not available when they were needed to remedy the shortage of labour in industry and agriculture. Some local authorities and military commanders accordingly began to use threats as a way of encouraging women to go out to work: women receiving the family allowance who were not working were to undergo a fresh means test in order to determine whether they were 'really' entitled to benefit.[67] The central government let the local authorities have their way,[68] although it refused to compel 'warrior wives' to go out to work.[69] In a decree dated 6 March 1917 the Reichskanzler instructed the authorities to avoid 'any pettiness' in dealing with family allowances, because

the men who are fighting at the front and daily risking their lives for the fatherland are entitled to be free of cares about their people back home. They must go in the knowledge that their families, for whom they are now unable to provide themselves, are not in need, but are receiving everything they require for their livelihood.

Family allowance was thus to be withheld only 'after mature and thorough examination' and after all other possible ways of influencing the women concerned had failed.[70]

In larger towns and districts it was not so easy for the authorities to monitor the income and fitness for work of every single woman, and accordingly there developed a different practice towards women in receipt of the family allowance. Here the authorities tried to persuade these women either to remain in work or look for a job by taking only part of their earnings into account when calculating the scale of the allowance. For now the notoriously low rates of pay for women were wreaking their vengeance: they were turning out to be a clear obstacle to mobilisation. Family allowance was in many cases below subsistence level, but there again women's wages were often not much more than subsistence. If the difference between family allowance and earnings was not very great and if, in addition, part of that difference had to be spent on transport, increased wear and tear on clothes, child minders and so on, then it made little sense economically for women to go out to work. As early as December 1914, factory inspectors in Mönchen-Gladbach pointed out that if seamstresses, to take a particular example, received 40 marks in war allowance each month, but could only earn around 60 marks by working, then 'it did not suit them' to work for the sake of an extra 20 marks per month, and they therefore proposed that low-paid women like these should be granted half their allowance.[71] In this case too, the central government left it to the local authorities to make their own rulings, although it also proposed that, as a matter of principle, half the total earnings should be disregarded.[72]

However, that half of their earnings were disregarded was insufficient to motivate these women to carry on or start working[73] and it also provoked strong indignation from those affected – not least the husbands who had been called up.[74] As a result, the practice of taking earnings into account had more of a negative effect on the mobilisation of women for war work. Speaking in retrospect, Marie-Elisabeth Lüders, the director of the Frauenreferat in the Kriegsamt, acknowledged that many women

were kept from working by the practice, generally established by the Prussian local authorities, of counting earnings towards family allowances. Understandably, the women felt that the practice of disregarding the first 50 per cent of earnings when calculating allowance was really a stoppage, and they felt that they were being penalised for wanting to work; in many cases it led directly to women giving up work they had already started, because after deductions, their income was hardly an appropriate reward for the work they did or for their readiness to sacrifice running their homes in an orderly manner.[75]

Conclusion

In summary, the following points may be made about women's work in Germany in the First World War. The war did not usher in an excessive growth in female employment, although it did shift the emphasis of women's work. Women workers transferred from other industries to war industry and they switched from non-industrial occupations, domestic service in particular, to factory work. A good deal of the displacement of women's work within industry between 1914 and 1918 was subsequently reversed when many women, especially those working in jobs and industries which before the war had been predominantly male preserves, were made redundant as soon as the war was over.[76] It is scarcely surprising, therefore, that there are hardly any visible long-term effects of this wartime displacement. Nor was the trend which had already made itself visible before the war, the increase in the number of women working in industries expanding as a result of the armaments boom, such as the metal, engineering, electrical and chemical industries, appreciably reinforced, in the long run, by the war. This is attested by the results of the employment censuses. Table 10.10 shows that the rate of increase in female employment, measured in terms of the distribution of women in the various industrial sectors, could scarcely be termed impressive. In addition it must be borne in mind that the rate of increase of female employment over the period spanning the First World War is overemphasised as a result of the longer intervals between one census and the next.

On the other hand, the departure of women from domestic service during the war did continue a long-term trend; the decline of service as a source of employment.[77] Those women whom wartime conditions forced into paid employment for the first time did not all enter industry by any means; they often resorted to homework. In doing so, they obeyed the logic implicit in their role as family workers; whatever work they did had to fit in with their family obligations. Women stayed away from the war industry for two reasons; because the amount of labour it took to look after a family rose considerably as the war went on and because, as a result of the collapse of the consumer goods market, a higher income could not bring about a significant reduction in the required amount of labour. The increase in homework and

Table 10.10. *Women employed in industries associated with the armaments industries as a percentage of all women employed*

Employment sector	1882	1895	1907	1925
Metal production and metal working	0.1	0.2	0.2	0.4
Engineering and vehicles	0.0	0.1	0.2	1.3
Electrical and precision engineering	0.1	0.3	0.8	2.4
Chemicals	0.2	0.5	0.8	1.6

Source
Walter Müller, Angelika Willms, Johann Handl, *Strukturwandel der Frauenarbeit 1880–1980*, Frankfurt/Main and New York, 1983, p. 136

the intensification of housework indicate that in many respects the First World War gave rise to anachronistic developments. These were by no means marginal to the direction of change in the economy but rather served to shape the overall war economy. The 'modern' aspects of the war economy for example, industrial mass production, and the application of new techniques, could function only on the basis of the extra work done by women in the home. After the collapse of the consumer goods market, and as money depreciated in value, this extra work provided the foundation upon which family survival rested, and thus constituted the material bedrock of wartime society. The state had to take into account the eminently important function of women as family workers. This it did by setting up a system of benefits which, although parsimonious, had a significant impact on the family and society. At the same time, though, this system thwarted the authorities in their efforts to encourage more women to work in the arms industry.

The dilemma posed by women's double burden, normally a 'private problem' of the women and families in question, became a public dilemma for wartime employment policy. The 'solution' did not come until the war was over. The absence of armaments contracts and the return of male survivors from the front put an end to the shortage of labour. The dilemma posed by women's double burden could be 'privatised' once more.

Notes

I would like to thank Marc Chinca for the care he devoted to the translation of this chapter.

1 Marie-Elisabeth Lüders, in *Jahrbuch des Bundes deutscher Frauenvereine 1917*, Berlin, 1917, pp. 7ff.
2 Stefan Bajohr, *Die Hälfte der Fabrik: Geschichte der Frauenarbeit in Deutschland*

1914–1945, Marburg, 1979, p. 101; also pp. 119, 127; see also Gisela Losseff-Tillmanns, *Frauenemanzipation und Gewerkschaften*, Wuppertal, 1978, pp. 179ff.; Barbara Greven-Aschoff, *Die bürgerliche Frauenbewegung in Deutschland 1894–1933*, Göttingen, 1981, p. 151; Jürgen Kocka, *Facing total war: German society 1914–1918*, trans. B. Weinberger, Leamington Spa, 1984, p. 19; Paul Umbreit, 'Die deutschen Gewerkschaften im Kriege' in Paul Umbreit and Charlotte Lorenz (eds.), *Der Krieg und die Arbeitsverhältnisse*, Stuttgart, 1928, p. 88. For reasons of space further references which support the assumption that female employment increased during the First World War have not been given. In general, it must be said that it has been customary to make a tacit assumption that there was such an increase in women's work during the First World War. It has sufficed simply to mention the phenomenon and to assert that any more exact examination of the facts is trivial and unnecessary. Now in studies where women's war work is not the chief object of interest but only a marginal theme, it is perfectly legitimate to take on board what passes for established fact. However, it is reasonable to expect that studies devoted to women's work in the First World War should question whether there was indeed an increase in the proportion of women in the labour force. None of the existing studies does so. Bajohr, *Die Hälfte der Fabrik*, does not challenge the standard interpretation. Other specialist studies do not even mention it, and thereby do not call it into question either; in some cases it is present as an unspoken insinuation; cf. Anneliese Seidel, *Frauenarbeit im Ersten Weltkrieg als Problem der staatlichen Sozialpolitik, dargestellt am Beispiel Bayerns*, Frankfurt, 1979; Ursula von Gersdorff, *Frauen im Kriegsdienst 1914–1945*, Stuttgart, 1969; Charlotte Lorenz, 'Die gewerbliche Frauenarbeit während des Krieges' in P. Umbreit and C. Lorenz, *Der Krieg*, pp. 307–91.

3 On this, see 'Der Anteil der Frau an der Sozialversicherung', *Archiv für Frauenarbeit*, 5, 1917, pp. 143–57, 196–217, in particular 143ff., and *Reichsarbeitsblatt*, 16, 1918, pp. 656f.

4 Quite apart from the fact that this indicator was chosen because it is used in support of the argument that the war brought about an above average rise in female employment, there are good grounds for considering that the insurance agency reports do provide an accurate picture of the trends in female employment. The increase in women's work as revealed by the three employment censuses carried out before the war correlates closely with the increase in the numbers of women paying insurance contributions (coefficient of correlation 0.999). Whereas the employment censuses report the number of women in employment as rising, from 7,794,000 in 1882 to 8,219,000 in 1895, and 9,742,000 in 1907, the number of women insured rose from 1,195,662 in 1889 to 1,690,326 in 1895, and to 3,166,756 in 1907. See for the former Walter Müller, Angelika Willms and Johann Handl, *Strukturwandel der Frauenarbeit 1880–1980*, Frankfurt, 1983, p. 35, and for the latter *Statistik des Deutschen Reiches*, new series, vol. 189, Berlin, 1921, p. 55*. While it would be dangerous to presume on the evidence of a correlation coefficient over no more than three cases, the correlation suggests nevertheless that there is a close connection between developments in each series of figures. It cannot be proven that this parallel development continued into the war, though by and large it must have done so. The under-registration of insurance contributors does not appear to have distorted the overall picture of the rate of increase to any considerable extent. How-

ever, one cannot exclude the possibility that the under-recording of the fluctuating number of woman workers might have led to a slight underweighting in the insurance statistics of the increase in female employment. There are, however, no figures available to eliminate this possible source of error. Contemporary employment statistics did not perceive any under-registration.

5 The index numbers in Table 10.1 are not strictly correct, because the number of insurance offices reporting fluctuated slightly from month to month. However, random samples which have been adjusted to eliminate error show that the index numbers in Table 10.1 still provide a genuine picture; cf. *Reichsarbeitsblatt*, 16, 1918, pp. 657ff.

6 As the extension of compulsory insurance to servants and agricultural workers came into force on 1 January 1914, this modification was ignored when calculating the rates of increase. For the purposes of Table 10.2, all women paying contributions were included by contrast with Table 10.1 which includes only those for whom insurance was compulsory. This does not detract from the comparability of the rates of increase in any way, because for both groups the trends were similar, cf. *Reichsarbeitsblatt*, 14, 1916, p. 736, and 'Der Anteil der Frau', pp. 145, 148. Curiously enough, there has been no previous attempt to take the very trivial step of comparing wartime and pre-war rates of increase. Contemporary interpretations of insurance statistics always drew comparisons with the number of contributors in mid-1914. Such comparisons naturally did not reveal the pre-war rate of increase; see *Reichsarbeitsblatt*, 14, 1916, pp. 734–42, 985–9 and 16, 1918, pp. 656–61 and 17, 1919, pp. 71–4. Studies of women's work which appeared after the First World War continue to make the same statistical comparison; see the specialist studies cited in note 2.

7 *Die Kriegsvolkszählungen vom Jahre 1916 und 1917 in Bayern, Beiträge zur Statistik Bayerns*, 89, published by the Regional Office of Statistics, Munich, 1919, pp. 131ff.

8 *Reichsarbeitsblatt*, 18, 1920, pp. 62ff. The index numbers are based on reports from selected firms, usually larger ones, where the numbers of women at work rose more sharply than in industry overall. They thus exaggerated the increase in female employment. The essence of the calculation was to multiply the number of women workers by the number of shifts worked in the last two full weeks in the month in question.

9 *Die Frauenarbeit in der Metallindustrie während des Krieges, dargestellt nach Erhebungen im August/September des Vorstandes des Deutschen Metallarbeiter-Verbandes*, Stuttgart, 1917, p. 12.

10 This figure is higher than that given in Table 10.3 because it also includes the category 'no profession/self-employed, without profession'.

11 The especially high number of new female workers in agriculture does not reflect genuinely new arrivals. In this category were recorded all the female dependants of conscripted farmers who had already been working on the land before but had been registered as dependants rather than as workers.

12 In the 1st Bavarian Army Corps alone – the military administrative district which included Munich, Upper and Lower Bavaria, Augsburg and Swabia – the number of women working in firms involved in war-related industries and with 50 employees and over, rose from 1304 before the war to 11,499 in February 1917. In the 3rd Bavarian Army Corps – embracing, amongst other places, the towns of Nuremberg, Erlangen and Fürth – the corresponding numbers were

32,926 before the war and 61,169 in February 1917. See Hauptstaatsarchiv/ Kriegsarchiv Munich (hereafter HStA/Kr) MKr 14198: Survey of workers in war industry in firms with 50 employees or more (as on 15 February 1917).

13 Sample surveys of the composition of the labour force in war industries in other states of the Reich yield a very similar result. See for instance *Der Arbeitsnachweis in Deutschland*, 3, 1915/16, no. 5, p. 98; Annual Report of the Factory Inspectorate in the districts of Stettin and Stralsund in *Jahresberichte der Gewerbeaufsichtsbeamten und Bergbehörden für die Jahre 1914–18*, official edition, prepared by the Reich Office of Statistics, vol. 1, Berlin, 1920, p. 280. The movement of women into industry from a variety of sectors of the economy is implied by the fact that the employment of women in some sectors – e.g. the textile industry, minerals, leather and rubber manufacture – declined during the war; see *Reichsarbeitsblatt*, 18, 1920, pp. 62ff. A further indication that women moved from non-industrial work to war industry is the decrease in the number of domestic servants during the war. For instance, on 1 October 1918 there were 20,584 female servants insured with the Allgemeine Ortskrankenkasse in Munich (i.e. 17 per cent of all women contributors), while on 1 July 1914 there had still been as many as 31,491 (31 per cent of all female contributors), see *Arbeitsverhältnisse und Organisation der häuslichen Dienstboten in Bayern, Beiträge zur Statistik Bayerns*, vol. 94, Munich, 1921, p. 14. The migration of women from agriculture into industry is not registered in the statistics. Nevertheless, it must have been considerable. Military and civil authorities issued decrees forbidding migration into the cities and banning the employment in town of workers who had come in from the countryside (see, for instance, Prussian War Ministry to Deputy General Headquarters, 27 March 1917, Zentrales Staatsarchiv Potsdam (hereafter ZStA Potsdam) Reichsfinanzministerium 46104, pp. 6ff., as well as Bavarian War Ministry, 28 March, 4 May and 6 June 1917, HStA/Kr MKr 14197, MKr 14201, Deputy General Headquarters of the 1st Bavarian Army Corps Munich 873). Nonetheless, these prohibitions seem to have met with little success; cf. Bavarian Interior Ministry to District Police Authorities, 27 February 1918, HStA/Kr MKr 14201 and the collected monthly reports of the Deputy General Headquarters, 3 February 1917, Bundesarchiv/ Militärarchiv Freiburg (hereafter BA/MA) RM 3/4670, p. 7. The flight of women off the land made itself felt most of all around the centres of industrial production for the war; cf. minutes of a discussion concerning the setting up of War Economic Offices, 18 January 1917, BA/MA RM 31/1003, pp. 17ff.

14 See for example Bajohr, *Die Hälfte der Fabrik*, pp. 124ff. Gabriele Wellner, 'Industrie arbeiterinnen in der Weimarer Republik', *Geschichte und Gesellschaft*, 7, 1981, pp. 534–54, in particular p. 538; Greven-Aschoff, *Die bügerliche Frauenbewegung*, p. 256, n. 11.

15 Goetz Briefs, 'Entwicklung und Verfassung der Hauswirtschaft innerhalb der Volkswirtschaft' in Briefs et al. (eds.), *Die Hauswirtschaft im Kriege, Beiträge zur Kriegswirtschaft*, vol. 25, Berlin, 1917, p. 30 and *passim*. On the deterioration of living conditions and the breakdown of economic management see Kocka, *Facing total war*, pp. 16–26, 40–52 and Gerd Hardach, *The First World War 1914–1918*, London, 1977, pp. 112–20. Ute Daniel, 'Frauen in der Kriegsgesellschaft 1914–1918; Arbeiterfrauen in Beruf, Familie und innerer Politik des Ersten Weltkriegs', dissertation, Bielefeld, 1986, pp. 211–73.

16 Collected monthly reports of the Deputy General Headquarters, 3 May 1917, p. 28, BA/MA RM 3/4670.

17 Briefs, 'Entwicklung und Verfassung der Hauswirtschaft', p. 34.

18 Klaus Dieter Schwarz, *Weltkrieg und Revolution in Nürnberg*, Stuttgart, 1971, p. 157.

19 Food rationing began in January 1915 when coupons were introduced for bread and flour. In the course of 1916 almost all basic foodstuffs were put on ration; Hardach, *First World War*; cf. the contribution by Armin Triebel, above, chapter 5 for further information on the effect of rationing on the composition of family budgets in wartime.

20 Irma von Blanquet, 'Die Kriegsernährungswirtschaft der Stadt Kassel und ihre Lehren für die öffentliche Lebensmittelversorgung', dissertation, Cologne, 1923, pp. 63ff.

21 Collected monthly reports of the Deputy General Headqaurters, 3 April 1917, BA/MA RM 3/4670, p. 44.

22 Martha Voss-Zietz, 'Praktische Hauswirtschaft im Kriege' in Briefs et al. (eds.), *Die Hauswirtschaft*, pp. 55, 60; Marie-Elisabeth Lüders, *Das unbekannte Heer. Frauen kämpfen für Deutschland*, Berlin, 1937, pp. 75ff.

23 Voss-Zietz, 'Praktische Hauswirtschaft', pp. 53ff. Monthly report of the Deputy General Headquarters Saarbrücken, 3 April 1917, BA/MA PH 2/72. See also 'Die Ziegenhaltung in Preußen 1913 bis 1916' and 'Kaninchenzucht in Preußen während der Kriegszeit', both in *Zeitschrift des Preußischen Statistischen Landesamtes*, 58, 1918, Berlin, 1919, pp. 36*ff. for evidence for the increased keeping of small animals during the war.

24 Voss-Zietz, 'Praktische Hauswirtschaft', p. 60.

25 Collected monthly reports of the Deputy General Headquarters, 3 February 1918, p. 40, BA/MA RM 3/7794.

26 von Blanquet, 'Die Kriegsnährungswirtschaft', p. 45.

27 Reports of the Bavarian Factory Inspectorate, mid-1915; Hauptstaatsarchiv/ Abteilung 2 Munich MH 15956, *passim* and *Jahresberichte der Gewerbeaufsichts-beamten*, *passim*. Related observations on women's work are in part reproduced in *Archiv für Frauenarbeit*, 7, 1919, pp. 152ff. See, too, the report of a discussion held in the (Prussian) War Ministry on 11 December 1915, p. 1, concerning the possible further enlistment of homeworkers in the production of war supplies, Staatsarchiv Münster (hereafter StA Münster) Oberpräsidium 4123, p. 344.

28 An extremely vivid picture of the uneven development of homework is painted by the *Jahresberichte der Gewerbeaufsichtsbeamten*, *passim*.

29 Extracts from *Jahresberichte der Gewerbeaufsichtsbeamten* in *Archiv für Frauen-arbeit*, 7, 1919, pp. 155ff.; Emmy Ludwig, *Die Unterstützungsabteilung des Badischen Landesvereins vom Roten Kreuz und die Badische Kriegsarbeitshilfe*, Karlsruhe, 1918, pp. 83ff.

30 Report of the factory inspectorate in Hamburg, *Jahresberichte der Gewerbeauf-sichtsbeamten*, vol. 3, p. 18.

31 *Ibid.*, vol. 1 (Prussia), pp. 871, 873. Of the women homeworkers employed in September 1918, roughly 5,000 were doing sewing work for the army; the others who worked for textile firms were, for the most part, also engaged in work for the military.

32 The explanations rooted in women's living and working conditions provide only a partial answer and there were further relevant factors, for example, the hostility

of many employers to taking on women, and so on, which cannot be gone into here. See Ute Daniel, 'Fiktionen, Friktionen und Fakten: Frauenlohnarbeit im Ersten Weltkrieg' in Gunther Mai (ed.), *Arbeiterschaft 1914–1918 in Deutschland*, Düsseldorf, 1985, pp. 277–323.

33 The Kriegsamt was set up in 1916. It was charged with responsibility for resources, raw materials, food and labour [translator].

34 Marie-Elisabeth Lüders, *Volksdienst der Frau*, Berlin, 1917, p. 100.

35 See the plan of action for the Frauenarbeitszentrale; Appendix 2 to the Kriegsamt decree concerning the organisation of women's work by the Kriegsamt, 16 January 1917, reproduced in von Gersdorff, *Frauen im Kriegsdienst*, pp. 129ff.

36 Lüders, *Das unbekannte Heer*, pp. 122ff., and also 'Mitteilungen aus der Arbeit der Frauengruppe beim Kriegsersatz- und Arbeitsdepartement, erstattet zur 3. Tagung des Nationalen Ausschusses für Frauenarbeit im Kriege am 22./ 23.4.1918', p. 3, HStA/Kr, MKr 14389. C. Lorenz, 'Die gewerbliche Frauenarbeit', pp. 319–26. On the administrative structure of the Kriegsamt in general, see Gerald D. Feldman, *Army, industry and labor in Germany 1914–1918*, Princeton, NJ, 1966, pp. 189–94, 306ff., *passim*.

37 On the development of factory welfare see Frieda Wunderlich, 'Fabrikpflegerinnen', *Archiv für Frauenarbeit*, 8, 1920, pp. 93–131, and by the same author, *Fabrikpflege: Ein Beitrag zur Betriebspolitik*, Berlin, 1926; Else Zodtke-Heyde, 'Fabrikinspektorinnen und Fabrikpflegerinnen', *Archiv für Frauenarbeit*, 6, 1918, pp. 10–27. See also a paper delivered at a conference of Prussian civil servants and trade officials on 4 March 1909 by Dr Czimatis, a government official: 'Empfiehlt es sich, auf die gewerblichen Unternehmer einen Einfluß zur Anstellung sog. Fabrikpflegerinnen auszuüben?', StA Münster, Oberpräsidium 4123.

38 Wunderlich, 'Fabrikpflegerinnen', p. 101.

39 Seidel, *Frauenarbeit*, p. 160.

40 On this see Daniel, 'Fiktionen', which studies the political and institutional obstacles which confronted the Kriegsamt and other government departments concerned with the mobilisation of women for war work.

41 After some initial mistrust, women workers seem to have been very well-disposed indeed towards factory nurses, insofar as they ever got to see them; cf. the extracts from the annual reports of the Factory Inspectorate which appeared in *Archiv für Frauenarbeit*, 7, 1919, pp. 160–6. The Bavarian Feldzeugmeisterei, the department charged with the supervision of munitions factories, confirmed that the 20 factory nurses in the Bavarian state armaments works had had a positive effect on the morale of women workers, see Feldzeugmeisterei to Bavarian Ministry for Military Affairs, 18 January 1919, HStA/Kr, MKr 14391. The overall activity of the Frauenreferate and the women in charge of them correspondingly received a degree of recognition from the authorities. When after the war it was discussed whether the Frauenreferate should be dissolved or retained, many Prussian governmental districts were in favour of retention; see the transcripts of the replies given in early 1919 by regional presidents/ commissars for demobilisation to a survey on this question, in the unpublished papers of Marie-Elisabeth Lüders, Bundesarchiv Koblenz (hereafter BA Koblenz) NL 151, 160, *passim*.

42 Lüders, *Das unbekannte Heer*, pp. 101ff.

43 Hermann Schäfer, *Regionale Wirtschaftspolitik in der Kriegszeit: Staat, Industrie und Verbände während des Ersten Weltkriegs in Baden*, Stuttgart, 1983, pp. 91ff.

44 Prussian Ministry of the Interior to regional presidents, 4 February 1916, Staatsarchiv Detmold (hereafter StA Detmold) M1IE/2803. From the central funds made available by the Bundesrat on 18 November 1915 for the assistance of unemployed textile workers – assistance was subsequently extended to textile homeworkers, garment workers and employees in other trades hit by production restrictions – local authorities received a refund of at least half of their expenditure in this area, backdated to 1 October 1915. Prussia paid its local authorities a further third.

45 *Der Arbeitsnachweis in Deutschland*, 3, 1915/16, p. 80.

46 Figures derived from, Association of Westphalian employment agencies to members of the Committee for combating the consequences of unemployment in the Westphalian textile industry, 4 December 1915, StA Münster, Oberpräsidium 4124; Association of Westphalian employment agencies: Minutes of a meeting held on 31 August 1915 concerning unemployment in the textile industry, *ibid*.

47 *Der Arbeitsnachweis in Deutschland*, 4, 1916/17, p. 84.

48 Figures taken from, Ministry of the Kingdom of Saxony for External Affairs to Reich Treasury, 7 October 1915, ZStA Potsdam, Reichsministerium des Innern 1055. It is possible that the calculations were rounded up a little, since there was a measure of financial interest in exaggerating the degree of unemployment rather than understating its extent.

49 On this see Regional President Arnsberg to Chief President Westphalia, 24 January 1916, and Association of Westphalian employment agencies: minutes of a meeting of the Committee for combating the consequences of unemployment in the Westphalian textile industry, held on 19 January 1916, both documents in StA Münster, Oberpräsidium 4124; Deputy General Headquarters of the 6th Army Corps Breslau to Prussian War Ministry, 28 October 1916, HStA/Kr, MKr 12689; collected monthly reports of the Deputy General Headquarters, 3 January 1918, p. 31, BA/MA RM3/v.7794, *Der Arbeitsnachweis in Deutschland*, 3, 1915/16, p. 80.

50 War reserves and labour department to Kriegsamtsstelle Karlsruhe, 17 February 1917, Generallandesarchiv Karlsruhe (hereafter GLA Karlsruhe) 456 EV 8/111.

51 Deputy General Headquarters of the 6th Army Corps Breslau to Prussian War Ministry, 28 October 1916, HStA/Kr, MKr 12689; Regional President, Minden to Chief President, Westphalia, 20 December 1915; Association of Westphalian employment agencies, 4 December 1915: Report on the survey conducted in October of unemployment in the Westphalian textile industry, both documents in StA Münster, Oberpräsidium 4124.

52 Cf. for instance, Prussian Minister for Trade and Industry to Chief Presidents, 23 July 1915. Prussian War Ministry/Abteilung für Zurückstellungswesen to Deputy General Headquarters, 28 July 1915, both documents in StA Münster, Oberpräsidium 4124.

53 Prussian Minister for Trade and Industry, 5 December 1916, reproduced in *Der Arbeitsnachweis in Deutschland*, 4, 1916/17, pp. 74ff.

54 Schäfer, *Regionale Wirtschaftspolitik*, pp. 115–20, 181–210.

55 See, for instance, Hans Horse, 'Maßnahmen zur Behebung der durch den Krieg entstandenen Arbeitslosigkeit in Krefeld', *Der Arbeitsnachweis in Deutschland*, 2, 1914/15, p. 206.

56 Rudolf Zesch, *Was ist geschehen zur Ermöglichung der Arbeit von Ungelernten und Frauen in der gesamten Schwer-, Maschinen- und chemischen Industrie und im Handwerk?*, Berlin, March 1933, BA/MA MSG 779/780, p. 3.

UTE DANIEL

57 On the law, its preceding history and implementation see Margarete Hoffmann, 'Das Gesetz betreffend die Unterstützung von Familien in den Dienst eingetretener Mannschaften vom 28.2.1888/4.8.1914 und seine Anwendung', unpublished dissertation, Berlin, 1918, *passim*.

58 Paul Hirsch, 'Die Kriegsfürsorge der deutschen Gemeinden', *Annalen für soziale Politik und Gesetzgebung*, 4, 1916, p. 263.

59 Minutes of a discussion about family allowances between the Reich Home Office, federal governments, trade unions, representatives of industry, association of municipal authorities and others, held on 11 November 1915, ZStA Potsdam, Reichsministerium des Innern 12094, pp. 212ff. Going by the results of the war census of 5 December 1917, according to which the population of Germany was 62,615,275, with 14,850,186 households (including institutions) (see *Hauptergebnisse der Volkszählung im Deutschen Reich am 5.12.1917*, prepared by the economic department of the War Food Office, Berlin, 1918, p. 2), the proportion of households or families receiving allowance would have come to almost one-third of the total, that of individual persons to a good sixth. As the war progressed, this proportion rose even further, especially in the bigger cities. In early 1918 26.4 per cent of the population of Düsseldorf were receiving family allowance, in Barmen the figure was 28.5 per cent. See Jürgen Reulecke, 'Städtische Finanzprobleme und Kriegswohlfahrtspflege', *Zeitschrift für Stadtgeschichte, Stadtsoziologie und Denkmalpflege*, 1, 1975, pp. 48–79, esp. 70.

60 Information on family allowance payments made by the central government, Zentrales Staatsarchiv Merseburg (hereafter ZStA Merseburg) Rep.77, Tit.332g, Nr. 27, Beiheft 3, Bd 1–7 (author's calculations). For comparison the total state income in Prussia from taxes and running the state railways (net profits) between January 1914 and December 1918 came to 6,223,733,310 marks; calculated on the basis of *Statistisches Jahrbuch für den Preußischen Staat*, 16, 1920, p. 320. The centrally funded portion of the payments made by all the federal states together in August 1915 came to 93.4 million marks; for August 1916 the sum was 128.3 million marks (the amount of 225,000 marks for Lübeck was added on by the authorities as an estimate): information on family allowance expenditure, ZStA Potsdam, Reichsministerium des Innern 12129, pp. 68ff.

61 All figures are inclusive of the 100 per cent supplement paid by the City of Berlin, Hoffman, 'Das Gesetz', pp. 134ff.

62 *Ibid.*

63 The municipal authorities put pressure on landlords to lower rents and granted rent support to 'warrior families', which was paid directly to the landlord on the condition that he reduced the rent. In many towns rent tribunals were established which had powers of veto over notices to quit or rent increases; see Ludwig Preller, *Sozialpolitik in der Weimarer Republik*, Kronberg and Düsseldorf, 1978, p. 67 and Walter Bierbrauer, 'Die Einwirkung des Krieges und der Nachkriegszeit auf die Wohnbautätigkeit, unter besonderer Berücksichtigung von Rheinland und Westfalen', unpublished dissertation, 1921, pp. 23ff.

64 For instance, according to a survey of its members conducted by the Association of German Steel Industrialists 237 iron and steel works paid about 33 marks per month per person to dependants of their conscripted employees in the first year of the war, 1914–15; Philipp Fabian, 'Kriegshilfe der deutschen Eisen- und Stahlindustrie', *Stahl und Eisen*, 7, 1916, pp. 1–4; see also *Jahresberichte der Gewerbeaufsichtsbeamten, passim*.

65 This line of differentiation is emphasised, for example, in the reports of mayors and rural administrators to the Regional President, Düsseldorf, about the progress of mobilisation in August 1914. Hauptstaatsarchiv Düsseldorf (hereafter HStA Düsseldorf) Regierung Düsseldorf 14911, pp. 199–287. One important qualification is that the income of most families, whether or not they were in receipt of the family allowance, could only be said to suffice for the purchase of rationed consumer goods; the prices of non-rationed and black market goods lay far beyond their financial means; cf. the even less optimistic view of the standard of living of the urban working class taken by Armin Triebel, above, chapter 5.

66 District Office of the Kingdom of Bavaria, Augsburg to Deputy General Headquarters of the 1st Bavarian Army Corps Munich, 19 December 1916, HStA/Kr, Stellvertrentendes Generalkommando I. Bayerisches Armeekorps München, 980.

67 Kriegsamtsstelle Munich to Bavarian Kriegsamt, 15 August 1917, HStA/Kr, MKr 14384; collected monthly reports of the Deputy General Headquarters, 3 May 1917, BA/MA RM3/4670, pp. 27ff. See also *Vorwärts*, 1 August 1915 and 21 October 1916, *Berliner Tageblatt*, 13 October 1916 and 13 June 1917, *Deutsche Tageszeitung*, 3 March 1917.

68 The Social Democrats had demanded that the Reich government put a stop to this practice, which they denounced as 'forced labour for warriors' wives' (see *Vorwärts*, 1 August 1915 and 21 October 1916) but the government refused; ZStA Potsdam, Reichsministerium des Innern 12092, p. 121 (Philipp Scheidemann (SPD) to Reich Home Office, 25 June 1915) and p. 332 (Secretary of State for the Interior to Scheidemann, 9 August 1915); in the same archive, Reichsministerium des Innern 12097, p. 284 (Prussian Minister for the Interior to Reich Chancellor, 25 August 1916).

69 Amongst others, the military leadership demanded that soldiers' wives be made to work. Cf. Hindenburg to Reich Chancellor, 13 September 1916, reproduced in Richard Sichler and Joachim Tiburtius, *Die Arbeiterfrage, eine Kernfrage des Weltkrieges: Ein Beitrag zur Erklärung des Kriegsausgangs*, Berlin, n.d. (1925?), pp. 105–8.

70 Reich Chancellor/Reich Home Office, 6 March 1917 (transcript), HStA/Kr, Stellvertretendes Generalkommando I. Bayerisches Armeekorps München, 882; published in *Norddeutsche Allgemeine Zeitung*, 8 March 1917, and elsewhere.

71 Factory Inspectorate Mönchen-Gladbach to Regional President, Düsseldorf, 2 December 1914, HStA Düsseldorf, Regierung Düsseldorf 15058. Similar cases in Hoffmann, 'Das Gesetz', pp. 324, 338ff.

72 Commissarial discussion in Reich Home Office, 7 July 1917, ZStA Merseburg, Rep.120 BB VII 1, Nr. 3i, Bd. 2, pp. 337–46; Reich Chancellor/Reich Home Office, 6 March 1917 and 14 August 1917, HStA/Kr, Stellvertretendes Generalkommando I. Bayerisches Armeekorps München, 882.

73 War reserves and labour department to federal governments, 13 July 1918, HStA/Kr, Stellvertretendes Generalkommando I. Bayerisches Armeekorps München, 882.

74 Agnes von Harnack, one of the most prominent figures in the official campaign to promote the movement of women into war work reported that in her conversations with former German prisoners of war in spring 1918, the latter felt that the practice of taking wages into account when calculating the family allowance was unjust. One of the men declared: 'I wrote to my wife, who told you to work, when you knew you'd have your allowance cut'. Harnack's report of her visit to

Warsaw on behalf of the War Press Department, 25 March–5 April 1918, BA Koblenz, NL 151, 165.

75 Marie-Elisabeth Lüders, *Die Entwicklung der gewerblichen Frauenarbeit im Kriege*, Munich and Leipzig, 1920, p. 23.

76 See Richard Bessel, ' "Eine nicht allzu grosse Beunruhigung des Arbeitsmarkts": Frauenarbeit und Demobilmachung in Deutschland nach dem Ersten Weltkrieg', *Geschichte und Gesellschaft*, 9, 1983, pp. 211–29; Paul Prange, 'Die Demobilmachung des Arbeitsmarkts im Deutschen Reich nach Beendigung des Weltkriegs 1914/18', unpublished dissertation, Würzburg, 1923; Josef Müller, 'Die Regelung des Arbeitsmarkts in der Zeit der wirtschaftlichen Demobilmachüng', unpublished dissertation, Erlangen, 1923; Elisabeth Martha Gravert, 'Der Einfluß der wirtschaftlichen Demobilmachüng auf die Entwicklung der Frauenarbeit', unpublished dissertation, Hamburg, 1924–5.

77 Domestic servants represented 40.0 per cent of all employed women in 1882, 34.4 per cent in 1895, 26.2 per cent in 1907 and 21.7 per cent in 1925. See Müller, Willms and Handl, *Strukturwandel*, p. 136.

11
Women and work in wartime Britain

Deborah Thom

In 1916, Mrs Churchill wrote in her book *Women's War Work*, 'It is one of the virtues of war that it puts the light which in peacetime is hid under a bushel in such prominence that all can see it'.[1] Her sense of war bringing women's contribution into the light, making them visible, was widely shared. In addition, the coincidence of the end of the war with the granting of the vote to women over thirty made contemporaries see wartime occupations as intrinsically emancipatory, because they had previously been done by men. Mrs Fawcett, a leading suffragist, argued that, 'The war revolutionised the industrial position of women. It found them serfs and left them free.'[2]

Mary Macarthur, a trade union leader, wrote in 1918,

Of all the changes wrought by war, none has been greater than the change in the status and position of women, but it is not so much that woman herself has changed but that man's perception of her has changed.[3]

Some have shared this view despite the light of hindsight. Professor Marwick, in particular, has propounded the view that women's consciousness was irrevocably changed by war.[4] Others have argued that there was change, but it was short-term because of the dominance of ideology or male hostility, expressed through men's trade unions.[5] There is some explanatory force in this argument, but it does not sufficiently explain the nature of the change that took place in employment or the ease of eviction from war occupations once the war was over and women's own agreement with this process. Women's attitudes are one factor, another is the shaping of the introduction of women into war work by pre-war attitudes and a third is the added emphasis given by war to women as mothers.[6]

The ideological shaping of women's work before the war

Women were not the serfs of Mrs Fawcett's description though their labour was the subject of concern and debate before the war. The 1911 census recorded about one-third of all women as doing some paid work. These figures are inadequate in many ways. Much domestic work would not be recorded in the census for a variety of reasons. For example, the taking in of washing, charring or child-minding might not be relayed by the head of the household. It is also difficult to know how many women would have wanted work in peace-time because women were grossly under-recorded in the data on unemployment. The largest single category of women's work was domestic service and this was not covered by the National Insurance scheme. As most Labour Exchanges did not do much placement in service, women were disinclined to register as unemployed.[7] The second largest category of women's employment was work in the textile trades and here the trade was 'half-recumbent' by 1914.[8] Women were involved in demands to extend the use of women's labour. They participated in the 'Right to Work' campaign of 1908. They argued that women had claimed more sickness benefit than men because their working conditions were bad, not because of female incapacity. Feminists campaigned for access to professions and education, and, for manual workers, that there should be protective legislation. In some trades they wanted exclusion from work altogether, as in the case of some chemicals for example, particularly lead. In other trades, associated with low-paid women's work, they wanted minimum wage levels, fixed by Trade Boards or 'Fair Wages' agreements. This work was often concentrated in particular regions and restricted to a few occupations where the majority of the workforce, as in the textile and clothing trades, were women. Campaigns on the issue of women's employment were important in informing attitudes to it. They tended to have a dual focus in that they either demanded admission to all jobs on the grounds of egalitarianism or, alternatively, insisted that society's need for fit mothers and children should be a primary factor in legislating or regulating employment or wages. These demands could, and did, come into contradiction but their effect was to emphasise the social determinants of women's work.

The ideological component in descriptions of women working was evident in the views of organisations of, or for, working women – the women's trade unions. The image of women's work was based on their concentration in the 'sweated trades'. The paradigm, particularly in graphics or photographs, was the women chainmakers who had fought and won a strike for minimum Trade Board wages in 1911. They had paraded through Britain's largest cities, notably London, carrying the chains they made – a disturbing double image of strength and skill allied to industrial slavery.[9] The pressure groups who agitated on behalf of working women were not only central to the formation of the image of the working woman; they were to be centrally concerned with the introduction of women into 'new' areas of work in the war economy. A small group met under a variety of different labels, wrote the commentaries on women's labour and discussed and campaigned for maternity benefits, factory inspection, and against low wages for women and sweating as a part of the larger phenomenon of 'women's work'. The reference to 'women's work' was deliberately ambiguous, including as it did women's domestic labour as well.[10] Women trade unionists were closely linked with the network of anti-sweating campaigners, the infant welfare movement and the constitutional suffragists, in the National Union of Women's Suffrage Societies and the Adult Suffrage Association. They shared the belief of Anna Martin of the National Union.

The rearing of the child crop is, confessedly, the most vital to the nation of all its industries, being that which alone gives to other industry any meaning or importance; but although its quality is occasioning grave concern, no attempt has been made to apply . . . principles to those on whose care and devotion it necessarily depends.[11]

Married women workers provided the particular focus for this philanthropic concern; they were also most subject to the limiting factors on women's 'emancipation' through employment. They predominated in women's trades; where almost by definition low wages were earned, and, as the chief woman factory inspector noted, they were mostly tied to one area by their families, and employed,

in poor or underpaid industries and in towns and districts where women are largely employed without a sufficient balance of men's staple industries to enable the husband or father to be the main breadwinner of the family.[12]

Their work was not extra to the family budget, the 'pin-money' of popular journalism. In such areas, and in cities of high unemployment, they were often the main wage-earners. A Fabian Women's Group survey concluded that one-third of all women workers were supporting dependants. It was not a sample scientifically collected and probably overestimated the number of women breadwinners but it certainly reflected reality in the areas of high female participation in the labour force, Lancashire, Belfast and Dundee.[13] Such results showed the commitment of married women to paid employment but they also demonstrated the connection between women's work and low wages, which was one of the reasons for male trade-union hostility to women in the workplace.

At the same time as the Fabian Women's Group, the Women's Industrial Council, the National Union of Women's Suffrage Societies and the Women's Trade Union League were investigating the living conditions of working women and the social reasons for low wages, working women were themselves beginning to agirate over conditions of work. The years before the war were marked by a steady increase in women's organisations of all types but particularly in women's trade unions. This growth was partly the result of increased organising work by a few female members of the Independent Labour Party; for example, Julia Varley for textile workers and the metalworkers in the Midlands, Ellen Wilkinson among Co-operative employees, Margaret Bondfield among shop assistants and above all Mary Macarthur and Gertrude Tuckwell through the National Federation of Women Workers and the Women's Trade Union League.[14] It also reflected increased demand from women workers themselves, politicised by feminism and labour unrest. Women leaders used the arguments of trade unionism as education, as preparation for marriage and for citizenship Their trade unionism was, if the word can be used, maternalist. Trade-union demands were put into the context of the family, or domestic life, rather than the life of the workplace. Margaret Bondfield, for example, enjoined a meeting of Labour women, 'Every mother should get her girl a union card.'[15] Much of the organisation was achieved as a result of strike action and only then calling in a union official. Union leaders pointed out to employers that union membership was as likely to prevent strikes as initiate them.[16] Here the image of the defenceless woman worker was tempered by the recognition that women's inexperience meant they could be more subversive of the established order – which might be industrial militancy or quietism.

This agitation allied to the raising of the 'woman question' in the parliamentary sphere had a cumulative effect. Gender came to the forefront of public discussion. Trade union organisations, those most closely concerned with women's employment, added their voice to those of others campaigning for support of motherhood, the vote and divorce law reform. Trade unions concentrated on national welfare issues (including low pay) and thereby diminished the amount of public attention that could be devoted to the specific occupational problems of women workers. The effect was also to reinforce the notion that women were inherently deficient as workers. They were deficient because they were inhibited by family responsibilities, and because they were physically weaker and lacked a tradition of work expertise except in certain forms of employment where they had not competed on equal terms with men.

Trade unionism protected women from their own inadequacies, it was argued, and thereby benefited the male majority by ensuring that they would not be undercut by low wages and undermined by worsening conditions.[17] Equal pay was demanded by some women on the grounds that their work was of equal worth; but the supplementary argument that it would eradicate the social evils of low wages for women, high infant mortality and prostitution, remained. All these social evils were threats to a good family life, and originated in the existing conditions of women's work. As a result working women were discussed in 1914 as potential or actual mothers rather than as workers, let alone specific kinds of workers.

Women's work in wartime: myth and reality

The effect of the war was to accentuate the trends of social thought current in the pre-war period. This happened in two phases; the first covered the five month period of unemployment at the beginning of the war, and the second which lasted about a year, the negotiation of the replacement of men by women. The textile trade contracted by 43 per cent in the first five months of the war, clothing manufacture by 21 per cent, women being particularly badly affected by lay-offs and short-time working. Large numbers of domestic servants and needleworkers were sacked as consumption fell.[18] The 'sacrifice' expected of households where servants were employed was often interpreted as the release of servants for war work but there was, as yet, no war work for women. The question of women's employment became the problem of women's unemployment. The belief that women were likely to accept inadequate conditions of work at low wages through a combination of ignorance, docility and patriotism was thoroughly reinforced by high unemployment among women, accentuated by the mobilisation of the volunteer army, the British Expeditionary Force, when many women were to be seen on the streets and at the railway stations, saying goodbye. The League of Decency and Honour and several other organisations counselled prudence and self-restraint[19] but others realised that social order could be better provided by removing unemployed women from the temptation of the streets, particularly in transit and billeting areas. Working women's organisations were particularly worried by the threat that wartime unemployment posed to good relations with the wider trade union movement. Feminist organisations were divided about the war itself and the most militant unconstitutional suffragettes, the Women's Social and Political Union, became active proponents of the wartime recruitment of men as soldiers and women as their replacements in the workplace.[20] However, the women who were already unemployed played no part in this and many were in an impoverished situation from which there was no apparent escape. In a piece of notable class collaboration Mary Macarthur was recruited by Queen Mary to run the Queen's Work for Women Fund. Its motto was 'Women's help for women'. The fund amassed substantial funds and ran workrooms which were forbidden to compete with commercial manufacture but could make good the loss of some German goods, such as toys and artificial flowers, retrain factory workers in domestic skills for their own homes, which in one instance involved cradles from orange boxes, and 're-moralise' the unemployed by running herb gardens. The women in them were explicitly neither trained nor made self-supporting. They were removed from the labour market for 15 weeks and thereby it was hoped from the 'abyss of destitution'.[21]

In fact as early as November 1914 there were signs of some expansion in employment opportunities for women. The greatest expansion was in clerical and shop assistant work. In these sections the process of 'feminisation' had already been under way before the war but the numbers of clerical staff were to increase further during the war due to the increased volume of paper work in all spheres of administration. This development was contested by some male workers but, for a variety of reasons, their protests aroused little public interest or concern. In the first place, clerical unions were weak at the beginning of the war and had very little control over job definition or hiring practices. Secondly, most of the women taken on were not replacements but extra workers. Finally, and most importantly, the 'feminisation' of clerical and shop work aroused no social concerns. Office and shop work was clean, respectable and presented no obvious threat to gynaecological health. They drew on women's innate qualities. As one National Union of Women's Suffrage Societies writer said, there were some jobs for which women are 'naturally suited' and she adduced civil service clerk, teacher or salesman as examples.[22] Such work was also generally undertaken by single women, since marriage bars (dismissal on marriage) had operated before, and was seen as appealing particularly to women's interest in 'meantime' work to fill in the years between school and marriage. Women's work had been described as 'meantime' before the war, even, as Mary Macarthur had argued, as good preparation for housewifery. 'The working girl has good habits, she is industrious and thrifty.'[23]

What was contentious to both the general public and representatives of women workers alike was the employment of women on new forms of arduous manual labour. One journalist wrote,

The extremist feminist in her wildest moments would not advocate dock-labouring, mining or road-digging as suitable employment for women.[24]

Some feminists had, in fact, drawn attention to the rigours of domestic work for example, the lifting of heavy weights of water and the prolonged stooping involved in the scrubbing of stairs but this was ignored. The TUC discussed the issue of women's employment very fully in 1915 and approved a motion which expressed the basis of the objection to manual work for women as well as the attempt to define processes as suitable for men or women. The motion is worth citing as the attitude it enshrined came to dominate discussion on women's work in wartime.

That in order to sustain the physique of Britain and to prevent physical degeneration, no relaxation of Trade Union rules shall lead to the employment of women on work of a character unsuited by
1 carrying or turning over weights, or operated by heavy foot pressure;
2 employment on hot or dusty trades in which lime, oil, grease, fires and or emery are used;
3 or on heavy machinery producing fatigue, or such machines where often male employment produces a large number of accidents.[25]

This list went unheeded in that all these conditions were broken on occasion but the consensus on 'proper' work for women was not a cynical bow to prevailing ideology. Rather the TUC in this list was expressing genuine fears as to how far the needs of the state might override the needs of society. Trade unionists, particularly women, believed that their knowledge of industrial processes was greater than that of government and that their duty lay in presenting such information and thereby preserving the nation's health. They became reconciled to women working in industry *even on these processes* because it was temporary, because welfare services were provided and because tasks were, to some extent, reorganised to reduce the adverse effects on women's health. They also saw this concession as a necessary price for the greater consultation involved in the wartime negotiation between management, government and trade union representatives over when, where and if dilution and substitution should take place. Dilution meant the replacement of skilled men by semi-skilled or unskilled workers; substitution meant the replacement of one semi-skilled or unskilled worker by another, usually in both cases thereby increasing the number of women in the workplace. Last of all very few women did in fact do very much new 'unsuitable' work. The majority were to work throughout the war on work defined as 'women's' processes. Those who did undertake heavy, outdoor work were explicitly there for the duration only.

Dilution and substitution

The government had started the war without a labour policy. The dual problem arising from its need of both men and munitions resulted in the creation of one, but it was little dignified by theoretical notions. Women were accepted reluctantly as a source of labour after other groups were shown to be inadequate. Belgian refugees were used but there were not enough. Imperial subjects were too expensive to transport.[26] Women were demanding the right to contribute and Lloyd George used their demands to sponsor a 'Right to Serve' march organised by Mrs Pankhurst. Under the caption 'The British Lion is awake, so is the Lioness' the newsreels of this march were shown in 3,000 cinemas. Some criticised the complete disregard of the march organisers for the rights of displaced men or replacement women as employees but it was the marchers' rhetoric of service by all women that dominated government propaganda and journalists' descriptions as well as administrative arrangements. Women were to volunteer as women, rather than on the basis of particular qualifications whether of labour experience, age, marital status or education. In the summer of 1915 the Women's War Register was set up, primarily to provide a workforce in munitions factories.[27] Unions had agreed to the process of dilution to make good the shortage of skilled engineers and to protect the existing workforce from attempts to lower wages, speed up rates of production or alter working procedures. The government began to monitor the movement of labour in order to control the processes of production, *particularly dilution*, rather than to investigate the labour market *per se*. As a result the labour force figures were designed to demonstrate the success of dilution and substitution in the years 1915–17. They were figures for trends rather than absolute totals, since they were submitted only by those employers in large firms. The *Labour Gazette* published monthly dilution totals based on these returns which were the source for most published surveys of the extent and effects of dilution on women (cf. Appendices 11.1 and 11.2).

All new female employees were inclined to be subsumed under the title of substitute, if not dilutee, although they were in many industries not replacements at all but extra workers. Such women were also likely to be described as though all came straight from the home, without history or knowledge of employment. Any figures of employment require careful scrutiny but those provided by the British government in the First World War need it more than most. There was the sustained growth in the numbers of women in the workforce (as the totals reproduced in Appendix 11.2 confirm) but since the base of July 1914 was a period of high unemployment for women (particularly in the textile industry) the amount of growth seems larger than would be shown by a longer view. Wartime is given the credit for many changes that were already underway so that dilution and substitution should take their place among other trends which influenced the level of women's employment as opposed to being considered as its sole determinants. Some of the changes are only indirectly attributable to the war because it was a time of full employment while others were distorted by the war but fundamentally unaffected by it, for example, the deskilling of work on the typewriter. Trade unions had assented to dilution in exchange for a commitment to restore the pre-war situation immediately the war ended. Women's representatives and most general unions had not participated in either the initial discussions or the final agreements over dilution since the agreements were not for them but for the men they 'replaced'. All such workers were defined as replacements, and increasingly the word 'dilution' became a synonym for the introduction of women. Pay for dilutees was regulated by the Treasury Agreement of May 1915,

The Agreement stated shall not adversely affect the rates customarily paid for the job, and the rates paid shall be the usual rate of the district for this class of work.[28]

This agreement did not cover all cases because of the difficulty of defining 'district', 'customarily' and 'usual' above all at a time when the number of jobs had suddenly multiplied thereby changing the essential character of the task. By 1916 pay was being decided by the sex of the worker. Women on men's work were given a minimum time rate of £1 for a 48-hour week, which protected learners and those on inadequate old machines since they could not fix them themselves. This commitment to 'equal pay' was entirely expedient. It was not designed to attract women into war work or as a recognition of 'worth' but was solely intended to win over men's unions to the process of dilution. Nor in practice was it paid. Employers were, in the event, much more resistant to Circular 447 of 1917 which was designed to fix a minimum rate for women on women's work, since it cost them much more.[29]

Labour mobility

Any assessment of the impact on women of their waged work in wartime needs to begin with an assessment of their reasons for seeking work. The official histories of the Ministry of Munitions tend to assume that munitions factories were successful in attracting and keeping women workers because of the availability of welfare services and stricter regulation of the work environment when the potential workforce as the population in general were enthused with patriotic fervour.[30] However, state intervention in employment, equal pay and welfare provision were not mentioned by any of some sixty former munitions workers whom I have interviewed. Nor does the chronology of changes in employment in general bear this out. A leading civil servant, Humbert Wolfe, who wrote later on labour policy of the time, said that more entered the workforce before their wages were protected than did so afterwards. July 1916 did see the largest number of additional women entering the workforce – according to the government statistics published in the *Labour Gazette*. However, there is no evidence that these were all new workers, since severe shortages of labour in 'traditional' women's trades indicate that much of this movement was from one form of employment into another. What was new and took some time to bring about was the eviction of men from their occupations. In fact, it was only during the course of the year July 1916–June 1917 that women came to contribute nearly half of the workforce (see Table 11.1).[31]

Table 11.1. *Trends in female employment, 1914–18*

Period, measured from July	Women entering the workforce (000s)	Females in workforce (%)
1914–15	382	—
1915–16	563	26.5
1916–17	511	46.9
1917–18	203	46.7

Source
IWM.EMP.4.282. Standing Joint Committee of Women's Industrial Organisation, *The position of women after the war*, p. 4

In any event, women's wages were protected by law only in those industries defined as munitions industries; trade union power alone provided a protection in those trades where dilution had been agreed between unions and management, like the boot and shoe trade or the Co-operative Employees.[32] And in the munitions industries the government did not begin to be a producer in its own right, in the national factories, until 1916.

As was pointed out above, the first phase of the move of women into the workforce was not principally into industry at all, nor into male jobs but into clerical and commercial occupations. By 1915 the textile trades had begun to pick up the trade lost at the onset of war and take on more workers as they diversified into serge and khaki, the new workers being all women, as had mainly been the case before. By July 1916 the privately owned munitions factories and the arsenals were in full production and had expanded considerably, so that in that summer the largest number of new entrants to industry were to be found in textile factories (see Appendix 11.1) while the largest proportion of growth was in the government's own armaments factories (cf. Table 11.2).[33]

These additional women had entered the workforce following a variety of individual decisions. Government posters had characterised the work as 'Do your Bit, Replace a Man for the Front' so that the life of the factory worker was not portrayed as such, but as war service. Government had attempted to see all women as a vast 'reserve army of labour' but women's own experience of work, locality and family role ensured that there was no easy match between labour needs and supply. Male unemployment encouraged many men to enlist and the women, conscious of low pay and harsh physical conditions at work, not unnaturally found mobility and munitions work that much more attractive. On the other hand engineering areas like outer London, Birmingham, Leeds and Clydeside had a large number of men in reserved occupations as skilled engineers or shipbuilders whose wives had a

Table 11.2. *Number of women employed in July 1914 and July 1916*

Economic sector	Women employed		Increase 1914–16 (000s)
	July 1914 (000s)	July 1916 (000s)	
All industry	2,117	2,479	362
Commercial occupations	454	652	198
Banking and finance	9.5	39.5	30
Professional	67.5	82.5	15
Hotels	175	194	19
Agriculture	130	196	66
Transport	15	46	31
Civil Service	60	108	48
Arsenals (dockyards)	2	71	69
Local government	184	212	28
Totals	3,214	4,080	866

Source
As Table 11.1.

laborious domestic life rendered more laborious by wartime shortages but a higher household income which kept them out of the labour market. Their daughters meanwhile simply replaced domestic service with war service in their local factory, a familiar environment in that when younger they had often taken their fathers, uncles, or brothers their lunch. The mobility of war service mimicked the pre-war mobility of domestic service for the group of young women aged between sixteen and twenty. Government encouragement made the workplace accessible, gave respectability to the industrial environment and encouraged a choice of industrial employment but it did not create the underlying need for work which had been so evident in the pre-war agitation. Of sixty interviewees 'My country needed me' was mentioned only once directly, just twice was the patriotic form used 'I wanted to do my bit', in all three cases by domestic servants.

Within factories and offices there were greater differences in attitude between women in the same workplace than had been the case before the war, differences that were not submerged but emphasised by the different ways in which they dealt with the experience. Management at the outset of the war was inexperienced in the organisation of socially mixed groups of women but soon learnt to sort them by social class as well as industrial experience and so on. In some factories, for example, explosives work went to married women because they were considered sensible and 'steady'; in others it went to girls because of the suspected gynaecological hazards of work with chemicals. The best-paid jobs in engineering tended to go to those with family connections in the workshop; sewing jobs to those from the needleworking trades; bullet-making, inspection and gauging to the blue-eyed. A survey of one munitions factory showed that about one-third had found work through the help of friends or relations, another third had simply turned up at the factory gates to be taken on, leaving only the final third to be supplied directly from government Labour Exchanges.[34] In Scotland, Ireland and Wales there was more travel far from home, analogous to male military recruitment, but such young women often caused massive problems for management. The diary of one woman police officer mentions one outstanding example. She left the Woolwich Arsenal partly because she could not stand the 'dirty, stinking, swearing people' but found her North Wales factory as difficult. Girls from the Rhondda were always 'getting up strikes' and full of 'socialistic speeches'; girls from Ireland started a riot by singing Fenian songs and casting aspersions on the Tommies. They had to be sent back to Ireland covered in mud after a pitched battle.[35] Such experience seems to have been rare but it demonstrates as the statistics on labour mobilisation do not, the many forms of 'mobilisation' and the variety of experiences behind the term 'war work'.

It is questionable how many of these women workers who entered new jobs during the war were replacing a man. The machinery of dilution gave a misleading impression of wholesale replacement of skilled men by women in the factories. Dilution officers toured the country to demonstrate the efficiency of women workers and the ease with which skilled work could be reorganised for the unskilled. They mounted exhibitions of photographs both of machines and of women actually at work. The Imperial War Museum's photographs were a product of the new detailed attention to work processes that dilution encouraged.[36] The War Office produced a pair of handbooks on dilution and sent 40,000 out to employers.[37] The result was a developing iconography of the working woman which emphasised the novel, the exceptional and the photogenic. Often the pictures showed work that was not new but was only performed by women in some parts of the country, pithead work for example.[38] It is also significant that the Imperial War Museum's collections of documents and photographs on women's work were assembled with the specific intention of showing what women had contributed to the war effort.[39] The consequence, intentional or otherwise, was to emphasise discontinuity, since there was no material extant to compare women's contributions to the economy before the war. Part of the light coming out from under the bushel represented what was newly perceived, rather than itself new.

It is impossible to estimate how many married women were working for

Plate 6. A young woman in engineering. The image of the woman war worker: fragile, heroic, with an immense machine under her control, alone.

the first time. The Ministry of Munitions certainly thought that there were additional married women who could be drawn into employment. In 1916 the report on labour said,

Although the women who would normally be engaged in industrial work are now all fully occupied, there are large reserves of women, principally married, who have had previous industrial experience and who could be utilised in special circumstances.[40]

However, both oral evidence and the reports on factories prepared by welfare supervisors, now at the Imperial War Museum, contradict this impression. There were no such reserves, most married women who had any experience of industrial life had entered factory work as soon as openings became known or available. The wives of members of the armed forces were frequently in great need. Dependants' allowances were low, took some time to come through and were administered by committees more used to giving out charitable doles.[41] Much of the 'new' labour of the second half of the war came from women entering employment for the first time because of their age and not through the removal of social inhibitions.

Plate 7. Young woman and old man in a rope works. This kind of photograph which contrasted the contribution of the woman and the man was not used in propaganda about women's capacities.

The production process and the welfare of female workers

The organisation of production is depicted in the unpublished official history of the Ministry of Munitions in the same way as the organisation of labour mobility and on this account much historical work has been based. The operation is described as a clearly theorised, disciplined affair – especially the development of welfare systems. In practice the welfare system did not even operate in every factory run by the Ministry of Munitions let alone in the 'controlled' factories for which the Ministry provided only management expertise and welfare, or in manufacture in general. The dangers of TNT poisoning and the chewing of cordite that was common at the time, were both dealt with as problems of production, affecting output, rather than as an industrial disease.[42] However, the care devoted to the health of munition workers did provide a large amount of valuable information about the significant impact that improvements in workers' welfare could have on the level of production. Successive reports of the Health of Munition Workers' Committee demonstrated clearly that good seating, lighting, washrooms and canteens helped to keep output high and rising.[43]

These technical issues were of especial concern to commentators on women's health. Thus, Dr Janet Campbell concluded her report on physiological factors and employment by arguing that much of the work done in wartime had been less injurious to health than domestic work, particularly the open-air forms of work. Posterity, or as she described it 'the germ plasm', would be unaffected by the employment of women.[44] There had been limited experiments with providing for pregnancy, breast-feeding and an immediate return to work with a lighter work-load but only one factory in Leeds had run a scheme for women to stay on while bearing their children that included all these features. Many factories had crèches, which munitions factories could run with the aid of subsidies. This was not viewed as anything other than a short-term expedient to attract and keep workers. Crèches do not seem to have been very popular in areas where such facilities would have been unfamiliar, though in areas where it was customary for married women to be employed, they were well supported and women argued that they should be kept on after the war. Janet Campbell, who surveyed nursery provision for the Ministry of Reconstruction, asked Medical Officers of Health to report on nurseries. Most disliked them on the grounds that they encouraged mothers to work, but some pointed out that they were better than child-minders to whom mothers who needed to work would turn in their absence.[45]

Women's reaction to the issue of welfare depended critically on the nature of the welfare on offer. Canteens were popular. For many women, particularly married women, it was the first time they had been able to sit down for a full meal on a regular basis. Uniforms, washrooms, lighting and seating were only noticed if deficient. Since welfare workers were employed primarily, 'To ensure good time-keeping',[46] they could be seen either as helpful, humanising the factory, or, alternatively, as disciplinary, reflecting another face of management. Trade Unions were suspicious of welfare. As Mary Macarthur said, 'There is no word more hated among women workers of today than welfare'.[47] However, the way in which many women reacted to the new environment of the factory was often crucially determined by the particular characteristics of the welfare system. Until 1917 nearly all agitation among women was over issues of supervision and welfare, most commonly combined in demands to keep or sack welfare supervisors. In Armstrong–Whitworths in Newcastle there was a major strike which began as 'the tea-break strike' and spread to become a strike of women for work-shop representation. The result was a ten-minute tea break, a welfare system, some new lavatories and union recognition and organisation. Yet one of the leaders of that agitation could not recall ever having met one of the welfare workers.[48]

Male militants have been much analysed and described in the industries of wartime Britain. Women's militancy has gone unrecognised, apart from the equal pay agitation of 1918.[49] Yet although employers lauded female docility, eagerness and dexterity during the introduction of dilutees in 1915–16 they were as enthusiastic in deploring their poor time-keeping, lack of commitment to work and low productivity when called upon to assess women's employment in 1918 for the Hills Committee (of the Ministry of Reconstruction) and the War Cabinet Committee on Women in Industry. A part of the explanation for this change of heart lay in the way in which working women did in some respects behave no differently from men. They learned to use the same industrial weapons as men, whether organised in trade unions or not, and they began to organise in trade unions in larger numbers. Mrs Blanco White in a very interesting piece of evidence to the War Cabinet Committee saw the process in two ways. One was class mingling. The old hands, she said, discouraged eager workers from staying, corrupting those that did. The other was the women's union, the National Federation of Women Workers, which made them discontented with their lot, with which otherwise they were perfectly content.[50] Women's trade union membership grew from 437,000 in 1914 to 1,209,000 in 1918 – a much faster rate of growth than their proportionate membership of the workforce (see Appendix 11.1). Certainly the confidence to organise, the money to pay the subscription and the need to prevent exploitation were all accentuated by war conditions, but these abilities and aspirations were not new and partly continued trends which had been set in motion before the war.[51] However, much of the wartime organisation could not continue after the war because it was in the hands of the National Federation of Women Workers which turned itself into what amounted to a union of women war workers, and was committed to the removal of all dilutees after the war. In so doing the Federation paid a high price for acceptance into the wider world of trade unions, in that they helped to perpetuate the secondary status of the working woman.

The demobilisation of the women workers

The end of the war came before 1918 for some women workers. The first demobilisations for them followed on the closure of the Russian Front. As Churchill, then Minister of Munitions, said to his staff,

The War Office are blamed like Pharaoh of old, because they will not let the people go. Our difficulty is we cannot let the people stay. We have actually succeeded in discharging nearly a million persons, the bulk of whom did not want to go.[52]

Just as the beginning of the war had turned nearly all women into potential war workers, now nearly all women were assumed to have been war workers. Married women, it was assumed, should revert to their previous occupation 'in the home'. The TUC supported the demand for 'mothers' pensions', as a speaker argued in 1919 using military terms and biological description,

If we have got to have an A1 nation we must protect the mothers . . . I honestly think that the institution of pensions for mothers would go a long way towards checking the race suicide that is going on.[53]

She used the pre-war language of social degeneration to argue for a concept of motherhood that, it was argued, war had supported not undermined. The Hills Committee also argued on similar lines. Although the Committee acknowledged that married women would continue to work and that they should not be prevented from doing so, they added a telling rider that women should be discouraged from doing work that was itself injurious to health – like fur pulling, rag picking and gut scraping on the grounds that,

The primary function of women in the state must be regarded, it is not enough to interfere with her service in bearing children, and the care of infant life and health, but she must be safeguarded as home-maker for the nation.[54]

To this end this report recommended exclusion from unhealthy trades and the aware of mothers' pensions and equal pay. Equality of pay was assumed to exclude women effectively from manual work because employers would prefer to employ men.

The policy of the Ministry of Labour also effectively excluded married women from employment. They were not allowed onto the few occupational training schemes set up after the war. They were denied 'out-of-work donation' as 'not genuinely seeking work' if they turned down employment because of domestic obligations. No woman could refuse domestic service work on the grounds that she had another trade as a war worker. Even the limited opportunities offered by 'alternative work', the production of peacetime goods in the war factories, were available only to the widowed mothers of large families. After some pressure from Lilian Barker, the former woman welfare superintendent at the Woolwich Arsenal, the Ministry did provide some domestic training either to turn factory girls into domestic servants or into housewives and mothers. A leaflet for the scheme stated,

A call comes again to the women of Britain, a call happily not to make shells or fill them so that a ruthless enemy can be destroyed but a call to help renew the homes of England, to sew and to mend, to cook and to clean and to rear babies in health and happiness, who shall in their turn grow into men and women worthy of the Empire.[55]

Women's war work: a reassessment

As far as the 'working woman' was concerned the 'experience of war' was ambiguous. Women had demonstrated that they could do work requiring physical strength. They had heaved coal and driven trams. One group of women navvies had built a shipyard. They had demonstrated dexterity and skill. Women had used the new technique of arc welding and built aeroplanes and airships and were employed on the sub-divided tasks of engineering. Dilution had not been achieved in the bastions of male trade unionism, the shipyards and the building of heavy artillery. Women formed the majority of the workforce in fuses and cartridges which had been women's work before the war but they remained dependent on male tool-setters in work on shells. Some had considerable experience of the supervision of a large number of workers in war factories but it was supervision of women on temporary war work. Despite frequent demands from workers themselves and their organisations very few women had been trained in general skills. When 'blind alley' jobs were perceived as a problem, the problem was only for boys, not for women. Individual women managed to 'beat the system' and learn skills, make their own tools and set their own machines, but it seems to have been more common among boys who missed the normal apprenticeship scheme because of the war but could pass as time-served men after the war when no woman could.[56]

Many women were ambivalent about war work, because it produced death-dealing objects. The prize-winning essay in a projectile factory magazine expressed this,

Only the fact that I am using my life's energy to destroy human souls gets on my nerves. Yet on the other hand, I'm doing what I can to bring this horrible affair to an end. But once the War is over, never in creation will I do the same thing again.[57]

They were not ambivalent about work in factories. Most of the sixty women interviewed recalled the work of wartime as a happy time because of the friendships they had formed, the wages, the amusements in the factory such as hair competitions, football matches, concerts and running jokes. They would have welcomed a chance to have continued to work in a factory but on another product. In the event, most of the interviewees out of 50 women war workers were reluctantly forced back into domestic service but there were several women who, through their war work, had lost the chance to train as servants, and found later that this option was no longer available because they were too old, too work-roughened or viewed with suspicion as an ex-factory worker.

Some employers learnt a different lesson from the war. Food production, light engineering and clothing expanded in the inter-war years using female labour, often organised on the same principles by the same managerial group who had organised the war. At a higher level the same phenomenon could be observed. Mary Macarthur, Margaret Bondfield, and Julia Varley continued to be active in labour or trade union politics; Clara Collet, Adelaide Anderson and Dr Janet Campbell pursued careers in the civil service; while the Fabian women, Beatrice Webb, Barbara Drake and Mrs Hutchins continued campaigning. The influence of all these on the quality of public debate on topics concerning women and the family was increased by the war but they did not, as Philip Abrams has argued, severely distort the politics of the reconstruction against the interests of organised labour because they shared the same concerns for the re-establishment of family life.[58] The activities of these prominent women suggest increased self-confidence and a new perception of work but not total emancipation.

The same is true of the question of equal pay. War wages are one of the issues on which published sources are least reliable. The major source is the War Cabinet Committee on Women in Industry which was set up to propitiate striking transport workers who demanded equal pay in the summer of 1918. The importance the government attached to the Report's verdict that government had kept its promise to preserve wage levels is evident from the attempt that was made to prevent Beatrice Webb issuing her minority report.[59] The Committee's Report concluded that most women had not in fact done men's work, but that when they had taken over a particular job from a man they had achieved about two-thirds his level of output. Beatrice Webb, however, argued in her Ministry report that although they had been doing the men's work, women had not received the men's pay. The evidence given by employers and managers was contradictory, often vitiated by their desire to report on the general principles of the employment of women rather than to record actual wage levels. Such comparisons as were made were of doubtful value. The availability of labour, the number of hours worked and work organisation were all different in wartime. Inexperience was frequently confused with gender. Few witnesses compared women with the boys beside whom they worked, and if they did, it was only to contrast their respective levels of ambition in munitions factories where most boys were deployed.

Clearly women on average earned less than men. They received cost-of-living bonuses later and these were lower than those offered to their male counterparts. Even the women working at exactly the same tasks as men did not in general receive equal pay. Just a few achieved equal pay rates by negotiation through a Special Arbitration Tribunal for women's pay and conditions. For example, in the Woolwich Arsenal, the biggest factory, only three small groups had equal pay, two after strike action; crane drivers, inspectors and wages clerks. Most women on engineering processes had to pass on some of their wages to the skilled engineer who set their tools. Their earnings, though, much higher than they had been before the war, averaging about 30s. a week against 11s. 6d. a week, pre-war, were still only approximately half of comparable male earnings. Wages rose in industries other than war production too, though it took longer than in munitions factories. Agitation by women for increased wages accompanied the first layoffs of women workers in the autumn of 1917. Men lent support to these demands because, as the Ministry of Munitions' secret report on labour noted cynically, they thought it would ensure fewer women would be employed after the war.[60] The women I interviewed considered that their wages had been sufficient for their needs. Although a few complained of differentials between groups of women, in general it was felt that the inequality of sacrifice between workers and soldiers rendered such complaints immoral.

Conclusion

Women's war work did not affect women evenly. Their experiences of work differed according to occupation, family responsibilities, previous work experience, education and where they lived. Munitions work dominated the records and obscured both the continuities and long-term change elsewhere, The rhetoric of war gives a seductive completeness to a period in which demand for labour fluctuated and the relative power of women and women's organisations changed. War experience was not simply an anticipation of later developments, either in general or for individuals. The absence of training, of permanent alterations in the organisation of production, of any change in the relationships of power within the workforce or in relation to the employers ensured that women did not keep jobs specifically designated as war work. The Restoration of Pre-War Practices Bill took jobs away from working-class women while middle-class women benefited from the Sex Disqualification Removals Act (which applied to the professions). Skilled occupations performed by women in wartime were taken on after the war by men even when in a few cases they had been completely new jobs.

The effect of war work was to demonstrate that women were capable of a great variety of tasks; it did not demonstrate that they should be able to do them. Indeed the war had shown women capable of great sacrifice in the name of a wider community than the household, a higher form of motherhood in the factory, and the result was to underline women's determination by their gender.[61] Women themselves talk proudly of their war contribution to this day, but as that, not as a part of a working life. It was factors external to the workplace that led to the sense of independence and 'traditional' values could therefore be reasserted once the workplace closed its doors to women. The one female occupation changed by the war was domestic service. There were still as many servants as before the war but the nature of the work had changed.[62] Most of the former war workers whom I interviewed had returned to domestic service after the war; far fewer lived in, far fewer worked in a large household. They felt a far greater capacity to resist exploitation than before, and had learned from the war that 'I could just move on if I didn't like the place'. War had not challenged for them, or in general, the sexual division of labour nor the notion of the male breadwinner. These roles were only suspended for the duration and then only in some households.

Because concern for women workers had been based on their womanhood, their highest service to the nation, war service, had emphasised what they had in common. Their welfare provision, the comments on their success as labourers, their willingness to abandon experience and trade union principles – all these had made it seem possible to say that women had been changed by war-work *en masse*. The women interviewed considered they had been changed, but as often as not for the worse or in ways which they would rather not have suffered. They agreed with Mrs Churchill about the light of wartime but regretted its immediate removal. They disagreed with Mrs Fawcett; most were too young to vote until the 1924 election at least. Above all, they disagreed with Mary Macarthur, their post-war world saw war work as something of the past, specific to wartime and leading to no subsequent improvement. They had changed but the war had not improved their working lives.

Appendix 11.1
Percentage of women in workforce, July 1914 and November 1918

Sectors are listed in order according to the percentage of women in the workforce in July 1914.

	July 1914		November 1918	
Rank order	Employment sector	Women in workforce (%)	Women in workforce (%)	Rank order
1	Hospitals (civil and military)	100	100	1
2	Tailoring, shirtmaking, dressmaking	78	84	2
3	Hosiery	75	82	3[a]
4	Teachers (local authority)	73	82	3[a]
5	Other clothing trades (except boots and shoes)	72	79	5
6	Linen, jute and hemp	70	76	7[a]
7	Tobacco	68	78	6
8	Silk	67	73	9
9	Stationery, cardboard boxes, pencils, gum, ink	66	76	7[a]
10	Textile: miscellaneous trades	62	72	10
11[a]	Rope and twine	60	66	12[a]
	Cotton	60	71	11
13	Woollen and worsted	56	62	15
14[a]	Lace	54	64	14
	All other food trades	54	59	17[a]
16	Hotels, public houses, cinemas, theatres, etc.	48	66	12[a]
17	Brushmaking	45	60	16
18	Sugar, confectionery, jam, bread, biscuits	44	54	21[a]
19	Chemicals, drugs, explosives, matches, tar distilling	40	39	36[a]
20	China and earthenware	39	56	20
21	Rubber	37	59	17[a]
22	Precious metals	36	53	23[a]
23	Other trades	35	53	23[a]
24	Clothing trades, boots, shoes and slippers	34	47	26[a]
25[a]	Paper and wallpaper	31	44	28[a]
	Printing, bookbinding, newspaper printing and publishing	31	41	33[a]
27	Commerce	29	54	21[a]
28	Miscellaneous metal trades (incl. ordnance and small arms)	28	42	32
29	Hardware and hollow ware	27	43	30[a]

Appendix 11.1 (*cont.*)

		July 1914	November 1918	
Rank order	Employment sector	Women in workforce (%)	Women in workforce (%)	Rank order
30	Civil Service (Post Office)	24	53	23[a]
31	Wood trades: basket and wicker work	22	41	33[a]
32[a]	Leather trades	20	44	28[a]
	Textile: dyeing and bleaching	20	30	41[a]
	Chemical trades (except chemicals, drugs, dyes, explosives, matches, tar distilling)	20	39	36[a]
35[a]	Electrical engineering	17	39	36[a]
	Cutlery and edged tools	17	26	46[a]
	Non-ferrous metals	17	28	44[a]
38	Municipal services (except teachers, tramways, gas, water, electricity)	14	26	46[a]
39	Tinplate	13	20	51
40[a]	Saw milling, joinery, cabinet making	12	30	41[a]
	Other professions (persons employed by accountants, solicitors, etc., mainly clerks)	12	37	39
42	Manufacture of alcoholic and other drinks	11	28	44[a]
43[a]	Agriculture	10	14	54
	Glass	10	24	49
45[a]	Cycles, motors and aircraft	8	32	40
	Civil service (excl. Post Office)	8	59	17[a]
47[a]	Grain milling	5	26	46[a]
	Bricks and cement	5	17	52
	Banking and finance	5	43	30[a]
50[a]	Engineering other than electrical and machine	3	21	50
	Factories, dockyards, arsenals, etc.	3	47	26[a]
52[a]	Railways	2	11	55[a]
	Vehicles (other than cycles, motors and aircrafts)	2	16	53
	Municipal tramways	2	41	33[a]
	Other transport	2	10	58[a]
56[a]	Iron and steel	1	11	55[a]
	Shipbuilding and marine engineering	1	7	59[a]
	Building trades	1	7	59[a]

Appendix 11.1 (*cont.*)

| | | July 1914 | November 1918 | |
| | | Women in workforce (%) | Women in workforce (%) | |
Rank order	Employment sector			Rank order
	Mines and quarries	1	1	61
	Gas, water and electricity (public and private)	1	11	55[a]
	Tramways and omnibuses	1	30	41[a]
	Docks and wharves	0	0	62[a]
	All sectors	23.6	37.7	—
	Employed women	3,277,000	4,940,000	—

[a]Tied ranks
Source
A. W. Kirkaldy (ed.), *British labour replacement and conciliation 1914–21*, London, 1921, Table XIII

Appendix 11.2
Index of trend in female employment July 1914–November 1918

Rank order	Employment sector	Women employed November 1918 (1914 = 100)	Women entering sector as percentage of all women entering employment since July 1914[b]
1	Factories, dockyards, arsenals, etc.	11,227	14.7
2	Tramways and omnibuses	2,325	0.5
3	Civil service (excl. Post Office)	2,140	6.1
4	Municipal tramways	1,583	1.1
5	Gas, water and electricity (public and private)	1,500	0.8
6	Iron and steel	1,147	2.1
7	Engineering other than electrical and marine	842	5.4
8	Cycles, motors and aircraft	809	4.7
9	Banking and finance	789	3.9
10	Vehicles (other than cycles, motors and aircraft)	633	0.5
11[a]	Grain milling	550	0.5
	Railways	550	3.2
13	Other transport	457	1.0
14	Building trades	443	1.4
15	Electrical engineering	350	2.4
16	Miscellaneous metal trades (incl. ordnance and small arms)	338	6.9
17	Chemicals, dyes, explosives, matches, tar distilling	295	2.5
18	Hospitals (civil and military)	242	2.8
19	Rubber	227	1.1
20	Other professions (persons employed by accountants, architects, solicitors, etc., mainly clerks)	222	1.3
21	Leather trades	218	1.2
22	Chemical trades (other than chemicals, drugs, dyes, explosives, matches, tar distillery)	216	1.3
23	Saw milling, joinery, cabinet making	209	2.1
24	Civil service (Post Office)	198	3.6

Appendix 11.2 (*cont.*)

Rank order	Employment sector	Women employed November 1918 (1914 = 100)	Women entering sector as percentage of all women entering employment since July 1914[b]
25	Rope and twine	197	0.5
26	Mines and quarries	186	0.4
27	Glass	185	0.2
28	Manufacture of alcoholic and other drink	183	0.9
29	Commerce	177	23.1
30	Non-ferrous metals	176	0.8
31	Bricks and cement	162	0.2
32	Brush making	150	0.3
33[a]	Cutlery and edged tools	145	0.2
	Hardware and hollow ware	145	0.8
35	Municipal services (excl. teachers, tramways, gas, water, electricity)	139	1.3
36	Shipbuilding and machine engineering	135	1.7
37	Tobacco	131	0.6
38[a]	Textile dyeing and bleaching	129	0.4
	Textile: miscellaneous trades	129	0.4
40	Precious metals	125	0.3
41	Hotels, public houses, cinemas and theatres, etc.	123	2.5
42	Clothing trades: boots, shoes, slippers	121	0.7
43[a]	Other trades	119	0.2
	Agriculture	119	0.9
45	Paper and wallpaper	117	0.2
46	Hosiery	113	0.5
47	China and earthenware	109	0.2
48	Teachers (local authority)	108	0.7
49	Woollen and worsted	103	0.3
50	Sugar, confectionery, jam, bread and biscuits	102	0.1
51[a]	Tinplate	100	0.0
	Silk	100	0.0
53	All other food trades	98	−0.1
54	Linen, jute and hemp	97	−0.2
55	Printing, bookbinding, newspaper printing and publishing	93	−0.4

Appendix 11.2 *(cont.)*

Rank order	Employment sector	Women employed November 1918 (1914 = 100)	Women entering sector as percentage of all women entering employment since July 1914[b]
56[a]	Tailoring, shirtmaking, dressmaking and millinery	90	−2.2
	Stationery, cardboard boxes, pencils, gum, ink	90	−0.2
58	Cotton	84	−4.0
59	Other clothing trades (except boots and shoes)	82	−1.9
60	Lace	81	−0.2
61	Wood trades: basket and wicker work	70	0.0
62	Docks and wharves	—	0.0
	All sectors	151	100.0
	No. of women employed November 1918	4,940,000	
	No. of women entering employment July 1914– November 1918		1,663,000

[a] Tied ranks
[b] Minus values indicate movement out of sector
Source
See Appendix 11.1

Notes

1 Lady Randolph Churchill (ed.), *Women's war work*, London, 1916, p. 10.
2 M. G. Fawcett, *The women's victory and after*, London, 1920, p. 106.
3 Marion Phillips (ed.), *Women and the Labour Party*, London, 1918, p. 18.
4 Arthur Marwick, *Women at war*, London, 1977, states the case most strongly.
5 Heidi Hartmann, 'Capitalism, patriarchy and job segretation by sex', in Zillah Eisenstein (ed.), *Capitalist patriarchy and the case for socialist feminism*, New York, 1978. Gail Braybon, *Women workers in the First World War*, London, 1981.
6 Deborah Thom, 'The ideology of women's work in Britain 1914–24, with specific reference to the NFWW and other trade unions', unpublished PhD for the CNAA at Thames Polytechnic, 1982, has a fuller version of this thesis.

7 Census report. *Report on occupations*, PP 1913, lxxxviii, Cmd 7018. Kenneth Brown, *Labour and unemployment, 1900–1914*, Newton Abbot, 1971, notes women's involvement in the Right to Work agitation. N. K. Buxton and D. Mackay, *British employment statistics, a guide to sources and methods*, Oxford, 1977, point out the general inadequacy of the relation between statistics for unemployment and employment and exclusions under the National Insurance scheme but ignores the question of women. Under-recording is suggested by the different findings of oral historians and the regional variation in numbers registered as unemployed according to industry as well as close qualitative studies as in B. L. Hutchins, *Women in modern industry*, London, 1915, and Clementina Black, *Married women's work*, London, 1915.

8 S. D. Chapman, *War and the cotton trade*, Oxford, 1915, p. 9.

9 Annual Report, National Federation of Women Workers, 1911, pp. 186–8; Sarah Boston, 'The chainmakers of Cradley Heath', BBC TV Norwich, 1977, mostly based on materials in the Gertrude Tuckwell collection at the TUC (GT).

10 These groups included the Fabian Women's Group, the Women's Labour League, the Women's Industrial Council and the Women's Trade Union League.

11 Anna Martin, *The mother and social reform*, London, 1913, p. 7.

12 Adelaide Anderson, *Women in the factory*, London, 1922, p. 161.

13 Ellen Smith, *Wage-earning women and their dependants*, London, 1911.

14 Teresa Olcott, 'The women's trade union movement', *London Journal*, 2, (1976); Sheila Lewenhak, *Women in trade unions*, London, 1977; Sarah Boston, *Women workers and the trade union movement*, London, 1980; all based to some extent on Barbara Drake, *Women in trade unions*, London, 1920.

15 Woolwich Pioneer, 5 May 1916.

16 Drake, *Women in trade unions*, p. 46.

17 Deborah Thom, 'The "bundle of sticks": women, trade unionists and collective organisation before 1918' in Angela John (ed.), *Unequal opportunities. Women's employment in Britain 1800–1918*, Oxford, 1986.

18 Fabian Women's Group, *The war, women and unemployment*, London, 1915.

19 This organisation was set up by the National Union of Women Workers which demonstrates in itself one major shift of wartime as it was an organisation of unwaged social workers to promote the 'social, civil, moral and religious welfare of women', GT, 17 November 1914.

20 Roger Fulford, *Votes for women*, London, 1958. E. Sylvia Pankhurst, *The Suffragette movement*, London, 1931.

21 Mary Agnes Hamilton, *Mary Macarthur*, London, 1925, p. 138; Kathleen Woodward, *Queen Mary*, London, 1927, p. 190; *Interim Report of the Women's Employment Commission*, PP 1914–1916, xxxviii, Cd 7848, pp. 4–11. Pankhurst Collection, Institute for the Study of Social History, Amsterdam, minute books of East London Federation of Suffragettes, 1915 (exact date unclear), report of a delegation to Mary Macarthur.

22 *Spectator*, 19 September 1914.

23 GT, *Lancashire Post*, 17 May 1915.

24 *New Age*, 19 August 1914, the start of a correspondence lasting into 1915.

25 GT 531, reports of the 1915 TUC, *Evening Times and Echo*, 11 September 1915.

26 Lynden Macassey, *Labour policy – false or true*, London, 1922. Mary Hammond, *British labor conditions and legislation during the war*, New York, 1919. Humbert Wolfe, *Labour supply and regulation*, Oxford, 1923, p. 77.

27 David Lloyd George, *War memoirs*, London, 1933. Christopher Addison, *Politics from within*, London, 1924, and Munitions records at the Public Record Office (PRO.MUN) 5.70.26., 11 August 1915.
28 G. D. H. Cole, *Trade unionism and munitions*, Oxford, 1923; James Hinton, *The first shop stewards movement*, London, 1973.
29 Barbara Drake, Historical introduction to the *Report of the War Cabinet on women in industry*, PP 1919, xxl, Cmd 135, p. 108.
30 Official History of the Ministry of Munitions, unpublished, vol. 6.
31 Wolfe, *Labour supply and regulation*, p. 169.
32 Imperial War Museum, Women's Work Collection, Employment (IWM.EMP), 19, file of dilution agreements lodged with the Board of Trade, 1916–17.
33 IWM.EMP. 4.28[2].
34 *Labour Gazette*, monthly produced by the Board of Trade for Labour Supply. Thom, 'The ideology of women's work', interviews, for allocation procedure. See also D. Thom, 'Women workers in the Woolwich Arsenal in the First World War', *Oral History*, 8 (Autumn 1978), and Thom, 'Nice girls and rude girls' in Raphael Samuel (ed.), *Patriotism and the making of the national identity*, London, 1988.
35 IWM. Documentary section. Diary of Gabrielle West. I am grateful to Jean Liddiard for this reference.
36 Many of the photographs exhibited were taken by Horace Nicholls who produced much telling wartime imagery on women's work.
37 Horace Nicholls (cf. note 36) took many of the photos for two War Office booklets for employers *Women's work in munitions* and *Women's work in non-munitions industries*, London, December 1916.
38 Angela John, *By the sweat of their brow*, London, 1984.
39 IWM.WMP.1. memo from F. H. Durham to Miss Conway in 1919 insisted that the exhibits should stress achievements in wartime.
40 PRO.MUN.2.27, 5 February 1916.
41 E. Sylvia Pankhurst, *The home front*, 1932, pp. 78–82.
42 Deborah Thom and Antonia Ineson, 'Women workers and TNT poisoning' in Paul Weindling (ed.), *A social history of occupational health*, London, 1985.
43 Reports of the Health of Munition Workers' Committee, PP 1916, xxiii, Cd 1185; *Memorandum on the employment of women*, PP 1917–18, xiii, Cd 8511, *Interim Report*; PP 1918, xii, Cd 9065, *Final Report*.
44 *Report of the War Cabinet Committee on women in industry, Medical Memorandum*, PP 1919, xxxi, Cmd 135.
45 Ministry of Reconstruction papers at British Library of Economic and Political Science, Box 4, document 90.
46 Antonia Ineson, interviews.
47 She added 'They don't like being done good to', IWM typed manuscripts of evidence to the War Cabinet on Women in Industry, (IWM.TE), 4 October 1918.
48 Thom, interviews, Grace Robson.
49 The full literature on this subject was first evoked by Hinton, *Shop Stewards movement*, and is summarised in Alastair Reid's contribution to this volume, above, chapter 7.
50 IWM, TE, 12 October 1918, evidence of Mrs Blanco White.
51 Thom, 'The "bundle of sticks"'.
52 PRO, MUN.5.55, 24 February 1918.
53 1919 TUC report cited by G. Braybon, *Women workers*, p. 199.

54 *Report of the Women's Employment Committee for the Ministry of Reconstruction*, PP 1918, xiv, CD 9239, p. 60.
55 Ministry of Labour leaflet, IWM.Emp.80, as cited by M. Kozak, 'Women munition workers during the First World War with special reference to engineering', unpublished PhD, University of Hull, 1977, p. 379.
56 Thom, 'The ideology of women's work', chapter 7.
57 IWM, Mun.28.
58 Thom, 'Women workers in the Woolwich Arsenal'; Thom, 'Nice girls and rude girls'.
59 Philip Abrams, 'The failure of social reform, 1918–1920', *Past and Present*, 24 (1963).
60 Beatrice Webb, Diary (at the LSE) entries for 21 November 1918 and 8 September 1919.
61 MUN 2.16, 31 August 1918, the report of the War Cabinet Committee on Women in Industry shows this very clearly.
62 Health of Munition Workers Committee, Memo 4, 1916. Pam Taylor, 'Daughters and mothers – maids and mistresses. Domestic service between the wars' in N. Clarke, C. C. Critcher and R. Johnson (eds.), *Working class culture*, London, 1979.

IV
SOCIAL POLICY AND
FAMILY IDEOLOGY

12
Pronatalism and the popular ideology of the child in wartime France: the evidence of the picture postcard

Marie-Monique Huss

This chapter presents part of a study of the popular ideology of Frenchness in France at the time of the First World War. This ideology formed a complex system and was expressed in a variety of ways, with various stresses and implications, but one of its main features was the central role which it gave to the child. Particularly during the war, children were not only the medium through which harsh adult realities could be made more palatable (as in representations of children's war games; they were the core of patriotism itself, the future of the nation, precisely what the brave *poilus*,[1] those 'enfants de la patrie', were fighting for. Just as, at the front, the most crucial problem was felt to be one of insufficient numbers, so, on the home front, Frenchness seemed to be under attack because not enough babies were being born. Thus numerous examples of child breeding and rearing presented as 'the other trench', 'the other duty', 'the other front', are to be found. It seems that in French popular culture the quality of Frenchness was almost indissociable from the idea of quantity.

In this chapter consideration will be given to only one source of popular culture, although a very rich one in the context of the war: picture postcards. However, before explaining the reasons for this choice and analysing what this kind of document can tell us about popular attitudes towards the family and the nation, it is worth recalling the intellectual background provided by explicit discussion of pronatalism among the elites.

The pronatalist debate among the elites

The fear of population decline in France and the pronatalism that came with it have recently been studied by P. E. Ogden and myself[2] and by J. Winter,[3] whose work offers a comparison with other European countries. For a study of the politics of population during the Third Republic, R. Tomlinson's PhD thesis,[4] should be consulted. Mention should also be made of Ronsin's *La Grève des ventres*[5] which, while focusing on neo-Malthusian propaganda in nineteenth- and twentieth-century France, nevertheless addresses the problem of the fear of population decline.

The most striking feature to emerge from the above research is the seemingly enormous gap between, on the one hand, a vocal elite made up of doctors, politicians, moralists and intellectuals, with a passionate pronatalist ideology and, in many cases, an articulate programme, and, on the other hand, the majority of French people who seem to have remained indifferent to the pleas for more children. However, during the 1914–18 period, with the nation under threat, it seems that this gap between the elites and the masses was much reduced, at least on the ideological level, if not in terms of reproductive behaviour. In my view, one important source of evidence for this facet of the *Union sacrée* is provided by the picture postcards of the period which it will be the main purpose of this article to examine.

First, however, let us briefly describe the vocal pronatalist elite. Concern about the fall of the birth rate in France began to be expressed before 1870 with the appearance of, for example, Raudot's *De la décadence de la France* in 1849, and Le Play's *La Réforme sociale* in 1864, but intensified after defeat in the Franco-Prussian War. The rate of publication on the subject increased in the 1890s and remained high up to and during the First World War. Among the 50 or so books published on the problem of depopulation in these decades, no less than five were written by Dr Jacques Bertillon.[6] There were a number of eloquent titles such as *Crimes of the bedchamber*, *The suicide of a race*, *Morality based on demography* and *Birth control and the defence of the nation*.[7] Boverat's book, *Patriotisme et paternité*,[8] is particularly representative of this kind of literature, presenting, as it does, the duty to repopulate more as a male responsibility ('paternité') than a female one. This imbalance was hardly corrected by the authors of *Maternité et féminisme*,[9] two men who asserted that 'the child is woman's only *raison d'être*'.[10] With self-proclaimed feminists like these, who needed male chauvinists?

Even a feminist paper, written by women, like *Le Féminisme intégral*, which in July 1913 had expressed virulent opposition to populationist demands made on women, found this stance untenable in wartime and, anxious not to be thought unpatriotic, urged its readers, in an editorial entitled 'Le Devoir intégral' (December 1915), to accept the duty of providing 'children, lots of children to fill the gaps'. It is likely, then, that there were few dissident voices when Doleris and Bouscatel appealed to French women to 'replace our glorious dead and regenerate a new France'.[11]

Most pronatalist authors came from the professional classes: doctors

(Bertillon, Doleris), lawyers (Allemane), politicians (Bureau, Piot), economists (Ch. Gide, Leroy-Beaulieu), journalists and writers like Vuillermet, Bourget and Emile Zola. Students of the period will appreciate that such names are by no means confined to the extreme right or to a lunatic fringe, but include respected scholars and well-known socialists. The case of Zola, champion of the oppressed, whose massive didactic novel *Fécondité* was published in 1899, is indicative of how wide an appeal pronatalist ideas had in pre-war France, right across the spectrum of political opinion, at least among the elites.

Apart from writing books, these pronatalist authors promoted their ideas by giving lectures, sending articles to the general press, publishing their own news-sheets, disrupting 'neo-Malthusian' meetings and suing the speakers, lobbying politicians and creating pressure groups. Associations were set up in an attempt to involve the masses in the pronatalist movement.

Since the beginning of the century three kinds of pressure group had been working with similar aims but appealing to different sorts of motivation. In addition to strictly pronatalist associations like the Alliance nationale pour l'accroissement de la population française, motivated by the fear of depopulation, there were family associations such as the Ligue populaire des pères et mères de familles nombreuses, whose main motivation was social welfare, and 'moralistic' associations like the Ligue française pour le relèvement de la moralité publique, whose crusade was against contraception, abortion and promiscuity – all referred to as 'pornography'. What sort of echo did these three main strands of pronatalism – populationist patriotism, the welfare preoccupation and the morality issue – find in the picture postcard which, as will be argued below, was a significant expression of popular culture at the time?

In the imagery of the wartime picture postcard one of these strands was clearly dominant. The moralistic theme was absent: instead there was an endorsement of male sexual pleasure. Girls should do all they could to make the fighting man happy, 'le poilu est amoureux, sachez donc le rendre heureux', as one card published by Dix typically put it. The social welfare theme was taken up mostly in posters such as those published by the Red Cross on child care and infant mortality. The fear of depopulation, on the other hand, with all that it implied for the armies of tomorrow and the future of the nation in general was, as will be shown, one of the great patriotic themes of the picture postcard. Indeed, so well established was the positive image of the child that a British card representing a baby having a tantrum with the caption 'another tyrant disturbing the peace of the world' was 'mistranslated' for the French market so as to read 'maman, je ne veux past être boche' ('Mummy, I don't want to be a Hun'), as if to reflect French reluctance to regard children as tyrants.[12]

Ogden's current research on early membership of the Alliance nationale pour l'accroissement de la population française shows its very slow progress between 1896 and 1913 to a membership of 1,321. Considering the relatively rapid increase which took membership to 5,248 by the end of 1917, Tomlinson comments that this rise occurred 'despite the disruption created by the conflict'.[13] Indeed, far from being a hindrance, the war stimulated support for the pronatalist cause, precisely because of the immediate and violent threat it posed to Frenchness and French values, a threat which brought into the homes of French men and women the demographic realities behind the statistics. As Doleris put it at the time, 'we must above all think of Life, speak of Life, while war sows death'.[14]

This is not to say that such bodies as the Alliance nationale were not doing their utmost to produce the most vivid propaganda, such as the 'two against five' posters and postcards[15] or the poster of the map of Europe and its population of which over one million copies were produced and circulated.[16] But there is a problem with this kind of propaganda. It emanated from a small number of activists and was distributed down the social pyramid free of charge to chosen recipients – journalists, politicians, schoolteachers – eventually, perhaps to reach the masses whose role had been totally passive. How are we to decide whether people regarded these images as reflecting their views and their culture, as 'speaking their language'? This is where the picture postcards of the period provide a useful missing link, because of the way the postcard market functioned in general and, more particularly, because of the function of picture postcards in wartime.

Production, function and representativeness of the picture postcard in wartime

Postcard production at the time of the war was characterised by the large number of publishers and by considerable differences in the scale and nature of their operations. In the 'patriotic fantasy' genre alone, which is of special concern and which will be defined more closely in the third part of the chapter, my research to date has revealed more than 70 different publishers (listed in Appendix 12.1). They vary in size and respectability from large and fairly reputable fine art publishers, like I. M. Lapina, whose main line of business was religious and artistic reproductions, to successful businessmen in the light erotic genre, such as Katz of Rueil, and small highstreet photographers/tobacconists like Boulanger who, when unable to find an older model for a posed scene, had to resort to sticking a white beard on a young man.[17]

Indeed, the amateurishness of some of these postcards gives an indication not only of the small scale of the organisation behind them (although in response to demand they might manage to work at high capacity and produce large numbers) but also of the family nature of many businesses: they were part of the market they served[18] and had no difficulty speaking its language.

A much better guarantee, however, of the representativeness of the attitudes expressed in these postcards is the fact that they had to be bought by, and appeal to, an entirely individualised market. Millions of individual trips to the tobacconist's or the village shop resulted in feedback about what did or did not sell. In spite of copyright, successful postcards were shamelessly imitated by other publishers and the copyright owner would print and launch a new series exploiting the successful theme.

There were, no doubt, certain limits to the representativeness of these postcards. Perhaps consumers rarely found a card which really expressed their feelings and had to choose the least inappropriate or objectionable of the selection available. Censorship during the war may have made finding an adequate postcard more difficult. I do not, however, believe that such considerations seriously limit the representative value of the postcard. Far from decreasing during the war, the yearly production of picture postcards multiplied by three and, according to Neudin,[19] 20,000 different illustrated postcards were published during the period.

This might seem to be an obvious response to the needs of eight million mobilised men and their families. It should be noted, however, that in wartime, competition in the postcard market was not just between publishers since, in order to sell, they had to compete with the state military postcard which, although not illustrated, was issued free to soldiers and in cheap packs of ten to their families. Thus, the decision to send a picture postcard had even more significance than before the war, not less. Free postage to and from the front may have been an encouragement to send more correspondence of any sort. The fact that letters from the front could be opened by the censor may have removed some of the reservations that people had towards postcards as being less intimate: even a sealed letter could be read by a stranger. Another consideration which worked in favour of postcards, but not specifically of picture postcards, was the need to keep up a constant flow of short messages. Members of the family would take it in turns to write so as to keep up the soldier's morale.[20] In the words of a French machine gunner in 1917 'correspondence is an essential part of the soldier's survival kit and comes halfway between bread and wine in the order of values',[21] a feeling faithfully echoed by the postcard artist Morinet who depicted the cook and the military postman as the soldier's best friends.[22] For his part, the soldier needed to reassure the family, if only with one word, that he was still alive, at a time when three days without news led people to fear the worst.[23]

But there were specific factors which made the picture postcard a particularly popular means of communication. There was the need for light relief from both the tedium and horror of war. The picture postcard, as opposed to the state subsidised military card, was a small gift for the recipient, a kind of surprise, and many postcards actually portray what one would have liked to send or receive: a girl emerging from a postal parcel[24] or a banknote for 1,000 kisses payable to the receiver.[25] Another problem of wartime correspondence was that one was always saying the same thing: 'life goes on at home', 'I am alright', 'we pray for you', etc. The picture postcard helped give a new slant, a wittier or more poetic version of a repeated message.

A typical production of the period was the postcard which required careful reading and diverted the recipient's attention from other concerns for as long as possible. Some of the cards fulfilling this function were composite cards, visually similar to the comic strips of the period, and contained a number of miniature pictures, each with its own (often ambiguous) caption. In this genre the realities of trench life were leavened with erotic *double entendre*, as in 'Les armes de l'amour',[26] 'Les menus du cuistot'[27] and the 'Langage des tranchées' series (a sort of illustrated dictionary of trench slang).[28] Others provided ambiguous images or 'enigmas', in which the reader was invited to discover hidden pictures within the immediately apparent picture.[29] Others again contained a verbal enigma in which incompatible meanings were held irresolvably together. 'Ma victoire est dans les choux' (Plate 8) is both a typical example of this genre and evidence of the popular preoccupation with the birth rate which is our central theme. The caption, which translates literally as 'My victory is in the cabbages' can be understood in two mutually exclusive ways. On the one hand, 'dans les choux' is a colloquial phrase which indicates failure: in this reading, Wilhelm acknowledges that his victory is 'up the spout'. Visually, however, the cabbage had another immediately perceivable meaning: in French popular culture baby boys came from cabbages, an association reinforced by countless postcards and posters of the period.[30] Thus, Wilhelm's scrutiny of the cabbage, from which no child emerges, gave a totally different meaning to the caption. Victory would be his if the French cabbage remained barren. In addition to the time it took to decipher them, such cards would be shown to friends in the trenches or to visitors at home, therefore serving a social function and associating the absent one with one's own present life. The problem of what to say was of course made more acute by the awareness of censorship, a point illustrated by a card entitled 'Correspondance militaire', which shows a soldier writing home and bears the legend: 'We have come from . . . ; we're on our way to . . . (I'm not allowed to tell you where)'.[31] The awareness of censorship made 'fantasy' type postcards preferable since topographical ones would not be sent from the front without the identifiable features being inked over by the censor.

Other reasons, connected not with the war but with the period in general, made people prefer to send a picture postcard. For example, the level of illiteracy[32] or at least lack of confidence in one's own writing and spelling, made the pre-written message of the picture postcard a convenient alternative. Finally, it should be mentioned that in the decades preceding the war postcard collecting had become a craze.[33] Comments such as 'this is another card for your collection' are often found on the back of picture postcards sent during the war. here again the card served as a present to be chosen with loving care.

In the face of competition, further increased by the state-subsidised cards, manufacturers were quick to respond to the special demands of the new market created by the war. In the 'patriotic fantasy' genre, one way in which they appealed to people was by depicting a wide range of tailor-made family links and relationships which one might have with the soldier at the front. For example, the 'to the beloved' theme catered for a broad spectrum of varying degrees of intimacy and respect which enabled the sender to choose the appropriate postcard for, say, a wife, a girl friend, or a *marraine* (literally a godmother, but in wartime a female correspondent).[34] The 'to my dear father' variety offered a wide choice, representing either son or daughter, or both, and all age groups from infancy to school-leaving age.[35] In the 'to our son' category, were variously depicted more or less elderly parents, peasants

Plate 8. 'My victory is in the cabbages.'

poorly dressed and praying,[36] or members of the middle classes, the father with an elegant moustache reading his paper.[37] The many versions of the 'to the defender of the nation' theme covered other relationships too, with cards also produced for brothers and nephews.

A whole imagery of the nation could well be drawn from these cards, but what is of particular interest here is the care taken by so many manufacturers to reflect the public's view of itself. Indeed, the fact that individuals often recognised themselves in the people pictured is evidenced by senders' comments on either the back or the front of the card.[38]

No doubt it was relatively easy to identify with the stock relationships presented by the postcards, but did this identification extend to their ideological content? The publishers were in business and cards were an important part of their livelihood. They must have taken care to present purchasers with a view of France, of themselves and of their role in the war which was acceptable. Some publishers may have wanted not to reflect but to model opinion, whether from patriotism or some other personal conviction. Even so, they would have had to operate within certain limits of acceptability, given the highly competitive nature of the market. However, to avoid the danger of giving too much weight to what might be the isolated view of an individual, I have regarded as unrepresentative any theme which is confined to the work of one publisher alone. Another limitation which might have affected the ability of postcards to reflect public attitudes is the fact that they were subject to censorship prior to publication: they could not be subversive. However, the comments of the censors on postcards whose publication was not approved during the year 1916 would suggest that censorship of postcards was handled leniently.[39] Cards were occasionally sent back for modification but were rarely rejected outright: in either case, the reasons given for the censor's disapproval tended to be that the cards were incompetent, coarse, obscene or too frivolous. There were next to no cases of postcards being rejected because of their subversiveness. Some were even censured for being over-zealous and excessive in their degradation of the enemy. In one case the censor rejected a postcard described as 'child urinating in Prussian helmet' (6 April 1916). Yet on other days the censor must have been more lenient, as dozens of such cards survive.[40] On 18 April 1916 a subversive card representing a baby emerging naked and vulnerable from an egg into a scene of battlefield slaughter and saying 'if this is life I prefer to go back inside' was dealt with very lightly, the censor suggesting that it should be resubmitted with a different caption.[41]

It would appear, then, that 'la tyrannique Anastasie', as the censor was popularly referred to, was not particularly tyrannical as far as picture postcards were concerned. In any case, to the extent that they expressed a genuine patriotism, postcards in the categories selected for study hardly justified the censor's attention. It is likely, of course, that there were other postcards which I have been unable to consult because they were censored; and there were probably many more which were published but are lost because they have been dispersed or destroyed. Nevertheless, the number of postcards which I have seen to date (in the H. Leblanc collection at Nanterre, at the Bibliothèque Forney, Paris, and at the Imperial War Museum, London) or have in my own collection,[42] is considerable enough to justify the claim that they provide if not a total picture at least a fair reflection of popular attitudes, particularly on the themes of babies and the family. Moreover, because of the fragmented nature of its production and publication and the individualised way in which it was bought, the picture postcard offers, in my opinion, a particularly faithful record of popular ideology and sensibility.

The 'patriotic fantasy' card

'Patriotic fantasy' and 'sentimental patriotism' are the headings used by French postcard dealers to describe that well-represented category of wartime picture postcard which made an appeal to personal feeling and patriotic sentiment by more varied and imaginative means than those used in purely naturalistic genres such as the documentary card (photographs of ruined cathedrals, marching armies and field kitchens) or the military regalia card (faithful depictions of uniforms, colours and insignia). The 'patriotic fantasy' genre used many techniques such as posed photography against backdrops, photomontage and drawing, sometimes combining them. Photomontage, in particular, made it possible to bring together on one postcard people or concepts which would otherwise be separated.[43] Another feature of the genre, particularly interesting in the present context, was the poetic or humorous caption or verse.

The ideological value of the family was more or less present in a multitude of postcards but is perhaps best encapsulated in 'Français, voilà ce que tu défends' ('Frenchman, this is what you are defending', Plate 9), in which a cradle occupies the centre of the foreground surrounded by the wife and grandparents, with a farm in the background and a village church in the distance, the whole scene framed by a tricoloured map of France. 'La chère maison' (Home, sweet home')[44] also stresses the importance of the cradle. Similarly, 'le rêve idéal'[45] includes the baby as part of the dream of the sentimental *poilu*. In 'Ceux de L'arrière'[46] only children are shown in order to represent the home front. Among the many postcards which featured members of families or family scenes, the focus in this section will be on those in which the theme of repopulation, the duty of young couples to procreate, and the presentation of children as the future of the nation were fairly

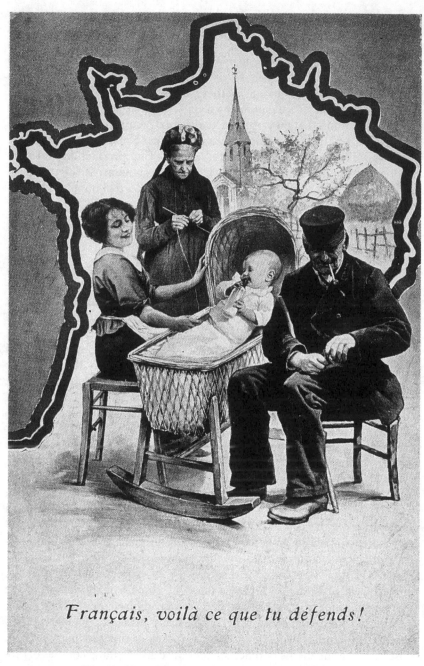

Français, voilà ce que tu défends!

Plate 9. 'Frenchman, this is what you are defending.'

explicit. For the sake of clarity I will first consider representations of the couple, and, more specifically, of masculine and feminine roles in the task of repopulation, before moving to a discussion of representations of children, both infants and those of school age.

COUPLES

The representation of couples about to do their reproductive duty had already appeared before the war. Puns on lovemaking ('s'aimer') and sowing ('semer') which totally identify love with procreation were particularly frequent. In one example, the foreground scene of a couple embracing is linked to a pastoral background full of babies by the encouraging caption 'Qui s'aime récolte!' ('Reap as you love/sow').[47] A wartime version of this theme, entitled 'Permission agricole' ('Agricultural leave'), shows the *poilu* joyfully reunited for the sowing season with his wife on the farm: the result of their labours, a baby *poilu* complete with kepi and rifle, appears as a radiant inset.[48] In another image from the rural world, the rabbit – not conventionally noted for its courage – becomes a war hero simply by virtue of its prodigious fertility. In one of a series of cards exploiting this theme, a rabbit dressed as a *poilu* points to his numerous offspring and proudly proclaims: 'C'est à moi, tout ça . . . et j'ai encore la mère!' ('They're all mine . . . and I've still got the mother!').[49]

The weapons and machinery of war itself were sometimes linked with the pronatalist theme in a visually surprising manner. One card shows a couple using a tank as their love nest to the dismay of the terrified German army; the caption, 'Tout pour la victoire' ('Everything for victory') indicates that everything is part of the war effort, including the couple's lovemaking and its possible results.[50]

Exhortations to marriage, not just for personal fulfilment but as the basis for repopulation were often featured, as in 'Ne restons pas vieux garçons. Travaillons pour la repopulation' ('Don't let's stay bachelors all our lives. Let's do our bit for repopulation', Plate 10). Although obviously romantic in its visual style, and somewhat tongue-in-cheek in its caption, this card goes beyond mere playfulness: whichever girl the *poilu* chooses, the purpose is marriage, and, clearly shown as a reward, framed in a ring of flowers, is a smiling, bouncing baby.[51] The full patriotic significance of marriage is brought out more solemnly by a card (Plate 11) in which Joffre himself, a figure somewhere between father and God, commonly referred to as 'notre père qui êtes au front' ('our father who art at the front'),[52] marries a young couple in the trenches. The caption makes it clear that their union was to be regarded as an act of service: 'Vous servez deux fois la France' ('You do France a twofold service').

The association of virility with weapons in pronatalist cards predates the

Plate 10. 'Let's do our bit for repopulation.'

Plate 11. 'You do France a twofold service.'

war. In 'Le fusil à répétition' ('The self-reloading rifle'; seven well-wrapped babies dangle from the weapon's barrel beneath the caption: 'ça c'est bon pour la repopulation' ('it's just what we need for repopulation').[53] The glorification of the *poilu*'s masculinity and a sense of duty encouraged post-card artists to use every possible variation on this theme: the erotic prowess of the gunner, the grenadier and the infantryman with his bayonet,[54] were exploited with gusto, the French colloquialism 'tirer un coup' (to have sexual intercourse from the male point of view – literally, 'to fire a shot') giving rise to a whole series of *double entendres*. 'Un bon coup de baïonnette' 'A good thrust', Plate 12) is an explicitly pronatalist card showing three healthy babies attached to a bayonet as the successful results of the soldier's patriotic thrusts, accompanied by the comment: 'Bravo *poilu*'. A scroll explained that the *poilu* had been given a six-day leave and sent home on special duty ('en service commandé').

The soldier's leave was itself a frequent source of inspiration, not only exploited for its romantic and erotic value, but promoted as a rare occasion to repopulate France. The 'service commandé' caption often appears, stressing that leave was a kind of military mission, a part of active service during which future cohorts were to be produced. In 'Les quatre jours', as the *poilu* bursts into the conjugal home, his wife rushes into his arms with the words: 'Enfin tu vas te reposer!' ('At last you will get some rest!') and the military style of his reply conveys the urgency of his mission: 'Impossible.

Plate 12. 'A good thrust.'

Service commandé: Préparation de la classe 36'.[55] In 'Qui vive?' ('Who goes there?', Plate 13) a *poilu* knocking at a door identifies himself as 'Permissionnaire . . . service commandé'.

Clearly he has not come home for a rest either: his thoughts are on fatherhood, as is illustrated by the two vigorous babies emerging from his shoulder bag, potential lives within him, which embody another answer to the question 'Qui vive?', literally 'Anyone alive?'.[56] 'Les suites d'une permission'[57] shows a young mother wearing a kepi and proudly holding 'the results of a leave', two beautiful babies. In 'Souvenir d'une permission', a baby emerges from a *poilu*'s helmet, hanging from a coat hook at home, next to his belt and bayonet.[58] In 'Le permissionnaire', it is not just sweet nothings that the loving couple are talking about, but whether the baby they are about to conceive for France should be a boy and become a soldier; this is the *poilu*'s preference: 'J'aimerais mieux un fils pour en faire un soldat'.[59] In popular language the expression 'un petit permissionnaire' thus had a special meaning: not so much a little soldier on leave as the baby conceived during the leave, as in General Mangin's advice to a soldier to go on leave and give his wife a 'petit permissionnaire'.[60]

The next occasion for the soldier to show initiative in performing his 'other duty' was to come at the end of the war. Demobilisation inspired postcard producers with erotic possibilities but duty was stressed as well. 'Après la victoire l'autre devoir' features an ideal post-war scene, the reunited family already comprising a toddler and a babe in arms, with several tiny heads emerging from cabbages in the background. The caption stresses that the two patriotic duties, fighting and providing the next generation for France, were of equal importance.[61] 'L'heure du retour' ('Homecoming') simply shows a couple kissing, but with the reminder: 'Songez que le foyer est triste sans enfants' ('Remember that a home is sad without children').[62] 'L'après-guerre: la poiluculture'('After the war: *poilu*-growing', Plate 14) is a humorous fantasy on the post-war repopulation theme and depicts couples visiting a *poilu*-growing establishment, half-farm, half-brothel (lovemaking is visible through each window) in whose grounds can already be seen a rich crop of young *poilus*.[63]

Women's role in the war effort was sometimes limited to that of hero's plaything and many cards invited them to be more welcoming, in a sort of imaginary nationwide extension of the field brothel.[64] Sometimes, however, their efforts to bring up the family were shown as a form of mobilisation, and they became 'nos chères mobilisées'.[65] In a number of cards which exhorted women to bear children for France, attempts were even made, albeit discreetly, to refer visually to pregnancy, traditionally a taboo subject in popular iconography. In 'Allons mesdames, travaillez pour la France' ('Come on ladies. Work for France', Plate 15) the wife's helmet indicates

Plate 13. 'Who goes there?'

that pregnancy (significantly both advertised and modestly covered by the sandwich-board) was to be seen as her active service. A series, published in 1915, shows three elegant female allegories of Russia, England and France, which represent different national priorities; Russia stands for Resistance, England for Justice, but France is biologically a woman ('La Française'), her ballooning skirt and full breasts inviting the audience to see Marianne as pregnant, an interpretation reinforced by the pronatalist caption (Plate 16).[66] This comparison between nations expresses an awareness of France's demographic weakness combined with patriotism in the unexpected style of the fashion drawing. In another fashion card, an elegant woman in a négligé finds a baby soldier inside an Easter egg; this time the pronatalist message was applied to Belgium and the caption reads: 'A *son* is what you need, golden-haired Flemish girl, to repopulate Flanders and defend it again'.[67]

CHILDREN

An even greater variety of postcards were produced on the subject of children themselves, in particular babies. Before the war there was already an abundance of postcards based on popular myths about where babies come from; brought by storks, or found in cabbages or roses, for boys and girls respectively.[68] There were also encouraging, pronatalist cards in which babies were offered, as if on a 'cash and carry' basis, each one with its selling

Plate 14. 'After the war: *poilu*-growing.'

Plate 15. 'Come on, ladies. Work for France.'

Plate 16. 'France: 1915.'

point.[69] Babies were also presented as household necessities (no home was complete without several of them)[70] or as available in specialised bazaars, lotteries and farms.[71] Associated with such fantasies were often ideologically loaded captions like: 'No more couples without children, make your own choice, or adopt a child'.[72]

Following the outbreak of war, the arrival of babies became even more uncertain and the traditional motifs were adapted to the new circumstances. The stork tradition will be considered first. Coming from the east, in particular from Alsace, storks already had a strong patriotic flavour in the context of the *Revanche*. On their wings they bring both babies and victory. Typically, a winged allegory contributes to this victory by pouring babies out of a cornucopia.[73] With the admiration for flying aces the stork myth was updated into an aviation fantasy: babies, often referred to as *graine de poilu* (literally 'soldier seed', a newly coined phrase meaning both the son of a soldier and the soldier of the future), are delivered by aeroplane.[74] In 'L'aéroplane du bonheur' this airborne delivery is the result of a happy leave in which 'time flew'.[75] 'Nous arrivons, nous voilà',[76] in which baby reinforcements appear, this time borne upon the telegraph wires above the fields of France, is a particularly striking example of how these fantasy post-cards went far beyond coy explanations of sexual reality to suggest a whole undercurrent of national concern. It is as if the French nation, like those believers in the cargo cults of the Pacific, were scrutinising the skies for signs of hope in the form of babies which, given the desperate family situations imposed by the war, could only arrive, like manna, from heaven.

As for the cultivation of cabbages, much more important than roses for the armies of the future, the addition of the *graine de poilu* caption made all the pre-war variations on this theme more topical. Publication continued, therefore, of cards representing the baby-farm,[77] the courting couple cultivating cabbages (but with the man now in uniform),[78] the healthy female gardener[79] and the baby emerging from a cabbage (but now in military dress).[80]

Other cards had babies streaming into a barracks and emerging in uniform ('Registration of the young *poilus*', Plate 17) or active in a military encampment.[81] Babies not only appeared as soldiers but were themselves attached to weapons, as in Revanche 309 which shows an array of shells, each containing a baby, with the caption: 'Des canons! des munitions! C'est nous qui serons les gardiens de la nation'.[82] In a less discordant patriotic image, the Tricolour was widely used to wrap up wartime babies.[83]

Students of French demography are familiar with the deeply indented pyramids which depict the age structure of France after the First World War. People born between 1915 and 1918 are still referred to as 'les classes creuses' ('the depleted cohorts'), as a glance at any standard work on the population of twentieth-century France will attest. It seems that this depletion was immediately and widely perceived. Particularly in 1915 and 1916, when the number of births fell to an all-time low, a great deal of attention and concern was devoted to the 'classe 35' and the 'classe 36', the military cohorts which these babies would form when called up, at the age of 20. The abundance of postcards on the subject is really remarkable, as indeed is the fact that to date I have not seen any card of this type produced before 1915. Even cards which refer to earlier cohorts were produced after the number of births plummeted in 1915.

Of the cards devoted to the 'classe 35',[84] 'Hélas, j'arrive trop tard' ('Alas I'm too late', Plate 18) is a vivid representation of how tragic the lack of past and present babies was felt to be. Its pronatalism is tinged with pessimism. However, the conscript of 1935 being breast-fed on another card is accompanied by a much more hopeful legens: 'He won't have to go to war, thanks to the brave soldiers of 1915'.[85] The precious few babies of the 1935 cohort, having aroused so much interest by their arrival, were then shown to be thriving.[86] The genre proved popular and cards were produced for the 'classe 36' ('*Poilu* seed 1916. Long live the class of 36', Plate 19)[87] and the 'classe 37'.[88]

If the stages of conception, birth and infancy occupied a special place in popular imagery, children of school age, especially primary school age, were

Plate 17. 'Registration of the young *poilus*.'

Plate 18. 'Alas, I'm too late.'

Plate 19. '*Poilu* seed 1916. Long live the class of 36.'

also the subject of a large number of cards, in which playing and learning, both at home and at school, were used as a vehicle for patriotic sentiment. Representation of their games, not surprisingly, reflected adult preoccupations. This even extended to the current concern with the birth rate, a preoccupation which in a number of cards children were portrayed as sharing. In fact, most of the variations on the pronatalist theme encountered in postcards representing adults have a child-focused equivalent. The soldier's leave, which he must put to good use with his wife, as an extension of military duty, is the theme of a humorous card by Poulbot featuring his famous urchins.[89] In a variant of the baby-farm fantasy,[90] children playing mothers and fathers are already tending a crop of tiny helmeted *poilus* emerging from a cabbage patch. The patriotic message is reinforced by the children's kepi, Tricolour, wooden sword and toy horse. 'Après le bataille', a miniature representation of post-war demographic reconstruction, shows a little boy who has given up his army of toy soldiers to look after a baby doll.[91]

Future parents, boys of this age are also future soldiers, a role illustrated by countless cards. Frequently shown expressing the wish to fight 'comme papa',[92] these miniature *poilus* also complain that their war games are not real enough.[93] Girls can only be such figures as Marianne, Liberty, Joan of Arc or Alsace and Lorraine,[94] otherwise they have to content themselves with holding the flag[95] or praying to God to change them into boys 'so that they may go and beat the Hun'.[96] Strangely enough little girls are rarely presented in the more active role of nurse.[97] Giving inspiration rather than acting is the lot of the female: 'Jeu de garçon, rêve de fillette'[98] shows heroic potential for the boy, the girl's part being limited to dreaming of the young hero. Boys on the other hand, have a whole array of uniforms and military attributes at their disposal.[99] The captions are worth noting: 'La France de demain', 'Jeune France', 'le futur défenseur du pays'. The theme of children, not just as children, but as the future of the nation, goes well beyond the need to cater for a market which included children. Presented as depositaries of essentially French values, children became values in themselves; this is one of the most pervasive tenets of popular ideology at the time.

In a world dominated by war, military cohort numbering was also applied to children of school age (although, as we have seen, this did not occur before 1915). These children are referred to as the 'classes futures'[100] or, more specifically, as the fresh conscripts of the 'classe 29'[101] and the 'classe 24', already at school and training for war in the playground.[102] 'Les poilus de la 6ème' ('The *poilus* of the sixth class = first form', Plate 20) plays on the double meaning of the word 'classe' (military cohort and school year) and portrays first formers in the secondary school giving way to boisterous

Plate 20. 'The *poilus* of the first form.'

patriotism under the benevolent eye of a master who has just been teaching 'la France'.

The pupil and future citizen-soldier are not simply roles which the word 'classe' makes it possible to confuse; at a more profound level they were felt to be inseparable, the one a necessary precursor of the other. Many post-cards, whether or not referring explicitly to the classroom (cf. Plate 21, 'Genius children, is a French talent'),[103] reflect the ideology of the national school of the Third Republic and its teaching of patriotic values. In a way they are themselves part of this 'enseignement de la patrie',[104] with their edifying examples of youthful bravery, sense of duty and love of country. In choosing and buying a card for a child, whether the child was to be the sender or the recipient,[105] adults were thus reinforcing this teaching, which indeed they had themselves received. After the *lois Jules Ferry* (1881–2) school became a common experience for whole age cohorts, with common curricula, readers (like the famous *Tour de France par deux enfants*)[106] and textbooks.[107] By the time of the war, most adults had had this experience which was therefore a common reference not only within a cohort but also across generations. Whether or not publishers were determined to produce propaganda, in speaking about 'la patrie', they used the language and images through which it had been taught to them, and which were common currency, instantly recognisable by all. Such themes as the heroic resistance of the Gauls[108] or of lion-hearted Belfort,[109] the loss of Alsace-Lorraine,[110] the writing of the *Marseillaise*,[111] and the national heroes of the past, Joan of Arc[112] and Napoleon[113] (of whom Joffre, in particular, appeared as a modern version),[114] were part of the child's life. Indeed, one important aspect of the family, as shown on many postcards, was that it was an extension of school, a place where 'la patrie' was taught. There is no shortage of parents pointing to pictures of Joffre or Napoleon, or to maps of France,[115] Joffre himself sometimes appears in the home with a message of encouragement[116] and children's homework, particularly on maps of Europe or Alsace, is pre-sented as an act of solidarity with the front.[117] Thus, the wartime picture postcard underlines the close relationship between family and school, and, more generally, between family and nation, the family being the place where the next generation is not only conceived and bred, but taught and prepared for its future duties. In this respect, the evidence of the picture postcard con-firms the results of other research into the way primary school moulded the self-image of the French nation.[118]

Comparisons with Germany and Britain

This analysis of popular images of the child in wartime picture postcards would be incomplete without some attempt to provide a comparative

Le Génie, mes enfants, est un don bien français. 54

Plate 21. 'Genius, children, is a French talent.'

perspective, however briefly. Do the postcard productions of other belligerent nations suggest that other ways of presenting children and parenthood were possible, at a time when patriotism and nationalism were such powerful factors?

If one considers images of children and parenthood in the postcard production of Germany and Great Britain one remarkable fact becomes evident: France seems to have had much in common with its enemy Germany while its British ally provides a striking contrast.

Germany had many producers of postcards and was an important exporter of postcards before the war. Its wartime production included many 'multiple baby' cards with a pronatalist flavour, as well as patriotic and sentimental family scenes.[119] Although there are differences in tone, German cards favouring a more pious brand of sentimentality while erotic wit plays a more important part in French cards, much of the German production could have been adapted for the French market by simple translation and change of uniform. Britain, however, with its strong 'Malthusian' tradition,[120] contrasts sharply with both France and Germany. In the humorous genre which was such a popular category of British wartime postcard, children are often presented negatively and babies, in particular, are frequently depicted as bawling menaces.[121] Fathers of large families, far from being heroes, are figures of fun, either victims of a fate worse than death or feckless scroungers.[122] Only months after the carnage on the Somme, infanticide could be presented as a joke and even associated with the front by means of a caption quoting the popular military song, 'Pack up your troubles in your old kit bag' (Plate 22)[123] – a far cry from the French card (Plate 16) which associated the *Marseillaise* with the message: 'let us replace the losses in our ranks'. It is true that there was a pronatalist current in Britain, albeit limited in influence, which did find some expression in postcards. Such cards, however, are striking in their dourness and severity, stressing duty to the exclusion of both sexual enjoyment and parental fulfillment.[124] 'Now is the time to do our utmost' (Plate 23) is a good example, with its empty and unwelcoming cradle and its lack of any human presence.

Conclusion

To return to France itself, the study of the popular ideology of the child in wartime would require the evidence of the picture postcards examined in this paper to be set against a wider spectrum of production which would include children's books, the popular press, songs, and so on. I nevertheless believe that because picture postcards were the means of so much family communication during the war, they are privileged documents which

Plate 22. 'Pack up your troubles in your old kit bag.'

present a view of the family, the child, and the nation which was not just propaganda from above, but reflected popular conceptions adhered to in great numbers by the public itself. As for the specific question of pronatalism, by the end of the war the problem was no longer the gap between the ideologies of the elites and the masses, but between widely accepted pronatalist ideology, on the one hand, and demographic behaviour which appeared largely untouched by this ideology, on the other.

The significance of such an ideology cannot, however, be adequately gauged by reference to fertility patterns alone. Quite apart from the difficulty of determining the extent, if any, of this kind of influence, such a narrowly pragmatic approach would ignore what is perhaps the most important feature of the wartime ideology of the child: the possibility which that ideology provided of incorporating the abstract and public values of patriotism with the most intimate aspects of personal and family life. Even people who had no intention or possibility of having children, because of, for instance, their age or marital status, could still participate in this child-centred culture, whose social function clearly went much further than mere pronatalism. The child *topos* acted as a kind of shibboleth: by showing concern for *dénatalité* and talking about procreation and babies, even in a tone of *gauloiserie*, people were joining in an assertion of Frenchness and showing themselves to be genuine 'enfants de la patrie'.

Plate 23. 'Now is the time to do our utmost.'

Appendix 12.1

The use of picture postcards as a source involves practical difficulties apart from those of interpretation. In particular, there is no easy way of determining the full range of postcards in existence or the complete extent of a publisher's output. Although postcard collecting has led to the production of postcard catalogues these can never be as authoritative as stamp catalogues which take their information about date, origin and numbers printed from centralised national issuing agencies.

In order to establish the usual quantities printed during the war, the copyright records were consulted despite the fact that they had not been centralised and were known to be incomplete. A production of 5,000 or 10,000 copies of one title was typical in 1914 and from 1915 onwards printings of 100,000 or more, sometimes followed by reprintings of similar size, were by no means rare. For example, I.M.L. no. 2433 (note 67) had an initial printing of 100,000. One way of establishing the extent and precise nature of a publisher's production would, of course, be to consult the publisher's own records. However, tracing such records, assuming they exist, would be an endless task given the highly fragmented nature of postcard production.

Dating is also often problematic, although references to Verdun, tanks, particular military cohorts, demobilisation, etc., enable one to be reasonably precise. Otherwise the written message (if there is one) sometimes provides an extra clue, as does the postmark, if legible. Given the buoyancy of the market during the war, postcards were usually sent within a few months at most of publication, although this cannot be stated with certainty for any one postcard. It can safely be assumed, however, that unless otherwise indicated, all the cards referred to in this article date from 1914–18.

The list which follows gives the names or trade marks of 75 French postcard publishers whose cards were consulted during the preparation of this chapter, and by its size supports the comments made about the fragmented nature of production.

A.C.A. (Artige), A.G. (A. Girard), A.N. (A. Noyer), A, TErnois, F.G., Calife, Cecil (S.I.D.), Ch. Bertholomier et Cie., Croissant, Devambez, Devena, Dix, Dora, D.U.M., E. Brocherioux, Edition Lorraine, E.L.D. (Deley or E. Le Deley), E.M., Etoile, F. Bouchy, Fauvette, Fides, France, Furia (L'atelier d'art photographique), Gaspard Chiroutre, Geo, G. L. Hermine, Gloria, G. Mathière (G.M.T.), Idéa, I.M.L. (I. Lapina), Irsa, J. Bouveret, J. Courcier, J.K. (A. H. Katz or A.H.K.), J.M.C., J.M.T., Kiss, Kisa, La Favorite, La Pensée, L'As, Laureys, L.H., L.V. Cie, L.V.G.. Luc, L.U.X., M., Maison de la Bonne Presse, Mésange, Mug, Myosotis (E.M.E.), Myrkad, N.D., Neo-Phot., Novelta, Par tous Pour tous, Patrie, Patriotic, P.H., Photo Dangereux (St. Martin), P.J.G. (P. et J. Gallais), P.R., Pro Patria (L.G. Pro Patria), R.D., Revanche, Rex (V.P.Ed.), R.I.P., Rob, S.E., S.J.M., Suzy, W., W.A., W.D.

Notes

I wish to express my thanks to Madame Migliorini of the BDIC and Mr M. Moodie of the Imperial War Museum for their assistance and for enabling me to photograph material in their collections.

1 *Poilu*, literally meaning hairy, i.e. virile and brave, was the standard term for the French soldier of the 1914–18 war.

2 P. E. Ogden and M. M. Huss, 'Demography and pronatalism in France in the 19th and 20th centuries', *Journal of Historical Geography*, 8 (1982), 283–98.

3 J. M. Winter, 'The fear of population decline in Western Europe, 1870–1940' in R. W. Hiorns (ed.), *Demographic patterns in developed societies*, London, 1980, see also, J. M. Winter and M. S. Teitelbaum, *The fear of population decline*, New York, 1985.

4 R. Tomlinson, 'The politics of *dénatalité* during the French Third Republic, 1890–1940', unpublished PhD thesis, Cambridge, 1984.

5 F. Ronsin, *La Grève des ventres*, Paris, 1980.

6 A doctor by training, Jacques Bertillon became head of the Bureau des Statistiques. An ardent pronatalist, he was one of the founders of the Alliance nationale pour l'accroissement de la population française. The five books in question were *Calcul de la mortalité des enfants du premier âge*, Paris, 1887; *De la mortalité par âge avant la naissance*, Paris, 1893; *De la dépopulation de la France et des remèdes à y apporter*, Paris, 1896; *Le Problème de la dépopulation*, Paris, 1897; *La Dépopulation de la France, ses conséquences, ses causes, mesures à prendre pour la combattre*, Paris, 1911.

7 L. Toesca, *Les Crimes de l'alcôve*, Auxerre, 1911; Vuillermet, F.-A., *Le Suicide d'une race*, Paris, 1911; A. Dumont, *La Morale basée sur la démographie*, Paris, 1901; P. Bureau, *La Restriction volontaire de la natalité et la défense nationale*, Paris, 1913.

8 F. Boverat, *Patriotisme et paternité*, Paris, 1913. Boverat was another ardent pronatalist and member from its early days of the Alliance nationale pour l'accroissement de la population française. In the inter-war years he was its General Secretary and most prolific propagandist and political lobbyist.

9 The title of a series of lectures given during the war by J. Doleris and J. Bouscatel; see *Néomalthusianisme. Maternité et féminisme. Education sexuelle*, Paris, 1918.

10 *Ibid.*, p. 23.

11 Doleris and Bouscatel, *Néomalthusianisme*, p. 73.

12 Postcard published by Inter-art Co., Red Lion Square, London WC (Patriotic series VII, no. 846). My copy of this card was sent in May 1915.

13 R. Tomlinson, 'The politics of *dénatalité*', p. 117.

14 Doleris and Bouscatel, *Néomalthusianisme*, pp. 73–4.

15 There were a number of variations on the 'two against five' theme, all of which showed two French soldiers outnumbered by the German enemy; a typical caption reads: 'For every two potential soldiers born in France, Germany produces five. Raising the birth rate is for France a matter of life and death'. An example of this material is reproduced in R. Tomlinson, M. M. Huss and P. E. Ogden, 'France in peril', *History Today*, 35 (April 1985), p. 25.

16 I am indebted to P. E. Ogden for this information.

17 N. Boulanger, Gloria no. 59. Caption: 'Allons . . . petit gars! Vengeons-les!' (grandfather exhorts grandson to avenge fallen Frenchmen).

18 This characteristic is illustrated by the publisher's depiction of his own shop in the Laureys postcard described in note 23.

19 J. and G. Neudin, *L'Argus international des cartes postales de collection*, annual publication, Paris, 1983.

20 The soldier waiting for news from home was itself a frequent subject of the picture postcard. For example, a postcard published by Laureys (no. 961), with

the caption: 'Write soon, see how we run when the bugle sounds the arrival of the mail', showed soldiers running enthusiastically towards the field post office.

21 Quoted by J.-N. Jeanneney, 'Les archives de contrôle postal aux armées (1916–18). Une source précieuse pour l'histoire contemporaine de l'opinion et des mentalités', *Revue d'histoire moderne et contemporaine*, 15 (1968), p. 218.

22 Patriotic no. 1104.

23 For example, a card sent from Verdun on 15 December 1916 (my collection) bears the message: 'still alive at 4.30, terrible fighting, we are advancing'. The anxiety of those waiting at home was itself often represented on the picture postcard. One example (Laureys no. 660) shows the inhabitants of a neighbourhood (all of them women) anxiously lining the street and leaning out of windows as the postman appears in the distance. Significantly the publisher also chose to represent his own shop (Etablissements Laureys) as part of this suffering community.

24 Patriotic, for example, published two such cards: no. 1173 ('A nos poilus, le colis désiré') and for the British army market no. 1205 ('A surprise for Tommies').

25 E.M. no. 235.

26 'The weapons of love' (J.K. no. 2111): four scenes in which a *poilu* (the general term for the French soldier of 1914–18 cf. above note 1) explains to a young woman how to use different weapons.

27 'The cook's specialities' (J.K. no. 2099): a number of scenes exploiting the use of food as a metaphor for sex. Significantly, the pronatalist theme was not felt to conflict with this erotic context and one scene ('le petit salé aux choux') represents a baby emerging from a cabbage (the French equivalent of the gooseberry bush) to the evident approval of a *poilu*, with the legend 'souvenir de permission' (the result of a leave).

28 G.M.T. nos. 716/1–5. Areas covered by these cards include food, the different branches of the army and the parts of the body; one card (no. 71/5) is entirely devoted to that most long-suffering part of the conscript's body, the feet. Even in this unpromising context, the pronatalist message finds a place. Contrasting with the clumsy adult footwear a baby's bootees occupy the centre of the card with the fond comment 'pour les petons du poilu de la classe 36' ('for the tootsies of the *poilu* of 1936'). The key concept of military 'classe' will be discussed on pp. 348–9.

29 Already a traditional genre in nineteenth-century popular imagery, the 'enigma' is often found in picture postcards from the 1890s onwards. A particularly relevant example in the present context (Enigma no. 149) represents the head of a bearded *poilu* accompanied by the instruction to look for the future soldier of 1937 ('Cherchez la classe 37'). When the card is turned upside down, a baby, the *poilu*'s contribution to a future army, appears in his helmet.

30 For example there are 19 different representations in my collection alone. Revanche nos. 303 and 307; Cecil no. 2014; Lapina: 'La Bonne Graine' (artist Sager); J.K. nos. 2044, 2099 and 2112; L'as: 'La Poiluculture'; Patriotic no. 1089; Furia nos. 420/4 and 372/3; E.M. no. 339; W. (Lemaire) no. 6201; Rex no. 1302; PC no. 4123; Mug nos. 257 and 665; Lotus no. 566; Dix no. 879/2.

31 Published by the Red Cross (no. 59), from a drawing by G. Scott, the famous illustrator of the weekly *L'Illustration*.

32 C. Dyer, *Population and society in twentieth century France*, London, 1978, p. 49.

33 There were even specialised journals for collectors.
34 E.g. Patriotic no. 1062 (respectful); Dix no. 630/2 (more enterprising); G.L. no. 403 (conjugal/romantic); W. no. 6227 (conjugal/homely); Patriotic no. 1172 (the soldier's first meeting with his correspondent).
35 For example, one publisher, Dix, alone, brought out no. 87 (girl of about 5), no. 192/2 (boy of about 4), no. 187/3 (girl of about 8), no. 147/1 (boy of about 8).
36 Dix no. 214/4.
37 Furia no. 447/2.
38 For example, cards featuring the joys of the next leave are often to be found with the initials of sender and recipient written above the heads of the protagonists.
39 'Cartes postales interdites par le service des périodiques du bureau de la presse (Ministère de la Guerre), 1916', manuscript consulted at the Bibliothèque de Documentation Internationale Contemporaine (BDIC), Nanterre. Equivalent documents for other years of the war are not in the BDIC holdings and are presumed by the library to have been lost or burnt. Unfortunately there is no detailed information about the recruitment, numbers and work-load of censors responsible for picture postcards either in published sources or in the records held at the BDIC. Information on censorship of other kinds of material can be found in M. Berger and P. Allard, *Les Secrets de la censure pendant la guerre*, Paris, 1932; see also L. Gabriel-Robinet, *La Censure*, Paris, 1965, pp. 146–56, and A. Ducasse, J. Meyer and G. Perreux, *Vie et mort des français, 1914–1918*, Paris, 1962, pp. 275–7.
40 E.g. Patriotic no. 1058.
41 I located the offending card (Croissant no. 164) in the Henri Leblanc collection (BDIC), but have found no resubmitted version to date.
42 The H. Leblanc collection was started in 1914 with the intention of preserving one copy of all ephemera published from the beginning of the war. It was later donated to the nation and enlarged by the addition of public archives like those of the Préfecture de Police de la Seine. Although it was never able to achieve its aim of total comprehensiveness, it holds no less than 60,000 picture postcards for the period 1900–20 (many from the war years), and is described by S. Zeyons in his reference work *Les Cartes postales*, Paris, 1979, as the most complete collection of First World War postcards (p. 98). The Bibliothèque Forney and the Imperial War Museum have a collection of several thousand postcards each from this period. My own collection, although more limited (approximately 500 cards) is the result of a highly selective process: for each card acquired dozens were consulted in private collections and in the stocks of postcard dealers in France and England.
43 For example, in the foreground women are shown knitting pullovers at home for the soldier who appears in the background suffering from the cold in the trenches (Gloria no. 79; Lapina no. 1841; E.L.D. no. 30; Revanche no. 134). Similar treatment unites letter-writer (Patriotic no. 1133; A.C.A. no. 2129; L.L.D. no. 7), day-dreamer (J.K. no. 9493), well-wisher (Patriotic no. 1034) and person praying (La Pensée no. 26; Furia no. 316; Geo no. 1008; Pro Patria no. 107) with the absent object of their thoughts.
44 Fides no. 1014.
45 J.K. no. 9493.
46 Maison de la Bonne Presse no. 106.
47 Mug no. 901.
48 G. Mathière no. 16 (signed C. H. Léo). The caption reads: 'Elle: C'est pour les

semailles que tu viens? Lui: Oui, Margot, et je crois qu'on va *"semer"* sérieuse-ment!' ('She: Have you come back for the sowing season? He: Yes, Maggie, and I think we're going to get some real sowing/loving done'). For the same pun see also Dix no. 425 and several unnumbered cards from the H. Leblanc collection (classified under 'Femme pendant la guerre, I'). Another typically *gaulois* pun is offered by the phrase 'sur le front' ('at the front' or 'on the forehead') when combined with the verb 'baiser' ('to kiss' or, colloquially, 'to make love to'): thus a particular erotic exploit of the *poilu* is to 'baiser sa femme sur le front' (several postcards classified under 'Vie du soldat, II', H. Leblanc collection).

49 Alpha no. 11. Relevant here are the positive connotations of the French 'mon lapin', a term of endearment, and 'un chaud lapin', an admiring description of a man's sexual capacities, which contrast with the negative connotations of the English expression 'to breed like rabbits.' The distaste for fertility evinced by this phrase and amply reflected in the British picture postcard will be discussed briefly at the end of the chapter. Another feature of the 'rabbit' card is the sub-ordinate role attributed to the female in the activity of procreation (cf. note 56).

50 Furia no. 1761/4. My copy of this card was sent on 2 July 1917, when tanks were still a relatively recent innovation.

51 The way in which the baby is portrayed is very important. I have seen many (mostly British) postcards in which the baby seems to be a punishment for love rather than a reward and the card serves as a cautionary tale. In one example of this particularly British genre a baby placed upon the last page of a book rep-resents 'The end of a love story' (signed T. Gilson, no. 800, publisher unknown). Other examples are discussed at the end of this chapter.

In a similar vein to Plate 10, 'Qui choisir?' ('Whom shall I choose?', Rex no. 1299) showed a young soldier facing a difficult choice among seven pretty girls. The caption stresses that this is not just a frivolous quest for pleasure but that the satisfaction of founding a family is at stake: 'Fonder une famille est un destin bien doux'.

52 There was a whole lay republican religion that was particularly marked during the war. Many of the most popular religious prayers and texts were transposed to fit patriotic figures and ideals. Joffre was a particularly revered figure and there were several versions of the Lord's prayer and the creed addressed to him. One version of the Lord's prayer, originally from a trench news-sheet, is quoted by General Weygand in 'La Presse des tranchées, 1914–18', *Histoire de la presse française*, vol. II, Lausanne, 1965, p. 425. It was also published as a postcard (I.M.L. no. 2182) as was the full text of the creed, 'Je crois en Joffre le père tout-puissant . . .' (D.U.M., 'Le Credo du soldat en 1915'). Other texts in this vein include the Ten Commandments (postcard by D.U.M., 1915) of which the tenth is pronatalist ('La France tu repeupleras'), and the *De profundis*, etc. This will be the subject of a future article.

53 'Ça, c'est bon pour la repopulation', Rex no. 2100. A very similar card, both in style and content, but dating from about 1919–20, shows 'la canne à Papa' ('Daddy's stick') with babies dangling from it and the caption: 'Pour repeupler, il n'y a que ça' ('to repopulate you can't beat it', Rex no. 1301, from P. E. Ogden's collection). Both these cards are reproduced in Tomlinson, Huss and Ogden, 'France in peril', p. 27.

54 La Favorite no. 2601. A.H.K. no. 308, J.K. no. 2111, I.M.L. no. 2127.

55 'Impossible. Special mission: must prepare class of 36' (G. Mathière no. 15, signed Ch. Leo).

56 This postcard is particularly rich in Freudian implications, as was pointed out by L. Jordanova and K. Figlio in particular following the initial presentation of my paper at the Cambridge conference on the European family and the First World War. The babies are presented as totally in the male's gift, his bag, a sort of scrotum, replacing the mother's womb. The total exclusion of the mother from the process of procreation can be read as a compensation for the *poilu*'s feeling of exclusion from the family cell and from the strong mother-child bonds being established without him (and possibly against him) while he is at the front. The fact that one baby is about to suck not the mother's breast but the *poilu*'s wine flask supports this reading. For a contrasted British wartime image of fatherhood see Plate 22.

57 Patriotic no. 1105.

58 Dix no. 442.

59 I.M.L. no. 2347.

60 G. Perreux, *La Vie quotidienne des civils pendant la guerre de 1914–18*, Paris, 1966, p. 328.

61 No. 15 (visé Paris), publisher unknown. Many similar postcards used the family as a symbol of reconstruction (e.g. Carrey no. 4) as did posters for war and reconstruction loans from 1915 onwards.

62 H. Leblanc collection ('Femme pendant la guerre, I'), publisher unknown. A British postcard with a similar title offers a striking contrast: three soldiers, realising that their wives have babes in arms and that their homes are turning into nurseries, retreat in disarray ('When the boys come home', C.P.C. Series 472).

63 This card was a development of the well-represented pre-war 'farming/fishing for babies' genre (e.g. Mug no. 257, Dix no. 879, Rex no. 4713, Furia no. 420).

64 One box in the H. Leblanc collection ('Femme pendant la guerre, I') contains numerous examples of this fantasy.

65 Title of a poem by A. Soriac, soldier in the 277th regiment, printed on a postcard (publisher unknown). Many cards illustrate this theme: for example, the 'La Femme du mobilisé' series (B.G. no. 702) shows women bravely looking after their families, in town and country settings.

66 S.J.M. (no number).

67 I.M.L. no. 2433. This extension of the pronatalist theme to friendly nations also applied to England and the United States (as in the 'graine de *poilu*', 'graine de Tommies', 'graine de Sammies' series, Dix nos. 1282/4/5/6).

68 E.g. 'graine de choux' (P.C. no. 4123) and 'Le Rosier d'amour' (V.A.P. no. 105).

69 E.g. Mug no. 185; pinned on babies are such captions as 'I never cry', 'Real bargain', 'Always smiling'.

70 E.g. Th.E.L. no. 1067 ('Article de ménage').

71 E.g. Rex no. 987 ('Loterie des bébés'); Rex no. 1201 ('Grand bazar des bébés'); Gloria no. 423 ('La Ferme aux bébés').

72 E.g. Mug no. 257 ('La Ferme aux bébés') and 'Choisissez et adoptez' (Bergeret, no number). The French childless couple, often represented disapprovingly as selfish and shortsighted, contrasts sharply with British representations: such couples are wise or fortunate and can look down with pity on enslaved parents (see note 122).

73 'Cigognes porte-bonheur' (Dix no. 796/4). The caption reads: 'Chères cigognes d'Alsace . . . Apportez la victoire, avec ces beaux bébés'.

74 J.K. no. 2044.

75 'Les jours de permission se sont vite envolés, mais leur souvenir refleurira l'an prochain, dans les beaux choux pommés de France' (Patriotic no. 1089). An interesting comparison can be made here with a similar postcard (Mésange no. 552) adapted by its French publisher for the 'Tommy' market. The usual pronatalist caption has been replaced by 'Happy birthday', assumed more likely to appeal to the British.

76 'We're coming, here we are' (Mug no. 300). The words of the French caption, borrowed from the trumpet song of the opera *Carmen*, were very recognisable at the time and underline the martial and hopeful connotations of the babies' arrival.

77 Furia no. 420/4.

78 Revanche no. 307.

79 'La Bonne Graine' (signed Xavier Sager, I.M.L., no number).

80 W.A. no. 6201.

81 E.M. no. 186.

82 'More guns! more munitions! We will be the guardians of the nation!' This card is reproduced in A. Kyrou, *L'Age d'or de la carte postale*, Paris, 1966, p. 69.

83 La Pensée no. 85; Furia no. 346; Dix no. 132; Patriotic nos. 1113 and 1142.

84 Patriotic nos. 1079 and 1119; A.N. no. 2977; I.M.L. no. 2349; Mug nos. 640 and 665; Croissant no. 82.

85 Croissant no. 82.

86 'La classe 35 se fortifie' (Patriotic no. 1126)

87 'Il est de la classe 36' (Par tous, Pour tous no. 113); 'Classe 36: petit poussin deviendra coq' (I.M.L. no. 2349); 'Vive la classe 36' (Mug no. 755).

88 'Cherchez la classe 37' (Enigma no. 149); 'Hardi la classe 37' (Cecil no. 2014); 'Vive la classe 37' (La Pensée no. 536).

89 A. Ternois (Poulbot no. 20). Poulbot's drawings were so successful in creating a type that his name has become a generic term in French for an urchin.

90 E.M. no. 339.

91 Devambez no. 10.

92 'Comme papa, graine de poilu' (Patriotic no. 1174; 'Comme papa, je fais le salut militaire' (La Pensée no. 74); 'Le fils à papa' (Patriotic no. 1107); 'Je voudrais comme toi défendre le pays' (J.K. no. 9454).

93 'Petit patriote' (Dix no. 122); 'Pan . . . sale boche: qu'est-ce que tu prends' (Gloria no. 192/2); 'Je voudrais un gros tambour' (E.M. no. 20); 'Je saurai te défendre' (W.D. no. 1127); 'Je voudrais bien tuer un Prussien' (J.M. No. 568); 'Avec des vrais petits boches' (Poulbot no. 1915, Devambez no. 60); 'Je veux foncer comme un poilu au travers des Germains' (Furia no. 372/3).

94 A.C.A. no. 2032; Dix nos. 120 and 2001/5; La Pensée no. 54; P.J. no. 317; J. Courcier no. 205. In this allegorical category girls are often a little older.

95 J.K. no. 9408; J.M.T. no. 116.

96 An unusual postcard in the style of a devotional image, 'La prière des petites filles' (signed Ch. de Bussy 1914, Ch. Bertholomier et Cie., no number), shows three little girls kneeling in prayer in an idealised French landscape with the caption: 'Dieu . . . Chagez-nous vite en grands garçons pour qu'on aille battre les boches'.

97 Idéa no. 52; J.K. no. 9589.

98 Idéa no. 63.

99 J.K. no. 9408; J.M.T. no. 116; A.C.A. nos. 2079 and 2167; Furia no. 357.

100 W.D. no. 1228.
101 'Nous sommes les conscrits de la classe vingt-neuf/Hurrah pour nos succès! Le matériel est neuf' (M. no. 1108).
102 'La classe 24 s'entraîne avec ardeur!!' (J. Bouveret, no number).
103 La Pensée no. 54; J.K. no. 9391; Revanche no. 171. The card reproduced here as Plate 12.2 encapsulates most of the themes of classroom patriotism (cf. note 104): a teacher dressed as a *poilu*, flags, the Michelettian caption, 'le génie mes enfants est un don bien français', underlining the universality of French values (a point reinforced by the globe), and the figure of Joffre in the background, endorsing the whole scene.
104 The phrase belongs to Michelet, who in 1846 described the national school of the future as a place 'où l'on n'apprendrait rien d'autre que la France' (*Le Peuple*, Paris, 1974, p. 240). This conception was largely implemented by the schools of the Third Republic, in which disciplines like French, history, geography and even natural science became vehicles for civic instruction.
105 From the messages written on the back of cards featuring children it seems that most were sent by adults to children, and a much smaller proportion by children to adults but even in these cases it is likely that the child's choice was guided by an adult. I have found no evidence of cards both sent and received by children.
106 G. Bruno, *Le Tour de France par deux enfants*, Paris, 1886. There were numerous subsequent editions (209 by 1891) and the work was still in use at the time of the Second World War. The same applies to Lavisse and Vidal de la Blache (note 107).
107 E. Lavisse, *Histoire générale à l'usage des candidats au certificat d'études primaires*, Paris, 1884 and *Histoire de France depuis les origines jusqu'à la révolution*, Paris, 1900–11; P. Vidal de la Blache, *Etats et nations de l'Europe*, Paris, 1889 and *Tableau de la géographie de la France*, Paris, 1903.
108 Revanche no. 108.
109 P.H. no. 317.
110 Kiss no. 726; S.E. no. 303; La Pensée no. 26; Dix no. 383; J.K. no. 9391; Revanche no. 171; Courcier no. 205.
111 Rex no. 4101; Mésange no. 117; J.K. no. 9559.
112 Dix nos. 118, 120, 1662, 2001.
113 A.N. no. 1489; Mug no. 532; Etoile no. 1054; Kisa (no number), Lapina no. 188.
114 Myosotis no. 102, L.D. no number (signed Roger Broders).
115 Dix no. 200/2; Etoile no. 1054; E.M. no. 16; S.E. no. 3103.
116 J.K. no. 9417.
117 J.M.T. no. 128.
118 P. Nora, 'Ernest Lavisse: son rôle dans la formation du sentiment national', *Revue historique*, 228 (1962), pp. 73–106; A. Prost, *Histoire de l'enseignement en France, 1800–1967*, Paris, 1968; Jeanneney, 'Les Archives de contrôle'.
119 German postcards in this style are reproduced in S. Zeyons, *Le Roman-photo de la grande guerre: les cartes postales bleu horizon*, Paris, 1976. For general background on the strength of the German postcard industry see J. Fraser, 'Propaganda on the picture postcard', *The Oxford Art Journal*, 3 (October 1980), 39–47. My own research has not been systematic, nor can I claim to have seen as great a number of German postcards as I have French.
120 'Malthusian' is used here with the meaning it has in the context of the French

pronatalist debate described above on pp. 329–32: being in favour of a reduced family size and birth rate, in contrast to pronatalists who favoured an increased family size.

121 Although portraits of pretty babies were published, infants in the humorous genre of the period were overwhelmingly presented as a burden, their faces disfigured by tears of tantrums. Many cards have ironic captions such as 'They grew in beauty side by side, they filled one's home with glee' (Victor no. 11, probably immediately pre-war), 'Suffer little children to come unto me' (The Regent no. 2631) and 'The kingdom within your eyes' (Bamford no. 1007, early post-war); others include more direct comments such as 'A bachelor's nightmare' (The Newest, series 444) or 'Clicked' (T. Gilson no. 915) beneath a miserable Tommy with two howling babies in his arms.

122 'And I always wanted to be a father' (Inter-Art no. 5117) shows a father enslaved in the nursery; 'England expects every man to do his duty' (Corona no. 1071) has a henpecked weakling leading ten children along a street; a beggar carries a placard 'I am blind and the father of six children by a horrible accident' (H.B. no. 769). In the immediate post-war period a childless couple (contrast note 72) looks down on a miserable father struggling with seven children: 'Yes, that man got the V.C. – he risked his life in France several times!'; 'I'm not surprised at that', comes the reply: dying in the trenches was obviously nothing compared with the horrors of fatherhood. The 'scrounger' theme appears associated with parenthood in a post-war card (D. Constance no. 996) in which another puny father, pushing a pram and dragging two more children along behind him, admits: 'We must keep having 'em. My wife's maternity benefit is the only income I've got!'

123 The card reproduced here as Plate 22 (The Regent no. 2598, postmarked November 1917) is not at all exceptional. 'Shall I drown 'em or give 'em to the cat' (Ludgate no. 1043) expresses similar infanticidal sentiments. Less murderous, but just as 'anti-baby' was the theme of castration. One card shows the gooseberry bush being chopped down with an axe as a response to the three screaming babies it has already produced (Inter-Art, 'girlie' series no. 532, signed Fred Spurgin) while on another card (W. E. Mack no. 1413) a pair of shears is brandished with the threat 'Sumfin's going to happen to that gooseberry bush!' Milder, but still significant, is the 'return to sender' theme as in another McGill card (D. Constance no. 2224) which suggests sending the baby back and keeping the stork as a pet.

124 In the same vein 'Both British Bre(a)d' (W. & K. no. 4280), a card in dull sepia monochrome, baldly juxtaposes a loaf of bread and a loaf-sized baby. The caption explains that 'both these two things (sic) were underrated before the war and are now appreciated'. Two McGill cards in the 'One six one' series refer explicitly to shortages in military manpower: a stork responds to a recruitment poster ('1000000 more men wanted') with the words 'I'd better get busy' but there is no human presence on the card (no. 169). In no. 164, the most enthusiastic example of popular pronatalism in a British postcard found to date, a plain, fat young mother with three children emphasises the self-sacrifice involved: 'What I'm doing for my country!' Sentimental family scenes can also be found but usually with only one or two children and no hint of more to come.

13
Eugenics and pronatalism in wartime Britain

Richard A. Soloway

Pronatalism in Britain during the First World War was characterised by an intensification of demographic anxieties and a rapid expansion of the maternal and child welfare campaign launched in the pre-war decade. The encouragement of greater fertility and the preservation of infant life as pronatalist goals had in large part been stimulated by the relentless decline in the birth rate that had started in the late 1870s and was already of pressing concern by the opening of the new century.

The gloomiest of Edwardian prognosticators saw in this phenomenon clear signs of 'race suicide', but even people of less apocalyptical disposition were aware of the mounting anxieties provoked by countless references to 'empty cradles' and 'silent nurseries.'[1] Such imagery lay behind a wide array of ideas and proposals that could broadly be described as pronatalist. They came from socialists, trade unionists, feminists, politicians, clergymen, physicians, philanthropic aristocrats and businessmen and a host of other social critics and reformers.

This essay explores a frequently overlooked aspect of the pronatalist campaign by examining the uneasy alliance of the newly emerging eugenics movement, with its faith in biological determination and selective reproduction, with the environmentally oriented pronatalist drive for non-selective social reform. British eugenics, despite its aspirations and intentions, was from its inception less an objective science than a biological way of thinking comparatively and qualitatively about classes and accounting for differences between them primarily in hereditarian rather than in social or cultural terms. The problem of reconciling imperfectly understood, popularised laws of heredity with the persuasive claims of environmental reformers plagued eugenics throughout its history. It contributed to the division of the movement into what Daniel Kevles has described as 'mainline' eugenics, which prevailed before and during the First World War, and 'reform' eugenics which increasingly came to dominate in the inter-war years. The first, stressing as it did the predominance of hereditary unit characters through which 'like begets like', concentrated upon class and race. The second, strengthened by important advances in genetics and a more sophisticated understanding of the complex interactive role of environment, or nurture, turned to wider considerations focusing on populations rather than on classes or races. The new language reflected the reform eugenists' belief that valuable characteristics were to be found in most social groups, and that the best in human variation was to be encouraged.[2]

Kevles persuasively argues that the discovery that people were so infinitely complex in their biochemistry that it was impossible to determine the genetic outcome of their reproductive behaviour, coupled to the recognition that genes were continually being altered by environment, seriously undermined mainline eugenics. By the mid-1930s it was generally recognised to be 'a farrago of flawed science'.[3] This was undoubtedly true within the scientific community where eugenics had always struggled to acquire credibility and found itself increasingly undermined by the genetical sciences it had done so much to promote.

But eugenics was much more than a would-be science; it was, as Michael Freeden has recognised, also a social ideology with an eclectic appeal that cut more widely across the social and political spectrum than has been appreciated. Although usually associated with conservative middle-class, professional interests on the right, eugenics also appealed to a variety of progressive social reformers in the centre and on the left who found portions or aspects of the eugenic ideology relevant to their interests.[4] They selectively integrated them into their own reform agenda without necessarily allying themselves with the wider eugenic cause.[5] Ultimately that cause, despite the new, reformist directions taken by eugenics in the inter-war period, remained more heavily burdened by its mainline, class-oriented, hereditarian origins than Kevles and Freeden have recognised in their important studies.

As this essay contends, those mainline origins, stressing as they did the domination of nature over nurture, seriously limited the ability of the Eugenics Education Society, founded in 1907, to translate its socio-scientific ideology into an effective social policy that could reverse pre-war patterns of differential class fertility.[6]

During the First World War the Society's pronatalist efforts to create and preserve an 'A1' population exposed the scientific and political limitations of the eugenic approach to 'race reconstruction'. For the first time eugenists were forced to confront the practical consequences of promoting a selective population strategy based upon qualitative assumptions of hereditary fitness that ran counter to the predominant nurturing, environmentalist beliefs of other pronatalists and most other social reformers.

The pre-war history of the infant and maternal welfare movement in Britain is well known, and after 1914 local authorities, reinforced by an extensive network of voluntary organisations, markedly increased their efforts to ensure that the size and well-being of future generations would be adequate to fill the depleted 'racial coffers'.[7] Despite the persistent objections of some eugenists like Karl Pearson, by the outbreak of the war the evidence strongly indicated that most infant and childhood deaths were not the inevitable result of inherent defects, but were a consequence of prenatal and postnatal environmental conditions that could be improved. Infant mortality had been gradually declining since the beginning of the century, and, encouraged by this progress, predictions during the war as to the number of additional babies who might be saved by the implementation of more extensive interventionist programmes ranged from one to three thousand a week.[8]

Eugenists, who, in their singular way, were the truest of all pronatalist believers, were troubled by the direction taken by the burgeoning pronatalist campaign. While they shared the concerns of the pronatalist movement about the declining birth rate, eugenists were much more troubled about the class differential patterns of that decline. As a result their relationship to the pronatalist campaign had been tentative at best before 1914, weakened by serious disagreements over the relative contribution of nature and nurture and the importance of quality over quantity in the rebuilding of the race after decades of diminished fertility. The special circumstances of the war did not resolve the issue, but did prod many eugenists and the Eugenics Education Society to consider a more inclusive theory of causation that would allow a somewhat greater role for environmental factors. It led them, mainly for tactical, pragmatic reasons, to join with widely diverse groups and individuals in the pronatalist camp to try to save the lives of as many children as possible, however questionable their pedigree.

At the same time eugenists did not lose sight of the primacy of inheritance and they carried on a unique and separate pronatalist campaign to ensure that the heritable qualities of British fighting men would be passed on to as many of the next generation as possible. This uneasy compromise survived into the post-war period where it was, to a limited extent, reinforced by the growth of reform eugenics. But the persistence of class-specific hereditarian dogma within the eugenics movement, while not as absolute as Greta Jones has argued in her rebuttal of Freeden's thesis, was nevertheless stronger and more enduring than a reading of Kevles or Freeden would suggest.[9] Even though genetics had by 1914 demonstrated that heredity was the result of an unpredictable complex mixture of genes, most eugenists continued to believe that inherited characteristics, however polygenetic in origin and imperfectly understood, were still predominant in the determination of individual and class fitness. It was a conviction, however modified by social reformers, that seriously restricted the ability of eugenics to move very far from the margins of British social thought and policy during the First World War and after.

This attempt to escape from marginality had been a concern of a number of prominent early eugenists and eugenic sympathisers, such as Sidney Webb, Caleb Saleeby and Major Leonard Darwin, the Eugenic Education Society's president from 1911 to 1928. Without denying the predominance of heredity over environment in the formation of individuals, classes and races they had argued in opposition to Pearson and other extreme hereditarians that the relative contribution of each factor was still too uncertain to justify taking unpopular stands against social reforms.[10] Even if the true eugenic reformer did not deny the primacy of 'natural eugenics' over 'nurtural eugenics', Saleeby insisted in 1914 that under no circumstances should that primacy be held out as an alternative to improving the social conditions that would aid in the rearing of healthy, sound children and the weeding out of 'race poisons' that could injure the germ plasm.[11]

Saleeby, a physician and charter member of the Eugenics Education Society, was well aware that many of his eugenist colleagues condemned the infant and maternal welfare movement for interfering with natural selection and encouraging a dangerous increase in 'the lowest types of careless, thriftless, dirty and incapable families'. While admitting that it would probably have been better if some children had never been born, he repeatedly denounced the 'better-dead' school of 'class eugenics' for twisting Darwinism into a weapon against humane social reform.[12]

If Leonard Darwin, the eminent naturalist's youngest son, was more ambivalent than Saleeby about the role of nurture in 'race reconstruction', he agreed that unless eugenists could reconcile their differences they were in danger of isolating themselves from the mainstream of social reform where, with their unique perspective, they rightly belonged. He had long been sensitive to the charge that eugenics was merely a pseudoscientific rationalisation for class prejudice and tried to persuade unyielding hereditarians that, as the heated dispute between Mendelians and biometricians illustrated, not enough was yet known about heredity to measure its contribution. What was certain, however, Darwin warned eugenists in 1916, was that there could be no heredity without environment, and unless they became more concerned with it they would have little say in shaping postwar society.[13]

The issue, as Darwin's complaints indicate, was not settled by the war.

The soaring casualty lists, added to an even sharper decline in fertility, were, however, sufficient to convince a majority of the Eugenics Education Society that for the immediate future at least, prudence and patriotism required the preservation of quantity as well as the promotion of quality. The result was an uneasy, tenuous alliance of the eugenics movement with the diverse reform elements that comprised the maternal and child welfare movement.

Eugenists recognised that most pronatalist schemes were unconcerned with genetic factors. Race quality to advocates of maternal and child welfare centres, milk depots, day nurseries, health visitors, domestic hygiene and maternity bonuses was a secondary consideration. Even then it was not something achieved by selective breeding, but by improved living standards and social conditions. Eugenists, by contrast, generally believed that environmental conditions were largely an outcome of inherited capacity. Improving the quality and efficiency of the race could best be accomplished by promoting higher fertility among those classes who had a statistically greater probability of being endowed with valuable genetic traits. In practice this meant the skilled working classes, and, more importantly, the middle classes.

Initially the alliance with environmentally centred pronatalists meant that the Eugenics Education Society joined with other groups across the political spectrum in lobbying for passage of such legislation as the compulsory Notification of Births (Extension) Act (1915), the Maternal and Child Welfare Act (1918), as well as for the establishment of a Ministry of Health (1919), that Saleeby had advocated in 1915 as a vital war measure.[14] After extensive debate and considerable disagreement among council members, the Society also agreed in 1917 to join with the National Association for the Prevention of Infant Mortality and some ninety other organisations in support of the first National Baby Week.[15] On this, as on previous occasions, Darwin acknowledged that he shared many of the reservations expressed by eugenists about the racial consequences of such indiscriminate activity. The alternative, however, would be the alienation of the Eugenics Education Society from nearly all other important social reform organisations planning the reconstruction of British society. Even before the war eugenists had been accused of being undemocratic, Darwin recalled; they did not want to add to that the charge of being unpatriotic.[16]

In contrast to their repeated pre-war complaints about the cost and futility of expanding social welfare services, eugenists now quietly acquiesced in a tenfold increase in local expenditure for such services, and had little comment about the doubling of maternity and child welfare centres throughout the country.[17] They recognised that the fearful destruction of 'young and lusty life', as Walter Long, President of the Local Government Board described it in 1915, had made the preservation of babies a form of patriotic war work.[18] The importance of filling 'racial cradles' faster than 'racial coffins' took on an urgency that only the most foolhardy questioned.

Eugenists found some comfort in the rationalisation that since 'the most intelligent parents will be those likely to avail themselves of facilities offered for their help . . . particularly the mothers . . . their children will tend to survive.'[19] At the same time, however, eugenists acknowledged that the percentage of the 'submerged tenth', the lowest strata of society, was also bound to increase. They hoped that their efforts to encourage greater fertility among the surviving A1 population, whose numbers were severely depleted by the dysgenic effects of combat, would in part affect the qualitative imbalance.

From the opening months of the war, eugenists predicted that because of its voluntary system of recruitment Britain would inevitably suffer racially more than other nations. It would be the young men 'of strongest character, possessing the most love of adventure, the greatest initiative, the keenest and fittest [who] will lay themselves out to be reduced in numbers.' Since these heroic qualities were presumably inheritable, Darwin feared that the pattern of casualties would substantially reduce the number of males 'amongst the class from which it is most desirable that [Britain] should produce the stock of the future', and whose rate of reproduction for a generation before the war had already been dangerously low. By the time voluntary enlistment gave way to conscription in 1916, with its dubious eugenic advantage of random rather than self-selective losses among A1 males, much of 'the cream of the race' had already been skimmed off. Not only would these men of 'special racial value' be unable to father valuable offspring, eugenists complained, but an even greater proportion of future generations would be produced by the surviving, inferior C3 types and worse whose physical and mental disabilities rendered them unfit for combat.[20]

These considerations made it difficult for some members to condone the Eugenic Education Society's decision to support pronatalist welfare programmes. Darwin, who was not unsympathetic to their dilemma, agreed that we must 'keep harping on the inequality of men as regards their inborn qualities, and we must keep repudiating environmental reform as a practical method insuring racial progress in the future'. But, he added, it must be done with moderation and an understanding that the times dictated a balance between the population requirements of the present and its racial composition in the future.[21]

If eugenists for practical, tactical reasons were prepared to accommodate themselves to wartime political and social realities, they were also determined to pursue their own pronatalist strategy of race reconstruction during the war to revitalise the fertility of whatever remained of the fittest classes.

That strategy involved the adoption of highly selective pronatalist financial inducements such as family bonuses or allowances, expanded maternity benefits and tax remissions, especially for officers and non-commissioned officers. Before the war, eugenists had been exceedingly suspicious of these and other schemes if there was any possibility that they might encourage the poor to have more children. Proposals for the direct endowment of mother-hood, or wages based upon family size received a particularly frosty recep-tion in eugenic circles.

Had it been possible to weight benefits in a way that encouraged only 'worthy parentage' eugenist objections might have evaporated.[22] But in the absence of such assurances it was more promising to recommend tax reforms for 'potential parents of sound stock' whose income was sufficient to bring them under tax obligations in the first place. It was a strategy that coincided with the eugenic belief that economic success correlated closely with innate ability. It would also, of course, exclude the majority of the labouring poor, whose income fell below the minimum rates, from any financial inducement to have more children. Consequently when, in his contentious budget of 1909, David Lloyd George introduced income tax child allowances of £10 for parents with income between £160 and £500, Saleeby described him as 'the first eugenist amongst modern statesmen' and the precedent was not forgotten.[23]

Complaints about the burden of rising taxation on the 'better classes' had become commonplace in the pre-war decade when the rate rose from a modest 8d. in the pound to 1s. 2d. These costs, plus the increased expenses of rearing and educating children, were widely held to be major reasons for the later marriages and smaller families of the responsible, tax-paying classes. The huge costs of the war quickly magnified the problem and pro-voked continual pleas for meaningful relief for families with children.

The prestigious National Birth Rate Commission, which strongly sup-ported the maternal and child welfare campaign, recommended in its 1916 report on the causes of declining fertility that joint incomes be taxed at a lower rate, and that educational bonuses and substantial tax remissions be at least given to families whose income was below £700 a year. With eugenic considerations in mind, it added that condemnation of the reckless poor, who had too many offspring, should be balanced with denunciations of the selfish rich, who had too few, and urged that bachelors, in particular, be taxed more heavily.[24] Walter Long assured a deputation from the Com-mission that the Local Government Board was sympathetic and promised to support legislation to reduce taxation as a stimulus to larger families. The Finance Act of 1916 did provide some relief for families with more than two children and incomes under £800.[25]

It was not surprising that the Eugenics Education Society welcomed the recommendations of the National Birth Rate Commission since several of its members, starting with Darwin, provided testimony. Others adorned the Commission's roster, including the Dean of St Paul's, William Inge, who served as chairman. But the Society's council was also worried that patriotic appeals for a general increase in the birth rate were not selective enough. With the Germans calling for ten million more children, there was a danger that the British nation might be panicked into indiscriminate reproduction. It was therefore imperative, eugenists repeatedly argued, that the government do everything possible to see that the fittest people had adequate inducements to rebuild as much of the population as possible from their able ranks.

Shortly before the outbreak of the war the Society's council, at Darwin's urging, had begun calculating the effects of taxation on the low fertility of the professional middle classes with the intention of providing sympathetic politicians with its findings.[26] The war gave new urgency to the project and between 1914 and 1918 proposal followed proposal asking the government to lighten the tax burden on people by such measures as dividing total family income by the number of family members and taxing each individually at the lower rate. People of substantial income would quickly seize upon the advantages of having more children and many middle-class and skilled working-class families would fall into the same low- or non-taxable brackets enjoyed by their economic, and, presumably, genetic, inferiors. In addition, the council proposed that maternity costs and the total expenses for educating children be deductible from income, and, in the case of education, from death duties as well.[27]

Discussions of tax reform during the war were frequently punctuated by the eugenically inspired charges of people like Sidney Webb that the rates fell most heavily upon the classes who should have the most children, but presented no impediment to 'the thriftless and irresponsible, the reckless and the short-sighted of all grades' so that 'the community now breeds fastest from its socially least desirable stocks'.[28] However much eugenists applauded Webb's sentiments they realised that the war had made it even more unlikely that any policy of direct, class-specific inducements to fertility stood a chance of being implemented. Tax reform as a part of reconstruction seemed to be the only hope.

Sir Hamar Greenwood, the Liberal MP and future Chief Secretary for Ireland, agreed when in 1918, at the urging of the Eugenics Education Society, he introduced an amendment to the Finance Act allowing income for tax purposes to be divided into equal shares on the basis of family size.[29] Angered by men and women who delayed or did not marry at all when the race was in such peril, Greenwood also contemplated a regressive levy on bachelors and spinsters. His amendment was received sympathetically by the Chancellor of the Exchequer, Andrew Bonar Law, who concurred that it would 'encourage healthy men and women to multiply' for the 'future of the race', but the loss to the Treasury would be too great while the war was still being fought. He promised, however, that it would be taken up in future considerations of finance.[30]

Tax reform was perhaps the most important ingredient in the eugenist's pronatalist recipe for race reconstruction, but it was not the only one. Another was the establishment of the Professional War Relief Committee to assist the wives of 'professional' and 'creative' men with the delivery and care of racially valuable children while their husbands were at the front. The Committee established a number of maternity homes, including one in J. Pierpont Morgan's London mansion where 242 infants were delivered during the war years.[31] It was no more than a token gesture in the face of the 'dysgenic elimination' of hundreds of thousands of potential fathers whose loss, the Regius Professor of Natural History at Aberdeen, J. Arthur Thompson, warned in 1915, would lead to a qualitative 'maternal depression' and the overproduction of 'under-average types' by men who were unfit to serve.[32] To minimise this possibility, Saleeby told the National Birth Rate commission, 'some of us are trying to encourage the men as far as possible to marry before they go'.[33] *The Eugenics Review* praised the Archbishop of Canterbury's sensible decision to reduce marriage fees for servicemen and urged the government to accede to the prelate's suggestion that the marriage licence duty be temporarily waived.[34] 'If there is patriotism in dying for our country', Thompson reasoned in 1915, 'there is a conceivable patriotism in marrying for her and in bearing children for her'.[35]

The marriage rate, which had hovered around 16 per 1,000 for several years, jumped sharply to over 20 per 1,000 in the first year of the war before declining to an average of about 15 per 1,000 for the duration. Darwin hoped that officers and noncommissioned officers comprised the largest proportion of those rushing to the altars and registry offices. Quality, he cautioned, must not be lost in the eagerness for quantity.[36] At least 200,000 couples were estimated to have wed because of the urgency of the times, nowhere near enough to compensate for the number of marriages calculated to have been discouraged, delayed or destroyed by the prolonged conflict. In addition, despite the surge in marriages in 1914–15, the birth rate continued to plummet another 26 per cent, reaching 17.7 per 1,000, the lowest figure ever recorded, in 1918. Even more disturbing, the ratio of children born to married women between the ages of 15 and 45 decreased by 30 per cent.[37]

To induce men to marry and sire offspring before leaving for the front, the Eugenics Education Society petitioned the War Pensions Committee to guarantee that living or posthumous children would be properly looked after and educated in the event of their fathers' death. In the same melancholy vein the Society led the way in trying to persuade the public that however horrible their wounds, most 'broken soldiers' were still capable of fathering healthy children. As Dr J. Murray Leslie told the Institute of Hygiene in 1916, the physical and psychological deformities suffered by the disabled soldier were not genetically transmissible, although such beliefs were still widespread.[38] Earlier the geneticist, R. A. Fisher, reminded 'the lonely women who would espouse these men that the injuries of war last but for one generation'. Their children, he assured them, would receive 'as a natural dower, a constitution unimpaired, and the power to become all that their father might have been'.[39]

Compared to their 'racial worth', eugenists complained, the odds were stacked too heavily against the wounded, who frequently required a great deal of personal care, were physically unattractive and reduced to living on an inadequate pension.[40] Nevertheless they still constituted a racial reservoir of several hundred thousand genetical, if no longer physical, A1 recruits in the campaign against racial deterioration. Some suggested that the most promising of the veterans be awarded 'eugenic stripes' to be worn on their uniforms to make them more attractive to potential brides.[41] Eugenic spokesmen tried in vain to persuade the beleaguered War Pensions Committee to grant generous tax allowances, tax rebates and educational expenses to wounded men who married and attempted to raise a family. At the same time, however, no compensation was to be given to men invalided out of the forces for illnesses not connected to combat. It would only encourage 'the reproduction of bad heritable tendencies'. The addition of a section on hereditary disability to the official 'Medical Reports on Invalid Soldiers' would, eugenists insisted, further ensure that the medical boards did not inadvertently subsidise the proliferation of the unfit.[42]

The 'broken soldiers' of the First World War not only represented a putative sperm bank for the reconstruction of the race, but their importance to eugenic pronatalists was magnified by the effect of the war on the sex ratio. Although on average 104 male children were born for every 100 females, the mortality of the former was approximately 14 per cent higher, and in some areas as much as 30 per cent.[43] The 'vital superiority' of girls was further confirmed when, after 1915, the recording of stillbirths revealed that the stillbirth mortality sex differential was as large as 40 per cent.[44]

These figures greatly strengthened the position of those pronatalists, including, occasionally, eugenists like Saleeby, who argued that wastage of life between conception and birth was not only greater than in infancy, but constituted a scale of male mortality approaching that encountered on the battlefield.[45] Antenatal care began to play a larger role in the thinking of pronatalists who, from 1915 on, increasingly recognised that thousands of babies could be saved through their mothers. The realisation that the nine months before birth were perhaps as critical as the three months that followed, led to the better care of pregnant women as an adjunct to the main goal of child welfare.[46] Saleeby, who had been a student in Edinburgh of Dr John Ballantyne, the leading authority in Britain on antenatal pathology, was aware of the importance of prenatal care in reducing the high rates of miscarriage, stillbirth and infant mortality. He had made little headway, however, in persuading his eugenist colleagues that such losses were not a 'natural and healthy process . . . a rather merciful elimination of infants not fit to live'. It was a view also widely held in medical circles until the war. This 'lie of lies', as Saleeby described it, had cost the nation millions of potential recruits who were now desperately needed, and whose loss, coupled to those on the battlefield, would, even after victory, leave Britain with a more serious sex imbalance than ever.[47]

The problem of surplus women that had troubled the Victorians took on new importance during the war. In 1914 there was already an 'excess' of more than 1,300,000 females, the largest imbalance in Europe. Projections varied about the likely effects of war losses on this 'sex disproportion', but most agreed that the difference would probably reach at least three million, with more than half the surplus in the marriageable, fecund age brackets.[48]

Under such calamitous circumstances much of the rhetoric of the maternal and child welfare campaign singled out the importance of saving male infants. The Carnegie Trust report on maternal and child welfare in 1917 calculated that had the annual wastage of male infant life during the last 50 years been no greater than at present, 'at least 500,000 more men would have been available for the defence of the country today'.[49] One of the welfare campaign's strongest supporters, Arthur H. D. Acland, was typical in his mourning the 'waste of large numbers of fine, strong men-babies who are born splendidly healthy and ready to do their share for their country some day'. In endorsing the 'Life Saving in War Time' drive of the National League for Physical Education and Improvement, Acland hoped that the infant mortality rate could be halved to about 50 per 1,000.[50] It might not alter what Sir Bernard Mallet, the Registrar General, President of the Royal Statistical Society and future President of the Eugenics Society, described in 1918 as 'a rise in the sex proportion so marked and sustained over so long a period', but any reduction in the number of prenatal and postnatal infant deaths would at least diminish the absolute loss of male lives that had become especially precious after 1914.[51]

Many pronatalists assumed, despite the decline in infant mortality, that the surge in female employment during the war would endanger the advances made since the opening of the century. With married women constituting 40 per cent of the swollen female workforce, there was a good deal of thoughtful consideration and, sometimes, hysterical rhetoric about the consequences for children and the race.[52] The lower fertility and higher infant mortality of the textile districts, where female labour was prevalent, had been observed for decades and criticism of working mothers and the infant welfare and mothercraft movement had intensified in the pre-war years.[53] During the war, three government committees and several unofficial bodies examined contradictory evidence and reached different conclusions about the seriousness of the problem.[54] It was an issue that transcended political and social ideologies; Labour Party spokesmen and socialists were as concerned about the effects of female employment on 'racial health' as were Liberals and Conservatives.[55]

With the exception of Saleeby, who found himself increasingly uncomfortable in the Eugenics Education Society, most eugenists were not particularly concerned with a problem that primarily affected the working classes. Citing the close correlation between high rates of infant mortality and the number of working mothers in Bradford and other industrial centres, Saleeby described their labour as 'a fundamental sin against the laws of life'. Although he had been a supporter of education and votes for women before the war, he now felt that anything that might sap their procreative energies and divert them from their primary task of childbearing and childrearing was unacceptable.[56]

Most eugenists, however, were more worried about the implications of an expanded female workforce for middle- and lower middle-class women whose heritable qualities were presumed to be, on the average, well above those of their working-class sisters. On the eve of the war, *The Eugenics Review* complained about the unwillingness of the London County Council and the Post Office to hire or retain married women, a policy widely enforced by educational and civil service authorities as well. Many of these women, the *Review* contended were 'eugenically able' and their ability to work might be the difference between their remaining single or being able to marry young and to raise at least a small family. Since the 'ennobling of marriage' was a fundamental eugenic goal, anything that discouraged talented and efficient women, who were also probably superior in energy and intellectual capacity, from marrying, was a serious mistake. The excess of females over males was already depriving the race of many promising mothers; nothing should be done to compound that loss.[57]

As the demands of the war increased the need for female workers, other eugenists like R. A. Fisher and C. A. Stock worried that the working-class model, with its 'lower quality' of marriage, would become established among the eugenically better classes and therefore urged a continuation of restrictive policies. There was no evidence that a woman's earning capacity, in contrast to that of a man's, was a measure of 'eugenic excellence', they reasoned, nor was it especially useful in domestic life. Far from encouraging eugenic marriage, the elimination of barriers to the employment of non-working-class married women would interfere with the different 'spheres of capability and excellence' that made such marriages valuable. The specialisation provided by sex and the finer female traits that advanced the race would be wasted if women joined men in the economic quest.

While welcoming the widest possible education and outlook for women, Fisher and Stock kept in mind 'the inherently different standard of selection to be applied to the two sexes'. That selection would become blurred if, as was frequently true of the industrial classes, both husband and wife worked. It would mean a radical change in the ideals of marriage among the eugenically superior classes and a tendency towards a lower standard of domestic and racial responsibility that would result in even fewer children being born to the genetically select.[58]

Given the elevated focus of their class preoccupations, eugenists were not inclined to pay much heed to the fears of workers and union leaders that women might be employed as blacklegs or cheap labourers who threatened to displace men permanently in the workforce. They did, however, share a concern about the preservation of a patriarchal society with the husband in the traditional role of breadwinner. Both eugenist and non-eugenist alike worried about the future of the family if gender roles continued to become confused and they talked a great deal about the importance of the quality of motherhood in the rebuilding of the race. Eugenists, of course, had a different agenda for the accomplishment of this goal than did the *Labour Woman* when it stressed the primacy of motherhood over work, or when Mary Macarthur, the most prominent female trade unionist, urged wives to stay home with their children. 'Women have done some wonderful work', she conceded, 'but a baby is more wonderful than a machine gun. I believe that the hand that rocks the cradle will still be a power when the other is only a hateful memory'.[59] The problem for the eugenist was how to increase substantially the probability that the infant in that cradle would be genetically fit.

Although eugenists continued to express reservations about the indiscriminate nature of the maternal and child welfare campaign, most recognised that it was, for better or for worse, an inescapable and integral part of wartime pronatalism that would remain an important feature of post-war reconstruction. But the war also forced eugenists to conclude that the race was perhaps stronger and more efficient than pre-war diagnoses had revealed. Far from crumbling under the German onslaught, the population had proven to be extraordinarily resilient and productive. As a result, there was a greater willingness on the part of the eugenically minded to acknowledge that while inherited ability was still distributed more heavily among the successful classes, it also extended to a wider range of the populace than had been realised before the war. It was a eugenic way of saying that all classes had done their part.

If the war forced the Eugenics Education Society to compromise with nurtural pronatalism and lend its support to official and voluntary programmes for maternal and infant care, it remained an uneasy association. In the Society's annual report for 1917–18, Darwin noted that eugenists were for now at least generally in agreement on the need for improved social conditions. He welcomed efforts to promote infant welfare, better housing and expanded maternity assistance to bring out the 'good qualities' of the race once they were produced by parents of finer stock.[60]

Although the report tried to gloss over the conflict within eugenics over the relative contribution of nature and nurture that wartime considerations had obscured, it failed to reconcile the contradictions and, after 1918, the Society quietly backed away from its uncomfortable alliances. Saleeby, who had played a major role in forging the fragile links of those alliances, remained, along with several others, committed to them and soon withdrew from the Society's affairs. Eight years after the end of hostilities, the Society's council was still trying to reconcile the ambiguous mix of hereditarian and environmentalist ideologies that divided the faithful. It finally agreed in 1926 on a compromise 'Practical Engenic Policy' acknowledging that while many immediate benefits might be derived from changes in the environment, it was probably best if the Society took no position on the matter. The council instead encouraged those members who wished to do so to co-operate as individuals with the 'innumerable existing bodies already striving to improve human surroundings'.[61]

The Society for its part continued to advance positive pronatalist schemes for selective tax rebates to encourage 'the fertility of superior types'. It also cautiously endorsed the post-war campaign for family allowances so long as payments were 'directly proportional to the scale of earnings of the parents' to ensure that the 'best stock' would receive the most.[62] But the Society was never able to agree on the best way to achieve this goal and its council in 1934 rejected the recommendations of a sub-committee established to formulate an acceptable policy.[63] In reality the enormous number of casualties in the war coupled, despite a brief post-war surge, with the continued fall in the birth rate, convinced many architects of race renewal that no pronatalist scheme would ever succeed in 'creating a superman' or in reversing differential fertility enough to be able to halt the slide towards deterioration.[64] Consequently, as eugenists became less confident in their ability to propagate a sizeable racial elite from positive inducements, they increasingly turned from selective pronatalism to negative policies such as sterilisation, and, more importantly, birth control, to curtail the proliferation of the unfit and gradually raise the qualitative level of the general population.[65]

Eugenic pronatalism, with its Galtonian dream of promoting higher fertility among the so-called fitter classes, had reached its peak during the war. But the Eugenics Education Society, for largely pragmatic, tactical reasons, had also grudgingly added the preservation of infant life and maternal and child welfare to its elitist agenda of race reconstruction. It was a troublesome decision born of wartime anxieties and the uncertain promise that the more limited innate talents of the lower classes could, in the right environment, be enhanced. Although it continued to follow the progress of various maternal and infant care organisations and to send representatives to some of their conferences, the Society, throughout the 1920s and most of the 1930s, showed little interest in renewing its wartime support of their activities, despite numerous invitations to do so.

Many individual members, however, were active in such groups as the National Association of Maternity and Child Welfare Centres, the National Association for the Prevention of Infant Mortality and the National Baby Week Council, but the Eugenic Society's council only agreed to join the parent organisation, the National Council for Maternity and Child Welfare, on the eve of the Second World War.[66] Then, as in 1914, it was a tactical decision prompted in part by renewed depopulation fears, political necessity and patriotic obligation. In addition, however, by 1939 the hereditarian determinism of mainline eugenics, with its qualitative delineation of class characteristics, had, as Kevles has shown, been considerably moderated by the rise of reform eugenics with its greater acceptance of the interaction of environment and heredity on classes and populations.

Nevertheless, a strong element of class-specific eugenics continued to pervade popular eugenic thought at the same time as its scientific foundations were crumbling. Without denying new genetic revelations that people were biochemically far more variable than recognised a generation earlier, and that all classes were susceptible to hereditary problems, the legatees of mainline eugenics continued to talk about 'predominant tendencies' and 'degrees of inheritance' evident in particular classes. Before and during the war they had hoped to reinforce those 'tendencies' and 'degrees' closely identified with the middle and upper end of the social scale. When, after the war, the scientific, social and political realities dashed their hopes, they increasingly turned their attention to preventing dysgenic growth at the lower end of that scale. It was a decision that removed eugenics even further from the mainstream of pronatalism which, in the inter-war years, continued to promote a variety of environmentally centred policies and programmes to improve the health and well-being of mothers and children.[67]

RICHARD SOLOWAY

After 1931, the Eugenic Society's new secretary, C. P. Blacker, was able, at the cost of several resignations, to attract to the organisation a number of able men and women who shared his reformist views and recognised that inherited ability was only one of several factors affecting the health and intelligence of the population. Confronted with dire predictions about the imminence of depopulation if the birth rate continued to fall, these recruits were willing to support numerous pronatalist recommendations to make family life healthier and financially more attractive even for the populous working classes.[68]

Blacker found, however, that the close correlation of biological fitness with social class was too deeply ingrained in eugenic thought to be easily displaced. This, as he knew all too well, made eugenics appear to the public to be a haven for 'cranks, misguided enthusiasts and irresponsible propagandists' who camouflaged their class prejudices as science and stultified the cause they were trying to espouse. The result was a 'profound distrust of the whole eugenic movement'.[69] But many of the more progressive eugenists as well, including Blacker, continued to identify a disproportionate amount of inherited defect in that sector of the lower classes who made up the eugenically defined 'social problem group' identified in the inter-war years.[70] In the final analysis, reform eugenists substantially moderated but were unable to eliminate the conflict between hereditarian and environmentalist opinion that had troubled the eugenics movement since its founding and which it had first tried to reconcile in the intensive, co-operative, pronatalist atmosphere of the First World War.[71]

A few progressive eugenists like Saleeby had warned before that war 'directly the eugenist begins to talk in terms of social classes (as Mr. Galton has never done), he is skating on thin ice'.[72] It was a lesson that eugenics never entirely learned, neither in the First World War nor after. Despite its scientific pretensions and selective affinities with progressive social reform movements, eugenics in Britain to a large extent remained what its ambivalent, pronatalist campaign revealed it to be during the war – an often ambiguous, biological, class-conscious way of thinking about contemporary issues and problems rather than a realistic, politically and scientifically credible programme to solve them.

Notes

1 For a fuller discussion of the public reaction to the birth rate statistics see R. A. Soloway, *Birth control and the population question in England, 1877–1930*, Chapel Hill, 1982, chs. 1–2.
2 D. J. Kevles, *In the name of eugenics: genetics and the uses of human heredity*, New York, 1985, pp. 173–5.

3 *Ibid.*, pp. 164, 251.

4 M. Freeden, 'Eugenics and progressive thought: a study in ideological affinity', *The Historical Journal*, 22 (1979), 645–71. On the social composition of the eugenics movement see D. MacKenzie, 'Eugenics in Britain', *Social Studies of Science*, 6, 1976, pp. 499–532 and 'Karl Pearson and the professional middle class', *Annals of Science*, 36 (1976), 125–43.

5 M. Freeden, 'Eugenics and ideology', *The Historical Journal*, 26 (1983), 959–62.

6 On the founding of the Society see L. A. Farrall, *The origins and growth of the English eugenics movement, 1865–1925*, New York, 1985, ch. 6.

7 See for example J. Lewis, *The politics of motherhood. Child and maternal welfare in England, 1900–1939*, London, 1980; and G. F. McCleary, *The maternity and child welfare movement*, London, 1935.

8 Parliamentary Papers, *Forty-Fifth Annual Report of the Local Government Board. Supplement in continuance of the Report of the Medical Officer of the Board for 1915–16. Containing a Report on Child Mortality at Age 0–5*, 1917–18, Cd 8496, vol. XVI, Pt I, and Carnegie United Kingdom Trust, *Report on the physical welfare of mothers and children. England and Wales*, London, 1917, vol. I, pp. 1–4. Also *Parliamentary Debates* (Commons), 5th series, 14 November 1917, vol. 99, cols. 386–7; 19 November, col. 862; 22 July 1918, vol. 108, cols. 1450–1; (Lords), 1 May 1919, vol. 34, col. 448.

9 G. Jones, 'Eugenics and social policy between the wars', *Historical Journal*, 25 (1982), 717–28. For his reply see Freeden, 'Eugenics and ideology'. See also G. R. Searle, 'Eugenics and class' in C. Webster (ed.), *Biology, medicine and society*, Cambridge, 1981, pp. 239–40.

10 Pearson insisted that the influence of environment, or nurture, was no more than an insignificant one-fifth to one-tenth that of heredity. See K. Pearson, *Nature and nurture – the problem of the future. A Presidential address at the annual meeting of the Social and Political Education League, April 28, 1910*, London, 1910, p. 27; S. Webb to K. Pearson, 16 November 1909 in Karl Pearson Papers, University College, London, 888/2; C. W. Saleeby, *The methods of race regeneration*, New York, 1911, pp. 11–12; *Eugenics Review*, 5 (1913), 154.

11 C. W. Saleeby, *The progress of eugenics*, London, 1914, pp. 28–31.

12 C. W. Saleeby, *Parenthood and race culture. An outline of eugenics*, New York, 1910, pp. 25–8; also 'The nurture of the race' in *Report of the Proceedings of the National Conference on Infant Mortality at St George's Hotel*, Liverpool, 1914, pp. 140–6.

13 L. Darwin, 'Heredity and environment: a warning to eugenists', *Eugenics Review*, 8 (1916), 93–122. For a discussion of the quarrel between Mendelism and biometrics see L. Farrall, 'Controversy and conflict in science: a case study – the English biometric school and Mendel's laws', *Social Studies of Science*, 5 (1975), 269–301.

14 See Eugenics Education Society (hereafter EES), Council Minutes, 13 November 1917; 14 May, 8 June 1918. Eugenics Society Library, London. Also *Parliamentary Debates* (Lords), 7 July 1918, cols. 928–9.

15 EES, Council Minutes, 16 January, 13 February, 17 April 1917. The Society allotted £100 for exhibits.

16 *Eugenics Review*, 8 (1917), 306–7, 314; also The National Council of Public Morals (hereafter NCPM), *The declining birth-rate, its causes and effects. Being the report and the chief evidence taken by the National Birth-Rate Commission, instituted*

with official recognition by the National Council of Public Morals – for the promotion of race regeneration – spiritual, moral and physical, London, 1916, pp. 127–31.

17 M. Palmer, *Life-saving. A campaign handbook. The Infant Welfare Propaganda Committee of the National League for Physical Education and Improvement*, London, 1916, pp. 85, 95–7; G. F. McCleary, *Maternal and Child Welfare*, London, 1934, pp. 12, 18–19; Lewis, *Politics of motherhood*, p. 34. Also *Parliamentary Debates* (Commons), vol. 105, 1918, cols. 1742–3. The number of welfare centres increased from 650 to nearly 1300.

18 *Parliamentary Debates* (Commons), vol. 73, 1915, cols. 617, 625.

19 *Eugenics Review*, 9 (1917), 107.

20 *Ibid.*, 1 (1914), 197; 7 (1915), 92–6.

21 *Ibid.*, 8 (1916), 112.

22 See for example *The Sociological Review*, 3 (1910), 278–9.

23 Saleeby, *The methods of race regeneration*, pp. 31–2. Eugenists were more critical of the modest maternity allowances provided in the 1911 National Insurance Act for being too indiscriminate and threatening paternal responsibility.

24 NCPM, *Declining birth-rate*, pp. 77–80. The NCPM followed up its report with a petition in 1917 calling for tax relief based upon educational allowances for parents of middle and higher incomes.

25 *The Times*, 29 June 1916. The exemption for children was raised from £10 to £25 and a man with a wife and two children was not taxed on income below £200.

26 EES, Council Minutes, 15 May, 17 June 1914.

27 *Ibid.*, 6 July 1916, 9 October, 3 November 1917.

28 National Birth-Rate Commission, *Problems of population and parenthood, being the second report of and the chief evidence taken by the National Birth-Rate Commission, 1918–1920*, New York, 1920, p. 65. Webb had long advocated the endowment of motherhood for the 'best members of the middle and upper artisan classes'. See S. Webb, *The decline in the birth-rate*, London, 1907, pp. 16–17.

29 EES, Council Minutes, 14 May 1918. The council first tried to get Sir John Simon, the former Liberal attorney general and home secretary, to introduce the measure.

30 *Parliamentary Debates* (Commons), 4 June 1918, vol. 106, cols. 1513–16. See also *Eugenics Review*, 10 (1918), 85–7.

31 EES, Council Minutes, 15 September 1914, 21 October 1915. Also *Eugenics Review*, 6 (1914), 200–3; 8 (1917), 359.

32 *Ibid.*, 7 (1915), 9.

33 NCPM, *Declining birth-rate*, p. 415. Also EES, Council Minutes, 23 March 1915 and *Eugenics Review*, 7 (1915), 2–10.

34 *Eugenics Review*, 6 (1915), 286.

35 *Ibid.*, 7 (1915), 9.

36 *Ibid.*, p. 101.

37 Parliamentary Papers, *Registrar General's 82nd Report*, 1920, Cmd 1017, pp. 5–6.

38 *The Times*, 5 April 1916.

39 *Eugenics Review*, 7 (1915), 102.

40 *Ibid.*, p. 202.

41 *Ibid.*, 9 (1917), 15.

42 EES, Council Minutes, 16 May 1916. See also *The Times*, 5 April 1916 and *Eugenics Review*, 9 (1917), 2–9, 15.

43 Palmer, *Life-saving*, p. 18; *Eugenics Review*, 10 (1918), 79; Registrar General, *82nd Report*, p. 5.

44 *Child Study*, 9 (1916), 22–3.

45 *Ibid.*

46 Lewis, *Politics of motherhood*, pp. 16, 33–5, 40, 50.

47 *Child Study*, 9 (1916), pp. 25, 27–8.

48 J. Marchant, *Birth rate and empire*, London, 1917, pp. 138–9; *Eugenics Review*, 10 (1918), 136.

49 Carnegie UK Trust, *Report on the physical welfare of mothers and children. England and Wales*, London, 1917, vol. I, p. 1.

50 *The Times*, 7 April 1916.

51 *Eugenics Review*, 10 (1918), p. 78. Mallet joined the Eugenics Education Society after his retirement as Registrar General and succeeded Darwin as president in 1928.

52 G. Braybon, *Women workers in the First World War*, London, 1981, pp. 118–25.

53 C. Dyhouse, 'Working-class mothers and infant mortality in England, 1895–1914', *The Journal of Social History*, 12 (1978), 248–67. See also *Report of the proceedings of the National Conference on Infant Mortality, 1906*, London, 1906.

54 Parliamentary Papers, *Final Report of the Health of Munition Workers Committee*, 1918, Cd 9065, vol. XIII; *Report of the Women's Employment Committee*, 1918, Cd 9239, vol. XIV; *Report of the War Cabinet Committee on Women in Industry*, 1919, Cmd 135, vol. XXXI. See also Palmer, *Life-saving*, pp. 31–2.

55 Braybon, *Women workers*, pp. 122–3.

56 *Ibid.*, p. 119. See also, R. A. Soloway, 'Feminism, fertility and eugenics in Victorian and Edwardian England' in S. Drescher, D. Sabean and A. Sharlin (eds.), *Political symbolism in modern Europe*, New Brunswick, NJ, 1982, pp. 121–45.

57 *Eugenics Review*, 6 (1914), 154–6.

58 *Ibid.*, 6 (1915), 313–15.

59 M. Macarthur, 'The woman trade unionist's point of view' in Marion Phillips (ed.), *Women and the Labour Party*, London, 1918, pp. 18–19; *The Daily News*, 15 August 1917; Lewis, *Politics of motherhood*, p. 80; Braybon, *Women workers*, pp. 120–5, 149.

60 Eugenics Education Society, *Tenth Annual Report 1917–18*, London, 1918, p. 4.

61 Eugenics Society, *Annual Report 1925–26*, London, 1926, p. 6. The Eugenics Education Society changed its name to The Eugenics Society in 1926.

62 ES, Annual Report 1925–6, p. 5; ES, Council Meeting Minutes, 9 October 1929. Also J. Macnicol, *The movement for family allowances, 1918–45*, London, 1980, ch. 4.

63 Eugenics Society, Minutes of the Council, 3 July 1934.

64 *Eugenics Review*, 16 (1924), 96–7.

65 Soloway, *Birth control*, pp. 199–202.

66 ES, Council Meeting Minutes, 16 May 1939; Executive Committee Minutes, 4 July 1939. The outbreak of the war delayed the Society's affiliation until October. Executive Committee Minutes, 7 November 1939.

67 For pronatalism in the inter-war years see Lewis, *Politics of motherhood*, chs. 4–6 and J. Macnicol, *The movement for family allowances*, chs. 2–6.

68 On the fear of depopulation see E. Charles, *The twilight of parenthood. A biological study of the decline of population growth*, London, 1934; G. Leybourne, 'An esti-

mate of the future population of Great Britain', *Sociological Review*, 36 (1934), 130–8.

69 C. P. Blacker, *Eugenics in retrospect and prospect*, Occasional Papers on Eugenics, 1, London, 1950, pp. 25–6; 'Birth control and eugenics' in *Nineteenth Century*, 3 (1932), 476.

70 See E. J. Lidbetter, *Heredity and the social problem group*, vol. I, London, 1933; Sir B. Mallet, 'The social problem group', *Eugenics Review*, 23 (1931), 203–6.

71 For criticism of the persistence of hereditarian determinism in eugenics see L. T. Hogben, *Genetic principles in medicine and social science*, London, 1931, ch. 8; *Nature and nurture*, London, 1939, ch. 1.

72 Saleeby, *Parenthood and race culture*, p. 118.

14

'Pregnancy is the woman's active service.' Pronatalism in Germany during the First World War

Cornelie Usborne

When in 1895 August Bebel, the leader of the German Social Democratic Party (SPD) compared women's death in childbirth to men's death in battle, he was greeted with derision.[1] But when twenty years later another prominent Social Democrat, Alfred Grotjahn, Professor of Social Hygiene in Berlin, expressed similar thoughts, he was taken very seriously indeed. In a widely quoted pamphlet published in 1915 Grotjahn suggested that reproduction was the 'only female contribution to war and military power which equals . . . men's wartime national service'. The task of replenishing the population after losses incurred during the war was 'indispensable for our national ascendency'.[2] Grotjahn later regretted the nationalistic tone of this publication[3] but the idea that 'women blessed with many children' were a precondition of military success was widely shared at the time.[4] This eulogy of motherhood stemmed from the belief that *Volkskraft* (population strength) was fundamental to Germany's military and economic success. The continued decline in the German birth rate caused considerable anxiety which increased with the outbreak of war.

The fear of national decline

In fact national fertility was declining in all other western European countries, and both the French and the English birth rates were lower than the German. But it was the rate at which demographic changes were taking place in Germany that aroused such fear in German political circles. In 1916, the Prussian Minister of the Interior, who with his predecessor was responsible for initiating a wide-ranging policy to reverse the fertility trend, put it to the Prussian Diet like this: 'in 1876 we had reached the peak of 40.9 live births per 1,000 inhabitants. This rate has declined to 28.2 by 1912 . . .'. Or,

389

in the words of another official in the same Ministry: 'France took seventy years to lower her birth rate by 8 per 1,000, we needed only twelve years.'[5] Since the proportion of married women of reproductive age had actually increased and non-marital fertility, though high by European standards, remained steady at about 9 per cent, it was clear that the decline in the national fertility rate was largely a result of fewer children within marriage.[6] Furthermore, family limitation which had been thought of as the preserve of the professional classes, particularly doctors and lawyers, now seemed to be spreading to the lower classes.[7]

According to the earliest official report on the implications of the declining birth rate in 1911, the phenomenon was 'not alarming considering the equally decreasing death rate',[8] but after the outbreak of war the discussion, official and unofficial, assumed a more urgent and often hysterical note. Moreover, the wartime powers of the military authorities and the growing regimentation of public life offered the Wilhelmine state an opportunity to intervene in decisions of family size and sexuality which today would be regarded as an intolerable interference with basic human rights. Since German wartime policies were pronatalist, attempting above all to stimulate the birth rate, this obviously had serious implications for women. The attack on the decline in the birth rate was three-pronged, legal, material and ideological, hammered out by inter-ministerial commissions, Reichstag select committees and had the support of the government and the Kaiser. It was a policy formulated by men and directed at women. The attempt to reverse the downward demographic trend was never a comprehensive policy with an inner logic and cohesion but more a hurried compromise between many factions with widely differing views both within parliamentary and governmental committees.[9] As a result it was a policy of small steps often unco-ordinated, contradictory and unrealistic. More importantly, it was for the most part never enacted because the revolution of 1918 turned out the government and ended the monarchy before any major bills had become law. Denise Riley has demonstrated the difficulty in 'grasping the full force of what can be loosely referred to as a climate of pronatalist opinion'[10] particularly if there are no obvious effects such as a rise in the fertility rate.

But it would be wrong to dismiss German wartime pronatalism as irrelevant rhetoric. A number of coercive measures, often harmful to women, were introduced, while social welfare programmes lagged far behind. Even policies which remained at the planning stage are worth investigating because of their possible psychological effect. They also reveal important male assumptions about women's social role which often clashed with women's own views. The reaction to a lower fertility rate at a time when there was no danger of national extinction cannot be explained solely in rational terms and suggests that there were deeper anxieties at work in the minds of population planners. The new freedom that many women derived by separating sex from procreation contradicted the traditionally accepted attitude to a double standard of sexual morality by which women fell into the category of whore or *Hausfrau*. The use of birth control smacked of revolt against the accepted roles of dominant man and passive woman within family life and was felt to jeopardise the entire social fabric.

The proposals to stimulate the birth rate by material inducements and improvements in the welfare system were impressive and included tax relief for large families, a salary structure for state employees that would enable them to have families earlier, better housing and substantial 'maternity protection'. But despite continued pressure from the SPD and even the Kaiser's personal encouragement for wide-ranging social measures, it was the legal sanctions against birth control and venereal diseases which were given precedence. As the Chancellor, von Bethmann-Hollweg, pointed out, sanctions were easier to enact and probably had more immediate effect.[11] They were also, of course, much cheaper.

Repressive sanctions

It was as a result of the Chancellor's pressure that a number of states banned the practice of publishing the addresses of couples to be married in registry offices so that they could no longer be sent catalogues of contraceptives.[12] Surveillance of contraceptive sales and advertising had been stepped up in some places even before the war[13] but from 1915 onwards the military authorities sharpened the existing legal restrictions by prohibiting the display and advertising of contraceptives and abortifacients, information about them and even their sale by door-to-door salesmen.[14] There were moves to requisition rubber contraceptives so that the rubber could be re-used for war purposes. Condoms were exempted as prophylactics against venereal diseases and were in fact recommended to soldiers and easily available.[15] Female contraceptive devices, although equally prophylactic, were not exempt. As a consequence many inconsiderate husbands were known to have infected their wives.

The double standard of sexual morality of Wilhelmine society condoned and even encouraged male promiscuity. Women alone were held accountable for prostitution. Under German criminal law prostitution was state-regulated which meant that registered prostitutes under police surveillance were subjected to regular medical checks while their male customers suffered no such control. During the war, the military authorities tightened control of prostitutes. Every serviceman who had contracted venereal disease was to give the name of the woman with whom he had had sex. In fact any woman alleged to have had relationships with several men during one month, whether she had received money or not, could be 'registered' as a prostitute after only two warnings. It was not unknown for completely innocent girls to be denounced.[16] In 1916 the Prussian Minister of the Interior issued mandatory regulations for abortions performed by physicians. This must have affected many women since doctors had previously interpreted the law more liberally.[17] A year later the Prussian Minister of Justice urged state prosecutors in Prussia and elsewhere to 'punish with severity' women who underwent abortions and to 'suppress their natural sympathy', advice which seems to have been heeded.[18]

The most far-reaching and controversial attempt to intervene in personal decisions on reproduction came in 1918 when the government introduced three bills. Although the governmental changes in October of that year and the revolution in November led to their being shelved, all three were passed by the Upper House, the Bundesrat, and the first two by the Reichstag Select Committee on Population Questions. They would have become law as a matter of routine had a little more time been available. They are so revealing in their intent that they deserve closer attention.[19]

The first 'population' bill concerned venereal disease which was thought (probably wrongly) to have increased enormously amongst the troops during the war. Venereal disease was considered a threat to the birth rate because it caused sterility[20] and could be transmitted to unborn children. The bill provided, amongst other things, a penalty of three years' imprisonment 'for anybody who had sex knowing . . . that he or she suffered from VD'. In effect this bill was much more likely to protect men than women since only 'female persons commercially trading in vice' could be forced to undergo a medical examination and compulsory treatment. The bill did not contain a similar clause for men, because, as the President of the Reich Health Office put it, a compulsory medical examination for them 'would be too deep an intrusion into family affairs and violate confidentiality between doctor and patient'.[21] Men were merely encouraged to consult venereal disease advice centres the first of which had opened in 1914. It is true that in a special clause to be included in the venereal disease bill, suggested by the Reichstag Select Committee on Population, soldiers found to be suffering from venereal disease could be retained by the army during demobilisation for treatment. But to spare them embarrassment it was suggested that all soldiers with any infectious disease should be retained.[22]

The second bill was designed to stop all public access to contraception. It banned the manufacture, import, sale and advertising of all contraceptives. In effect, it singled out female birth control because condoms as prophylactics were exempted. The ban extended to abortifacients, previously not covered by legislation, and to advertisement of abortion services. Even printed material with oblique references to birth control was no longer to be available. The preamble to the bill declared its intention to halt the spread of contraceptive practices, which formerly had been restricted to extra-marital sex, but were now being made use of by married couples who were 'healthy, economically secure, and often even newly-wed'.[23] This bill was the second attempt to outlaw contraception and encountered much opposition and ridicule from physicians, socialists and feminists. Many doctors, particularly with a knowledge of birth control practices, described the bill as unrealistic. One trade union paper ridiculed it as an attempt to turn German women into 'breeding machines and mother-animals' and in the Prussian Diet the socialist Liebknecht accused the government of forcing women to bear 'future soldiers' by measures which amounted to 'protecting the bayonet inside the womb'.[24]

The last bill concerned abortion and sterilisation. It sought to curb the alleged dramatic rise of abortions and voluntary sterilisations by limiting the legal grounds on which doctors could perform both operations to the saving of health or life. It also prohibited any non-medical practitioner such as nature therapists from performing an abortion. Medical confidentiality was to be abandoned by prescribing compulsory notification of the name and address of any woman who had undergone a therapeutic abortion or sterilis-ation , because as the preamble put it, 'the general welfare of the state has to have precedence over women's feelings'.[25]

The three bills were to be discussed on the floor of the Reichstag before finally becoming law in November 1918, but the revolution foiled this most determined attempt by the government to counteract the refusal by 'healthy women to bear children as a moral and patriotic duty'.[26] Apart from a motion in the Reichstag in 1930[27] there was never again an attempt to ban contraceptives. In December 1918 two decrees were issued which pre-scribed compulsory treatment of all persons suspected of suffering from venereal disease. In 1927 a law which was significantly different from the 1918 bill was passed to combat venereal disease and repeal the prostitution regulation. It was welcomed by physicians and declared a moral victory by feminists who had been campaigning since the 1890s for the abolition of state-regulated prostitution. During the Weimar Republic the abortion law was made not harsher but milder and there was considerable support for the campaign to legalise abortion.

The three bills reflected and reinforced a climate of opinion which saw individuals as objects of planning for a growing *Volk*, but it was women who were the main target of repressive measures. Pronatalists repeatedly stressed that they were concerned with the common rather than the individual good and pointed to *Pflichtwillen* (voluntary duty) of the individual towards the community. They used a rhetoric full of biological terms which obscured the clash between the interests of the individual woman seeking to control her fertility and of the state, the body politic, wishing to impose unlimited reproduction. The *Volk* was described as an 'organic body' made up of 'the cells of individual families' implying a fusion of citizen and state. By describing the family as 'seed', as a 'fountain of youth' (*Jungbrunnen*) which would rejuvenate *Volkskraft*, as a *Pflanzschule* (nursery) of the community, the image of growth and expansion as a natural process was persuasively linked to family size and birth rate. The falling fertility was not, in pronatalist terminology, an expression of changing social needs or individual aspirations and least of all of a necessary female strategy. Instead it was described as a *Zellenkrankheit* (cell disease), even as a 'cancerous growth' and a 'degeneration of the *Volkskörper*'.[28] This use of biological language and emphasis on the *Volk* betrays an underlying interest in eugenics which is, in more explicit terms, curiously missing from official population directives. It was of course recognised that national fertility decline was a problem of a differential birth rate, with the lower classes multiplying faster than the upper classes. The potential 'dysgenic' effects did not go unnoticed. There were indeed several schemes for 'selective breeding' which involved encouraging only those commonly regarded as of 'sound heredity' to produce children and discouraging or even preventing those considered genetically 'unfit' from reproduction. But these were mostly proposed by members of the medical profession and received little or no support from government agencies. In fact, qualitative population measures played a very minor role in official thinking, which was obsessed with increasing *Volkskraft* quantitatively.

Positive incentives

The concern to stimulate the birth rate undoubtedly gave a strong impetus to social policy, particularly in the field of maternal and child welfare. This implied a public recognition of the value of children and of women's burden of childbirth and childrearing. The SPD in particular, pressed for improvements in the maternity allowance and child welfare provisions, for laws protecting women working in factories and for the improved status for unmarried mothers and their children.[29] The Social Democrats, conscious of numerous attacks from conservative circles who held them responsible for neo-Malthusian propaganda amongst the working class, found the proposals for an extension of social security a convenient excuse for backing the government's policy. Positive measures reconciled socialists to a programme inspired by imperialism and largely aimed at the working classes because they shared the government's concern with a declining birth rate, albeit for different reasons. The SPD's ambiguous attitudes towards birth control had become obvious in the famous 'birth strike' episode of 1913. While it was clear that many working-class families considered numerous children a disadvantage, socialist leaders had publicly rejected birth control as a method of solving the social question and demanded more proletarian children as 'soldiers for the revolution'.[30]

The earliest and by far the most important of all material inducements for childbearing was the introduction, in 1914, of the *Kriegswochenhilfe*, the wartime maternity allowance for expectant and recent mothers. In 1915 it was extended to unmarried women who could prove that the father of their child was in active service.[31] In fact, children born out of wedlock benefited most noticeably from positive population measures, although this was less a reflection of humanitarian concerns than a pragmatic attempt to keep alive the 180,000 or so 'illegitimate' children born annually whose chance of surviving the first year of life was only half that of children born within marriage.[32] In 1915 entitlement to the war allowance and to the state pension paid to servicemen's families was extended to include any 'illegitimate' dependants. Together with gradual increases in the numbers of maternal and infant welfare centres, these measures constituted real improvements, but should not deflect attention from the many grandiose schemes which were discussed in endless government and parliamentary committees, approved by the Chancellor and sometimes pressed for by the Kaiser but which were never realised. Reasons for this must remain a matter for speculation but resistance by the Finance Minister obviously occurred and lack of determination must surely have been another factor, particularly if the slow progress of positive 'cures' is compared with the speed with which the major 'repressive' measures were whipped through parliament.[33]

The ideological campaign

Population planners had always pinned hope on an ideological campaign to encourage women to have more children. This was obviously much cheaper than positive social policy and in the nationalistic atmosphere of the war stood a good chance of success. Von Lobell, the Prussian Minister of the Interior spoke of 'a holy task . . . to rouse the entire people', and Krohne, his senior official, of a 'moral crusade'. By posing fertility control as a moral question, pronatalists received the backing of the churches.[34] But the idea that birth control would encourage promiscuity was probably genuinely believed as well. It was, in part at least, also a reaction to the 'New Ethics' of the League for the Protection of Motherhood[35] whose campaign for the legal equality and social acceptance of single mothers was interpreted as a campaign for 'free love'. Franz Hitze, for example, a leading social reformer and Centre Party delegate in the Reichstag, who had been responsible for the founding of the Select Committee on Population, was convinced that the continued trend of reproductive behaviour would lead to a 'shock to the moral order'. He called any act to prevent conception 'a sacrilege . . . a revolt against nature' and a way of 'denuding marriage of its moral dignity'.[36]

This view was by no means confined to Catholics. By controlling the size of her family a woman challenged the traditional image which portrayed her as 'the product and prisoner of her reproductive system'.[37] Contraception presented many women with the possibility of new roles and a new autonomy that interfered with the conventional notion of women as passive and submissive, and disturbed, it was feared, the balance of power between husband and wife. The notion of dominant wives would have appeared particularly threatening to men in a country whose civil law afforded women no legal equality and actually prescribed female sexual submission at any time the husband might demand. The separation of sex from procreation implied that women like men could enjoy intercourse without fear of the consequences. The mediaeval notion of women as sexually voracious had been revived in the 'scientific' literature of the nineteenth century. This alluded to the innate sexual powers of women which could, unless kept in check, become dangerous. Especially in middle-class moral terms, female sexuality was respectable only within marriage and when reserved for procreation. Birth control, by providing the chance of 'safe' sensual pleasure could, it was felt, turn wives into whores, or, in the words of the pronatalists, 'into wild animals', 'mere objects of lust' and 'slaves of their desire'.[38]

But the ideological campaign also played on nationalistic feelings. Grotjahn was not alone in this. Because he believed that modern contraceptives were there for good, he appealed to women's patriotism to keep up their 'will to motherhood' and to behave 'generatively responsibly' to the community.[39] The women's movement, girls' higher education and women's employment came under attack as 'counter-productive' to women's true role as housewife and mother. Women with academic education in particular were accused of subnormal fecundity, their brains having somehow destroyed their reproductive genes.[40] Intellectual training was also said to harden women's characters, which were by nature soft and emotional; it would impair their capacity to transmit 'the spirit of maternity and family values'.[41]

If this implied a belief in the innate female qualities of motherliness and domesticity, the public campaign to improve standards of housekeeping and mothercraft suggested otherwise. Girls from the poorer section of the community were said to lack the essential 'art of prudent housewifery' without which proletarian households would necessarily display 'filth and disorder', driving husbands to drink and children into neglect.[42] The attempts by politicians to improve standards in the poorer homes should not be confused with the attempts by the women's movement to professionalise housework or by socialist feminists to free working women from some of their domestic duties by planning communal kitchens.[43] State agencies who talked about 'mothercraft' had other things in mind. It was not rare that, without reference to social and economic conditions, 'ignorant working-class mothers' and 'dirty midwives' were made scapegoats for the appallingly high infant mortality rate. One authority, in Munich, accused midwives of causing annually 'serious illness or even the death of at least 480,000 babies'.[44] Pronatalists aimed their campaign for domesticity also at the increasing number of women employed outside the home, a trend considered an important contributory factor to the demographic decline but of no significance for the economy. Grotjahn called female paid labour 'irrelevant to national production but fatal for population growth'.[45]

However, the aim of taking women out of the labour market and keeping them at home to serve husband and *Volk* proved to be just one of the many contradictions between the hopes of population planners and the realities of war. The government failed to reconcile its conflicting demands on women to be productive in war industries and reproductive at home. Despite the strong appeal for women to stay with their children, there was never enough financial support for women actually to do so. Neither the wartime allowance nor the state pension given to needy servicemen's families were ever large enough to live on, nor were they meant to be.[46] Even the much-praised maternity allowance lagged behind the level of sickness benefit and far behind the average weekly wage that an unskilled female labourer could earn. Thus these schemes generally failed to convince women to stop work and lose earnings.

Married women and mothers with young children joined the industrial labour force during the war in great numbers. Military authorities as well as private entrepreneurs pressurised women to take up positions that servicemen had left vacant. Because of the desperate labour shortage, workers were selected chaotically, irrespective of family status, age, health, training or location. This meant that many mothers with young babies ended up in jobs quite unsuitable for them.[47] The employment of well over two million women in the war industries, many married with children, made indeed a mockery of the official 'eulogy' of motherhood, particularly since many women worked in heavy industry where, according to at least one informed critic, the physical demands of the work were beyond them. Furthermore, an emergency decree of 4 August 1914 had effectively abolished the laws protecting female labourers and working days of up to twelve hours and long night shifts became the norm rather than the exception. It was quite usual for women with children of pre-school age to volunteer for night work in order 'to be free' during the day to supervise their children.[48]

Reports of increasing maternal morbidity and evidence of rising maternal and infant mortality, particularly during the last two years of the war, reflect the hardship that many women and their children must have endured.[49] But maternal illness and death never featured prominently in pronatalist discussions. Despite SPD pressure to re-introduce female work protection laws, to reinstate factory inspectors and employ women factory welfare officers, the occasional appeal by the Kaiserin herself and an attempt in 1917 by the War Ministry to investigate the conditions of female workers, little, if anything, seems to have happened. Women's welfare was not one of the government's priorities as the following incident underlines. In October 1917, during questioning in the Reichstag population committee, a government spokesman admitted that the increasingly unfavourable working conditions for women had meant 'a serious deterioration of the health of mothers of the *Volk* and had impaired any prospect of population growth', *but*, he went on, protection of motherhood was less important than maximising production in the armament industries.[50]

The feminist response

So far we have looked at male responses to the decline in the birth rate, which portrayed women as 'silent' victims. This was, however, far from the truth. Women were, on the contrary, actors and not just recipients of directives even if their responses to state policies were not always easy to discover or interpret. Those women who were most outspoken and whose public utterances are comparatively well-recorded were leaders of the women's movement and, as such, probably not representative of ordinary women. Even this organised feminist reaction is difficult to evaluate. Such statements as we have frequently conflict one with another, sometimes sharply refuting, sometimes lending support to the official prescriptions. For the most part, however, women's views go unrecorded in official reports. Their reactions are, as Riley has put it, 'oblique', appearing 'in the field of political speech as silence, absence of challenge, indirection.'[51] Statements by feminists need careful interpretation for a number of reasons to do with the manner in which women reacted to attacks made on them, the wartime political climate, and the special conditions of censorship; also we must be aware of the many different meanings that the word 'motherhood' has for different people.

It was quite normal for pronatalists to denigrate the women's movement as 'a movement of spinsters' inciting women against marriage and motherhood. A prominent physician and sexual scientist accused women's emancipation of having caused a 'masculinisation of women', which implied both degeneration of fecundity and perversion of sexuality.[52] In particular, the radical sex reform organisation, the League for the Protection of Motherhood and its president, Helene Stöcker, were under attack for their 'New Ethics' and for their campaign for access to contraception and legalised abortion. Within the moderate Federation of German Women's Associations (BdF), opinions on birth control were divided. But even in this predominantly middle-class organisation a radical wing had, as early as 1908, demanded a repeal of the abortion law.[53] Socialist women leaders had, during the 'birth strike' discussions, publicly dismissed neo-Malthusianism[54] but were nevertheless suspect in pronatalist circles because of their emphasis on the emancipatory effect of women's paid labour. It is no wonder therefore that feminists frequently defended themselves by pointing out their own belief in maternity. Gertrud Bäumer, president of the BdF, for example, spoke of the need 'to strengthen the sacred will to motherhood' and Luise Zietz, from the left wing of the SPD, called maternity 'women's natural duty towards family and society'.[55]

Wartime censorship had brought a number of feminists, especially those involved in pacifist campaigns, into trouble and even into prison. It also acted as a severe restraint on any public criticism of government policies. In the circumstances it is surprising how frequently and with what outspokenness feminists criticised population planning. Many of them ridiculed the fact that women, who were the subject of pronatalism, were, with a few exceptions, not officially consulted, and that policy-making was left to 'old professors and bachelor politicians discussing female ignorance of housekeeping and the importance of breastfeeding'.[56] The bills to outlaw contraceptives and venereal disease came under particularly strong attack. Marie Stritt of the BdF called it a 'degradation of and an assault on women' and, like many others, described the government's tactics as 'compulsory conception' (Gebärzwang). For the same reason the social democratic leaders held a number of meetings in order to protest against the 'intolerable interference with the free right of women's self-determination'.[57] Members of the women's movement were also united in their disapproval of the militaristic line adopted by pronatalists who, as Helene Stöcker put it, expected women to 'bear live munition'.[58]

On the other hand many prominent women, particularly from the BdF, used, perhaps even invented, the concept of 'pregnancy as women's active service'.[59] What are we to make of this? Do phrases like this suggest genuine support for the war effort? Did women simply ape male slogans even when they were as crude as these? Many women were certainly affected by the general patriotic fervour which followed the outbreak of war and which inspired the concept of Burgfrieden, the truce between organised labour and the government. Like many British suffragists, many German women engaged in the movement for female emancipation welcomed the temporary suspension of war between the sexes when the fatherland was at risk. The enormous support by the women's movement for the National Women's Service is proof of this. But even though very few feminists questioned the need for a growing population and some might well have supported the government's attempts to stimulate the birthrate for patriotic reasons, there was more to it than that. By using a language which men would understand and listen to, women could turn male arguments and anxieties into advantages for themselves. Rosa Kempf, a suffragist and member of the BdF, in an influential sociological journal, described 'women's sacrifice to the fatherland' (in bearing and raising children) as equal to men's military service, even in war, because maternal deaths in childbirth during war and peace would equal the number of war victims.[60] Kempf was not suggesting that women *ought* to have children but was pointing to the dangers of pregnancy and childbirth which had received so little attention in the debate over population. Certainly, whenever feminists pledged their support for 'a healthy population increase', they linked this to a demand for better social and economic conditions in family life.

The frequent use of the concept of 'motherhood' in the public discourse poses additional problems for the historian. It is comparatively easy to recognise the prescriptive intentions of male pronatalists encouraging maternity but more difficult to understand feminists' motives when they enthused about motherhood, implying that it was also women's highest fulfilment. Even the radical socialist Clara Zetkin, not known for sentimentality, applauded 'motherliness' as a quality innate in women which gave them a special aptitude for caring.[61] The ideal of the 'emancipated woman' and the notion of women as more caring and peace-loving than men have always been two parallel strands of feminism. There is therefore no easy interpretation of feminists' own eulogy of motherhood. Was this, as has been suggested, a defeat for the 'new woman' and a retreat into the narrow confines of *Kinder, Küche, Kirche*?[62] Or should we consider it to have been a conscious strategy by women, especially of the middle classes, to gain equality in public life by an attempt to 'politicise and professionalise the female sphere of unpaid work'? Was this stress on motherhood guided by the hope to 'humanise society' and to improve women's status within the society by an 'organised' and 'extended' motherhood?[63]

Popular birth control practices

If printed accounts of the views of women's leaders pose problems of interpretation, the responses of ordinary women and men to the population question and fertility control are even more difficult to trace and evaluate. For the most part the historian has to turn to statistics, judicial files, police reports and medical surveys which are all indirect accounts compiled for quite different reasons. The continued fall in the German birth rate suggests that the blandishments of government and the press in their campaign against the 'two-child system' had little effect.[64] The views of ordinary German families, when recorded, showed considerable independence from the official line. In 1916 Max Marcuse, a Berlin dermatologist and sex researcher, investigated 300 marriages by interviewing soldiers who were being treated for venereal disease in a military hospital.[65] They were predominantly from the rural and urban working class and belonged to different religious denominations. They gave their views on family size and birth control and also gave details of their own occupations and those of their wives and their parents. This study reveals two striking facts: the dramatic demographic change from large to small family within just one generation and the clear conviction of the majority that social advancement and family limitation were interlinked. The couples who were the subject of the investigation originated from families where seven or more children were not abnormal yet their own marriages had an average number of only 2.4 conceptions and 1.1 children, although in some cases, of course, the family was not yet complete. To quote a typical case, there was the 37-year-old transport worker from a family of nine with a 39-year-old wife, who ran a fruit stall, from a family of 13. They had had sexual relations for ten years, been married for four but had not had any children, only one miscarriage.[66]

The interest in and use of birth control is very noticeable. Of the 300 couples, 210 used some form of preventive measures and the most frequent reason for limiting a family was 'getting on in life'. In marked contrast to the language of the pronatalists who referred to children as *Kindersegen* (being blessed with children), the interviewees described children as a 'burden', 'too expensive' and a 'hindrance to enjoyment'. One man, a waiter and father of four, felt he was ridiculed for having a large family and a 27-year-old mechanic, married to a shop assistant for five years, but still childless, proudly called his a 'modern marriage' and said, 'any fool can have a child, but it takes a bit more to have none'.[67] Very few of the servicemen put their wives' health as the prime motivation for birth control. By contrast, the 1913 report of a woman factory inspector in Saxony referred to the concern felt by many women workers about the effect of frequent childbirth. Too many children would 'render women prematurely old, sick and unfit' to work and enjoy life.[68]

The different approach of men and women to birth control is clearly shown by comparing this survey with two earlier surveys of 600 women just prior to the First World War. One was conducted in 1914 by O. Polano, a Professor of Gynaecology in Würzburg, Bavaria on 500 women of mostly lower-class origin and predominantly Catholic. The other, again by Marcuse, during 1911–13, involved 100 women married to manual workers in Berlin.[69] Both studies confirm that significantly more couples practised conception control than did not. Sixty-seven per cent of the 467 married women in Polano's sample and 64 per cent of the women in Marcuse's study used some form of birth control. Marcuse found it easy to obtain information from women patients; men were much more reluctant to speak and in many cases feigned ignorance. At least 23 men held their wives alone responsible for family limitation. A few expressed opposition. There was also a callous lack of concern by husbands newly infected with venereal disease who admitted regular unprotected sex with their wives. Many husbands fathered children when drunk but found little wrong with it.[70] By contrast, only two of the hundred women indicated a 'fatalistic' approach to childbirth. A comparison of attitudes expressed and methods used suggests that working-class women were more determined than their husbands to avoid unwanted children. This difference of opinion hinted at marital tension and this was openly admitted by at least one wife. Another woman aged only 24 who had had two children in quick succession preferred her husband to 'go to other women' rather than risk another pregnancy. A third, 28 years old, had only submitted to intercourse 'six or eight times during the last three years and then only because the husband became violent'.[71] Several women admitted to using contraception without their husbands' knowledge and sometimes against their will.

There were, however, signs of co-operation between husband and wife because the most frequent method of birth control was *coitus interruptus*[72] which required a certain agreement on sexual behaviour and family size. Withdrawal had been maligned by the medical profession for allegedly causing nervous exhaustion in men, sexual neurasthenia and hysteria in women. But when questioned about this one agricultural labourer replied 'I don't believe it, because then everybody would be ill.'[73] It is easy to see why this most trditional method was so popular. It was widely known even in rural societies, an important factor considering that access to birth control information was curtailed by the obscenity clause in the penal code. *Coitus interruptus* needed no forethought or preparation, was convenient and practical. It did not involve getting out of bed in freezing conditions and crowded housing disturbing other family members who, in working-class homes, often shared the parental bedroom. But most important, it was free. The prevalence of withdrawal made nonsense of the government's plans to increase national fertility by banning manufacture and sale of contraceptives. Many physicians were quick to point this out.[74]

By contrast with withdrawal, the condom was used very rarely: only 57 of the 293 servicemen, and only 14 husbands of the Berlin women used it. In the Polano survey of 500 women the condom was only mentioned in 13 cases. In the soldiers' case this is particularly surprising since medical personnel in the army taught prophylactic methods. There were, however, several reasons why the condom was apparently little used amongst the lower-classes. It was said to limit sexual pleasure and cause physiological disorders. It was also associated with prostitution. To use a condom success-fully men also needed self-discipline and forethought. Condoms were also very expensive costing six marks and more per dozen in 1914. This meant that they were out of the reach of the ordinary labourer whose weekly wage, by 1915, was not more than 20 marks.[75]

Both *coitus interruptus* and the condom required male co-operation. Con-sidering many husbands' lack of interest in birth control why did not more women use female contraception? The diaphragm, which had been invented in Germany as early as 1838 and successfully used since the 1870s, was regarded by many medical experts as both reliable and safe.[76] Yet, if the soldiers can be believed, only 29 of their wives used the diaphragm and only 5 of the Berlin women and none in Polano's survey. Again the price could have been decisive. By March 1920, admittedly at a time of inflation, they were sold for as much as 20 or 30 marks, and there was the additional cost of fitting and regular check-ups by a doctor.[77] Furthermore, in the absence of women doctors many women would have been reluctant to consult male doctors over such an intimate matter, that is if they were able to find a doctor qualified and willing to help. Women would naturally have turned to midwives, many of whom were known to insert these devices although they were officially prohibited from doing so.[78]

It was precisely in this area of safe female contraception that working-class wives were hardest hit by the tightening up of birth control laws and police surveillance. They had to rely on incidental information in health manuals with obscure titles or follow the advice of mail order catalogues, pedlars and back street chemists who put profit before all else. But even these irregular channels were increasingly under attack, driving contraceptive information more and more underground.[79] The result was that most working-class wives were ill-informed and ill-advised and resorted to methods which were either unreliable or dangerous, often putting their health and even their lives at risk. Marcuse's Berlin survey reflects this dilemma. Of those women who used barrier methods, two used cotton sponges, notorious for their failure rate, two used a metal cervical cap inserted by a midwife, in one case causing serious infection, and two used stem-pessaries. These pessaries were intra-cervical devices which were known to have caused many deaths especially since women usually inserted them without expert help.[80]

The most popular female contraception was post-coital douching. Syringes used for this were comparatively easily obtainable from chemists or even supplied through the local sick fund as sanitary equipment. According to contemporary accounts they were an enormous commercial success, selling at between 4 and 50 marks during the war. Despite enticing names such as *Ladies' friend*, *Ritter St Georg* or *Gloria*, however, they proved as inconvenient as they were inefficient. Of the 17 users in Marcuse's Berlin sample, eight had to have abortions. Syringes were also potentially dangerous as they could easily be converted into abortion instruments by attaching a long thin glass catheter. Although numerous attempts were made to declare the simple syringe illegal and ban it from open sale, it was the converted model (*Mutterrohre*) used as an abortifacient that concerned the authorities most.[81]

The very high incidence of abortion in the two Marcuse studies confirms the impression gained from a number of judicial records that abortion continued to play a major part in regulating working-class family size. Better-off women also practised abortion but they had the opportunity of discreet help from their family doctors. Unmarried women who had aborted featured less in trials. This is surprising if we consider that they could not usually conceal abortions as miscarriages, like married women, and were therefore easier to detect as 'culprits'. The typical abortion case was in fact a married woman of between 30 and 40, with two or more children, who had completed her family. Abortion was not just the last desperate attempt to prevent an unwanted child when all else had failed. For many women, particularly the least privileged, it was an alternative to birth control and not thought of as abnormal or criminal. Marcuse expressed his surprise at the matter-of-fact way in which 41 of his 100 Berlin women described their abortions. The dichotomy beween the harsh abortion law and the popular perception was often commented on by physicians with working-class patients.[82] Even amongst the educated, abortion and contraception were often considered identical and the same instruments or potions could act as contraceptive or abortifacient. In the absence of pregnancy tests, the distinction between abortion and 'bringing on' a late period was genuinely blurred. Many women accused of a criminal abortion were in fact later found not to have been pregnant.[83] The law described abortion in scientific terms often far removed from reality as it presented itself to the ordinary woman. In legal language abortion was the act of 'killing a foetus in the womb'. Most women aborted when they were only two or three months pregnant and did not consider the little clot of blood as a 'foetus' and their act of 'making the blood come back', or *kippen* (tipping) had, in their eyes, nothing to do with murder, especially when the operation was performed in the very early stages when, according to traditional beliefs, the foetus was not yet ensouled.[84]

Most abortions were induced by women themselves by 'natural' methods such as jumping from tables and chairs, taking hot baths or carrying heavy objects. They would also drink herbal teas and traditional potions for inducing abortion or use a combination of these, frequently achieving the desired result.[85] If these methods failed some would resort to mechanical interference with knitting needles and the like, often with fatal consequences. Or they would turn to outside help. The typical 'commercial' abortionist was a 'wise woman' of the neighbourhood or a midwife or nature healer in the vicinity. To cite just one example: in 1914 Frau K. was accused of abortion by the public prosecutor in Düsseldorf. She was 24, Catholic and married to an industrial labourer. It is not known whether she had children. When she found that she was pregnant she turned for help to Frau E. who lived in the same block of flats. Frau E. offered a bed and fetched Frau T. who also lived in the same building. Frau T., 29, Protestant, was married to a railway worker. She had often helped with abortions before in order to earn a little additional money. She had a good record and was also successful this time using Frau K.'s own syringe. Frau T. received five marks and the syringe as a present. This incident was freely discussed amongst the women in the neighbourhood where everybody seemed to accept it as good news. The police got to hear about it only because of the personal grievance of a woman who had lost her flat to Frau K.[86]

Commercial abortions were of course not always so successful or so cheap. There are many other cases where 'wise women' charged up to 50 marks and more and where the syringe injured the womb and caused the death of the abortee. The danger of amateur abortionists was, however, often exaggerated in official and popular accounts because it was precisely those cases in which the patient died or needed emergency treatment which came to the prosecutor's notice. Abortion accidents were thus over-represented in judicial files. Although physicians lobbied to monopolise this operation, medically induced abortions were not necessarily always safer. This sad truth was revealed to an astonished public in a famous court case in 1917 involving Henkel, Professor of Gynaecology at the University of Jena, who was also director of the University Women's Hospital. Henkel had aborted many women privately and in his public ward but only his sick fund patients were scrutinised and prosecuted. He was accused of having carried out abortions without the accepted medical grounds on 54 women. He was also accused of serious medical negligence, causing the death of several women by operating in unhygienic conditions. In one case a woman who had just breakfasted was rushed to the operating table because Henkel wanted to impress a minor German prince with his surgical skills and no other patient was found to be available.[87] Henkel was by no means a special case in that he was acquitted of most charges, simply losing his clinical post but remaining a member of the medical faculty. The authorities were less concerned about the fact that some of his patients had died than that he had carried out voluntary sterilisation in 31 cases. In fact, it was this case that motivated the government to include sterilisation regulations in the bill of 1918 to outlaw abortion.

Because abortion was widely accepted by the working-class community, the dark figure of criminal cases which never came to light was bound to make it impossible to judge illegal abortion frequency. Yet population planners continued to refer confidently to estimates which were based on slender evidence but proved to be political dynamite. By 1915 the criminal abortion rate was said to be between 30,000 and half a million per year, depending on which medical estimates were used: the higher figure was usually quoted in government papers causing an 'abortion scare' in official circles. Yet, if national abortion estimates were highly speculative, a number of small-scale studies by medical statisticians such as Freudenberg in Berlin and Roesle in Magdeburg and the personal experiences of physicians like Marcuse, Grotjahn and Max Hirsch suggest that by the First World War abortion was very widespread and on the increase.[88] It seems fair to conclude that abortion was a major, possibly even the most important, factor in the long-term decline of the German birth rate.

The failure of pronatalism and the cult of maternity

With the benefit of hindsight it is clear that German pronatalists were fighting a losing battle. They had to contend not, as they thought, with a temporary and reversibly moral trend, but with deeper processes associated with industrialisation. The sharp decline in the birth rate reflected dramatic social and economic changes which transformed Germany in little more than forty years from a pre-industrial into a modern nation.[89] The pronatalists fought, as it were, the symptoms rather than the disease. It is difficult to determine how far they were aware that the complex interconnection between industrialisation and demographic change was undermining their attempts to change reproductive behaviour. What seems clear is that pronatalism was advocated with considerable urgency. It was hoped that national fertility could be boosted by increasing state intervention in personal decisions about procreation and sexuality. The SPD and women's movement resisted such state interference and campaigned to give precedence over coercive measures to welfare provisions and material incentives for large families. But both groups, for varying reasons, applauded the concept of pronatalism. In lending their support to government policy which promised social improvement but actually concentrated on suppressing birth control, they supported a programme which was detrimental to both the working class and the female sex. It is also clear that attempts to stimulate the birth rate failed. Neither persuasion nor threats produced larger families for the fatherland. The fertility rate continued to fall until the 'demographic transition' was complete by the 1931–5 period.[90]

There was also a serious flaw in the population programme itself: the conflicting demand on women to be at the same time productive both in the war economy and in reproduction. The harsh wartime conditions under which so many lived made a mockery of official celebration of motherhood. The proposals for curbing the practice of birth control and abortion in the population bills of 1918 were totally unrealistic. The most popular method of preventing conception was *coitus interruptus* which was beyond police control, a point repeatedly made by socialists and doctors. To try and stamp out birth control by outlawing contraceptive devices was, as one physician put it, as illogical as 'banning pistols in order to prevent suicide'.[91] Abortion, largely self-induced, was similarly immune to legal restrictions. The existing abortion law was, as we have seen, already out of tune with popular views of abortion and had failed to deter the many thousands of women who had abortions every year. There was no reason to believe that a law based on the 1918 bill would have curtailed abortion habits any more successfully. The desire to keep families small was overwhelmingly the most important underlying cause of the declining birth rate, far more significant than either the technology of birth control and abortion or legal prescription. Why then did the government pursue its misguided policy? We cannot be sure, but it seems probable that the three bills of 1918 designed to tighten the regulation of venereal disease, contraception, abortion and sterilisation were a tactical manoeuvre aimed at placating those who regarded the continuous fall in fertility as the result of moral corruption, and to reassure those who equated a low birth rate with military weakness. Although it seems unlikely that the 'compulsory motherhood' policy had any significant impact on national fertility, the policy did have serious consequences for women who wanted to control their reproductive ability. Denied access to adequate contraception, many women were driven to abortion. But in the absence of legal medical abortion women depended on self-help. This was accompanied by risks to health and life. There was also considerable fear of detection and prosecution. Even though the majority of cases were probably undiscovered, many hundreds of women went to prison every year for having undergone an abortion.[92]

Internationally, from the late nineteenth century high fertility was seen as a sign of national 'virility' and power. Naturally Germany was concerned that it would fall behind in the population race – as France had done. But this does not explain the hysterical terms in which the decline of the birth rate was discussed. The German nation was obviously not in danger of extinction with a fertility rate well above replacement level: the population was in fact continuing to grow. It is likely that the 'demographic crisis' was itself a product of masculine ideology and was used by men to preserve their status which was threatened by the practice of birth control, since by freeing women from some of the burden of childbearing and motherhood, those who were determined to be equal partners with men in both the family and society at large acquired a new self-refpect. Men saw this as a rebellion against women's 'traditional' role of mother and housewife. The ability to separate sexuality from procreation shocked many men because it was a danger to the double standards of morality. To borrow a phrase from Anneliese Bergmann, female sexuality was permitted only in two forms: as *Fortpflanzung ohne Lust* or *Lust ohne Fortpflanzung*, for 'procreation without pleasure' or 'pleasure without procreation'.[93] Anything that would disturb this delicate balance between illicit and permitted sexuality was seen as a threat to the patriarchal family and to the entire fabric of society.

During the Weimar Republic there was a significant shift in population policy away from crude pronatalism to a new emphasis on qualitative improvement of the future generations, a change of attitude that was accompanied by an increasing acceptance of eugenic ideas preparing the way for the racist laws of National Socialism. The ideology of motherhood and domesticity continued to be a strong undercurrent in the Weimar years and eventually merged into the sexist policies after 1933 of compulsory sterilisation for women regarded as eugenically 'unfit' and compulsory motherhood for those of eugenic 'value'. The Nazis once again postulated motherhood as a duty for the *Volk*. The slogan was: 'Every childbirth . . . is a battle, a battle waged for the existence of her people.'[94]

Notes

Thanks to Anneliese Bergmann, Richard Bessel, Helen Boak, Elisabeth Croll, Clive Emsley, Karin Hausen, Lyndal Roper, Peter Usborne, Bernard Waites, Noelle Whiteside and Jenny Willis. Research was made possible by grants from the Open University and the German Historical Institute.

1 Amy Hackett, 'The politics of feminism in Wilhelmine Germany 1890–1918', unpublished PhD thesis, Columbia University, 1976, p. 928.
2 Alfred Grotjahn, *Der Wehrbeitrag der deutschen Frau*, Bonn, 1915, p. 3.
3 D. V. Glass, *Population policies and movements in Europe*, Oxford, 1940, p. 313.
4 E.g. Max von Gruber, *Ursachen und Bekämpfung des Geburtenrückganges im Deutschen Reich*, Munich, 1914; J. Borntrāger, 'Der Geburtenrückgang in Deutschland, seine Bewertung und Bekämpfung', *Veröffentlichungen aus dem Gebiete der Medizinalverwaltung*, vol. I, no. 3, 1912; Franz Hitze, *Geburtenrückgang und Sozialreform*, Mönchen-Gladbach, 1917.
5 Geheimes Staatsarchiv Preussischer Kulturbesitz Berlin-Dahlem (GSA Dahlem), Rep 84a, Prussian Ministry of Justice, 865, proceedings of the Prussian Diet, 25 February 1916, pp. 1007, 1010.
6 John E. Knodel, *The decline of fertility in Germany, 1871–1939*, Princeton, 1974, p. 246; see also Stadtarchiv Köln (SA Köln) Abt. 424, no. 502, Bl. 124, report

by the Statistical Office in Cologne, 3 October 1912, pointed to the increased proportion of married women, from 47.5 per cent in 1890 to 52.1 per cent in 1910.

7 SA Köln, Abt. 424, no. 502, Bl. 142, report of the meeting of the health commission of Cologne by mayor of Cologne, 26 October 1912; Zentrales Staatsarchiv Potsdam (ZSA Potsdam), R. Min.d.I, 9342, Bl. 7, 'Denkschrift über die Ursachen des Geburtenrückganges', Berlin, 1915, pp. 35, 38.

8 Zentrales Staatsarchiv Merseburg (ZSA Merseburg), Min.f. H.u.G, Nr. 65.I, 'Bericht über die Verhandlungen der erweiterten Wissenschaftlichen Deputation für das Medizinalwesen', Berlin, 1912, p. 67.

9 For example cf. Bundesarchiv Koblenz (BA Koblenz), R 86, 2379 'Niederschrift über die kommissarische Beratung', 26 May 1916. Grotjahn also expressed views in *Geburtenrückgang und Geburtenregelung*, Berlin, 1914, such as the eugenic usefulness of contraception which received little support in government circles.

10 Denise Riley, ' "The free mothers": pronatalism and working women in industry at the end of the last war in Britain', *History Workshop*, 11 (1981), p. 60.

11 GSA Dahlem, Rep 84a, 866, Bl. 31, letter by the Reich Chancellor to all Ministers of State, 5 June 1917.

12 Staatsarchiv Dresden (STA Dresden), Aussenmin., 8582, Bl. 13, Saxon Embassy to Foreign Minister, 30 March 1914; Ulrich Linse, 'Arbeiterschaft und Geburtenentwicklung im deutschen Kaiserreich von 1871', *Archiv für Sozialgeschichte*, 12 (1972), p. 264.

13 GSA Dahlem, Rep. 84a, 865, Bl. 1, letter by the Prussian Minister of the Interior to public prosecutors, 1 September 1913; for examples of increased police surveillance: Haupstaatsarchiv Düsseldorf (HSA Düsseldorf), Reg. Dü, Kreisarzt Dü, Bl. 35, report by police headquarters Düsseldorf, 20 December 1913.

14 The existing law, paragraph 184, section 3a of the penal code, prescribed imprisonment up to one year and/or a fine for the display, recommendation or advertising of objects 'intended for indecent (*unzüchtig*) use'. According to a decision by the Reich law court of 11 June 1912 'the use of contraceptives is "indecent" . . . because sexual intercourse with contraception is "indecent"', quoted in Kurt Bendix (ed.), *Geburtenregelung*, Berlin, 1928, p. 21. For various military decrees see Bayerisches Haupstaatsarchiv, Kriegsarchiv München (KA München), St GKdo 1771 and MKr 967. For attempt to requisition rubber contraceptives: ZSA Merseburg, Rep. 76, Nr. 2017, Bl. 82.

15 See the Reichstag discussion of the successful distribution of condoms during the war which included vending machines for soldiers: Reichstag, 256th session, 21 January 1927, p. 8677. Venereologists, in particular, supported the use of condoms as prophylactics, see below the contribution of Paul Weindling, chapter 15. Weindling also discusses how doctors used the campaign against venereal disease to advance their role in the regulation of public health.

16 KA München, St Gko 966, *Volkswart*, October 1916; StGko 967. For similar regulations in Britain see Lucy Bland, 'In the name of protection: the policing of women in the First World War' in C. Smart and J. Brophy (eds.), *Women-in-Law*, London, 1985.

17 The German criminal law (paragraphs 218–20) prescribed penal servitude for any woman who had an abortion and for any person helping to procure it. If an abortion resulted in the death of the woman penal servitude for not less than ten years, or for life, was prescribed for the abortionist. There was no provision for

therapeutic abortions but in practice many physicians terminated pregnancies on medical grounds. As a result the Prussian Medical Advisory Committee published guidelines limiting medical grounds, see BA Koblenz R 86, 2379, *Niederschrift*, 26 May 1916.

18 ZSA Potsdam, R.Min.d.I., 9344, Bl. 110, letter by Prussian Minister of Justice 13 April 1917.

19 SA Dresden, Aussenmin. 8644, 'Gesetzentwurf zur Bekämpfung der Geschlechtskrankheiten', and 'Gesentzentwurf betr. Verkehr mit Mitteln zur Verhinderung von Geburten', Bundesrat no. 322, 8 November 1917; 'Gesetzentwurf gegen Unfruchtbarmachung und Schwangerschaftsunterbrechung', Bundesrat no. 148, 22 June 1918. The first two bills were passed by the Bundesrat and presented to the Reichstag on 20 February 1918 which passed them to the select committee (Reichstag no. 1287). They were to be discussed on the floor of the Reichstag in November 1918. The third bill was passed in the Bundesrat on 4 July 1918. It was presented to the Reichstag on 6 July 1918 (Reichstag no. 1717) which passed it on without discussion to the select committee.

20 The preamble to the venereal disease bill stated an estimated loss of 100,000 children a year as a result of gonorrhoea and blamed the existence of the 300,000 childless couples on this disease: Preamble, Bl. 10.

21 ZSA Potsdam, Reichstag, 441, Bl. 27, statement by president of the Reich Health office in the Reichstag, 29 November 1916. For difference of opinions about compulsory notification see GSA Dahlem, R 84a, 866, Bl. 31, letter by Reich chancellor to all ministers of state, 5 June 1917.

22 ZSA Potsdam, R.Min.d.I., 9350, Bl. 5, report of Reichstag select committee for population questions, n.d.

23 ZSA Potsdam, R.Min.d.I., 9350, Bl. 72.

24 ZSA Potsdam, R.Min.d.I., 9343, *Deutsche Arbeit*, n.d. GSA Dahlem, Rep 84a, 865, Bl. 71a, Prussian Diet, 3 March 1916, p. 1328.

25 ZSA Potsdam, R.Min.d.I., 9350, Bl. 143.

26 SA Dresden, Aussenmin., 8644, preamble to the bill outlawing abortion and sterilisation, no. 148, Bl. 132.

27 Reichstag no. 1741, 13 March 1930, motion by the National-Sozialistische Deutsche Arbeiterpartei (NSDAP) for a law 'to protect the nation'. This prescribed penal servitude for anybody who 'limits the natural fertility of the German *Volk* with artificial means' and the same for anybody promoting fertility control.

28 F. Burgdörfer, 'Familienpolitik und Familienstatistik' in *Zur Erhaltung und Mehrung der Volkskraft*, Arbeiten einer vom ärztlichen Verein Münchens eingesetzten Kommission, Munich, 1918, pp. 69, 72; Hitze, *Geburtenrückgang*, p. 1; Proceedings of the Prussian Diet, 23 February 1914, p. 2783 quoted by Anneliese Bergmann, 'Von der "unbeflekten Empfängnis" zur "Rationalisierung des Geschlechtlebens"' in J. Geyer-Kordesch and A. Kuhn (eds.), *Frauenkörper, Medizin, Sexualität*, Düsseldorf, 1986, p. 127. J. Bornträger, 'Der Geburtenrückgang', p. 166. Cf. Paul Weindling's account of the organicist ideology, below, chapter 15.

29 GSA Dahlem, Rep. 84a, Bl. 180i–k, Proceedings of the Prussian Diet, 17 February 1917, pp. 3695–702.

30 For attacks on the SPD which allegedly spread birth control propaganda: e.g. Bornträger, 'Der Geburtenrückgang', pp. 27, 46; SA Köln, Abt. 424, 502, Bl. 103, conference of health commission, Cologne, 5 July 1912; for a fuller

account of attitudes towards the SPD see Linse, 'Arbeiterschaft'; for an account of the 'birth strike' see Kurt Nemitz, 'Julius Moses und die Gebärstreikdebatte 1913', *Jahrbuch des Instituts für deutsche Geschichte*, 2 (1973), 321–35; Anneliese Bergemann, 'Frauen, Männer, Sexualität und Geburtenkontrolle. Die Gebärstreikdebatte der SPD im Jahre 1913' in Karin Hausen (ed.), *Frauen suchen ihre Geschichte*, Munich, 1983, pp. 81–108.

31 This comprised a contribution to the cost of confinement and any medical expenses, a daily sum for maternity leave for eight weeks and a breast-feeding allowance for a maximum of 12 weeks. The plan had the support of a wide variety of groups ranging across much of the political spectrum, see Paul Weindling's contribution, chapter 15, p. 423.

32 *Statistisches Jahrbuch des deutschen Reiches*, 47, Berlin, 1928, p. 56: in 1913 the legitimate mortality rate was 14.2 per 100 live births, the illegitimate rate was 23.7 per cent.

33 GSA Dahlem, Rep. 84a, Bl. 31, letter by the Reich chancellor to all ministers of state, 5 June 1917.

34 ZSA Merseburg, Rep. 120, Nr. 65, Bl. 291, proceedings of the Prussian Diet, 25 February 1916, p. 1009; for responses by Protestant and Catholic representatives in politics see Martin Fassbender, *Des deutschen Volkes Wille zum Leben*, Freiburg, 1917.

35 The League (Bund für Mutterschutz) was founded in January 1905 by leading feminists including Helene Stöcker, Marie Stritt, Ruth Bré and Maria Lischneska, physicians such as Alfred Blaschko, sexologists such as Max Marcuse, Auguste Forel and Magnus Hirschfeld, and economists such as Walter Sombart. It soon had 400 members some of whom were prominent public figures with an interest in welfare for mothers, particularly unmarried mothers. The campaign for a 'New Ethics' comprised a radical programme for sexual reform, including demands for dissemination of birth control information, legalised abortion and a recognition of love without marriage. For accounts of the League see Richard J. Evans, *The feminist movement in Germany 1894–1933*, London, 1976; Christel Wickert et al., 'Helene Stöcker and the Bund für mutterschutz', *Women's Studies International Forum*, 5 (1982), 611–17; Amy Hackett, 'The German women's movement and suffrage, 1890–1914: A study of national feminism' in R. Bezucha (ed.), *Modern European Social History*, Lexington, Mass., 1972. For official disapproval of the League: ZSA Merseburg, Rep. 120, Nr. 65, I, Bl. 44 and Rep. 77, 662, No. 123, Bl. 2, letter by secretary of Kaiserin to president of Prussian Police 8 March 1905 urging him to ban the League.

36 Hitze, *Geburtenrückgang*, p. 11.

37 C. Smith-Rosenberg and C. Rosenberg, 'The female animal: medical and biological views of woman and her role in nineteenth-century America', *Journal of American History*, 60 (1973), 332–56, esp. p. 335. This analysis of earlier American biological arguments typifies later German ideology very well.

38 Opinions on these lines were, for example, expressed by the Centre Party delegate von Steinaecker in the Prussian Diet, quoted by A. Bergmann, 'Frauen, Männer, Sexualität', p. 97; Hitze, *Geburtenrückgang*, p. 11; Bornträger, 'Der Geburtenrückgang', p. 96; Karl Kautsky, *Vermehrung und Entwicklung in Natur und Gesellschaft*, Stuttgart, 1910, p. 251, quoted in Linse, 'Arbeiterschaft', p. 224.

39 Grotjahn, *Wehrbeitrag*, p. 23. See also Paul Weindling, below, chapter 15, pp. 428–9, on the ideas of Friedrich Naumann.

40 For example, by Ernst Bumm, *Über das Frauenstudium*, Berlin, 1917, quoted in Robert Lennig, Max Hirsch, Sozialgynäkologie und Frauenkunde', unpublished medical dissertation, Free University of Berlin, 1977, p. 41.

41 ZSA Merseburg, Rep. 120, Nr. 65, I, Bl. 295b.

42 Hitze, *Geburtenrückgang*, p. 33.

43 E.g. Henriette Fürth, *Die Hausfrau*, Munich, 1914; Lily Braun, 'Reform der Hauswirtschaft', 1901, quoted in Gisela Brinker-Gabler (ed.), *Frauenarbeit und Beruf*, Frankfurt, 1979, pp. 275–84.

44 ZSA Potsdam, R.Min.d.I., 9345, Bl. 477v.

45 Grotjahn, *Wehrbeitrag*, p. 25. The figure of 400,000 married women factory workers given by Grotjahn was disputed in a critical review of his pamphlet in the journal of the Motherhood League, *Die Neue Generation*, 1/2, 1918, p. 47. This suggested that by 1907 there were at least 700,000 married women workers, a figure which had increased enormously by 1917. For a more detailed account see Christa Zeitler, 'Die wirtschaftliche und berufliche Lage der erwerbstätigen Frauen in Deutschland seit 1914', unpublished PhD, University of Nuremberg, 1951.

46 KA München, StGKdo 980, letter Munich Stadtmagistrat, 18 December 1916; *Schwäbische Volkszeitung*, 3 April 1917.

47 Marie-Elisabeth Lüders, *Das unbekannte Heer. Frauen kämpfen für Deutschland*, Berlin, 1926, p. 97. However, a sharply different interpretation of the pattern of women's work in wartime Germany is provided above by Ute Daniel. She not only claims that overall there was no excessive increase in female employment during the war but also that the most spectacular increase occurred not in the wary industries but in work that could be performed in the home and be combined with family responsibilities, see above, chapter 10, esp. pp. 267, 269, 278 and Table 10.3.

48 Marie-Elisabeth Lüders, 'Die Entwicklung der gewerblichen Frauenarbeit im Krieg', *Schmollers Jahrbuch*, 44 (1920), p. 264.

49 ZSA Merseburg, Rep. 120, Nr. 65, I, Bl. 398, report of the inter-departmental commission on the declining birth rate, 17 March 1916. This admitted that by 1916 at least 6,500 women died annually in childbirth, the equivalent of 18 mothers a day and five to six times as many remained seriously ill. According to Friedrich Prinzing, *Handbuch der medizinischen Statistik*, Jena, 1931, p. 106, maternal mortality (without puerperal fever) rose from 17.8 per 10,000 births in 1901–10 to 21.6 per 10,000 in 1916–20 while deaths caused by puerperal fever increased even more dramatically, from 16.9 per 10,000 births in 1911–15 to 25.1 per 10,000 in 1916–20. The director of the Berlin youth office claimed puerperal deaths had increased by 50 per cent during the war, see *Die Gleichheit*, 30 August 1919, p. 217. A broader survey of trends in female mortality has more recently been undertaken by Adelheid Gräffin zu Castell in 'Die Auswirkungen des Krieges auf die Sterblichkeit des weiblichen Geschlechts im Deutschen Reich am Beispiel Preussens', unpublished paper given at the Cambridge Conference on the European family and the First World War, September 1983. This study revealed that female mortality in Prussia rose considerably during the war: in the 15–20 age group from 32.1 per 1,000 in 1910–14 to 54.2 per 1,000 in 1915–19; in the 20–5 age group from 42.0 per 1,000 to 65.8 per 1,000; for those aged 25–30 from 50.1 per 1,000 to 75.9 per 1,000. On the other hand, in Prussia the infant mortality rate declined during the early years of the war although it increased dramatically during the 'crisis years' of 1917/18. Mortality caused by hereditary

weakness rose: for male infants from 40.4 per 1,000 live births in 1913–14 to 41.2 in 1918, for female infants from 33.3 per 1,000 live births to 35.2. Mortality caused by pneumonia, influenza and respiratory diseases rose for male infants from 18.9 per 1,000 live births to 36.1 for female infants from 15.8 per 1,000 live births to 30.5.

50 GSA Dahlem, Rep. 84a, 886 Reichstag printed matter no. 1087, 5 October 1917; Ursula von Gersdorff, *Frauen im Kriegsdienst 1914–1945*, Stuttgart, 1969, document no. 70, p. 223; KA München, MKr 14383, Kriegsamtstelle Nürnberg to war ministry 24 March 1917.

51 Riley, '"The free mothers"', p. 61.

52 See, for example, Max von Gruber, *Ursachen*. BA Koblenz, R 86, 2373, 3, *Die Post*, Berlin, 7 August 1912, leading article by Professor Dr Langemann of Kiel accusing the women's movement of being a movement of spinsters with 'selfish, emancipatory ideas' out to 'destroy marriage and the family'. Otto Krohne, responsible for drafting the 1915 memorandum on the declining birth rate for the Prussian Ministry of the Interior also usually attacked the women's movement, for example, in the report of the German conference for population questions in Darmstadt, November 1916, pp. 26–7 in BA Koblenz, R 86, 2373, 12. See also A. von Moll,*Handbuch des Sexualwissenschaften*, Leipzig, 1912, quoted in Max Marcuse, *Wandlungen der Fortpflanzungs-Gedanken und -Willens*, Bonn, 1918, p. 68. For a more extensive treatment on von Moll's attitudes see Marcus Wawerzonnek, *Implizite Sexualpädagogie in der Sexualwissenschaft 1886–1933*, Cologne, 1984.

53 For the League for the Protection of Motherhood see note 35; for the BdF see Richard Evans, *The feminist movement*, p. 193. He puts membership by 1912 at about 280,000. The BdF was a loose federation of most women's organisations of the middle-class moderate feminist movement. For attempts by radical members within the BdF to repeal paragraph 218 of the abortion law, see Evans, p. 133. In Evans's view, from around this time onwards the BdF became increasingly more moderate and conservative. For a different interpretation see Irene Stoehr, 'Organisierte Mütterlichkeit' in K. Hausen (ed.), *Frauen suchen ihre Geschichte*, Munich, 1983, pp. 221–49 and Elisabeth Meyer-Renschhausen, 'Das radikal traditionelle Selbstbild', *Geschichtsdidaktik*, 10, 2 (1985), 129–48.

54 Rosa Luxemburg rejected it as an appeal to 'the frivolity, stupidity and mental laziness of the masses' and Clara Zetkin declared that 'history demonstrated that aspiring classes had not won by their quality but by the mass of their numbers', quoted by Bergmann in K. Hausen (ed.), *Frauen suchen ihre Geschichte*, p. 94, For an account of the socialist women's movement see Richard J. Evans, *Sozialdemokratie und Frauenemanzipation im deutschen Kaiserreich*, Berlin, 1979, Jean H. Quataert, *Reluctant feminists in German Social Democracy 1885–1917*, Princeton, 1979 and Jacqueline Strain, 'Feminism and political radicalism in the German Social Democratic movement 1890–1914', PhD, University of California, 1964.

55 ZSA Potsdam, R.Min.d.I., 9353, *Der Tag*, 30 October 1915, reported speech by Gertrud Bäumer; Zietz is quoted in *Die Gleichheit*, vol. 27, 8 December 1916.

56 Gertrud Bäumer, 'Bevölkerungspolitik und Kindersegen', in Gertrud Bäumer (ed.), *Weit hinter den Schützengräben*, Jena, 1916, p. 188.

57 Amy Hackett, 'The politics of feminism', p. 938; ZSA Merseburg, Rep. 76, 2013, Bl. 45, *Vorwärts*, 18 April 1918, report on the SPD women's protest meeting.

58 Helene Stöcker, *Moderne Bevölkerungspolitik*. Kriegshefte des Bundes für Mutterschutz, Berlin, 1916, p. 7.

59 E.g. Gertrud Bäumer, 'Der Krieg und die Frau', *Der deutsche Krieg*, Politische Flugschriften, 15, Stuttgart and Berlin, 1914, p. 19; M.-E. Lüders, *Das unbekannte Heer*, p. 63.

60 Rosa Kempf, 'Das weibliche Dienstjahr', *Archiv für Sozialwissenschaft und Sozialpolitik*, 41 (1916), p. 424.

61 *Die Gleichheit*, 27, 8 December 1916.

62 Jean Quataert, 'The German socialist women's movement 1890–1918', PhD, University of California, 1974.

63 Irene Stoehr, 'Organisierte Mütterlichkeit', pp. 221–49.

64 The birth rate declined dramatically during the war, reaching its lowest point of 13.9 per 1,000 by 1917. See *Statistisches Jahrbuch des deutschen Reiches*, 42, Berlin, 1921/22, p. 37. See also R. Spree, 'The German petite bourgeoisie and the decline of fertility: some statistical evidence from the late 19th and early 20th centuries', *Historical Social Research*, 22 (April 1982), 15–49.

65 Max Marcuse, *Der eheliche Präventivverkehr. Seine Verbreitung, Verursachung und Methodik, Dargestellt und beleuchtet an 300 Ehen*, Stuttgart, 1917.

66 Marcuse, *Präventivverkehr*, case no. 196.

67 Marcuse, *Präventivverkehr*, for example case nos. 22, 31, 172.

68 SA Dresden, Aussenmin., 8582, Bl. 2, report by a woman factory inspector.

69 Otto Polano, 'Beitrag zur Frage der Geburtenbeschränkung', *Zeitschrift für Geburtshilfe und Gynäkologie*, 79 (1917), 567–78. In the sample there were 33 single women; the rest were married to unskilled and skilled manual workers. 114 were married to peasants, 68 to state employees. 350 were Catholics, 83 Protestants, 30 represented mixed marriages and 4 were Jewish. 77 per cent of the mixed marriages used contraception as did 75 per cent of the Jews, 73 per cent of the Protestants and 64 per cent of the Catholics. Max Marcuse, 'Zur Frage der Verbreitung und Methode der wilkürlichen Geburtenbeschränkung in Berliner Proletarierkreisen', *Sexualprobleme*, 9 (November 1913), 752–80; see also R. P. Neumann, 'Working-class birth control in Wilhelmine Germany', *Comparative Studies in Society and History*, 20 (1978), 408–28.

70 Marcuse, *Präventivverkehr*, case nos. 26, 86, 194.

71 Marcuse, 'Zur Frage', nos. 18, 78, 71.

72 In Polano's study of all women using birth control 280 (84 per cent) relied solely on *coitus interruptus*, of whom 20 were unmarried; another 37 used this method together with douching. Of the 100 Berlin women who used birth control 23 (46 per cent) relied on *coitus interruptus*. Amongst the 300 soldiers who used birth control 130 (64 per cent) used this method, 52 of these in conjunction with other methods.

73 Marcuse, *Präventivverkehr*, no. 90.

74 For example, Marcuse, 'Zur Frage', p. 778; Polano, 'Beitrag', p. 578; Grotjahn, *Geburtenrückgang*, pp. 103ff.

75 Grotjahn, *Geburtenrückgang*, p. 99. For weekly wages see *Statistisches Jahrbuch*, 42, 1921/22, p. 307.

76 It was first invented by the Berlin physician F. A. Wilde and further developed by the Flensburg physician Mensinga who wrote about his own survey in 1881. The diaphragm was usually referred to as the 'Mensinga diaphragm'. It was adopted by the first Dutch birth control clinic and arrived in Britain via Holland, hence the name 'Dutch cap'. The cervical cap was invented by the Viennese

gynaecologist Kafka and was also in use in Germany. Physicians like Grotjahn recommended the diaphragm as a female contraceptive, the condom as a male preventive method if contraception was necessary for health reasons, see Grotjahn, *Geburtenrückgang*, p. 88.

77 See Grotjahn, *Geburtenrückgang*, p. 94; HSA Düsseldorf, Reg. Dü, 43053, advertisement, March 1920.

78 Most German universities only admitted female students after 1908; as a result there were only 82 women doctors by 1909, see *Die Ärztin*, 7 (1931), p. 70. For evidence that midwives inserted diaphragms see, for example, SA Köln, Abt. 424, Nr. 502, report by health commission, 5 July 1912, specifically a statement by a midwife that physicians sent women to them for this purpose, and that 'those midwives who refuse to help with contraceptives have very few patients'.

79 See SA Köln, Abt. 424, no. 502, Bl. 202, circular letter by Regierungspräsident to all Landräte and police chiefs, 21 January 1916, which called for tighter surveillance of the sale of health manuals with birth control and abortion information; ZSA Potsdam, R.Min.d.I, 9346 Saxon memorandum on population policy which singled out books on nature therapy for suppression because they contained contraceptive instructions; see also ZSA Merseburg, Min.f.H.u.G., no. 65, I, Bl. 125 which mentioned such obscure titles as *The new cure* by Platen or *New nature therapy* by Bilz. These were apparently selling in millions and regarded as dangerous because of their section on 'prevention of offspring'. For evidence that authorities sought to enforce the obscenity law against birth control pamphlets see ZSA Potsdam, R.Min.d.I., 9346, Bl. 286.

80 ZSA Potsdam, R.Min.d.I., 9351, expert opinion by Prussian Medical Advisory committee, 27 October 1923.

81 BA Koblenz, R 86, 2373, vol. 12, Dr med Hanssen (paediatrician in Kiel), 'Die Abnahme der Geburtenzahlen in den verschiedenen Bevölkerungsklassen', *Archiv für soziale Hygiene*, 7, 4 (1912), p. 393. He found syringes amongst many of his working-class patients who bought them from a hawker dressed in women's clothes. For evidence of the popularity of syringes: ZSA Potsdam, R.Min.d.I., 9344, Bl. 76v, petitions to Prussian Diet, 1916, Vereinigung für Familienwohl and HSA Düsseldorf, Reg. Dü., 43053, Bl. 486, letter by Medical Officer of Health, Bornträger, to Chief Public Prosecutor Düsseldorf, 3 January 1916. For evidence of police raids on chemists displaying syringes see SA Köln, Abt. 424, no. 502, in 1912 several chemists were fined 120 marks; also Bl. 186 decree by Oberpräsident 25 March 1914. For attempts to ban *Mutterrohre* see BA Koblenz, R 86, 2379, 1, Proceedings of the Prussian Diet, 1 March 1918, p. 7976.

82 For example by Max Hirsch, *Fruchtabreibung und Präventivverkehr im Zusammenhang mit dem Geburtenrückgang*, Würzburg, 1914.

83 According to the criminal law attempted abortion was an offence even if it was carried out with unsuitable means and the woman was not pregnant; for examples of women prosecuted who were not pregnant at the time of their attempted abortion, see Landesarchiv Berlin (LA Berlin), Rep. 58, no. 2138.

84 Such beliefs were also held by women in Basle at that time, see Annamarie Ryter, 'Abtreibung in Basel zu Beginn des Jahrhunderts' in *Die ungeschriebene Geschichte*, Dokumentation 5. Historikerinnentreffen, Vienna, 1984, pp. 289–97.

85 L. Lewin, *Die Fruchtabtreibung durch Gifte und andere Mittel. Ein Handbuch für Ärzte und Juristen*, Berlin, 1922, mentions a large number of different herbal

remedies and other methods traditionally used to induce abortions. For England see Barbara Brookes, 'The illegal operation: abortion, 1919–39' in *The sexual dynamics of history*, London, 1983.

86 HSA Düsseldorf, Reg. Dü, 38892, 1st public prosecutor Düsseldorf, 10 December 1914, prosecution against Frau K., Frau T., and Frau E.

87 ZSA Potsdam, R.Min.d.I, 9345; BA Koblenz, R 86, 2379, Bd. 1, various newspaper cuttings reporting case; letter exchange between Reich Minister of the Interior and president of the Reich Health office, November 1917.

88 Karl Freudenberg, 'Berechnungen zur Abtreibungsstatistik', *Zeitschrift für Hygiene und Infektionskrankheiten*, 104 (1925), 529–50; Max Hirsch, 'Zur Statistik des Aborts', *Zentralblatt für Gynäkologie*, part I, no. 3, part II, no. 43, 1918; E. Roesle, 'Die Magdeburger Fehlgeburtenstatistik', *Archiv für soziale Hygiene und Demographie*, 1, 3 (1925/6), 26–195.

89 Knodel, *The decline of fertility*, pp. 3, 4.

90 *Ibid.*, p. 52. See also Jill Stephenson, *Women in Nazi society*, London, 1975, pp. 50–1 and her ' "Reichsbund der Kinderreichen": the League of Large Families in the population policy of Nazi Germany', *European Studies Review*, 9 (1979), 351–75, esp. p. 369: '. . . the revival achieved in the German birthrate in the 1930s under Nazi rule was fully compatible with fluctuations in the rate after the Great War and also in the 1950s and 1960s, and can therefore not be considered a reversal of the long-term decline in German fertility from the 1870s'.

91 Attributed to Alfred Blaschko, quoted in Magnus Hirschfeld, *Geschlechtskunde*, vol. II, Stuttgart, 1928, p. 428.

92 GSA Dahlem, Rep. 84a, 8232, Bl. 89, Reich criminal statistics, prosecutions for abortion according to clause 218 prescribing penal servitude for up to five years for any woman who underwent an abortion and for any person helping to procure the abortion. In 1913 1,809 persons (women and their accomplices) were tried, 1,467 convicted of whom 570 were sentenced to between three and twelve months imprisonment, 769 to under three months imprisonment, but 83 to over one year's imprisonment and 45 to penal servitude for an unspecified length. Criminal statistics do not differentiate between women and their accomplices.

93 I am indebted for this idea to Anneliese Bergmann, 'Von der "unbefleckten Empfängnis" ', p. 146, who adapted the phrase originally taken from Christine Woesler de Panafieu, 'Das Konzept von Weiblichkeit als Natur- und Machinenkörper' in Barbara Schaeffer-Hegel and Brigitte Wartmann (eds.), *Mythos Frau-Projektionen und Inszenierungen im Patriarchat*, Berlin, 1984, pp. 244–66.

94 See Gisela Bock, *Zwangssterilisation im Nationalsozialismus. Studien zur Rassenpolitik und Frauenpolitik*, Opladen, 1986 and her 'Racism and sexism in Nazi Germany: motherhood, compulsory sterilization, and the state', *Signs*, 8 (1983), 400–21. The Nazi slogan is quoted in Leila Rupp, 'Mothers of the *Volk*: The image of women in Nazi ideology', *Signs*, 3 (1977), 362–79.

15

The medical profession, social hygiene and the birth rate in Germany, 1914–18

Paul Weindling

During the First World War the welfare of mothers and children, and the control of chronic diseases became national priorities. Officials responded to long-term processes of social and demographic change, by advocating new objectives in wartime social policy. The war marked a turning-point, because public health officials stressed that chronic diseases like tuberculosis and VD posed greater social problems than acute infectious diseases. Even more threatening than this 'epidemiological transition' was the 'demographic transition'. There was widespread concern over the decline in the hitherto high birth rate, and over high rates of infant mortality. Pre-war efforts to improve infant care had not compensated for the decline in the birth rate. During the war, national mortality rates exceeded the birth rate. This brought about a crisis in public health: civilian health and the birth rate became issues of national survival.[1]

Underlying these perceptions of demographic and health conditions were changes in the relations between the state and the medical profession. Concern with welfare resulted in a restructuring of the public health administration and in closer relations between the state and medical profession. Theories of 'social hygiene' redefined the authority of the state and medical profession over family welfare. Social hygiene focused on fertility, child health and chronic diseases. Housing, work, nutrition and sexuality were the objects of medical surveys and public health regulations. The medical profession extended its powers and professional opportunities, and the state benefited by the reduction of controversial social issues to the value-neutral terms of medical science.

Medicalisation and militarisation, 1900–14

Intervention in family health violated the official premise that welfare was not the responsibility of the state. The Prussian Ministry of Justice defended the legislation that medicine was a free trade, and that the practitioner and therapy were matters of individual choice. Not until the Weimar constitution was the state obliged to uphold the health of the family. Yet in the decade before 1914, state medical authorities attempted to improve family health. Reforming officials looked to the public for support, and state-approved medical and welfare organisations were launched. The medical profession was responsive, at a time when it was discarding an individualistic and liberal concept of professional freedoms. The profession claimed the status of a corporation or *Stand* and argued that it should be granted a state monopoly over medicine, so as to curb the competition of nature therapists and limit the powers of the sick funds.

Conflicts arose between the Prussian Ministries of Finance and Justice (defending health as the responsibility of the individual) on the one side, and the medical administration on the other. Social hygiene was supported by a broad political spectrum of social reformers, and by medical and military interests. The conservative view was that the state ought, at most, to educate citizens about health risks, and that all humanitarian issues, including the health of the family, were matters for private philanthropy. But some leading officials and politicians like Althoff, Berlepsch, Bethmann Hollweg, and Posadowsky-Wehner considered that an improvement in public health was a national priority. They aimed to counter socialist accusations that poverty bred disease. The state would attempt the administrative centralisation of welfare in Kreisfürsorgeämter, or district health centres, under state medical officers. It was a policy that aimed to defeat the socialist demand for Stadtgesundheitsämter, or municipal health centres, and to give priority to rural areas whence the nation's population resources were to be replenished.

The Prussian Medical Department was reorganised. Medically qualified administrators were appointed. This accounted for differences in outlook from that of the legally trained officials. In 1899 the first full-time state medical officers were appointed in Prussia. When the Department was transferred to the Ministry of the Interior in 1911, the medical profession welcomed a newly appointed, medically qualified director, Martin Kirchner. Other medical officials included Eduard Dietrich, responsible for infant health, and Otto Krohne, who oversaw midwifery. They directed the attention of the Minister of the Interior to the declining birth rate. That Dietrich, Kirchner and Krohne participated in a multitude of public health and medical organisations meant that they acted as mediators between the medical profession and the state. Policy-making committees like the Scientific Committee for Medical Affairs ensured consensus between the profession and the state over health and population policies.[2]

Intervention in family health involved reform of the state's medical auxiliaries of medical officers and midwives. Indirect methods were to co-ordinate the resources of sick funds, municipalities, doctors and welfare organisations. Family health was subjected to new national organisations that were technically independent of the state, but worked to reinforce the Imperial social order. The health campaigns beginning in the 1890s can be compared to the rise of the Navy League and other nationalist associations. The middle class were offered new outlets for voluntary welfare work that would bring prestigious contacts with officials, aristocrats and military dignitaries, and the rewards of official honours. District officials were to 'voluntarily' set up and co-ordinate welfare organisations. In TB dispensaries, it was expected that 'the sisters should do the visiting, the doctors the examining, and the local official, with the mayor's help, should do the organising'.[3] It was hoped that a fitter population would result for the eventuality of war.

Such fusion of social interests in welfare was a type of medical *Sammlungspolitik* or the politics of national integration. It was supported by the activities of Friedrich Althoff, *Ministerialdirektor* (Chief Secretary of the Education Ministry) where the Prussian Medical Department was located until 1911. He took a leading role in promoting the Anti-TB League and in organising a network of dispensaries and outpatient clinics throughout the metropolis for tuberculosis, mother and child health, and later, for cancer and alcoholism. The dispensaries were controlled by a committee of leading medical specialists, state officials and other dignitaries.[4] It was a model organisation, stretching down to local sub-committees, and imitated throughout Germany. In 1899 the first TB dispensary opened, and by 1910 there were 320. In 1905 the first infant care dispensary opened, and by 1915 there were 1,000. The war saw the rapid implementation of VD clinics.

The dispensaries were staffed by the Vaterländische Frauenvereine (Patriotic Women's Association), a branch of the Red Cross. The Empress was patron and a banker, Fritz Behring, the leading organiser of this patriotic women's league. Its most rapid expansion coincided with the founding of dispensaries, and by 1915 it had 700,000 members in 2,019 branches. In 1899 the Red Cross established a section for family welfare, which ran many children's homes, holiday colonies and sanatoria. Officials, like Eduard Dietrich of the Prussian Medical Department, supervised these activities. The patriotic ideology of the German Red Cross meant that in the years prior to the war, welfare activities amounted to a peace-time mobilisation for health care, which could be readily adapted to the needs of a society at war. In 1914 the appointment of the Imperial Commissioner and Military Inspector of Voluntary Health Care completed official control over a massive and diverse system of welfare.[5]

Bethmann Hollweg's pre-war administrative experience led him to see welfare organisations as supplementing the state, and he took a special interest in infant welfare. At a 1906 conference on welfare, he praised charities' 'freie Tätigkeit im Behördeorganismus' (free activity in the official body).[6] Welfare organisations flourished because they could tap public support beyond the normal capacity of the state, and dislodge interests within the state opposed to the extension of health benefits.[7] National priorities in the infant welfare campaign were shown by the founding of the Kaiserin Auguste Viktoria-Haus between 1905 and 1909 as a central institution for research and education in infant care. Its patrons included the Empress, her advisor Carl von Behr-Pinnow, Althoff, Bethmann Hollweg, and leading paediatricians.[8] Preservation of infant lives was to maintain Germany as a world power. It was a point made by a conference on the birth rate organised by the Haus in September 1913. Paediatricians became concerned with the 'natural number' of children in a family, and with higher mortality resulting from poor feeding and 'illegitimacy'.[9]

Medical specialists were led towards the problem of the declining birth rate by recognising that the strengthening of the family had preventive medical value. Early marriage was prescribed as a preventive remedy against venereal disease and alcoholism.[10] Alcoholism was denounced as impeding breast-feeding, and as a cause of pathological behaviour that might end in venereal disease or in crime. Professional interests motivated doctors' campaigns: for it was argued that unlicensed practitioners were a threat to family health, as well as ineffective in treating venereal disease, and that they also undertook abortions.

The prospect of war heightened concern with the physical condition of the population. The army favoured direct state intervention to promote the health of mothers and children. In 1914 the army demanded state district health centres on social hygienic principles. The War and Education Ministries had a long-standing interest in school health services, because of their prime military importance. By 1913 there were 2,000 school doctors in Prussia.[11] In January 1914 the military medical authorities issued a memorandum on school health that was the basis for wartime planning for social hygiene. It recommended early diagnosis and regular medical examinations, and hoped that the Jungdeutschlandbund would organise these in rural areas. Ultimately, the army hoped for an integrated system of dispensaries and school health services, co-ordinated by district health centres. These would provide much needed facilities in rural areas where voluntary resources were not available.

War fever infected health officials. Krohne, who conducted the Prussian survey on the declining birth rate, addressed a student meeting on 29 January 1914. He elaborated a programme of social hygiene to raise the birth rate. He believed that an inevitable struggle lay ahead, when new territory for settlements would be gained. It would mark a turning-point in the trend in the birth rate, by engendering the national spirit that was so lacking in the 'two-child system'. The survey on the birth rate had alerted doctors to an 'epidemic' of criminal abortions. Krohne concluded from the reports of medical officials, doctors' associations, provincial medical colleges, and from gynaecological societies that infertility was not caused by racial degeneration. The causes were complex owing to regional differentials in fertility. Overall he discerned a voluntary limitation of numbers of children. For this moral failing, the selfless nationalism of war was to be a cure.[12]

1914–18. Centralisation and co-ordination

During the war the informal state control over welfare was increasingly centralised. The hitherto covert and fragmented population policy, supported by health officials and public health reform associations, became explicit. Social hygiene became a means of unifying the diverse initiatives of national associations, municipalities and sick funds, and ensuring the co-operation of the medical profession. Although medical officials congratulated themselves that the infant mortality rate fell, at least initially, there was an alarming increase in adult mortality. Food shortages resulted in severe ill health. Among the worst hit group were school children. Here low mortality concealed high morbidity. That the birth rate continued to fall, and could no longer be offset by increased life expectancy, meant that policies to improve family health became urgent. The war meant that health officials hoped that opposition within other ministries to family-oriented policies could now be overcome, and that the strikes and boycotts of militant doctors against the sickness funds would cease in a new conciliatory spirit of the *Burgfrieden*, or the wartime political truce.

An important element of the patriotic 'ideals of 1914' was a healthier society.[13] The expectation was not of a Social Darwinist survival of the fittest, but of a primarily moral and nationalist regeneration of the family. The materialist culture of France and Britain was synonymous with the worst features of industrial and urban Germany. France was condemned as the embodiment of the two-child system, and as ravaged by alcoholism, nervous diseases and by the *morbus gallicus* on a scale far worse than Germany. War was an opportunity for the nation to purge itself of the materialism that brought on these diseases. The war could provide an antidote to the threat of Germans being demographically swamped by the larger

Slav families in the East, with new territories for the settlement of large German families.

Measures imposed during mobilisation expressed this medical optimism. Consumption of alcohol and tobacco was placed under strict control, as threatening military efficiency.[14] Active military service was glorified as healthier than urban life. The fresh air and exercise of the front meant that it could be a vast open-air sanatorium. Another indicator of health was the fall in the number of mental patients, and a decrease in suicides.[15] Even food shortages were regarded as beneficial, as declining rates of diabetes, obesity and jaundice were recorded.[16]

The medical profession enthusiastically mobilised. About 24,000 out of 33,000 male doctors served. Leading university professors, who were often reserve officers, set an example by quickly reporting for duty. Months and years elapsed before the army realised that gynaecologists and obstetricians were more useful in a university clinic than at the front.[17] Experts in social hygiene signed manifestos on German war aims. Pan-Germanist annexation of territories was supported by the Munich professor of hygiene Max von Gruber, by the paediatrician Arthur Schlossmann, by the venereologist Adolf Neisser, and by the professor of hygiene Rudolf Abel, who until 1915 was a medical official.[18]

The first priorities were medical examination of recruits, the organisation of field hospitals, and the prevention of epidemics at the front. Hygienic regulations were to be strictly observed as in the case of the provision of latrines. Confidence was unflinching in the recent German bacteriological triumphs over epidemic diseases. Typhus was controlled by de-lousing. Dysentery and typhoid that could be spread by inadequate sanitation were kept in check. Cholera – spilling over from Russia – was contained. Advances in antiseptics meant that a relatively low rate of 3 per cent mortality occurred among the 10 million field hospital patients. The warning of medical demographers that epidemics resulting from wars could cause greater loss of life than military action was well-heeded.[19]

As the war proceeded, greater concern was aroused by the health of soldiers' families. State medical authorities defended the health of families with methods of social hygiene like dispensaries, health propaganda, and family income supplements. Military medical authorities communicated their concerns to the High Command and Prussian War Ministry. Venereal disease had the highest incidence of all infections that afflicted the army. Medical officials sought to convince the Staatsministerium (Ministry of State) of the need for a population policy. The army pressed for action from civilian authorities with regard to maternity allowances for soldiers' wives, the control of venereal disease, and improving school medical services. By 1916 the army supported the demand for a comprehensive population policy.[20] What follows here is an account of how family allowances, VD prevention, measures to improve midwifery and school health were part of a strategy for a comprehensive social welfare and population policy.

Campaigners for financial subsidies for families won a swift victory in December 1914 with maternity benefits being granted to soldiers' wives. Whereas in the Reichsversicherungsordnung (Imperial Insurance regulations) of 1911 maternity benefits were discretionary, mandatory maternity benefits marked a stage in the advance to family insurance for a worker's dependants. The benefits were extended during the war to single-parent families.[21] It was a move towards the realisation of the demands of the Bund für Mutterschutz (League for the Protection of Motherhood) for improving the conditions of the 'illegitimate', of progressive sick funds which were keen to promote preventive medicine, of socialists and of Naumann's social liberalism. The state insurance offices, which had contributed towards the costs of dispensaries, were sympathetic to sick funds providing additional family benefits despite falling insurance contributions during the war.[22] But the Prussian Finance Ministry resisted plans for altering taxation to benefit large families, and so checked the advance of social hygiene into the realm of state finance.

Military pressure was effective on public health issues like venereal disease prevention. The state had first discussed clinics at the Reich Health Council in 1908. Only in 1911 did venereal disease become a statutory obligation of sick funds. In January 1914 the first advisory clinic financed by a Landesversicherungsamt (Provincial Insurance Office) was opened in Hamburg. During the War a national system of VD clinics was established to provide free consultation on the model of TB dispensaries. Treatment by doctors in a private practice was to be paid for by an insurance office.[23] The Governor General of the occupied territories in Belgium, von Bissing, brought it to the attention of the Reich Insurance Office that the incidence of venereal disease was far higher in troops not at the front.[24] On 14 June 1915 the Prussian War Ministry decreed that all leaving the army were to have a health examination; soldiers with venereal disease were to be placed under the supervision of a welfare centre. The Chancellor, Bethmann Hollweg, showed that more than just military efficiency was at stake, when in March 1915 he called for vigorous state intervention to defend the health and numbers of future generations.[25]

In December 1915 conferences on venereal disease prevention were held by the authorities in Belgium and by the Prussian Ministry of the Interior. Experts in social hygiene like Blaschko and Neisser were summoned to both conferences. That Blaschko was Secretary and Neisser President of the Anti-VD Society exemplify how the policies of a reforming pressure group could achieve considerable influence. Social hygienists impressed on the military that venereal disease accounted for a loss of 60 births per 100 marriages, and 100,000 babies each year had hereditary syphilis.[26] Venereologists successfully defended the value of condoms as prophylactics against venereal disease. The medical advisors demanded that venereal disease control be a medical rather than primarily a police responsibility, and that there should be compulsory medical treatment of soldiers and prostitutes. Doctors' demands were realised in the decree of 11 December 1918, which was regarded as a stage towards achieving a monopoly of treatment for venereal disease.[27] The medical profession's powers represented a victory over nature therapists as well as eroding the voluntaristic principles of health care that had prevailed in Imperial Germany. The state and army distributed the propaganda of the Anti-VD Society. Venereal disease prevention exemplifies the state centralisation of hygienic measures that occurred during the war.[28]

Concern to prevent degeneration of the family motivated state intervention in infant and child health. By 1916 it was calculated that Germany had 'lost' 680,000 births in the course of the war on the basis of the pre-war high, albeit falling, birth rate. By 1917 the Prussian Statistical Office calculated that Germany had lost one and a half million births. It feared that by 1936 only 235,000 infants would survive the first year of life in comparison to 620,000 in 1914.[29] Lowering the infant mortality rate was to compensate for the decline in births. Remedies were the improvement of midwifery, and infant feeding practices, and the training of children's nurses. The state regarded midwifery reform as the best means of raising standards of infant care. Plans for reform, which had foundered because of opposition from the Finance Ministry in 1902 and 1908, re-surfaced. Doctors frequently criticised midwives for their ignorance, and accused them of performing criminal abortions.[30]

The remedy suggested by the Association of German Midwives was to raise their professional status by improved training, higher income, recognition as state officials rather than as *nicht beamtete Medizinalpersonen* (non-official paramedical personnel), and legislating for their compulsory attendance at all births. Midwives interpreted lack of state support for the final demand as implying a preference for doctors to attend births especially in prosperous families.[31] Otherwise medical officials supported their demands, but planned to restrict where midwives could practise. Increased supervision by police and medical officers would ensure that midwives were of good character and prevent illegal abortions.[32] An even distribution of midwives would remedy the considerable regional variations in infant mortality.[33]

In order to improve hospital clinics, the state carried out surveys of obstetric facilities in 1914, 1915 and 1918. Despite recognition of a growing public preference for hospital births, the Prussian Ministry of the Interior favoured home births supervised by a midwife as preferable to district maternity hospitals.[34] At the Inter-ministerial Committee on the Birth Rate in February 1916, the Finance Ministry opposed midwifery reform. But the Agriculture Ministry championed the cause of midwifery on the grounds that it would improve rural health. In July 1916 a survey of midwifery was conducted so as to see whether a district midwife or other types of financial subsidies were necessary.[35] Grants were made to each province to educate midwives so that they could train mothers in methods of infant care. Midwives were to be alerted as to their patriotic responsibilities in working to offset the declining birth rate, and about the nation's economic and military plight in the absence of healthier babies.[36] The Association of German Midwives in 1917 requested state subsidies for courses on social science and hygiene, so that midwives could contribute to the new population policy.[37] Medical officials felt that midwives could reduce numbers of still births and a maternity mortality rate which produced 65,000 deaths a year.[38] But when a law for the reform of midwifery was drawn up in 1917, it encountered the same opposition from the Ministry of Finance as in 1908. The Ministry of the Interior was forced to continue with its policies of re-educating midwives and increasing supervision by medical officers.[39]

The centralisation of resources to combat infant mortality found expression in the increasing state reliance on the Kaiserin Auguste Viktoria-Haus. It exerted influence through a widespread network of infant care clinics, milk depots and local associations for maternal welfare.[40] Behr-Pinnow continued to mediate between the Emperor and Empress, ministerial officials and paediatricians. He condemned ignorant mothers as responsible for 200,000 deaths a year. He recommended that all districts should have an integrated system of clinics under the control of a medical officer and that the state should educate girls for motherhood.[41] Health officials took up his demand that all districts with over 30,000 inhabitants should have infant care and maternal advice clinics. As in other areas of social hygiene, which it was proposed to administer or directly subsidise by the state, the Finance Ministry objected: it considered infant health a charitable issue which was beyond the needs of a war economy and thus beyond the competence of the state. In the end, the most that was achieved was an increase in subsidies to infant welfare organisations.[42]

The Kaiserin Auguste Viktoria-Haus contributed to the transition from voluntary work to a new professional ethos. It raised standards in training infant nurses by instigating a professional exam in May 1917.[43] The Haus prepared the official textbook based on the principles of social hygiene, emphasising the responsibility of nurses to supervise not only a child's physical condition, but also its character and sexuality.[44] Officials regarded child nursing as a suitable occupation for women from 'better families' to develop their experience in war nursing as a career.[45] The Bund deutscher Frauenvereine (Federation of German Women's Associations) protested on 19 August 1917 that the new state regulations confused domestic infant care, public service, and the nursing of sick children. Women doctors were excluded from the examining commission as they were from most doctors' war services. The criticisms revealed the new hierarchy of control envisaged with medical officers in charge of nurses recruited from the ranks of the Vaterländische Frauenvereine.[46] Marie Baum of the Bund Deutscher Frauenvereine objected that the motive for combining nursing care of sick and healthy children in the domestic and public spheres was to incorporate these functions in the district welfare centres that were the state's main aim. These would undermine the independence of voluntary organisations. At the Inter-ministerial Committee on the Birth Rate, Anna von Gierke emphasised the need to give women social workers administrative training so that they could have the status of officials rather than remain ancillaries.[47]

The war ushered in a more compassionate attitude to the problems of single mothers. When the Kaiser recognised the urgent need for a population policy on 14 October 1916, he stressed that measures should be devised to improve the chances of survival of the 'illegitimate'. It was recommended that medical officers supervise and instruct foster parents in methods of infant care.[48] Health officials relaxed their animosity against artificial feeding and became concerned with the unhygienic design of babies' bottles and with the quality of the milk supply.[49]

School health was a major component of population policy. Children were among the worst-off social groups. The extension of medical supervision of school children became urgent. Malnutrition resulted in an increase of rickets, stomach and intestinal disorders, and hunger oedema.[50] Medical officers were censured for having undertaken surveys of the extent of hunger among children because socialists had produced devastating criticisms of health and nutritional conditions by using sick fund and factory inspectorate statistics.[51] The state administration emphasised the need for central controls over the food supply. Health officials and physiologists like Max Rubner took an optimistic view that the nation could withstand short-term food shortages, despite the rise in mortality from infectious diseases. Tuberculosis rose to a level reached 25 years previously.[52]

As the military situation worsened, officials urged implementation of population policies. The diverse areas of reform like venereal disease control and infant health measures required a co-ordinated strategy of social reform, accompanied by an extension of the responsibilities of doctors and public health officials. The tenor of the debate increased in nationalistic fervour with the glorification of Germanic family life. Such a heightening of phraseology can be seen in the reports on the birth rate drafted by the Prussian Medical Department in 1912, 1915 and 1917. They were reinforced by a military report in 1918, advising that ethical, material and '*völkisch*' reserves be mobilised for a comprehensive population policy. The Chief of Staff in 1918 made urgent recommendations regarding infant health, and suggested that dermatology and paediatrics should be incorporated into medical education.[53] It marked the high point of official support for a population policy based on social hygiene.

The Inter-ministerial Committee on the Birth Rate held 15 sessions between 13 October 1915 and 3 February 1917. Because rural health (the topic of the first session) was a major priority, the support from other ministries increased. By contrast, in 1912 the Prussian Ministers for Finance and Trade had objected that the state survey on the birth rate implied criticisms of government neglect of urban living conditions. Rural areas had high infant and adult mortality rates (higher than in many cities). This differential provided the Prussian Medical Department with a reason for its programme of state centralisation, which would be consistent with the wishes of powerful landed interests. The number of full-time medical officers was to be increased, as 86 per cent of the existing 520 officers were part-time appointments. Kreisfürsorgeämter were already established in Cologne, Düsseldorf and Potsdam, and it was hoped that these could provide the basis of a social hygienic solution to the declining birth rate. It was important that such officers should come under the auspices of the central government rather than those of the municipalities. Kirchner disliked the municipal health departments (as much as socialists favoured these), although certain state medical officers had dual appointments with municipalities.[54]

Despite the support of the Kaiser and Staatsministerium, the principal instrument of a successful population policy, that of subsidies for large families, was successfully blocked by the Finance Ministry. On the Committee were several economists invited by the Medical Department. Their expertise was to be used on a sub-committee for taxation reforms giving fiscal benefits for the 'child rich'. Each time such proposals were raised, they were quashed by the Finance Ministry, which insisted on its exclusive prerogative over fiscal matters. The 1917 report on the birth rate was unable to discuss taxation reform other than in the most general terms. The Ministry of Justice had consistent reservations over any extension of doctors' and midwives' responsibilities. Despite the policy-making discussions, the state was slow to implement legislation. The medical authorities remained dependent on the voluntary co-operation of doctors, insurance and welfare organisations. Their co-operation could only be maintained under war conditions of intense nationalism. But the disastrous wartime food shortages, rising adult mortality, and the inability of state officials to agree on co-ordinated measures defeated the population policy.

Organicist ideology and social hygiene

The closer links between the medical profession and the state were expressed by a shared organicist ideology. It showed how social hygiene and nationalism had become intertwined. Medical and demographic conditions were regarded as barometers of patriotism. Statistics and commentaries on health conditions were more ideological constructs than reflections of actual conditions. By focusing attention onto the declining birth rate, state medical authorities shifted debate away from the extent that social conditions caused ill health. Germany's enemies were blamed for social deprivation. Dietary deficiencies could be attributed to the enemy blockade. 'Child rich' families were by definition healthy families. These were threatened by 'epidemics' of abortions, harmful contraceptives and venereal disease. Official statistics of these immeasurable phenomena revealed the ideological commitments of their compilers. Organicist theories of the state were popularised. The state was conceptualised as an organism, the family as an elemental cell, and the decreasing family size as cancer or cellular degeneration. This implied that the professional expert and state medical officer had a patriotic duty to intervene over issues of family health. The hostility to small families indicates a new consensus on pronatalism, which was shared by the various family welfare organisations and public health officials. The war gave rise to a wholistic ideology that brought about state centralisation of the Red Cross, medical and welfare organisations, and an increased professionalism.[55]

Theories of social hygiene were based on eclectic combinations of medical, biological, social and ethical theories. The tone was set by the Christian socialism of Friedrich Naumann. He had long been urging welfare measures as necessary to strengthen military prowess. He considered that the birth rate was an index of national vitality (*Lebensbejahung des Volkes*). He inspired Alfons Fischer to organise a Propagandagesellschaft für Mutterschafts-versicherung (Propaganda Association for Maternity Insurance) in 1907 and the Badische Gesellschaft für soziale Hygiene (Baden Society for Social Hygiene) in 1916. The paediatrician, Arthur Schlossmann, greatly admired Naumann, and pioneered the training of children's nurses and benefits for 'child rich' families in Düsseldorf. Alfred Grotjahn was influenced by Naumann with regard to maternal insurance, but rejected Naumann's Christian moralising. Otto Krohne, the official organising population policy, approved of Naumann's views on the birth rate and on the responsibility of civil servants to have more children.[56]

Naumann's moral priorities influenced such officials. They were unsympathetic to attributing the decline in births to increasing poverty, apart from recognising the economic difficulties of the *Mittelstand* (middle class). Instead, a diagnosis was made in moral terms: that of *Überkultur* (excessive civilisation), of egoism and personal indulgence, of materialist socialism, and disregard for the higher interests of the nation. A moral diagnosis of the nation's ills underlay organicist analogies in war propaganda. The rationalism of the 'two-child system' was identified as an enemy characteristic. The antidote was to strengthen the woman's *Wille zum Kind* (maternal instinct). Naumann took an active interest in population policy, and addressed the opening meeting of the Society for Population Policy in 1915.

Naumann's emphasis on social integration was used to counter theories based on conflict, whether in the form of the class struggle or the Darwinian survival of the fittest. This can be seen in the views of leading university professors, who were self-elected spokesmen for the medical profession. They condemned eugenics and Social Darwinism. Ernst Bumm, the Berlin professor of gynaecology, criticised eugenic theories in his speech as Rector in 1916. The professor of anatomy, Oscar Hertwig, attacked the biological premises of the eugenicists but favoured an ethical and Christian view of the social organism in terms reminiscent of Naumann's belief in the need to fuse Darwin with Rousseau. The public debate on eugenics occurred simultaneously with a debate on eugenics within the state. The official memorandum on the birth rate drafted by Krohne rejected the theory that smaller families would improve the race. If the eugenic theory was correct, that one in six of the population was of a higher quality, then large numbers of children were necessary.[57] Naumann preached that civil servants should have larger families. Such remedies for the declining birth rate were intended to strengthen the existing social structure.

Racial hygiene and social hygiene overlapped with their common focus on reproduction. But only those eugenic solutions conforming to the moral precepts of Naumann's Christian nationalism were officially acceptable. The eugenicists were divided by bitter disagreements over issues like the admissibility of Aryan racial categories, and the value of abortion and sterilisation on racial hygienic grounds. Proposals like marriage certificates indicating whether the prospective partners suffered from venereal disease provoked disagreement over their effectiveness. State advisers like Blaschko and Behr-Pinnow, with affiliations to eugenic organisations, were critical of negative eugenics. Advocates of negative eugenics like Alfred Ploetz and Wilhelm Schallmayer were decisively rejected by medical officials like Dietrich, Kirchner and Krohne. The Munich Racial Hygiene Society developed connections with the Pan-German League. They demanded new territories for re-settlement of families. This was a further reason for official distrust, as the bellicose League clashed with government policy. The nationalist publisher, Julius Lehmann, was censured for works on venereal disease and attacks on Bethmann Hollweg.[58]

The defeat of negative eugenics occurred over official discussions of induced abortion and of marriage certificates. Leading gynaecologists and state officials allied against eugenics. In April 1914 the Prussian Scientific Committee for Medical Affairs demanded a tightening of controls on induced abortion, and in May 1917 the Ministry of Justice reiterated that induced abortion on racial or social grounds was illegal. That doctors could undertake abortions when there was a 'severe threat' to the health of the mother, was a vestige of state reliance on professional autonomy. The laxity with which a 'severe threat' could be interpreted came to be regarded as a loophole in the law. Medical officials hoped to secure registration of all abortions and a minimum of two doctors having to give permission. Prosecutions, as of the Jena professor of gynaecology, Max Henkel, showed how efforts were made to impose more stringent standards.[59] Sterilisation on eugenic or social grounds was also condemned. Serious consideration was given to renewed demands for marriage certificates as a means of preventing hereditary diseases. Certificates were a long-standing demand of the Bund für Mutterschutz and of eugenicists. Blaschko had shown that most cases of venereal disease among the married had been previously contracted. His finding influenced the Berlin Racial Hygiene Society to petition for marriage certificates. But Blaschko regarded even the lack of symptoms of infection as an unreliable indicator of venereal disease. Diagnostic difficulties persuaded the Reich Health Office to reject the proposal in December 1917. It preferred increased health education, and special advisory clinics.[60]

The emphasis on pronatalism rather than eugenics, meant that the state favoured associations for family welfare. Before the war, there were moved to subsidise large families like Polligkeit's Zentrale für kinderreiche Familien (Central Office for 'Child-rich' Families). During the war the numbers of such societies increased, and these coalesced after the war into the powerful Reichsbund für kinderreiche Familien (Reich League for 'Child-rich' Families). The state supported societies with a local basis. The Düsseldorf medical officer, Julius Bornträger, encouraged the formation of the Vereinigung für Familienwohl (Association for Family Welfare), which subsidised large families of more than seven children. After a number of towns had followed this example, the Vereinigung kinderreicher Familien und Witwen (Association for the Support of Large Families and Widows) was established in the Rhineland. Other regions followed this pattern.

National associations were inherently less efficient than local organisations in distributing welfare. Coinciding with the Inter-ministerial Committee on the Birth Rate, a Society for Population Policy was called into being on 19 October 1915. The charity organisation agency, the Zentral-stelle für Volkswohlfahrt, also held a major pronatalist conference on 'Die Mehrung und Hebung der Volkskraft' (the maintenance and growth of population) on 26–8 October. There was official dissatisfaction at these initiatives. The Zentralstelle placed too great an emphasis on eugenics, as its policies were influenced by two leading eugenicists, Ignaz Kaup and Max Christian. Officials distrusted the Society for Population Policy, although it attracted prominent politicians to its meetings. Its President was the economist Julius Wolf, who analysed the declining birth rate in terms of increasing rationalisation of personal values, and the Secretary was the Berlin sexologist Albert Moll. They were unable to convince state officials that the Society merited support. Behr-Pinnow wrote to the Prussian Minister of the Interior denouncing the Society, as he felt it had made too many compromises with radical women's leaders like Käthe Schirmacher, favouring birth control. The medical officials, Krohne and Robert Roesle criticised Wolf as a dilettante and the Society as unproductive. A reversal occurred in February 1916 when the Berlin theologian, Reinhold Seeberg, was appointed Chairman. He campaigned for a moral approach to the population question such as was favoured both by the state and churches. The Society accordingly was awarded an official subsidy.[61]

Conferences were a means of co-ordinating voluntary and professional efforts. Representatives of doctors' associations became prominent in the organisations for population policy. Hugo Dippe of the Association to Defend the Economic Interests of the Medical Profession (Hartmannbund) organised the conference, *Hausarzt und Bevölkerungspolitik* (family doctors and population policy) in 1916. In Munich, medical societies favoured eugenic demands for marriage certificates and in 1917 promoted a Kom-mission zur Erhaltung und Mehrung der Volkskraft (Commission for the Maintenance and Growth of the Population). The Darmstadt conference, on the reconstruction of German family life after the war, was an important meeting of different organisations. In Dresden, the Hygiene Museum organised travelling exhibitions on child health. The nationalism of the medical profession served professional ends by establishing the need to extend infant and family health measures.[62]

The war's strengthening of the ideology of the *Volksgemeinschaft* (com-munity of the nation or people), meant increased professional and state power over the family. Doctors and midwives were allotted increased responsibilities by a state anxious to promote welfare measures as an anti-dote to political discontents. However, the ideology of the *Volksgemeinschaft* was transformed by defeat, revolution and the redefinition and restructur-ing of the state. That influential medical officials remained in office, and that family health was a prominent feature in Weimar social policy should not obscure the major changes in attitudes and in the political and professional interest groups that came to influence state medical policies. A shift occurred away from moral to racial precepts after 1918. In the shock of defeat and revolution, demographic and medical statistics could be taken as indicators that the German nation might no longer survive. The optimism of statisticians, who had predicted a baby boom after the war, turned to despair: in 1919 the Prussian Statistical Office prophesied the extermination of the race. Medical officials condemned the enemies' trade embargo and peace conditions as 'a war of extermination against the German race'. The feared racial extermination meant positive eugenics and racial biology became means of national salvation. The biological nationalism that had been decisively rejected during the war was to provide authoritative guidelines for social policies that were to save the nation from destruction.[63] A shift occurred from Naumann's Christian humanitarianism, suiting a voluntary system of welfare, to biological values, that expressed the new ethos of scientifically trained professionals.

Each phase of the Republic was accompanied by a strengthening of the eugenic lobby in the new welfare state. The Treaty of Versailles was regarded as a demographic disaster. For example, medical officials considered that the loss of dairy cattle and consequent loss of milk would result in an inevitable surge of infant mortality. When troops occupied the Rhineland, national and racial concerns underlay measures to protect infant and child health. Eugenicists supported vicious propaganda against the non-European French soldiers, as polluting the race with the half-caste *Rheinlandbastarde* and causing sterility among Germans by spreading venereal disease.[64] Prussian statisticians estimated 'losses in births' as a result of the war, and calculated that in 1914–19 the Reich had 'lost' four million babies, a quarter of these because of sterility arising from venereal disease. Each baby was priced with a capital value of 8,330 marks, and thus the loss to 'the human economy' of the nation was substantial. The revolutionary tumults were diagnosed as the work of 'psychopaths', and a network of clinics was set up to root out supposedly hereditary mental abnormalities. Experts in social hygiene like Grotjahn pressed for the institutionalisation of those unfit to reproduce, and estimated that a third of the population were degenerate. Such theories were introduced into the prescribed training courses for doctors, nurses and social workers,[65] and social hygiene became a central feature of policies for pronatalism and positive eugenics designed to promote family health. Policies were determined by medically trained administrators. Social hygiene went with a reorientation of interests within the state. A new technocracy was in power.

That state centralisation of welfare measures was planned before 1914 indicates the importance of the expectation of war. The war saw rapid planning for a population policy, made all the more urgent by rising morbidity and mortality. Deaths alarmingly outstripped births. The medical profession, midwives, nurses and social workers all gained considerable professional advantages. Wartime population policies provided the opportunity of co-ordinating and centralising health measures dealing with diverse social sectors: rural and urban, infants, school children and mothers. They could all be placed in a co-ordinated scheme that was to strengthen the Imperial social order by extending medical and welfare facilities.

That the wartime policy was only a partial success was due to the entrenched opposition of other Ministries. A diversity of interests and policies became increasingly apparent in the state. Ironically, a population policy that aimed to reinforce the existing social order could not remove other fundamental features of that order. Obstacles included both the right of self-determination in the choice of a medical practitioner and in matters concerning the family, such as marriage, and the independence of corporate bodies representing the interests of the medical profession and the health insurance officials. Well-defined administrative divisions obstructed state intervention in welfare, or prevented a Ministry from using a medical rationale to institute family allowances.

The clash of interests within the state was symptomatic of how social hygiene was part of a broader process of socio-political change. It pointed the way towards a redefinition of the state and a realignment of social interests. There was a new stress on the primacy of the family in social policy. That the medical profession achieved greater prominence was part of a realignment of class and power relations in Germany. Professional interests gained a new technocratic hold on government. Public health officials and the medical profession extended their authority over issues of welfare and family size. The fusion of professional, state and military interests supported a socialised programme for public health and for the extension of welfare benefits. The welfare state, conceived amidst the destruction of war, was to embark on ambitious policies of social reconstruction during the Weimar Republic.

Notes

1 On the medical profession in the 1914–18 war see, W. Hoffmann, *Die deutschen Ärzte im Weltkriege*, Berlin, 1940. W. His, *Die Front der Ärzte*, Bielefeld and Leipzig, 1931. M. Kirchner, *Ärztliche Kriegs- und Friedensgedanken*, Berlin, 1918. G. Jeschal, *Politik und Wissenschaft deutscher Ärzte im ersten Weltkrieg*, Pattensen, 1978. On health conditions see F. Bumm, *Deutschlands Gesundheitsverhältnisse unter d. Einfluss d. Weltkrieges*, Stuttgart, 1928. For the demo-

graphic context see J. Knodel, *The decline of fertility in Germany, 1871–1939*, Princeton, 1974. P. Marschalck, *Bevölkerungsgeschichte Deutschlands im 19. und 20. Jahrhundert*, Frankfurt am Main, 1984.

2 Zentrales Staatsarchiv Dienststelle Merseburg (hereafter ZSTA Merseburg), Rep. 76 viii B, Nr 37, 38. Die wissenschaftliche Deputation für das Medizinalwesen, *25 Jahre preussischer Medizinalverwaltung seit Erlass des Kreisarztgesetz, 1901–1926*, Berlin, 1927. M. Stürzbecher, 'Otto Krohne', *Berliner Ärzteblatt*, 92 (1979), 697–8.

3 *Soziale Medizin und Hygiene*, 2 (1907), pp. 468, 637. W. zur Nieden-Rohwinkel, 'Die Tuberkulosefürsorge in den Landkreisen der Rheinprovinz', *Schmollers Jahrbuch*, 37 (1913), 103–18.

4 ZSTA Merseburg Rep 76 viii B, Nr 4155, Auskunfts- und Fürsorgestellen für Lungenkranken, Bl. 13–14. Rep. 76 viii B, Nr 1958, Zentralkomitee der Auskunfts- u. Fürsorgestellen für Lungenkranken u. Alkoholkranken und Krebskranken in Berlin. Rep. 92 Althoff A I Nr 227, Bl. 38. K. Strubel, W. Tetzner, W. Piechocki, *Zur Geschichte der Gründung des Zweigvereins zur Bekämpfung der Schwindsucht in der Stadt Halle am 15 Juni 1899*, Halle, 1974.

5 ZSTA Merseburg Rep 76 viii B, Nr 1704, Die Vaterländische Frauenvereine. Von Frankenberg, 'Beteiligung von Frauen an der Waisen- und Armenpflege in Braunschweig', *Soziale Reform und Medizin*, 2 (1907), 212–14. His, *Die Front*, p. 15.

6 ZSTA Merseburg Rep 76 viii B, Nr 2023, Die Schaffung eines Volkswohlfahrtsamts, Bl. 225, 243.

7 Staatsarchiv Potsdam Rep. 2 A I SW, Nr 756, Die Wohlfahrtspflege auf den Lande. G. Asmus (ed.), *Hinterhof, Keller und Mansarde. Einblicke in Berliner Wohnungselend 1902–1920*, Hamburg, 1982, p. 23. M. Fürst, 'Der Leipziger Verband und die Gesellschaft für Soziale Reform', *Soziale Medizin und Hygiene*, 2 (1907), 31–5. ZSTA Merseburg Rep. 77 Tit. 662, Nr 44 Beiakten 5 betr. den deutschen Verein für Volkshygiene.

8 BA Koblenz R 86, Nr 2376 Bd 1. ZSTA Potsdam 15.01, Nr 11974, 11982. ZSTA Merseburg Rep. 77 Tit. 662, Nr 123 Bund für Mutterschutz, Bl. 1–3.

9 ZSTA Merseburg Rep. 151 I C, Nr 9071, Bl. 259 Rep. 77 Tit. 662, Beiakten 9, Bl. 63–74. On legislation for infant care see M. Stürzbecher, 'Die Bekämpfung der Geburtenrückganges und der Säuglingssterblichkeit im Spiegel der Reichstagsdebatten 1900–1930', unpublished dissertation, Berlin, 1954. On factors affecting infant mortality see R. Spree, *Soziale Ungleichheit vor Krankheit und Tod*, Göttingen, 1981, pp. 49–92.

10 See, for example, H. Senator and S. Kaminer, *Krankheiten und Ehe. Darstellung der Beziehungen zwischen Gesundheitsstörungen und Ehegemeinschaft*, Berlin, n.d.

11 ZSTA Merseburg Rep. 76 viii B, Nr 2830 Hygiene in Schulen, Bl. 144. Nr. 2831, Bl. 15–31.

12 O. Krohne, *Die Beurteilung des Geburtenrückgangs vom volkshygienischen, sittlichen und nationalen Standpunkt*, Leipzig, 1914.

13 On the health benefits of war see: Bumm, *Gesundheitsverhältnisse*, vol. 1, pp. 58–60.

14 ZSTA Merseburg Rep. 76 viii B, Nr 1951, Bekämpfung der Truncksucht 1913–22.

15 ZSTA Merseburg Rep. 76 viii, B, Nr 1960, Bl. 77. Hoffmann, *Ärzte im Weltkrieg*, pp. 60, 64.

16 ZSTA Merseburg Rep. 76 viii B, Nr 2048 Hygiene in Schulen, Bl. 315.

17 W. Stoeckel, *Erinnerungen eines Frauenarztes*, Leipzig, 1980, pp. 86–7.
18 *Berliner klinische Wochenschrift*, 1915, p. 1383.
19 F. Prinzing, *Epidemics resulting from wars*, Oxford, 1916. His, *Die Front*, p. 13.
20 ZSTA Potsdam Rep. 15.01, Nr 9345, Massregeln gegen den Geburtenrückgang, Bl. 141.
21 Stürzbecher 'Bekämpfung', p. 45. For details of the benefits, see the contribution of Cornelie Usborne, above, chapter 14, p. 395.
22 ZSTA Merseburg Rep. 151 I C, Nr 9073, Bl. 280. ZSTA Merseburg Rep. 76 viii B, Nr. 4197, Bekämpfung der Geschlechtskrankheiten, Bl. 320. A fuller account of the insurance scheme and details on the numbers insured during the war years is provided above by Ute Daniel in chapter 10, especially Table 10.1. Cornelie Usborne, above, chapter 14, p. 395, argues that lack of determination on the part of those campaigning for positive measures to reverse the decline in the birth rate also explains in part the fact that the more expensive policies were never implemented.
23 ZSTA Potsdam 15.01, Nr 11869, Massregeln gegen Geschlechtskrankheiten, Bl. 31, 84–96.
24 On VD see H. C. Fischer and E. X. Dubois, *Sexual life during the World War*, London, 1937, pp. 357–98. M. Hirschfeld (ed.), *Sittengeschichte des Weltkriegs*, 2 vols., Leipzig and Vienna, n.d., vol. I, pp. 219–48.
25 ZSTA Potsdam 15.01, Nr 11868, Bl. 68.
26 *Massnahmen zur Bekämpfung der Geschlechtskrankheiten*, Brussels, 1915. ZSTA Potsdam 15.01, Nr 11868, Bl. 195–234. Nr 11869, Bl. 390. F. Tennstedt, 'Alfred Blaschko – das wissenschaftliche und sozialpolitische Wirken eines menschenfreundlichen Sozialhygienikers im Deutschen Reich', *Zeitschrift für Sozialreform*, 25 (1979), 513–23, 600–134, 646–67. ZSTA M Rep. 77 Tit. 662, Nr 44 Beiakten 4, Deutsche Gesellschaft für Bekämpfung der Geschlechtskrankheiten.
27 ZSTA Potsdam 15.01, Nr 11881. See also the contribution of Cornelie Usborne, above, chapter 14, p. 393.
28 S. Schmitz, *Adolf Neisser*, Düsseldorf, 1968, p. 57. P. Kaufmann, *Krieg, Geschlechtskrankheiten und Arbeiterversicherung*, Berlin, 1916.
29 ZSTA Merseburg Rep. 151 I C, Nr 9071, Bl. 327, 329. *Denkschrift des Ministers des Innern* . . . , Berlin, 1917, pp. 5, 7, 50.
30 ZSTA Merseburg Rep. 76 viii B, Nr 2766, Sorge um die Erhaltung der Neugeborenen, Bl. 103.
31 Staatsarchiv Dresden, Ministerium des Innern, Nr 15249, Das Hebammenwesen, Bl. 88–92.
32 Staatsarchiv Dresden, Ministerium des Innern, Nr 15248, Bl. 78–9.
33 GStA Dahlem Rep. 84a, Nr 10995, Bl. 111.
34 ZSTA Merseburg Rep. 76 viii B, Nr 1734, Schaffung von Entbindungsanstalten. Nr 1735, Bl, 90, 100.
35 ZSTA Merseburg, Rep. 151 I C, Nr 8892. Rep. 76 viii B, Nr 2766, Bl. 118. Nr 1443, Bl. 82.
36 ZSTA Merseburg Rep. 76 viii B, Nr 1415, Bl. 106, 152.
37 *Ibid.*, Bl. 220.
38 GStA Dahlem Rep. 84a, Nr 865, Bl. 67.
39 ZSTA Merseburg Rep. 76 viii B, Nr 1416. Decree of 5 January 1918. Nr 1443, Bl. 158–61. Rep. 161 I C, Nr 9071, Bl. 233. *Denkschrift über die Ursachen des Geburtenrückganges*, Berlin, 1915, p. 47.

PAUL WEINDLING

40 A. Peiper, *Chronik der Kinderheilkunde*, Leipzig, 1951, p. 109.
41 ZSTA Merseburg Rep. 76 viii B, Nr 2766, Sorge um die Erhaltung der Neugeborenen, Bl. 164, 1945–8.
42 ZSTA Merseburg Rep. 76 viii B, Nr 2803, Bl. 2–5.
43 ZSTA Merseburg Rep. 76 viii B, Nr 2791, Ausbildung von Säuglingspflegerinnen, Bl. 53–5, 117, 144. 2.2.1, Nr 24546, Bl. 3. Staatsarchiv Dresden Ministerium des Innern, Nr 15221, Ausbildung von Säuglingspflegerinnen, Bl. 328. ZSTA Potsdam 15.01, Nr 1 1974, Bl. 147.
44 ZSTA Merseburg Rep. 76 viii B, Nr 2791, Bl. 203–5.
45 *Ibid.*, Bl. 198.
46 *Ibid.*, Bl. 136–9. Rep. 76 viii B, Nr 1704, Bl. 167–8.
47 M. Baum, 'Die Staatliche Anerkennung von Säuglingspflegerinnen. Bemerkungen zu dem Erlass des Ministeriums des Innern von 31.iii.1917', *Deutsche medizinische Wochenschrift* (1917), 913–15. 23 September 1916, Ministerialkommission zur Geburtenrückgangsfrage.
48 8 April 1916, Ministerialkommission zur Geburtenrückgangsfrage.
49 ZSTA Merseburg Rep. 76 viii B, Nr 2789. Nr 2051, Volksgesundheitliche Fragen während des Krieges.
50 ZSTA Merseburg Rep. 76 viii B, Nr 2051, Bl. 16.
51 *Ibid.*, Bl. 208–396. M. Kirchner, 'Kriegsernährung und Volksgesundheit', *Berliner Lokalanzeiger*, 6 November 1916, Rep. 76 viii B, Nr 2079, Bl. 30–4.
52 *Denkschrift*, Berlin, 1917, pp. 32–3. *Stenographische Bericht der Verhandlungen des Reichstag*, 1918, 5346, 10 June 1918.
53 *Denkschrift über die Ursachen des Geburtenrückgangs und die zur Bekämpfung desselbes etwa in Betracht zu ziehenden Massnahmen*, Berlin, 1912. *Denkschrift über die Ursachen des Geburtenrückganges und die dagegen vorgeschlagenen Massnahmen. Bearbeitet im Ministerium des Innern*, Berlin, 1915. *Denkschrift des Ministers des Innern über die Ergebnisse der Beratungen der Ministerialkommission für die Geburtenrückgangsfrage*, Berlin, 1917.
54 ZSTA Merseburg Rep. 76 viii B, Nr 1998, Die Geburtenrückgang, Bl. 87. *Denkschrift*, 1917, pp. 28–31.
55 D. V. Glass, *Population policies and movements in Europe*, Oxford, 1940, pp. 270–3. A Mendelsohn-Bartholdy, *The war and German society, the testament of a liberal*, New Haven, 1937, pp. 135, 139. Cf. Cornelie Usborne's account of the pronatalist campaign for a growing *Volk*, particularly their stress on the common, rather than on the individual good, above, chapter 14, p. 396. For an analysis of the transition from liberalism to collectivism, see P. Weindling, *Health, race and German politics from National Unification to Nazism*, Cambridge, 1989.
56 ZSTA Potsdam 15.01, Nr 11982 Musteranstalt zur Bekämpfung der Säuglingssterblichkeit. On Naumann see T. Heuss, *Friedrich Naumann*, Stuttgart and Tübingen, 1949, pp. 206, 314. A. Fischer, 'Der Frauenüberschuss. Eine sozialhygienische Betrachtung Naumannscher Aufsätze', *Hilfe*, 17 (1911). K.-D. Thomann, *Alfons Fischer [1873–1936] und die Badische Gesellschaft für soziale Hygiene*, Cologne, 1980. P. J. Weindling, 'Soziale Hygiene, Eugenik und medizinische Praxis', *Argument – Sonderband*, 119 (1984), 6–20.
57 P. J. Weindling, 'Theories of the cell state in Imperial Germany' in C. Webster (ed.), *Biology, medicine and society 1840–1940*, Cambridge, 1981, pp. 99–155. E. Bumm, *Über das deutsche Bevölkerungsproblem. Rede zum Antritt des Rektorats . . .* , Berlin, 1916. P. J. Weindling, 'Cell biology and Darwinism in

Imperial Germany: the contribution of Oscar Hertwig', PhD, London University, 1982. P. J. Weindling, *Darwinism and Social Darwinism in Imperial Germany*, Stuttgart, 1988.

58 ZSTA Merseburg Rep. 76 Va Sekt 2 Tit. 12, Nr 83, Bd. 12, Bl. 275. Bd. 13, Bl. 5.

59 The case is discussed in detail by Cornelie Usborne, above, chapter 14, p. 405. and on proposed legislation to curb abortion, see pp. 393, 407.

60 *Berliner klinische Wochenschrift*, 1918, Nr 1. ZSTA Potsdam, Nr 9379. 'Vorberatung über die Frage des Austausches von Gesundheitszeugnissen vor der Eheschliessung, 23 September 1917' in Rott Sammlung, FU Berlin. ZSTA Merseburg 2.2.1., Nr 24546, Bl. 101–5.

61 Rep. 76 viii B, Nr 2002, Bl. 3. Rep. 169 C 17, Nr 26, Bl. 2. ZSTA Potsdam 15.01, Nr 9344, Bl. 51 2. BA Koblenz R 86, Nr 2387 Wolf on 27 May 1915, and condemnation by Roesle. ZSTA Potsdam 15.01, Nr 9350, Bl. 90. ZSTA Merseburg Rep. 76 viii B, Nr 4388 Ausstellungen.

62 ZSTA Merseburg Rep. 76 viii B, Nr 2002, Bl. 199 re. Hausarzt und Bevölkerungspolitik conference.

63 ZSTA Merseburg Rep. 76 viii B, Nr 2049, Bl. 153.

64 R. Pommerin, *Sterilisierung der Rheinlandbastarde: das Schicksal einer farbigen deutschen Minderheit*, Düsseldorf, 1979.

65 On socialist health strategies see: E. Hansen et al., *Seit über einem Jahrhundert . . . Verschüttete Alternativen in der Sozialpolitik*, Cologne, 1981. P. J. Weindling, 'Shattered alternatives in medicine. [Essay review of the Verschüttete Alternativen Project]', *History Workshop*, 16 (1983), 152–6. A. Labisch, 'Die gesundheitspolitischen Vorstellungen der deutschen Sozialdemokratie von ihre Gründung bis zur Parteispaltung (1863–1917)', *Archiv für Sozialgeschichte*, 16 (1976), 325–70. D. S. Nadav, *Julius Moses und die Politik der Sozialhygiene in Deutschland*, Gerlingen, 1985. On public health and eugenics see, P. J. Weindling, 'Die Preussische Medizinalverwaltung und die "Rassenhygiene", 1905–1933', *Zeitschrift für Sozialreform* (1984), 675–87. A. Labisch and F. Tennstedt, *Der Weg zum 'Gesetz über die Vereinheitlichung des Gesundheitswesens'*, Düsseldorf, 1986.

16

Männerbund versus the family: middle-class youth movements and the family in Germany in the period of the First World War

Jürgen Reulecke

Almost all social groups participated in the controversial discussion which took place in Germany after the First World War concerning the 'crisis of the family' and its consequences for the state and society. At the outset we must draw a distinction between the propositions of the various ideologies and the objective changes that had occurred in the structure and socio-economic condition of the family since the end of the nineteenth century, because this discussion was determined to a significant extent by ideology. Most advocates of a restoration of the conventional family ideal as well as most critics of the bourgeois family were not primarily interested in the family itself but rather in using it in connection with strategies aimed at the attainment of far more extended goals. Thus, for example, the family was attacked from both the left and the right in terms of its role within bourgeois–capitalist society.

In the discussions revolving around this topic a noticeable generational differentiation can be observed especially in the bourgeois camp, from left-wing liberals to the extreme right. Representatives of the older generations wanted to overcome the crisis with a carefully directed youth policy and with measures to revitalise the family so that it would once again become the centre of bourgeois life. In contrast the ideas which increasingly appealed to the young generation placed a very different emphasis on the need to heal the wounds of German society (*Volkskörper*) and simultaneously, to reform German self-confidence at least to its pre-war level. The older generation, from a position of comparative economic and social security, demanded an expansion of welfare work and family aid, eugenic measures of every sort, improvement of the educational system, and the dissemination of information about diverse biological and moral dangers threatening the family. They also called for the extension of measures for the preservation of morals among youth (*Jugendbewahrungsmassnahmen*) and the like. Meanwhile, representatives of the younger generation put their faith in the self-healing powers ostensibly inherent in youth itself. They placed their trust in a new youth movement which, with energy, determination and enthusiasm, would conquer the world of 'philistines' and inaugurate a 'living renewal' of a conventional, degenerate society. To the extent that the ideologists who promulgated this doctrine commented in any positive way about the family, they reduced its function essentially to its biological and race-preserving aspects. They considered the family to be almost exclusively the realm of the woman where, according to her natural destiny, she should care for healthy and vigorous offspring. On the other hand, the entirety of political life, especially in times of upheaval and of the struggle of society for self-preservation and the 'new creation of the fantastic' (*Neuschöpfung des Unerhörten*), took place in the masculine realm (Männerbund – men's league), whose 'militant advance troop' was the young men's troop (Jungmannschaft).[1] Männerbund and Jungmannschaft constituted the family's counterpart; they created and secured the framework in which the family could develop and fulfill its tasks for the people's community (*Volksgemeinschaft*).

These attitudes on their own, representing, as they do central points of National Socialist ideology of the family and the men's leagues (Männerbünde, suffice to reveal the significant generational differences in the discussion of the crisis of the bourgeois family. This chapter deals with the roots and precursors of this ideology, which was itself involved in a process of continuous development during the 1920s. These connections are, in my opinion, of great importance for German history in the inter-war period and for our understanding of the advance of National Socialism. Further, it would be interesting to discover whether parallel occurrences and developments can be observed in other states in this period. The reaction of nationalist circles to the experience of the First World War and the German defeat had an important role to play in this connection. The war, as seen in retrospect in 1933, had led to the 'rebirth of indispensable but forgotten and decayed powers of [child] rearing',[2] primarily in the form of the 'heroic men's league' (*der heroische Männerbund*).

In the search for the origins of this ideology the years around 1900 are clearly critical. This period, of such importance in the evolution of both positive and negative trends, was dominated in particular by a crisis of self-confidence in the educated middle classes.[3] Formerly the progressive driving force of the transformation of German society, this middle class recognised an ever-growing discrepancy between the enormous progress in the technical–economic sphere on the one hand and the unsolved, critical problems in the political–social sphere on the other.[4] Responses varied: there were some attempts at reform but there also emerged escapist trends of all kinds, especially ones leading to new myths and cults in the hope of finding a new meaning in an overly complicated world. The growing mood of uncertainty showed itself in internal and external aggressiveness as well as in a surge of criticism of 'civilisation'. Emotions and passions increasingly infected political discussion and threats perceived by individuals were inflated into dangers confronting the whole of society.

Younger people appeared to constitute one of the dangers threatening the system. No longer were they prepared to blindly transmit the ideals, values and norms of the older generation. Instead youth came increasingly to question the traditional structures of authority and meaning.[5] In addition to the impact on the world of work, the challenge of youth made itself felt especially in the bourgeois family which corresponded to an ever-decreasing degree to their ideal of the family life-style. According to their notions, the ideal family was one maintained by the authority of the father, and where there was a clear separation of all familial roles and seclusion from other social realms.[6] A number of critics of the family and campaigners for a reform of life-styles turned this thinking in a positive direction with the simple declaration that 'youth' were society's paradigm. Here, the term 'youth' did not so much refer to a stage of biological transition on the way to adulthood but rather to a myth and concomitantly to a code for setting out on a better future, regardless of its form.[7] The main thrust of this ideology, which would become much more blatant in the 1920s, had already been formulated by one of its spokesmen, Moeller van den Bruck, in 1904: 'A change of blood is necessary for the Nation, a revolt of the sons against the fathers, the replacement of the old by the young'.[8] Two years earlier the sociologist and folklorist Heinrich Schurtz had described the organisational form which was supposed to constitute the basis of such a revolution against the older generation. Using social forms among primitive peoples as his reference point, he outlined in his book, *Altersklassen und Männerbünde*[9] ('Age groups and men's leagues') a social form in opposition to that of the family where Schurtz held the woman ultimately dominated. In the Männerbund, the male character would be unfettered.

Meanwhile, some elements within the young generation had resisted all attempts to contain them, including the regulatory intentions of Wilhelminian youth welfare agencies, which various interests together with the state had developed since the 1890s with the express purpose of taming and integrating restless youth into society. In opposition to the 'official' youth organisations, they founded their own autonomous movement which spread rapidly throughout Germany, Austria and Switzerland: the so-called

'Wandervogel'.[10] Functioning usually as groups of young males, although at first there were a few mixed groups, these youths set themselves two objectives: the first practical, marking a physical retreat from the city, the second ideological, symbolising a departure from what they considered the ossified and mendacious Wilhelminian 'plush culture' (*Plüschkultur*). In teams of boys of about the same age under the direction of a leader a few years older, they set out to create a utopia of new human beings.

The ideological sub-structure of this movement was at first not very distinct. It united all kinds of heterogeneous aspirations, including those elements which would become dominant after the First World War. The climax of the pre-war youth movement was a great gathering on top of the Hohe Meissner, a mountain near Kassel. It was here that in October 1913, the representatives of the various independent groups, total abstainers, reformist educators, reformers of life-style and 'people's educators' (*Volkserzieher*) agreed upon the famous 'Meissner formula' which has to this day remained the cornerstone of the philosophy of the youth movement. The Freideutsche Jugend ('Free German Youth'), as they were termed, called for the creation of a moral force rather than for concrete action.[11] Accordingly they wanted 'to shape their lives on their own terms, with their own responsibility, according to their inner concept of truthfulness.' The goal of the founding generation was to create a 'new, noble German youth culture'. This community of youth and comradeship was to confront the loathsome conventions propagated by bourgeois families and the schools. The Freideutsche Jugend questioned whether the family should exercise its hitherto explicit function of guiding young people to maturity and preparing them for their role as adults. Only the task of 'rearing' (*Aufzucht*) small children and girls was supposed to be left to the family. By contrast, it was proposed that the education and upbringing of adolescent young men should take place in communities resembling religious orders and in the so-called Freien Schulgemeinden (Free School Communities). In these organisations they were to be prepared for their mission in society under the challenging guidance of a leader, removed from the corrupting influence of metropolitan civilisation. In fact, there were a number of experiments of this nature of which the best-known was the Free School Community in Wickersdorf under the direction of Gustav Wyneken.[12]

The most controversial, but in this connection the most important, Wandervogel ideologist before the war was the student Hans Blüher. In 1912 at the age of 23, he published an original review and interpretation of the Wandervogel.[13] Although his interpretation was only shared by some sections of the Wandervogel and Freideutschen movements, it had a great deal of influence, especially after the end of the war when the bourgeois youth movement re-constituted itself. Blüher interpreted the awakening of youth since 1900 exclusively as a 'passionate movement of masculine youth' and, since passion could not exist without Eros, as being simultaneously an 'erotic phenomenon'. For Blüher, this phenomenon found its purest expression in masculine friendship leagues (Bünde).[14] The Männerbund alone could liberate a man in order to realise his complete creative activity, while the family had a negative effect upon him because it put him at the mercy of the 'predominance of the woman'. The actual elite of the nation (*Volk*) must therefore, attend the Männerbund and seek to attain 'the felicity of human society . . . available in the Männerbund and only in that setting'.[15]

At first, the First World War had the effect of postponing the crisis of the German bourgeoisie. Fostered by propaganda asserting the national identity in a world of enemies, a new sense of unity appeared in a society temporarily swayed by the illusory hope that a non-partisan, uniform and powerful *Volksgemeinschaft* could emerge from the war's bath of purification. Consequently, the war provided a significant impetus to the dissemination of the Männerbund concept. The war offered the chance to test manliness and at the same time provided the context in which the effeminate 'French' (*welsche*) civilisation could be defeated. Manly virtues were in demand: courage and toughness, loyalty and iron will, comradeship, love of the *Volk*, readiness for action and self-sacrifice. War poetry, soldiers' songs, tales of heroes and propaganda from the front all had the same theme: the boy or the young man happy, yet serious, leaving his mother, his lover or his family and hastening to meet his fate and to prove himself a man in the 'storm of steel' (*Stahlgewitter*). The intoxicating and completely irrational aspect of this scene is clearly expressed in the following war poem of Heinrich Zerkaulen (born in 1892).[16]

> Aus zieh ich meiner Jugend buntes Kleid
> und werf es hin zu Blumen, Glück und Ruh.
> Heiss sprengt das Herz die Brust mir breit,
> der Träume Türen schlag' ich lachend zu.
>
> Ein nacktes Schwert wächst in die Hand hinein,
> der Stunden Ernst fliesst stahlhart durch mich hin.
> Da steh ich stolz und hochgereckt allein
> im Rausch, dass ich ein Mann geworden bin!
>
> [I am discarding the colourful clothes of my youth
> and throw them away at flowers, fortune and peace.
> In excitement my heart rends asunder my broad chest.
> I joyfully slam the door on my dreams.
>
> A naked sword grows into my hand.
> The earnestness of the hour flows through me and is as strong as steel.
> Then I stand proudly erect on my own,
> intoxicated by the knowledge that I have become a man!]

In the trench community at the front the great hour of the Männerbund finally arrived. In the battle of Langemarck, in Flanders, new regiments with many Wandervögel as volunteers in their ranks, stormed to their deaths with the German national anthem on their lips. This event helped to create a new myth with which the succeeding generation would be sent into another world war a quarter of a century later.[17]

The image of the front-line soldiers as heroes outlived the war and the defeat to remain one of the worst legacies of war. It reinforced the so-called *Dolchstosslegende* (the myth of the 'stab in the back') and the demagogical contention that the German army had been 'unconquered in the field'. Many soldiers, especially the younger ones, had found an emotional home in soldierly comradeship. Disillusioned, they returned home in 1918 and 1919 and could not adjust to daily life: 'Flee home, those without a home, into the grey future the grey army is pulling . . .', is the feeling expressed in a poem by the volunteer Fritz Woike, born in 1890.[18] It was into this post-war emotional vacuum that the Freikorps settled as did other new para-military organisations offering the uprooted front-line soldiers new support and meaning through the perpetuation of the militant male community. The unrest in Bavaria and Saxony, in the Ruhr area and in Silesia drew their attention, supplying them with opportunities to prove themselves. They were also involved in many of the spectacular political murders during the early years of the Weimar Republic. Recent studies into the psychology of Freikorps members have revealed how significant was the ideal of male communities not only for the units as a whole but also for the actions of the individual Freikorps warrior.[19] It is also significant that there was a tendency for such units to form around outstanding officers of the former Imperial Army. These men were able to capture the imagination and hence the obedience of their juvenile adherents by a display of 'charisma' and leadership qualities.

The implementation of the ideology of the Männerbund after the Revolution of 1918/19, did not, however, take place solely in the realm of the Freikorps but exerted its influence over much of the bourgeois youth movement which had entered its second phase. Although some organisations continued to allow girls to be members and despite the existence of independent Bünde designed exclusively for younger females, the masculine character of the youth movement became increasingly dominant.[20] Both the outward appearance and the organisational structure of the groups began to conform to a set pattern: in particular a greater insistence on discipline and due respect for the hierarchy of command within the organisation. The wearing of uniforms and the insistence on ideology affected, therefore, both outward appearance and inner orientation. Whereas the pre-war Wandervogel were small groups characterised by a relaxed co-operative atmosphere, spontaneity and colourful variety and their communal experiences consisted mainly in group hiking trips, after the war the central organisational form and associated paradigm became the Bund. The Bund was a type of self-contained youth state where the term 'youth' did not refer to the biological age group but rather to all those 'whose actions pointed toward the future'.[21] Insofar as it was divided into Jungenschaft, Jungmannschaft and Mannschaft, it encapsulated a number of generations. One can characterise the Bund in its ideal form as an aristocratic organisation, hierarchically based on estates, a counter-model to the unloved, cold and discredited parliamentary system.[22] Very few Bünde gave the Republic their unequivocal support or were willing to defend it during the final phase of the Weimar Republic.

All of this demonstrates that it is no longer appropriate to speak of the youth movement in the narrow sense but rather as a movement dominated by young adults attempting to create enthusiasm among youth for their ideological and more or less diffuse political and other 'world-changing' doctrines. The organisation of the individual leagues was hierarchical. In essence, this meant that the small group or 'Horde' took the place of the bourgeois family. Here the leader, who was not elected but who selected his followers himself, was dominant. The bourgeois family as well as the Männerbund or Jungenbund were based on the principle of command and obedience, but whereas the familial role of the rather was legitimised by tradition, which demanded that the sons subordinate their wishes to his authority, the leaders of the individual groups of young males as well as the leader of the entire Bund won their authority through their charisma.[23] The devotion of their adherents stemmed from a harmony of minds, friendship and voluntary loyalty, which, however, could be renounced at any time. The way in which a charismatic leader selected his disciples was regarded as a 'mystery', in which Eros, the emotional attachment, and Logos, the cogently represented value system, were in harmony.[24]

There should, therefore, be little cause for surprise that many kinds of myths, cult forms, symbols and rituals were of central significance for the inner cohesion of the Bund's community. It is typical that during the period of reorganisation in 1919 and 1920, the thoughts of Hans Blüher with their evocation of male eroticism, experienced a revival which he himself incited by publishing on 'state building by man'.[25] Yet (and here he has often been misunderstood), he did not connect the erotic interpretation of the relationship between the leader and his followers with any sexual expression. Instead, he had in mind a purely spiritual, philosophical, 'platonic' set of relationships.[26] To swear allegiance to the leader meant, at least for his disciples, to participate in an elitist blood brotherhood which constituted the image of a new and better *Volksgemeinschaft* which would be realised in the future. The leader embodied most clearly the league's idea (*Bundesidee*) and endeavoured to set a most attractive and convincing example.[27] The old Germanic clans, mediaeval chivalry, the Deutschritterorden, sometimes the lives of the seventeenth-century mercenaries, the *lansquenets*, and briefly later, those of the Cossacks served as the Bund's idealised precursors, providing models which youths could imitate, more or less lightheartedly. The folk-songs or students' songs of the Wandervogel were replaced by old or adapted horsemen's, soldiers', *lansquenets'* and pirates' songs, which could usually be sung while marching. In place of fiddles, flutes or mandolins which were common in the Wandervogel, fanfares and drums now set the tone of the great parades, which had come into fashion. Besides the extended excursions, which led some groups as far as the Black Sea and to Lapland, the bivouacs, during which the league's leader held military-style reviews (*Heerschau*), grew in importance. Under the influence of the Boy Scout Movement (Pfadfinderbewegung), which merged with *bündische* Youth, there was a growth in the popularity of cross-country running as well as in the wearing of insignia, uniformed clothing and competitive sports in camp life. Above all, these bivouacs transmitted to the members of the Bund, the feeling of being active combatants in an uprising of youth against the world of the older generation, a revolt which was destined to succeed.

The bourgeois '*bündische*' Youth Movement was, in its extreme form, almost exclusively an urban phenomenon and never comprised much more than between 3 and 5 per cent of the male population aged between ten and eighteen. The magnetism of their ideas, and the impact of their outward appearance and style were nevertheless immense and influenced in numerous ways the large youth associations of the different religious denominations, the sports clubs and youth groups sponsored by political parties and also the working-class youth organisations.

Only the socialist youth movement attempted to develop counter-models to the Männerbund with its charismatic leadership, but even they borrowed some of the forms of the bourgeois youth movement.[28] Although the 'Red Falcons' also organised large camps, they fashioned them into 'Republics of Children' in which democratic life patterns were to be practised in conscious contrast to the anti-democratic and latently militaristic camp rules of the *bündische* Youth. From the camp communities of boys and girls, they elected, for example, both a camp parliament and a camp mayor, through which they learned co-determination and joint responsibility. Moreover, education at the camp was not intended to supplant the role of the family and allow daily problems to be ignored. On the contrary, the education programme was supposed to help youths develop skills and insights which would have positive effects on proletarian families and the living conditions of the workers, through encouraging the workers of the next generation to perceive themselves as a class.[29]

The fact that it was particularly the younger generation of the bourgeois middle classes, usually pupils and students, who were infected with the *bündische* ideas, owed much to their feeling of insecurity which intensified dramatically after the First World War and during the period of inflation, and represented in a more critical form the crisis of the German bourgeoisie. The initial protests of the bourgeoisie faced with a decline in both their wealth and status rapidly developed into panic under the post-war conditions.[30] The progressive erosion of the certainties of bourgeois society, which had a particularly powerful impact on the middle-class family with its clear differentiation of roles, led occasionally to a manic search for a new identity, which would provide both short-term security and strategies of long-term survival. In short, what they sought was a new home. For the younger generation, therefore, the eclipse of the father was answered by the *Führer* cult and the 'crisis of the family' by the escape to the Männerbund.

The mood appeared to change somewhat as the Weimar Republic entered its quite phase from 1924 to 1929. Most Freikorps units disbanded or were smashed by the police. Others organised themselves and survived. Touring the country as the 'Ekkehard Acting Troop', the former Freikorps Rossbach spread propaganda about the preservation of German culture which they assumed was under attack.[31] Other Freikorps leaders founded extreme right-wing youth leagues (Jungenbünde) which adopted the forms of the *bündische* youth. Viking Youth, Schill Youth and the Young Oberland League had the intention of spreading Freikorps thinking and the spirit of the heroic front-line soldier among young people. The same impulse lay behind the founding of the Hitler Youth. In 1925, following an initial, brief period between 1922 to 1923 as the 'Jungsturm Adolf Hitler', the Hitler Youth was formed by the twenty-one-year-old Kurt Gruber. Its ultimate name was given it a year later at the National-Sozialistische Deutsche Arbeiterpartei convention in Weimar.[32] Shortly afterwards, a National Socialist students' league and a pupils' league were formed.

In the 1924–9 period, discussions of the 'proper' role for youth became less emotionally charged. In these years the main weakness of the *bündische* youth, ironically called the 'splitting fungus', appeared to have been overcome. In 1925, the different Bünde were amalgamated into the largest autonomous youth league of the Weimar period; by 1929 the 'Deutsche Freischar' had approximately 12,000 members, 15 per cent of whom were girls.[33] The moderate leadership of the Freischar decided not to pursue the Männerbund concept to its fullest extent and from this more realistic assessment of the possibilities for *bündisch* education of youth, began to repress the hitherto apolitical attitude widespread in the older groups. According to one of their journals in 1926, what was required was not 'a parade of adolescent boys playing soldier (and) politically inclined young men . . . but rather the lively drive of those willing to declare themselves for the new Reich and its laws'.[34] They adopted the motto that youth was the forerunner of humanity (*Menschentum*) and that a 'Reich of youth' could, therefore, be of no higher value.[35] Under the leadership of Ernst Buske, who died in 1930, the Deutsche Freischar developed activities which were among the most remarkable of any emanating from the German youth movement. Their activities embraced adult education and seminars concerning political questions, contacts with working-class youth, a variety of cultural initiatives for youth, debates with contemporary educationalists and even the construction of volunteer work camps as youth unemployment rose drastically from 1929. Finally, the Deutsche Freischar gave direct support to the German State Party (Deutsche Staatspartei), founded in 1930 with the parliamentary system in apparent decline, as a last attempt to strengthen the middle of the political spectrum through reforms from within. In the event, the rapidity of this decline, together with the economic cricis, the heightening tension of the political home front and the tremendous growth of extremist parties, guaranteed the failure of such schemes.

In the hothouse climate of the early 1930s the Männerbund concept, the call for a strong leader, the Langemarck Myth, and the idealisation of youth as a revolutionary force that alone could lead the way out of misery, were all transformed into a radicalism more extreme than any that had emerged since 1918 and 1919. This is not the place to discuss in detail the facets of this renaissance. In this connection, however, it was significant that the two combat groups of the National-Sozialistische Arbeiterpartei (NSDAP), the Sturm Abteilung (SA), and the Schutz Staffeln (SS) offered a new home not only to the former Freikorps warriors and combat veterans but also to those adolescents from the lower or declining middle class who found themselves in a desperate situation with little prospect of amelioration. The National Socialists did this by adopting a great number of the demands of the former front-line soldiers together with the *bündische* ideology in a special form of 'piracy' which they also employed successfully in many other areas. National Socialist educationalists and ideologists concerned with the family even made the Männerbund concept the basis of their notions, which also stressed racism, antisemitism and the ideology of *Blut und Boden*.

The National Socialist position was that the family was no longer the 'basic unit' of the state but merely 'the natural beginning which (had to) be continued somewhere else'.[36] On the contrary, the state originated in the league of free men, associated in the Männerbund which was charismatically organised and radically opposed to the family.[37] If a man did not find his place and his duty in the Bund, his fighting virtues would never develop. Otherwise, his only option, as the National Socialist 'philosopher' Alfred Baeumler put it, was to become 'a matter-of-fact businessman, a servant of women, or a dull family man'.[38] Since combat 'always is the vital spark' and a people no longer able to fight were doomed to destruction, it was the intention that the Männerbund, inspired with 'heroic enthusiasm', should become the central structural principle of the National Socialist state. By contrast, to quote Rosenberg, 'The woman (or) the family will be either annexed or excluded; her ability to sacrifice [herself] will be forced into service of one kind', by which was meant attention to the wishes of the male fighters.[39] The idea was that the woman should be the 'keeper of the natural strength of the people, the keeper of the purity of the race and the race's true mores'.[40] A man's only actual emotional tie was love of his own people for which he would be willing to sacrifice himself. These objectives were particularly those of the Jungmannschaft. Hitler's remark that he wanted a new youth to be brought into being: 'violent, haughty, undaunted and cruel'[41] expresses this aim, as does the Hitler Youth motto 'live in truth, fight death defiantly, die laughing!'.[42] The terrible consequences of this doctrine are well known; its effectiveness may be judged not only from the biographies of individual National Socialists but also from many other sources of this period. An especially ugly example is provided by the career of the concentration camp commander, Rudolf Höss.[43]

To conclude, let us simply reiterate that the Männerbund concept, despite the diversity of original interpretations, took on a distinct direction through the Freikorps, following the experiences of the war and the postwar period. In the *bündische* Youth, the concept remained alive in the form of the *Lebensbund* (life community) ideology. This lost influence in the latter half of the 1920s. In the final phase of the Weimar Republic, however, the idea of the Bund experienced a remarkably widespread renaissance, particularly after it was adopted by the National Socialists and extended to fit in with their ambitions. The function of the Männerbund was construed by the National Socialists in a radical, militant and racist manner and served, along with the even more indistinct *Volksgemeinschaft* ideology, as a suggestive and emotive basis for the entire National Socialist programme. The anti-familial and anti-feminine thrust of the concept of the Männerbund was, from the beginning, one of its crucial elements. Under National Socialism it found its most extreme expression, despite its co-existence with a social policy which at times pretended to be both pro-family and pro-women.[44]

Notes

1 Horst Becker, *Die Familie*, Leipzig, 1935, pp. 56ff. My own position is set out in my contribution to Thomas Koebner, Rolf-Peter Janz and Frank Trommler (eds.), *Mit uns zieht die neue Zeit, Der Mythos Jugend*, Frankfurt am Main, 1985, pp. 199–223.
2 Karl Friedrich Wurm, *Deutsche Erziehung im Werden. Von der pädagogischen

Reformbewegung zur völkischen und politischen Erziehung, Berlin, 1933; cited here in the fourth edition, Berlin, 1938, p. 136.

3 On this see Klaus Vondung, 'Zur Lage der Gebildeten in der Wilhelminischen Zeit' in Klaus Vondung (ed.), *Das Wilhelminische Bildungsbürgertum*, Göttingen, 1976, pp. 20–33.

4 This account and the succeeding section rely heavily on Thomas Nipperdey, 'Probleme der Modernisierung in Deutschland', *Saeculum*, 30 (1979), esp. pp. 300ff.

5 See Jürgen Reulecke, 'Bürgerliche Sozialreformer und Arbeiterjugend im Kaiserreich', *Archiv für Sozialgeschichte*, 22 (1982), 299–329.

6 Heidi Rosenbaum, *Formen der Familie*, Frankfurt am Main, 1982, esp. pp. 376ff.

7 Walter Ruegg, 'Jugend und Gesellschaft um 1900' in Walter Ruegg (ed.), *Kulturkritik und Jugendkult*, Frankfurt am Main, 1974, pp. 47–59, esp. p. 52.

8 Arthur-Moeller van den Bruck, *Die Deutschen*, vol. 1, *Verirrte Deutsche*, 3 vols., Minden, 1904, p. 142.

9 Heinrich Schurtz, *Altersklassen und Männerbünde. Eine Darstellung der Grundformen der Gesellschaft*, Berlin, 1902.

10 Over the years a large number of publications have appeared on the history of the middle-class youth movement. The statements in the text on the Wandervogel are based above all on the work of Gerhard Ziemer and Hans Wolf, *Wandervogel und Freideutsche Jugend*, Bad Godesberg, 1961. See also John R. Gillis, *Geschichte der Jugend*, Weinheim and Basle, 1980, esp. pp. 155ff.

11 Walter Z. Laqueur, *Die deutsche Jugendbewegung. Eine historische Studie*, Cologne, 1962, p. 44.

12 On Wyneken see Ziemer and Wolf, *Wandervogel*, pp. 423ff., and Laqueur, *Jugendbewegung*, pp. 66ff.; see also the paper by Gustav Wyneken, 'Die neue Jugend. Ihr Kampf um Freiheit und Wahrheit in Schule und Elternhaus' in his *Religion und Erotik*, Munich, 1914, and his *Was ist Jugendkultur?*, Munich, 1914.

13 Hans Blüher, *Wandervogel. Geschichte einer Jugendbewegung*, Part II, Berlin, 1912. The third part appeared in 1914 under the title *Die deutsche Wandervogelbewegung als erotisches Phänomen*.

14 Blüher, *Werke und Tage*, Munich, 1953, p. 181.

15 Blüher, *Führer und Volk in der Jugendbewegung*, Jena, 1924, p. 8.

16 Herbert Böhme (ed.), *Rufe in das Reich. Die heldische Dichtung von Langemarck bis zur Gegenwart*, Berlin, 1934, p. 11.

17 Cf. Wolfgang Paul, *Das Feldlager. Jugend zwischen Langemarck und Stalingrad*, Esslingen, 1978, p. 84.

18 Quote from Böhme, *Rufe in das Reich*, p. 33; see also the lines of Otto Paust (born 1897), *ibid.*, p. 34. 'We look strange around the home, do not belong with comfort and pleasure, do not belong with man's daily concerns, on us is still a kiss of death.'

19 On this see esp. Klaus Theweleit, *Männerphantasien*, 2 vols., Frankfurt am Main, 1977, vol. 2.

20 Hermann Giesecke, *Vom Wandervogel bis zur Hitlerjugend. Jugendarbeit zwischen Politik und Pädagogik*, Munich, 1981, pp. 104ff. The principal authority on the middle-class youth movement of the 1920s is Felix Raabe, *Die bündische Jugend*, Stuttgart, 1961. See also Laqueur, *Jugendbewegung*.

21 Noted by Walter Rathenau as cited in the journal *Junge Menschen*, 3, vol. 13/14, July 1922, p. 177.

22 On this see Giesecke, *Wandervogel bis Hitlerjugend*, pp. 94ff.
23 Cf. for example, the revealing statement in a journal of June 1920. 'We have faith in the unknown, in our communal life-style out of which the leader arises to instruct his people.' Werner Kindt, *Die deutsche Jugendbewegung 1920 bis 1933. Die bündische Zeit*, Cologne, 1974, p. 837.
24 Blüher, *Führer und Volk*, p. 7.
25 See for example Blüher, *Die Rolle der Erotik in der männlichen Gesellschaft. Eine Theorie der menschlichen Staatsbildung nach Wesen und Wert*, 2 vols., Jena, 1917, 1919; new edn Stuttgart, 1962.
26 Cf. Ziemer and Wolf, *Wandervogel*, pp. 420ff.
27 Giesecke, *Wandervogel bis Hitlerjugend*, pp. 101ff.
28 *Ibid.*, pp. 108ff., see also Erich Eberts, *Arbeiterjugend 1904–1945. Sozialistische Erziehungsgemeinschaft – Politische Organisation*, Frankfurt am Main, 1980, esp. pp. 59ff. On the succeeding paragraph see Ferdinand Brandecker, 'Erziehung durch die Klasse für die Klasse. Zur Pädagogik der Kinderfreundebewegung in Deutschland 1919–1933' in Manfred Heinemann (ed.), *Sozialisation und Bildungswesen in der Weimarer Republik*, Stuttgart, 1976, pp. 167–86.
29 Giesecke, *Wandervogel bis Hitlerjugend*, p. 123.
30 Of critical importance in this connection is Heinrich August Winkler, 'Vom Protest zur Panik. Der gewerbliche Mittelstand in der Weimarer Republik' in his *Liberalismus und Antiliberalismus*, Göttingen, 1979, pp. 99–109; see also Jürgen Kocka, *Die Angestellten in der deutschen Geschichte 1850–1980*, Göttingen, 1981, esp. pp. 142–70.
31 Theweleit, *Männerphantasien*, p. 41.
32 On the origins of Hitlerjugend see Peter D. Stachura, *Nazi Youth in the Weimar Republic*, Santa Barbara, 1975; also Hans-Christian Brandenburg, *Die Geschichte der HJ*, 2nd edn, Cologne, 1982, and Arno Klönne, *Jugend im Dritten Reich*, Cologne, 1982, pp. 15ff.
33 Data from Rudolf Kneip, *Jugend in der Weimarer Republik. Handbuch der Jugendverbände 1919–1938*, Frankfurt am Main, 1974, pp. 75ff.
34 As quoted by Kindt, *Die deutsche Jugendbewegung*, p. 234.
35 Laqueur, *Jugendbewegung*, p. 163.
36 Becker, *Familie*, p. 1349.
37 Alfred Baeumler, *Männerbund und Wissenschaft*, Berlin, 1934, consulted here in its second edn, Berlin, 1943, p. 42; cf. the analogous interpretation offered by the chief ideologist of the National Socialists, Alfred Rosenberg, *Der Mythus des 20. Jahrhunderts*, Munich, 1930, pp. 485, 493.
38 Baeumler, *Männerbund und Wissenschaft*, p. 42.
39 Rosenberg, *Mythus*, p. 493.
40 Becker, *Familie*, p. 138.
41 Cited in Hermann Rauschning, *Gespräche mit Hitler*, Zurich and New York, 1940, p. 237.
42 Quoted in the *Kalender der deutschen Jugend 1936*, Bayreuth, 1935, p. 176.
43 See Martin Broszat (ed.), *Kommandant in Auschwitz, Autobiographische Aufzeichnungen des Rudolf Höss*, Munich, 1936. This relationship was also very marked in the case of the chief of the SS, Heinrich Himmler; see Heinrich Fraenkel and Roger Manvell, *Himmler. Kleinbürger und Massenmörder*, Frankfurt am Main and Berlin, 1965.
44 On this see Tim Mason, 'Women in Germany, 1925–1940: family, welfare and work', *History Workshop*, 1 (1976), 74–113, and 2 (1976), 5–32: cf. also Dörte

Winkler, *Frauenarbeit im Dritten Reich*, Hamburg, 1977, and Gisela Bock, 'Frauen und ihre Arbeit im Nationalsozialismus' in Annette Kuhn and Gerhard Schneider (eds.), *Frauen in der Geschichte*, Düsseldorf, 1979, pp. 113–49.

Bibliography

Abelshauser, W. 'Verelendung der Handarbeiter? Zur sozialen Lage der deutschen Arbeiter in der grossen Inflation der frühen zwanziger Jahre' in H. Mommsen and W. Schulze (eds.), *Vom Elend der Handarbeit*, Stuttgart, 1981

Abrams, P. 'The failure of social reform 1918–1920', *Past and Present*, 24 (1963)

Addison, C. *Politics from within*, London, 1924

Adler, E. 'Das Arbeitsrecht im Kriege' in F. Hanusch and E. Adler, *Die Regelung der Arbeitsverhältnisse im Kriege*, Vienna, 1927

Amalgamated Engineering Union. *Financial Report*, 1931

Amdur, K. *Syndicalist legacy*, Urbana-Champaign, Illinois, 1986

Anderson, A. *Women in the factory*, London, 1922

Anderson, M. *Family structure in nineteenth-century Lancashire*, Cambridge, 1971

Annuaire statistique de la Belgique et du Congo belge, Quarante-sixième à cinquantième année, 1913–1915, 46 (1922)

Asmus, G. (ed.), *Hinterhof, Keller und Mansarde. Einblicke in Berliner Wohnungselend 1902–1920*, Hamburg, 1982

Atwater, W. O. and Bryant, A. P. *The chemical composition of American food materials*, US Department of Agriculture, Bulletin No. 28, revised edn, Washington, 1906

Avondts, G. and Scholliers, P. *Prices and house rents in Ghent and budget inquiries in the nineteenth and twentieth centuries*, vol. 5 of the series, *Textile workers in Ghent in the nineteenth and twentieth centuries*, Brussels, 1981

Baeumler, A. *Männerbund und Wissenschaft*, Berlin, 1943

Bajohr, S. *Die Hälfte der Fabrik: Geschichte der Frauenarbeit in Deutschland 1914–1945*, Marburg, 1979

Barnett, M. *British food policy during the First World War*, London, 1984

Baudhuin, F. *Histoire économique de la Belgique, 1914–1939*, Brussels, 1946

Baum, M. 'Die staatliche Anerkennung von Säuglingspflegerinnen. Bemerkungen zu dem Erlass des Ministeriums des Inneren von 31.iii.1917, *Deutsche medizinische Wochenschrift* (1917)

Bäumer, G. 'Bevölkerungspolitik und Kindersegen' in G. Bäumer (ed.), *Weit hinter den Schützengräben*, Jena, 1916

'Der Krieg und die Frau', *Der deutsche Krieg*, Politische Flugschriften, 15, Stuttgart and Berlin, 1914

Becker, H. *Die Familie*, Leipzig, 1935
Becker, J.-J. *1914. Comment les Français sont entrés dans la guerre*, Paris, 1977
  'Dalla sorpresa alla protesta: classi popolari francesi di fronte alla guerra (1914–
  1918)', *Movimento operaio e socialista*, 20 (September–December 1982)
  La première guerre mondiale, Paris, 1985
  The Great War and the French people, trans. A. Pomerans, Leamington Spa, 1986
*Beiträge zur Kenntnis der Lebenshaltung im dritten Kriegsjahre. Auf Grund einer
  Erhebung des Kriegsausschusses für Konsumenteninteressen*, Sondarheft zum
  Reichs-Arbeitsblatt 17, Berlin, 1917
*Beiträge zur Kenntnis der Lebenshaltung im vierten Kriegsjahre. Auf Grund einer
  Erhebung des Kriegsausschusses für Konsumenteninteressen*, Sonderheft zum
  Reichs-Arbeitsblatt, 21 Berlin, 1919
Bendix, K. (ed.), *Geburtenregelung*, Berlin, 1928
Benjamin, W. *Über den Begriff der Geschichte* in *Illuminationen. Ausgewählte
  Schriften*, Frankfurt, 1977
Berger, M. and Allard, P. *Les Secrets de la censure pendant la guerre*, Paris, 1932
Bergmann, A. 'Frauen, Männer, Sexualität und Geburtenkontrolle. Die
  Gebärstreikdebatte der SPD im Jahre 1913' in Karin Hausen (ed.), *Frauen
  suchen ihre Geschichte*, Munich, 1983
  'Von der "unbeflekten Empfängnis" zur "Rationalisierung des Geschlecht-
  lebens"' in J. Geyer-Kordesch and A. Kuhn (eds.), *Frauenkörper, Medizin,
  Sexualität*, Düsseldorf, 1986
Bertillon, J. *Calcul de la mortalité des enfants du premier âge*, Paris, 1887
  De la Mortalité par âge avant la naissance, Paris, 1893
  De la Dépopulation de la France et des remèdes à y apporter, Paris, 1896
  Le Problème de la dépopulation, Paris, 1897
  *La Dépopulation de la France, ses conséquences, ses causes, mesures à prendre pour la
  combattre*, Paris, 1911
Bessel, R. ' "Eine nicht allzu grosse Beunruhigung des Arbeitsmarkts": Frauen-
  arbeit und Demobilmachung in Deutschland nach dem Ersten Weltkrieg',
  Geschichte und Gesellschaft, 9 (1983)
Beveridge, W. H. *British food control*, London, 1928
*Bewegung der Bevolkerung in den Jahren 1914 bis 1919, Statistik des Deutschen Reichs,
  Band 276*, Berlin, 1922
Bierbrauer, W. 'Die Einwirkung des Krieges und der Nachkriegszeit auf die
  Wohnbautätigkeit, unter besonderer Berücksichtigung von Rheinland und
  Westfalen', unpublished dissertation, 1921
Black, C. *Married women's work*, London, 1915
Blacker, C. P. 'Birth control and eugenics', *Nineteenth Century*, 3 (1932)
  Eugenics in retrospect and prospect, Occasional Papers on Eugenics, 1, London,
  1950
Blanquet, I. von. 'Die Kriegsernährungswirtschaft der Stadt Kassel und ihre Lehren
  für die öffentliche Lebensmittelversorgung', unpublished dissertation,
  Cologne, 1923
Bland, L. 'In the name of protection: the policing of women in the First World War'
  in C. Smart and J. Brophy (eds.), *Women-in-law*, London, 1985
Blot, J. 'La Sarthe, un département de l'arrière pendant la grande guerre', MA, Uni-
  versity of Le Mans, 1976
Blüher, H. *Wandervogel. Geschichte einer Jugendbewegung*, Part II, Berlin, 1912
  Die Rolle der Erotik in der männlichen Gesellschaft. Eine Theorie der menschlichen

Staatsbildung nach Wesen und Wert, 2 vols., Jena, 1917, 1918, new edn, Stuttgart, 1962

Führer und Volk in der Jugendbewegung, Jena, 1924

Werke und Tage, Munich, 1953

Board of Education. *Annual Report of the Chief Medical Officer of the Board of Education 1910*, PP 1911, xvii, Cd 5925

Annual Report of the Chief Medical Officer of the Board of Education 1915, PP 1916, viii, Cd 8338

Annual Report of the Chief Medical Officer of the Board of Education 1917, PP 1918, ix, Cd 9206

Annual Report of the Chief Medical Officer of the Board of Education 1919, PP 1920, xv, Cmd 995

Annual Report of the Chief Medical Officer of the Board of Education 1920, PP 1921, xi, Cmd 1522

Board of Trade. *Consumption and cost of food in workmen's families in urban districts in the United Kingdom*, PP 1905, lxxxiv, Cd 2337

Report of the state of employment in the United Kingdom in July 1918

Bock, F. 'L'Exubérance de l'Etat en France de 1914 à 1918', *Vingtième Siècle*, 1 (July 1984)

Bock, G. 'Frauen und ihre Arbeit im Nationalsozialismus' in Annette Kuhn and Gerhard Schneider (eds.), *Frauen in der Geschichte*, Düsseldorf, 1979

'Racism and sexism in Nazi Germany: motherhood, compulsory sterilization, and the state', *Signs*, 8 (1983)

Zwangssterilisation im Nationalsozialismus. Studien zur Rassenpolitik und Frauenpolitik, Opladen, 1986

Böhme, H. (ed.), *Rufe in das Reich. Die heldische Dichtung von Langemarck bis zur Gegenwart*, Berlin, 1934

Bond-Howard, J. 'The Syndicat des Métalurgistes de Bourges during the 1914–1918 war: a study of a minoritaire trade union', PhD, London, 1985

Bonfield, L., Smith, R. and Wrightson, K. (eds.), *The world we have gained*, Oxford, 1986

Bonnefoy, J. M. 'Les mineurs de Montceau, les mines et les métallurgistes de Chalon sur Saône pendant la grande guerre', MA, University of Dijon, 1974

Bornträger, J. 'Der Geburtenrückgang in Deutschland, seine Bewertung und Bekämpfung', *Veröffentlichungen aus dem Gebiete der Medizinalverwaltung*, 1 (1912)

Boston, S. *Women workers and the trade union movement*, London, 1980

Botz, G. *Gewalt in der Politik*, Vienna, 1976

Boverat, F. *Patriotisme et paternité*, Paris, 1913

Bowley, A. L. 'The measurement of changes in the cost of living', *Journal of the Royal Statistical Society*, new series, 82 (1919)

Prices and wages in the United Kingdom, 1914–1920, Oxford, 1921

Some economic consequences of the Great War, London, 1927

Brandecker, F. 'Erziehung durch die Klasse für die Klasse. Zur Pedägogik der Kinderfreundebewegung in Deutschland 1919–1933' in Manfred Heinemann (ed.), *Sozialisation und Bildungswesen in der Weimarer Republik*, Stuttgart, 1976

Brandenburg, H.-C. *Die Geschichte der HJ*, 2nd edn, Cologne, 1982

Braun, A. *Haushaltungs-Rechnungen Nürnberger Arbeiter. Ein Beitrag zur Aufhellung der Lebensverhältnisse des Nürnberger Proletariats*, Nuremberg, 1901

Braybon, G. *Women workers in the First World War*, London, 1981

Breller, L. *Sozialpolitik in der Weimarer Republik*, Kronberg and Düsseldorf, 1978

Briefs, G. 'Entwicklung und Verfassung der Hauswirtschaft innerhalb der Volks-wirtschaft' in G. Briefs, Marthe Voss-Zeitz and Maria Stegemann-Runk (eds.), *Die Hauswirtschaft im Kriege (Beiträge zur Kriegswirtschaft)*, 25, Berlin, 1917

Brinker-Gabler, G. (ed.), *Frauenarbeit und Beruf*, Frankfurt, 1979

Brookes, B. 'The illegal operation: abortion, 1919–39' in *The sexual dynamics of history*, London, 1983

Broszat, M. (ed.), *Kömmandant in Auschwitz, Autobiographische Aufzeichnungen des Rudolf Höss*, Munich, 1936

Brown, K. *Labour and unemployment, 1900–1914*, Newton Abbot, 1971

Bruck, A.-M. van den. *Die Deutschen, vol. 1, Verirrte Deutsche*, Munden, 1904

Brunet, J. P. *Saint-Denis la ville rouge*, Paris, 1980

Bruno, G. *Le Tour de France par deux enfants*, Paris, 1886

Bry, G. *Wages in Germany 1871–1945*, Princeton, NJ, 1960

Bumm, E. *Über das deutsche Bevölkerungsproblem. Rede zum Antritt des Rektorats …*, Berlin 1916

Über das Frauenstudium, Berlin, 1917

Bumm, F. *Deutschlands Gesundheitsverhältnisse unter d. Einfluss d. Weltkrieges*, Stuttgart, 1928

Bunzel, J. (ed.), *Geldentwertung und Stabilisierung in ihren Einflüssen aur die soziale Entwicklung Österreichs* (Schriften des Vereins zur Sozialpolitik 169), Vienna, 1925

Burchardt, L. 'The impact of the war economy on the civilian population of Germany during the First and Second World Wars' in W. Deist (ed.), *The German military in the age of total war*, Leamington Spa, 1985

Bureau, P. *La Restriction volontaire de la natalité et la défense nationale*, Paris, 1913

Burgdörfer, F. 'Familienpolitik und Familienstatistik' in *Zur Erhaltung und Mehrung der Volkskraft*, Arbeiten einer vom ärtzlichen Verein Münchens eingesetzten Kommission, Munich, 1918

Burk, K. *Britain, America and the sinews of war, 1914–1918*, London, 1985

(ed.) *War and the state*, London, 1983

Burnett, J. *Plenty and want*, London, 1979

Buxton, N. K. and Mackay, D. *British employment statistics, a guide to sources and methods*, Oxford, 1977

Callow, A. B. *Food and health*, Oxford, 1938

Carls, S. D. 'Louis Loucheur: a French technocrat in government, 1916–1920', PhD, Minnesota, 1982

Carnegie United Kingdom Trust. *Report on the physical welfare of mothers and children. England and Wales*, 2 vols., London, 1917, vol. I

Carre, J. J., Dubois, P. and Malinvaud, E. *La Croissance française, un essai d'analyse économique causale de l'après-guerre*, Paris, 1972

Cavignac, J. *La classe ouvrière bordelaise face à la guerre (1914–1918)*, Bordeaux, 1976

Census of England and Wales, 1911. Part I. Occupations and industries, PP 1913, lxxxviii, Cd 7018

Chapman, S. D. *War and the cotton trade*, Oxford, 1915

Charles, E. *The twilight of parenthood. A biological study of the decline of population growth*, London, 1934

Charrier, D. 'La vie quotidienne des Nantais pendant la première guerre mondiale', MA, University of Nantes, 1978

Churchill, Lady Randolph (ed.) *Women's war work*, London, 1916

Citroën, A. 'L'organisation de travail, les règles de l'hygiène et du repos dans l'usine moderne', *La Science et la Vie*, 6 (1917–18)

Clapham, J. H. *An economic history of modern Britain: machines and national rivalries (1887–1914)*, Cambridge, 1938

Clegg, H. A. *A history of British trade unions since 1889. Volume II 1911–1933*, 2 vols., Oxford, 1985

Coale, A. 'The decline of fertility in Europe since the French revolution' in S. H. Behrmann (ed.), *Fertility and family planning*, Ann Arbor, 1965

Cohen, Y. 'Quand les masses viennent au syndicat: moralisation et représentativité', *Révoltes logiques*, 5 (1979)

Cole, G. D. H. *Trade unionism and munitions*, Oxford, 1923
Workshop organisation, Oxford, 1923

Colinet, R. 'Un site industriel: Nouzonville. Une dynastie industrielle de la métallurgie ardennaise: les Thomé', MA, University of Nancy II, 1979

Collinet, P. and Stahl, P. *Le Ravitaillement de la France occupée*, Paris–New Haven, 1928

Commission exécutive de la Fédération des Métaux, séance du 6 juin 1917, Procès-verbal déposé au Centre de Recherches des Mouvements sociaux et du syndicalisme de l'Université de Paris-1

Coyner, S. *Class patterns of family income and expenditure during the Weimar Republic*, New Brunswick, 1975

Crew, D. F. 'German socialism, the state and family policy, 1918–33', *Continuity and Change*, 1 (1986)

Cronin, J. E. 'Labour insurgency and class formation: comparative perspectives on the crisis of 1917–1920 in Europe' in J. E. Cronin and C. Sirianni (eds.), *Work, community and power*, Philadelphia, 1983

Cross, G. 'Towards social peace and prosperity: the politics of immigration in France during the era of the First World War', *French Historical Studies*, 11 (1980)

Daline, V. *Hommes et idées*, Moscow, 1983

Daniel, J. 'La vie quotidienne à Rennes et en Ille et Vilaine de juillet 1918 à juin 1919', MA, University of Rennes II, 1977

Daniel, U. 'Fiktionen, Friktionen und Fakten: Frauenlohnarbeit im Ersten Weltkrieg' in Gunther Mai (ed.), *Arbeiterschaft 1914–1918 in Deutschland*, Düsseldorf, 1985
'Frauen in der Kriegsgesellschaft 1914–1918; Arbeiterfrauen in Beruf, Familie und innerer Politik des Ersten Weltkriegs', unpublished dissertation, Bielefeld, 1986

Dantan, A. 'Le développement de l'industrie dans les cantons de Sotteville et de Grand-Couronne 1914–1939', *Etudes Normandes*, 24 (July–December 1974)

Darwin, L. 'Heredity and environment: a warning to eugenists', *Eugenics Review*, 8 (1916)

Davidson, R. 'The Board of Trade and industrial relations 1896–1914', *Historical Journal*, 21 (1978)

Declas, G. 'Recherches sur les usines Berliet (1914–1949)', MA, University of Paris-I, 1977
'Les usines Berliet 1895–1921' in *De Renault Frères constructeurs d'automobiles à Renault Régie Nationale*, 110, June 1979

De Lannoy, Ch. 'Quelques données rétrospectives sur les prix de détail à Bruxelles de août 1914 à octobre 1918', *Revue du Travail*, 1919

Delorme, R. and André, C. *L'Etat et l'économie, un essai d'explication et de l'évolution des dépenses publiques en France 1870–1980*, Paris, 1983

Denkschrift des Ministers des Innern über die Ergebnisse der Beratungen der Ministerial-kommission für die Geburtenrückgangsfrage, Berlin, 1917

Denkschrift über die Ursachen des Geburtenrückgangs und die zur Bekämpfung desselbes etwa in Betracht zu ziehenden Massnahmen, Berlin, 1912

Denkschrift über die Ursachen des Geburtenrückgangs und die dagegen vorgeschlagenen Massnahmen. Bearbeitet im Ministerium des Innern, Berlin, 1915

Depretto, J. P. and Schweitzer, S. V. *Le Communisme à l'usine*, Roubaix, 1984

Dereymez, J. W. 'Les usines de guerre (1914–1918) et le cas de la Saône et Loire', *Cahiers de Histoire*, 26 (April–June 1981)

Deutsch, J. 'Radikale Strömungen'. *Der Kampf*, 11/12 (February 1918) *Geschichte der österreichischen Arbeiterbewegung*, Vienna, 1947

Dewey, P. E. 'Food production and policy in the United Kingdom, 1914–1918', *Transactions of the Royal Historical Society*, 5th series, 30 (1980)

'Military recruiting and the British labour force during the First World War', *Historical Journal*, 27 (1984)

Didier, M. 'Recherches pour servir à l'histoire des établissements Bessonneau à Angers des origines à 1939', MA, Paris-I, 1976

Dogliani, P. 'Stato, imprenditori e manodopera industriale in Francia durante la prima guerra mondiale', *Rivista di storia contemporanea*, 30 (1982)

'Guerra e mobilizatione industriale in Francia' in G. Procacci (ed.), *Stato e classe operaia in Italia durante la prima guerra mondiale*, Milan, 1983

Doleris, J. and Bouscatel, J. *Néomalthusianisme. Maternité et féminisme. Education sexuelle*, Paris, 1918

Dooghe, G. 'De bevolking', *Twintig eeuwen Vlaanderen*, part 8, Hasselt, 1978

Drake, B. Historical introduction, *Report of the War Cabinet on women in industry*, PP 1919, xxl, Cmd 135

Women in trade unions, London, 1920

Drummond, J. C. and Wilbraham, A. *The Englishman's food: a history of five centuries of English diet*, revised edn, London, 1957

Dubreuil, H. *La Vraie Cassure*, Paris, Comité de défense syndicaliste, 1917

Employeurs et salariés en France, Paris, 1934

Ducasse, A., Meyer, J. and Perreux, G. *Vie et mort des Français, 1914–1918*, Paris, 1962

Dumont, A. *La Morale basée sur la démographie*, Paris, 1901

Dupin, C. *Forces productives et commerciales en France*, Paris, 1827

Dyer, C. *Population and society in twentieth century France*, London, 1978

Dyhouse, C. 'Working-class mothers and infant mortality in England, 1895–1914', *The Journal of Social History*, 12 (1978)

Eberts, E. *Arbeiterjugend 1904–1945. Sozialistische Erziehungsgemeinschaft – politische Organisation*, Frankfurt am Main, 1980

'Einkommen und Lebenshaltung. Die Erhebungen des Kriegsausschusses für Konsumenteninteressen über die Lebenshaltung im Kriege, Die Erhebung vom April 1916', *Reichs-Arbeitsblatt*, 15 (1917)

Eltzbacher, P. (ed.), *Die deutsche Volksernahrung und der englische Aushungerungs-plan. Eine Denkschrift von Friedrich Aereboe*, Braunschweig, 1914

Englander, D. and Osborne, J. 'Jack, Tommy and Henry Dubb: the armed forces and the working class', *Historical Journal*, 21 (1978)

Eockhout, P. van den and Scholliers, P. 'De hoofdelijke voedselconsumptie in Belgie, 1831–1939', *Tijdschrift voor sociale geschiedenis*, 8 (1983)

'Die Erhebung vom Juli 1916', *Reichsarbeitsblatt*, 15, 1917

Evans, R. J. *The feminist movement in Germany 1894–1933*, London, 1976

Sozialdemokratie und Frauenemanzipation im deutschen Kaiserreich, Berlin, 1979

Erhebung von Wirtschaftsrechnungen minderbemittelter Familien im Deutschen Reiche, Berlin, 1909

Fabian, P. 'Kriegshilfe der deutschen Eisen- und Stahlindustrie', *Stahl und Eisen*, 7 (1916)

Fabian Women's Group. *The war, women and unemployment*, London, 1915

Farrall, L. A. *The origins and growth of the English eugenics movement, 1865–1925*, New York, 1985, ch. 6

'Controversy and conflict in science: a case study – the English biometric school and Mendel's laws', *Social Studies of Science*, 5 (1975)

Fassbender, M. *Des deutschen Volkes Wille zum Leben*, Freiburg, 1917

Favre-Le van Ho, M. 'Un milieu porteur de modernisation: travail et travailleurs vietnamiens en France pendant la première guerre mondiale', PhD dissertation, École des Chartes, Paris, 1986

Fawcett, M. G. *The women's victory and after*, London, 1920

Federn, P. *Psychologie der Revolution – Die vaterlose Gesellschaft*, Leipzig, 1919

Feinstein, C. H. *National income, expenditure and output of the United Kingdom 1855–1965*, Cambridge, 1972

Feldman, G. D. *Army, industry and labor in Germany 1914–1918*, Princeton, NJ, 1966

Felician, J. 'Remarques sur le travail des femmes dans les Bouches du Rhône pendant la première guerre mondiale' in *Colloque sur l'histoire de sécurite sociale*, Paris, 1985

Ferguson, M. 'The family budgets and dietaries of forty labouring class families in Glasgow in war time', *Proceedings of the Royal Society of Edinburgh*, 37 (1916–17)

Ferro, M. *The Great War 1914–1918*, London, 1970

Festy, P. 'Effets et répercussions de la première guerre mondiale sur la fécondité française', *Population*, 39 (1984)

Final Report of the Health of Munition Workers Committee, PP 1918, xiii, Cd 9065

Fischer, A. 'Der Frauenüberschuss. Eine sozialhygienische Betrachtung Naumannscher Aufsätze', *Hilfe*, 17 (1911)

Fischer, H. C. and Dubois, E. X. *Sexual life during the World War*, London, 1937

Flux, A. W. 'Our food supply before and after the war', *Journal of the Royal Statistical Society*, new series, 93 (1930)

Forty-fifth Annual Report of the Local Government Board. Supplement in Continuance of the Report of the Medical Officer of the Board for 1915–16. Containing a Report on Child Mortality at Age 0–5, PP 1917–18, xvi, Cd 8496

Frachon, B. *Pour la C.G.T.*, Paris, 1981

Fraenkel, H. and Manvell, R. *Himmler, Kleinbürger and Massenmörder*, Frankfurt am Main and Berlin, 1965

Frankenberg, D. von. 'Beteiligung von Frauen an der Waisen- und Armenpflege in Braunschweig', *Soziale Reform und Medizin*, 2 (1907)

Fraser, J. 'Propaganda on the picture postcard', *The Oxford Art Journal* 3 (October 1980)

Die Frauenarbeit in der Metallindustrie während des Krieges, dargestellt nach Erhebungen im August/September des Vorstandes des Deutschen Metallarbeiter-Verbandes, Stuttgart, 1917

Freeden, M. 'Eugenics and progressive thought: a study in ideological affinity', *Historical Journal*, 22 (1979)

'Eugenics and ideology', *Historical Journal*, 26 (1983)

Freiherr von Bardolff, C. *Soldat im alten österreich. Erinnerungen aus meinem Leben*, Vienna, 1936 and 1943

Freud, S. Introduction to 'Zur Psychoanalyse der Kriegsneurosen'. *Internationale psychoanalytische Bibliothek*, 1 (1919)

Freudenberg, K. 'Berechnungen zur Abtreibungsstatistik', *Zeitschrift für Hygiene und Infektionskrankheiten*, 104 (1925)

Freundlich, E. 'Die Frauenarbeit im Kriege' in F. Hanusch and E. Adler (eds.), *Die Regelung der Arbeitsverhältnisse im Kriege*, Vienna, 1927

Fridenson, P. 'Automobile workers in France and their work, 1914–83' in S. L. Kaplan and C. J. Koepp (eds.), *Work in France*, Ithaca, NY, 1986

(ed.) *1914–18: L'Autre front*, Paris, 1977

Frois, M. *La Santé et le travail des femmes pendant la guerre*. Paris, 1926

Fulford, R. *Votes for women*, London, 1958

Fürst, M. 'Der Leipziger Verband und die Gesellschaft für Soziale Reform', *Soziale Medizin und Hygiene*, 2 (1907)

Fürth, H. *Die Hausfrau*, Munich, 1914

Gabriel-Robinet, L. *La Censure*, Paris, 1965

Gallie, D. *Social inequality and class radicalism in France and Britain*, Cambridge, 1983

Gallois, J. 'Quelques aspects de la vie en France pendant la guerre de 1914–1918 vus à travers *L'Illustration* et quelques autres périodiques', MA dissertation, University of Reims, 1977

Gay, G. *The commission for relief in Belgium: Statistical review of relief operations*, Stanford, 1925

von Gersdorff, U. *Frauen im Kriegsdienst 1914–1945*, Stuttgart, 1969

Giddens, A. *The class structure of the advanced societies*, London, 1981

Giesecke, H. *Vom Wandervogel bis zur Hitlerjugend. Jugendarbeit zwischen Politik und Pädagogik*, Munich, 1981

Gill, D. and Dallas, G. *The unknown army*, London, 1986

Gillis, J. R. *Geschichte der Jugend*, Weinheim and Basle, 1980

Gittins, D. *Fair sex, family size and structure, 1900–39*, London, 1982

Glass, D. V. *Population policies and movements in Europe*, Oxford, 1940

Godfrey, J. F. *Capitalism at war. Industrial policy and bureaucracy in France 1914–1918*, Leamington Spa, 1987

Godfroid, H. 'Les oeuvres sociales à l'usine', *Chimie et Industrie* (September–October 1918)

Goetz, B. 'Entwicklung und Verfassung der Hauswirtschaft innerhalb der Volkswirtschaft' in Briefs G., et al., *Die Hauswirtschaft im Kriege*, Beiträge zur Kriegswirtschaft 25, Berlin, 1917

Goux, J. P. *Mémoires de l'enclave*, Paris, 1986

Gratz, G. and Schüller, R. *Der wirtschaftliche Zusammenbruch Österreich-Ungarns*, Vienna, 1930

Gravert, E. M. 'Der Einfluß der wirtschaftlichen Demobilmachung auf die Entwicklung der Frauenarbeit', unpublished dissertation, Hamburg, 1924–5

Greven-Aschoff, B. *Die bürgerliche Frauenbewegung in Deutschland 1894–1933*, Göttingen, 1981

Grossheim, H. *Sozialisten in der Verantwortung. Die Französischen Sozialisten und Gewerkschaften im ersten Weltkrieg 1914–1917*, Bonn, 1978

Grotjahn, A. *Geburtenrückgang und Geburtenregelung*, Berlin, 1914
Der Wehrbeitrag der deutschen Frau, Bonn, 1915

Gruber, M. von. *Ursachen und Bekämpfung des Geburtenrückganges im Deutschen Reich*, Munich, 1914

Guilbert, M. *Les Fonctions des femmes dans l'industrie*, Paris, 1966

Guillaume, J. C. *Guillet. Histoire d'une entreprise 1847–1879*, Auxerre, 1986

Gunther, E. 'Haushalt des kleinen Mittelstandes und der Arbeiter', *Schmollers Jahrbuch*, 34 (1910)

Haber, L. R. *The poisonous cloud*, Oxford, 1986

Hackett, A. 'The German women's movement and suffrage, 1890–1914: A study of national feminism' in R. Bezucha (ed.), *Modern European Social History*, Lexington, Mass., 1972
'The politics of feminism in Wilhelmine Germany 1890–1918', PhD, Columbia University, 1976

Hajnal, J. 'Age at marriage and proportions marrying', *Population Studies*, 7 (1953)

Haller, M. *Theorie der Klassenbildung und der sozialen Schichtung*, Frankfurt and New York, 1983

Hamilton, M. A. *Mary Macarthur*, London, 1925

Hammond, M. *British labor conditions and legislation during the war*, New York, 1919

Hansen, E., et al. *Seit über einem Jahrhundert . . . Verschüttete Alternativen in der Sozialpolitik*, Cologne, 1981

Hanssen, R. 'Die Abnahme der Geburtenzahlen in den verschiedenen Bevölkerungsklassen', *Archiv für soziale hygiene*, 7 (1912)

Hanusch, F. and Adler, E. (eds.) *Die Regelung der Arbeitsverhältnisse im Kriege*, Vienna, 1927

Hardach, G. *The First World War 1914–1918*, London, 1977
'Guerre, Etat et main d'ouevre', *Recherches* 13 (1978)

Hardy-Hémery, O. *De la croissance à la désindustrialisation*, Paris, 1984

Hartmann, F. *Die Heeresverpflegung (Beiträge zur Kriegswirtschaft* 11), Berlin, 1917

Hartmann, H. 'Capitalism, patriarchy and job segregation by sex' in Zillah Eisenstein (ed.), *Capitalist patriarchy and the case for socialist feminism*, New York, 1978

Hatry, G. 'Les délégués d'atelier aux usines Renault' in P. Fridenson (ed.), *1914–1918: l'autre front*, Paris, 1977
Renault usine de guerre 1914–1918, Paris, 1978
'Les rapports gouvernement, armée, industrie privée pendant la première guerre mondiale: le cas des usines Renault' in G. Canini (ed.), *Les Fronts invisibles*, Nancy, 1984

Hautmann, H. *Die Anfänge der linksradikalen Bewegung und der Kommunistischen Partei Deutsch-Österreichs 1916–1919*, 1970
'Hunger ist ein schlechter Koch' in G. Botz et al. (eds.), *Bewegung und Klasse. Studien zur österreichischen Arbeitergeschichte*, Vienna, 1978

Health of Munition Workers' Committee. Interim Report. Industrial efficiency and fatigue, PP 1917–18, xvi, Cd 8511

Health of Munition Workers' Committee. Memorandum on the employment of women, PP 1916, xxiii, Cd 8185

Henderson, H. D. *The Cotton Control Board*, Oxford, 1922
Henry, A. *Le Ravitaillement de la Belgique pendant l'occupation allemande*, Paris, 1924
Henry, L. 'Les Perturbations de la nuptialité résultant de la guerre de 1914–1918', *Population*, 20 (1966)
Herbig, E. 'Wirtschaftsrechnungen Saarbrücker Bergleute', *Zeitschrift für das Berg-, Hütten- und Salinen-Wesen in dem preussischen Staat*, 60 (1912)
Heuss, T. *Friedrich Naumann*, Stuttgart and Tübingen, 1949
Hinton, J. *The first shop stewards' movement*, London, 1974
Hirsch, M. *Fruchtabtreibung und Präventivverkehr im Zusammenhang mit dem Geburtenrückgang*, Würzburg, 1914
  'Zur Statistik des Aborts', *Zentralblatt für Gynäkologie*, part I, no. 3, part II, no. 43, 1918
Hirsch, P. 'Die Kriegsfürsorge der deutschen Gemeinden', *Annalen für soziale Politik und Gesetzgebund*, 4 (1916)
Hirschfeld, M. *Geschlechtskunde auf Grund dreissigjahr*, Stuttgart, 1928, vol. II
  (ed.), *Sittengeschichte des Weltkriegs*, 2 vols., Leipzig and Vienna, n.d., vol. 1
Hirschfeld, M. and Gaspar, A. (eds.), *Sittengeschichte des Ersten Weltkrieges*, Hanau, 1929
His, W. *Die Front der Ärzte*, Bielefeld and Leipzig, 1931
Hitze, F. *Geburtenrückgang und Sozialreform*, Mönchen-Gladbach, 1917
Hochard, J. 'Les origines françaises des allocations familiales avant 1920' in Comité d'histoire de la sécurité sociale (ed.), *Colloque sur l'histoire de la sécurité sociale*, Paris, 1984
Hoffman, M. 'Das Gesetz betreffend die Unterstützung von Familien in den Dienst eingetretener Mannschaften vom 28.2.1888/4.8.1914 und seine Anwendung', unpublished dissertation, Berlin, 1918
Horrman, W. *Die deutschen Ärzte im Weltkriege*, Berlin, 1940
Hoffmann, W. G., Grumbach, F. and Hesse, H. *Das Wachstum der deutschen Wirtschaft seit der Mitte des 19. Jahrhunderts*, Berlin, 1965
Hoffmann, W. G. and Müller, J. H. *Das deutsche Volkseinkommen*, Tübingen, 1959
Hogben, L. T. *Genetic principles in medicine and social science*, London, 1931
  Nature and nurture, London, 1939
Holtfrerich, C.-L. *Die deutsche Inflation 1914–1923. Ursachen und Folgen in internationaler Perspektive*, Berlin and New York, 1980
Hoover, H. *An American epic, vol. 1, The relief of Belgium and Northern France, 1914–1930*, Chicago, 1959
Horne, J. 'Le Comité d'Action (CGT–PS) et l'origine du réformisme syndical du temps de guerre (1914–1916)', *Le Mouvement Social*, 24 (1983)
  'Immigrant workers in France during World War I', *French Historical Studies*, 14 (1985)
Horse, H. 'Maßnahmen zur Behebung der durch den Krieg enstanenen Arbeitslosigkeit in Krefeld', *Der Arbeitsnachweis in Deutschland*, 2 (1914/15)
Hug, E. and Rigoulot, P. *Le croque-rave libertaire*, Paris, 1980
Humphreys, G. C. *Taylorism in France 1904–1920*, New York and London, 1986
Hutchins, B. L. *Women in modern industry*, London, 1915
Interim Report of the Women's Employment Commission, PP 1914–16, xxxviii, Cd 7848
Isserlis, L. 'Tramp shipping, cargoes and freights', *Journal of the Royal Statistical Society*, new series, 101 (1938)
Jahrbuch des Bundes deutscher Frauenvereine 1917, Berlin, 1917
Jeanneney, J.-N. 'Les archives de contrôle postal aux armées (1916–18). Une source

précieuse pour l'histoire contemporaine de l'opinion et des mentalités', *Revue d'histoire moderne et contemporaine*, 15 (1968)

Jeschal, G. *Politik und Wissenschaft deutscher Ärzte im ersten Weltkrieg*, Pattensen, 1978

John, A. *By the sweat of their brow*, London, 1984

(ed.) *Unequal opportunities. Women's employment in Britain 1800–1918*, Oxford, 1986

Jones, G. 'Eugenics and social policy between the wars', *The Historical Journal*, 25 (1982)

Jünger, E. 'Der Krieg als inneres Erlebnis' in R. Winter (ed.), *Auszüge aus seinen Schriften*, Frankfurt am Main, 1933

Kalender der deutschen Jugend 1936, Bayreuth, 1935

Kaufmann, P. *Krieg, Geschlechtskrankheiten und Arbeiterversicherung*, Berlin, 1916

Kautsky, K. *Vermehrung und Entwicklung in Natur und Gesellschaft*, Stuttgart, 1910

Kellogg, V. *Headquarters nights*, New York, 1919

Kempf, R. *Das Leben der jungen Fabrikmädchen in München*, Leipzig, 1911

'Das weibliche Dienstjahr', *Archiv für Sozialwissenschaft und Sozialpolitik*, 41 (1916)

Kertzer, D. I. *Family life in central Italy 1880–1910*, New Brunswick, NJ, 1984

Kevles, D. J. *In the name of eugenics: genetics and the uses of human heredity*, New York, 1985

Keynes, J. M. *The collected writings of John Maynard Keynes* (ed.) E. Johnson, vol. XVI, London, 1971

Kindt, W. *Die deutsche Hugendbewegung 1920 bis 1933. Die bündische Zeit*, Cologne, 1974

Kirchner, M. 'Kriegsernährung und Volksgesundheit', *Berliner Lokalanzeiger*, 6 November 1916

Ärztliche Kriegs- und Friedensgedanken, Berlin, 1918

Klenner, F. *Die österreichischen Gewerkschaften*, vol. 1, Vienna, 1951

Klönne, A. *Jugend im Dritten Reich*, Cologne, 1982

Kneip, R. *Jugend in der Weimarer Republik. Handbuch der Jugendverbände 1919–1938*, Frankfurt am Main, 1974

Knodel, J. E. *The decline of fertility in Germany, 1871–1939*, Princeton, 1974

Knorring, E. van. 'Strukturwandlungen des privaten Konsums im Wachstums-Prozess der deutschen Wirtschaft seit der Mitte des 19. Jahrhunderts' in Walther G. Hoffmann (ed.), *Untersuchungen zum Wachstum der deutschen Wirtschaft*, Tübingen, 1971

Knox, W. (ed.) *Scottish labour leaders, 1918–1939*, Edinburgh, 1984

Kocka, J. *Klassengesellschaft im Krieg. Deutsche Sozialgeschichte 1914–1918*, Göttingen, 1973

Die Angestellten in der deutschen Geschichte 1850–1980, Göttingen, 1981

Facing total war. German society 1914–1918, trans. B. Weinberger, Leamington Spa, 1984

Koebner, T., Janz, R.-P. and Trommler, F. (eds.) *Mit uns zieht die neue Zeit. Der Mythos Jugend*, Frankfurt am Main, 1985

Kozak, M. 'Women munition workers during the First World War with special reference to engineering', unpublished PhD thesis, University of Hull, 1977

Krohne, O. *Die Beurteilung des Geburtsrückgangs vom volkshygienischen, sittlichen und nationalen Standpunkt*, Leipzig, 1914

Kuczynski, J. *Die Geschichte der Lage der Arbeiter unter dem Kapitalismus*, vol. 4, Berlin, 1967

Kuczynski, R. and Zuntz, N. 'Deutschlands Nahrungs- und Futtermittel', *Allgemeines Statistisches Archiv*, 9 (1915)

Kuisel, R. F. *Capitalism and the state in modern France*, Cambridge, 1981

Kunz, A. 'Verteilungskampf oder Interessenkonsensus? Zur Entwicklung der Realeinkommen vom Beamten, Arbeitern und Angestellten in der Inflationszeit 1914–1924' in Gerald D. Feldman et al. (eds.), *Die deutsche Inflation. Eine Zwischenbilanz*, Berlin and New York, 1982

Kyrou, A. *L'Age d'or de la carte postale*, Paris, 1966

Labisch, A. 'Die gesundheitspolitischen Vorstellungen der deutschen Sozialdemokratie von ihre Gründung bis zur Parteispaltung (1863–1917)', *Archiv für Sozialgeschichte*, 16 (1976)

Labisch, A. and Tennstedt, F. *Der Weg zum 'Gesetz über die Vereinheitlichung des Gesundheitswesens'*, Düsseldorf, 1986

Landwehr, General. *Hunger, Die Erschöpfungsjahre der Mittelmächte 1917/18*, Vienna, 1931

Laqueur, W. Z. *Die deutsche Jugendbewegung. Eine historische Studie*, Cologne, 1962

Laslett, P. *Family life and illicit love in earlier generations*, Cambridge, 1977

Lavisse, E. *Histoire générale à l'usage des candidats au certificat d'études primaires*, Paris, 1884

Histoire de France depuis les origines jusqu'à la révolution, Paris, 1900–11

Die Lebenshaltung von 2,000 Arbeiter-, Angestellten- und Beamtenhaushaltungen. Erhebungen von Wirtschaftsrechnungen im Deutschen Reich vom Jahre 1927/28, Berlin, 1932

Lee, J. J. 'Administrators and agriculture: some aspects of German agricultural policy in the First World War' in J. M. Winter (ed.), *War and economic development: essays in memory of David Joslin*, Cambridge, 1975

Leed, E. J. *No man's land*, Cambridge, 1979

Lehmann, J. 'Untersuchungen über Gewicht, Grosse und Hämoglobingehalt des Blutes der Kinder einer Bürgerschule in Löbau', *Zeitschrift für Schulgesundheitspflege*, 33 (1920)

Leichter, K. *Frauenarbeit und Arbeiterinnenschutz in Österreich*, Vienna, 1917

Lennig, R. and Birsch, M. 'Sozialgynäkologie und Frauenkunde', unpublished medical dissertation, Free University of Berlin, 1977

Lenz, R. 'Die Lebensmittel-Zulagen für die schwerarbeitende Bevölkerung' in A. Stegerwald, R. Lenz, L. Wiernik, *Die Schwerarbeiterfrage* (*Beiträge zur Kriegswirtschaft 26/27*), Berlin, 1917

Lewenhak, S. *Women in trade unions*, London, 1977

Lewin, L. *Die Fruchtabtreibung durch Gifte und andere Mittel. Ein Handbuch für Ärzte und Juristen*, Berlin, 1922

Lewis, J. *The politics of motherhood. Child and maternal welfare in England, 1900–1939*, London, 1980

Leybourne, G. 'An estimate of the future population of Great Britain', *Sociological Review*, 36 (1934)

Lidbetter, E. J. *Heredity and the social problem group*, vol. I, London, 1933

Linse, U. 'Arbeiterschaft und Geburtenentwicklung im deutschen Kaiserreich von 1871', *Archiv für Sozialgeschichte*, 12 (1972)

Lloyd, E. M. H. 'Food and money: some reflections on changes in food consumption and farm prices', *Journal of Proceedings of the Agricultural Economics Society*, 10 (1953)

Lloyd George, D. *War memoirs*, 2 vols., London, 1933

Loewenberg, P. *Decoding the past. The psycho-historical approach*, Berkeley, 1985

Lojkine, J. and Viet-Depaule, N. *Classe ouvrière, société locale et municipalités en région parisienne*, Paris, 1984

Lorenz, C. 'Die gewerbliche Frauenarbeit während des Krieges' in P. Umbreit and C. Lorenz, *Der Krieg und der Arbeitsverhältnisse*, Stuttgart, 1928

Lorenz, E. H. 'The labour process and industrial relations in the British and French shipbuilding industries from 1880 to 1970', PhD, Cambridge, 1983

Losseff-Tillmanns, G. *Frauenemanzipation und Gewerkschaften*, Wuppertal, 1978

Lowe, R. 'The Ministry of Labour, 1916–1924: a graveyard of social reform', *Public Administration*, 52 (1974)

Lüders, M.-E. *Volksdienst der Frau*, Berlin, 1917

Das unbekannte Heer. Frauen kämpfen für Deutschland, Berlin, 1937

Die Entwicklung der gewerblichen Frauenarbeit im Kriege, Munich and Leipzig, 1920

'Die Entwicklung der gewerblichen Frauenarbeit im Kriege', *Schmollers Jahrbuch*, 44 (1920)

Ludwig, E. *Die Unterstützungsabteilung des Badischen Landesvereins vom Roten Kreuz und die Badische Kriegsarbeitshilfe*, Karlsruhe, 1918

Luquet, A. *La législation sur les loyers de guerre*, Paris, 1919

Macarthur, M. 'The woman trade unionist's point of view' in Marion Phillips (ed.), *Women and the Labour Party*, London, 1918

Macassey, L. *Labour policy – false or true*, London, 1922

McCleary, G. F. *The maternity and child welfare movement*, London, 1935

Maternal and child welfare, London, 1934

MacKenzie, D. 'Eugenics in Britain', *Social Studies of Science*, 6 (1976)

'Karl Pearson and the professional middle class', *Annals of Science*, 36 (1976)

McLean, I. *The legend of red Clydeside*, Edinburgh, 1983

Macnicol, J. *The movement for family allowances, 1918–45*, London, 1980

Magri, S. 'Le mouvement des locataires à Paris, 1919–1925', *Le Mouvement Social*, 27 (1986)

Maier, C. *Recasting bourgeois Europe*, Princeton, 1977

Mallet, Sir B. 'The social problem group', *Eugenics Review*, 23 (1931)

March, L. *Le Mouvement des prix et des salaires pendant la guerre*, Paris, 1925

Marchant, J. *Birth-rate and empire*, London, 1917

Marcuse, M. 'Zur Frage der Verbreitung und Methode der willkürlichen Geburtenbeschränkung in Berliner Proletarierkreisen', *Sexualprobleme*, 9 (November 1913)

Der eheliche Präventivverkehr. Seine Verbreitung, Verursachung und Methodik, dargestellt und beleuchtet am 300 Ehen, Stuttgart, 1917

Wandlungen des Fortpflanzungs-Gedankens und -Willens, Bonn, 1918

Marschalk, P. *Bevölkerungsgeschichte Deutschlands im 19. und 20. Jahrhundert*, Frankfurt am Main, 1984

Martin, A. *The mother and social reform*, London, 1913

Marwick, A. *The deluge. British society and the First World War*, London, 1966

Britain in the century of total war, London, 1970

Women at war, London, 1977

Mason, T. 'Women in Germany, 1925–1940: family, welfare and work', *History Workshop*, 1 (1976), and 2 (1976)

Massnahmen sur Bekämpfung der Geschlechtskrankheiten, Brussels, 1915
Matsumura, T. *The labour aristocracy revisited. The Victorian flint glass makers 1850–80*, Manchester, 1983
Meerwarth, M., Günther, A. and Zimmermann, W. (eds.) *Die Einwirkung des Krieges auf Bevölkerungsbewegung und der Lebenshaltung in Deutschland* (Wirtschafts- und Sozialgeschichte des Weltkrieges, Deutsche Serie (ed.) James T. Shotwell), Stuttgart and New Haven, 1932
Mellanby, K. *Can Britain feed itself?*, London, 1975
Mendelsohn-Bartholdy, A. *The War and German society, the testament of a liberal*, New Haven, 1937
Meyer-Renschhausen, E. 'Das radikal traditionelle Selbstbild', *Geschichtsdidaktik*, 10 (1985)
Michelet, J. *Le Peuple*, Paris, 1874
Middleton, T. H. *Food production in war*, Oxford, 1923
Ministère de l'Agriculture. *Consommation de la viande de boucherie*. Publication du Service des Associations et de la Statistique, Brussels, 1919–22
Mitford, M. R. *Our village*, London, 1936
Moll, A. von. *Handbuch des Sexualwissenschaften*, Leipzig, 1912
Moutet, A. 'La première guerre mondiale et le taylorisme' in M. de Montmollin and O. Pastré (eds.), *Le taylorisme*, Paris, 1984
'Ingénieurs et rationalisation 1914–1929' in A. Thépot (ed.), *L'ingénieur dans la société française*, Paris, 1985
Müller, J. 'Die Regelung des Arbeitsmarkts in der Zeit der wirtschaftlichen Demobilmachung', unpublished dissertation, Erlangen, 1923
Müller, W., Willms, A. and Handl, J. *Strukturwandel der Frauenarbeit 1880–1980*, Frankfurt, 1983
Nadav, D. S. *Julius Moses und die Politik der Sozialhygiene in Deutschland*, Gerlingen, 1985
National Birth-Rate Commission. *Problems of population and parenthood, being the second report of and the chief evidence taken by the National Birth-Rate Commission, 1918–1920*, New York, 1920
The declining birth-rate. Its causes and effects. Being the report and the chief evidence taken by the National Birth-Rate Commission, instituted with official recognition by the National Council of Public Morals – for the promotion of Race regeneration – spiritual, moral and physical, London, 1916
National Federation of Women Workers. *Annual Report*, 1911
Néant, H. (ed.) *La Sarthe 1914–1939*, Le Mans, 1979
Nemitz, K. 'Julius Moses und die Gebärstreikdebatte 1913', *Jahrbuch des Instituts für deutsche Geschichte*, 2 (1973)
Neudin, J. and G. *L'Argus international des cartes postales de collection*, Paris, 1983
Neumann, R. P. 'Working-class birth control in Wilhelmine Germany', *Comparative Studies in Society and History*, 20 (1978)
Nieden-Rohwinkel, W. zur. 'Die Tuberkulosefürsorge in den Landkreisen der Rheinprovinz', *Schmollers Jahrbuch*, 37 (1913)
Nipperdey, T. 'Probleme der Modernisierung in Deutschland', *Saeculum*, 30 (1979)
Nora, P. 'Ernest Lavisse: son rôle dans la formation du sentiment national', *Revue historique*, 228 (1962)
Oddy, D. and Miller, D. (eds.) *The making of the modern British diet*, London, 1976
Official History of the Ministry of Munitions, London, 1922
Ogden, P. E. and Huss, M. M. 'Demography and pronatalism in France in the 19th

and 20th centuries', *Journal of Historical Geography*, 8 (1982)

Olbrechts, R. 'La Population' in E. Mahaim (ed.), *Le Belgique restaurée. Etude sociologique*, Brussels, 1926

Olcott, T. 'The women's trade union movement', *London Journal*, 2 (1976)

Omnès, C. *De l'atelier au groupe industriel*, Paris, 1980

Oschmann, 'Der Einfluss der Kriegkost auf die Schulkinder, *Zeitschrift für Schulgesundheitspflege*, 30 (1917)

Oualid, W. and Picquenard, C. *Salaires et tarifs. Conventions collectives pendant la guerre (1914–1918)*, Paris, 1928

Palmer, M. *Life-saving. A campaign handbook. The Infant Welfare Propaganda Committee of the National League for Physical Education and Improvement*, London, 1916

Pankhurst, E. S. *The Suffragette movement*, London, 1931
The home front, London, 1932

Papayanis, N. *Alphonse Merrheim*, Dordrecht, 1985

Paul, W. *Das Feldlager. Jugend zwischen Langemarck und Stalingrad*, Esslingen, 1978

Peacock, A. and Wiseman, J. *The growth of public expenditure in the United Kingdom*, Cambridge, 1967

Pearson, K. *Nature and nurture – the problem of the future. A Presidential address at the annual meeting of the Social and Political Education League, April 28, 1910*, London, 1910

Peiper, A. *Chronik der Kinderheilkunde*, Leipzig, 1951

Peiter, H. D. 'Les patrons, les mutilés de guerre et la France', *Recherches*, 13 (1978)

Pelé, E. 'Le mouvement ouvrier lyonnais pendant la première guerre mondiale', MA, University of Lyon II, 1970

Pelling, H. *A history of British trade unionism*, London, 1972

Perreux, G. *La Vie quotidienne des civils pendant la guerre de 1914–18*, Paris, 1966

Perrot, M. 'La ménagère et la classe ouvrière', Vincennes colloquium on 'Les femmes et la classe ouvrière', December 1978
'La ménagère dans l'espace parisien au xixᵉ siècle', *Nouvelles annales de la recherche urbaine*, December 1980

Pfoser, A. 'Verstörte Männer und emanzipierte Frauen' in F. Kadrnoska (ed.), *Aufbruch und Untergang*, Vienna, 1982

Phillips, M. (ed.) *Women and the Labour party*, London, 1918

Pierenkemper, T. *Arbeitsmarkt und Angestellte im Deutschen Kaiserreich, 1880–1913*, Münster, 1989
'Die Einkommensentwicklung der Angestellten in Deutschland 1880–1913', *Historical Social Research*, 27 (1983)

Pirenne, H. *La Belgique et la guerre mondiale*, Paris–New Haven, 1928

Pirhofer, G. and Sieder, R. 'Zur Konstitution der Arbeiterfamilie im Roten Wien' in M. Mitterauer and R. Sieder (eds.), *Historische Familienforschung*, Frankfurt, 1982

Piven, F. and Cloward, R. *Regulating the poor. The functions of public welfare*, London, 1974

Plaschka, R. G., Haselsteiner, H. and Suppan, S. *Innere Front. Militärassistenz, Widerstand und Umsturz in der Donaumonarchie 1918*, Vienna, 1974

Pogge van Strandman, H. (ed.) *Walther Rathenau. Industrialist, banker, intellectual and politician. Notes and diaries 1907–1922*, Oxford, 1985

Polano, O. 'Beitrag zur Frage der Geburtenbeschränkung', *Zeitschrift für Geburtshilfe und Gynäkologie*, 79 (1917)

Pollard, S. *The development of the British economy 1914–1950*, London, 1962

Pollet, C. 'La vie quotidienne des Rouennais pendant la guerre de 1914–1918', MA, University of Rouen, 1974

Pommerin, R. *Sterilisierung der Rheinlandbastarde: das Schicksal einer farbigen deutschen Minderheit*, Düsseldorf, 1979

Prange, P. 'Die Demobilmachung des Arbeitsmarkts im Deutschen Reich nach Beendigung des Weltkriegs 1914/18', unpublished dissertation, Würzburg, 1923

Preller, L. *Sozialpolitik in der Weimarer Republik*, Kronberg and Düsseldorf, 1978

Prest, A. R. and Adams, A. A. *Consumers' expenditure in the United Kingdom 1900–1919*, Cambridge, 1954

Pribram, K. 'Die Sozialpolitik im neuen Österreich', *Archiv für Sozialwissenschaft und Sozialpolitik*, 48 (1920/21)

Prinzing, F. *Epidemics resulting from wars*, Oxford, 1916
Handbuch der medizinschen Statistik, Jena, 1931

Prost, A. *Les Anciens Combattants et la société française*, Paris, 1977
Histoire de l'enseignement en France, 1800–1967, Paris, 1968

Quante, P. 'Lohnpolitik und Lohnentwicklung im Kriege' in *Zeitschrift des Preussischen Statistischen Landesamtes*, 59 (1919)

Quataert, J. H. 'The German socialist women's movement 1890–1918', PhD, University of California, 1984
Reluctant feminists in German Social Democracy 1885–1917, Princeton, 1979

Raabe, F. *Die bündische Jugend*, Stuttgart, 1961

Rapport général sur le fonctionnement et les opérations du Comité National de Secours et d'Alimentation 1914–1919, 5 vols., Brussels, 1920–7

Rapport spécial sur le fonctionnement et les opérations de la section agricole du Comité National de Secours et d'Alimentation, 1914–1919, Brussels, 1920

Rauschning, H. *Gespräche mit Hitler*, Zurich and New York, 1940

Regional Office of Statistics, Munich. *Der Kriegs- Volkszählangen vom 1916 und 1917 in Bayern*, Beiträge zur Statistik Bayerns, 89, Munich, 1919
Die Frau der bayerischen Kriegsindustrie, Beiträge zur Statistik Bayerns, 92, Munich, 1920
Arbeitsverhältnisse und Organisation der häuslichen Dienstboten in Bayern, Beiträge zur Statistik Bayerns, 94, Munich, 1921

Reich Office of Statistics. *Jahresberichte der Gewerbeausichtsbeamten und Bergbehörden für die Jahre 1914–18*, vol. 1, Berlin, 1920

Reid, A. J. 'The division of labour in the British shipbuilding industry, 1880–1920', PhD, Cambridge, 1980
'Dilution, trade unionism and the state in Britain during the First World War' in S. Tolliday and J. Zeitlin (eds.), *Shop floor baragining and the State*, Cambridge, 1985
'The division of labour and politics in Britain, 1850–1920' in W. J. Mommsen and H.-G. Husung (eds.), *The development of trade unionism in Great Britain and Germany 1880–1914*, London, 1985

Reid, D. 'Guillaume Verdier et le syndicalisme révolutionnaire aux usines de Decazeville (1917–1920)', *Annales du Midi*, 96 (1984)
The miners of Decazeville, Cambridge, Mass., 1985

Rency, G. and Stassar, A. *La Belgique et la guerre, vol. I, La vie matérielle de la Belgique pendant la première guerre mondiale*, Brussels, 1920.

Renouvin, P. 'L'opinion publique et la guerre en 1917', *Revue d'histoire moderne et contemporaine*, 20 (1968)

Report of an enquiry by the Board of Trade into working-class rents, housing, retail prices and standard rates of wages in the principal industrial towns of Belgium, PP 1905, xcv, Cd 5065

Report of the Committee appointed to enquire into and report upon (i) the actual increase since June 1914, in the cost of living to the working classes, and (ii) any counterbalancing factors (apart from increases of wages) which may have arisen under war conditions, PP 1918, vii, Cd 8980

Report of the proceedings of the National Conference on Infant Mortality, 1906, London, 1906

Report of the Proceedings of the National Conference on Infant Mortality at St. George's Hotel, Liverpool, Liverpool, 1914

Report of the War Cabinet Committee on Women in Industry, PP 1919, xxxi, Cmd 135

Report of the Women's Employment Committee for the Ministry of Reconstruction, PP 1918, xiv, Cd 9239

Résultats statistiques du recensement général de la population, Mars 1911, Paris, 1913

Resurgam. La reconstruction en Belgique après 1914, Brussels, 1985

Reulecke, J. 'Städtische Finanzprobleme und Kriegswohlfahrtspflege', *Zeitschrift für Stadtgeschichte, Stadtsoziologie und Denkmalpflege*, 1 (1975)

'Bürgerliche Sozialreformer und Arbeiterjugend im Kaiserreich', *Archiv für Sozialgeschichte*, 22 (1982)

Riedl, R. *Die Industrie Österreichs während des Krieges*, Vienna, 1932

Riley, D. ' "The free mothers": pronatalism and working women in industry at the end of the last war in Britain', *History Workshop*, 11 (1981)

Robert, J.-L. 'Les luttes ouvrières en France pendant la première guerre mondiale', *Cahiers d'histoire de l'Institut de Recherches Marxistes*, 11 (1977)

'Nouveaux éléments sur les origines de P.C.F.', *Cahiers d'histoire de l'Institut de Recherches Marxistes*, 14 (1980)

La scission syndicale de 1921, Paris, 1980

'La CGT et la famille ouvrière 1914–1918, première approche', *Mouvement Social*, 22 (1981)

'Les "programmes minimums" de la CGT de 1918 et 1921', *Cahiers d'histoire de l'Institut de Recherches Marxistes*, 18 (1984)

Roesle, E. 'Die Magdeburger Fehlgeburtenstatistik', *Archiv für soziale Hygiene und Demographie*, 1 (1925/6)

Ronsin, F. *La grève des ventres*, Paris, 1980

Rosenbaum, H. *Formen der Familie*, Frankfurt am Main, 1982

Rosenberg, A. *Der Mythus des 20. Jahrhunderts*, Munich, 1930

Rossiter, A. 'Experiments with corporatist politics in Republican France, 1916–1939', DPhil, Oxon, 1986

Routh, G. *Occupation and pay in Great Britain 1906–60*, Cambridge, 1965

Rowntree, R. S. *Poverty. A study of town life*, London, 1901

Royal commission on the supply of food and raw material in time of war, PP 1905, xxxix, Cd 2643

Royal Society. *Food (War) Committee. The food supply of the United Kingdom, 1916*, London, 1916

The food supply of the United Kingdom, PP 1916, ix, Cd 8421

Rubenstein, W. D. 'Wealth, elites and the class structure of modern Britain', *Past and Present*, 76 (1977)

Rubner, M. 'Ernährungswesen' in F. Bumm (ed.), *Deutschlands Gesund-*

heitsverhältnisse unter dem Einfluss des Weltkriegs (Wirtschafts- und Sozialgeschichte des Weltkrieges. Deutsche Serie (ed.) James T. Shotwell), Stuttgart, 1928

Ruegg, W. 'Jugend und Gesellschaft um 1900' in W. Ruegg (ed.), *Kulturkritik und Jugendkult*, Frankfurt am Main, 1974

Rupp, L. 'Mothers of the *Volk*: The image of women in Nazi ideology', *Signs*, 3 (1977)

Ryter, A. 'Abtreibung in Basel zu Beginn des Jahrhunderts' in *Die ungeschriebene Geschichte*, Dokumentation 5. Historikerinnentreffen, Vienna, 1984

Safrian, H. and Sieder, R. 'Gassenkinder – Strassenkämpfer. Zur politischen Sozialisation einer Arbeitergeneration in Wien 1900 bis 1938' in L. Niethammer and A. Plato (eds.), *'Wir kriegen jetzt andere Zeiten'. Auf der Suche nach der Erfahrung des Volkes in nachfaschistischen Ländern*, Bonn and Berlin, 1985

Saleeby, C. W. *Parenthood and race culture. An outline of eugenics*, New York, 1910
The methods of race regeneration, New York, 1911
The progress of eugenics, London, 1914

Salmon, J. M. 'Essai sur là lutte ouvrière dans les usines de guerre de la region parisienne en 1917 et 1918', MA, University of Paris, 1967

Saul, K. et al. (eds.) *Arbeiterfamilien im Kaiserreich. Materialien zur Sozialgeschichte in Deutschland 1871–1914*, Königstein, 1982

Schaeffer-Hegel, B. and Wartmann, B. (eds.) *Mythos Frau Projektionen und Inszenierungen im Patriarchat*, Berlin, 1984

Schäfer, H. *Regionale Wirtschaftspolitik in der Kriegszeit: Staat, Industrie und Verbände während des Ersten Weltkriegs in Baden*, Stuttgart, 1983

Schepens, L. 'Belgie in de Eerste Wereldoorlog' in *Algemene Geschiedenis Nederlanden*, Bussum, 1979, vol. 14

Schmitz, S. *Adolf Neisser*, Düsseldorf, 1968

Schmucker, H. 'Die langfristigen Strukturwandlungen des Verbrauchs der privaten Haushalte in ihrer Interdependenz mit dem übrigen Bereichen einer wachsenden Wirtschaft' in F. Neumark (ed.), *Strukturwandlungen einer wachsenden Wirtschaft* (Schriften des Vereins für Sozialpolitik, new series, vol. 30/I), Berlin, 1964, vol. I

Scholliers, P. 'Verschuivingen in het arbeidersconsumptiepatroon, 1890–1930', *Revue belge d'histoire contemporaine*, 13 (1982)

Scholz, R. 'Ein unruhiges Jahrzehnt: Lebensmittelunruhen, Massenstreiks und Arbeitslosenkrawalle in Berlin 1914–1923' in Manfred Gailus (ed.), *Pöbelexzesse unde Volkstumulte in Berlin. Zur Sozialgeschichte der Strasse (1930–1980)*, Berlin, 1984

Schurtz, H. *Altersklassen und Männerbünde. Eine Darstellung der Grundformen der Gesellschaft*, Berlin, 1902

Schwarz, K. D. *Weltkrieg und Revolution in Nürnberg*, Stuttgart, 1971

Schweitzer, S. *Des engrenages à la chaîne*, Lyon, 1982

Searle, G. R. 'Eugenics and class' in C. Webster (ed.), *Biology, medicine and society*, Cambridge, 1981

Segalen, M. *Sociologie de la famille*, Paris, 1981

Seidel, A. *Frauenarbeit im Ersten Weltkrieg als Problem der staatlichen Sozialpolitik, dargestellt am Biespiel Bayerns*, Frankfurt, 1979

Senator, H. and Kaminer, S. *Krankheiten und Ehe. Darstellung der Beziehungen zwischen Gesundheitsstörungen und Ehegemeinschaft*, Berlin, n.d.

Sichler, R. and Tiburtius, J. *Die Arbeiterfrage, eine Kernfrage des Weltkrieges. Ein Beitrag zur Erklärung des Kriegsausgangs*, Berlin, n.d. (1925?)

Sieder, R. 'Bemerkungen zur Verwendung des Narrativinterviews für eine Geschichte des Alltags', *Zeitgeschichte*, 15 (1982)
'Gassenkinder', *Aufrisse*, 4 (1984)
'Geschichten erzählen und Wissenschaft treiben' in G. Botz and J. Weidenholzer (eds.), *Mündliche Geschichte und Arbeiterbewegung*, Vienna, 1984
'Housing policy, social welfare, and family life in "Red Vienna", 1919–1934', *Oral History*. The Journal of the Oral History Society, 13 (1985)
' "Vata, derf i aufstehn?" Childhood experiences in Viennese working-class families around 1900', *Continuity and Change*, 1 (1986)

Silverman, D. P. *Reconstructing Europe after the Great War*, Cambridge, Mass., 1982

Sköllin, H. 'Die Lebenshaltung minderbemittelter Familien in Hamburg im Jahre 1925' in H. Sköllin (ed.), *Statistische Mitteilungen über den Hamburgischen Staat*, 20, Hamburg, 1926

Sloterdijk, P. *Kritik der zynischen Vernunft*, Frankfurt, 1983, vol. 2

Smith, E. *Wage-earning women and their dependants*, London, 1911

Smith-Rosenberg, C. and Rosenberg, C. 'The female animal: medical and biological views of woman and her role in nineteenth-century America', *Journal of American History*, 60 (1973)

Soloway, R. A. *Birth control and the population question in England, 1877–1930*, Chapel Hill, 1982
'Feminism, fertility and eugenics in Victorian and Edwardian England' in S. Drescher, D. Sabean and A. Sharlin (eds.), *Political symbolism in modern Europe*, New Brunswick, NJ, 1982

Sorba, C. 'Edilizia popolare nella regione parigina: il caso dell' "Office Public d'Habitations à Bon Marché du Département de la Seine" (1915–1939)', *Storia Urbana*, 26 (1984)

Spree, R. *Soziale Ungleichheit vor Krankheit und Tod*, Göttingen, 1981
'The German petite bourgeoisie and the decline of fertility: some statistical evidence from the late 19th and early 20th centuries', *Historical Social Research*, 22 (1982)

Stachura, P. D. *Nazi youth in the Weimar Republic*, Santa Barbara, 1975

Stadthagen, H. *Die Ersatzlebensmittel in der Kriegswirtschaft (Beiträge zur Kriegswirtschaft 56–8)*, Berlin, 1919

Starling, E. H. *The feeding of nations*, London, 1919

Statistik des Deutschen Reiches, new series vol. 189, Berlin, 1921

Statistique de la France. Publiée par le ministère de l'Agriculture et du Commerce, Paris, 1846

Statistische Kommission der 'Gesellschaft der Freunde des vaterlandischen Schul- und Erziehungswesens' (ed.), *Haushaltungsrechnungen hamburgischer Volksschullehrer*, Hamburg, 1906

Statistisches Amt der Stadt Halle a/S, *Wirtschaftsrechnungen kleiner Haushaltungen in Halle a.S. und Umgebung 1909/10* (Beitrage zur Statistik der Stadt Halle a.S., 13), Halle, 1911

Statistisches Bundesamt. *Wirtschaftsrechnungen. Verbrauch in Arbeiterhaushalten 1937*, vol. I, Stuttgart and Mainz, 1960

Statistisches Jahrbuch des deutschen Reiches, 42, Berlin, 1921/22

Statistisches Jahrbuch des deutschen Reiches, 47, Berlin, 1928

Stegen, J. van der. 'Les Chinois en France, 1915–1929', MA, University of Paris X – Nanterre, 1974

Stein, M. B. 'The meaning of skill: the case of the French engine-drivers, 1837–1917', *Politics and Society*, 8 (1978)

Stein, V. 'Die Lage der österreichischen Metallarbeiter im Kriege' in F. Hanusch and E. Adler (eds.), *Die Regelung der Arbeitsverhältnisse im Kriege*, Vienna, 1927

Stenographische Bericht der Verhandlungen des Reichstage, 1918, 5364, 10 June 1918

Stephenson, J. *Women in Nazi society*, London, 1975

'"Reichsbund der Kinderreichen": the League of Large Families in the population policy of Nazi Germany', *European Studies Review*, 9 (1979)

Stöcker, H. *Moderne Bevölkerungspolitik*. Kriegshefte des Bundes für Mutterschutz, Berlin, 1916

Stoeckel, W. *Erinnerungen eines Frauenarztes*, Leipzig, 1980

Stoehr, I. 'Organisierte Mütterlichkeit' in K. Hausen (ed.), *Frauen suchen ihre Geschichte*, Munich, 1983

Stovall, T. E. 'The urbanization of Bobigny 1900–1939', PhD, University of Wisconsin at Madison, 1984

Strain, J. 'Feminism and political radicalism in the German Social Democratic movement 1890–1914', PhD, University of California, 1964

Strubel, K., Tetzner, W. and Piechocki, W. *Zur Geschichte der Gründung des Zweigvereins zur Bekämpfung der Schwindsucht in der Stadt Halle am 15 Juni 1899*, Halle, 1974

Stürzbecher, M. 'Die Bekämpfung des Geburtenrückganges und der Säuglingssterblichkeit im Spiegel der Reichstagsdebatten 1900–1930', unpublished dissertation, Berlin, 1954

'Otto Krohne', *Berliner Ärzteblatt*, 92 (1979)

Sulger-Buel, S. 'Les cantonnements féminins pendant la première guerre mondiale', MA, University of Paris–VII, 1976

Tawney, R. H. 'The abolition of economic controls, 1918–1921', *Economic History Review*, 13 (1943)

Taylor, P. 'Daughters and mothers – maids and mistresses. Domestic service between the wars' in N. Clarke, C. C. Critcher and R. Johnson (eds.), *Working class culture*, London, 1979

Tennstedt, F. 'Alfred Blaschko – das wissenschaftliche und sozialpolitische Wirken eines menschenfreundlichen Sozialhygienikers im Deutschen Reich', *Zeitschrift für Sozialreform*, 25 (1979)

Thébaud, F. *La Femme au temps de la guerre de 14*, Paris, 1986

Theweleit, K. *Männerphantasien*, vol. 2, Frankfurt am Main, 1977

Thom, D. 'Women workers in the Woolwich Arsenal in the First World War', *Oral History*, 8 (Autumn 1978)

'The ideology of women's work in Britain, 1914–1924, with specific reference to the NFWW and other trade unions', unpublished PhD thesis, Thames Polytechnic, 1982

'The "bundle of sticks"; women, trade unionists and collective organisation before 1918' in A. John (ed.), *Unequal opportunities. Women's employment in Britain 1800–1918*, Oxford, 1986

'Nice girls and rude girls' in R. Samuel (ed.), *Patriotism and the making of the national identity*, London, 1988

Thom, D. and Ineson, A. 'Women workers and TNT poisoning' in P. Weindling (ed.), *A social history of occupational health*, London, 1985

Thomann, K.-D. *Alfons Fischer [1873–1936] und die Badische Gesellschaft für sozial Hygiene*, Cologne, 1980

Thompson, G. W. *Short history of the Association of Engineering and Shipbuilding Draughtsmen*, London, 1934

Thompson, W. H. 'The food value of Great Britain's food supply', *The Economic Proceedings of the Royal Dublin Society*, II, no. 11, March 1916

Toesca, L. *Les Crimes de l'alcôve*, Auxerre, 1911

Tomlinson, R. 'The politics of *dénatalité* during the French Third Republic, 1890–1940', unpublished PhD thesis, Cambridge, 1984

Tomlinson, R., Huss, M. M. and Ogden, P. E. 'France in peril', *History Today*, 35 (1985)

Triebel, A. 'Differential consumption in historical perspective', *Historical Social Research*, 17 (1981)

'Ökonomie und Lebensgeschichte' in C. Conrad and H.-J. von Kondratowitz (eds.), *Gerontologie und Sozialgeschichte*, Berlin, 1983

Turner, J. 'The politics of "organized business" in the First World War' in J. Turner (ed.), *Businessmen and politics. Studies of business activity in British politics, 1900–1945*, London, 1983

Tyszka, C. von. 'Die Veränderungen in der Lebenshaltung städtischer Familien im Kriege' in *Archiv für Sozialwissenschaft und Sozialpolitik*, 43 (1916/17)

'Hunger und Ernahrung' in R. Allers (ed.), *Soziale Physiologue und Pathologie*, Berlin, 1927

Umbreit, P. 'Die deutschen Gewerkschaften im Kriege' in P. Umbreit and C. Lorenz (eds.), *Der Krieg und die Arbeitsverhältnisse*, Stuttgart, 1928

United Society of Boilermakers and Iron and Steel Shipbuilders. *Annual Report*, 1931

Vallin, J. *La Mortalité par génération en France, depuis 1899*, Institut National d'Etudes Démographiques, Travaux et Documents, Cahier no. 63, Paris, 1973

Vandenbroeke, C. 'Kwantitatieve en kwalitatieve aspecten van het vleesverbruik in Vlaanderen', *Tijdschrift voor sociale geschiedenis*, 8 (1983)

Vesselitsky, V. de. *Expenditure and waste: a study in war-time*, London, 1917

Veys, D. *Cohort survival in Belgium in the past 150 years*, Sociologische Studien en Documenten, vol. 15, Louvain, 1983

Vichniac, J. 'Industrial relations in historical perspective: a case study of the French iron and steel industry (1830–1921)', PhD, Harvard, 1981

Vidal de la Blache, P. *Etats et nations de l'Europe*, Paris, 1889

Volovitch, M. C. 'Essai sur l'évolution et la composition de la main d'oeuvre industrielle pendant la guerre de 1914–1918', MA, University of Paris, 1968

Völter, H. 'Die deutsche Beamtenbesoldung' in W. Gerloff (ed.), *Die Beamtenbesoldung im modernen Staat*, Munich and Leipzig, 1932

Vondung, K. 'Zur Lage der Gebildeten in der Wilhelminischen Zeit' in Klaus Vondung (ed.), *Das Wilhelminische Bildungsbürgertum*, Göttingen, 1976

Vorstand des Deutschen Metallarbeiter-Verbandes (ed.), *320 Haushaltungsrechnungen von Metallarbeitern*, Stuttgart, 1909, reprint (ed.) Dieter Dowe, Berlin and Bonn, 1981

Vorwärts-Verlag (ed.) *Um Friede, Freiheit und Recht! Der Jännerausstand des Innerösterreichischen Proletariats*, Vienna, 1918

Voss-Zietz, M. 'Praktische Hauswirtschaft im Kriege' in Voss-Zietz, M., et al., *Die Hauswirtschaft im Kriege, Beiträge zur Kriegswirtschaft*, 25, Berlin, 1917

Vuillermet, F.-A. *Le Suicide d'une race*, Paris, 1911

Waites, B. A. 'The effect of the First World War on class and status in England, 1910–20', *Journal of contemporary history*, 11 (1976)
    A class society at war, Leamington Spa, 1987
Wall, R. 'Inferring differential neglect of females from mortality data', *Annales de démographie historique*, 1981
    'Regional and temporal variations in the structure of the British household since 1851' in T. C. Barker and M. Drake (eds.), *Population and society in Britain 1850–1980*, London, 1982
    'Residential isolation of the elderly, a comparison over time', *Ageing and Society*, 4 (1984)
Wall, R., Laslett, P. and Robin, J. (eds.) *Family forms in historic Europe*, Cambridge, 1983
War Cabinet. Report for the year 1918, PP 1919, xxx, Cmd 325
War Office. *Women's work in munitions*, London, 1916
    Women's work in non-munitions industries, London, 1916
    Statistics of the military effort of the British Empire during the Great War 1914–1920, London, 1922
Wawerzonnek, M. *Implizite Sexualpädagogie in der Sexualwissenschaft 1886–1933*, Cologne, 1984
Webb, S. *The decline in the birth-rate*, London, 1907
Weindling, P. J. 'Theories of the cell state in Imperial Germany' in C. Webster (ed.), *Biology, medicine and society 1840–1940*, Cambridge, 1981
    'Cell biology and Darwinism in Imperial Germany: the contribution of Oscar Hertwig', PhD, London University, 1982
    'Shattered alternatives in medicine [Essay review of the Verschüttete Alternativen Project]', *History Workshop*, 16 (1983)
    'Die Preussische Medizinalverwaltung und die "Rassenhygiene", 1905–1933', *Zeitschrift für Sozialreform* (1984)
    'Soziale Hygiene, Eugenik und medizinische Praxis', *Argument – Sonderband*, 119 (1984)
    Darwinism and social Darwinism in Imperial Germany, Stuttgart, 1988
    Health, race and German politics from National Unification to Nazism, Cambridge, 1989
Wellner, G. 'Industrie-arbeiterinnen in der Weimarer Republik', *Geschichte und Gesellschaft*, 7 (1981)
Weygand, General. 'La Presse des tranchées, 1914–18', *Histoire de la presse française*, vol. II. Lausanne, 1965
Whitlock, B. *Belgium under the German occupation*, London, 1919
Wickert, C. et al. (eds.) 'Helene Stöcker and the Bund für Mutterschutz', *Women's Studies International Forum*, 5 (1982)
Wiener, M. J. *English culture and the decline of the industrial spirit 1850–1980*, Cambridge, 1981
Wiernik, L. *Die Arbeiterernährung in der Kriegsorganisation der Industrie (Beiträge zur Kriegswirtschaft*, 26/27), Berlin, 1917
Wilkinson, F. 'Collective bargaining in the steel industry in the 1920s' in A. Briggs and J. Saville (eds.), *Essays in labour history 1918–1939*, London, 1977
Wilson, T. *The myriad faces of war*, London, 1986
Winkler, D. *Frauenarbeit im Dritten Reich*, Hamburg, 1977
Winkler, H. A. 'Vom Protest zur Panik. Der gewerbliche Mittelstand in der Weimarer Republik' in his *Liberalismus und Antiliberalismus*, Göttingen, 1979

Winkler, W. *Berufsstatistik der Kriegstoten der österreichische-ungarischen Monarchie*, Vienna, 1919
Die Totenverluste der österreichisch-ungarischen Monarchie nach Nationalitäten, Vienna, 1919
Die Einkommensverschiebungen in Österreich während des Weltkrieges, Vienna, 1930
Winter, J. M. 'The impact of the First World War on civilian health in Britain', *Economic history review*, 2nd series, 30 (1977)
'The fear of population decline in Western Europe, 1870–1940' in R. W. Hiorns (ed.), *Demographic patterns in developed societies*, London, 1980
The Great War and the British people, London, 1985
Winter, J. M. and Teitelbaum, M. S. *The fear of population decline*, New York, 1985
Die wissenschaftliche Deputation für das Medizinalwesen, *25 Jahre Preussischer Medizinalverwaltung seit Erlass des Kreisarztgesetz, 1901–1926*, Berlin, 1927
Woesler de Panafieu, C. 'Das Konzept von Weiblichkeit als Natur- und Maschinenkörper' in Barbara Schaeffer-Hegel and Brigitte Wartmann (eds.), *Mythos Frau: Projektionen und Inszenierungen im Patriarchat*, Berlin, 1984
Wohl, R. *The generation of 1914*, Cambridge, Mass., 1979
Wolfe, H. *Labour supply and regulation*, Oxford, 1923
Woodward, K. *Queen Mary*, London, 1927
Wunderlich, F. 'Fabrikpflegerinnen', *Archiv für Frauenenarbeit*, 8 (1920)
Fabrikpflege: Ein Beitrag zur Betriegspolitik, Berlin, 1926
Wurm, K. F. *Deutsche Erziehung im Werden. Von der pädagogischen Reformbewegung zur völkischen und politischen Erziehung*, Berlin, 1938
Wyneken, G. 'Die neue Jugend. Ihr Kampf und Freiheit und Wahrheit in Schule und Elternhaus' in *Religion und Erotik*, Munich, 1914
Was ist Jugendkultur?, Munich, 1914
Zancarini, M. 'Etude du registre de la main d'oeuvre feminine aux Forges et Aciéries de la Marine de Saint-Etienne' in Université de Vincennes colloquium on 'Les femmes et la classe ouvrière', December 1978
Zeitler, C. 'Die wirtschaftliche und berufliche Lage der erwerbstätigen Frauen in Deutschland seit 1914', unpublished PhD, University of Nuremberg, 1951
Zesch, R. *Was ist geschehen zur Ermöglichung der Arbeit von Ungelernten und Frauen in der gesamten Schwer-, Maschinen- und chemischen Industrie und im Handwerk?*, Berlin, March 1933
Zeyons, S. *Le Roman-photo de la grande guerre: les cartes postales bleu horizon*, Paris, 1976
Les Cartes postales, Paris, 1979
Ziemer, G. and Wolf, H. *Wandervogel und Freideutsche Jugend*, Bad Godesberg, 1961
Zimmermann, W. 'Die Veränderungen der Einkommens- und Lebensverhältnisse der deutschen Arbeiter durch den Krieg' in Rudolf Meerwarth, Adolf Gunther and Waldemar Zimmermann, *Die Einwirkung des Krieges auf Bevolkerungsbewegung, Einkommen und Lebenshaltung in Deutschland (Wirtschafts- und Sozialgeschichte des Weltkrieges*, Deutsche Serie (ed.) James T. Shotwell), Stuttgart and New Haven, 1932
Zodtke-Heyde, E. 'Fabriksinspektorinnen und Fabrikpflegerinnen', *Archiv für Frauenarbeit*, 6 (1918)

BIBLIOGRAPHY

(faded and illegible text)

Index

Abel, Rudolf, 422
abortificients, 391, 392, 404–5, 415n, 416n
abortion, 331, 391, 392, 393, 399, 404–6, 407, 409n, 413n, 415n, 416n, 421, 424, 428, 429, 430, 437n
abortionists, 405–6
Abrams, Philip, 315
absenteeism, 58, 96–7, 102n, 212
Acland, H. D., 379
Adams, A. A., 213, 214, 219n
administrators: see bureaucracy; officials
adolescents, 236–8, 439–52
   see also children
adoption, 348
Adult Suffrage Association, 299
adulteration of food: see food, adulterated
affluence, 95–7
   see also standard of living
ageing, 69, 72–3
agriculture, 59–61, 103n, 111, 130, 140–2, 145, 151, 153, 155, 202, 203, 216, 262, 263, 269, 271–2, 273, 274, 276, 284, 289n, 290,n, 307, 319, 322
   see also farm labourers; farmers
aircraft industry, 56, 319, 321
Albert I (of Belgium), 151
albumen, 163, 169
alcohol consumption, 93, 94, 95–6, 106n, 133, 191n, 192n, 209, 212, 219n, 284, 333, 402, 419, 420
   manufacture, 319, 322, 421, 422
Algeria, 236
aliens, 95
Allemane, R., 331
Allgemeine Ortskrankenkasse, 290n

Alliance nationale pour l'accroissement de la population française, 331, 332, 360n
allied supply policy, 37, 239
allotments: see War Gardens Movement
Alsace, 348, 352, 354
Althoff, Friedrich, 418, 419, 420
Amalgamated Society of Engineers, 227–8
amusements, 171–4, 175, 176–7, 178–9, 182, 184, 186, 188, 189, 315
anaemia, 53–4, 101n
Anderlecht, 148
Anderson, Adelaide, 315
Angestellte: see workers, white collar
Annuaire Statistique de la Belgique, 141
Anti-VD Society, 423, 424
Antwerp, 140, 147, 149, 152, 153
apprenticeship, 238, 271n, 314
Apprenticeship and Skilled Employment Association, 58
Arbeiter- und Soldatenräte, 125
arbitration, 242, 316
Archiv für Frauenarbeit, 291n, 292n
armaments: see arsenals; munitions factories; war industries
Armistice, 10, 159, 202, 204, 237, 245, 255, 256
army, 420, 422–3, 424
   provisioning of, 140, 190n, 211, 213, 237, 281
   standing of, 127–8
   see also soldiers
arsenals, 55–6, 57, 306, 307, 319, 321
artificial flower making, 301
arts and crafts, 272
Asquith, H. H., 201–2

477

INDEX

Greenwich, 48
Greenwood, Sir Hamar, 376
Grenoble, 236, 241
Groener, General Wilhelm, 279
Grotjahn, Alfred, 389, 396, 397, 406, 409n, 411n, 415n, 428, 432
Gruber, Karl, 447
Gruber, Max von, 422
Guilbert, M., 265n
gum workers, 318, 323
gun powder industry: *see* munitions factories

Hackett, Amy, 411n
Hackney, 48
Hainaut, 149, 152
half pay, 94
Halle, 164–5
ham, 208, 215n, 218n
Hamburg, 164–7, 190n, 277, 423
Hammersmith, 48, 57, 94, 99n
Hampstead, 48
Handl, Johann, 288n
Hanusch, Ferdinand, 131
hardware and hollow ware workers, 318, 322
Harnock, Agnes von, 295n
harvests: *see* agriculture
Hausen, Karin, 408n
headship rate, 76–7
   see also household heads
health: *see* material and child welfare campaign; social policy; social workers
heating, cost of, 144, 145, 161, 167, 170, 174, 175, 212, 213
hemp workers, 318, 322
Henkel, 405, 430
heredity, 369–73, 378, 380, 38£, 382, 383, 384, 412n, 430, 432
Hertwig, Oscar, 429
Het Volk, 146
Hiebert, David, 5n, 137n
high status employment: *see* upper class
Himmler, Heinrich, 451n
Hindenburg Plan, 39, 162
Hinton, James, 222, 325n
Hirsch, Max, 406
Hirschfeld, Magnus, 109, 411n
Hitler, Adolf, 449
Hitler Youth, 447, 449
Hitze, Franz, 395
hoarding, 111, 143
Hoffman, Margarete, 294n
Hoffman, Walter G., 164n, 192n, 193n
Holborn, 48, 93
holidays, 126, 176n, 177n

Hollingsworth, T., 219n
Holtfrerich, Carl-Ludwig, 190n
home workers, 259, 268, 276–8, 283, 286–7, 291n, 293n, 412n
Horne, John, 245n
horses, 94, 111, 116, 155
Horvath, Willi, 123
hosiery workers, 318, 322
hospitals, 55, 142, 153, 238, 318, 321, 401, 405, 422, 424–5
Höss, Rudolf, 449
hotels and inns, 59–60, 272, 307, 318, 322
household equipment, 171–4, 175, 176–7, 182, 212
household heads, 74–93
household work, professionalisation of, 134
households, 62–6, 73–93
   composition, 74–93
   formation, 73, 76–7, 85, 90, 104n
   size, 63–5, 159
   structure, 65
   see also life cycle
housewifery: *see* women, home-keeping
housing, 37, 73, 76, 112, 133–4, 144, 145, 147, 164–7, 175, 182, 189, 191n, 193n, 212, 213, 219n, 222, 229, 230, 239, 240, 282, 284, 382, 405, 417
   see also rent control
Huk, Emil, 127
Hungary, 111
Huss, Marie-Monique, vii, 3, 98n, 266n, 329–67
Hutchins, Mrs B. L., 315, 324n
hygiene: *see* cleanliness

illegitimacy, 390, 395, 411n, 420, 423, 426
immorality, 45, 301, 343
Imperial War Museum, vii, 308, 310, 337, 359n, 362n
Independent Labour Party, 300
Indo-China, 236
industrial employment, 59–61, 135n, 147, 262–3, 269, 271, 290n, 307
   see also factories
industrial mobilisation: *see* war economy
industrial relations: *see* trade unions
industrialists, 39–40, 141, 161, 228, 230, 294n
infant mortality, 150, 152, 301, 331, 371, 378, 379, 380, 397–8, 411n, 412n, 413n, 417, 420, 421, 424–5, 427, 432, 434n
infanticide, 356, 367n
infirmaries, 241
   see also factory nurses